GROUP DYNAMICS

GROUP DYNAMICS

Research and Theory

THIRD EDITION

Edited by

DORWIN CARTWRIGHT
Professor of Psychology and Research Coordinator

ALVIN ZANDER
Professor of Psychology and Director
Research Center for Group Dynamics
University of Michigan

HARPER & ROW, PUBLISHERS
New York, Evanston, and London

GROUP DYNAMICS: *Research and Theory,* Third Edition

Library of Congress Catalog Card Number: 68–12274

Contents

Preface

The literature about groups goes back to the distant past. Careful research, however, has been known for only a few decades. Although man was slow in demanding that his working assumptions about the nature of group life be based upon objective evidence, his curiosity is no longer satisfied with speculation or the accumulated wisdom of personal experience. Today we demand facts. And, although all of us sometimes mistakenly take our untested prejudices to be facts, there is widespread recognition that a fact can be established only through careful use of objective methods of observation, measurement, and experimentation. The use of such methods to provide a dependable body of knowledge about groups has accelerated rapidly within recent years. Perhaps the most important reason for this development is the simultaneous acceptance of two propositions—that the health of democratic society is dependent upon the effectiveness of its component groups and that the scientific method can be employed in the task of improving group life.

A democratic society derives its strength from the effective functioning of the multitude of groups that it contains. Its most valuable resources are the groups of people found in its homes, communities, schools, churches, business concerns, union halls, and various branches of government. Now, more than ever before, it is recognized that these units must perform their functions well if the larger systems are to work successfully.

Awareness of the practical importance of something does not, however, lead automatically to its scientific investigation. The rise of research in group dynamics could occur only because people began to see that the scientific method can be applied to these important phenomena. Only after social scientists had made some progress in developing research techniques applicable to group life could there be mounted a systematic and empirical attack on the functioning of groups. Of critical importance was the development of techniques of observation for recording and classifying behavior in group settings, the demonstration that group phenomena can be created in the laboratory, and the invention of action-research with its emphasis upon the possibility of conducting genuine experiments in natural groups.

The recognition that techniques such as these can provide dependable findings about critical social problems resulted, immediately after World War II, in a great increase in the financial resources and the number of competent investigators available for research on groups. The conclusions and theoretical interpretations of this rapidly growing body of research were scattered throughout a variety of publications in several professional fields. By the early 1950's a great need had developed for a systematic summary of the results and for a handy collection of the more significant articles describing the methods and results of research on group dynamics.

The first edition of this book, published in 1953, was prepared in order to help meet these needs. When we decided to undertake this task, two alternative procedures presented themselves. We could try to write a systematic summary in a manner similar to the usual textbook, or we could compile a collection of the major publications in order to illustrate the variety of approaches, methods, and findings. The preparation of an integrated summary seemed to us to be premature. To achieve theoretical consistency, we would have had to omit important findings that did not then fit readily into a single theory and we would have had to present large segments of theory for which adequate empirical testing had not yet been provided. The second alternative seemed hardly better, however, for there was in fact a greater systematic relation among various research projects than would be evident from a mere stringing together of research articles. A middle course seemed best. We chose, therefore, a limited number of theoretically defined problems and presented representative publications from these areas. For each of these topics we prepared an introductory chapter designed to give a theoretical framework for relating the various articles to one another. The second edition, published in 1960, preserved this same structure for the book.

Since the publication of the earlier editions, research on groups has continued at an accelerated pace. Many new problems have been investigated, new techniques of research have been invented, and new theoretical formulations have been produced. A deeper understanding of the central problems of group dynamics and a firmer empirical basis for conclusions have also been achieved. Much of the work reported in the first and second editions has since been subjected to the test of replication or extension to new types of population and situation. The literature of group dynamics now contains a much larger number of monographs, books, and critical reviews of research and theory.

In preparing this third edition we have attempted to create a volume that reflects these various changes. Although the original structure is basically unaltered, considerable changes have been made. Fourteen articles in the second edition have been replaced by fourteen new ones. In adding new articles we have chosen those that, in our opinion, serve best as an introduction to a significant theoretical point of view or to an important line of empirical research and that combine well with others to round out a particular topic. The present edition contains eight chapters, written by us, whose objective is to place the large mass of empirical findings within a historical and theoretical perspective. It also includes four chapters, prepared especially for this volume, that summarize work done on more specialized problems. Of the thirty-five articles reprinted in the original edition, only thirteen are to be found in the present one.

The book is divided into seven parts. The first contains two chapters, prepared for this volume, that place the field of group dynamics within its larger context. They describe the theoretical and social origins of group dynamics and discuss the basic theoretical and methodological issues encountered by those working in the field. Each of the remaining sections begins with an introductory chapter in which we have tried to define the scientific nature of a particular problem and to point out ways in which research is beginning to add up to general principles. At the same time we have attempted to communicate some of the vitality of the field by stressing problems that need further study, by raising questions, and by suggesting hypotheses that soon may be tested. Each chapter also presents a bibliography of the more important related publications. The major sections of the book deal with the following topics: Part Two—the nature of groups and group membership; Part Three—the origin of group pressures and the operation of group standards; Part Four—the determinants and consequences of interpersonal power and influence within groups; Part Five—leadership and the performance of group functions; Part Six—motivational processes in groups and the nature of group goals; Part Seven—the structural properties of groups. It should be mentioned that many of the articles could well be located in any of several different sections because they deal with various phenomena simultaneously. Their present placement reflects our judgment of "best fit," but the reader may wish to consider the same article from different points of view. A brief overview of the field of group dynamics may be obtained by the consecutive reading of chapters 1, 2, 3, 11, 17, 24, 31, and 36.

The audience we have in mind for this volume is a broad one. We have tried to make the book useful to students in the various social sciences that are concerned with groups. At the same time we have been aware of the questions raised by consultants, teachers, and social engineers. Although this book does not attempt to tell such people how to apply group dynamics, many of the problems they meet daily are examined in the research reports included here. Experience with persons working in occupations that demand insight into group processes encourages us to believe that the more capable of them are quite prepared to employ theoretical explanations of group events in developing their programs.

This book is the product of the work of many people. We deeply appreciate the kindness of those who have given us permission to include their research reports. In preparing the introductory chapters we have drawn upon the work and ideas of many whose publications could not, for lack of space, be reprinted here. We have tried to give credit, but we are sure that sometimes we have forgotten the source of an idea. The pervasive influence of Kurt Lewin's work upon our thinking should be too obvious to require detailed citation. We are indebted in many ways to our colleagues and students, past and present, at the University of Michigan. Without their suggestions, stimulation, and support, neither the earlier editions nor this new one would have been possible.

DORWIN CARTWRIGHT
ALVIN ZANDER

October 1967
Ann Arbor, Michigan

PART ONE

INTRODUCTION TO GROUP DYNAMICS

1

Origins of Group Dynamics

If it were possible for the overworked hypothetical man from Mars to take a fresh view of the people of Earth, he would probably be impressed by the amount of time they spend doing things together in groups. He would note that most people cluster into relatively small groups, with the members residing together in the same dwelling, satisfying their basic biological needs within the group, depending upon the same source for economic support, rearing children, and mutually caring for the health of one another. He would observe that the education and socialization of children tend to occur in other, usually larger, groups in churches, schools, or other social institutions. He would see that much of the work of the world is carried out by people who perform their activities in close interdependence within relatively enduring associations. He would perhaps be saddened to find groups of men engaged in warfare, gaining courage and morale from pride in their unit and a knowledge that they can depend upon their buddies. He might be gladdened to see groups of people enjoying themselves in recreations and sports of various kinds. Finally he might be puzzled why so many people spend so much time in little groups talking, planning, and being "in conference." Surely he would conclude that if he wanted to understand much about what is happening on Earth he would have to examine rather carefully the ways in which groups form, function, and dissolve.

Now if we turn to a more customary perspective and view our society through the eyes of Earth's inhabitants, we discover that the functioning or malfunctioning of groups is recognized increasingly as one of society's major problems. In business, government, and the military, there is great interest in improving the productivity of groups. Many thoughtful people are alarmed by the apparent weakening and disintegration of the family. Educators are coming to believe that they cannot carry out their responsibilities fully unless they understand better how the classroom functions as a social group. Those concerned with social welfare are diligently seeking ways to reduce intergroup conflicts between labor and management and among religious and ethnic groups. The operation of juvenile gangs is a most troublesome obstacle in attempts to prevent crime. It is becoming clear that much mental illness derives in some way from the individual's relations with groups and that groups may be used effectively in mental therapy.

Whether one wishes to understand or to improve human behavior, it is necessary to know a great deal about the nature of groups. Neither a coherent view of man nor an advanced social technology is possible without dependable answers to a host of questions concerning the operation of groups, how individuals relate to groups, and how groups relate to larger society. When, and under what conditions, do groups form? What conditions are necessary for their growth and effective functioning? What factors foster the decline and disintegration of groups? How do groups affect the behavior, thinking, motivation, and adjustment of individuals? What makes some groups have powerful influence over members while other groups exert little or none? What characteristics of individuals are important determinants of the properties of groups? What determines the nature of relations between groups? When groups are part of a larger social system, what circumstances make them strengthen or weaken the more inclusive organization? How does the social environment of a group affect its properties? Questions like these must be answered before we will have a real understanding of human nature and human behavior. They must be answered, too, before we can hope to design an optimal society and bring it into being.

The student of group dynamics is interested in acquiring knowledge about the nature of groups and especially about the psychological and social forces associated with groups. Such an interest has, of course, motivated intellectual activities of thoughtful people for centuries. The earliest recorded philosophical literature contains a great deal of wisdom about the nature of groups and the relations between individuals and groups. It also contains a variety of specifications concerning the "best" ways of managing group life. During the period from the sixteenth through the nineteenth centuries there was created in Europe an impressive literature dealing with the nature of man and his place in society. In this literature one can find most of the major orientations, or "basic assumptions," which guide current research and thinking about groups. It is evident that the modern student of group dynamics is not essentially different in his interests from scholars writing at various times over the centuries. And yet, it is equally clear that the approach to the study of groups known as "group dynamics" is strictly a twentieth-century development; it is significantly different from that of preceding centuries.

What, then, is group dynamics? The phrase has gained popular familiarity since World War II but, unfortunately, with its increasing circulation its meaning has become imprecise. According to one rather frequent usage, group dynamics refers to a sort of political ideology concerning the ways in which groups should be organized and managed. This ideology emphasizes the importance of democratic leadership, the participation of members in decisions, and the gains both to society and to individuals to be obtained through cooperative activities in groups. The critics of this view have sometimes caricatured it as making "togetherness" the supreme virtue, advocating that everything be done jointly in groups that have and need no leader because everyone participates fully and equally. A second popular usage of the term group dynamics has it refer to a set of techniques, such as role playing, buzz-sessions, observation and feedback of group process, and group decision, which have been employed widely during the past decade or two in training programs designed to improve skill in human relations and in the management of conferences and committees. These techniques have been identified most closely with the National Training Laboratories whose annual training programs at Bethel, Maine, have become widely known. According to the third usage of the term group dynamics, it refers to a field of inquiry dedicated to achieving knowledge about the nature of groups, the laws of their development, and their interrelations with individuals, other groups, and larger institutions.

It is not possible, of course, to legislate how terms are to be used in a language. Nevertheless, it is important for clarity of thinking and communication to distinguish among these three quite distinct things which have been given the same label in popular discussions. Everyone has an ideology, even though he may not be able to state it very explicitly, concerning the ways in which group life should be organized. Those responsible for the management of groups and the training of people for participation in groups can fulfill their responsibilities only by the use of techniques of one sort or another. But there is no rigidly fixed correspondence between a particular ideology about the "ideal" nature of groups and the use of particular techniques of management and training. And it should be obvious that the search for a better understanding of the nature of group life need not be linked to a particular ideology or adherence to certain techniques of management. In this book we shall limit our usage of the term group dynamics to refer to the field of inquiry dedicated to advancing knowledge about the nature of group life.

Group dynamics, in this sense, is a branch of knowledge or an intellectual specialization. Being concerned with human behavior and social relationships, it can be located within the social sciences. And yet it cannot be identified readily as a subpart of any of the traditional academic disciplines. In order to gain a better understanding of how group dynamics differs from other familiar fields, let us consider briefly some of its distinguishing characteristics.

1. Emphasis on theoretically significant empirical research. We noted above that an interest in groups can be found throughout history and that such an interest cannot, therefore, distinguish group dynamics from its predecessors. The difference lies, rather, in the way this interest is exploited. Until the beginning of the present century those who were curious about the nature of groups relied primarily upon personal experience and historical records to provide answers to their questions. Not being burdened by the necessity of accounting for an accumulation of carefully gathered empirical data, writers in this speculative era devoted their energies to the creation of comprehensive theoretical treatments of groups. These theoretical systems, especially the ones produced during the nineteenth century, were elaborate and widely inclusive, having been created by men of outstanding intellectual ability. The list of names from this era contains such impressive thinkers as Cooley, Durkheim, Freud, Giddings, LeBon, McDougall, Ross, Tarde, Tönnies, and Wundt. Their ideas can still be seen in contemporary discussions of group life.

By the second decade of this century an empiricist rebellion had begun in social science, principally in the United States and especially in psychology and sociology. Instead of being content with speculation about the nature of groups, a few people began to seek out facts and to attempt to distinguish between objective data and subjective impression. Although rather simple empirical questions initially guided this research, a fundamentally new criterion for evaluating knowledge about groups was established. Instead of asking merely whether some proposition about the nature of groups is plausible and logically consistent, those interested in groups began to demand that the proposition be supported by reliable data that can be reproduced by an independent investigator. Major effort went into the devising and improving of techniques of empirical research that would provide reliability of measurement, standardization of observation, effective experimental design, and the statistical analysis of data. When, in the late 1930's, group dynamics began to emerge as an identifiable field the empiricist rebellion was well along in social psychology and sociology, and from the outset group dynamics could employ the research methods characteristic of an empirical science. In fact, group dynamics is to be distinguished from its intellectual predecessors primarily by its basic reliance on careful observation, quantification, measurement, and experimentation.

But one should not identify group dynamics too closely with extreme empiricism. Even in its earliest days, work in group dynamics displayed an interest in the construction of theory and the derivation of testable hypotheses from theory, and it has come progressively to maintain a close interplay between data collection and the advancement of theory.

2. Interest in dynamics and interdependence of phenomena. Although the phrase group dynamics specifies groups as the object of study, it also focuses attention more sharply on questions about the dynamics of group life. The student of group dynamics is not satisfied with just a description of the properties of groups or of events associated with groups. Nor is he content with a classification of types of groups or of forms of group behavior. He wants to know how the phenomena he observes depend on one another and what new phenomena might result from the creation of conditions never before observed. In short, he

seeks to discover general principles concerning what conditions produce what effects.

This search requires the asking of many detailed questions about the interdependence among specific phenomena. If a change of membership occurs in a group, which other features of the group will change and which will remain stable? Under what conditions does a group tend to undergo a change of leadership? What are the pressures in a group which bring about uniformity of thinking among its members? What conditions inhibit creativity among group members? What changes in a group will heighten productivity, lower it, or not affect it at all? If the cohesiveness of a group is raised, which other of its features will change? Answers to questions like these reveal how certain properties and processes depend on others.

Theories of group dynamics attempt to formulate lawful relations among phenomena such as these. As these theories have been elaborated, they have guided work in group dynamics toward the intensive investigation of such things as change, resistance to change, social pressures, influence, coercion, power, cohesion, attraction, rejection, interdependence, equilibrium, and instability. Terms like these, by suggesting the operation of psychological and social forces, refer to the dynamic aspects of groups and play an important role in theories of group dynamics.

3. Interdisciplinary relevance. It is important to recognize that research on the dynamics of groups has not been associated exclusively with any one of the social science disciplines. Sociologists have, of course, devoted great energy to the study of groups, as illustrated by investigations of the family, gangs, work groups, military units, and voluntary associations. Psychologists have directed their attention to many of the same kinds of groups, concentrating for the most part on the ways groups influence the behavior, attitudes, and personalities of individuals and the effects of characteristics of individuals on group functioning. Cultural anthropologists, while investigating many of the same topics as sociologists and psychologists, have contributed data on groups living under conditions quite different from those of modern industrial society. Political scientists have extended their traditional interest in large institutions to include studies of the functioning of legislative groups, pressure groups, and the effects of group membership on voting. And economists have come increasingly to collect data on the way decisions to spend or save money are made in the family, how family needs and relationships affect the size of the labor force, how goals of unions affect policies in business, and how decisions having economic consequences are reached in businesses of various kinds. Since an interest in groups is shared by the various social science disciplines, it is clear that any general knowledge about the dynamics of groups has significance widely throughout the social sciences.

4. Potential applicability of findings to social practice. Everyone who feels a responsibility for improving the functioning of groups and the quality of their consequences for individuals and society must base his actions upon some more or less explicit view of the effects that will be produced by different conditions and procedures. Anyone who is concerned with improving the quality of work in a research team, the effectiveness of a Sunday school class, the morale of a military unit, with decreasing the destructive consequences of intergroup conflict, or with attaining any socially desirable objective through groups, can make his efforts more effective by basing them on a firm knowledge of the laws governing group life.

The various professions that specialize in dealing with particular needs of individuals and of society have much to gain from advances in the scientific study of groups. One outstanding development in the more advanced societies during the past century has been the increasing differentiation undergone by the traditional professions of medicine, law, education, and theology. Today there are people who receive extensive training and devote their lives to such professional specialties as labor-management mediation, public health education, marriage counseling, human relations training, intergroup relations, social group work, pastoral counseling, hospital administration, adult education, public administration, psychiatry, and clinical psychology—just to mention a few. The professionalization of practice in these many areas has brought about a self-conscious desire to improve standards and the establishment of requirements for proper training. The major universities now have professional schools in many of these fields to provide such training. As this training has been extended and rationalized, members of these professions have become increasingly aware of the need for knowledge of the basic findings and principles produced in the social sciences. All of these professions must work with people, not simply as individuals but in groups and through social institutions. It should not be surprising, therefore, to find that courses in group dynamics are becoming more and more common in the professional schools, that people trained in group dynamics are being employed by agencies concerned with professional practice, and that group dynamics research is often carried out in connection with the work of such agencies.

In summary, then, we have proposed that group dynamics should be defined as a field of inquiry dedicated to advancing knowledge about the nature of groups, the laws of their development, and their interrelations with individuals, other groups, and larger institutions. It may be identified by four distinguishing characteristics: (a) an emphasis on theoretically significant empirical research, (b) an interest in dynamics and the interdependence among phenomena, (c) a broad relevance to all the social sciences, and (d) the potential applicability of its findings in efforts to improve the functioning of groups and their consequences on individuals and society. Thus conceived, group dynamics need not be associated with any particular ideology concerning the ways in which groups should be organized and managed nor with the use of any particular techniques of group management. In fact, it is a basic objective of group dynamics to provide a better scientific basis for ideology and practice.

CONDITIONS FOSTERING THE RISE OF GROUP DYNAMICS

Group dynamics began, as an identifiable field of inquiry, in the United States toward the end of the 1930's. Its origination as a distinct specialty is associated primarily with Kurt Lewin (1890–1947) who popularized the term group dynamics, made significant contributions to both research and theory in group dynamics, and in 1945 established the first organization devoted explicitly to research on group dynamics. Lewin's contribution was of great importance, but, as we shall see in detail, group dynamics was not the creation of just one person. It was, in fact, the result of

many developments that occurred over a period of several years and in several different disciplines and professions. Viewed in historical perspective, group dynamics can be seen as the convergence of certain trends within the social sciences and, more broadly, as the product of the particular society in which it arose.

The time and place of the rise of group dynamics were, of course, not accidental. American society in the 1930's provided the kind of conditions required for the emergence of such an intellectual movement. And, over the years since that time, only certain countries have afforded a favorable environment for its growth. To date, group dynamics has taken root primarily in the United States and the countries of northwestern Europe, although there have also been important developments in Israel, Japan, and India. Three major conditions seem to have been required for its rise and subsequent growth.

A SUPPORTIVE SOCIETY

If any field of inquiry is to prosper, it must exist in a surrounding society which is sufficiently supportive to provide the institutional resources required. By the end of the 1930's cultural and economic conditions in the United States were favorable for the emergence and growth of group dynamics. Great value was placed on science, technology, rational problem-solving, and progress. There was a fundamental conviction that in a democracy human nature and society can be deliberately improved by education, religion, legislation, and hard work. American industry had grown so rapidly, it was believed, not only because of abundant natural resources but especially because it had acquired technological and administrative "know how." The heroes of American progress were inventors, like Bell, Edison, Franklin, Fulton, and Whitney, and industrialists who fashioned new social organizations for efficient mass production. Although there had grown up a myth about the inventor as a lone wolf working in his own tool shed, research was already becoming a large-scale operation—just how big may be seen in the fact that private and public expenditures for research in the United States in 1930 amounted to more than $160,000,000 and increased, even during the depression years, to nearly $350,000,000 by 1940.

Most of this research was, of course, in the natural and biological sciences and in engineering and medicine. The idea that research could be directed profitably to the solution of social problems gained acceptance much more slowly. But even in the 1930's significant resources were being allotted to the social sciences. The dramatic use of intelligence testing during World War I had stimulated research on human abilities and the application of testing procedures in school systems, industry, and government. "Scientific management," though slow to recognize the importance of social factors, was laying the groundwork for a scientific approach to the management of organizations. The belief that the solution of "social problems" could be facilitated by systematic fact-finding was gaining acceptance. Thomas and Znaniecki (45) had, by 1920, demonstrated that the difficulties accompanying the absorption of immigrants into American society could be investigated systematically; several research centers had been created to advance knowledge and to improve practice with respect to the welfare of children; by the early 1930's practices in social work and juvenile courts were being modified on the basis of findings from an impressive series of studies on juvenile gangs in Chicago that had been conducted by Thrasher (46) and Shaw (40); and, enough research had been completed on intergroup relations by 1939 so that Myrdal (31) could write a comprehensive treatment of the "Negro problem" in America. Symptomatic of the belief in the feasibility of empirical research on social problems was the establishment in 1936 of the Society for the Psychological Study of Social Issues with 333 charter members. Thus, when the rapid expansion of group dynamics began after World War II, there were important segments of American society prepared to provide financial support for such research. Support came not only from academic institutions and foundations but also from business, the Federal Government, and various organizations concerned with improving human relations.

DEVELOPED PROFESSIONS

The attempt to formulate a coherent view of the nature of group life may be motivated by intellectual curiosity or by the desire to improve social practice. A study of the conditions

bringing the field of group dynamics into existence reveals that both of these motivations played an important role. Interest in groups and a recognition of their importance in society were apparent early among social scientists, who according to a common stereotype are motivated by idle curiosity. But it should be also noted that some of the most influential early systematic writing about the nature of groups came from the pens of people working in the professions, people whose motivation has often been said to be purely practical. Before considering the social scientific background of group dynamics, we will describe briefly some of the developments within the professions that facilitated its rise.

By the 1930's a large number of distinct professions had come into existence in the United States, probably more than in any other country. Many of these worked directly with groups of people, and as they became concerned with improving the quality of their practice they undertook to codify procedures and to discover general principles for dealing with groups. It gradually became evident, more quickly in some professions than in others, that generalizations from experience can go only so far and that systematic research is required to produce a deeper understanding of group life. Thus, when group dynamics began to emerge as a distinct field, the leaders of some of the professions were well prepared to foster the idea that systematic research on group life could make a significant contribution to their professions. As a result, several professions helped to create a favorable atmosphere for the financing of group dynamics research, provided from their accumulated experience a broad systematic conception of group functioning from which hypotheses for research could be drawn, afforded facilities in which research could be conducted, and furnished the beginnings of a technology for creating and manipulating variables in experimentation on groups. Four professions played an especially important part in the origin and growth of group dynamics.

Social Group Work. This profession should be mentioned first because it was one of the earliest to recognize explicitly that groups can be managed so as to bring about desired changes in members. Being responsible for the operation of clubs, recreational groups, camps, and athletic teams, group workers came to realize that their techniques of dealing with groups had important effects on group processes and on the behaviors, attitudes, and personalities of those participating in these groups. Although the objective of group work included such diverse purposes as "character building," "providing constructive recreation," "keeping the kids off the street and out of trouble," and, later, "psychotherapy," it gradually became evident that, whatever the objective, some techniques of group management were more successful than others. One of the earliest experimental studies of groups concerned the effects of several leadership practices on the adjustment of boys in their summer camp cabins (33). The wealth of experience acquired by group workers has been systematized by Busch (9), Coyle (11), and Wilson and Ryland (54). Group dynamics drew heavily on this experience at the outset, and group dynamicists have continued to collaborate with group workers on various research projects.

Group Psychotherapy. Although group psychotherapy is commonly considered a branch of psychiatry, the use of groups for psychotherapeutic purposes has grown up in other than strictly medical settings, the Alcoholics Anonymous movement being one outstanding example. In the development of a professional approach to psychotherapeutic work with groups, psychoanalytic theory has exerted the major, though not exclusive, influence. Freud's writing (especially his *Group Psychology and the Analysis of the Ego*) has set the tone, but many of the techniques for dealing with groups and much of the emphasis upon group processes have been contributed by people drawing from the field of group work—see, for example, the writings of Redl (37), Scheidlinger (39), and Slavson (43). A rather different tradition, although strongly psychoanalytic in its orientation, has grown up in England under the influence of Bion (7) and a group of people associated with the Tavistock Institute of Human Relations (53). An important feature of this approach is the application of psychoanalytic group work to "natural" groups in the military establishment, industry, and the community. Still another approach in group psychotherapy was established by the unusually creative and pioneering work of Moreno (30). His techniques of role-playing (more precisely, psychodrama and

sociodrama) and sociometry were among the earliest contributions to the field and have been of great value both in group psychotherapy and in research on group dynamics. Although many of the developments in group psychotherapy and in group dynamics have been simultaneous, the early work in group psychotherapy had a clear and distinct influence on the initial work in group dynamics. And the two lines of endeavor have continued to influence each other, as can be seen, for example, in the systematic treatment of group psychotherapy by Bach (3).

Education. The revolution in American public education that occurred in the first quarter of this century, influenced strongly by the writings of Dewey, broadened the conception of both the purposes and the procedures of education. The goal of education in the public schools became the preparation of children for life in society rather than merely the transmission of knowledge. "Learning by doing" became a popular slogan and was implemented by such things as group projects, extracurricular activities, and student government. Teachers became interested in instilling skills of leadership, cooperation, responsible membership, and human relations. It gradually became apparent that teachers, like group workers, were having to take actions affecting the course of events in children's groups and needed principles to guide these events toward constructive ends. A similar trend was developing simultaneously in adult education, where the problems were made even more apparent by the voluntary nature of participation in adult-education programs. There began to emerge the conception of the teacher as a group leader who affects his students' learning not merely by his subject-matter competence but also by his ability to heighten motivation, stimulate participation, and generate morale. Although controversy over this general approach to education has persisted up to the present time, the education profession had, by the late 1930's, accumulated a considerable fund of knowledge about group life. Group dynamics drew upon this experience in formulating hypotheses for research, and group dynamicists established close working relations with educators and schools of education. Both educational practice and research in group dynamics have benefited from this association.

Administration. Under this label is a whole cluster of specialties, all concerned with the management of large organizations. Included are such specific professions as business administration, public administration, hospital administration, and educational administration. Although each of these must develop expertise in its particular sphere of operation, all share the necessity of designing effective procedures for coordinating the behavior of people. For this reason, they share a common interest in the findings of social science. It might be expected, therefore, that systematic treatments of management would early come to a recognition of the importance of groups in large enterprises and that management practices for dealing with groups would become highly developed. Actually, the historical facts are rather different. Until the 1930's efforts to develop principles of management were remarkably blind to the existence of groups. One noteworthy exception is found in the writings of Mary P. Follett (13, 14), who after World War I attempted to construct a systematic approach to administration, and more generally to government, in which groups were recognized as important elements. Her ideas, however, gained little acceptance.

In fact, the individualistic orientation held sway until about 1933 when the first of several books by Mayo and his associates (27, 38) made its appearance. These publications reported an extensive program of research begun in 1927 at the Hawthorne plant of the Western Electric Company. The initial objective of this research was to study the relation between conditions of work and the incidence of fatigue among workers. A variety of experimental variations was introduced—frequency of rest pauses, length of working hours, nature of wage incentives—with the intention of discovering their influence on fatigue and productivity. It is to the great credit of these investigators that they were alert to the existence of effects not anticipated, for the important changes actually produced by their experiments turned out to be in interpersonal relations among workers and between workers and management. The results of this program of research led Mayo and his associates to place major emphasis on the social organization of the work group, on the social relations between the supervisor and his subordinates, on informal standards governing the behavior of members of the work group, and on the attitudes and motives of workers existing in a group context.

The impact of this research upon all branches of administration can hardly be exaggerated. Haire has described it in the following way (17, 376):

After the publication of these researches, thinking about industrial problems was radically and irrevocably changed. It was no longer possible to see a decrement in productivity simply as a function of changes in illumination, physical fatigue, and the like. It was no longer possible to look for explanation of turnover simply in terms of an economic man maximizing dollar income. The role of the leader began to shift from one who directed work to one who enlisted co-operation. The incentive to work was no longer seen as simple and unitary but rather infinitely varied, complex, and changing. The new view opened the way for, and demanded, more research and new conceptualizations to handle the problems.

Another important contribution to this new view of management was the systematic theory of management published in 1938 by Barnard (5), which was the product of his many years of experience as a business executive. Although this book did not put primary stress on groups as such, it placed human needs and social processes in the forefront of consideration. Barnard made it clear that management practice can be satisfactorily understood and effectively fashioned only if large organizations are conceived as social institutions composed of people in social interrelations.

The emergence of group dynamics in the late 1930's came, then, at the very time when administrators and organization theorists were beginning to emphasize the importance of groups and of "human relations" in administration. In subsequent years the findings from research in group dynamics have been incorporated increasingly into systematic treatments of administration, and a growing number of administrators have supported group dynamics research in various ways.

Before leaving the discussion of the role of the professions in the origin and growth of group dynamics, we should note that the developments reported here had counterparts to varying degrees in other areas of social practice, many of which were not highly professionalized. Special mention should be made of the support that has come from those concerned with providing a scientific basis for work in intergroup relations, public health, the military, religious education, community organization, and speech.[1]

DEVELOPED SOCIAL SCIENCE

In considering the conditions that stimulated the present approach to group dynamics within the social sciences, it is essential to recognize that this approach could originate only because certain advances had been accomplished in the social sciences at large. Thus, the rise of group dynamics required not only a supportive society and developed professions but also developed social sciences.

A basic premise of group dynamics is that the methods of science can be employed in the study of groups. This assumption could be entertained seriously only after the more general belief had gained acceptance that man, his behavior, and his social relations can be properly subjected to scientific investigation. And, any question about the utilization of scientific methods for learning about human behavior and social relations could not rise, of course, before the methods of science were well developed. It was only in the nineteenth century that serious discussions of this possibility occurred. Comte's extensive treatment of positivism in 1830 provided a major advance in the self-conscious examination of basic assumptions about the possibility of subjecting human and social phenomena to scientific investigation; and the controversies over evolutionary theories of man in the last half of the century resulted in a drastically new view of the possibility of extending the scientific enterprise to human behavior. Not until the last decades of the nineteenth century were there many people actually observing, measuring, or conducting experiments on human behavior. The first psychological laboratory was established only in 1879.

[1] For example, at the time Lewin established the Research Center for Group Dynamics at M.I.T., the American Jewish Congress created a related organization known as the Commission on Community Interrelations to undertake "action research" on problems of intergroup relations. And heavy financial support for research in group dynamics has come from the National Institute of Mental Health, the United States Navy and Air Force, and several large business organizations.

One can hardly imagine how group dynamics could have come into existence before the belief had taken root that empirical research can be conducted on groups of people, that important social phenomena can be measured, that group variables can be manipulated for experimental purposes, and that laws governing group life can be discovered. These beliefs gained acceptance only in recent years, though they had been advocated now and then by writers since the seventeenth century, and they are not universally held even today. There remain those who assert that human behavior does not operate according to laws, that important social phenomena cannot be quantified, and that experimentation on groups is impossible or immoral, or even both. William H. Whyte, Jr. (**52**), in his attack on "the organization man," has spoken most eloquently for those who remain skeptical about the applicability of the methods of science to the study of man. He defines *scientism* as "the promise that with the same techniques that have worked in the physical sciences we can eventually create an exact science of man." He identifies scientism as a major component of the Social Ethic which, in his opinion, is weakening American society. And, the tragedy of scientism, he maintains, is that it is based on an illusion, for "a 'science of man' cannot work in the way its believers think it can." Were such views to prevail, group dynamics could not thrive.

The Reality of Groups. An important part of the early progress in social science consisted in clarifying certain basic assumptions about the reality of social phenomena. The first extensions of the scientific method of human behavior occurred in close proximity to biology. Techniques of experimentation and measurement were first applied to investigations of the responses of organisms to stimulation of the sense organs and to modification of responses due to repeated stimulation. There was never much doubt about the "existence" of individual organisms, but when attention turned to groups of people and to social institutions, a great confusion arose. Discussion of these matters invoked terms like "group mind," "collective representations," "collective unconscious," and "culture." And people argued heatedly as to whether such terms refer to any real phenomena or whether they are mere "abstractions" or "analogies." On the whole, the disciplines concerned with institutions (anthropology, economics, political science, and sociology) have freely attributed concrete reality to supra-individual entities, whereas psychology, with its interest in the physiological bases of behavior, has been reluctant to admit existence to anything other than the behavior of organisms. But in all these disciplines there have been conflicts between "institutionalists" and "behavioral scientists."

The sharpest cleavage occurred in the early days of social psychology, naturally enough since it is a discipline concerned directly with the relations between the individual and society. Here the great debate over the "group mind" reached its climax in the 1920's. Although many people took part, the names of William McDougall and Floyd Allport are most closely associated with this controversy. At one extreme was the position that groups, institutions, and culture have reality quite apart from the particular individuals who participate in them. It was maintained that a group may continue to exist even after there has been a complete turnover of membership, that it has properties, such as a division of labor, a system of values, and a role structure, that cannot be conceived as properties of individuals, and that laws governing these group-level properties must be stated at the group level. A slogan reflecting this approach is the statement, attributed to Durkheim, that "every time a social phenomenon is directly explained by a psychological phenomenon, we may be sure that the explanation is false." In strong reaction to all this was the view, advanced most effectively by Allport, that only individuals are real and that groups or institutions are "sets of ideals, thoughts, and habits repeated in each individual mind and existing only in those minds" (**1**, 9). Groups, then, are abstractions from collections of individual organisms. "Group mind" refers to nothing but similarities among individual minds, and individuals cannot be parts of groups, for groups exist only in the minds of men.

It may appear strange that social scientists should get involved in philosophical considerations about the nature of reality. As a matter of fact, however, the social scientist's view of reality makes a great deal of difference to his scientific behavior. In the first place, it determines what things he is prepared to subject to empirical investigation. Lewin pointed out this fact succinctly in the following statement (**22**, 190):

Labeling something as "nonexistent" is equivalent to declaring it "out of bounds" for the scientist. Attributing "existence" to an item automatically makes it a duty of the scientist to consider this item as an object of research; it includes the necessity of considering its properties as "facts" which cannot be neglected in the total system of theories; finally, it implies that the terms with which one refers to the item are acceptable as scientific "concepts" (rather than as "mere words").

Secondly, the history of science shows a close interaction between the techniques of research which at any time are available and the prevailing assumptions about reality. Insistence on the existence of phenomena that cannot at that time be objectively observed, measured, or experimentally manipulated accomplishes little of scientific value if it does not lead to the invention of appropriate techniques of empirical research. As a practical matter, the scientist is justified in excluding from consideration allegedly real entities whose empirical investigation appears impossible. And yet, as soon as a new technique makes it possible to treat empirically some new entity, this entity immediately acquires "reality" for the scientist. As Lewin noted (**22**, 193), "The taboo against believing in the existence of a social entity is probably most effectively broken by handling this entity experimentally."

The history of the "group mind" controversy well illustrates these points. The early insistence on the reality of the "group mind," before techniques for investigating such phenomena were developed, contributed little to their scientific study. Allport's denial of the reality of the group actually had a strongly liberating influence on social psychologists, for he was saying, in effect, "Let us not be immobilized by insisting on the reality of things which we cannot now deal with by means of existing techniques of research." He, and like-minded psychologists, were then able to embark upon a remarkably fruitful program of research on the attitudes of individuals toward institutions and on the behavior of individuals in social settings. Although this view of reality was too limited to encourage the empirical study of properties of groups, it did stimulate the development of research techniques that subsequently made a broader view of reality scientifically feasible. Until these techniques were in existence those who persisted in attributing reality to groups and institutions were forced to rely on purely descriptive studies or armchair speculation from personal experience, and such work was legitimately criticized as being "subjective" since the objective techniques of science were rarely applied to such phenomena.

Development of Techniques of Research. Of extreme importance for the origin of group dynamics, then, was the shaping of research techniques that could be extended to research on groups. This process, of course, took time. It began in the last half of the nineteenth century with the rise of experimental psychology. Over the subsequent years more and more aspects of human experience and behavior were subjected to techniques of measurement and experimentation. Thus, for example, during the first third of this century impressive gains were made in the measurement of attitudes. Noteworthy among these were the scale of "social distance" developed by Bogardus (8), the comprehensive treatment of problems of scaling by Thurstone (47) and Thurstone and Chave (48), and the much simpler scaling technique of Likert (24). Parallel to these developments, and interacting with them, were major advances in statistics. By the late 1930's powerful statistical methods had been fashioned, which made possible efficient experimental designs and the evaluation of the significance of quantitative findings. These advances were important, of course, not only for the rise of group dynamics but for progress in all the behavioral sciences.

Within this general development we may note three methodological gains contributing specifically to the rise of group dynamics.

1. Experiments on individual behavior in groups. As noted above, research in group dynamics is deeply indebted to experimental psychology for the invention of techniques for conducting experiments on the conditions affecting human behavior. But experimental psychology did not concern itself, at first, with social variables; it was only toward the beginning of the present century that a few investigators embarked upon experimental research designed to investigate the effects of social variables upon the behavior of individuals. The nature of this early experimental social psychology has been described by G. W. Allport this way (2, 46):

The first experimental problem—indeed the only problem for the first three decades of experimental research—was formulated as follows: *What change in an individual's normal solitary performance occurs when other people are present?*

And, according to Allport, the first laboratory answer to this question came from Triplett (49), who compared the performance of children in winding fishing reels when working alone and when working together with other children. Triplett concluded from this experiment that the group situation tended to generate an increase in output of energy and achievement.

Of greater significance for the development of experimental social psychology was the work of Moede (28), begun at Leipzig in 1913, in which he undertook a systematic investigation of the effects of having several people take part simultaneously in a variety of the then standard psychological experiments. This work was influential in the development of social psychology primarily because Münsterberg called it to the attention of F. H. Allport and encouraged him to repeat and extend it. Allport (1) not only conducted several impressive experiments but also provided a theoretical framework for interpreting the findings. By 1935 Dashiell (12) was able to write a long summary of the work comparing behavior elicited when the subject was working in isolation and in the presence of others. Another important study of this era was that conducted by Moore (29) in which he experimentally demonstrated the influence of "expert" and "majority" opinion upon the moral and aesthetic judgments of individuals. These early experiments not only demonstrated the feasibility of conducting experiments on the influence of groups upon individual behavior; they also developed techniques that are still in use.

A somewhat different but closely related line of research attempted to compare the performance of individuals and of groups. In these studies, as illustrated by the work of Gordon (16), Watson (50), and Shaw (41), tasks were employed that could be performed either by individuals or by groups of people, and the question was asked whether individuals or groups did the better job. As it turned out, this question is unanswerable unless the conditions are further specified, but much was learned in seeking an answer.

All this work made it much more likely that such a field as group dynamics could develop by bringing groups into the laboratory. Although these early experiments did not, strictly speaking, deal with properties of groups, they made it evident that the influence of groups upon individuals could be studied experimentally, and they made it much easier to conceive of the idea of varying group properties experimentally in the laboratory.

2. Controlled observation of social interaction. One might think that the most obvious device for learning about the nature of group functioning would be simply to watch groups in action. Indeed, this procedure has been employed by chroniclers and reporters throughout history and has continued to be a source of data, perhaps most impressively as employed by social anthropologists in their reports of the behavior, culture, and social structure of primitive societies. The major drawback of the procedure as a scientific technique is that the reports given by observers (the scientific data) depend to such a high degree upon the skill, sensitivity, and interpretive predilections of the observer. The first serious attempts to refine methods of observation, so that objective and quantitative data might be obtained, occurred around 1930 in the field of child psychology. A great amount of effort went into the construction of categories of observation that would permit an observer simply to indicate the presence or absence of a particular kind of behavior or social interaction during the period of observation. Typically, reliability was heightened by restricting observation to rather overt interactions whose "meaning" could be revealed in a short span of time and whose classification required little interpretation by the observer. Methods were also developed for sampling the interactions of a large group of people over a long time so that efficient estimates of the total interaction could be made on the basis of more limited observations. By use of such procedures and by careful training of observers quantitative

data of high reliability were obtained. The principal researchers responsible for these important advances were Goodenough (15), Jack (19), Olson (34), Parten (35), and Thomas (44).

3. Sociometry. A somewhat different approach to the study of groups is to ask questions of the members. Data obtained in this manner can, of course, reflect only those things the individual is able, and willing, to report. Nevertheless, such subjective reports from the members of a group might be expected to add valuable information to the more objective observations of behavior. Of the many devices for obtaining information from group members one of the earliest and most commonly used is the sociometric test, which was invented by Moreno (30). During World War I, Moreno had administrative responsibility for a camp of Tyrolese displaced persons, and he observed that the adjustment of people seemed to be better when they were allowed to form their own groups within the camp. Later, in the United States, he undertook to check this insight by more systematic research on groups of people in such institutions as schools and reformatories. For this purpose he constructed a simple questionnaire on which each person was to indicate those other people with whom he would prefer to share some specified activity. It quickly became apparent that this device, and modifications of it, could provide valuable information about interpersonal attractions and repulsions among any collection of people. The data concerning "who chooses whom" could be converted into a "sociogram," or a picture in which individuals are represented by circles and choices by lines. Inspection of such sociograms revealed that some groups were more tightly knit than others, that individuals varied greatly in their social expansiveness and in the number of choices they received, and that cliques formed on the basis of characteristics such as age, sex, and race. In short, the sociometric test promised to yield valuable information about both individuals and interpersonal relations in groups. Although based essentially on subjective reports of individuals, the sociometric test provides quantifiable data about patterns of attractions and repulsions existing in a group. The publication by Moreno (30) in 1934 of a major book based on experience with the test and the establishment in 1937 of a journal, *Sociometry*, ushered in a prodigious

amount of research employing the sociometric test and numerous variations of it.

The significance of sociometry for group dynamics lay both in the provision of a useful technique for research on groups and in the attention it directed to such features of groups as social position, patterns of friendship, subgroup formation, and, more generally, informal structure.

BEGINNINGS OF GROUP DYNAMICS

By the mid-1930's conditions were ripe within the social sciences for a rapid advance in empirical research on groups. And, in fact, a great burst of such activity did take place in America just prior to the entry of the United States into World War II. This research, moreover, began to display quite clearly the characteristics that are now associated with work in group dynamics. Within a period of approximately five years several important research projects were undertaken, more or less independently of one another but all sharing these distinctive features. We now briefly consider four of the more influential of these.

EXPERIMENTAL CREATION OF SOCIAL NORMS

In 1936 Sherif (**42**) published a book containing a systematic theoretical analysis of the concept *social norm* and an ingenious experimental investigation of the origin of social norms among groups of people. Probably the most important feature of this book was its bringing together of ideas and observations from sociology and anthropology and techniques of laboratory experimentation from experimental psychology. Sherif began by accepting the existence of customs, traditions, standards, rules, values, fashions, and other criteria of conduct (which he subsumed under the general label, social norm). Further, he agreed with Durkheim that such "collective representations" have, from the point of view of the individual, the properties of exteriority and constraint. At the same time, however, he agreed with F. H. Allport that social norms have been too often treated as something mystical and that scientific progress can be achieved only by subjecting phenomena to acceptable techniques of empirical research. He proposed that social norms should be viewed

simultaneously in two ways: (*a*) as the product of social interaction and (*b*) as social stimuli which impinge upon any given individual who is a member of a group having these norms. Conceived in this way, it would be possible to study experimentally the origin of social norms and their influence on individuals.

In formulating his research problem, Sherif drew heavily upon the findings of Gestalt psychology in the field of perception. He noted that this work had established that there need not necessarily be a fixed point-to-point correlation between the physical stimulus and the experience and behavior it arouses. The frame of reference a person brings to a situation influences in no small way how he sees that situation. Sherif proposed that psychologically a social norm functions as such a frame of reference. Thus, if two people with different norms face the same situation (for example, a Mohammedan and a Christian confront a meal of pork chops), they will see it and react to it in widely different ways. For each, however, the norm serves to give meaning and to provide a stable way of reacting to the environment.

Having thus related social norms to the psychology of perception, Sherif proceeded to ask how norms arise. It occurred to him that he might gain insight into this problem by placing people in a situation that had no clear structure and in which they would not be able to bring to bear any previously acquired frame of reference or social norm. Sherif stated the general objective of his research as follows (**42**, 90–91):

. . . What will an individual do when he is placed in an objectively unstable situation in which all basis of comparison, as far as the external field of stimulation is concerned, is absent? In other words, what will he do when the external frame of reference is eliminated, in so far as the aspect in which we are interested is concerned? Will he give a hodgepodge of erratic judgments? Or will he establish a point of reference of his own? *Consistent* results in this situation may be taken as the index of a subjectively evolved frame of reference. . . .

Coming to the social level we can push our problem further. What will a group of people do in the same unstable situation? Will the different individuals in the group give a hodgepodge of judgments? Or will there be established a common norm peculiar to the particular group situation and depending upon the presence of these individuals together and their influence upon one another? If they in time come to perceive the uncertain and unstable situation which they face in common in such a way as to give it some sort of order, perceiving it as ordered by a frame of reference developed among them in the course of the experiment, and if this frame of reference is peculiar to the group, then we may say that we have at least the prototype of the psychological process involved in the formation of a norm in a group.

In order to subject these questions to experimental investigation, Sherif made use of what is known in psychology as the autokinetic effect. It had previously been shown in perceptual research that if a subject looks at a stationary point of light in an otherwise dark room he will soon see it as moving. Furthermore, there are considerable individual differences in the extent of perceived motion. Sherif's experiment consisted of placing subjects individually in the darkened room and getting judgments of the extent of apparent motion. He found that upon repeated test the subject establishes a range within which his judgments fall and that this range is peculiar to each individual. Sherif then repeated the experiment, but this time having groups of subjects observe the light and report aloud their judgments. Now he found that the individual ranges of judgment converged to a group range that was peculiar to the group. In additional variations Sherif was able to show that (**42**, 104).

When the individual, in whom a range and a norm within that range are first developed in the individual situation, is put into a group situation, together with other individuals who also come into the situation with their own ranges and norms established in their own individual sessions, the ranges and norms tend to converge.

Moreover, "when a member of a group faces the same situation subsequently *alone*, after once the range and norm of his group have been established, he perceives the situation in terms of the range and norm that he brings from the group situation" (**42**, 105).

Sherif's study did much to establish the feasibility of subjecting group phenomena to experimental investigation. It should be noted that he did not choose to study social norms

existing in any natural group. Instead, he formed new groups in the laboratory and observed the development of an entirely new social norm. Although Sherif's experimental situation might seem artificial, and even trivial, to the anthropologist or sociologist, this very artificiality gave the findings a generality not ordinarily achieved by naturalistic research. By subjecting a group-level concept, like social norm, to psychological analysis, Sherif helped obliterate what he considered to be the unfortunate categorical separation of individual and group. And his research helped establish among psychologists the view that certain properties of groups have reality, for, as he concluded, "the fact that the norm thus established is peculiar to the group suggests that there is a factual psychological basis in the contentions of social psychologists and sociologists who maintain that new and supra-individual qualities arise in the group situations" (**42**, 105).

SOCIAL ANCHORAGE
OF ATTITUDES

During the years 1935–39, Newcomb (**32**) was conducting an intensive investigation of the same general kind of problem that interested Sherif but with quite different methods. Newcomb selected a "natural" rather than a "laboratory" setting in which to study the operation of social norms and social influence processes, and he relied primarily upon techniques of attitude measurement, sociometry, and interviewing to obtain his data. Bennington College was the site of his study, the entire student body were his subjects, and attitudes toward political affairs provided the content of the social norms.

It was first established that the prevailing political atmosphere of the campus was "liberal" and that entering students, who came predominantly from "conservative" homes, brought with them attitudes that deviated from the college culture. The power of the college community to change attitudes of students was demonstrated by the fact that each year senior students were more liberal than freshmen. The most significant feature of this study, however, was its careful documentation of the ways in which these influences operated. Newcomb showed, for example, how the community "rewarded" students for adopting the approved attitudes. Thus, a sociometric-like test, in which students chose those "most worthy to represent the College at an intercollegiate gathering," revealed that the students thus chosen in each class were distinctly less conservative than those not so chosen. And, those students enjoying a reputation for having a close identification with the college, for being "good citizens," were also relatively more liberal in their political attitudes. By means of several ingenious devices Newcomb was able to discover the student's "subjective role," or self-view of his own relationship to the student community. Analysis of these data revealed several different ways in which students accommodated to the social pressures of the community. Of particular interest in this analysis was the evidence of conflicting group loyalties between membership in the college community and membership in the family group and some of the conditions determining the relative influence of each.

Newcomb's study showed that the attitudes of individuals are strongly rooted in the groups to which people belong, that the influence of a group upon an individual's attitudes depends upon the nature of the relationship between the individual and the group, and that groups evaluate members, partially at least, on the basis of their conformity to group norms. Although most of these points had been made in one form or another by writers in the speculative era of social science, this study was especially significant because it provided detailed, objective, and quantitative evidence. It thereby demonstrated, as Sherif's study did in a different way, the feasibility of conducting scientific research on important features of group life.

GROUPS IN STREET CORNER SOCIETY

The sociological and anthropological background of group dynamics is most apparent in the third important study of this era. In 1937 W. F. Whyte moved into one of the slums of Boston to begin a three and one-half year study of social clubs, political organizations, and racketeering. His method was that of "the participant observer," which had been most highly developed in anthropological research. More specifically, he drew upon the experience of Warner and Arensberg which was derived from the "Yankee City" studies. In various ways he gained admittance to the so-

cial and political life of the community and faithfully kept notes of the various happenings that he observed or heard about. In the resulting book, Whyte (51) reported in vivid detail on the structure, culture, and functioning of the Norton Street gang and the Italian Community Club. The importance of these social groups in the life of their members and in the political structure of the larger society was extensively documented.

In the interpretation and systematization of his findings, Whyte was greatly influenced by the "interactionist" point of view that was then being developed by Arensberg and Chapple, and that was subsequently presented by such writers as Chapple (10), Bales (4), and Homans (18). The orientation derived by Mayo and his colleagues from the Western Electric studies is also evident in Whyte's analysis of his data. Although he made no effort to quantify the interactions he observed, Whyte's great care for detail lent a strong flavor of objectivity to his account of the interactions among the people he observed. His "higher order" concepts, like social structure, cohesion, leadership, and status, were clearly related to the more directly observable interactions among people, thus giving them a close tie with empirical reality.

The major importance of this study for subsequent work in group dynamics was threefold: (a) It dramatized, and described in painstaking detail, the great significance of groups in the lives of individuals and in the functioning of larger social systems. (b) It gave impetus to the interpretation of group properties and processes in terms of interactions among individuals. (c) It generated a number of hypotheses concerning the relations among such variables as initiation of interaction, leadership, status, mutual obligations, and group cohesion. These hypotheses have served to guide much of Whyte's later work on groups as well as the research of many others.

EXPERIMENTAL MANIPULATION OF GROUP ATMOSPHERE

By far the most influential work in the emerging study of group dynamics was that of Lewin, Lippitt, and White (23, 25, Chap. 25). Conducted at the Iowa Child Welfare Research Station between 1937 and 1940, these investigations of group atmosphere and styles of leadership accomplished a creative synthesis of the various trends and developments considered above. In describing the background of this research, Lippitt noted that the issue of what constitutes "good" leadership had come to the fore in the professions of social group work, education, and administration, and he observed that, with the exception of the Western Electric studies, remarkably little research had been conducted to help guide practice in these professions. In setting up his theoretical problem, he drew explicitly on the previous work in social, clinical, and child psychology, sociology, cultural anthropology, and political science. And in designing his research, he made use, with important modifications, of the available techniques of experimental psychology, controlled observation, and sociometry. This work, then, relied heavily upon previous advances in social science and the professions, but it had an originality and significance which immediately produced a marked impact on all these fields.

The basic objective of this research was to study the influences upon the group as a whole and upon individual members of certain experimentally induced "group atmospheres," or "styles of leadership." Groups of ten- and eleven-year-old children were formed to meet regularly over a period of several weeks under the leadership of an adult, who induced the different group atmospheres. In creating these groups care was taken to assure their initial comparability; by utilizing the sociometric test, playground observations, and teacher interviews, the structural properties of the various groups were made as similar as possible; on the basis of school records and interviews with the children, the backgrounds and individual characteristics of the members were equated for all the groups; and the same group activities and physical setting were employed in every group.

The experimental manipulation consisted of having the adult leaders behave in a prescribed fashion in each experimental treatment, and in order to rule out the differential effects of the personalities of the leaders, each one led a group under each of the experimental conditions. Three types of leadership, or group atmosphere, were investigated: democratic, autocratic, and laissez faire.

In the light of present-day knowledge it is clear that a considerable number of separable variables were combined within each style of leadership. Perhaps for this very reason, however, the effects produced in the behavior of the group members were large and dramatic. For example, rather severe forms of scapegoating occurred in the autocratic groups, and at the end of the experiment the children in some of the autocratic groups proceeded to destroy the things they had constructed. Each group, moreover, developed a characteristic level of aggressiveness, and it was demonstrated that when individual members were transferred from one group to another their aggressiveness changed to approach the new group level. An interesting insight into the dynamics of aggression was provided by the rather violent emotional "explosion" which took place when some of the groups that had reacted submissively to autocratic leadership were given a new, more permissive leader.

As might be expected from the fact that this research was both original and concerned with emotionally loaded matters of political ideology, it was immediately subjected to criticism, both justified and unjustified. But the major effect on the social sciences and relevant professions was to open up new vistas and to raise the level of aspiration. The creation of "miniature political systems" in the laboratory and the demonstration of their power to influence the behavior and social relations of people made it clear that practical problems of group management could be subjected to the experimental method and that social scientists could employ the methods of science to solve problems of vital significance to society.

Of major importance for subsequent research in group dynamics was the way in which Lewin formulated the essential purpose of these experiments. The problem of leadership was chosen for investigation, in part, because of its practical importance in education, social group work, administration, and political affairs. Nevertheless, in creating the different types of leadership in the laboratory the intention was not to mirror or to simulate any "pure types" that might exist in society. The purpose was rather to lay bare some of the more important ways in which leader behavior may vary and to discover how various styles of leadership influence the properties of groups and the behavior of members. As Lewin put it (21, 74), the purpose "was not to duplicate any given autocracy or democracy or to study an 'ideal' autocracy or democracy, but to create set-ups which would give insight into the underlying group dynamics." This statement, published in 1939, appears to be the earliest use by Lewin of the phrase group dynamics.

It is important to note rather carefully how Lewin generalized the research problem. He might have viewed this research primarily as a contribution to the technology of group management in social work or education. Or he might have placed it in the context of research on leadership. Actually, however, he stated the problem in a most abstract way as one of learning about the underlying dynamics of group life. He believed that it was possible to construct a coherent body of empirical knowledge about the nature of group life that would be meaningful when specified for any particular kind of group. Thus, he envisioned a general theory of groups that could be brought to bear on such apparently diverse matters as family life, work groups, classrooms, committees, military units, and the community. Furthermore, he saw such specific problems as leadership, status, communication, social norms, group atmosphere, and intergroup rela-

tions as part of the general problem of understanding the nature of group dynamics. Almost immediately, Lewin and those associated with him began various research projects designed to contribute information relevant to a general theory of group dynamics. Thus, French conducted a laboratory experiment designed to compare the effects of fear and frustration on organized versus unorganized groups. Bavelas (6) undertook an experiment to determine whether the actual behavior of leaders of youth groups could be significantly modified through training. Later, Bavelas suggested to Lewin the cluster of ideas that became known as "group decision." With America's entry into the war, he and French, in association with Marrow (26), explored group decision and related techniques as a means of improving industrial production; and Margaret Mead interested Lewin in studying problems related to wartime food shortages, with the result that Radke together with others (20, 36) conducted experiments on group decision as a means of changing food habits.

SUMMARY

Group dynamics is a field of inquiry dedicated to advancing knowledge about the nature of groups, the laws of their development, and their interrelations with individuals, other groups, and larger institutions. It may be identified by its reliance upon empirical research for obtaining data of theoretical significance, its emphasis in research and theory upon the dynamic aspects of group life, its broad relevance to all the social sciences, and the potential applicability of its findings to the improvement of social practice.

It became an identifiable field toward the end of the 1930's in the United States and has experienced a rapid growth since that time. Its rise was fostered by certain conditions that were particularly favorable in the United States just prior to World War II. These same conditions have facilitated its growth here and in certain other countries since that time. Of particular importance among these has been the acceptance by significant segments of society of the belief that research on groups is feasible and ultimately useful. This belief was initially encouraged by a strong interest in groups among such professions as social group work, group psychotherapy, education, and administration. It was made feasible because the social sciences had attained sufficient progress, by clarifying basic assumptions about the reality of groups and by designing research techniques for the study of groups, to permit empirical research on the functioning of groups.

By the end of the 1930's several trends converged with the result that a new field of group dynamics began to take shape. The practical and theoretical importance of groups was by then documented empirically. The feasibility of conducting objective and quantitative research on the dynamics of group life was no longer debatable. And the reality of groups had been removed from the realm of mysticism and placed squarely within the domain of empirical social science. Group norms could be objectively measured, even created experimentally in the laboratory, and some of the processes by which they influence the behavior and attitudes of individuals had been determined.

The dependence of certain emotional states of individuals upon the prevailing group atmosphere had been established. And different styles of leadership had been created experimentally and shown to produce marked consequences on the functioning of groups. After the interruption imposed by World War II, rapid advances were made in constructing a systematic, and empirically based, body of knowledge concerning the dynamics of group life.

References

1. Allport, F. H. *Social psychology*. Boston: Houghton Mifflin, 1924.
2. Allport, G. W. The historical background of modern social psychology. In G. Lindzey (Ed.), *Handbook of social psychology*. Cambridge, Mass.: Addison-Wesley, 1954. Pp. 3–56.
3. Bach, G. R. *Intensive group psychotherapy*. New York: Ronald Press, 1954.
4. Bales, R. F. *Interaction process analysis*. Cambridge, Mass.: Addison-Wesley, 1950.
5. Barnard, C. I. *The functions of the executive*. Cambridge, Mass.: Harvard Univ. Press, 1938.
6. Bavelas, A. Morale and training of leaders. In G. Watson (Ed.), *Civilian morale*, Boston: Houghton Mifflin, 1942.
7. Bion, W. R. Experiences in groups, I–VI. *Human Relations*, 1948–1950, **1**, 314–320, 487–496; **2**, 13–22, 295–303; **3**, 3–14, 395–402.
8. Bogardus, E. S. Measuring social distance. *Journal of Applied Sociology*, 1925, **9**, 299–308.
9. Busch, H. M. *Leadership in group work*. New York: Association Press, 1934.
10. Chapple, E. D. Measuring human relations: An introduction to the study of interaction of individuals, *Genetic Psychology Monographs*, 1940, **22**, 3–147.
11. Coyle, G. L. *Social process in organized groups*. New York: Rinehart, 1930.
12. Dashiell, J. F. Experimental studies of the influence of social situations on the behavior of individual human adults. In C. C. Murchison (Ed.), *Handbook of social psychology*, Worcester, Mass.: Clark Univ. Press, 1935. Pp. 1097–1158.
13. Follett, M. P. *The new state, group organization the solution of popular government*. New York: Longmans, Green, 1918.
14. Follett, M. P. *Creative experience*. New York: Longmans, Green, 1924.
15. Goodenough, F. L. Measuring behavior traits by means of repeated short samples. *Journal of Juvenile Research*, 1928, **12**, 230–235.
16. Gordon, K. Group judgments in the field of lifted weights. *Journal of Experimental Psychology*, 1924, **7**, 398–400.
17. Haire, M. Group dynamics in the industrial situation. In A. Kornhauser, R. Dubin, & A. M. Ross (Eds.), *Industrial conflict*. New York: McGraw-Hill, 1954. Pp. 373–385.
18. Homans, G. C. *The human group*. New York: Harcourt, Brace, 1950.
19. Jack, L. M. An experimental study of ascendent behavior in preschool children. *Univ. of Iowa Studies in Child Welfare*, 1934, **9** (3).
20. Lewin, K. Forces behind food habits and methods of change. *Bulletin of the National Research Council*, 1943, **108**, 35–65.
21. Lewin, K. *Resolving social conflicts*. New York: Harper, 1948.
22. Lewin, K. *Field theory in social science*. New York: Harper, 1951.
23. Lewin, K., Lippitt, R., & White, R. Patterns of aggressive behavior in experimentally created "social climates." *Journal of Social Psychology*, 1939, **10**, 271–299.
24. Likert, R. A technique for the measurement of attitudes. *Archives of Psychology*, 1932, No. 140.
25. Lippitt, R. An experimental study of authoritarian and democratic group atmospheres. *Univ. of Iowa Studies in Child Welfare*, 1940, **16** (3), 43–195.
26. Marrow, A. J. *Making management human*. New York: McGraw-Hill, 1957.
27. Mayo, E. *The human problems of an industrial civilization*. New York: Macmillan, 1933.
28. Moede, W. *Experimentelle massenpsychologie*. Leipzig: S. Hirzel, 1920.
29. Moore, H. T. The comparative influence of majority and expert opinion. *American Journal of Psychology*, 1921, **32**, 16–20.

30. Moreno, J. L. *Who shall survive?* Washington, D. C.: Nervous and Mental Diseases Publishing Co., 1934.

31. Myrdal, G. *An American dilemma.* New York: Harper, 1944.

32. Newcomb, T. M. *Personality and social change.* New York: Dryden, 1943.

33. Newstetter, W., Feldstein, M., & Newcomb, T. M. *Group adjustment, a study in experimental sociology.* Cleveland: Western Reserve Univ., School of Applied Social Sciences, 1938.

34. Olson, W. C., & Cunningham, E. M. Time-sampling techniques. *Child Development,* 1934, **5,** 41–58.

35. Parten, M. B. Social participation among preschool children. *Journal of Abnormal and Social Psychology,* 1932, **27,** 243–269.

36. Radke, M., & Klisurich, D. Experiments in changing food habits. *Journal of the American Dietetics Association,* 1947, **23,** 403–409.

37. Redl, F., & Wineman, D. *Children who hate.* Glencoe, Ill.: Free Press, 1951.

38. Roethlisberger, F. J., & Dickson, W. J. *Management and the worker.* Cambridge, Mass.: Harvard Univ. Press, 1939.

39. Scheidlinger, S. *Psychoanalysis and group behavior.* New York: Norton, 1952.

40. Shaw, C. R. *The jack roller.* Chicago: Univ. of Chicago Press, 1939.

41. Shaw, M. E. A comparison of individuals and small groups in the rational solution of complex problems. *American Journal of Psychology,* 1932, **44,** 491–504.

42. Sherif, M. *The psychology of social norms.* New York: Harper, 1936.

43. Slavson, S. R. *Analytic group psychotherapy.* New York: Columbia Univ. Press, 1950.

44. Thomas, D. S. An attempt to develop precise measurement in the social behavior field. *Sociologus,* 1933, **9,** 1–21.

45. Thomas, W. I., & Znaniecki, F. *The Polish peasant in Europe and America.* Boston: Badger, 1918.

46. Thrasher, F. *The gang.* Chicago: Univ. of Chicago Press, 1927.

47. Thurstone, L. L. Attitudes can be measured. *American Journal of Sociology,* 1928, **33,** 529–554.

48. Thurstone, L. L., & Chave, E. J. *The measurement of attitude.* Chicago: Univ. of Chicago Press, 1929.

49. Triplett, N. The dynamogenic factors in pacemaking and competition. *American Journal of Psychology,* 1897, **9,** 507–533.

50. Watson, G. B. Do groups think more effectively than individuals? *Journal of Abnormal and Social Psychology,* 1928, **23,** 328–336.

51. Whyte, W. F., Jr. *Street corner society.* Chicago: Univ. of Chicago Press, 1943.

52. Whyte, W. H., Jr. *The organization man.* New York: Simon and Schuster, 1956.

53. Wilson, A. T. M. Some aspects of social process. *Journal of Social Issues,* 1951 (Suppl. Series 5).

54. Wilson, G., & Ryland, G. *Social group work practice.* Boston: Houghton Mifflin, 1949.

2

Issues and Basic Assumptions

An adequate understanding of the work in group dynamics requires viewing it in broad perspective. Three facts especially should be kept in mind. First, group dynamics became a specialized field of inquiry only in recent years. Its history is brief, and although its growth has been rapid, it has not yet reached full maturity. Second, group dynamics is concerned with intellectual problems that have puzzled man from earliest history. Contemporary discussions of group dynamics tend to invoke, consciously or unconsciously, one or another of the classic solutions to such problems. They are, moreover, the stuff of which social and political ideologies are made, and few people react to them with indifference. Third, group dynamics has roots in a wide range of traditionally separated fields. Contributions to the literature of group dynamics come from people with remarkably different backgrounds and training. Each author brings with him certain values which color his attitude toward groups, certain conceptions about which variables are the most important, certain beliefs about appropriate methods of research, and a particular vocabulary for describing groups and explaining why things happen as they do in groups.

In view of the youthfulness of the field and its heterogeneous origins, one must be prepared to encounter in it a wide array of values, theoretical orientations, basic assumptions, concepts, and methods. In a sense, group dynamics is in its adolescence, and like many adolescents it is testing out its capacities, trying out its newly acquired skills, but primarily seeking a coherent sense of self-identity. In this chapter we shall examine some of the basic issues that group dynamicists face in their efforts to achieve a systematic body of knowledge about groups.

PRECONCEPTIONS ABOUT GROUPS

In the classic discussions of social and political philosophy there persist two opposite views of the relation of man to society. In the one, individual man is imperfect or even evil, and social organization is required to do things he cannot do alone or to control his aggressive, selfish, and exploitative tendencies. Without cooperation, social organization, and groups of various kinds, man would not survive biologically, and without group standards, social values, and laws, or other means of controlling behavior, civilization would be impossible.

According to the opposite view, man is intrinsically good in what is called his "natural" condition, and social organization of all kinds is bad. The state, organization, or group only inhibit and corrupt the individual. Groups demand blind conformity, they encourage mediocrity, they generate regressive dependency, and they cling stubbornly and irrationally to the status quo. The emotional flavor of this extreme view may be illustrated in C. G. Jung's assertion that "when a hundred clever heads join a group, one big nincompoop is the result, because every individual is trammelled by the otherness of the others" (**24**, 80).

Contemporary discussions of modern society reveal these two conflicting evaluations of man and groups. And, unfortunately, the term group dynamics has become associated in some popular writings with the first of these. For example, in his critique of "the organization man," William H. Whyte, Jr. (**44**) asserts that this odious creature has been encouraged by group dynamicists, who have deified the group. Group dynamicists believe, according to such critics, that everything should be done by and in groups: individual responsibility is always bad, man-to-man supervision is bad, and even individual therapy is bad; the only good things are committee meetings, group decisions, group therapy, group think, and togetherness. In short, the group dynamicists are said to hold the classic view that individual man is imperfect or impotent while the group is good. Although this extreme position has undoubtedly been advocated by some people calling themselves "group dynamicists," it does not reflect accurately the views of most people working in this field.

Anyone responsible for the management of group life must make some working assumptions about the values that will be gained or lost as a result of any particular kind of group activity. But it is the essence of the researcher's task to attempt to determine empirically what these effects are in actuality. The group dynamicist who is dedicated to research refuses to begin his investigations by assuming he knows the answers. He cannot, of course, avoid making basic assumptions of various

sorts in his work, but these should merely guide his research so that he can better discover the true nature of group life. The basic assumptions held by most group dynamicists may be summarized by means of the following four propositions.

1. *Groups are inevitable and ubiquitous.* This is not to say that groups must maintain the properties they display at any given time in a particular society nor that every group that now exists should perpetuate itself, but one can hardly conceive of a collection of human beings living in geographical proximity under conditions such that it would be correct to assert that no groups exist and that there is no such thing as group membership. Even the most extreme individualists, such as the Beatniks, form groups that have their own language, heroes, hangouts, and distinctive dress. In fact, it is clear to social scientists that conformity is as extreme among such groups of nonconformists as anywhere in society.

2. *Groups mobilize powerful forces that produce effects of utmost importance to individuals.* A person's very sense of identity is shaped by the groups of significance to him—his family, his church, his profession or occupation. A person's position in a group, moreover, may affect the way others behave toward him and such personal qualities as his level of aspiration and self-esteem. Group membership itself may be a prized possession or an oppressive burden; tragedies of major proportions have resulted from the exclusion of individuals from groups and from enforced membership in groups.

3. *Groups may produce both good and bad consequences.* The view that groups are completely good and the view that they are completely bad are both based on convincing evidence. The only fault with either is its one-sidedness. An exclusive focus on pathologies or on constructive features leads to a seriously distorted picture of reality.

4. *A correct understanding of group dynamics (obtainable from research) permits the possibility that desirable consequences from groups can be deliberately enhanced.* Through a knowledge of group dynamics, groups can be made to serve better ends, for knowledge gives power to modify human behavior and social institutions.

The group dynamicist, then, who starts with these assumptions agrees with the individualist that groups do exert powerful influences on people and that these influences may be harmful to individuals, to the group itself, and to society at large. But he maintains that cooperative action is essential for the attainment of important objectives and that groups can be beneficial to individuals and to society. Instead of concentrating exclusively on the restrictive and inhibiting features of groups, the group dynamicist advocates the scientific study of groups and the individual's relations to groups with the belief that a better understanding of the nature of these will make it possible to devise groups and procedures better able to attain the legitimate goals of groups, to enhance the best values of society, and to enrich the personal resources of individuals.

PROBLEMS OF BOUNDING THE FIELD

Agreement among group dynamicists concerning these basic assumptions still leaves open many questions about best ways to proceed in the conduct of research and in the organization of findings into a coherent body of knowledge. Any particular study must make specific kinds of observations, classify these in certain ways, employ a definite set of terms in describing the findings, and propose some general principles to account for the relationships among variables. The choices made among these reflect each investigator's theoretical orientation. The student of group dynamics will quickly come to see that little general agreement has yet been achieved with respect to these issues and that, in fact, group dynamics possesses, fortunately or unfortunately, a multitude of concepts, theories, and proposals for relating group dynamics theory to more general theories of human behavior.

Those who are disturbed by this sometimes bewildering variety of approaches and by the broad scope of group dynamics have urged that the field be narrowed in some way. Three major criteria for bounding the field have been advocated.

KINDS OF GROUPS

Sociologists were early concerned with the problem of classifying groups. They had hoped they could provide a way of locating any specific group under a distinct category so that generalizations about the category would apply automatically to this specific group. Over the years, many different classificatory schemes have been proposed. A common procedure has been to select a few properties and to define "types" of groups on the basis of whether these properties are present or absent. Among the properties most often employed are: size (number of members), amount of physical interaction among members, degree of intimacy, level of solidarity, locus of control of group activities, extent of formalization of rules governing relations among members, and tendency of members to react to one another as individual persons or as occupants of roles. Although it would be possible to construct a large number of types of groups by combining these properties in various ways, usually only dichotomies have resulted: formal-informal, primary-secondary, small-large, Gemeinschaft-Gesellschaft, autonomous-dependent, temporary-permanent, consensual-symbiotic. Sometimes a rather different procedure has been advocated in which groups are classified according to their objectives or social settings. Accordingly, there are said to be work groups, therapy groups, social groups, committees, clubs, gangs, teams, coordinating groups, religious groups, and the like.

The identification of group dynamics with the study of any one of these kinds of groups, or a limited number of them, would seem to us to be unfortunate. Our reluctance to restrict the field in this way does not arise from any desire to minimize the importance of such things as group size, opportunity for physical interaction, degree of intimacy, and the rest as determinants of what happens in groups. In fact, it is because of the importance of these features that they should not be used to define the boundaries of a field of inquiry. Such important variables should be the center of attention!

To illustrate this point of view, we may consider the matter of group size. Would it be fruitful to construct a distinct branch of knowledge concerning, let us say, the two-person group? The research problems that could be feasibly investigated with respect to such groups are almost unlimited, and an individual investigator might want to study them intensively, perhaps even specializing in this work for a lifetime. But surely there would be dissatisfaction with a body of theory which was applicable only to two-person groups. Would general principles of this theory apply equally to three-person groups? If so, why restrict the theory so arbitrarily? If not, something very important about groups would have been neglected by concentrating exclusively on the two-person group. And if it is admitted that an arbitrary distinction should not be made between two-person and three-person groups, what size can be chosen that is less arbitrary? This question can be answered safely only on the basis of actual data. Only if it were determined empirically that one set of laws holds for groups up to some critical size and that a different set holds for larger groups would there be justification for establishing a boundary at this critical point.

Surprisingly enough, on the basis of available findings one would have more reason to draw a boundary between groups of two and groups of three than at any other critical size. Years ago, Simmel (38) pointed out some of the features not shared by two-person and three-person groups (for example, the possibility of forming coalitions), and a good deal of empirical work has been conducted on such distinctive properties of triads (see, for example, Caplow (7)). Still, it is clear from this research and from such treatments of dyads as that by Thibaut and Kelley (42) and by Foa (15) that both dyads and triads can be dealt with effectively in terms of theory developed from investigations of larger groups. Moreover, as shown by Converse and Campbell in Chapter 16, conceptions of group dynamics derived from research on rather small groups can be successfully applied to groups having members numbering in the millions. Until better empirical evidence becomes available to establish a fundamental discontinuity along the dimension of size, it would be unwise to use size to define the field of group dynamics.

The same line of reasoning holds when considering all the other criteria that have been proposed. Thus, it should not be assumed without good evidence that one set of laws applies to informal groups while another applies to formal ones, or that a single theoretical system cannot encompass face-to-face groups and organizations. Similarly, it should not be taken for granted that a special field of knowledge is required for groups having some particular objective.

One of the basic assumptions of group dynamics has been that general laws concerning group life can be discovered that will hold for such apparently different groups as a juvenile gang, the executive board of a YMCA, a jury, and a railroad maintenance crew. The essential feature of this point of view is its insistence that the various criteria that have been used to identify "types" of groups should be conceived as *variables* that may enter into a single general theory of groups. Approaching the field of group dynamics in this way, one will do research to discover how these variables affect group life. How, for example, does the size of a group affect its cohesiveness, the degree of specialization of its activities, the formality of its organization, or the nature of its leadership? How does the objective of a group influence the motivation of its members and the nature of their interactions? In research on such variables, the investigator is equally interested in variance and invariance; it is important for him to know both what things change and what things remain the same under variations in the size of groups or in the objectives of groups.

This conception of the field of group dynamics is obviously broad, and the task of constructing an empirically based general theory might seem almost overwhelming. Needless to say, only beginnings have been made; the number of variables to be studied is large, and the number of their combinations is enormous. Because of the magnitude of the task, research carried out to date has concentrated more on some aspects than others. For this reason, we must distinguish between the domain of knowledge aspired to and the nature of completed research. The assertion that group dynamics is concerned with small, informal, primary, or face-to-face groups would be accurate only as a description of prevailing trends in research undertaken to date, and even this description would be incorrect if it implied that work has been conducted exclusively on such groups. The studies reported in this book are concerned with a broad range of groups.

CONCEPTUAL SYSTEMS

Another way of limiting the field might be according to the use of a particular conceptual system. It has sometimes been proposed that, because of the close association of Kurt Lewin with the rise of group dynamics, adherence to the theoretical approach advocated by him should be taken as the defining characteristic of the field. This proposal, however, can be rejected readily because it would arbitrarily exclude many of the most important contributions to the understanding of group life. Lewin's general approach and specific concepts have exerted great influence on the study of group dynamics and may be expected to continue to do so, but it is antithetical to the nature of the scientific enterprise to enforce upon a field of inquiry any particular set of concepts or theories. If group dynamics were to be defined in this way, the result would be to create a multitude of fields each of which would be dealing with groups but by means of different concepts. And, worst of all, conceptual innovation within each would be discouraged since any major change of the theoretical approach that defined a field would mean leaving the field and setting up still another area of specialization. In principle, a field of inquiry should be defined in terms of the substantive problems it seeks to solve rather than according to the partial solutions achieved or concepts employed at any given time.

METHODS OF RESEARCH

One of the more dramatic aspects of the rise of group dynamics was its demonstration that important aspects of group life can be brought into the laboratory and subjected to controlled experimentation. The originality and power of some of these early laboratory experiments on "artificial" groups was quickly recognized, and many investigators began to use similar techniques. The popularity of the laboratory experiment has led some people to identify group dynamics with such research. But this criterion for bounding the field must also be rejected. Research methods are means for accomplishing some scientific objective; each method is particularly suited for revealing certain features of nature. If a field of inquiry were defined in terms of the use of a limited method, an extremely partial view of the proper subject matter of the field would result. As a matter of fact, it is fortunate that group dynamicists have employed a great variety of methods and are constantly inventing new ones.

We must conclude that none of these ways of bounding the field is satisfactory. Group dynamics must be identified by its desire to gain an understanding of the nature of group life. Rather than attempt to bound the field in some arbitrary way, attention would be better concentrated on the central theoretical and empirical problems involved in creating such an understanding.

THEORETICAL ORIENTATIONS

The student of group dynamics must be prepared to encounter and make constructive use of a wide variety of theoretical approaches. It is not possible to summarize here all of the many theoretical orientations to be found in the field. The different approaches derive from all the social sciences and reflect the many schools of thought within each. As an aid to identifying points of view and "placing" particular studies, we will list a few of the major orientations that have most influenced work in group dynamics. Then we will discuss some of the reasons for the great diversity of orientations and concepts and, finally, attempt to identify the more important theoretical issues that underlie all the different orientations. In reading the following list it should be understood that these are not schools of thought to which individuals belong; an investigator may be influenced, even in a single research project, by several of these orientations.

A LIST OF ORIENTATIONS

1. *Field theory.* This is the name given to the theoretical approach originated by Lewin (29). It derives this name from its basic thesis that behavior is the product of a field of interdependent determinants (known as life space or social space). The structural properties of this field are represented by concepts from topology and set theory, and the dynamic properties by means of concepts of psychological and social forces. For an overview of this approach reference may be made to articles by Cartwright (8, 9) and Deutsch (11). The chapters introducing each section of this book reflect a field-theoretical point of view.

2. *Interaction theory.* As developed especially by Bales (3, Chap. 30), Homans (23), and W. F. Whyte (43), this conceives of a group as a system of interacting individuals. The basic concepts of this approach are activity, interaction, and sentiment, and the attempt is made to construct all higher order concepts from these terms.

3. *Systems theory.* The view that a group is a system, adopted by the interaction theorists, is also found in a wide variety of forms in

other writings. These may be referred to as *systems theories*. Thus, "systems of orientation" and "systems of interlocking positions and roles" are central conceptions in the work stimulated by Newcomb (35); the notion of "communication system" has been widely employed in research following the leads of communications engineering (Chaps. 37 and 38); and the conception of a group as an "open system," derived from biology, may be found in the writings of Miller (33) and Stogdill (41). Systems theories place major emphasis on various kinds of "input" and "output" of the system, and they share with field theory a fundamental interest in equilibrating processes.

4. Sociometric orientation. Originated by Moreno (34) and elaborated by Jennings (25), this is concerned primarily with the interpersonal choices that bind groups of people together. The remarkably large quantity of research conducted within this orientation has been effectively reviewed by Lindzey and Borgatta (31), who point out that little systematic theory has yet resulted.

5. Psychoanalytic theory. Psychoanalytic theory focuses upon certain motivational and defensive processes within the individual and was first extended to group life by Freud (17). In more recent years, especially as a result of the growing interest in group psychotherapy, it has been elaborated in various ways by such writers as Bach (2), Bion (4, 5), Ezriel (12), Scheidlinger (37), and Stock and Thelen (40). Of especial relevance to group dynamics are its concepts of identification, regression, defense mechanisms, and the unconscious. Although comparatively little experimental or quantitative research on groups has been conducted within this orientation, concepts and hypotheses from psychoanalytic theory have permeated much of the work in group dynamics.

6. General psychology orientation. Since groups consist of individuals, it is to be expected that conceptions of human behavior developed in general psychology will be found in work on group dynamics. And, in fact, the influence of each of the major theories of motivation, learning, and perception can be seen. Perhaps the most influential of these to date has been a broad approach referred to as *cognitive theory*. This is not, strictly speaking, a theory but a point of view that insists on the importance of understanding how individuals receive and integrate information about the social world and how this information affects their behavior. Important contributions to the study of groups have been made within this orientation by Asch (1), Festinger (13, Chap. 10), Heider (21), and Krech and Crutchfield (27).

7. Empiricistic-statistical orientation. This maintains that the concepts of group dynamics should be discovered from statistical procedures, such as factor analysis, rather than constructed on *a priori* grounds by a theorist. Those working in this orientation make considerable use of the procedures developed in the field of personality testing. Good illustrations of this approach may be found in the writings of Borgatta, Cottrell, and Meyer (6), Cattell (10), and Hemphill (22), who have concentrated to date on ascertaining the orthogonal dimensions in terms of which groups can be characterized.

8. Formal models orientation. In sharp contrast to this last orientation is the work of a group of writers who have attempted to construct *formal models* with the aid of mathematics in order to deal rigorously with some rather limited aspects of groups. Although these models ordinarily contain some assumptions drawn from one or another of the social sciences, the emphasis is more on formal rigor than on comprehensive substantive theory. Examples of this approach may be found in publications of French (Chap. 42), Harary, Norman, and Cartwright (19), Hays and Bush (20), Rapoport (36), and Simon (39).

SOME SOURCES OF DIVERSITY

These, then, are some of the major approaches to the study of groups, and there are many others that could be enumerated. Although many of these appear to be in competition with one another, a careful study of them will reveal that the different theories and explanations do not actually contradict but instead augment and amplify one another. In order better to understand these various approaches and their interrelations, the reasons for the existence of so many theoretical orientations should be known.

Variety of Groups and Social Settings Investigated. It cannot be said of group dynamicists that they have confined their research to a narrow range of groups or to a limited segment of society. While it is true that they have conducted many studies on college students, they have also worked in a variety of other social settings. Thus, studies have been conducted on children in classrooms and summer camps, on military units, on committees and boards at all levels of business and government, on neighborhood groups, on voluntary groups as different from one another as labor unions and the League of Women Voters, on athletic teams, on therapy groups, on research teams, on international conferences, and on work groups in industry. In view of this great diversity it is only to be expected that different investigators will emphasize in their theorizing different phenomena and explanatory principles.

Differences in Social Problems Motivating Research. A project that is stimulated by interest in some social problem tends to concentrate on particular phenomena and social situations. An investigator who seeks to find ways of improving group efficiency may limit his attention to work groups and be especially concerned with the division of responsibilities among members, their acceptance of group goals, and the adequacy of their communication. A person who wishes to reduce intergroup conflicts may focus on sources of frustration, autistic hostility, and the transmission of stereotypes among group members. And the researcher who seeks to learn how to make groups more effective media for changing attitudes, behavior, or personal adjustment may pay special attention to group cohesiveness, social pressures generating conformity, and the emotional atmosphere created by trainers or therapists.

Number of Disciplines Contributing to the Field. People coming to the study of groups from different disciplines bring with them the special vocabularies of these disciplines and certain assumptions about the relative importance of various aspects of group life. Thus, a political scientist may be especially interested in social power and want to account for as much as possible in terms of this variable. An economist may believe that the dominant determinants are economic resources and technological skills. A sociologist may emphasize the place of the group in an organized society. An anthropologist may stress the importance of culture. A psychoanalyst may maintain that unconscious processes and ego defenses within group members are of the greatest significance. A psychologist may insist that events occurring in groups depend basically upon the way members view the group and the relationships among members.

The various circumstances surrounding the conduct of research generate a diversity of terminology and a variety of conceptions as to what the important determinants of group life are. Many of the more obvious disparities of terminology that derive from the special languages brought to the study of groups will undoubtedly be eliminated as research techniques become more standardized and as people from different disciplines become accustomed to communicating with one another about the same research material. And much of the disagreement as to which variables are the most important will disappear when it is realized that different writers are referring to different kinds of groups and social settings.

The understandable tendency of an investigator to generalize his findings from a particular setting to "groups in general" is another source of confusion. It is a legitimate objective of group dynamicists to construct a general theory applicable to all types of groups, but this does not mean that any particular finding will be applicable to all groups in all conceivable settings. The task of deriving general principles from diverse findings is a most difficult one. It is the essential nature of a general law that it specifies what effects may be anticipated under specified conditions. The achievement of such a law demands, therefore, that great care be exercised in specifying the conditions which generate any particular findings. Only confusion will result unless one is careful to determine what limits should be imposed upon findings from a particular type of investigation or a particular type of group. Such different findings, when properly conceived, can be made to supplement one another in a comprehensive theory.

SOME BASIC THEORETICAL ISSUES

All the conflicting points of view in group dynamics cannot, however, be eliminated by doing away with terminological misunderstandings or excessive zeal in generalizing from particular studies. Certain fundamental questions remain unanswered concerning the best ways to proceed in research and theorizing. Many genuine differences among the various approaches lie in the different answers people give to these questions. Four questions are of greatest importance: (*a*) What is the proper relation between data collection and theory building? (*b*) What are the proper objects of study and techniques of observation? (*c*) What are the basic variables that determine what happens in groups? (*d*) How can the many factors affecting group life be combined into a comprehensive conceptual system?

The development of any science seems to work progressively toward a satisfactory answer to the question of how data collection and theory building should be related. It appears that all the sciences have stemmed initially from armchair speculation; most can be traced back to a definite tradition in philosophy. For each developed science it can be said that at some point in history some people became dissatisfied with speculation and undertook to observe carefully and objectively the phenomena in question. Often the rebellion against speculation created an extreme position that ignored theory and let the data "speak for themselves." Finally, as a branch of science became more mature, theory building and data collection assumed a more interdependent relation to each other. In its advanced stage the scientific enterprise consists of developing hypotheses and theories from observations, checking these theoretical formulations by new observations and experiments, revising the hypotheses, checking these new hypotheses in new investigations, and so on over and over again. In the process, more and more comprehensive theoretical systems emerge, each part of which has a firm empirical basis.

As we saw in Chapter 1, research and theorizing in group dynamics illustrate this trend quite well. Until the beginning of the present century the study of groups was in the speculative era. Then the empiricist rebellion held sway, with most energy being devoted to "fact finding" and improving techniques of research. Finally, during the past three decades or so, group dynamics has entered progressively into the third stage of development, with more and more of its research being motivated by an interest in testing hypotheses that are "derived" from a larger body of theory. There do remain, however, genuine disagreements among those working in this third stage about the exact way in which testable hypotheses should be constructed.

Some investigators believe that such methodological problems as those of developing measuring instruments and of demonstrating their reliability should come before much theorizing. They hold that the empiricist era should not be left too rapidly for fear that premature theorizing will get the research into blind alleys. Those working in the empiricistic-statistical orientation, for example, maintain that the basic dimensions of groups should be revealed through such procedures as factor analysis in which a large sample of reliable measurements of group phenomena are analyzed to determine homogeneous factors. The sociometrists, too, have tended to concentrate upon the development of sociometric tests before building an elaborate theory of group structure. And the interactionists have devoted energy to creating standardized systems for recording and categorizing various kinds of interaction on the assumption that theorizing will develop more rapidly as a body of standardized "facts" is developed.

In sharp contrast are those who feel that in the past the collection of data has been inefficient because so few findings can be added up to a comprehensive formulation. They prefer to let theory exert a more guiding influence in the design of research. According to this second view one should not select devices for recording and measuring before one knows what it is that needs to be studied. Until the variables necessary for developing a given theory or testing a hypothesis have been defined, these investigators hold, one has no real basis for deciding whether to use an interaction chronograph, a sociometric test, a personality test, a certain questionnaire, or some other device.

If we take the view that group dynamics is ready for the third stage of scientific development in which theorizing and data collection mutually contribute to our understanding by a process of approximation, the conflicts between these two views do not seem irreconcilable. The collection of standardized data can help formulate theory, provided the data are not collected just because the standardized instrument is available. Similarly, each new formulation of a hypothesis may call for a refinement or revision of the data-gathering instruments. And it is certainly to be hoped that investigators will not invent new procedures when existing ones are satisfactory, because such innovation only serves to make it difficult to compare findings from one study to the next.

It is apparent, then, that the way a person attempts to solve the problem of data collection and theory building will greatly influence his selection of specific phenomena for investigation and his methods of research. Thus, for example, the investigator who believes that rigorous theorizing is dangerous at the present stage of development may prefer broad exploratory field studies in order to gain a more intuitive grasp of the variables with which subsequent theorizing should deal. On the other hand, an investigator who wants to test some restricted hypothesis derived from a theory or conceptual model may desire to conduct a rigidly controlled experiment in which some limited number of variables are varied systematically. The same investigator may choose one method in one study and quite a different one in another, depending upon his judgment of how well developed a given theoretical area is.

Because of the heterogeneous background of group dynamics and its recent history of being in the empiricist era, the phenomena selected for observation and measurement are quite diverse. As a result, different researchers may observe the same group discussion, let us say, and yet come out with widely different descriptions of what happened. One, who adheres to the interactionist orientation, will present a frequency distribution of the interactions for each of a set of categories of interaction. Another, who is primarily interested in sociometry and group structure, will relate his observations to the sociometric structure of the group. Another, who holds to the psychoanalytic orientation, will attempt in various ways to detect the prevailing emotional and unconscious determinants. And yet another, who adopts the view of cognitive theorists that perceptions and cognitions determine the events in groups, will describe the content of communication and the beliefs held by various members. If it were evident, as is often the case when different kinds of groups are being studied, that all these different descriptions actually point to different phenomena, there would be no insurmountable difficulty. The basic task would then be to determine how each of these aspects relates to the others both conceptually and empirically. But unfortunately it is not always clear to what degree these different descriptions may be different ways of

talking about exactly the same things. A great deal of work remains to be done before this problem can be solved, and much will be gained by broadening the range of data collected from the same groups. Many needless confusions would never arise if interaction records, sociometric tests, interviews, and projective tests, let us say, were all employed in the same research project. It would then become evident that all of these make important contributions to understanding a particular group, but it would also become possible to discover how these various kinds of data relate to one another empirically.

The most important task for group dynamics as it works in the third stage of scientific development is to establish a generally accepted set of basic variables and concepts having clear empirical and conceptual meanings. The essential problem may be posed in this way. The basic laws of group dynamics toward which all investigators are working are to be stated in terms of functional relations of the type: $x = f(y)$; x is a certain function of y. How are we to select and name the x's and the y's in our research? In working toward a resolution of this issue it is well to keep separate two of its aspects that are rather different. One part of the problem is to isolate the actual unitary variables or dimensions that make discernible differences. The other part consists of giving these variables appropriate names and conceptual properties.

The determination of unitary variables can be accomplished only by empirical work which discovers what regularities are invariably found among measurements and observations. Factor analysis and other methods of detecting invariant empirical associations can help here. The achievement of a common language of concepts that will permit the ordering of variables into a coherent conceptual system is more difficult. If the variables are to be employed in a conceptual system in such a way that derivations can be made to new empirical data and relations, then their conceptual properties must be clearly specified. These properties indicate the place of each variable in the conceptual system and the kinds of logical or mathematical operations that may be performed upon it.

Despite the importance of conceptual systems and models, at the present time there is no single language that all theorists will agree upon. Furthermore, there is little prospect that such a language will soon emerge. Fortunately, however, the conceptual systems that are currently in use are not completely incompatible with one another. In a general sense those who employ one set of terms can "understand" those who employ another, even though a dictionary of translations has not been worked out. This possibility of sensing when two differently oriented theorists are talking about essentially the same thing provides the way in which a generally agreed upon set of terms can be achieved. When two theorists can agree that they are talking sufficiently about the same thing that the same operational definition can be given to the differing terms, then a rigorous translation can be made between the two languages and eventually the two will become amalgamated as one.

At the present time most of the theoretically oriented research in group dynamics consists of specific investigations of how two or three variables are related to one another. Thus, one study may investigate how variations in the cohesiveness of a group affect the strength of pressures on group members toward homogeneity of opinions. Another may seek to determine how variations in cohesiveness affect members' readiness to express hostility. And yet another may examine how the degree of similarity of opinions affects the cohesiveness of the group. There have as yet been few efforts to put these variables together into one coherent theoretical system. A promising lead, however, has been provided by March and Simon (**32**), who have developed several "maps" which show how the relations among variables reported by different investigators may be combined. These maps make it clear that a fully adequate understanding of the determinants of group life will involve a specification of a network of causal relationships. One of their maps indicates, for example, that the extent to which goals are perceived as shared and the number of individual needs satisfied in the group jointly determine the frequency of interaction in the group, which influences the strength of identification with the group, which in turn affects the extent to which goals are perceived as shared and the number of individual needs satisfied in the group. In other words, there is a circular chain of causal interactions.

The field of group dynamics appears to be ready for rapid progress in the construction of such maps. As attention shifts from isolated

causal relations between variables taken two at a time to configurations of relations, a more penetrating understanding of the nature of group life will quickly emerge. And, as a result, the practical value of group dynamics theory will be greatly enhanced, since practitioners must be concerned, not with single relationships, but with the total ramifications that stem from the modification of any particular variable.

KINDS OF METHODS EMPLOYED

As one reviews the literature of group dynamics one cannot help but be impressed with the great ingenuity that has been employed in designing research. The phenomena of group life have been subjected to study by means of many different techniques, and each new publication brings the report of some methodological innovation. It may be helpful, therefore, to classify the various methods that have been more commonly employed and to describe the relative advantages and disadvantages of each. No single method, as we shall see, can be termed "the best" since the choice of method must be guided by the special objectives of each investigation. The only genuine issue, then, with respect to methods is whether a particular one is optimally suited to the objectives of a research project. To settle this question one must make a detailed examination of each objective and each method.

FIELD STUDY

Under this heading are investigations that subject some existing groups to study without in any way attempting to influence them. In fact, great care is often taken to assure that the investigator's presence has as little effect as possible upon the functioning of the group. W. F. Whyte's study of street corner society and Newcomb's study of Bennington College, two of the early investigations in group dynamics, represent the field study and illustrate some of the variety that may exist within the general method. While Whyte's major objective was to record carefully the events he observed and to report them faithfully, Newcomb sought to obtain quantitative data on several variables and to discover by statistical methods how these different variables were related to one another. The product of Whyte's study was a vivid account of the nature of street corner society, a rich case study for the student of group dynamics. Newcomb's report, while giving a description of certain features of student life at Bennington, concentrated more on showing relationships among variables (for example, how popularity was associated with the tendency to change attitudes).

Another example of the field study is given in Chapter 12, where Festinger, Schachter, and Back report the results of their study of the operation of group norms in a housing project. In this study it was found that certain attitudes and behaviors tended to be homogeneous among people living in the same court, that these were more homogeneous the more the residents reported that their friends lived in the same court, and that those individuals who differed from others in the same court tended not to be chosen by the others as friends. On the basis of these findings, the authors present the hypothesis that group standards existed in each court, that the strength of each standard depended upon the cohesiveness of the group of people living in the court, and that the price of deviation from the standard was rejection.

The major advantages and disadvantages of the field study may be seen in these examples. On the positive side, it can be employed with little disruption to the group and can provide a great variety of data. If these data are collected without bias, there can be little question as to the applicability of the findings to "real life." The information thus obtained is especially valuable in suggesting generalizations about the nature of group life. One major disadvantage of the field study is apparent in questions that must be raised concerning the typicality of the group studied. Can one, for example, safely assume on the basis of one study of a housing project that group standards will operate in the same way in such different groups as committees, families, and athletic teams, or even in all housing projects? The problem of typicality can be overcome whenever it is possible to study a representative sample of groups drawn from the universe of groups to which generalizations are to be made. But such procedures are costly and have seldom been used.

A more serious limitation of the field study is the difficulty encountered in interpreting the direction of causality from correlations. Does the correlation between the degree of homogeneity of attitudes within a court and the number of friends residing there indicate a tendency for people who like each other to influence each other toward similarity or a tendency for similar people to become friends or both? To answer this question, Festinger, Schachter, and Back subsequently subjected their hypotheses to more controlled experimentation in which interpersonal attraction was experimentally varied so that its effects on processes of influence could be determined. Although one can often make inferences about the direction of causality from certain configurations of correlations and from information about temporal sequences, a more direct study of the effects produced by experimentally manipulated variables is required to establish a confident interpretation of any correlation obtained from a field study.

NATURAL EXPERIMENT

Because of the limitations inherent in correlational procedures, all the sciences attempt, whenever possible, to subject their generalizations to experimental test. Although the same considerations apply in research on groups, there are certain difficulties in manipulating for experimental purposes any variables that might disrupt the life of the group. Fortunately, however, it is sometimes possible to take advantage of changes that are not produced by the investigator but occur in the normal course of events. When some new policy or procedure is introduced or when some critical event occurs in the environment of the group, an opportunity is given the researcher to discover what other things change as a result of this "experiment of nature."

The potential value of natural experiments may be seen in a study reported by Lieberman (30). Here, data from a field study were used to provide a base line against which to evaluate changes generated by a natural experiment in an appliance factory. In the original field study the rank-and-file workers were asked to fill out attitude questionnaires dealing with management and the union. During the next year, twenty-three of these workers were promoted to foremen and thirty-five were elected as union stewards. About fifteen months after the original study the questionnaires were re-administered to the workers who had changed positions and to a matched control group of workers who had not changed positions. By comparing the attitude changes that took place among the "experimental" and "control" subjects, the attitudinal effects of moving into the job of foreman and that of steward could be determined. These comparisons showed that those whose positions were changed underwent systematic modification in attitudes while those who experienced no change of position displayed little or none. The workers who were made foremen tended to become more favorable toward management, while those who were made stewards tended to become more favorable toward the union. The changes were more marked among the foremen than among the stewards. The correlation between position in the organization and attitudes toward the company and union that was found in the second round of measurements can be interpreted as indicating the influence of social position upon attitudes rather than showing that people were selected for positions on the basis of their attitudes. This interpretation is given added confidence by the fact that the data come from a natural experiment rather than simply a field study.

The major advantages of the natural experiment are that the researcher does not impose disruptive changes in the group under study, that changes of significance can be studied, and that the direction of causality can be inferred with considerable confidence. One disadvantage is that the researcher can study only those changes that happen to take place. Other limitations reside in the difficulties usually encountered in establishing adequate experimental controls. These controls were rather successfully set up in the study reported here, but often these cannot be readily established. One general problem lies in the fact that changes introduced by nature are often a result of other factors that may, themselves, influence the resulting course of events. In particular, when any introduced change is at the discretion of some individual or group of people, great care is required in interpreting the consequences produced by this change.

The essential requirements for a successful natural experiment are that appropriate data be collected both before and after the change being evaluated and that adequate comparisons of experimental and control conditions be made. Since changes are constantly occurring in groups, it is clear that much can be learned about the functioning of groups if provision is made for the systematic collection of relevant data. In view of the great promise of this kind of research, it is surprising that so little use has yet been made of it. As group dynamicists establish more enduring relationships with various groups in society, we may expect greater exploitation of natural experiments.

FIELD EXPERIMENT

In order to introduce greater control over the variables under investigation, social researchers have developed a technique known as the field experiment. It differs from the natural experiment primarily in the fact that now changes are introduced in the group with the explicit purpose of testing some hypothesis or evaluating the effectiveness of some innovation in methods of group management. The change is carefully designed to meet the requirements of the research problem and is put into effect under conditions that allow for controls and comparisons of properly comparable groups. Obviously, the cooperation of the group under investigation is required in order for the researcher to introduce such changes.

The experiments reported by Coch and French and by Siegel and Siegel in Chapters 26 and 5 are examples of the field experiment. In the Coch and French experiment, the research problem was stimulated by difficulties experienced rather commonly in industry when technical changes are introduced. The practice usually followed in the clothing factory where this experiment was done had been to introduce the new technical procedure, explain it to the employees, provide a "retraining allowance" on the piece rate, and train employees in the new method. The usual response from employees was one of suspicion, resistance, and hostility.

The researchers developed the hypothesis that introduction of new methods made the employees feel insecure, worry about whether the new piece rates would be fair, and resent the interference by management. These, in turn, resulted in the establishment of informal group standards to restrict production. The researchers reasoned further that if workers were allowed to participate in the design of new methods, they would resist less these new methods when introduced.

Several groups were selected to participate in the experiment. These groups were matched on the level of performance they had prior to the experiment and on the magnitude of change in the job that would be introduced. Three experimental conditions were established. The first, no participation, consisted of the usual procedure employed by the company. In the second, participation by representation, the employees were called together, told about the need for the change, and asked to select representatives from their group to work with the engineer in designing the new procedures. In the third, full participation, all members of the group were asked to work with the engineer in designing the new procedure.

Before the experimental treatment, all groups displayed an average rate of production that fluctuated slightly around 60 units per hour. After the new procedure was introduced, the no-participation group dropped in productivity to slightly less than 50 units and remained at this level for six weeks without any significant improvement. The group that experienced participation by representation dropped to about 45 units but returned to 60 units by the end of three weeks and leveled off at around 65 units thereafter. The group with full participation showed an initial drop to about 55 units and by the end of three weeks achieved a level slightly above 70 units, which it maintained indefinitely. At a later time, the people who had been in the no-participation group were changed to another new method by means of the full-participation procedure. These people showed this time the rapid increase in production displayed by those in the full-participation group initially.

Since the experimental manipulations were designed to test the hypothesis about participation and since it was administered so as to rule out spurious influences, we may conclude with reasonable confidence that the experimental treatments were in fact determinants of the observed changes in production.

In principle the field experiment has few drawbacks; it combines all the assets of the experimental method and the field study. But in actuality there are many problems involved in conducting experiments in field settings. It is one thing to speak abstractly about "manipulation of variables" and quite a different matter to put into actual practice the changes called for. In the first place, one cannot simply go to a group and introduce experimental changes; permission to do research must be obtained. Since the conditions conducive to granting such permission are not randomly distributed over all types of groups, great care must be exercised in generalizing findings from field experiments to all groups. But even after permission to conduct a field experiment has been granted, the researcher faces another serious problem. How is he to bring about the changes demanded by his research objective? Sometimes, as in the field experiment by Siegel and Siegel, the changes may be produced through slight modification of the usual procedures of management. But more often the changes require alterations in the customary behavior of key people. Can one hope, for example, to change the style of leadership of a group simply by telling the leader to behave differently? It is at this point that the social scientist most needs the collaboration of expert practitioners and people trained in the relevant professions. But, unfortunately, the development of an effective social technology depends to a considerable extent upon the accumulation of knowledge from research. Thus, at best, field experiments will have to be conducted with imperfect manipulation and control of variables until knowledge about group dynamics is more advanced. The feasibility of field experimentation should increase as work of all sorts in group dynamics progresses.

NATURAL GROUPS
IN THE LABORATORY

One modification of the field experiment has been to take natural groups from their usual setting and to place them under much more highly controlled, or artificial, conditions than is possible in the usual field experiment. To illustrate this procedure we shall describe briefly a study conducted by French and Snyder (16) on maintenance crews in the Air Force.

The broad objective of this study was to determine some of the factors that affect how much influence a noncommissioned officer actually has on the performance of his men. The factor of concern here is the degree to which the officer is liked by his men. The members of several crews at an Air Force base were administered questionnaires on which they were asked to indicate their personal feelings toward their officers. These replies provided information about the degree of liking for his officer that each man had developed in the normal course of living at the base. Somewhat later each officer and three of his subordinates participated in an experiment in which they worked together on two tasks under controlled conditions.

The first task was designed so that the noncommissioned officer would initially disagree with his men concerning the solution that the group should give to a problem. By carefully recording the interactions in the discussion and by measuring the changes brought about by the discussion, it was possible to determine how much influence the noncommissioned officer attempted and how successful he was in influencing his men. The results showed that well-liked officers, in comparison to those less well liked, attempted more to influence their men and succeeded more in doing so.

The second task was fashioned so that it would be possible to hold constant from group to group the amount of influence attempted by the noncommissioned officer. Would the better-liked officer be more successful in his influence even if he made precisely the same number and kind of influence attempts as the less well-liked officer? In order to answer this question, every officer left the room but communicated to his men by written notes asking his men to modify their behavior in certain ways. Although his men were not aware of it, the notes sent by the officer were identical in all groups. The results of this portion of the experiment revealed that a standard influence attempt coming from a better-liked officer resulted in greater actual influence than the same one coming from a less-liked officer.

It would have been virtually impossible to have determined the actual influence exerted by strictly equivalent attempts without introducing the kinds of controls possible only under laboratory conditions. And yet, by using natural groups it was possible to allow nature to generate stronger differences in interpersonal relations than is ordinarily possible in artificial groups. A major advantage of this method is that it permits the investigation of variables not easily created in the laboratory. Since its other advantages are essentially the same as those of other variations of the experimental method, we shall not repeat them here. However, one problem should be noted. The measured degree of liking of each man for his officer undoubtedly does not tell the entire story of the relationships between the two men. Thus, those groups with high attraction toward the officer may very well have been different from those with low attraction in

other ways as well. The correlation obtained between liking and influence may conceivably, therefore, reflect the operation of some of these associated features rather than liking itself. Whenever "nature" is allowed to generate independent variables, this problem of interpretation will arise.

ARTIFICIAL GROUPS IN THE LABORATORY

The desire to isolate variables and to manipulate them under conditions as controlled as possible has led social researchers to create groups in the laboratory and have them function under conditions created by the experimenter. It will be recalled that the early work by Sherif and by Lewin, Lippitt, and White made use of groups created for research purposes. Furthermore, these investigators went to great pains to subject the groups to conditions they set up. Over the succeeding years, many extensions and elaborations of this basic method have been made. As efforts have been directed toward exercising more and more control over variables, the conditions under which groups function in the laboratory have become increasingly "artificial," not resembling any conditions in "real life." Thus, in order to rule out uncontrolled effects of previous acquaintance among members, groups have been formed of strangers. And, in order to study various effects of communication among members, messages have been restricted to written notes so that these could be intercepted surreptitiously and previously prepared ones substituted. Probably the most extreme degree of control has been exercised in experiments where subjects are led to believe that they are members of a group with whom they can communicate only over an electronic intercommunication system but where, in actuality, they listen to a tape recording of a prepared interaction (see, for example, Chap. 9). In all of these experiments, the intent is not to create an exact replication of some type of circumstance found in society but instead to discover the effects produced by variations in abstractly defined variables.

The principal advantages of conducting experiments on artificial groups under laboratory conditions stem from the possibilities of controlling variables. When on the basis of research in field settings or on natural groups there remain questions about the direction of causality or about which of several simultaneously varying conditions are responsible for observed effects, research on artificial groups under laboratory conditions can provide much clearer answers. Only deficiencies in the experimenter's skill or ethical restraints prevent the manipulation of any variable of significance to the life of the groups, and the limitations of the method reside in these very considerations. The frequently voiced criticism that laboratory experiments are "artificial" is not accepted as valid by those conducting such research because only through such artificiality can commonly associated variables be studied in isolation. And, in rebuttal to criticisms of artificiality, proponents of this method point out that experiments in the physical sciences are at least as artificial, in this sense, as any conducted in group dynamics.

A major difficulty remains, nevertheless, in generalizing the results from laboratory research to groups in society. In the laboratory experiment only a few variables are manipulated at any given time while all the remainder are held constant at some level. Until a very great amount of research is completed it will not be possible to know the effects produced by all the possible combinations of variables. For this reason, caution is required in generalizing findings to situations where conditions exist that have not been investigated. Thus, to cite an obvious example, most laboratory experiments have been conducted on groups with an extremely short history. If a group's age influences the effects of other variables, it is safe to generalize from laboratory experiments only to young groups.

In an effort to overcome this difficulty a technique known as simulation has been introduced into some laboratory experiments. The purpose is to simulate real, or potentially real, conditions in which actual groups might find themselves. Thus, conditions might be created to resemble a bomb shelter or a space ship. Or groups might be formed and placed in a building designed to simulate an aircraft interceptor facility. Each experimental team would be provided with all of the electronic equipment available to such real teams. Then, various programs of messages would be introduced so as to resemble various circumstances that real teams might face. In this way it is possible to determine, for instance, what difficulties such teams working under real conditions might encounter and to test various methods of overcoming them. The possibilities of simulation are almost endless but, as noted by Guetzkow (18) in describing the possible use of simulation in the study of international relations, little use of it has yet been made except in certain military and business settings. Simulation is best suited for "developmental research," where the objective is to determine the effects that may be expected from combining a large number of variables in a single situation. To what extent the gamelike qualities of such settings affect the ability to generalize to real life has not yet been established.

CONCLUSIONS

It would be a mistake to maintain that any one of these different kinds of methods is the best. Findings and hypotheses derived from a study employing one method should serve to guide subsequent studies employing each of the other methods. Thus, field studies and natural experiments provide tentative conclusions that can be subjected to more rigorous test by more controlled experiments. And, at the same time, field studies and field experiments are needed to determine whether generalizations drawn from artificial situations and artificial groups can be safely applied in natural settings. The genuine issues of methodology deal essentially with tactics: What is the best method for a particular objective? Given a certain stage of development, how much effort should be devoted to general exploratory studies and how much should be directed to control of variables and precise quantification? These issues are matters of judgment, and only experience can determine which resolutions are the best.

GROUP DYNAMICS AND SOCIETY

All branches of science in the modern world are intimately related to society, as the construction of the atomic bomb so dramatically demonstrated to the physical scientists, but group dynamics has an especially close relationship. It of course shares with the natural sciences the fact that its findings may be used for good or evil purposes. It differs from them, however, in that its research materials are human beings and social groups. This difference has both technical and ethical consequences. For example, the group dynamicists cannot keep groups of people "on tap" the way a chemist keeps a supply of chemicals on his shelf or the way a biologist maintains a colony of experimental animals. Nor can he take a group of people and subject them to all sorts of conditions just to find out what happens. And the practical outcome of research in group dynamics is not a piece of hardware that can be installed by following a manual; it is instead a set of principles concerning the way people should arrange group procedures if they want to accomplish certain results. The methods and products of the group dynamicist, in short, constantly and inevitably involve him in society whether he wishes to be involved or not (26).

Some troublesome problems stem from this fact. We will now briefly consider three aspects of work in group dynamics that are especially dependent upon its relations with society: (a) formulating research problems, (b) conducting research, and (c) converting knowledge into practice.

FORMULATING RESEARCH PROBLEMS

Many factors influence the investigator's choice of a research problem and the way in which he formulates it. His disciplinary background and his general theoretical orientation, as we have seen, will affect his views of what variables are important, what kinds of data should be collected, what methods are most appropriate, and what concepts should be employed in his theoretical formulations. But, in addition, it must be recognized that he conducts his research in a particular society and is influenced by his participation in that society. Thus, for example, he holds certain values and is unlikely to design a research project whose major purpose would be a better understanding of how to undermine these values. And, since research costs money, he is dependent upon the opinions of society's financial gatekeepers as to what problems are worthy of support. Finally, since his research must be conducted on groups of people, he can investigate only problems these groups will allow him to study. It should be apparent, then, that the group dynamicist cannot formulate his research problems in a social vacuum, that the topics chosen for research are highly dependent upon the society in which he works. And, as we discovered in Chapter 1, the field of group dynamics has flourished only in certain countries.

These influences can be clearly seen in the accumulated research in group dynamics. It can hardly be an accident that so much research was conducted on the problem of conformity in the United States during the era of the McCarthy controversies. Nor is it an accident that in democratic societies so much emphasis has been placed on the problem of leadership. Similar influences can be detected in the great amount of work on group efficiency, the group as a source of resistance to change, and the consequences of groups on mental health.

We should not assume, however, that the group dynamicist exerts no influence upon the way society views the role of groups in society. To a considerable extent the generous financial support given to research in group dynamics by the military establishment, industrial organizations, and governmental agencies concerned with mental health is a result of the demonstration by group dynamicists that groups exert profound influences on matters of concern to these agencies and that research on groups can be productive. Furthermore, as group dynamicists have worked with professional people and practitioners of various kinds, they have helped these people see new ways in which research on groups can be ultimately beneficial to them.

Because of the close interaction between the researcher in group dynamics and those segments of society concerned with improving social practice, it is important that the nature of the researcher's contribution be clearly understood. If research in group dynamics is to be of genuine help in improving social practice, it must be conducted in a way such that it creates a significantly new understanding of the nature of group life. The achievement of this kind of understanding requires the group dynamicist to approach social phenomena in a way essentially different from that of the practitioner and to concentrate on a problem, attacking it from many different angles, until he understands it—not merely until the need for some particular administrative action has passed. A too great or too impatient concern for reaping the practical fruits of research will only reduce the chances of reaping any.

In examining the relations between the researcher and the practitioner, one encounters a disconcerting paradox: the very thing that makes the social researcher uniquely valuable causes him the greatest difficulty in gaining from practical-minded people the kind of support required to be valuable. The competent researcher differs from the competent practitioner mainly in the way he formulates problems and conceptualizes social phenomena. It is in this peculiar unconventionality that the group dynamicist's practical value lies. But it is here, too, that his difficulties arise.

Lewin (28) illustrated this requirement by suggesting that in order to achieve a fundamental understanding of minority problems one would have to investigate such apparently different matters as the interrelations between the blind and the seeing and between adults and children as well as between Negroes and whites or Catholics and Protestants. Minority problems, he asserted, should be viewed as but one example of the effect of group status on group living. If he is correct, those concerned with improving the lot of Negroes, the blind, or children have a stake in a co-ordinated program of research on the abstract problem of group status, as do those concerned with the welfare of the professional woman, the personnel department or the research staff in a business organization, the clinical psychologists in a mental health clinic, or the social scientist in the world of science.

It is for these reasons that the group dynamicist aspires to construct a general theory of groups and resists any attempt to define group dynamics in terms of some particular kind of group of social problem. Group dynamics will achieve such a fundamental view of group life and make its major practical contribution to society to the extent that its research problems are formulated according to the dictates of the phenomena themselves and in keeping with the requirements of theory building. Such a course means, however, that the group dynamicist will have to investigate in an integrated fashion phenomena and problems that to the practitioner may appear unrelated to one another. Moreover, the ultimate value of his research will be in fields of practice customarily viewed as having nothing to do with one another.

CONDUCTING RESEARCH

In the actual conduct of research the group dynamicist is bound to exert influences of one sort or another upon the groups he studies. Even in the field study, where he attempts to minimize this influence, the researcher establishes relationships that are bound to make a difference. For example, if he interviews or asks questions, he directs attention to certain phenomena, and people are unlikely to react to these in the same manner after his investigation. But more importantly, the question must be raised as to what will be done with his findings. If he learns anything of vital importance about the group, members will have a legitimate interest in knowing how this information is to be used. Since this question cannot be side-stepped, the researcher must be clear from the outset what understanding, implicit or explicit, exists concerning the role of his research in the administration of the group.

When the research design calls for experimental manipulation of variables, the investigator makes especially heavy demands on the group. Suppose, for example, that he wants to investigate the effects of different degrees of participation by group members in decisions of importance to the group and that he wants to do this by conducting field experiments on the locals of a labor union. Why should a union grant permission to introduce variations in the way it makes decisions? If the customary practice is for decisions to be made by the entire membership and the experiment calls for centralizing decision-making, then the experimenter may be asking the union to go against a strong democratic ideology. If the prevailing practice is for a few people to make decisions for the group and the experiment requires total participation in decisions, then the experimenter may be threatening the political power of this ruling clique. In any case, if the experimental changes are significant, the experiment is bound to be disruptive or even threatening. To justify such effects there would have to be some compensating gain from the research for the participants. In attempting to get the cooperation of groups the investigator appears to have two things to offer. He may try to persuade the group, or those with power to give permission, that they will benefit from sharing in the knowledge resulting from the experiment, or he may promise that the changes introduced by the experiment will produce consequences of immediate value. Although both considerations may, under certain circumstances, be both justified and persuasive, it should be evident that experiments can be conducted only on groups where conditions foster cooperation with the experimenter.

The problem of gaining access to the phenomena he wants to study creates certain ethical problems for the group dynamicist. Nearly everyone would agree that experiments, whether in the laboratory or in the field, should not be conducted when there is a possibility that harm might befall the subjects. But who is to decide what "harm" is? And who can legitimately grant permission for the conduct of experiments on groups of people? Although few would object to conducting research that has been approved by all participants on the basis of full knowledge of possible outcomes, the gaining of such approval would make it sometimes impossible to conduct the kind of research required. Is it legitimate for the management of a group to grant permission for research on the group? Some people would answer in the affirmative, since management is constantly making decisions and instituting procedures that affect all the members, but others have expressed the opinion that no one has the right to authorize experimentation or data collection on other people. An example of the complexity of the issue is provided by the controversy that arose a few years ago when it was revealed that recordings had been made of jury deliberations without the knowledge of the jurors but with the permission of the judge. Despite the fact that responsible lawyers believed that such research would contribute ultimately to strengthening the jury system, serious question remains as to whether concealed recording of data is ever justified.

The related problem of the use of deception arises in many investigations. It is especially difficult because there is good reason to believe that, if people know what the researcher is attempting to find out, this knowledge may influence the results of the research. The problem may be illustrated by the research of Festinger, Riecken, and Schachter (14), who wanted to study various effects of a dramatic disconfirmation of beliefs held in common by a group of people. They discovered a small group that would provide an unusual opportunity for studying these effects, since the members were prophesying the end of the world. The researchers wished to avoid exerting any influence on the group and felt that they could not candidly reveal their inter-

ests to the members. They decided, therefore, to join the group in the guise of believers. In this way they gained access to the phenomena they wished to observe. The ethical issue here is whether they were justified in employing this deception, even though they exercised great care in reporting their findings to conceal the identity of the group and the individuals involved. The same issue arises in a more general form in many laboratory experiments (see, for example, Chap. 13) where subjects are led to believe that others disagree with them concerning some matter of fact or opinion. Here the deception is employed as a means of manipulating a variable. Is this deception justified, even when the true nature of the experiment is explained to the subjects immediately after the experiment?

Obviously, universal consensus on issues like these cannot be achieved, but the researcher must be aware of these ethical problems and be prepared to forego research whenever serious questions of ethics are involved. It is clear that research on variables that are important to people and to society requires skill, diplomacy, and high ethical standards. Intellectual ability and a capacity for abstract thinking, which are requirements in any science, are not enough.

CONVERTING KNOWLEDGE INTO PRACTICE

Group dynamics is dedicated to advancing a basic understanding of group life. As noted above, if it is to succeed in this endeavor, its research problems must be formulated according to the demands of abstract theory rather than immediate, practical needs. Despite the different ways in which the researcher and the practitioner approach groups, the accumulated knowledge of group dynamics should provide a storehouse of information useful in the management of group life. Much has yet to be learned, however, about the most effective ways of converting basic knowledge into improved practice.

The group dynamicist can, of course, influence social practice in many ways. He can, for example, provide facts of value to those who take social action. His techniques for collecting data, such as the sociometric test, interaction recording, and interviewing, can be fruitfully employed as a tool for improving the efficiency of group functioning. And his concepts, such as cohesiveness, structure, and role, can help the practitioner think about events taking place in the groups with which he works. The teaching of group dynamics to people concerned not with research but with practice is based on the assumption that a knowledge of findings from research will aid in the practical affairs of groups. And there can be little doubt that social practice has benefited from having an increasing number of people acquainted with the findings of research on groups.

Still, there is reason to believe that new procedures will be needed before optimal use of knowledge in group dynamics is achieved. As basic knowledge has accumulated over recent years it has become increasingly evident that findings of basic research cannot simply be taken from the storehouse and put into use. Principles have to be converted into practices and procedures. There is a great need in the social sphere for an explicit attention to the process of invention and developmental research. The problem of converting basic

knowledge into social practice has not been that those working with groups have been timid or conservative when it comes to trying out new methods of management. The problem is that neither researchers nor practitioners have recognized sufficiently that a great deal of hard work must go into the process of making basic knowledge useful. If the experiences of natural science and engineering are any guide, a long period of developmental research—of pilot runs, evaluation, and redesign—is required before a dependable product can be attained. All too often in the world of social management we put into operation any procedure that is new and plausible without any test runs or evaluation of results. It is to be hoped that in the coming years we will witness the rise of a new specialty concerned directly with the challenging problems of how to invent, on the basis of firm general principles, new techniques of group life and how to evaluate their actual consequences before they are put into general practice.

SUMMARY

Group dynamics is a relatively young field, and it displays the characteristics of youth. It is experiencing rapid growth and seeking a sense of identity. The issues within the field can be better understood if viewed in this perspective.

The major issues of group dynamics concern the following matters: (*a*) preconceptions about the values to be gained or lost through group activities, (*b*) ways in which the field of group dynamics should be distinguished from other social science specializations, (*c*) the best theoretical orientation to employ in studying groups, (*d*) the use of the research methods that are most appropriate to research objectives, and (*e*) the relations that should be maintained between group dynamics and society.

The student of group dynamics, we have suggested, should not bring to his inquiry any preconception that groups are universally "good" or "bad." The more appropriate assumption is that groups may either facilitate or inhibit the attainment of desirable social objectives and that the task of research is to gain an understanding of the nature of group life so that desirable objectives may be more rationally sought by means of knowledge produced by research.

Although research that is properly labeled as group dynamics has tended to concentrate on small, informal, or primary groups, it would seem unwise to define the field as the study of any particular "type" of group. Similarly, it would be unwise to bound the field according to the use of a particular kind of research method or the adherence to a single theoretical orientation. No satisfactory citeria for bounding the field have yet been established, and group dynamics can be identified only by its central objective of gaining an understanding of the nature of group life.

The study of group dynamics has been guided by a great variety of theoretical orientations. Although this diversity of approaches and conceptual schemes may at times seem confusing, it reflects the youthfulness and vigor of the field. Efforts to achieve a coherent body of knowledge about groups must arrive at satisfactory answers to four questions: (*a*) What is the proper relation between data collection and theory building? (*b*) What are the proper objects of study and techniques of observation?

(*c*) What are the basic variables that determine what happens in groups? (*d*) How can the many factors affecting group life be combined into a comprehensive conceptual system? As work in group dynamics continues, progressively more satisfactory answers to these questions may be expected.

Investigators in group dynamics have displayed great ingenuity in devising methods of research. It would be a mistake to insist that any one of these is "the best." Each has advantages and limitations, and the basic problem is one of selecting the method most appropriate to the research objective and the stage of theoretical development in each problem area.

The methods and products of the group dynamicist constantly and inevitably involve him in society whether he wishes to be involved or not. The intimate relation between group dynamics and society is reflected in the formulation of research problems, in the conduct of research, and in the conversion of basic knowledge into practice. With respect to each of these matters the group dynamicist is influenced by and, in turn, influences society. In doing his work, therefore, the group dynamicist must possess not only intellectual ability and the capacity for abstract thinking but also social skill, sensitivity, and high ethical principles.

References

1. Asch, S. E. *Social psychology.* New York: Prentice-Hall, 1952.
2. Bach, G. R. *Intensive group psychotherapy.* New York: Ronald Press, 1954.
3. Bales, R. F. *Interaction process analysis.* Cambridge, Mass.: Addison-Wesley, 1950.
4. Bion, W. R. Experiences in groups, I–VI. *Human Relations,* 1948–1950; **1,** 314–320, 487–496; **2,** 13–22, 295–303; **3,** 3–14, 395–402.
5. Bion, W. R. Group dynamics: A re-view. *International Journal of Psychoanalysis,* 1952, **33,** 235–247.
6. Borgatta, E. F., Cottrell, L. S., & Meyer, H. J. On the dimensions of group behavior. *Sociometry,* 1956, **19,** 223–240.
7. Caplow, T. Further development of a theory of coalitions in the triad. *American Journal of Sociology,* 1959, **64,** 488–493.
8. Cartwright, D. A field theoretical conception of power. In D. Cartwright (Ed.), *Studies in social power.* Ann Arbor, Mich.: Institute for Social Research, 1959. Pp. 183–220.
9. Cartwright, D. Lewinian theory as a contemporary systematic framework. In S. Koch (Ed.), *Psychology: A study of a science.* Vol. 2. New York: McGraw-Hill, 1959.
10. Cattell, R. B. Concepts and methods in the measurement of group syntality. *Psychological Review,* 1948, **55,** 48–63.
11. Deutsch, M. Field theory in social psychology. In G. Lindzey (Ed.), *Handbook of social psychology.* Cambridge, Mass.: Addison-Wesley, 1954. Pp. 181–222.
12. Ezriel, H. A psychoanalytic approach to group treatment. *British Journal of Medical Psychology,* 1950, **23,** 59–74.
13. Festinger, L. *A theory of cognitive dissonance.* Evanston, Ill.: Row, Peterson, 1957.
14. Festinger, L., Riecken, H. W., & Schachter, S. *When prophecy fails.* Minneapolis: Univ. of Minnesota Press, 1956.
15. Foa, U. G. Behavior, norms, and social rewards in a dyad. *Behavioral Science,* 1958, **3,** 323–334.
16. French, J. R. P., Jr., & Snyder, R. Leadership and interpersonal power. In D. Cartwright (Ed.), *Studies in social power.* Ann Arbor, Mich.: Institute for Social Research, 1959. Pp. 118–149.
17. Freud, S. *Group psychology and the analysis of the ego.* London: Hogarth, 1922.
18. Guetzkow, H. A use of simulation in the study of inter-nation relations. *Behavioral Science,* 1959, **4,** 183–191.
19. Harary, F., Norman, R. Z., & Cartwright, D. *Structural models: An introduction to the theory of directed graphs.* New York: Wiley, 1965.
20. Hays, D. G., & Bush, R. R. A study of group action. *American Sociological Review,* 1954, **19,** 693–701.
21. Heider, F. *The psychology of interpersonal relations.* New York: Wiley, 1958.

22. Hemphill, J. K. *Group dimensions: A manual for their measurement.* Columbus: Ohio State Univ., Bureau of Business Research, 1956, No. 87.

23. Homans, G. C. *The human group.* New York: Harcourt, Brace, 1950.

24. Illing, H. A.   C. G. Jung on the present trends in group psychotherapy. *Human Relations,* 1957, **10,** 77–84.

25. Jennings, H. H. *Leadership and isolation.* New York: Longmans, Green, 1943.

26. Kelman, H. C. The social consequences of social research: A new social issue. *Journal of Social Issues,* 1965, **21** (3), 21–40.

27. Krech, D., & Crutchfield, R. S. *Theory and problems of social psychology.* New York: McGraw-Hill, 1948.

28. Lewin, K. The Research Center for Group Dynamics at Massachusetts Institute of Technology. *Sociometry,* 1945, **8,** 126–136.

29. Lewin, K. *Field theory in social science.* New York: Harper, 1951.

30. Lieberman, S. The effects of changes in roles on the attitudes of role occupants. *Human Relations,* 1956, **9,** 385–402.

31. Lindzey, G., & Borgatta, E. F. Sociometric measurement. In G. Lindzey (Ed.), *Handbook of social psychology.* Cambridge, Mass.: Addison-Wesley, 1954. Pp. 405–448.

32. March, J. G., & Simon, H. A. *Organizations.* New York: Wiley, 1958.

33. Miller, J. G. Toward a general theory for the behavioral sciences. *American Psychologist,* 1955, **10,** 513–531.

34. Moreno, J. L. *Who shall survive?* Washington, D.C.: Nervous and Mental Diseases Publishing Co., 1934.

35. Newcomb, T. M. *Social psychology.* New York: Dryden, 1950.

36. Rapoport, A. Mathematical models of social interaction. In R. D. Luce, R. R. Bush & E. Galanter (Eds.), *Handbook of mathematical psychology.* Vol. 2. New York: Wiley, 1963. Pp. 493–579.

37. Scheidlinger, S. *Psychoanalysis and group behavior.* New York: Norton, 1952.

38. Simmel, G. *The sociology of . . .* (Trans. by K. H. Wolff.) Glencoe, Ill.: Free Press, 1950.

39. Simon, H. A. *Models of man: Social and rational.* New York: Wiley, 1957.

40. Stock, D., & Thelen, H. A. *Emotional dynamics and group culture.* New York: New York Univ. Press, 1958.

41. Stogdill, R. M. *Individual behavior and group achievement.* London: Oxford Univ. Press, 1959.

42. Thibaut, J. W., & Kelley, H. H. *The social psychology of groups.* New York: Wiley, 1959.

43. Whyte, W. F., Jr. Small groups and large organizations. In J. H. Rohrer & M. Sherif (Eds.), *Social psychology at the crossroads.* New York: Harper, 1951.

44. Whyte, W. H., Jr. *The organization man.* New York: Simon and Schuster, 1956.

PART TWO

GROUPS AND GROUP MEMBERSHIP

3

Groups and Group Membership: Introduction

The social entity known as a group is an object of everyday experience. If we were to ask someone, say, a college student, to name the groups to which he belongs, he could respond readily. He might begin by listing certain clubs or organizations such as a fraternity, a dramatics club, or a student government organization. He might then tell us that he is a member of an athletic team and that he regularly "hangs around" with a particular bunch of fellows. He might recall that he attends classes with certain other students. Upon further questioning he might mention his family, his ethnic identification, his religious affiliation, and the political party of his choice. Similar questions addressed to other people would soon produce a long list of referents of the term group as employed in everyday language.

Social entities such as these constitute the subject matter of group dynamics. It is apparent that this subject matter is diverse, for groups display a great variety of properties. They differ in size, duration, objectives, activities, degree of formalization, internal structure, importance to their members, and in many other respects. Theories of group dynamics are concerned with interrelations among the properties of groups, how particular properties arise and vary, and how they affect group functioning, intergroup relations, and the lives of members.

Because of the multiplicity of properties possessed by groups, it is difficult to formulate a definition of *group* that encompasses the full variety of groups encountered in society and still provides a clear distinction between those social entities to be called "groups" and those to be given some other name. We begin the chapter with a discussion of this problem of definition. We then consider the relations that may exist between a person and a group. Next we examine some of the conditions that bring about the formation of groups. And we conclude by considering the kinds of properties that may be legitimately attributed to groups.

DEFINITION OF GROUP

The following definition, given by Brodbeck, serves to identify the broad class of social entities commonly referred to as groups (**5**, 2):

> A group is an aggregate of individuals standing in certain descriptive (i.e., observable) relations to each other. The kinds of relations exemplified will, of course, depend upon, or determine, the kind of group, whether it be a family, an audience, a committee, a labor union, or a crowd.

Certain features of this definition should be noted. The elements of a group are individuals; the membership of a group is a set of people. But it is not true that any arbitrary collection of people, such as all students whose last names begin with a given letter, constitute a group. For a set of people to qualify as a group, they must be related to one another in some definite way.

This point of view has been developed further by Lewin (**27**, 184).

> Similarity between persons merely permits their classification, their subsumption under the same abstract concept, whereas belonging to the same social group means concrete, dynamic interrelations among persons. A husband, a wife, and a baby are less similar to each other, in spite of their being a strong natural group, than the baby is to other babies, or the husband to other men, or the wife to other women. Strong and well-organized groups, far from being fully homogeneous, are bound to contain a variety of different sub-groups and individuals. It is not similarity or dissimilarity that decides whether two individuals belong to the same or different groups, but *social interaction or other types of interdependence*. A group is best defined as *a dynamic whole based on interdependence rather than on similarity*.

In keeping with the approach advanced by Brodbeck and Lewin, we adopt the following definition: a group is a collection of individuals who have relations to one another that make them interdependent to some significant degree. As so defined, the term group refers to a class of social entities having in common the property of interdependence among their constituent members.

Groups differ greatly in the nature and magnitude of interdependence among their members. An audience at a concert is a group, albeit a weak and transitory one, for each member's reactions (for example, applause, laughter, or restlessness) depend to some degree upon the reactions of all the others. Such an audience might become a highly interdependent group for a period of time if someone were to shout "fire." A collection of people who are striving to attain a common goal also constitutes a group, since goal-relevant behavior on the part of each person affects the others' likelihood of goal attainment. And if a set of people are treated in a homogeneous way by society because of race or religion or for some other reason, they may come to identify with one another and thereby become an interdependent group. Finally, the members of a family ordinarily compose an especially strong group because of their high degree of interdependence with respect to a variety of matters of great importance to them all.

Most definitions of group found in the literature of group dynamics are more restrictive than the one adopted here. Typically, an author selects certain relations or other properties that are of special interest to him and then sets these up as criteria for the existence of a group. As a result, there are many apparently conflicting definitions. From our point of view, these various definitions simply identify different kinds of groups, and little is to be gained from arguments over which is the "true" one. It is instructive, nevertheless, to examine some of these definitions, for they reveal several attributes of groups that investigators have felt to be of particular importance.

Many theorists have been especially interested in a form of interdependence known as interaction and have made it an essential part of their definition of a group. Two people are said to be engaged in interaction if the behavior of each directly affects that of the other. The following definition, proposed by Homans, makes interaction the sole criterion for the existence of a group and provides an operational means for deciding whether two people are members of the same group (**21**, 84).

> A group is defined by the interaction of its members. If we say that individuals A, B, C, D, E, . . . form a group, this will mean that at least the

following circumstances hold. Within a given period of time A interacts more with B, C, D, E, . . . than he does with M, N, L, O, P, . . . , whom we choose to consider outsiders or members of other groups. B also interacts more often with A, C, D, E, . . . than he does with outsiders, and so on for the other members of the group. It is possible just by counting interactions to map out a group quantitatively distinct from others.

If a collection of people engages in interaction frequently and over an extended period of time, it is likely that their interactions will become patterned, that they will develop expectations concerning one another's behavior, and that they will come to identify one another as members of the same social entity. As Merton noted, such consequences of interaction have often been incorporated into the definition of a group (33, 285–286).

It is generally understood that the *sociological* concept of a group refers to a number of people who interact with one another in accord with established patterns. This is sometimes phrased as a number of people having established and characteristic social relations. The two statements are, however, equivalent, since "social relations" are themselves patterned forms of social interaction, enduring sufficiently to become identifiable parts of a social structure.

One objective criterion of a group [is] . . . "frequency of interaction."

A second criterion of a group . . . is that the interacting persons *define themselves* as "members," i.e., that they have patterned expectations of forms of interaction which are morally binding on them and on other "members," but not on those regarded as "outside" the group.

The correlative and third criterion is that the persons in interaction be *defined by others* as "belonging to the group," these others including fellow-members and non-members.

An essentially similar orientation, though expressed in different terminology, has been set forth by Newcomb (34, 3):

For social psychological purposes, at least, the distinctive thing about a group is that its members share norms about something. The range covered by the shared norms may be great or small, but at the very least they include whatever it is that is distinctive about the common interests of the group members—whether it be politics or poker. They also include, necessarily, norms concerning the roles of the group members—roles which are interlocking, being defined in reciprocal terms. . . . These distinctive features of a group—shared norms and interlocking roles—presuppose a more than transitory relationship of interaction and communication.

A different sort of interdependence has been emphasized by writers in the psychoanalytic tradition, who are more concerned with the psychological aspects of groups than with interaction or its products. The following statement by Scheidlinger describes this orientation (37, 137–138):

According to [Freud], two or more people constitute a psychological group if they have set up the same model-object (leader) or ideals in their superego, or both, and consequently have identified with each other. Redl postulated that group formation occurs also when several individuals have used the same objects as a means of relieving similar internal conflicts. Furthermore, the leader might be an object of identification on the basis of the group member's love for him, or fear of him—an object of the group member's love or aggressive drives, or both. As a result of these common ties to the leader, all of which might operate together in any one group, the affective bonds among the individuals come into being.

Other psychologists have focused attention upon the gratification that members derive from belonging to a group. They argue that unless a collection of people, in their relationships, provides some degree of satisfaction to each member, the collection will not remain a distinctive social entity. This point of view is expressed in the following definition by Bass (4, 39):

We define "group" as a collection of individuals whose existence as a collection is rewarding to the individuals.

The motivational aspects of groups have also been stressed by Deutsch in a careful analysis of cooperative and competitive interrelations (see Chap. 35). He assumes that individuals have goals whose attainment may depend upon the actions of others, and he distinguishes two types of such motivational interdependence, which he labels "promotive" and "contrient." According to Deutsch, two people are promotively interdependent if the progress of each toward his goal makes it more likely that the other will reach his goal; they are contriently interdependent if one's progress reduces the likelihood that the other will attain his. Having developed these distinctions, Deutsch then offers the following definitions (Chap. 35, 467–468):

A sociological group exists (has unity) to the extent that the individuals composing it are pursuing promotively interdependent goals.
    A psychological group exists (has unity) to the extent that the individuals composing it perceive themselves as pursuing promotively interdependent goals.

Deutsch's distinction between sociological and psychological groups points to another important feature that groups may possess. It is evident that if a collection of people is sufficiently interdependent, the resulting unity may be perceived by the members and others. Clearly, groups may exist as objects in the perceptions and cognitions of individuals. Such cognitions have sometimes been employed as criteria for the existence of a group, as illustrated by the following definition by Smith (**40**, 227):

We may define a social group as a unit consisting of a plural number of separate organisms (agents) who have a collective perception of their unity and who have the ability or tendency to act and/or are acting in a unitary manner toward the environment.

Perhaps the most restrictive definition to be found in the literature is that given by Bales, who wished to identify precisely the kind of social entity he was studying in the laboratory and to encourage restraint in generalizing findings to social entities not possessing the specified properties (**3**, 33).

A small group is defined as any number of persons engaged in interaction with one another in a single face-to-face meeting or series of such meetings, in which each member receives some impression or perception of each other member distinctive enough so that he can, either at the time or in later questioning, give some reaction to each of the others as an individual person, even though it be only to recall that the other was present.

If, as we propose, the term group is used to refer to any collection of interdependent peo-ple, then it is evident that each of the definitions just considered, by requiring certain forms of interdependence or other properties, designates a particular kind of group. These definitions taken together provide a list of attributes that have impressed various theorists as being especially important features of groups. It seems likely, then, that when a set of people constitutes a group, one or more of the following statements will characterize them: (*a*) they engage in frequent interaction; (*b*) they define themselves as members; (*c*) they are defined by others as belonging to the group; (*d*) they share norms concerning matters of common interest; (*e*) they participate in a system of interlocking roles; (*f*) they identify with one another as a result of having set up the same model-object or ideals in their superego; (*g*) they find the group to be rewarding; (*h*) they pursue promotively interdependent goals; (*i*) they have a collective perception of their unity; (*j*) they tend to act in a unitary manner toward the environment.

It is an empirical question whether certain clusters of these characteristics tend to be found together—whether, for example, frequent interaction does in fact generate shared norms and a system of interlocking roles, or whether people who find a group rewarding are likely to pursue promotively interdependent goals. The larger the number of these attributes possessed by a set of people, and the greater their strength, the closer the collection would seem to come to being a "full-fledged" group.

RELATIONS BETWEEN A PERSON AND A GROUP

In considering any given individual and a particular group it is evident that there are many possible relationships between them. The person may be a member, or not. He may depend upon the group to some degree to provide things he values. He may find the prospect of membership attractive or repulsive, and the group, in turn, may accept or reject him. His membership, or nonmembership, may be voluntary or involuntary. He may belong simultaneously to several groups, and these memberships may be more or less compatible with one another. Finally he may use the group as a reference in forming his beliefs or attitudes, in steering his behavior, and in evaluating himself, the treatment he receives, and other people. These and other person-group relations can have important consequences for both the person and the group.

MEMBERSHIP

It follows from our definition of group that anyone who belongs to a particular group is affected in some way by the fact of membership. We should expect the effects of membership on a person to be greater the stronger the "group character" of the set of individuals constituting the group.

This expectation has been confirmed by the results of a laboratory experiment conducted by Zander, Stotland, and Wolfe (49). These investigators created two kinds of groups differing in their degree of unity, each group being composed of female college students who were unacquainted with one another prior to the experimental session. In one kind of group to generate high unity the subjects were seated facing one another around a small circular table so that the configuration of the group was clear. The experimenter gave a short speech on the importance of groups in daily living and on the properties usually required for a collection of persons to be considered a group. He informed the participants that they would be competing against other groups and asked them to select a name for their group. In the other kind of group, in the low-unity condition, the subjects were asked to sit "just anywhere," the chairs and tables being scattered around the room in a haphazard fashion. The experimenter did not use the word "group" but referred to the subjects simply as "you girls." He made no mention of the importance of groups nor of the properties that groups may have. He gave the assemblage a number instead of asking them to choose a group name, and he told them that they would be competing with persons in other experimental sessions.

All groups were given the same task, which was concerned with good taste in dressing. The girls were to select color schemes for a number of complete outfits appropriate to various occasions and to assign specific colors to the various items of clothing making up each outfit. Each girl worked on the task alone in a separate cubicle. After the task was completed the experimenter scored the products and combined the scores to yield a single group score. Half of the groups were told that

they had succeeded, that their score was "second from the top so far." The other half of the groups were informed that they "didn't do too well, since they were third from the bottom." A questionnaire was then distributed to each member asking, among other things, that she rate herself on a number of characteristics or abilities.

The results of this experiment show clearly that the degree of group unity affects members' reactions to group success or failure. In the high-unity groups, members of groups that failed rated themselves significantly lower than members of groups that succeeded, while in the low-unity groups, members of groups that failed and members of groups that succeeded were not significantly different in their self-evaluations. It is interesting to note further that the number of self-ratings affected by group failure was greater for subjects in the high-unity groups. Apparently, the higher the unity, the greater the proportion of the self that becomes involved in the group and is affected by identification with the group.

The groups said to have high unity in this experiment were clearly weaker than most groups encountered in everyday life, and yet their effects on members were not trivial. Natural groups found in society ordinarily have a much higher degree of interdependence with respect to a wider range of matters and endure for vastly longer periods of time. An individual's membership or nonmembership in a natural group may therefore be expected to have profound significance for him. The groups to which an individual belongs or does not belong—a fraternity, a work group, a recreation club, a religious body, an ethnic group, a political party, or even a therapy group—basically affect the kind of person he is.

A person who is a member of a group is said to be "in" the group, to be located within its boundaries. But it is clear that membership does not necessarily engage the entire person; it may have significance for only certain segments of his life. Groups differ greatly in the amount of the person involved in membership. The impact of the Tuesday Night Poker Club on its most devoted member may be confined to his behavior on Tuesday night and to his attitudes and beliefs concerning poker. Membership in a labor union may have implications mainly in the economic sphere of a person's life. Other groups, such as a family, a military unit, a therapy group, or an ethnic group, may involve major portions of their members' lives. The particular parts of a person that are engaged by membership will affect both the functioning of the group and its significance for members.

DEPENDENCE

Membership often makes an individual dependent upon the group for many of the things he needs. The members of a nuclear family are usually highly dependent upon it for the provision of food, shelter, affection, security, and other resources required for effective living. The members of a labor union are dependent upon it—the effectiveness of its bargaining, the nature of its social welfare programs, and the progressiveness of its leadership—for their level of income, conditions of work, and security in old age. The members of professional societies and trade associations may depend primarily upon the publications of these groups for information related to their occupational roles. And the self-esteem of the members of an ethnic group depends in large part upon its status in society. We see, then, that dependence, its nature and degree, is an important aspect of the relation between a person and a group.

ATTRACTION AND ACCEPTANCE

An individual's relation to a group is said to be that of *positive attraction* if he is motivated to become or to remain a member, that of *negative attraction* if he desires not to belong, and that of *neutral attraction* if he is indifferent to membership. A group whose members are related to it by a high degree of positive attraction is said to be highly cohesive. Such a group is likely to be "strong" in the sense that it has the capacity to retain members, to mobilize their energies in support of group goals, and to bring about adherence to group standards. The concept of group cohesiveness, which has proved to be of great value in theories of group dynamics, will be discussed at some length in Chapter 7.

Jackson (**23**) has employed the relation of attraction together with that of acceptance to identify certain more complex relations between a person and a group. He defines acceptance as the degree to which the group employs role prescriptions to influence an individual's behavior. Positive acceptance means that the members of a group see the individual as subject to the sanctions attendant upon adherence to or deviation from group norms. Neutral acceptance means that members are indifferent to or tolerant of the individual's conformity to group norms. And negative acceptance means that members treat the individual as not belonging to the group, that they exclude him from membership. Full "psychological membership" is said to obtain when a person is both positively attracted to the group and positively accepted by it. "Psychological nonmembership" is characterized by neutral attraction together with neutral acceptance. "Marginal membership" exists when a person who is accepted as a member feels indifferent to membership. And a "rebellious relationship" arises when an accepted individual desires not to belong to the group. Jackson's analysis of these and the other possible combinations of attraction and acceptance makes it clear that these two features of a person's relation to a group can have significant consequences for both the person and the group involved in the relationship.

VOLITION

The possibility that a person may be a member of a group to which he does not want to belong has led many theorists to distinguish between "voluntary" and "nonvoluntary" membership. Although it is not easy to arrive at a fully satisfactory definition of these two terms, the distinction clearly refers to a fundamental aspect of the relation of membership. The inmates of a prison are usually highly interdependent and thus constitute a group even though they would prefer not to belong. A child ordinarily has no choice regarding his membership in a family, and his parents may be forced to remain members of the family because of religious or legal prohibitions against divorce. An individual may be assigned to a particular group regardless of his wishes simply because he possesses certain visible characteristics such as skin color, sex, or a particular disability. And a worker may stay with a company only because the costs of leaving, in terms of seniority rights and pension benefits, are high.

These examples make it evident that there are various conditions generating nonvoluntary membership. A person may be forced to remain in a group because others treat him as a member, because no other alternatives are available to him, or because of excessive costs he will incur if he withdraws. If an individual wishes to leave a group but remains for any of these reasons, he will experience frustration and deprivation. A group composed of such people will possess distinctive characteristics, many of which will create problems for its effective functioning. It should be noted, however, that compulsory membership is not necessarily accompanied by negative attraction. A collection of individuals who are forced to belong to the same group may develop a high degree of cohesiveness and pride in membership. The creation of member loyalty is a challenging problem to the leadership of such groups.

Another type of person-group relation is that of involuntary nonmembership. This relation arises when someone is excluded from membership in a group to which he desires to belong. Such rejection can have devastating consequences for the rejected person, and many people go to great extremes to avoid it. The conditions determining the effects of involuntary nonmembership have not been systematically studied, but an interesting beginning has been made by Snoek (41), who investigated the reactions of college students who had just learned that they had been excluded from participation in a bridge club to which they had applied for membership. He found that a person who is told that he has been rejected will maintain his desire to be a member and will try to win the approval of other members if the rejection is based on some criterion that affects his self-evaluation, such as his lack of ability or the fact that the members do not like him. But his desire to become a member of the group will be reduced and he will not try to become more acceptable to others if the rejection is based on some characteristic he cannot change, such as being of the wrong sex for the group.

A more detailed discussion of the nature of "open" and "closed" groups and of nonvoluntary membership is given by Ziller (50) and by Thibaut and Kelley (43).

MULTIPLE MEMBERSHIP

In thinking about the relations between a person and a group, it is important to remember that any given individual is a member of several groups. His relationships to these groups may be compatible with one another or they may create conflicts of some kind. A "conflict of interest" may arise if, for example, a member of a committee that awards research grants is also a member of a research group applying for a grant. Conflicts of interest are not at all uncommon whenever a coordinating, or executive, committee is composed of representatives of subordinate groups.

If a person is a member of two groups having distinctive norms or values, each may be expected to exert conformity pressures on him. Since an individual will ordinarily find it distasteful to be subjected to conflicting social pressures, we should expect to find a tendency for people to avoid combinations of memberships that are incompatible in this sense. Thus, a member of a civil rights organization is likely not to belong also to the John Birch Society, and a member of a politically active labor union is likely to identify with a political party whose programs are compatible with the ideology of the union.

It is possible, nevertheless, for a person to find himself in two groups with quite contradictory norms. A businessman may go to his church on Sunday and listen to a sermon concerning the way to deal with his fellow men and heartily endorse these views. On Monday he may attend a session of the Society for Sharp Business Practices and embrace the opposed opinions of this group just as readily. Although membership in different groups may create dilemmas and contradictions for the individual, it is commonly observed that the majority of people function efficiently as members of many groups. Often they may be only vaguely aware of the inconsistencies of their beliefs, acting in accord with the standards of the group that is most salient at the moment or managing to resolve the conflicts without being aware of them at all.

Some roles place their occupants unavoidably in a position of overlapping membership. The modern industrial foreman, as an example, is formally a member of management but informally a member of the work group on the shop floor. Where the standards of these two groups differ, which shall he follow? The school superintendent, as a further illustration, is a member of the school board and a member of the school faculty. Gross, Mason, and McEachern (18) show that the conflicts arising for a superintendent because of his middleman position are often resolved by his adherence to the standards of a third group, his professional association of peers.

In a study of foreign visitors, Watson and Lippitt (46) observed that the stranger finds many people reacting to him only as a representative of his home country and that the new environment challenges the assumptions of the old. The visitor must try to meet this challenge as a necessary condition for interaction with the hosts and for his own peace of mind. He feels the need to conform to his present group while feeling loyalty to the groups "back home." Zajonc (47) reports that strangers who are frustrated by the difficulty in conforming turn to aggression against the new behavior or beliefs they have tried to adopt. Their aggression is facilitated by their social position as a stranger and diminishes their original need to conform to their new environment while increasing their desire to behave as people do "back home."

Killian (26) has vividly described how overlapping loyalties and "cross pressures" can become a keen conflict for an individual when he is forced to choose among them in some emergency such as a community disaster. Killian found that in such a situation previously nonconflicting memberships suddenly presented the person with the necessity of making a choice difficult for him—between, for example, caring for his family and seeking to help his fellow workers. Each person tended to offer help to the group that was most important or attractive to him. The effects of overlapping membership have also been examined by Gerard (15), who allowed groups in a laboratory experiment to arrive at a unanimous decision concerning the best solution for a social problem. A week later he placed the members in different groups, where they found the decision of their previous groups opposed by their new colleagues, who were paid participants assigned the task of disagreeing with the subjects. Pressures to change were resisted in the latter groups to the degree that the former groups were attractive to the members.

The memberships in other groups held by the members of a particular group may have various consequences for its functioning. They may create conflicts of loyalty and inhibit concerted group action. But they may also be a source of creativity and innovation by bringing to the group heterogeneous points of view and a variety of information and values. Multiple group membership may also increase the group's capacity for action by providing a wide range of "contacts" and liaison with other groups that can assist the group in meeting its objectives.

The nature and extent of multiple memberships can have important consequences also for the larger social system of which the groups are a part. Some of these consequences have been examined by Coleman (9) in a theoretical analysis of community conflicts related to such matters as fluoridation of water, public school policies, racial integration, and reform of city government. He notes that conflicts become acute when issues become polarized so that individuals or groups become identified with one of two opposing sides; if the community is organized in a way such that few people have multiple group memberships, it is relatively easy for the groups to line up on one of two opposing sides. If, however, there are many overlapping memberships, people belonging to two groups, each aligned with an opposing side, experience cross-pressures; in this case the conflict is localized within groups and within individuals having multiple memberships. Attempts to reconcile the conflicts should arise and thus counteract any tendency for the controversy to become a polarized community issue.

The deliberate use of overlapping group memberships as a technique in the management of organizations has been advocated by Likert (28). He argues that an organization will function best when its personnel function not as individuals but as members of highly effective work groups with high production goals. To coordinate the activities of these groups and to achieve a coherent total system, they should be linked together through people who hold overlapping group memberships. The superior in one group is the subordinate in the next group, and so on throughout the organization. It should be evident that this conception of management relies heavily upon an adequate performance of the "linking pin" function by those who hold overlapping memberships.

The quality of relations between any two groups may be expected to depend on the degree to which they have members in common. At one extreme is the condition of disjoint membership where no one is a member of both groups. If two such groups come into contact with each other, the possibilities of conflict, rivalry, and misunderstanding would seem to be numerous. At the other extreme, all members of one group, the subgroup, are also members of the other, the encompassing group, and relations between the two will depend to a considerable degree upon the position of the subgroup within the inclusive one. Between these extremes are the many cases of multiple membership already considered.

REFERENCE GROUPS

Theoretical accounts of the formation, maintenance, and change of attitudes, especially attitudes toward the self, frequently employ the concept of reference groups. This term was first used by Hyman (**22**) in an analysis of the ways in which an individual forms a conception of his status in society. Hyman proposed that, since status is defined by one's position relative to other people, a person's view of his status depends upon the particular group of people he compares himself with—his reference group. Hyman was able to demonstrate that changes in an individual's judgment of his status can be brought about by changes in his reference group. The concept was subsequently used effectively by investigators in the U. S. War Department (**42**) to account for variations in morale, and especially feelings of deprivation, among American soldiers during World War II.

With the passage of time, the concept of reference group has acquired a progressively broader meaning so that now it is commonly used to denote any group to which an individual relates his attitudes. A person whose attitudes are dependent upon, shaped by, or anchored in a particular group has a reference relation to that group. Kelley (**24**) has noted that reference groups so conceived may serve two rather different functions. He calls the first of these the *comparison function* and states that "a group functions as a comparison reference group for an individual to the extent that the behavior, attitudes, circumstances, or other characteristics of its members represent standards or comparison points which he uses in making judgments and evaluations" (**24**, 413). This function is the one Hyman emphasizes and would seem to be primarily involved in the social influences on an individual's perception, cognition, and level of aspiration as studied by Sherif (**39**), Chapman and Volkmann (**7**), Festinger (**11**), and Asch (**2**). Kelley refers to the second function as the *normative function* and asserts that "a group functions as a normative reference group for a person to the

extent that its evaluations of him are based upon the degree of his conformity to certain standards of behavior or attitude and to the extent that the delivery of rewards or punishments is conditional upon these evaluations" (**24**, 413). This function would seem to be operative in the processes of social pressure considered in Part Three of this book. Kelley notes that these two functions will frequently, but not always, be served by the same group.

It is important to observe that the reference relation and the membership relation are not necessarily identical. A student's orientation toward scholarship may be affected by the norms of a senior honorary society as a result either of his membership in the society or of his desire to become a member. And, in forming a judgment of the equity of his compensation, an employee may compare his salary with that of others in his work group or with the salaries paid to employees of another company in the community. In Chapter 5, Siegel and Siegel present data from two situations, one in which the individual's reference group and membership group are the same and one in which they are different.

Of the many groups known to an individual, only a few ordinarily serve as reference groups, and the conditions determining the choice of reference group are far from completely understood. There is evidence to suggest, however, that a person is more likely to refer his attitudes to a particular group the more strongly he is oriented toward membership in that group. If this orientation is positive, so that he desires membership in the group, he is likely to employ it as a positive reference and attempt to become similar to its members with respect to the characteristics that distinguish them as a group. But if the idea of membership is repulsive, the reference is likely to be negative, and he will try to maximize differences between himself and the group's members. Many other factors are undoubtedly involved in the selection of reference groups, and systematic research is needed to provide a fuller understanding of the nature of the reference relation between persons and groups.

FORMATION OF GROUPS

Any group in society originated at some point in time, and its formation was determined by a particular set of conditions. Why do groups form? How does it happen that a certain collection of individuals comes to constitute a group? In view of the tremendous diversity of groups, it seems unlikely that there is a simple answer to these questions. The reasons for the formation of a family, a committee, an adolescent gang, a business association, a church, and an ethnic group would appear to have little in common. It is possible, nevertheless, to identify three rather different kinds of circumstances under which groups come into existence: (*a*) A group may be created deliberately by one or more people in order to accomplish some objective. (*b*) A group may be formed spontaneously by the people who come to participate in it. (*c*) A collection of individuals may become a group because they are treated in a homogeneous way by other people.

DELIBERATE FORMATION

The basic condition for the deliberate creation of a group is the judgment by one or more people that a collection of individuals can accomplish some purpose (or do so at a level of efficiency) not otherwise possible. It is not necessary, of course, that this judgment be valid, as witnessed, for example, by the high rate of bankruptcy among business enterprises. The purposes envisaged by the founders of groups are diverse, but they may be classified under a few general headings that serve to designate certain types of groups.

1. Work groups. The objective in forming a work group is to perform some task more efficiently through the pooling and coordination of the behavior and resources of a collection of individuals. A prototypic example is the entrepreneur who establishes a small company to manufacture a product. Another example is the formation of an expedition to explore the Antarctic, to climb Mount Everest, or to land on the moon. Work groups of one sort or another are found extensively in any society.

2. Problem-solving groups. The fundamental purpose of many groups such as research teams, commissions, task forces, and certain kinds of committees is to arrive at a solution to a problem. The rational basis for forming them is the belief that a solution will be attained more efficiently, discarded sooner for a better one, or adopted more readily when a collection of people work on the problem together than when it is assigned to a single individual or several working independently. Everyday experience makes it plain, however, that such rational assessment does not always

underlie the formation of problem-solving groups and that they are often created simply because the procedure is customary or because no one individual is willing to assume responsibility. Unfortunately, few general rules have been established for determining the conditions under which a group is a superior means for problem-solving, although the search for such rules has occupied social scientists for many years. Work directed toward this end has nevertheless produced valuable findings that have been summarized by Kelley and Thibaut (**25**), Lorge *et al.* (**29**), Maier (**31**), Collins and Guetzkow (**10**), and Hoffman (**20**). Several promising models of problem-solving groups have been constructed too (**30, 44, 48**).

3. Social-action groups. The desire to influence the course of events in society, combined with the realization that individuals acting alone can rarely exert much influence, frequently leads to the creation of social-action groups. Political life abounds with such groups —parties, lobbies, citizens committees, trade associations, veterans organizations, civil rights groups—and much of the business of politics consists in processes of accommodation among their demands and pressures (**45**).

4. Mediating groups. In a complex society many groups are created with the purpose of coordinating the activities of other groups, distributing resources among them, or reconciling conflicting interests. Often, though not always, such groups are composed of representatives of those affected by their decisions. Examples of this type of group are coordinating councils such as a council of social agencies, interdepartmental committees in a bureaucracy, arbitration boards, committees of the United Nations, and the Supreme Court.

5. Legislative groups. Much of anyone's behavior is governed by rules, regulations, laws, or policies set up by the decisions of groups whose basic purpose is to formulate such legislation. The decisions of a board of directors establish policies for a business organization that affect its operation and effectiveness. The deliberations of a university senate result in regulations governing the behavior of the faculty. And governmental legislative bodies arrive at decisions that become part of a body of law. Summaries of research on decision-making by groups are given by March and Simon (**32**), Collins and Guetzkow (**10**), and Gore and Dyson (**17**).

6. Client groups. During any twenty-four-

hour period thousands of groups hold meetings whose purpose is to "improve" in some way the members of these groups, who may be seeking help with alcoholism, drug addiction, obesity, mental illness, delinquency, poor academic performance, or a disability. They may be in search of guidance in coping with new or difficult situations related to the choice of a career, the birth of a child, retirement, or the rearing of children without a marital partner. They may wish to increase their sensitivity to human relationships, to improve their skills of leadership, or to learn how to win friends and influence people. They may desire to become better informed about foreign affairs, race relations, religion, literature, or the arts. Or they may be looking for an opportunity to develop a hobby or to engage in some form of recreation. The creation of groups of this sort by a social agency rests on the assumption that the performance of such services is more effective or efficient if the "clients" are treated as groups rather than as individuals.

SPONTANEOUS FORMATION

Many groups arise, not because someone has deliberately created them to accomplish an objective, but because people expect to derive satisfaction from associating together. Groups such as friendship cliques, informal clusterings within a formal organization, social clubs, and juvenile gangs usually have this sort of origin. Since the formation is based on voluntary interpersonal choices, the group's composition is determined by processes of mutual consent—each member wants to be in the relationship and each is accepted, or at least is not rejected, by the others. Such groups are often quite informal, with shifting boundaries and few explicit goals or tasks, but they may develop a stable structure, take on certain tasks, and even acquire recognized legal status, as illustrated by a family established through marriage as the result of courtship.

A basic condition for the spontaneous formation of a particular group is that the individuals involved have sufficient contact with one another to become acquainted. The probability that two people will become acquainted tends to increase with the frequency that they find themselves in physical proximity. Thus, spontaneously formed groups tend to be composed of individuals who reside near one another, work in geographical proximity, "hang out" on the same street corner, or are thrown together by other activities in their daily lives. Marriage partners are likely to have resided within a few blocks of each other or to have gone to the same school. Juvenile gangs are composed largely of boys from the same neighborhood. And social groups tend to contain members who reside in the same area or who have become acquainted through occupational or other activities.

A dramatic documentation of the effects of the physical layout of a housing project upon the composition of spontaneously formed groups has been provided by Festinger, Schachter, and Back (13). They found that the distance a resident lived from others in the project and the fortuitous arrangement of sidewalks, mailboxes, stairways, and other facilities that controlled his likelihood of having contact with others were important determinants of the people he made friends with. Well over half of all friendships reported by residents of the project were with people living in the same building or court. Thus, the composition of social groups within the project was heavily determined by its architectural features. It should be pointed out, however, that since the residents were married students and their families, they constituted a rather homogeneous population. Gross differences among residents in values, interests, age, education, or occupation would undoubtedly have attenuated the effects of physical proximity on group formation.

Because the spontaneous formation of a group from a particular collection of acquaintances involves the development of interpersonal attractions among them, the composition of such groups may be expected to depend upon conditions that determine such attractions. Although these conditions are only partially understood, several have been especially emphasized in the literature. Heider (19) and Newcomb (35) have proposed that a person will tend to be attracted to another if he believes that the other's attitudes and values are similar to his own. Moreover, this attraction will be stronger the more important the attitudes and values are to the person. In an intensive study of the development of interpersonal attractions among male college students residing in a small dormitory, Newcomb found that he could predict rather well the emergence of friendship ties on the basis of certain tests of attitudes and values administered before the students became acquainted.

He concludes that "following but not before adequate opportunity for pair members to become familiar with each other's attitudes, pair attraction is predictable from actual agreement" (**35**, 96). Data collected in other settings generally support the hypothesis that people are attracted to one another when they believe that they hold important attitudes and values in common.

To theorists writing in the psychoanalytic tradition, spontaneous group formation depends upon conditions that generate interpersonal identification. Freud (**14**) maintained that two or more people come to identify with one another when they have substituted one and the same object—a leader or "leading ideal"—for their ego ideal. Subsequent writers have proposed that a collection of people come to identify with one another, and thus form a group, when they employ the same objects as a means for relieving similar internal conflicts. A related view is advanced by Cohen (**8**) in his analysis of the formation of lower-class delinquent gangs when he asserts that boys who despair of meeting society's standards of success are drawn together by their common adoption of values that they can satisfy but that are antithetical to those of society at large. A more detailed analysis of the operation of interpersonal identifications in the formation and functioning of groups is presented by Janis in Chapter 6.

A rather different conception has been developed by theorists who see group formation as resulting from advantages people believe they will obtain from group membership. Thibaut and Kelley (**43**) propose that when two or more people come in contact with one another they engage in an exploratory process of "testing out" one another to discover the gains and costs they would incur from maintaining an active relationship. According to this view, groups arise when a number of people find that their needs interrelate in a way such that they all can gain sufficient satisfaction from continued interaction.

Most people have social needs that can be satisfied only by interaction with other people. These affiliative tendencies, which provide much of the motivation for group formation, appear to have a variety of sources. Schachter (**36**) has demonstrated, for example, that when individuals are subjected to an anxiety-arousing situation many, but not all, experience a heightened desire to be with other people. He argues that the reduction of anxiety brought about by the presence of others derives in part, at least, from the fact that each person helps the other to define the nature of their emotional upset and locate the appropriate responses to it. Festinger (**12**, Chap. 14) has argued in a similar vein that groups tend to construct a single view of the world—a social reality—that people employ to validate their beliefs about their environment and themselves when an independent check is not possible or readily available. And Scott (**38**) has proposed that similar processes operate with respect to values, that people tend to validate their views of what is morally right by referring them to the norms and standards of respected groups. We should expect, then, to find groups especially prevalent among a collection of people characterized by a high state of anxiety or uncertainty concerning the validity of their beliefs and values. The great incidence of groups among adolescents would seem to be consistent with this expectation.

EXTERNAL DESIGNATION

For some groups the original impetus to their formation derives neither from the desire to accomplish an objective nor from the needs of those who become members but from the fact that certain people are treated in a homogeneous manner by others. The number of ways in which a population can be categorized is, of course, very large. People can be placed into categories on the basis of the color of their skin, hair, or eyes or their age, sex, height, weight, ability, place of birth, language, hobbies, occupation, income, education, religion, and many other attributes. Under certain conditions, which unfortunately are not well understood, one or more of these personal traits become socially relevant, and individuals possessing them are clustered into perceptual or cognitive categories such as teenagers, older people, women, motorcyclists, hillbillies, migrants, cripples, "the poor," college graduates, artists, Negroes, Jews, Mormons, or people who speak a distinctive language. Others behave toward people in these categories on the basis of their inclusion in the category; perceptual or cognitive segregation leads to behavioral segregation. The members of a socially defined category find that certain kinds of behavior are expected of them and that certain opportunities are available to them or denied them simply because of their membership in the category. Interdependence among members develops because society gives them "a common fate."

Although it is clear that often groups form because of this sort of external designation, the nature of the processes involved and the conditions generating them are understood only in broad outline. What determines whether a particular personal trait will become a socially significant basis for categorization? Why are people so often segregated on the basis of age, sex, skin color, and education and so seldom segregated according to such visible characteristics as eye color and height? And, once a socially significant category has developed, what determines the responses of those placed in it? Under what conditions does the experience of a common fate lead to the emergence of such group properties as cohesiveness, norms or standards, goals, and role differentiation? Although there has been much speculative writing, remarkably little systematic research has been devoted to providing definitive answers.

PROPERTIES OF GROUPS

The study of group dynamics is concerned with phenomena that arise when a collection of individuals has become, for whatever reason, sufficiently interdependent to be called a group. Its goal is the construction of systematic theory to account for these phenomena, their determinants, effects, and interrelationships. Any such theory must, of course, contain concepts referring to the phenomena that are to be explained by the theory. What concepts are suitable for inclusion in a theory of groups? What properties may be properly attributed to a group?

Questions of this sort have been a source of endless controversy throughout the history of social science; they reached a peak in the 1920's in the debate over the concept of group mind.[1] At that time the fundamental issue was conceived as a question concerning the "reality" of groups. On the one side were those who argued that a group has existence over and above that of the individuals who

[1] For a retrospective account of this controversy and an assessment of its current status, the reader is referred to an interesting article by F. H. Allport (1).

compose it and that this entity has attributes distinct from those of its members. According to this view, it is entirely meaningful to say that a group convenes, thinks, decides, solves problems, achieves solidarity, becomes organized and has a role structure, a culture, or a system of values. Those on the other side of the debate maintained that only individuals have reality and that any term purported to describe a group has no concrete empirical referent. Only individuals can think, decide, and act; the attribution of such characteristics to a collection of people was said to have no firm empirical basis and to involve the twin fallacies of "reification" and "personification."

To most contemporary theorists, arguments about "reality" seem fruitless. A term like group mind is currently in disrepute, not so much because of reservations about the reality of groups, but because of its deficiencies as a scientific concept. It has never been clearly defined; neither its conceptual properties nor its empirical referents have been satisfactorily established. A term like group size, however, though referring to a collection of people is readily accepted, since it is not difficult to conceive of feasible operations for ascertaining the number of people to be considered members of any particular group. According to the current view, any concept that is clearly defined, both conceptually and operationally, is a suitable candidate for inclusion in a theory of groups, whether it refers to a single person or to a collection of individuals.

During the early stages of theory building, the terms used to describe groups are drawn chiefly from everyday language and research problems tend to be stated in these terms. What are the determinants of group loyalty? What are the effects of different styles of leadership upon group effectiveness? What accounts for differences in persistence toward the attainment of group goals? Even though such terms as group loyalty, style of leadership, group effectiveness, and group goal serve reasonably well in ordinary communication, it is exceedingly difficult to specify their exact empirical referents and they may remain ambiguous and have only limited value as theoretical concepts. Theoretical progress depends to a considerable degree upon success in clarifying the empirical referents of terms employed in the description of groups.

Suppose that we want to study the problem-solving of committees. We might decide to characterize each committee under investigation according to its level of "intelligence." How should we proceed? What sorts of measurements of "group intelligence" should we employ? What exactly do we mean by this term? Two rather natural possibilities come to mind. We might administer an intelligence test to all the members of the committees and employ the average score for each committee as a measure of its intelligence. Or we might ask each committee to work as a group on a series of problems graded according to difficulty and then characterize the intelligence of each on the basis of its success in solving these problems. These two procedures give basically different empirical meanings to the term "group intelligence." The first refers to a characteristic of each member of the group taken separately, whereas the second refers to a property of the group considered as a whole. Each procedure results in a clear operational definition, but the meaning of the term is quite different depending upon which one is used.

Cattell (6) has proposed that the terms used to describe a group may refer to any of three "panels of group description": (*a*) characteristics of the individuals who constitute its membership (population variables), (*b*) attributes of the collection of members considered as a whole (syntality variables), and (*c*) relationships existing among the members of the group (structural variables). The first definition of "group intelligence" suggested above, by referring to the average intelligence of the members of the group, employs a population variable. The second, by referring to the performance of the group as a whole, uses a syntality variable. If we were to ask the members of a group to fill out a sociometric test and use the indicated interpersonal likes and dislikes to characterize the group's "affect structure," we would be employing a structural variable.

The language used to describe groups has many terms used also to describe individuals. For this reason needless confusion results unless care is exercised to make explicit the panel of group description to which any such term refers. If we say that a group is "friendly," do we intend to assert that it is composed of friendly people (a population variable), that its policies are supportive of the interests of other groups (a syntality variable), or that the interpersonal relationships among its members are characterized by friendliness (a structural variable)? Is the term "authoritarian group"

meant to refer to one whose members score high on a test of authoritarianism or to one with a centralized pattern of authority relationships among its members? By "a high-status group" do we wish to refer to one whose members occupy respected positions in a community or to one whose activities make it highly valued in comparison with other groups? And if we speak of the "age" of a group, are we referring to the mean age of its members or to the length of time elapsed since the group's formation? Identification of the panel of group description to which any term refers helps to clarify its intended empirical meaning and is a first step toward giving it an operational definition.

The development of a systematic theory of the phenomena of group life is, of course, an ongoing process involving a progressive refinement of the concepts contained in the theory. This refinement demands a simultaneous concern for theoretical and operational requirements. Unless the investigator has at least a general notion of the theoretical use of a concept, he has no basis for selecting a suitable operational definition. And even the most elegant theory remains an empty formalism unless it has a firm operational underpinning. As research progresses a body of findings emerges each of which fits into a general theoretical scheme, and concepts acquire an increasingly precise meaning both theoretically and operationally. The task of research is to refine these terms and to extend the empirical applicability of the developing theoretical formulation.

A GENERAL THEORETICAL SCHEME

The selection of materials from the literature of group dynamics and their clustering into major sections of this volume have been guided by a broad theoretical orientation whose principal features are briefly described in the following paragraphs. This theoretical scheme has made it possible to organize a large segment of the literature into a reasonably coherent structure so that theoretical interrelations among the reported findings can be better apprehended. An unfortunate consequence of this procedure is the exclusion of certain bodies of research not readily fitted into the theoretical scheme. It is to be hoped that future work will result in the construction of a theoretical system capable of ordering a larger portion of the total body of findings concerning the nature of groups.

The selections in Part Two define the nature of groups and group membership. As indicated above, a group is conceived as a set of people whose relationships make them interdependent. A group has a "boundary" of membership, and a variety of consequences follow for a person, depending upon whether he is located "inside" or "outside" a particular group. In addition, a group may have a dynamic character—forces may operate on an individual to bring him toward or take him away from location in the group. These forces are reflected by the tendency for persons to move into a group, to leave or resist leaving, or to encounter resistance in attempting to cross the group's boundary of membership. The constellation of such forces for any given group determines its "cohesiveness."

Part Three discusses the pressures to uniformity in groups. Interdependent people are likely to engage in some degree of communication and to refer their beliefs, values, and behavior to those of others in the group. Out of such interaction the members tend to develop a common set of beliefs, or "social reality," and normative expectations, or "group standards." It is assumed that the magnitude of a person's tendency to accept these depends upon his degree of attraction to membership in the group. Thus, the "power" of a group to influence its members is related to its cohesiveness. A person who persistently deviates from a group's predominant beliefs or values will tend to be rejected by other members of the group.

Part Four deals with the determinants and consequences of power and influence in groups. As the members of a group engage in interaction, they exert some degree of influence on one another. A person's capacity to influence others and to shape the course of events in the group constitutes his "power" in the group. There are several qualitatively different bases of an individual's power, and these may be expected to affect both his behavior and that of others toward him. Groups differ with respect to the bases of power afforded to members and the distribution of power among members.

Part Five defines leadership and discusses the performance of group functions. A group may be conceived as existing in an environment and as having a location in that environment. Some locations are more favorable for the group than others. Certain acts, which may be performed by one or more members of the group, have the effect of changing the group's location within its environment. If a person's behavior moves the group toward more favorable locations or improves the group's capacity to do so, he exercises "leadership" in the group. It is possible, in principle, for any member of a group to perform acts of leadership, but groups may be expected to differ considerably in the actual distribution of such acts among members. The nature of this distribution has widespread effects on other aspects of the group's functioning.

Part Six describes the nature of motivational processes in groups. Individual members tend to develop preferences for the group's location in its environment. These personal goals for the group may enter into a process of "group decision" from which a "group goal" emerges. A group's procedure for decision-making—which members are allowed to participate, the rules for combining individual preferences into a group goal, and the like—affects the nature of the goal selected and the motivation of members to contribute to the group's goal-directed activities. Groups may succeed or fail in achieving their goals, with a variety of consequences for group functioning and for the self-esteem of members.

Finally, Part Seven defines the structural properties of groups. The members of a group tend to develop a variety of interpersonal relationships, having some degree of stability, which constitute the group's structural properties. Some of the more important of these relationships are interpersonal liking (yielding a "sociometric structure"), communication (giving a "communication network"), task-related interaction (generating a "work structure"), and interpersonal influence (forming a "power structure"). Properties of these structures, such as their degree of centralization, connectedness, and stratification, affect group functioning, and a member's position in each structure will influence the amount of satisfaction he derives from membership.

OVERVIEW OF RESEARCH REPORTED IN PART TWO

The material presented in this section focuses on some of the basic relationships that may exist between a person and a group. The first selection is by Zajonc (Chap. 4), who reviews research directed toward answering one of the earliest questions raised in experimental social psychology: What are the consequences upon a person's behavior that derive from the sheer physical presence of other individuals? He examines two basic situations. In the first, the individual under investigation performs some task in front of an audience of passive spectators; in the second, he performs the task in the presence of others who are also engaged in the same activity. How does the individual's performance differ in each situation from his performance when working in isolation? The results summarized by Zajonc show that even under such conditions of weak interdependence the presence of others can produce marked effects upon a person's behavior.

The person-group relations of "membership" and "reference" are examined by Siegel and Siegel (Chap. 5) in their report of a natural experiment designed to study attitudinal changes occurring among female college students after a change of residence. At the beginning of the experiment all students expressed a desire to be assigned for the coming year to the same residential group; they had the same reference group. Since it was not possible to satisfy all these preferences, a random "drawing" was held with the result that some girls became members of their reference group and others did not. Attitude measurements taken before and after this change of membership revealed that a subject's change in attitude was a function of both the norms of her new membership group and her reference group. The greatest change took place when the imposed membership group was initially nonpreferred but subsequently came to serve as a reference group.

In Chapter 6, Janis examines the causes and consequences of "identification" with a group. On the assumption that these phenomena will be revealed most vividly under conditions of extreme danger, he draws upon research and observations conducted during World War II. He shows how the anxieties arising from combat heighten group identification and documents a variety of striking consequences that follow from identification.

The concept of group cohesiveness, which has come to have a central place in theories of group dynamics, refers to the person-group relation of "attraction to membership." In Chapter 7, Cartwright discusses problems involved in measuring group cohesiveness and in refining its theoretical meaning. He lists several features of groups that have been shown to affect attraction to membership and reports findings from research on the consequences of group cohesiveness.

In Chapter 8, Radloff presents results from an experiment designed to test the hypothesis that a person's needs for self-evaluation regarding the correctness of his opinions arouse affiliative tendencies in him. The findings support the view that individuals may come to depend upon groups for the social validation of their beliefs and that such dependence is often a source of attraction to group membership. Radloff also presents data indicating that the affiliative responses of subjects who were first-born or only children are more strongly affected by varying evaluative needs than are those of later born subjects.

The two final chapters are concerned with the applicability of the theory of cognitive dissonance to social behavior. The core notion of the theory is that "the simultaneous existence of cognitions which in one way or another do not fit together (dissonance) leads to effort on the part of the person to somehow make them fit better (dissonance reduction)." Aronson and Mills (Chap. 9) reason, in keeping with this conception, that if a person has undergone an unpleasant initiation to gain admission to a group, his cognition that he has gone through an unpleasant experience for the sake of membership is dissonant with a cognition that there are things about the group that he does not like. One way for the person to reduce such dissonance, they argue, is to heighten his evaluation of the attractiveness of the group. They present evidence showing that individuals who undergo an unpleasant initiation do, in fact, find the group more attractive than do persons who become members without going through a severe initiation. These results have been replicated under somewhat different conditions by Gerard and Mathewson (16). In Chapter 10, Festinger and Aronson discuss more generally the ways in which group interaction may be both a source of dissonance and a means of reducing dissonance.

References

1. Allport, F. H. A structuronomic conception of behavior: Individual and collective I. Structural theory and the master problem of social psychology. *Journal of Abnormal and Social Psychology*, 1962, **64**, 3–30.
2. Asch, S. E. Studies of independence and conformity: I. A minority of one against a unanimous majority. *Psychological Monographs*, 1956, **70** (9, Whole No. 416).
3. Bales, R. F. *Interaction process analysis*. Cambridge, Mass.: Addison-Wesley, 1950.
4. Bass, B. M. *Leadership, psychology, and organizational behavior*. New York: Harper, 1960.
5. Brodbeck, M. Methodological individualism: Definition and reduction. *Philosophy of Science*, 1958, **25**, 1–22.
6. Cattell, R. B. New concepts for measuring leadership in terms of group syntality. *Human Relations*, 1951, **4**, 161–184.
7. Chapman, D. W., & Volkmann, J. A. A social determinant of the level of aspiration. *Journal of Abnormal and Social Psychology*, 1939, **34**, 225–238.
8. Cohen, A. K. *Delinquent boys*. Glencoe, Ill.: Free Press, 1955.
9. Coleman, J. S. *Community conflict*. Glencoe, Ill.: Free Press, 1957.
10. Collins, B. E., & Guetzkow, H. *A social psychology of group processes for decision-making*. New York: Wiley, 1964.
11. Festinger, L. Wish, expectation, and group performance as factors influencing level of aspiration. *Journal of Abnormal and Social Psychology*, 1942, **37**, 184–200.
12. Festinger, L. A theory of social comparison processes. *Human Relations*, 1954, **7**, 117–140.
13. Festinger, L., Schachter, S., & Back, K. *Social pressures in informal groups*, New York: Harper, 1950.
14. Freud, S. *Group psychology and the analysis of the ego*. London: Hogarth, 1922.
15. Gerard, H. The anchorage of opinions in face-to-face groups. *Human Relations*, 1954, **7**, 313–325.
16. Gerard, H. B., & Mathewson, G. C. The effects of severity of initiation on liking for a group: A replication. *Journal of Experimental Social Psychology*, 1966, **2**, 278–287.
17. Gore, W. J., & Dyson, J. W. (Eds.) *The making of decisions*. New York: Free Press of Glencoe, 1964.
18. Gross, N., Mason, W. S., & McEachern, A. W. *Explorations in role analysis: Studies of the school superintendency role*. New York: Wiley, 1958.
19. Heider, F. *The psychology of interpersonal relations*. New York: Wiley, 1958.
20. Hoffman, L. R. Group problem solving. In L. Berkowitz (Ed.), *Advances in experimental social psychology*. Vol. 2. New York: Academic Press, 1965. Pp. 99–132.
21. Homans, G. C. *The human group*. New York: Harcourt, Brace, 1950.
22. Hyman, H. H. The psychology of status. *Archives of Psychology*, 1942, No. 269.
23. Jackson, J. M. A space for conceptualizing person-group relationships. *Human Relations*, 1959, **12**, 3–15.
24. Kelley, H. H. Two functions of reference groups. In G. E. Swanson, T. M. Newcomb, & E. L. Hartley (Eds.), *Readings in social psychology*. New York: Holt, Rinehart, and Winston, 1952. Pp. 410–414.
25. Kelley, H. H., & Thibaut, J. W. Experimental studies of group problem solving and process. In G. Lindzey (Ed.), *Handbook of social psychology*. Cambridge, Mass.: Addison-Wesley, 1954. Pp. 735–785.
26. Killian, L. The significance of multiple-group membership in disaster. *American Journal of Sociology*, 1952, **57**, 309–314.
27. Lewin, K. *Resolving social conflicts*. New York: Harper, 1948.
28. Likert, R. *New patterns of management*. New York: McGraw-Hill, 1961.
29. Lorge, I., *et al.* A survey of studies contrasting the quality of group performance and individual performance, 1920–1957. *Psychological Bulletin*, 1958, **55**, 337–372.
30. Lorge, I., & Solomon, H. Two models of group behavior in the solution of Eureka-type problems. *Psychometrika*, 1955, **20**, 139–148.

31. Maier, N. R. F. *Problem-solving discussions and conferences: Leadership methods and skills.* New York: McGraw-Hill, 1963.
32. March, J. G., & Simon, H. A. *Organizations.* New York: Wiley, 1958.
33. Merton, R. K. *Social theory and social structure.* (Rev. ed.) Glencoe, Ill.: Free Press, 1957.
34. Newcomb, T. M. Social psychological theory. In J. H. Rohrer & M. Sherif (Eds.), *Social psychology at the crossroads.* New York: Harper, 1951. Pp. 31–49.
35. Newcomb, T. M. *The acquaintance process.* New York: Holt, Rinehart, and Winston, 1961.
36. Schachter, S. *The psychology of affiliation.* Stanford: Stanford Univ. Press, 1959.
37. Scheidlinger, S. *Psychoanalysis and group behavior.* New York: Norton, 1952.
38. Scott, W. A. *Values and organizations.* Chicago: Rand McNally, 1965.
39. Sherif, M. *The psychology of social norms.* New York: Harper, 1936.
40. Smith, M. Social situation, social behavior, social group. *Psychological Review,* 1945, **52,** 224–229.
41. Snoek, J. D. Some effects of rejection upon attraction to a group. *Journal of Abnormal and Social Psychology,* 1962, **64,** 175–182.
42. Stouffer, S. A., et al. *The American soldier.* Vols. I–II. *Studies in social psychology in World War II.* Princeton, N.J.: Princeton Univ. Press, 1949.
43. Thibaut, J. W., & Kelley, H. H. *The social psychology of groups.* New York: Wiley, 1959.
44. Thomas, E. J., & Fink, C. F. Models of group problem solving. *Journal of Abnormal and Social Psychology,* 1961, **68,** 53–63.
45. Truman, D. *The governmental process.* New York: Knopf, 1951.
46. Watson, J., & Lippitt, R. *Learning across cultures.* Ann Arbor, Mich.: Institute for Social Research, 1955.
47. Zajonc, R. B. Aggressive attitudes of the "stranger" as a function of conformity pressures. *Human Relations,* 1952, **5,** 205–216.
48. Zajonc, R. B., & Smoke, W. H. Optimal task assignments for group performance. In N. F. Washburne (Ed.), *Decisions, values, and groups.* New York: Macmillan, 1962. Pp. 279–290.
49. Zander, A., Stotland, E., & Wolfe, D. Unity of group, identification with group, and self-esteem of members. *Journal of Personality,* 1960, **28,** 463–478.
50. Ziller, R. C. Toward a theory of open and closed groups. *Psychological Bulletin,* 1965, **64,** 164–182.

4

Social Facilitation

ROBERT B. ZAJONC

Most textbook definitions of social psychology involve considerations about the influence of man upon man, or, more generally, of individual upon individual. And most of them, explicitly or implicitly, commit the main efforts of social psychology to the problem of how and why the *behavior* of one individual affects the behavior of another. The influences of individuals on each others' behavior which are of interest to social psychologists today take on very complex forms. Often they involve vast networks of interindividual effects such as one finds in studying the process of group decision-making, competition, or conformity to a group norm. But the fundamental forms of interindividual influence are represented by the oldest experimental paradigm of social psychology: social facilitation. This paradigm, dating back to Triplett's original experiments on pacing and competition, carried out in 1897 (**37**), examines the consequences upon behavior which derive from the sheer presence of other individuals.

Until the late 1930's, interest in social facilitation was quite active, but with the outbreak of World War II it suddenly died. And it is truly regrettable that it died, because the basic questions about social facilitation—its dynamics and its causes—which are in effect the basic questions of social psychology, were never solved. It is with these questions that this article is concerned. I first examine past results in this nearly completely abandoned area of research and then suggest a general hypothesis which might explain them.

Research in the area of social facilitation may be classified in terms of two experimental paradigms: audience effects and co-action effects. The first experimental para-

From *Science*, 1965, **149**, 269–274. Reprinted by permission of the author and the American Association for the Advancement of Science. Copyright 1965 by the American Association for the Advancement of Science. Preparation of this article was supported by grants from the Office of Naval Research and the National Science Foundation.

digm involves the observation of behavior when it occurs in the presence of passive spectators. The second examines behavior when it occurs in the presence of other individuals also engaged in the same activity. We shall consider past literature in these two areas separately.

AUDIENCE EFFECTS

Simple motor responses are particularly sensitive to social facilitation effects. In 1925 Travis (35) obtained such effects in a study in which he used the pursuit-rotor task. In this task the subject is required to follow a small revolving target by means of a stylus which he holds in his hand. If the stylus is even momentarily off target during a revolution, the revolution counts as an error. First each subject was trained for several consecutive days until his performance reached a stable level. One day after the conclusion of the training the subject was called to the laboratory, given five trials alone, and then ten trials in the presence of from four to eight upper-classmen and graduate students. They had been asked by the experimenter to watch the subject quietly and attentively. Travis found a clear improvement in performance when his subjects were confronted with an audience. Their accuracy on the ten trials before an audience was greater than on any ten previous trials, including those on which they had scored highest.

A considerably greater improvement in performance was recently obtained in a somewhat different setting and on a different task (6). Each subject (all were National Guard trainees) was placed in a separate booth. He was seated in front of a panel outfitted with 20 red lamps in a circle. The lamps on this panel light in a clockwise sequence at 12 revolutions per minute. At random intervals one or another light fails to go on in its proper sequence. On the average there are 24 such failures per hour. The subject's task is to signal whenever a light fails to go on. After 20 minutes of intensive training, followed by a short rest, the National Guard trainees monitored the light panels for 135 minutes. Subjects in one group performed their task alone. Subjects in another group were told that from time to time a lieutenant colonel or a master sergeant would visit them in the booth to observe their performance. These visits actually took place

about four times during the experimental session. There was no doubt about the results. The accuracy of the supervised subjects was on the average 34 percent higher than the accuracy of the trainees working in isolation, and toward the end of the experimental session the accuracy of the supervised subjects was more than twice as high as that of the subjects working in isolation. Those expecting to be visited by a superior missed, during the last experimental period, 20 percent of the light failures, while those expecting no such visits missed 64 percent of the failures.

Dashiell (11), who, in the early 1930's, carried out an extensive program of research on social facilitation, also found considerable improvement in performance due to audience effects on such tasks as simple multiplication or word association. But, as is the case in many other areas, negative audience effects were also found. In 1933 Pessin (28) asked college students to learn lists of nonsense syllables under two conditions, alone and in the presence of several spectators. When confronted with an audience, his subjects required an average of 11.27 trials to learn a seven-item list. When working alone they needed only 9.85 trials. The average number of errors made in the "audience" condition was considerably higher than the number in the "alone" condition. In 1931 Husband (17) found that the presence of spectators interferes with the learning of a finger maze, and in 1933 Pessin and Husband (29) confirmed Husband's results. The number of trials which the isolated subjects required for learning the finger maze was 17.1. Subjects confronted with spectators, however, required 19.1 trials. The average number of errors for the isolated subjects was 33.7; the number for those working in the presence of an audience was 40.5.

The results thus far reviewed seem to contradict one another. On a pursuit-rotor task Travis found that the presence of an audience improves performance. The learning of nonsense syllables and maze learning, however, seem to be inhibited by the presence of an audience, as shown by Pessin's experiment. The picture is further complicated by the fact that when Pessin's subjects were asked, several days later, to recall the nonsense syllables they had learned, a reversal was found. The subjects who tried to recall the lists in the presence of spectators did considerably better than those who tried to recall them alone.

Why are the learning of nonsense syllables and maze learning inhibited by the presence of spectators? And why, on the other hand, does performance on a pursuit-rotor, word-association, multiplication, or a vigilance task improve in the presence of others?

There is just one, rather subtle, consistency in the above results. It would appear that the emission of well-learned responses is facilitated by the presence of spectators, while the acquisition of new responses is impaired. To put the statement in conventional psychological language, performance is facilitated and learning is impaired by the presence of spectators.

This tentative generalization can be reformulated so that different features of the problem are placed into focus. During the early stages of learning, especially of the type involved in social facilitation studies, the subject's responses are mostly the wrong ones. A person learning a finger maze, or a person learning a list of nonsense syllables, emits more wrong responses than right ones in the early stages of training. Most learning experiments continue until he ceases to make mistakes—until his performance is perfect. It may be said, therefore, that during training it is primarily the wrong responses which are dominant and strong; they are the ones which have the highest probability of occurrence. But after the individual has mastered the task, correct responses necessarily gain ascendency in his task-relevant behavioral repertoire. Now they are the ones which are more probable—in other words, dominant. Our tentative generalization may now be simplified: audience enhances the emission of dominant responses. If the dominant responses are the correct ones, as is the case upon achieving mastery, the presence of an audience will be of benefit to the individual. But if they are mostly wrong, as is the case in the early stages of learning, then these wrong responses will be enhanced in the presence of an audience, and the emission of correct responses will be postponed or prevented.

There is a class of psychological processes which are known to enhance the emission of dominant responses. They are subsumed under the concepts of drive, arousal, and activation (13, 32, 39). If we could show that the presence of an audience has arousal consequences for the subject, we would be a step further along in trying to arrange the results of social-facilitation experiments into a neater package. But let us first consider another set of experimental findings.

CO-ACTION EFFECTS

The experimental paradigm of co-action is somewhat more complex than the paradigm involved in the study of audience effects. Here we observe individuals all simultaneously engaged in the same activity and in full view of each other. One of the clearest effects of such simultaneous action, or co-action, is found in eating behavior. It is well known that animals simply eat more in the presence of others. For instance, Bayer (5) had chickens eat from a pile of wheat to their full satisfaction. He waited some time to be absolutely sure that his subject would eat no more, and then brought in a companion chicken who had not eaten for 24 hours. Upon the introduction of the hungry co-actor, the apparently sated chicken ate two-thirds again as much grain as it had already eaten. Recent work by Tolman and Wilson (34) fully substantiates these results. In an extensive study of social-facilitation effects among albino rats, Harlow (16) found dramatic increases in eating. In one of his experiments, for instance, the rats, shortly after weaning, were matched in pairs for weight. They were then fed alone and in pairs on alternate days. Figure 1 shows his results. It is clear that considerably more food was consumed by the animals when they were in pairs than when they were fed alone. James (18, 19, 20), too, found very clear evidence of increased eating among puppies fed in groups.

Perhaps the most dramatic effect of co-action is reported by Chen (10). Chen observed groups of ants working alone, in groups of two, and in groups of three. Each ant was observed under various conditions. In the first experimental session each ant was placed in a bottle half filled with sandy soil. The ant was observed for six hours. The time at which nest-building began was noted, and the earth excavated by the insect was carefully weighed. Two days afterward the same ants were placed in freshly filled bottles in pairs, and the same observations were made. A few days later the ants were placed in the bottles in groups of three, again for six hours. Finally, a few days after the test in groups of three, nest-

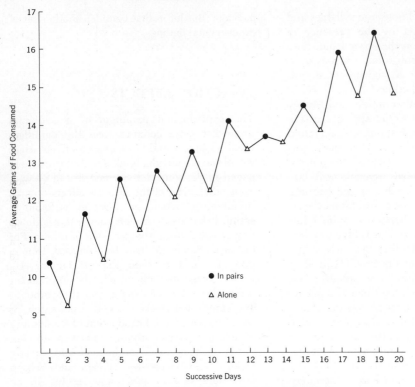

FIGURE 1. Feeding of isolated and paired rats. [From Harlow, **16**]

building of the ants in isolation was observed. Figure 2 shows some of Chen's data.

There is absolutely no question that the amount of work an ant accomplishes increases markedly in the presence of another ant. In all pairs except one, the presence of a companion increased output by a factor of at least 2. The effect of co-action on the latency of the nest-building behavior was equally dramatic. The solitary ants of session 1 and the final session began working on the nest in 192 minutes, on the average. The latency period for ants in groups of two was only 28 minutes. The effects observed by Chen were limited to the immediate situation and seemed to have no lasting consequences for the ants. There were no differences in the results of session 1, during which the ants worked in isolation, and of

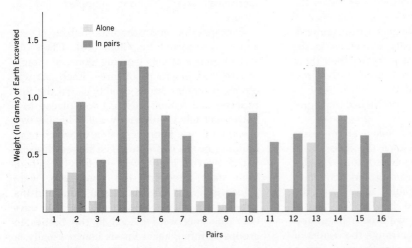

FIGURE 2. Nest-building behavior of isolated and paired ants. [From Chen, **10**]

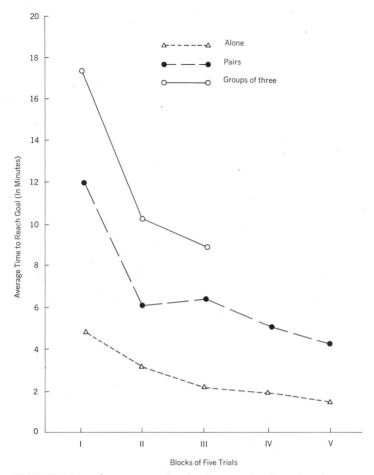

FIGURE 3. Maze learning in isolated and grouped cockroaches. [From Gates & Allee, **14**]

the last experimental session, where they again worked in solitude.

If one assumes that under the conditions of Chen's experiment nest-building *is* the dominant response, then there is no reason why his findings could not be embraced by the generalization just proposed. Nest-building is a response which Chen's ants have fully mastered. Certainly it is something that a mature ant need not learn. And this is simply an instance where the generalization that the presence of others enhances the emission of dominant and well-developed responses holds.

If the process involved in audience effects is also involved in co-action effects, then learning should be inhibited in the presence of other learners. Let us examine some literature in this field. Klopfer (**21**) observed greenfinches—in isolation and in heterosexual pairs—which were learning to discriminate between sources of palatable and of unpalatable food. And, as one

would by now expect, his birds learned this discrimination task considerably more efficiently when working alone. I hasten to add that the subjects' sexual interests cannot be held responsible for the inhibition of learning in the paired birds. Allee and Masure (**2**), using Australian parakeets, obtained the same result for homosexual pairs as well. The speed of learning was considerably greater for the isolated birds than for the paired birds, regardless of whether the birds were of the same sex or of the opposite sex.

Similar results are found with cockroaches. Gates and Allee (**14**) compared data for cockroaches learning a maze in isolation, in groups of two, and in groups of three. They used an E-shaped maze. Its three runways, made of galvanized sheet metal, were suspended in a pan of water. At the end of the center runway was a dark bottle into which the photophobic cockroaches could escape from the noxious light. The results, in terms of time required to reach the bottle, are shown in Figure 3. It is clear from the data that the solitary cockroaches required considerably less time to learn the maze than the grouped animals. Gates and Allee believe that the group situation produced inhibition. They add, however (14, 357):

The nature of these inhibiting forces is speculative, but the fact of some sort of group interference is obvious. The presence of other roaches did not operate to change greatly the movements to different parts of the maze, but did result in increased time per trial. The roaches tended to go to the corner or end of the runway and remain there a longer time when another roach was present than when alone; the other roach was a distracting stimulus.

The experiments on social facilitation performed by Floyd Allport (3) in 1920 and continued by Dashiell (11), in 1930, both of whom used human subjects, are the ones best known. Allport's subjects worked either in separate cubicles or sitting around a common table. When working in isolation they did the various tasks at the same time and were monitored by common time signals. Allport did everything possible to reduce the tendency to compete. The subjects were told that the results of their tests would not be compared and would not be shown to other staff members, and that they themselves should refrain from making any such comparisons.

Among the tasks used were the following: chain word association, vowel cancellation, reversible perspective, multiplication, problem solving, and judgments of odors and weights. The results of Allport's experiments are well known: in all but the problem-solving and judgments test, performance was better in groups than in the "alone" condition. How do these results fit our generalization? Word association, multiplication, the cancellation of vowels, and the reversal of the perceived orientation of an ambiguous figure all involve responses which are well established. They are responses which are either very well learned or under a very strong influence of the stimulus, as in the word-association task or the reversible-perspective test. The problem-solving test consists of disproving arguments of ancient philosophers. In contrast to the other

tests, it does not involve well-learned responses. On the contrary, the probability of wrong (that is, logically incorrect) responses on tasks of this sort is rather high; in other words, wrong responses are dominant. Of interest, however, is the finding that while intellectual work suffered in the group situation, sheer output of words was increased. When working together, Allport's subjects tended consistently to write more. Therefore, the generalization proposed in the previous section can again be applied: if the presence of others raises the probability of dominant responses, and if strong (and many) incorrect response tendencies prevail, then the presence of others can only be detrimental to performance. The results of the judgment tests have little bearing on the present argument, since Allport gives no accuracy figures for evaluating performance. The data reported only show that the presence of others was associated with the avoidance of extreme judgments.

In 1928 Travis (36), whose work on the pursuit rotor I have already noted, repeated Allport's chain-word-association experiment. In contrast to Allport's results, Travis found that the presence of others decreased performance. The number of associations given by his subjects was greater when they worked in isolation. It is very significant, however, that Travis used stutterers as his subjects. In a way, stuttering is a manifestation of a struggle between conflicting response tendencies, all of which are strong and all of which compete for expression. The stutterer, momentarily hung up in the middle of a sentence, waits for the correct response to reach full ascendancy. He stammers because other competing tendencies are dominant at that moment. It is reasonable to assume that, to the extent that the verbal habits of a stutterer are characterized by conflicting response tendencies, the presence of others, by enhancing each of these response tendencies, simply heightens his conflict. Performance is thus impaired.

AVOIDANCE LEARNING

In two experiments on the learning of avoidance responses the performances of solitary and grouped subjects were compared. In one, rats were used; in the other, humans.

Let us first consider the results of the rat experiment by Rasmussen (30). A number of albino rats, all litter mates, were deprived of water for 48 hours. The apparatus consisted of a box containing a dish of drinking water. The floor of the box was made of a metal grille wired to one pole of an electric circuit. A wire inserted in the water in the dish was connected to the other pole of the circuit. Thirsty rats were placed in the box alone and in groups of three. They were allowed to drink for five seconds with the circuit open. Following this period the shock circuit remained closed, and each time the rat touched the water he received a painful shock. Observations were made on the number of times the rats approached the water dish. The results of this experiment showed that the solitary rats learned to avoid the dish considerably sooner than the grouped animals did. The rats that were in groups of three attempted to drink twice as often as the solitary rats did, and suffered considerably more shock than the solitary subjects.

Let us examine Rasmussen's results somewhat more closely. For purposes of analysis let us assume that there are just two critical responses involved: drinking, and avoidance of contact with the water. They are clearly incompatible. But drinking, we may further assume, is the dominant response, and, like eating or any other dominant response, it is enhanced by the presence of others. The animal is therefore prevented, by the facilitation of drinking which derives from the presence of others, from acquiring the appropriate avoidance response.

The second of the two studies is quite recent and was carried out by Ader and Tatum (1). They devised the following situation with which they confronted their subjects, all medical students. Each subject is told on arrival that he will be taken to another room and seated in a chair and that electrodes will be attached to his leg. He is instructed not to get up from the chair and not to touch the electrodes. He is also told not to smoke or vocalize, and is told that the experimenter will be in the next room. That is all he is told. The subjects are observed either alone or in pairs. In the former case the subject is brought to the room and seated at a table equipped with a red button which is connected to an electric circuit. Electrodes, by means of which electric shock can be administered, are attached to the calf of one leg. After the electrodes are attached, the experimenter leaves the room.

From now on the subject will receive ½ second of electric shock every 10 seconds unless he presses the red button. Each press of the button delays the shock by 10 seconds. Thus, if he is to avoid shock, he must press the button at least once every 10 seconds. It should be noted that no information was given him about the function of the button, or about the purpose of the experiment. No essential differences are introduced when subjects are brought to the room in pairs. Both are seated at the table and both become part of the shock circuit. The response of either subject delays the shock for both.

The avoidance response is considered to have been acquired when the subject (or pair of subjects) receives less than 6 shocks in a period of 5 minutes. Ader and Tatum report that the isolated students required, on the average, 11 minutes, 35 seconds to reach this criterion of learning. Of the 12 pairs which participated in the experiment, only 2 reached this criterion. One of them required 46 minutes, 40 seconds; the other, 68 minutes, 40 seconds! Ader and Tatum offer no explanation for their curious results. But there is no reason why we should not treat them in terms of the generalization proposed above. We are dealing here with a learning task, and the fact that the subjects are learning to avoid shock by pressing a red button does not introduce particular problems. They are confronted with an ambiguous task and told nothing about the button. Pressing the button is simply not the dominant response in this situation. However, escaping is. Ader and Tatum report that 8 of the 36 subjects walked out in the middle of the experiment.

One aspect of Ader and Tatum's results is especially worth noting. Once having learned the appropriate avoidance response, the individual subjects responded at considerably lower rates than the paired subjects. When we consider only those subjects who achieved the learning criterion and only those responses which occurred *after* criterion had been reached, we find that the response rates of the individual subjects were in all but one case lower than the response rates of the grouped subjects. This result further confirms the generalization that, while learning is impaired by the presence of others, the performance of learned responses is enhanced.

There are experiments which show that learning is enhanced by the presence of other learners (15, 38), but in all these experiments, as far as I can tell, it was possible for the subject to *observe* the critical responses of other subjects and to determine when he was correct and when incorrect. In none, therefore, has the co-action paradigm been employed in its pure form. That paradigm involves the presence of others, and nothing else. It requires that these others not be able to provide the subject with cues or information as to appropriate behavior. If other learners can supply the critical individual with such cues, we are dealing not with the problem of co-action but with the problem of imitation or vicarious learning.

PRESENCE OF OTHERS AS A SOURCE OF AROUSAL

The results I have discussed thus far lead to one generalization and to one hypothesis. The generalization which organizes these results is that the presence of others, as spectators or as co-actors, enhances the emission of dominant responses. We also know from extensive research literature that arousal, activation, or drive all have as a consequence the enhancement of dominant responses (32). We now need to examine the hypothesis that the presence of others increases the individual's general arousal or drive level.

The evidence which bears on the relationship between the presence of others and arousal is, unfortunately, only indirect. But there is some very suggestive evidence in one area of research. One of the more reliable indicators of arousal and drive is the activity of the endocrine systems in general, and of the adrenal cortex in particular. Adrenocortical functions are extremely sensitive to changes in emotional arousal, and it has been known for some time that organisms subjected to prolonged stress are likely to manifest substantial adrenocortical hypertrophy (31). Recent work (27) has shown that the main biochemical component of the adrenocortical output is hydrocortisone (17-hydroxycorticosterone). Psychiatric patients characterized by anxiety states, for instance, show elevated plasma levels of hydrocortisone (7, 8). Mason, Brady, and Sidman (26) have recently trained monkeys to press a lever for food and have given these animals unavoidable electric shocks, all preceded by warning

signals. This procedure led to elevated hydrocortisone levels; the levels returned to normal within one hour after the end of the experimental session. This "anxiety" reaction can apparently be attenuated if the animal is given repeated doses of reserpine one day before the experimental session (24). Sidman's conditioned avoidance schedule also results in raising the hydrocortisone levels by a factor of 2 to 4 (22). In this schedule the animal receives an electric shock every 20 seconds without warning, unless he presses a lever. Each press delays the shock for 20 seconds.

While there is a fair amount of evidence that adrenocortical activity is a reliable symptom of arousal, similar endocrine manifestations were found to be associated with increased population density (33). Crowded mice, for instance, show increased amphetamine toxicity—that is, susceptibility to the excitatory effects of amphetamine—against which they can be protected by the administration of phenobarbital, chlorpromazine, or reserpine (22). Mason and Brady (25) have recently reported that monkeys caged together had considerably higher plasma levels of hydrocortisone than monkeys housed in individual cages. Thiessen (33) found increases in adrenal weights in mice housed in groups of ten and 20 as compared with mice housed alone. The mere presence of other animals in the same room, but in separate cages, was also found to produce elevated levels of hydrocorti-

TABLE 1. *Basal Plasma Concentrations of 17-Hydroxycorticosterone in Monkeys Housed Alone (Cages in Separate Rooms), Then in a Room with Other Monkeys (cages in Same Room).*

Subject	Time	Concentration of 17-hydroxycorticosterone in caged monkeys (μg per 100 ml of plasma)	
		In separate rooms	In same room
M-1	9 A.M.	23	34
M-1	3 P.M.	16	27
M-2	9 A.M.	28	34
M-2	3 P.M.	19	23
M-3	9 A.M.	32	38
M-3	3 P.M.	23	31
Mean	9 A.M.	28	35
Mean	3 P.M.	19	27

SOURCE: Leiderman and Shapiro (23, 7).

TABLE 2. *Variations in Urinary Concentration of Hydrocortisone over a Nine-Day Period for Five Laboratory Monkeys and One Human Hospital Patient.*

Subjects	Amounts excreted (mg/24 hr)								
	Mon.	Tues.	Wed.	Thurs.	Fri.	Sat.	Sun.	Mon.	Tues.
Monkeys	1.88	1.71	1.60	1.52	1.70	1.16	1.17	1.88	
Patient		5.9	6.5	4.5	5.7	3.3	3.9	6.0	5.2

SOURCE: Leiderman and Shapiro (**23**, 8).

sone. Table 1, taken from a report by Mason and Brady (**25**), shows plasma levels of hydrocortisone for three animals which lived at one time in cages that afforded them the possibility of visual and tactile contact and, at another time, in separate rooms.

Mason and Brady also report urinary levels of hydrocortisone, by days of the week, for five monkeys from their laboratory and for one human hospital patient. These very suggestive figures are reproduced in Table 2 (**25**). In the monkeys, the low weekend traffic and activity in the laboratory seem to be associated with a clear decrease in hydrocortisone. As for the hospital patient, Mason and Brady report (**25**, 8), "he was confined to a thoracic surgery ward that bustled with activity during the weekdays when surgery and admissions occurred. On the weekends the patient retired to the nearby Red Cross building, with its quieter and more pleasant environment."

Admittedly, the evidence that the mere presence of others raises the arousal level is indirect and scanty. And, as a matter of fact, some work seems to suggest that there are conditions, such as stress, under which the presence of others may lower the animal's arousal level. Bovard (**9**), for instance, hypothesized that the presence of another member of the same species may protect the individual under stress by inhibiting the activity of the posterior hypothalamic centers which trigger the pituitary adrenal cortical and sympathetico-adrenal medullary responses to stress. Evidence for Bovard's hypothesis, however, is as indirect as evidence for the one which predicts arousal as a consequence of the presence of others, and even more scanty.

SUMMARY AND CONCLUSION

If one were to draw one practical suggestion from the review of the social-facilitation effects which are summarized in this article he would advise the student to study all alone, preferably in an isolated cubicle, and to arrange to take his examinations in the company of many other students, on stage, and in the presence of a large audience. The results of his examination would be beyond his wildest expectations, provided, of course, he had learned his material quite thoroughly.

I have tried in this article to pull together the early, almost forgotten work on social facilitation and to explain the seemingly conflicting results. This explanation is, of course, tentative, and it has never been put to a direct experimental test. It is, moreover, not far removed from the one originally proposed by Allport. He theorized (**4**, 261) that "the sights and sounds of others doing the same thing" augment ongoing responses. Allport, however, proposed this effect only for *overt* motor responses, assuming (**4**, 274) that "*intellectual* or *implicit responses* of thought are hampered rather than facilitated" by the presence of others. This latter conclusion was probably suggested to him by the negative results he observed in his research on the effects of co-action on problem solving.

Needless to say, the presence of others may have effects considerably more complex than that of increasing the individual's arousal level. The presence of others may provide cues as to appropriate or inappropriate responses, as in the case of imitation or vicarious learning. Or it may supply the individual with cues as to the measure of danger in an ambiguous or stressful situation. Davitz and Mason (**12**), for instance, have shown that the presence of an unafraid rat reduces the fear of another rat in stress. Bovard (9) believes that the calming of the rat in stress which is in the presence of an unafraid companion is mediated by inhibition of activity of the posterior hypothalamus. But in their experimental situations (that is, the open field test) the possibility that cues for appropriate escape or avoidance responses are provided by the co-actor is not ruled out. We might therefore be dealing not with the effects of the mere presence of others but with the considerably more complex case of imitation. The animal may not be calming *because* of his companion's presence. He may be calming *after* having copied his companion's attempted escape responses. The paradigm which I have examined in this article pertains only to the effects of the mere presence of others and to the consequences for the arousal level. The exact parameters involved in social facilitation still must be specified.

References

1. Ader, R., & Tatum, R. Free-operant avoidance conditioning in individual and paired human subjects. *Journal for Experimental Analysis of Behavior*, 1963, **6**, 357–359.
2. Allee, W. C., & Masure, R. H. A comparison of maze behavior in paired and isolated shell parakeets (*Melopsittacas undulatus*, Shaw). *Physiological Zoology*, 1936, **22**, 131–156.
3. Allport, F. H. The influence of the group upon association and thought. *Journal of Experimental Psychology*, 1920, 3, 159–182.
4. Allport, F. H. *Social psychology*. Boston: Houghton Mifflin, 1924.
5. Bayer, E. Beitrage zur zweikomponentheorie des hungers. *Zeitschrift für Psychologie*, 1929, **112**, 1–54.
6. Bergum, B. O., & Lehr, D. J. Effects of authoritarianism on vigilance performance. *Journal of Applied Psychology*, 1963, **47**, 75–77.
7. Bliss, E. I., Sandberg, A. A., & Nelson, D. H. Normal levels of 17 hydroxycorticosteroids in peripheral blood of man. *Journal of Clinical Investigation*, 1953, **32**, 818–823.
8. Board, F., Persky, H., & Hamburg, D. A. Psychological stress and endocrine functions; blood levels of adrenocortical and thyroid hormones in actively disturbed patients. *Psychosomatic Medicine*, 1956, **18**, 324–333.
9. Bovard, E. W. The effect of social stimuli on the response to stress. *Psychological Review*, 1959, **66**, 267–277.
10. Chen, S. C. Social modification of the activity of ants in nest-building. *Physiological Zoology*, 1937, **10**, 420–436.
11. Dashiell, J. F. An experimental analysis of some group effects. *Journal of Abnormal and Social Psychology*, 1930, **25**, 190–199.
12. Davitz, J. R., & Mason, D. J. Socially facilitated reduction of a fear response in rats. *Journal of Comparative and Physiological Psychology*, 1955, **48**, 149–151.
13. Dufy, E. *Activation and behavior*. New York: Wiley, 1962.
14. Gates, M. F., & Allee, W. C. Conditioned behavior of isolated and grouped cockroaches on a simple maze. *Journal of Comparative Psychology*, 1933, **15**, 331–358.
15. Gurnee, H. The effect of collective learning upon the individual participants. *Journal of Abnormal and Social Psychology*, 1939, **34**, 529–532.
16. Harlow, H. F. Social facilitation of feeding in the albino rat. *Journal of Genetic Psychology*, 1932, **41**, 211–221.
17. Husband, R. W. Analysis of methods in human maze learning. *Journal of Genetic Psychology*, 1931, **39**, 258–277.
18. James, W. T. Social facilitation of eating behavior in puppies after satiation. *Journal of Comparative and Physiological Psychology*, 1953, **46**, 427–428.
19. James, W. T. The development of social facilitation of eating in puppies. *Journal of Genetic Psychology*, 1960, **96**, 123–127.
20. James, W. T., & Cannon, D. J. Variation in social facilitation of eating behavior in puppies. *Journal of Genetic Psychology*, 1955, **87**, 225–228.
21. Klopfer, P. H. Influence of social interaction on learning rates in birds. *Science*, 1958, **128**, 903–904.
22. Lasagna, L., & McCann, W. P. Effect of tranquilizing drugs on amphetamine toxicity in aggregated mice. *Science*, 1957, **125**, 1241–1242.

23. Leiderman, P. H., & Shapiro, D. (Eds.), *Psychobiological approaches to social behavior.* Stanford: Stanford Univ. Press, 1964.

24. Mason, J. W., & Brady, J. V. Plasma 17-hydroxycorticosteroid changes related to reserpine effects on emotional behavior. *Science,* 1956, **124,** 983–984.

25. Mason, J. W., & Brady, J. V. The sensitivity of psychoendocrine systems to social and physical environment. In P. Leiderman and D. Shapiro (Eds.), *Psychobiological approaches to social behavior,* Stanford: Stanford Univ. Press, 1964.

26. Mason, J. W., Brady, J. V., & Sidman, M. Plasma 17-hydroxycorticosteroid levels and conditioned behavior in the Rhesus monkey. *Endocrinology,* 1957, **60,** 741–752.

27. Nelson, D. H., & Samuels, L. T. Method for determination of 17-hydroxycorticosteroids in blood. *Journal of Clinical Endocrinology,* 1952, **12,** 519–526.

28. Pessin, J. The comparative effects of social and mechanical stimulation on memorizing. *American Journal of Psychology,* 1933, **45,** 263–270.

29. Pessin, J., & Husband, R. W. Effects of social stimulation on human maze learning. *Journal of Abnormal and Social Psychology,* 1933, **28,** 148–154.

30. Rasmussen, E. Social facilitation in albino rats. *Acta Psychologica,* 1939, **4,** 275–294.

31. Selye, H. General adaptation syndrome and diseases of adaptation. *Journal of Clinical Endocrinology,* 1946, **6,** 117–130.

32. Spence, K. W. *Behavior theory and conditioning.* New Haven, Conn.: Yale Univ. Press, 1956.

33. Thiessen, D. D. Population density, mouse genotype, and endocrine function in behavior. *Journal of Comparative and Physiological Psychology,* 1964, **57,** 412–416.

34. Tolman, C. W., & Wilson, G. F. Social feeding in domestic chicks. *Animal Behavior,* 1965, **13,** 134–142.

35. Travis, L. E. The effect of a small audience upon eye-hand coordination. *Journal of Abnormal and Social Psychology,* 1925, **20,** 142–146.

36. Travis, L. E. The influence of the group upon the stutterer's speed in free association. *Journal of Abnormal and Social Psychology,* 1928, **23,** 45–51.

37. Triplett, N. The dynamogenic factors in pacemaking and competition. *American Journal of Psychology,* 1897, **9,** 507–533.

38. Welty, J. C. Experimental explorations into group behavior of fishes: A study of the influence of the group on individual behavior. *Physiological Zoology,* 1934, **7,** 85–128.

39. Zajonc, R. B., & Nieuwenhuyse, B. Relationship between word frequency and recognition: Perceptual process or response bias? *Journal of Experimental Psychology,* 1964, **67,** 276–285.

5

Reference Groups, Membership Groups, and Attitude Change

ALBERTA ENGVALL SIEGEL AND SIDNEY SIEGEL

In social psychological theory, it has long been recognized that an individual's *membership groups* have an important influence on the values and attitudes he holds. More recently, attention has also been given to the influence of his *reference groups:* the groups in which he aspires to attain or maintain membership. In a given area, membership groups and reference groups may or may not be identical. They are identical when the person aspires to *maintain* membership in the group of which he is a part; they are disparate when the group in which the individual aspires to *attain* membership is one in which he is not a member. It has been widely asserted that both membership and reference groups affect the attitudes held by the individual (4).

The present study is an examination of the attitude changes which occur over time when reference groups and membership groups are identical and when they are disparate. The study takes advantage of a field experiment which occurred in the social context of the lives of the subjects, concerning events considered vital by them. The subjects were not aware that their membership and reference groups were of research interest; in fact, they did not know that the relevant information about these was available to the investigators.

The field experiment permitted a test of the general hypothesis that both the amount and the direction of a person's attitude change over time depends on the attitude norms of his membership group (whether or not that group is chosen by him) and on the attitude norms of his reference group.

This hypothesis is tested with subjects who shared a common reference group at the

From *The Journal of Abnormal and Social Psychology*, 1957, **55**, 360–364. Reprinted by permission of the authors and the American Psychological Association. The study was supported by grants from the Committee for the Study of American Values at Stanford University and from the Stanford Value Theory Project.

time of the initial assessment of attitudes. They were then randomly assigned to alternative membership groups, some being assigned to the chosen group and others to a non-chosen group. Attitudes were reassessed after a year of experience in these alternative membership groups with divergent attitude norms. During the course of the year, some subjects came to take the imposed (initially nonpreferred) membership group as their reference group. Attitude change after the year was examined in terms of the membership group and reference group identifications of the subjects at that time.

THE FIELD EXPERIMENT

The subjects of this study were women students at a large private coeducational university. The study was initiated shortly before the end of their freshman year, when they all lived in the same large freshman dormitory to which they had been assigned upon entering the university. At this university, all women move to new housing for their sophomore year. Several types of housing are available to them: a large dormitory, a medium-sized dormitory, several very small houses which share common dining facilities, and a number of former sorority houses which have been operated by the university since sororities were banished from the campus. These latter are located among the fraternity houses on Fraternity Row, and are therefore known as "Row houses." Although the Row houses are lower in physical comfort than most of the other residences for women, students consider them higher in social status. This observation was confirmed by a poll of students (5, 205), in which over 90 per cent of the respondents stated that Row houses for women were higher in social status than non-Row houses, the remaining few disclaiming any information concerning status differences among women's residences.

In the Spring of each year, a "drawing" is held for housing for the subsequent year. All freshmen must participate in this drawing, and any other student who wishes to change her residence may participate. It is conducted by the office of the Dean of Women, in cooperation with woman student leaders. Any participant's ballot is understood to be secret. The woman uses the ballot to rank the houses in the order of her preference. After submitting this ballot, she draws a number from the hopper. The rank of that number determines the likelihood that her preference will be satisfied.

In research reported earlier (5), a random sample was drawn from the population of freshman women at this university, several tests were administered to the persons in that sample, and (unknown to the subjects) their housing preferences for the forthcoming sophomore year were observed by the investigator. The subjects were characterized as "high status oriented" if they listed a Row house as their first choice, and were characterized as "low status oriented" if they listed a non-Row house as their first choice. The hypothesis under test, drawn from reference group theory and from theoretical formulations concerning authoritarianism, was that high status orientation is a correlate of authoritarianism. The hypothesis was confirmed: freshman women who listed a Row house as their first choice for residence scored significantly higher on the average in authoritarianism, as measured by the E-F scale (1, 2) than did women who listed a non-Row house as their first choice. The present study is a continuation of the one described, and uses as its subjects only those members of the original sample who were "high status oriented," i.e., preferred to live in a Row house for the sophomore year. In the initial study (5), of the 95 subjects whose housing choices were listed, 39 were "high status oriented," i.e., demonstrated that the Row was their reference group by giving a Row house as their first choice in the drawing. Of this group, 28 were available to serve as subjects for the follow-up or "change" study which is the topic of the present paper. These women form a homogeneous subsample in that at the conclusion of their freshman year they shared a common membership group (the freshman dormitory) and a common reference group (the Row). These subjects, however, had divergent experiences during their sophomore year: nine were Row residents during that year (having drawn sufficiently small numbers in the housing drawing to enable them to be assigned to the group of their choice) and the other 19 lived in non-Row houses during that year (having drawn numbers too large to enable them to be assigned to the housing group of their choice).

E-F scores were obtained from each of the

28 subjects in the course of a large-scale testing program administered to most of the women students at the university. Anonymity was guaranteed to the participants, but a coding procedure permitted the investigators to identify each respondent and thereby to isolate the subjects and compare each subject's second E-F score with her first.

To prevent the women from knowing that they were participating in a follow-up study, several procedures were utilized: (*a*) many persons who had not served in the earlier study were included in the second sample, (*b*) the testing was introduced as being part of a nation-wide study to establish norms, (*c*) the test administrators were different persons from those who had administered the initial tests, (*d*) persons who informed the test administrator that they had already taken the "Public Opinion Questionnaire" (E-F scale) were casually told that this did not disqualify them from participating in the current study.

The women had no hint that the research was in any way related to their housing arrangements. Testing was conducted in classrooms as well as in residences, and all procedures and instructions were specifically designed to avoid any arousal of the salience of the housing groups in the frame of reference of the research.

The annual housing drawing was conducted three weeks after the sophomore-year testing, and, as usual, each woman's housing ballot was understood to be secret. In this drawing, each subject had the opportunity to change her membership group, although a residence move is not required at the end of the sophomore year as it is at the end of the freshman year. If a subject participated in this drawing, the house which she listed as her first choice on the ballot was identified by the investigators as her reference group. If she did not, it was evident that the house in which she was currently a member was the one in which she chose to continue to live, i.e., was her reference group. With the information on each participant's residence choice at the end of her freshman year, her assigned residence for her sophomore year, and her residence choice at the end of her sophomore year, it was possible to classify the subjects in three categories:

A. Women (*n* = 9) who had gained assignment to live on the Row during their sophomore year and who did not attempt to draw out of the Row at the end of that year;

B. Women (*n* = 11) who had not gained assignment to a Row house for the sophomore year and who drew for a Row house again after living in a non-Row house during the sophomore year; and

C. Women (*n* = 8) who had not gained assignment to a Row house for the sophomore year, and who chose to remain in a non-Row house after living in one during the sophomore year.

For all three groups of subjects, as we have pointed out, membership group (freshman dormitory) and reference group (Row house) were common at the end of the freshman year. For Group A, membership and reference groups were identical throughout the sophomore year. For Group B, membership and reference groups were disparate throughout the sophomore year. For Group C, membership and reference groups were initially disparate during the sophomore year but became identical because of a change in reference groups.

As will be demonstrated, the Row and the non-Row social groups differ in attitude norms, with Row residents being generally more authoritarian than non-Row residents. From social psychological theory concerning the influence of group norms on individuals' attitudes, it would be predicted that the different group identifications during the sophomore year of the three groups of subjects would result in differential attitude change. Those who gained admittance to a Row house for the sophomore year (Group A) would be expected to show the least change in authoritarianism, for they spent that year in a social context which reinforced their initial attitudes. Group C members would be expected to show the greatest change in authoritarianism, a change associated not only with their membership in a group (the non-Row group) which is typically low in authoritarianism, but also with their shift in reference groups, from Row to non-Row, i.e., from a group normatively higher in authoritarianism to a group normatively lower. The extent of attitude change in the members of Group B would be expected to be intermediate, due to the conflicting influences of the imposed membership group (non-Row) and of the unchanged reference group

(Row). The research hypothesis, then, is that between the time of the freshman-year testing and the sophomore-year testing, the extent of change in authoritarianism will be least in Group A, greater in Group B, and greatest in Group C. That is, in extent of attitude change, Group A < Group B < Group C.

RESULTS

GROUP NORMS

From the data collected in the large-scale testing program, it was possible to determine the group norms for authoritarian attitudes among the Row and the non-Row women at the university. The E-F scale was administered to all available Row residents ($n = 303$) and to a random sample of residents of non-Row houses ($n = 101$). These women were sophomores, juniors, and seniors. The mean E-F score of the Row women was 90, while the mean E-F score of the non-Row was 81. The E-F scores of the two groups were demonstrated to differ at the $p < .001$ level ($x^2 = 11.1$) by the median test (**6**, 111–116), a nonparametric test, the data for which are shown in Table 1.

TABLE 1. *Frequencies of E-F Scores Above and Below Common Median for Row and Non-Row Residents*

	Residents of non-row houses	Residents of row houses	Total
Above median	36	166	202
Below median	65	137	202
Total	101	303	404

ATTITUDE CHANGE

The central hypothesis of this study is that attitude change will occur differentially in Groups A, B, and C, and that it will occur in the direction which would be predicted from knowledge of the group norms among Row and non-Row residents in general. The 28 subjects of this study had a mean E-F score of 102 at the end of their freshman year. The data reported above concerning authoritarianism norms for all women residing on campus would lead to the prediction that in general the subjects would show a reduction in author-

itarianism during the sophomore year but that this reduction would be differential in the three groups; from the knowledge that Row residents generally are higher in authoritarianism than non-Row residents, the prediction based on social group theory would be that Group A would show the smallest reduction in authoritarianism scores, Group B would show a larger reduction, and Group C would show the largest reduction. The data which permit a test of this hypothesis are given in Table 2.

TABLE 2. *Freshman-Year and Sophomore-Year E-F Scores of Subjects*

Group	End of Freshman Year	End of Sophomore Year	Difference
	108	125	−17
	70	78	−8
	106	107	−1
	92	92	0
A	80	78	2
	104	102	2
	143	138	5
	110	92	18
	114	80	34
	76	117	−41
	105	107	−2
	88	82	6
	109	97	12
	98	83	15
B	112	94	18
	101	82	19
	114	93	21
	104	81	23
	116	91	25
	101	74	27
	121	126	−5
	87	79	8
	105	95	10
C	97	81	16
	96	78	18
	108	73	35
	114	77	37
	88	49	39

The Jonckheere test (**3**), a nonparametric *k*-sample test which tests the null hypothesis that the three groups are from the same population against the alternative hypothesis that they are from different populations which are ordered in a specified way, was used with these data. By that test, the hypothesis is confirmed at the $p < .025$ level.

DISCUSSION

Substantively, the present study provides experimental verification of certain assertions in social group theory, demonstrating that attitude change over time is related to the group identification of the person—both his membership group identification and his reference group identification. The hypothesis that extent of attitude change would be different in the three subgroups of subjects, depending on their respective membership group and reference group identifications, is confirmed at the $p < .025$ level; in extent of change in authoritarianism, Group A < Group B < Group C, as predicted.

Another way of looking at the data may serve to highlight the influence of membership groups and reference groups. At the end of the freshman year, the members of Groups A, B, and C shared the same membership group and the same reference group. During the sophomore year, those in Group A shared one membership group while those in Groups B and C together shared another. From membership group theory, it would be predicted that the extent of attitude change would be greater among the latter subjects. This hypothesis is supported by the data (in Table 2): by the Mann-Whitney test (6, 116–127), the change scores of these two sets of subjects (Group A versus Groups B and C together) differ in the predicted direction at the $p < .025$ level. This finding illustrates the influence of *membership* groups on attitude change. On the other hand, at the conclusion of the sophomore year, the women in Groups A and B shared a common reference group while those in Group C had come to share another. From reference group theory, it would be predicted that attitude change would be more extensive among the subjects who had changed reference groups (Group C) than among those who had not. This hypothesis is also supported by the data (in Table 2): by the Mann-Whitney test, the change scores of these two sets of subjects (Groups A and B together versus Group C) differ in the predicted direction at the $p < .05$ level. This finding illustrates the influence of *reference* groups on attitude change. Any inference from this mode of analysis (as contrasted with the main analysis of the data, by the Jonckheere test) must be qualified because of the nonindependence of the data on which the two Mann-Whitney tests are made, but it is mentioned here to clarify the role which membership and reference groups play in influencing attitude change.

The findings may also contribute to our understanding of processes affecting attitude change. The imposition of a membership group does have some effect on an individual's attitudes, even when the imposed group is not accepted by the individual as his reference group. This relationship is shown in the case of Group B. If the person comes to accept the imposed group as his reference group, as was the case with the persons in Group C, then the change in his attitudes toward the level of the group norm is even more pronounced.

Methodologically, the study has certain features which may deserve brief mention. First, the study demonstrates that it is possible operationally to define the concept of reference group. The act of voting by secret ballot for the group in which one would like to live constitutes clear behavioral specification of one's reference group, and it is an act whose conceptual meaning can be so directly inferred that there is no problem of reliability of judgment in its categorization by the investigator. Second, the study demonstrates that a field study can be conducted which contains the critical feature of an experiment that is usually lacking in naturalistic situations: randomization. The determination of whether or not a woman student would be assigned to the living group of her choice was based on a random event: the size of the number she drew from the hopper. This fact satisfied the requirement that the treatment condition be randomized and permitted sharper inferences than can usually be drawn from field studies. Third, the test behavior on which the conclusions of this study were based occurred in a context in which the salience of membership and reference groups was *not* aroused and in which no external sanctions from the relevant groups were operative. This feature of the design permitted the interpretation that the E-F scores represented the participant's internalized attitudes (4, 218). Finally, the use of a paper-and-pencil measure of attitude and thus of attitude change, rather than the use of some more behavioral measure, is a deficiency of the present study. Moreover, the measure which was used suffers from a well-known circularity, based on the occurrence of pseudo-low scores (1, 771; 5, 221–222).

SUMMARY

In the social context of the lives of the subjects, and in a natural social experiment which provided randomization of the relevant condition effects, the influence of both membership and reference groups on attitude change was assessed. All subjects shared a common reference group at the start of the period of the study. When divergent membership groups with disparate attitude norms were socially imposed on the basis of a random event, attitude change in the subjects over time was a function of the normative attitudes of both imposed membership groups and the individuals' reference groups. The greatest attitude change occurred in subjects who came to take the imposed, initially nonpreferred, membership group as their reference group.

References

1. Adorno, T. W., *et al. The authoritarian personality.* New York: Harper, 1950.
2. Gough, H. G. Studies of social intolerance: I. Some psychological and sociological correlates of anti-Semitism. *Journal of Social Psychology,* 1951, **33**, 237–246.
3. Jonckheere, A. R. A distribution-free *k*-sample test against ordered alternatives. *Biometrika,* 1954, **41**, 133–145.
4. Sherif, M., & Sherif, C. W. *Groups in harmony and tension.* New York: Harper, 1953.
5. Siegel, S. Certain determinants and correlates of authoritarianism. *Genetic Psychology Monographs,* 1954, **49**, 187–229.
6. Siegel, S. *Nonparametric statistics: For the behavioral sciences.* New York: McGraw-Hill, 1956.

6

Group Identification Under Conditions of External Danger

IRVING L. JANIS

It has long been known that when people are exposed to external danger they show a remarkable increase in group solidarity. That is, they manifest increased motivation to retain affiliation with a face-to-face group and to avoid actions that deviate from its norms. The importance of primary group factors was not fully appreciated until converging observations were made by psychiatrists, psychologists, and sociologists during World War II. These observations indicated that the average combat soldier's willingness to engage in hazardous combat duty depended largely on group identification. The term "group identification," although not rigorously defined, has been used to designate a set of preconscious and unconscious attitudes which incline each member to apperceive the group as an extension of himself and impel him to remain in direct contact with the other members and to adhere to the group's standards.

In the present paper, I shall focus on a set of intriguing theoretical problems concerning the causes and consequences of group identification—problems which can be illuminated by examining situations of extreme danger. Why is it that exposure to external danger has such a marked effect on the solidarity of a face-to-face group? What are the preconscious and unconscious mechanisms that underlie the strengthening of group ties under conditions of danger? What are the favorable and unfavorable consequences of group identification?

My interest in these problems dates back to the last months of World War II. As psychologists in a morale research organization of the U. S. Army, my colleagues and I conducted a large number of intensive interviews with American combat soldiers in the European Theater. Time and again we encountered instances when a man failed to act in accordance with his own self-interests in order to ward off separation fears or guilt

From the *British Journal of Medical Psychology*, 1963, **36**, 227–238. Reprinted by permission of the author and the *British Journal of Medical Psychology*.

about "letting the other guys down." For example, soldiers who had performed well in combat sometimes refused to accept a promotion if it entailed being shifted to another group. Men who were physically ill, or suffering from acute anxiety symptoms, avoided going on sick call and struggled against being withdrawn from combat because they did not want to be separated from their unit. Severe casualty cases, after being sent to a hospital in the rear, developed intense guilt feelings concerning their comrades at the front and sometimes went A.W.O.L. from the hospital or replacement depot in order to return to the front in an attempt to rejoin their comrades.

During the year and a half following the end of the war, the opportunity arose to check my observations against the findings from a variety of other sources of morale data, while working on a large social psychological study of World War II, in collaboration with Samuel Stouffer and others. This collaborative work, which was subsequently published in a volume entitled *The American Soldier: Combat and Its Aftermath* (14) is one of the main sources of empirical data on the behavior of combat groups used in preparing the present paper. I have also examined carefully the extensive psychiatric literature bearing on emotional aspects of the behavior of combat soldiers, including some reports about those in the British Army and German Army as well as the American Army.

In formulating hypotheses about the causes and consequences of group identification, I have also taken into account parallel phenomena on group solidarity encountered in my research investigations on the way people react when they are facing objective threats of body damage and annihilation. One investigation, reported in a book on *Air War and Emotional Stress* (8), involved surveying the existing evidence on civilian reactions to wartime dangers during World War II. A more recent series of studies published a few years ago in a book on *Psychological Stress* (9) was focused on psychological aspects of *surgery* and was based on my psychoanalytic observations as well as behavioral studies of surgical patients.

My formulations and illustrations concerning group identification in the present paper are based mainly on the studies of surgical patients and the studies of wartime danger situations. However, most, if not all, of the hypotheses seem to be applicable to *any* face-to-face group that is exposed to *any* common source of external stress. One of the values of concentrating on group behavior under the conditions of extreme physical danger is that we can sometimes see quite clearly the manifestations of basic psychological processes. The same processes may occur in a much more subtle form in the group behavior of people who face the common threats of everyday social life, such as loss of esteem from fellow workers or friends, disapproval from one's employer, and all the various signs of potential failure, humiliation, and loss of status that typically give rise to social anxiety in clinically normal people.

Most of the hypotheses to be presented are based on psychoanalytic theory and make use of concepts derived from clinical psychoanalytic observations. Scattered throughout the extensive psychoanalytic literature on ego ideals, super-ego functions, object relations, and related topics, there are numerous case study observations that seem relevant for specifying the unconscious determinants of group behavior in normal, as well as neurotic, adults. Major sources for such material are Freud's classical contributions to group psychology, Flugel's monograph on *Man, Morals, and Society* (3) and Fritz Redl's studies of antisocial adolescent gangs (10, 11).

The hypotheses I have singled out are ones that appear to be highly plausible in the light of the existing evidence. But, since the observations come primarily from studies of extreme danger situations, it must be emphasized from the outset that we cannot be at all certain about how far these hypotheses can be generalized. Perhaps some of them apply only when there is actual danger of annihilation combined with a host of severe deprivations of the type seldom encountered by anyone except in wartime. All such questions concerning the verification and generality of the hypotheses obviously must remain open until more systematic evidence becomes available from further research.

TRANSFERENCE REACTIONS

According to Freud's (5) theory of group behavior, much of the motivation for group solidarity comes from the strong emotional bonds established between each member and the leader. Freud speaks of "transference" reactions toward the idealized leader who, as a parent surrogate, provides the main impetus to a group for sharing common ideals and standards of conduct.

Certain regressive features of unconscious transference reactions toward authority figures become quite apparent whenever one observes people who are exposed to severe reality dangers, especially when there is a threat of mutilation or annihilation. I have been strongly impressed by manifestations of unconscious dependency needs not only among combat soldiers but also among civilians when they are exposed to the warnings of wartime bombing attacks or peacetime disasters or to the more personalized threats of illness and surgery. One of the main hypothetical constructs which seems to be useful in accounting for the upsurge of these dependency reactions is the *reactivation of separation anxiety.* We know, of course, that exaggerated fears of being abandoned by the parents arise early in life, especially on occasions when the child feels ill, injured, or unable to escape from threatened pain. Such fears persist in latent form in adulthood and underlie the characteristic changes in the social behavior of persons exposed to danger: they show increased interest in establishing close affiliation with any available primary group and they *seek to be reassured that the significant persons in their lives will not leave them or break preexisting affectionate ties.* This fear-ridden type of dependency is likely to develop toward any authority figures who are perceived to be in a position to increase or decrease their chances of warding off the danger. I refer to such persons as "danger-control authorities." These authorities tend to be over-idealized and misperceived in a variety of ways, under the influence of deep-seated attitudes and expectations derived from early life experiences. Here I refer mainly to those experiences in which one or both parents had been perceived by the child as being responsible for the onset and termination of suffering and pain.

The manifestations of transference on the part of normal adults who face serious external dangers are remarkably parallel to those shown by psychoneurotic patients undergoing psychoanalysis, especially during critical periods of treatment when the analyst becomes momentarily an authority figure to whom the patient's own superego functions have been assigned (**12**, 156–158). Persons in both types of situations overestimate the power of the authority figure and become preoccupied about whether his intentions are good or bad. They also become extraordinarily sensitive to his demands, continually attempting to do and say things that will please him, reacting with bitter disappointment at any apparent slights, and becoming depressed or aggrieved whenever they are not in communication with him.

In addition to the foregoing dependency phenomenon induced by reality threats, the propensity to develop affectionate ties with an authority figure and with comrades is probably augmented whenever a group is socially isolated. For example, soldiers in combat are far removed from their parents, siblings, and all those other persons back home who may have played a significant role in satisfying their emotional needs. Similarly, patients in a surgical ward are separated from their families and friends except for rather brief visits. Transference reactions, under these conditions, become a matter of psychological *replacement,* an unconscious means of enabling the missing family members to become symbolically present. Thus, the company commander or the surgeon is likely to become a symbolic representative of the father, and a fellow soldier or fellow patient may become a substitute for an older or younger brother. The individual will then unconsciously respond to the parent substitute and the sibling substitute in some of the same ways that he used to respond to the original object.

If this unconscious substitutive process occurs at a time when external dangers foster strong dependency needs, the individual is especially likely to undergo a partial regression in his dealings with the surrogate persons. This entails what Erik Erikson has described as a "blurring of an adult-relationship through the transfer upon it of infantile loves and hates, dependencies, and impotent rages" (**1,** 94).

Perhaps the most essential feature of transference from the standpoint of group dynamics is the tendency to overestimate the power of the surrogate person, which heightens sensitivity to his expressions of approval and disapproval. When a conscientious officer is unconsciously regarded as a father surrogate, the men under his command will be strongly motivated to accept his orders and to adhere to the group standards, if only to maintain the approval of a man who is now endowed with the attributes of a significant authority figure from the past.

REASSURANCE NEEDS

Next we shall consider additional *needs for reassurance* that are directly stimulated by external danger and that are satisfied through interaction with fellow members of the primary group. Studies of combat soldiers provide exceptionally rich material on this aspect of group psychology.

In morale surveys during World War II, we found that many soldiers said they would not want to be shifted to any other unit because they felt *safer* with their own group. For example, a wounded veteran of combat in North Africa said: "The fellows don't want to leave when they're sick. They're afraid to leave their own men—the men they know. Your own outfit —they're the men you have confidence in. It gives you more guts to be with them."

Now when a soldier says that "it gives you more guts" to be with the men in your own outfit, it is not merely because of the increase in actual protection he consciously anticipates. External threats foster increased reliance on the group by arousing a variety of basic psychological needs for reassurance, some of which are, of course, preconscious, or unconscious.

At least temporary emotional relief seems to be obtained not merely from the occasional serious discussions in which the men implicitly promise to "stick by" each other in the event of injury or dire need. They also tell each other jokes and tall stories about how badly things are going; they exchange banter concerning their poor chances of survival; and they engage in many other forms of "kidding around" that are heavily tinged with gallows humor.

Whether serious or humorous, these informal interchanges among members of a combat team probably touch off a number of different reassurance mechanisms, all of which can contribute to the alleviation of fear.

1. From the affective expressions as well as the content of his team-mate's comments, the individual soldier can quickly come to realize that they must be suffering from essentially the same worries, longings, and conflicts as himself. The damage to a man's self-esteem is minimized by the opportunity to perceive that

other men are equally frightened—that they too have strong wishes to escape from hazardous assignments and are equally unsure of their own capacity to live up to the masculine ideals of not being a "sissy."

2. By openly expressing his private fears and confessing his weaknesses to one or more empathic listeners, the individual may gain emotional rapport similar to that occurring in the early sessions of psychotherapy. Here the crucial factor may be the permissive social atmosphere of the work group, which provides an opportunity for mutual self-revelations with relatively little danger of being censured or humiliated.

3. When a man airs his private fears and grievances he will sometimes elicit comments from others which have a corrective effect on his appraisals of the external dangers. The more experienced combat veterans, despite their general proclivity for conveying a very black picture, would often "wisen up" the green replacements in their units. For example, many men entered combat with vague paranoid-like fears about the possibility of being shot by their own military authorities, partly because they thought this would be the prescribed punishment if they were to fail to carry out a suicidal mission ordered by an uninformed or inhuman commander. But combat soldiers in the U. S. Army gradually came to realize that in actual practice offenders were not executed. The popular notion that American combat men were facing a choice of possible death from the enemy versus certain death if they refused to fight was a grossly unsubstantiated myth. Informal group discussions between fresh replacements and the more experienced members of the combat team probably served a reality-testing function, exploding such myths and correcting other exaggerated notions about the dire consequences of deviating from military regulations, as well as clearing up misconceptions about the strength of the enemy and about the devastating power of the enemy's weapons.

4. When a soldier knows that his group is facing severe danger and that his own life as well as the lives of his comrades is at stake, he becomes extremely sensitive to being treated impersonally, as a mere cog in a machine. In military service, however, it frequently happens that the men in operational units are subjected to seemingly arbitrary and impersonal treatment by officers in higher

headquarters. During World War II, for example, a high percentage of combat men, after having spent weeks or months in overcrowded replacement depots, felt they had been badly "kicked around" by the military organization and were acutely aware of being treated as an expendable item. By becoming an accepted comrade the individual soldier can counteract, to some extent, the disturbing perception of himself as a *passive victim* at the disposal of an impersonal military organization whose high officers can make drastic decisions with little or no regard for the value of his life. The attractiveness of the local work group becomes greatly enhanced as the individual encounters the first acts of friendship on the part of his team-mates and immediate superiors, which reassure him that he *still counts as a person.* Moreover, once the men begin sharing their feelings about the Army organization, they soon acquire the illusion that the work group has the power to see to it that its members will not be neglected or maltreated by higher headquarters.

In so far as the soldier's needs for reassurance are satisfied by interpersonal relationships with his comrades, he becomes strongly dependent upon his work group to counteract his dysphoria. Thus the individual becomes strongly motivated to behave in such a way that the others will continue to accept him as a member in good standing. The threat of the group's disapproval or rejection, therefore, becomes all the more effective in suppressing any inclinations to deviate from the group norms.

The "sharing of fear" in combat units—in the many different forms which have just been described—probably enables many soldiers to adapt 'to severe stresses that they otherwise might not be able to withstand. In *Psychological Stress* (9), I have reported similar phenomena from studies of surgical patients. The evidence from these studies strongly suggests the following general proposition: when a person's anticipatory fears have been stimulated to a *moderate* degree before being exposed to actual stress stimuli, there is less likelihood of his being overwhelmed, or becoming resentful toward danger-control authorities, than if his anticipatory fears have *not been at all stimulated* during the precrisis period. For the purpose of conceptualizing the normal processes of inner psychological preparation, I have introduced the term "work of worrying," as a construct analogous to the "work of mourning." The work of mourning usually begins

after object loss has occurred, whereas the work of worrying starts *before* a blow strikes, as soon as a person becomes convinced that he is facing a potential danger or loss.

The same book contains a detailed account of various situational factors (such as exposure to accurate warning information from an authority figure) that help a person to go through all the steps involved in completing the work of worrying and a number of hypotheses are presented concerning the ways in which this type of inner preparation can enable a person to adapt more adequately to a painful reality situation. For the present, it will suffice to call attention to the likelihood that the opportunity to talk about one's fears in a permissive group setting—and the opportunity to hear the members of the group verbalize fears similar to one's own—may have a long-range prophylactic effect. In other words, sharing one's fears with others may facilitate the development of adaptive defences and thereby reduce the chances of being traumatized if one is subsequently exposed to the actual harassments of severe danger.

MOURNING AND INTROJECTION

We turn now to a major source of military stress, which sets in after the emotional ties to the leader and to other members of the face-to-face group have become firmly established—namely, the repeated loss of buddies and of a succession of leaders who are members of the combat soldier's "family circle."

When a combat unit sustains casualties, a number of readjustive mechanisms can be discerned among the survivors, which appear to counteract group demoralization. One such mechanism involves unconscious identification with the men who had become casualties. As is frequently observed in psychoanalytic studies of civilian cases, the mourning soldier uses the mechanism of "introjection" to build up a substitute object within himself. In one way or another he changes his behavior to resemble the lost object. The characteristics taken over by the mourner, of course, include moral standards and ego ideals as well as physical characteristics. Fenichel (2) asserts that this process of introjection is a normal component of mourning, becoming a pathological depression only when it involves a prolonged period of "regression to orality," with a predominance of sadomasochistic tendencies that go beyond an attempt merely to undo the loss. (I shall return to the problem of pathological mourning later on.)

Psychoanalytic studies of "normal" reactions to the loss of a father figure indicate that the post-bereavement identification entails much more compulsive conformity with the standards of the man after he is dead than when he was alive. Flugel (3) points out that a live parent figure can be influenced by the individual into giving his approval to new patterns of behavior, and thus the internalized code need not be inflexible when new circumstances are encountered; but, when he is no longer alive, he cannot be persuaded or cajoled into giving his approval, nor can he offer forgiveness for minor deviations from his standards. Flugel says: "What psychoanalysts have sometimes called 'postponed obedience' to dead parents may be a harder discipline than obedience to a living parent" (3, 188).

In a closely knit combat group, the same type of "postponed obedience" seems to occur following the loss of a leader or comrade. An unconscious form of attitude change occurs which has the effect of markedly increasing adherence to all those group norms which were manifestly valued by the dead man. To a lesser extent, the same type of compensatory attitude change is to be expected when a leader or comrade has been removed from the unit because of a promotion to a new position of greater responsibility.

The foregoing comments about mourning reactions suggest that the blood price paid by units in active combat may contribute a powerful unconscious source of motivation to group conformity. However, there is a compulsive quality that characterizes the conformity behavior arising from introjection, which might sometimes interfere with the effectiveness of group performances. It is necessary, therefore, to examine the unfavorable as well as the favorable consequences of introjection and to attempt to predict the conditions under which the alternative consequences are likely to occur.

REACTIVE DEPRESSION AND THE "OLD SERGEANT" SYNDROME

One clear-cut type of adverse reaction which has been repeatedly reported pertains to the small percentage of combat personnel who developed a pathological form of depression. Like the normal mourner, the depressed soldier seems to be attempting to undo the loss and to keep the missing person symbolically present; but he becomes almost exclusively preoccupied with these efforts, showing little or no interest in any aspect of his daily life. There is a well-known set of incapacitating symptoms of anxiety-mixed-with-depression which has been labelled the "old sergeant" syndrome. (This name was used because the most striking cases occurred among non-commissioned officers who were old in combat experience.) The syndrome consists of a progressive deterioration in attitudes and performance, including a gradual decrease in mental efficiency, loss of self-confidence in ability to cope with danger, withdrawal from current social activities, apathy, and intense guilt feelings. According to Sobel (13), who has given the classical account of it, this syndrome occurred during World War II in "well-motivated, previously efficient soldiers, as a result of the chronic and progressive breakdown of their normal defenses against anxiety in long periods of combat." The same syndrome was observed in a high percentage of psychiatric casualties in combat divisions fighting in Korea during 1950–51 (6).

The symptoms comprising this syndrome usually do not appear during the first month or two of combat, which is the period when group identification becomes intensified. However, as the subsequent months go by, and as casualties mount, friendships become sharply restricted to a few "old timers" who started out together in the original unit. This restriction in the formation of friendship ties evidently arises because the battle veteran fears a repetition of the painful reactions he has repeatedly experienced when he lost his closest friends in combat. It is during this later phase that symptoms of chronic anxiety and depression make their appearance, insidiously developing into the "old sergeant" syndrome. As more and more members of the original group become casualties, the survivors become more and more inhibited with respect to forming new attachments, precisely because they have developed an attitude of defensive *detachment* toward the here-and-now combat group. The old sergeant no longer perceives himself as an integral part of the entire fighting group, although he may retain a sense of identification with a few of its original members. The latter, however, are men who, like himself, have become apathetic, inefficient, and "beat up." As a result, his conception of the group no longer serves to bolster his self-confidence.

The fact that these men develop the classical symptoms of depression suggests that an unconscious process has occurred whereby they regress from object relations to a pathological form of incorporation. In order to account for this process, it is necessary to emphasize one aspect of the normal work of mourning that is often neglected, namely, the process of seeking for and finding *substitute persons in reality* who will replace the lost object.

In *Mourning and Melancholia,* Freud (4) alludes to this process. When describing the pathological features of melancholia, he mentions in passing that *normal* adaptation to the loss of a cherished object involves not merely the withdrawal of cathexis from the lost object but also the *transference of cathexis to a new object.* This he regards as the normal pathway that is abandoned by the depressed patient, who reacts solely by incorporating the lost object into his own ego.

At the beginning of this paper, I introduced the assumption that the soldier's attachment to his leader and to others in his work group comes about partly as a result of the normal type of transference that enables him to replace his own absent family members and other loved persons he reluctantly had to leave behind. During the first few months of combat, this normal type of transference continues to take place to the surviving members of the group and leads to a heightened cathexis of the existing group. That is, the love and affection that had formerly been attached to the lost comrades is transferred to newcomers and to others in the existing combat group. Evidently, in order for this re-cathexis of the existing group to occur, the mourner must be able to seek and accept *substitute* objects in reality who will enable him to compensate for the lost gratifications and the lost emotional ties. But then the substitutes, in turn, are lost—often at a time when the work of mourning for the first lost object is not yet complete—and so a new painful loss is added to the original one. The mourner then seems to become wary of finding any new substitutes and begins to show a self-preoccupying process of identification with the dead.

This pathogenic development seems to involve a regressive process that could be considered as a form of *reactive narcissism.* I suspect that two sources contribute to this reaction. First, the loss of comrades through injury and death may be unconsciously equated to being *abandoned* by them at a time when they are sorely needed. Case studies of surgical patients strongly suggest that, in a situation of prolonged stress, the absence of any affectionate person (no matter how legitimate or excusable his absence is known to be at the conscious level) will unconsciously tend to reactivate childhood episodes of profound grief in which the parent's temporary absence during a period of illness or suffering was experienced by the child as an abandonment. Secondly, the longer the duration of suffering and deprivation, the greater the likelihood that the leader and other members of the group will be unconsciously perceived as failing to use their power to terminate the suffering. In effect, like a small child, the sufferer gradually becomes more and more angry at those he feels are supposed to protect him from harm because they haven't yet made the enemy—or any of the other bad things—go away. These two factors—the repeated *loss* of members of the group combined with prolonged *continuation* of danger and suffering—give rise to an aggrievement reaction. This reaction heightens the intensity of the individual's ambivalence toward the remaining members of the protective group, which probably sets in motion the regressive process, fostering the more pathological form of introjection that we see in the "old sergeant" syndrome. As Freud puts it, "the conflict due to ambivalence gives a pathological cast to mourning and forces it to express itself in the form of self-reproaches to the effect that the mourner himself is to blame for the loss of the loved object, i.e. that he had willed it" (4, 251).

DELINQUENT BEHAVIOR

The remainder of this paper will be devoted to another type of unfavorable consequence of group identification—mutual support for delinquent behavior. Freud and other psychoanalysts have pointed out that war conditions tend to create a "war superego" in soldiers, which is a type of auxiliary super-ego that permits the men to express a variety of impulses ordinarily held in check, thus overriding the "normal peace ego." In his book on *Group Psychology,* Freud states (5, 85):

For the moment it [the group] replaces the whole of human society, which is the wielder of authority, whose punishments the individual fears, and for whose sake he has submitted to so many inhibitions. It is clearly perilous for him to put himself in opposition to it, and it will be safer to follow the example of those around him and perhaps even "hunt with the pack." In obedience to the new authority he may put his former "conscience" out of action, and so surrender to the attraction of the increased pleasure that is certainly obtained from the removal of inhibitions.

We know that the members of a highly cohesive group sometimes support each other in ignoring authoritative demands from outside the group and participate in delinquent actions without experiencing the intense feelings of social anxiety and guilt that would obviously develop if each man were alone. Redl and Wineman (11) have specified the following factors as necessary conditions for the "contagious effect" of delinquent or countermores behavior in a peer group: (a) an initiator must openly "act out" in such a way that he obviously gratifies an impulse that the rest of the members have been inhibiting; (b) the initiator must display a lack of anxiety or guilt; (c) the other members who perceive the initiator's actions must have been undergoing for some time an intense conflict with respect to performing the forbidden act; i.e., they must have such a strong urge to commit the act that they were just barely able to inhibit its release prior to the initiator's demonstration. Thus, according to Redl and Wineman (11) it is the sudden perception of fearless and guiltless enjoyment of what they have been longing to do that sways the members of a group to become psychologically infected by a delinquency-carrier.

While caught up in a group epidemic of delinquency, the members will commit sadistic and narcissistic acts that later on, after the atmosphere of shared excitement has subsided, evoke feelings of remorse, apprehension, and loss of self-esteem. Following any single episode of wayward group behavior, the intensity of an individual member's dysphoric reaction and the degree to which his inhibitory controls are re-established will depend partly on what the other members of the group do and say about it.

Psychoanalytic observers have called attention to the numerous ways in which the members of a cohesive group *share the guilt* so as to ward off or minimize their dysphoric reactions. "Sharing the guilt" refers to a complex set of mechanisms whereby internalized standards are temporarily set aside or modified as a consequence of interaction with others in a primary group. Each member of the group experiences some relief from knowing that "I am not the only one who did it." Fenichel (2) assumes that this relief occurs as a result of a "quasi-projection" mechanism: a guilty person who places the blame on his entire group is displaying an attenuated form of projection ("all of us did it, not just me"). This involves much less distortion of reality than the more extreme projections in which the blame is placed entirely on other people ("they are responsible, I had nothing to do with it").

In addition to a quasi-projection mechanism, it seems to me that there are other psychological processes which also enter into the sharing of guilt:

1. Denial of dysphoric affect and reaction formations against guilt are probably facilitated when the group members openly communicate to each other a manifest attitude of tough-minded indifference concerning immorality, especially when everyone continues to act as though he accepts at face value the carefree manner with which moral scruples are being ignored.

2. In a group atmosphere where the members are speaking nonchalantly about the morally objectionable things they have done, there are frequent opportunities for a surreptitious form of confession, for those who are seeking to unburden themselves of unacknowledged guilt.

3. Seeing and hearing others in the group talk unembarrassedly about participation in a collective spree can also have the effect of reinforcing an illusory belief of ethical validity ("it must be O.K. if everyone else admits doing it"). And, at the same time, it also fosters an illusory sense of being protected against the power of the punitive authorities ("we're all in this together, so they can't punish any of us").

4. After collectively committing serious acts of violence, the members' retrospective accounts to each other may help them to arrive at a convincing set of rationalizations to exculpate themselves. For example, they can excuse the damage they created by agreeing that "it was an accident." Or they can justify themselves for maltreating innocent victims by developing the shared belief that "they had it coming to them." A major type of guilt-evading rationalization that seems to be especially common both in military units and in adoles-

cent gangs is the belief that one's own offenses are excused if some other person was the initiator of the forbidden behavior: "we didn't start it so we're not responsible."

From what has already been said it is apparent that intra-group communications can facilitate the formation of rationalizations in two ways: first, since the members share a common need for finding excuses for the offense, they can *pool their inventive resources* to arrive at a much better case for themselves than any one person would be able to think up himself; secondly, when all members show signs of accepting any alleged explanation for the offense, their *unanimity lends authenticity* to the excuse, furnishing the same type of consensual validation that is commonly accepted by most people as grounds for believing explanations about impressive events in their daily lives ("if everyone says so, it must be true").

In this connection, it is important to note that the same group influences that enable scrupulous men to overcome their inhibitions and become "good" soldiers may, later on, lead to their becoming "bad" soldiers and "bad" citizens.

The combat soldier is required to overcome his internal restraints against violent acts and, in order to do so, he relies more and more upon the support of the combat group. As inner controls based on personal conscience become partially replaced by outer controls based on signs of group approval or disapproval, the members are likely to support each other not only in connection with the release of hostility toward the enemy but with respect to other forms of gratification as well. For example, if the members adopt an informal code of regularly maltreating captured soldiers, and share the same rationalizations for warding off the accompanying guilt feelings, it becomes an easy step to accept and rationalize similar maltreatment of enemy *civilians* ("They have it coming to them for all the atrocities their side has committed against our side"). The least inhibited member of the military group then feels quite safe in initiating new forms of countermores activity in captured towns—such as looting private homes, misusing military food supplies to force old people to give up their jewellery or other hidden possessions, and applying pressure on young women to submit sexually. A contagious effect is then likely to occur among the other men in the

unit, who have also been longing to obtain the same types of gratification during the long periods of extreme privation. As each man participates in more and more antisocial behavior, an acculturation process takes place, so that the inhibitory power of his former moral scruples is increasingly weakened.

The military group, then, serves an *initiating* function, in that it provides powerful incentives for releasing forbidden impulses, inducing the soldier to try out formerly inhibited acts which he originally regarded as morally repugnant. In addition, the military group furnishes a social milieu which *facilitates the unlearning of inhibitions*. It is especially in connection with the latter function that the various mechanisms of sharing the guilt enter in. With the help of the other men in his unit, the soldier who is burdened with guilt following a first violation will gradually take over the group-sanctioned rationalizations, projections, and reaction formations that enable his guilt to subside to a relatively low level.

FACTORS FOSTERING A DEVIANT INFORMAL CODE

When we examine the various documented instances of military violations on the part of local units, we obtain some clues pertinent to the following general question, which has considerable practical as well as theoretical implications: *Under what conditions will a cohesive local group provide mutual support for violations of the norms of the superordinate organization with which it is affiliated and develop an informal code of its own that opposes the organization's code?*

One major factor that must be taken into account was implied in my earlier statements about transference, namely, the attitudes conveyed by the local leader. Obviously, when a primary work group has a leader who openly opposes the demands of the organization, the chances are greater that the group will develop an informal code that deviates from the organizational norms. However, it is unwarranted to assume that a group of soldiers is wholly passive with respect to accepting a local leader's influence. If an officer encourages his men to perform acts that are extreme violations of the rules of the military organization—for example, shirking a dangerous assignment, engaging in looting, or selling military supplies on the black market—the group members may reject his demands and spontaneously turn to an informal leader who induces much less conflict. Thus, it is essential to examine the influence of a local leader with anti-army attitudes in relation to other factors that also enter into the picture when the members of a local unit undergo a conflict of the type under discussion.

Taking account of observations bearing on dissident behavior in industrial and political organizations, as well as the military studies already cited, I shall now attempt to draw some inferences concerning the conditions under which the members of a local group will mutually support each other in repeatedly violating the organization's norms. A number of important factors can be discerned, which appear to be major determinants of delinquent behavior in situations where the members of a military unit mutually support each other in taking advantage of opportunities for shirking their duties, for seeking personal aggrandizement, and for indulging in antisocial sexual exploits.

The following four conditions seem to be the most obvious antecedents of persistently deviant behavior on the part of a local unit: (*a*) most men in the unit have specific grievances against the superordinate organization, and feel resentful toward the top leadership for neglecting their needs, for inflicting unnecessary deprivations or for imposing extraordinarily harsh demands which menace their personal welfare; (*b*) the members perceive their group as having no channel open for communicating their grievances to the top levels of the hierarchy or are convinced that such communications would be wholly ineffective in inducing any favorable changes; (*c*) the organization is perceived as having little or no opportunity for detecting the deviant behavior in question; and (*d*) one or more central persons in the local unit communicates disaffiliative sentiments to the others and sets an example, either by personally acting in a way that is contrary to the organization's norms or by failing to use his power to prevent someone else in the same group from doing so.

The psychological conditions just described could be seen quite clearly among American occupation troops stationed in disorganized German cities at the end of World War II. I encountered a series of extreme examples in a study (7) conducted among American infantrymen stationed in Berlin during the summer of 1945, at a time when the entire population was suffering from an acute food shortage. Both the interviews and direct observations indicated that a very high percentage of the men were violating military regulations (and the moral code of their society) in taking advantage of their economic power over the starving Berliners. Most of the American soldiers were regularly profiteering on the black market (e.g., exchanging a few candy bars for a Leica camera) and were openly purchasing sexual partners (e.g., soliciting girls at public places by holding up a can of C-rations or a candy bar). The men who had been stationed in Berlin for less than ten days appeared to express more guilt feelings about exploiting the hungry civilians than the men who had been on occupation duty in Berlin for a longer period of time. At night in the barracks there were bull sessions in which one could observe the ways in which they were "sharing the guilt." In their group discussions, the men encouraged each other to continue seeking out the rare opportunities afforded by being stationed in the starving city and spoke about the "reasons" why the German people deserved to be mistreated and why much of the blame for their exploitation could be placed on the Russian occupying forces, whose mistreatment of the Berliners in the eastern zone was said to be far worse than the Americans'.

Much of the exploitative behavior was instigated by combat veterans, who felt that they had already done more than their share and were resentful about not being sent back to the United States promptly. Furthermore, the men perceived themselves as being isolated to an unusual degree from the main headquarters of the U. S. Armed Forces in Europe (especially since they knew that the western sector of Berlin was only a small island in Russian-controlled territory). The social disorganization that characterized the entire city was such that most American soldiers felt there was little chance of being detected in black marketeering or in other illegal activities by the Berlin police, by the U. S. military police, or by any authorities in the U. S. Army. It is not known to what extent the leaders of the local units actually encouraged the men to indulge in illegal activities, but there is little question that the non-commissioned officers, and to some extent the commissioned officers, actively participated in such activities themselves. Thus, it seems likely that all four conditions were present and contributed to the development of an informal code such that the men felt relatively free to give in to the temptation to exploit the starving German population, thereby violating not only the policies of the U. S. Army, but also the humanitarian ethical norms of the western democratic nations.

In conclusion, I wish to state once again my expectation that the hypotheses concerning the conditions under which group identification will lead to "sharing the guilt" and the development of a deviant group code of behavior will prove to be applicable to many non-military groups in civilian life. I have the same expectation with respect to the potential applicability of the other hypotheses I have presented concerning transference toward the leader, the reassurances gained by group members from sharing their fears, and the heightened cathexis of the group that results from mourning for lost members. Essentially the same psychological processes that we see in *extreme form* in combat groups may occur in groups of factory employees, white collar workers, and professional men at times when they are facing the external dangers of financial insecurity or social censure. All of us can think of well-known examples of how outstanding artists, composers, writers, and scientists, before they gained recognition, have banded together and mutually supported each other against the scorn and derision of their community. We sometimes discern comparable instances of mutual support occurring in ordinary work groups, friendship cliques, and families at times of stress or bereavement.

Perhaps the main value of formulating hypotheses about the processes of group identification in extreme danger situations, as I stated at the outset, is that we become alerted to look for similar processes, which may be manifested in much less obvious ways, in our subsequent observations and research on other primary groups.

References

1. Erikson, E. H. The first psychoanalyst. In B. Nelson (ed.), *Freud and the twentieth century.* New York: Meridian, 1957. Pp. 79–101.

2. Fenichel, O. *The psychoanalytic theory of neurosis.* New York: Norton, 1945.

3. Flugel, J. *Man, morals, and society.* New York: International Universities Press, 1945.

4. Freud, S. *Mourning and melancholia.* London: Hogarth, 1917.

5. Freud, S. *Group psychology and the analysis of the ego.* London: Hogarth, 1922.

6. Glass, A. J. Psychotherapy in the combat zone. *American Journal of Psychiatry,* 1954, **110,** 725–731.

7. Janis, I. L. Morale attitudes and social behavior of American soldiers in post-war Berlin. Unpublished memorandum for the European Theater of Operations, Information and Education Division, Research Branch, 1945.

8. Janis, I. L. *Air war and emotional stress.* New York: McGraw-Hill, 1951.

9. Janis, I. L. *Psychological stress.* New York: Wiley, 1958.

10. Redl, F. Group emotion and leadership. *Psychiatry,* 1942, **5,** 573–596.

11. Redl, F., & Wineman, D. *The aggressive child.* Glencoe, Ill.: Free Press, 1957.

12. Sandler, J. On the concept of super-ego. *The psychoanalytic study of the child.* Vol. 15. New York: International Universities Press, 1960.

13. Sobel, R. The "old sergeant" syndrome. *Psychiatry,* 1947, **10,** 315–321.

14. Stouffer, S., et al. *The American soldier.* Vol. 2. *Combat and its aftermath.* Princeton, N. J.: Princeton Univ. Press, 1949.

7

The Nature of Group Cohesiveness

DORWIN CARTWRIGHT

The term group cohesiveness has come to have a central place in theories of group dynamics. Although different theorists attribute somewhat different conceptual properties to the term, most agree that group cohesiveness refers to the degree to which the members of a group desire to remain in the group. Thus, the members of a highly cohesive group, in contrast to one with a low level of cohesiveness, are more concerned with their membership and are therefore more strongly motivated to contribute to the group's welfare, to advance its objectives, and to participate in its activities. Cohesiveness contributes to a group's potency and vitality; it increases the significance of membership for those who belong to the group.

Group cohesiveness has been investigated from two points of view—as a dependent variable and as an independent variable. Studies of the first type have undertaken to ascertain the conditions that bring about various levels of cohesiveness, whereas those of the second type have investigated the effects of different levels of cohesiveness upon the group and its members. These two lines of investigation taken together have contributed significantly to our understanding of this basic aspect of group life, but a theoretical integration of the total body of findings has yet to be achieved.

In this chapter we draw upon this research in an attempt to construct a general formulation of the nature of group cohesiveness, its determinants, and its consequences. Our approach may be described with the help of Figure 1, the details of which will become evident throughout the course of the chapter. We employ the definition advanced by Festinger (Chap. 14), who states that group cohesiveness is "the resultant of all forces acting on members to remain in the group." These forces are determined jointly by certain properties of the group and by certain characteristics of the members which, in conjunction, can be conceived as the immediate determinants of cohesiveness. These forces, in turn, have various effects that constitute the consequences of group cohesiveness. Thus, if a study shows that there is a positive correlation between the

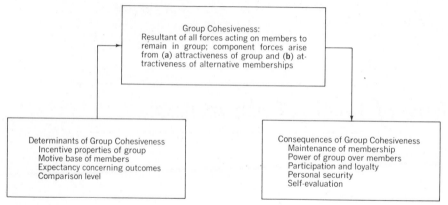

FIGURE 1. A scheme for analyzing group cohesiveness.

degree of interpersonal liking among the members of a group and the strength of group norms, we attempt to account for this relationship by showing how interpersonal liking creates forces on members to remain in the group and how these forces contribute to the power of a group over its members.

The resultant force acting on a member to remain in a group has at least two types of components: (*a*) forces that derive from the group's attractiveness and (*b*) forces whose source is the attractiveness of alternative memberships.[1] Most investigators have equated the term cohesiveness with "attraction to group," focusing mainly upon the first component of the resultant force acting on members to remain in the group. As a result, the literature on group cohesiveness contains, for the most part, investigations of attraction to, or satisfaction with, group membership. As might be expected in the early stages of research, a great variety of devices have been used to measure attraction and satisfaction. Therefore, before considering further the nature of group cohesiveness, we will review briefly the measuring devices more commonly employed. This should serve also to convey an impression of the meaning of the term group cohesiveness as actually used in research.

[1] The complete set of forces determining whether a member will remain in a group may contain, in addition, forces against leaving the group that result from costs associated with leaving or from other restraints. We do not include these in our conception of cohesiveness, but it is important to recognize that they may influence the findings obtained in research on cohesiveness.

APPROACHES TO MEASURING GROUP COHESIVENESS

Five major approaches to the problem of measuring group cohesiveness have established a claim for serious consideration. Each is plausibly related to the definition of cohesiveness, and each has produced meaningful relations between its type of measurement and other properties of groups that might be expected to be associated with cohesiveness.

INTERPERSONAL ATTRACTION AMONG MEMBERS

On the assumption that a group will be more attractive the more its members like one another, some investigators have constructed indexes designed to measure the extent of interpersonal attraction among members. Thus, for example, Dimock (3, 118) compared the cohesiveness of adolescent clubs by means of a "friendship index," which is the ratio of the number of selections made within a club, when each member is asked to name his ten best friends, to the number that could possibly have been chosen within the club.

A rather similar sociometric index was employed by Festinger, Schachter, and Back (Chap. 12) in a study of informal groups in a housing project. These investigators asked the residents of each court to name their friends who lived in the entire community and then calculated the proportion that "in-own-court" choices were out of the total number of friends mentioned. They obtained a rank order correlation, across courts, of −.53 between this index and the percentage of the court's residents who deviated from its norms concerning attitudes and behavior. If it is assumed that cohesiveness provides a group with power to influence its members, this correlation suggests that the index is a reasonably good measure of cohesiveness.

It should be noted, however, that this index makes use of the "density" of choices within a group and ignores their patterning. But one might expect different configurations of the same number of choices to result in quite different degrees of group cohesiveness. Thus, for example, mutual choices may reflect attraction to a dyad that contributes little, if at all, to the cohesiveness of the entire group. To explore this possibility, Festinger, Schachter, and Back adjusted their index by counting only half of the reciprocated "in-own-court" choices. With this rather arbitrary adjustment, the correlation with the percentage of deviates in each court changed from $-.53$ to $-.74$. This result suggests that measures of cohesiveness based on interpersonal bonds might be improved by a more refined structural analysis.

A slightly different way of assessing interpersonal attraction was employed by Bovard (2) in a study comparing two styles of college teaching, labeled "group centered" and "leader centered." After forty-two hours' experience with a particular style of teaching, each student rated every other student in his class on an eleven-point scale of degree of liking. It was found that those in the group-centered class gave a higher average rating of fellow students than did those in the leader-centered class. Bovard also conducted an experiment designed to measure pressures to uniformity in each class and found that members of the group-centered class were more ready to alter their cognitions in the direction of a common norm.

These results and those of Festinger, Schachter, and Back support the view that cohesiveness gives a group power to influence its members, but they do not provide a basis for determining which method of measuring cohesiveness is superior. For a more detailed discussion of the problems of measuring cohesiveness in terms of interpersonal attraction, the reader is referred to a critical review of the literature by Lott and Lott (22).

EVALUATION OF A GROUP AS A WHOLE

A second approach to measuring cohesiveness focuses upon the group as an entity rather than interpersonal relations and develops indexes from members' evaluations of the group. Bovard employed this approach, in addition to the one described above, when he asked each student to rate his liking for the class as a whole. As before, he obtained a higher average rating for the group-centered class than for the leader-centered one, but the mean rating was more favorable when the object evaluated was the class as a whole than when it was another member. Moreover, the difference between the two types of rating was greater for the group-centered class.

Two different scales to measure each person's attraction to his work group were employed by Jackson (17) in an investigation conducted among staff members of a child welfare agency. One was based upon questions about the amount of benefit the respondent felt he was receiving from membership in the group, and the other was derived from questions about his attraction to the people in the group. The two scales were found to correlate .61 and to relate to other variables in a similar, though not identical, way. This study, along with that of Bovard, suggests that evaluations of group members and of the group as a whole tend to go together but that they are not precisely the same. Systematic research has yet to be done to discover the conditions affecting the association between these two types of evaluation.

The possibility that members of a group may be able to perceive its cohesiveness and to communicate this to others is suggested by research conducted by Mann and Baumgartel (23), who asked employees of a public utility whether or not they endorsed the statement, "Our crew is better than others at sticking together." Among white-collar workers, 62 percent of those with a low rate of absence endorsed the statement, whereas only 21 percent of those with a high rate did so. This result suggests the value of further exploration of the use of group members as informants about the cohesiveness of their groups.

CLOSENESS OR IDENTIFICATION WITH A GROUP

Questions designed to reveal how strongly members identify with a group or feel personally involved in it have been used by some researchers to measure group cohesiveness. Converse and Campbell (Chap. 16) report findings illustrative of this approach from a study of the 1956 presidential election. They wished to test the hypothesis that large groups in society, such as Catholics, Jews, Negroes, and trade-union members, display more distinctive voting patterns the more their members identify with them. Toward this end they constructed a scale of member identification based on responses to the following questions: (*a*) Would you say you feel pretty close to (for example, Negroes) in general or that you don't feel much closer to them than you do to other kinds of people? (*b*) How much interest would you say you have in how (for example, Negroes) as a whole are getting along in this country? If it is assumed that this scale measures group cohesiveness and that the distinctiveness of a group's voting pattern arises from the group's ability to influence its members, the results of this study lend additional support to the hypothesis that cohesiveness gives a group power to influence its members.

The question, "How strong a 'sense of belonging' do you feel you have to the people you work with?" was used to construct an index of the cohesiveness of work groups in a study reported by Indik (**16**). This index correlated $+ .41$ with a measure of ease of communication within the group and $- .30$ with the group's absence rate. An eight-item scale of personal involvement in a group was administered to groups of college students by Sagi, Olmstead, and Atelsek (**36**), who found that those students who voluntarily dropped their group membership over a period of six months had significantly lower values on this scale than those who remained members of the group.

The pattern of findings from studies such as these indicates that measurements of personal involvement, interest, identification, and sense of belonging tap at least one important component of group cohesiveness.

EXPRESSED DESIRE TO REMAIN IN A GROUP

A fourth approach makes direct use of our conceptual definition of group cohesiveness in that it asks members to indicate the strength of their desire to remain in the group. The following questions, used by Schachter (Chap. 13) to test the success of experimental manipulations intended to create different degrees of cohesiveness, have been employed also by many other investigators: (*a*) Do you want to remain a member of this group? (*b*) How often do you think this group should meet? (*c*) If enough members decide not to stay, so that it seems this group might discontinue, would you like the chance to persuade others to stay? Schachter found, as have most others, that an index constructed from these questions distinguishes between groups that on other grounds are presumed to differ in cohesiveness.

Reasoning that members might not always respond candidly to such direct questions, Libo (**21**) developed a picture-projective test. Libo reasoned that the immediate social environment of an individual influences his feelings and that these, in turn, will be reflected in stories written about the pictures when the test is administered in a meeting of a group. He found that the test distinguishes rather well between subjects who, when subsequently left free to choose, remain in the group and those who leave. The test also correlates highly with the measure of cohesiveness based on Schachter's three direct questions.

COMPOSITE INDEXES

Research employing the four approaches just described has generated a variety of devices for measuring cohesiveness. Each, taken alone, has been shown to relate to other phenomena in a manner generally consistent with expectations derived from theoretical conceptions of the nature of group cohesiveness. The recognition that cohesiveness may have diverse manifestations has led some investigators to construct composite indexes.

One such index was developed by Seashore (**39**) from a questionnaire administered to the employees of a large manufacturing firm. Each person was asked the following questions about his work group: (*a*) Do you feel that you are really a part of your work group? (*b*) If you had the chance to do the same kind of work for the same pay in another work group how would you feel about moving? (*c*) How does your work group compare with other work groups at (name of company) on each of the following points? The way the men get along together. The way the men stick together. The way the men help each other on the job. Seashore computed intercorrelations among the answers and found them all to be positively correlated, with values ranging from .15 to .70. He then constructed a single index of cohesiveness which related meaningfully to several indicators of phenomena assumed to be consequences of cohesiveness.

A rather different composite index, based on seven questions concerning feelings of devotion to one's group, was constructed by Scott (38) in a longitudinal study of ten college fraternities and sororities. He found that those who left the organizations during the course of a year had significantly lower mean scores at the beginning of the year than did those who remained. Moreover, pledges as a group scored higher than actives, and younger actives scored higher than seniors, presumably indicating a progressive disenchantment with these organizations. It is important to note, however, that Scott found virtually no correlation between this index of group attraction and the average interpersonal attraction among members. Scott interprets this result to mean that for these organizations group attraction was not based in any significant degree upon interpersonal liking.

A study by Hagstrom and Selvin (12) casts further light upon the problem of constructing composite indexes of group cohesiveness. These investigators gave questionnaires to female college students living in twenty sororities, dormitories, boarding houses, and co-ops. Nineteen items, thought to be relevant to group cohesiveness, were used to construct aggregative measures for each living unit. Intercorrelations among these items across groups were almost entirely positive and rather high. A factor analysis revealed two factors that together account for most of the variation in scores. On the basis of the loadings, the two factors were labeled "social satisfaction" and "sociometric cohesion." Hagstrom and Selvin believe that the first factor measures the instrumental attractiveness of groups —the degree to which they provide opportunities for making friends, having dates, and participating in social life. The second factor, they feel, measures intrinsic attractiveness—the degree to which members are attracted to close personal association with others in the group. They conclude from observations and other measurements on these groups that different combinations of these two types of attractiveness produce important differences in the nature of group functioning.

The studies reported thus far reveal a general tendency for various indicators to be positively correlated, at least across broad ranges of items. Unfortunately, the research literature is not univocal in this regard. Gross and Martin (11), in an investigation of thirteen residential units for female students, found no substantial positive correlation among three different indicators of cohesiveness. And in a study of eleven student groups, Eisman (6) obtained no significant positive correlations among five different measures. Moreover, a replication of the Eisman study on Dutch female students, conducted by Ramuz-Nienhuis and Van Bergen (31), produced rather similar results.

It is difficult to know how best to interpret these conflicting findings. The bulk of the evidence strongly supports the view that each approach has produced indicators tapping something appropriately identified as group cohesiveness. Moreover, cohesiveness, as measured in these various ways, is meaningfully related to other features of groups. Measuring instruments, when appropriately tailored to fit particular situations, do yield significant results. On the other hand, it is clear that the correlations among various indicators are not consistent across all groups and situations. A standard all-purpose procedure for measuring group cohesiveness does not yet exist. This state of affairs, though disconcerting, is not really unexpected, for the development of measuring instruments cannot proceed much in advance of a basic understanding of the nature of the phenomena to be measured. Theory and measurement must advance together. Toward this end, we next examine more closely the nature of the determinants of attraction to a group.

DETERMINANTS OF ATTRACTION TO A GROUP

What determines how much a person will be attracted to a particular group? We propose that, in most general terms, attraction to group for a given individual will depend upon his assessment of the desirable and undesirable consequences attendant upon membership in the group. Simon, Smithburg, and Thompson (42) adopt this general view in their theory of organizational survival, one of whose postulates is stated as follows: "Each participant will continue his participation in an organization only so long as the inducements offered him are as great or greater (measured in terms of *his* values and in terms of the alternatives open to him) than the contribution he is asked to make." In a similar way, Thibaut and Kelley (45) analyze attraction to group in terms of the rewards and costs to an individual that are entailed by group membership. Apart from other considerations, an individual will be more attracted to a group the more favorable to him are the outcomes he expects to derive from membership.

Implicit in formulations such as these is the assumption that a person's attraction to a group is determined not simply by the characteristics of the group but also by his view of how these characteristics relate to his needs and values. Thus, for example, a group engaged in a contest with other groups might yield rewards to a self-confident individual with a strong achievement orientation but costs to a timid person with a high fear of failure. A person's actual attraction to the group may be expected to depend upon the magnitude of the rewards or costs afforded by the group but also upon his assessment of the likelihood that he will in fact experience them as a result of membership. Attraction to group depends, then, upon the expected value of the outcomes linked to membership.

One additional determinant of attraction to a group has been emphasized by Thibaut and Kelley (45). They assert that in evaluating the expected outcomes of group membership a person employs a standard, called the comparison level, against which he compares the expected outcomes of membership. This comparison level derives from his previous experience in groups and indicates the level of outcomes he aspires to receive from membership. He will be more attracted to the group the more the level of expected outcomes exceeds his comparison level.

We propose, then, that a person's attraction to a group is determined by four interacting sets of variables: (*a*) his *motive base for attraction*, consisting of his needs for affiliation, recognition, security, money, or other values that can be mediated by groups; (*b*) the *incentive properties of the group*, consisting of its goals, programs, characteristics of its members, style of operation, prestige, or other properties of significance for his motive base; (*c*) his *expectancy*, the subjective probability, that membership will actually have beneficial or detrimental consequences for him; and (*d*) his *comparison level*—his conception of the level of outcomes that group membership should provide.

With the help of such a formulation several interesting derivations become possible. If, for example, a person joins a group with the expectation of fulfilling certain personal needs but these change while he is a member, the attractiveness of the group will decrease for him unless the group is able to fulfill the new needs equally well or better. It is possible, of course, for an individual's needs to be modified through experience in the group. Indeed, some groups deliberately attempt to change the needs of their members. Sometimes such groups "lure" members into joining, by promising certain inducements, and then work on the member to develop other needs and interests that are considered more important to the group. Just how these conversions of motivation take place, though, is far from clearly understood.

Broad social conditions may modify the needs of large segments of the population more-or-less simultaneously. When such changes take place, we should expect the attractiveness of certain types of groups to be affected accordingly. Thus, it has been suggested that the postwar increase in church membership and attendance resulted from popular anxieties and insecurities brought about by the advent of the atomic age.

In an ingenious program of research, Schachter (37) studied the effects of experimentally induced states of anxiety on the desire to be with other people, which he calls "affiliative tendencies." His results show clearly that a state of anxiety leads to the arousal of affiliative tendencies. In attempting to account for the results of this research, Schachter concludes (37, 132):

It appears theoretically rewarding to formulate this body of findings as a manifestation of needs for anxiety reduction and of needs for self-evaluation; that is, ambiguous situations or feelings lead to a desire to be with others as a means of socially evaluating and determining the "appropriate" and proper reaction.

It would be expected, then, that when the members of a group encounter threatening or ambiguous situations, their attraction to the group will increase unless, perhaps, they believe the group itself to be the source of their disturbance.

Over the course of time the properties of a group may change so as to alter its incentive properties for its members. Thus, for example, a social club may become active in local politics and thereby become less satisfying to those members previously attracted by its friendly social activities. A group riven by a conflict for leadership may become more attractive when one of the contenders withdraws from the group. And a student organization primarily devoted to opposing some policy of the school's administration, if successful in effecting a change, may suddenly lose its attractiveness for those members with a dominant need to rebel against authority.

Even if the incentive properties of a group and the motive bases of its members remain unchanged, the group's attractiveness may be expected to vary with a member's subjective probability that he will actually experience rewards or costs from membership. Consider, for example, an individual who joins a group because he places high value on its purposes—perhaps on such goals as combatting prejudice, getting out the vote, or improving local business practices. If he comes to believe that the chances of achieving this end are slight—perhaps because of inefficiency in the group, poor leadership, friction, lack of money, or any of a number of reasons—he will become less attracted to the group.

The subjective probability of need satisfaction was demonstrated by Ross and Zander (35) to affect the desire of employees to remain in a business organization. These investigators measured the strength of members' needs for autonomy, recognition, fair evaluations, and the like, and obtained the workers' estimates of the probability that these needs would be satisfied by continued employment in the company. After a reasonable number of these employees had resigned, the scores of those who had left were compared with the scores of matched persons who had remained. The strength of the needs was found to be essentially the same for those who resigned and for the continuing workers, but those who stayed in the company had reported a greater likelihood that their needs would be fulfilled than had those who departed.

From the assumption that a person employs his own comparison level in evaluating the expected outcomes of group membership, it follows that determinants of the comparison level are also determinants of the attractiveness of a group. In their discussion of the nature of the comparison level, Thibaut and Kelley (45, 80–99) suggest a variety of such determinants. It will be possible here only to describe their general approach and to indicate some of the ways in which an individual's comparison level affects his attraction to a group.

According to Thibaut and Kelley, a person's comparison level is "some modal or average value of all the outcomes known to him (by virtue of personal or vicarious experience), each outcome weighted by its salience." Thus, if we hold salience constant, a person who has experienced superior outcomes in other groups will have a higher comparison level in the present group than will a person who has experienced generally inferior outcomes. And, the greater number of satisfying memberships a person has, the more he will demand from membership in any particular group.

In support of this conception, Thibaut and Kelley cite data from studies of the American soldier in World War II, reported by Stouffer *et al.* (43). Thus, for example, better-educated soldiers were found to be less satisfied with their status and opportunities for promotion than were less-educated soldiers. Presumably, each soldier was comparing the outcomes to him from army life with those previously enjoyed as a civilian. Noncombat soldiers in rear areas overseas were found, also, to be more satisfied with army life than were noncombat troops in the United States. This surprising finding can be explained if we assume that the salient comparison for the overseas troops was the life of the combat soldier, whereas for those in the United States it was that of the civilian population.

It should be noted that the ability of a group to meet the desires of an individual may not be totally dependent upon occurrences within the group itself. Group membership may provide access to certain gratifications obtainable outside the group that are not available to the nonmember. Thus, Hagstrom and Selvin (12) found college girls to be attracted to certain social groups because membership made it easier for them to have dates and to engage in campus activities. Similarly, Rose (34) states that the major benefit members say they derive from belonging to a large union local is that it obtains higher wages and job security for them. It should be noted, however, that membership in a group may also have negative effects by limiting the satisfactions a person can receive from activities outside it. A telephone operator on a night shift, for example, cannot participate in normal family life or be available for dates with friends. The extent to which a job interferes with family or community activities may be as important in reducing attraction to the organization as lack of satisfaction on the job (35).

The ways in which changes in an environment may determine the ability of voluntary organizations to meet members' needs have been vividly described by Eisenstadt (5) in a study in Israel immediately after it became a nation. While the country had been a British mandate, most organizations had had certain typical characteristics: they were closely related to various social movements or political parties; they performed functions of vital importance within the community such as guard duty, defense, medical aid, social welfare, education, and agriculture; they were connected with the social and political centers of the government; and they conceived of themselves as realizing the ideal of national rebirth. Thus, most of the groups enabled their members to participate in the civic life of the country and to feel that they were contributing to its development. Moreover, through participation in these groups the members received recognition and prestige in the community. When Israel became a nation there was rapid centralization of power and services in the hands of the government and an accompanying increase in the value placed upon power. As a result of these changes, voluntary associations lost their former usefulness, and members' interest in active political and social life dwindled. Instead of being concerned with social action, voluntary associations in the new nation became pressure groups, philanthropic societies, and social clubs, all having little connection with the government. The new voluntary groups provided little fulfillment of needs for action and achievement and primarily helped members to understand social or political problems, to promote points of view, and to encourage sociability.

INCENTIVE PROPERTIES OF GROUPS

In our formulation of the determinants of attraction to groups it is assumed that certain properties of a group have potential motivational significance for the people who come in contact with it. But a given property of a group will have incentive value for a particular person only if it is appropriate to his motive base. Thus, if we ask what properties of a group will affect its attractiveness, we must refer, at least implicitly, to the motivational characteristics of the people involved. Unfortunately, these characteristics have not been studied systematically in research on the incentive properties of groups. Great care must be exercised, therefore, in generalizing the results obtained from any particular collection of people. With this caution in mind, we turn now to a summary of findings concerning the properties of groups that influence their attractiveness.

ATTRACTIVENESS OF MEMBERS

As noted in our discussion of the problem of measuring group cohesiveness, many investigators have assumed that an individual will be more attracted to membership in a group the more he likes its members. The evidence in support of this assumption is sufficiently convincing to lead Lott and Lott (22) to define cohesiveness as "that group property which is inferred from the number and strength of mutual positive attitudes among the members of a group." But since measures of interpersonal attraction do not always correlate significantly with other indicators of the attraction to group, we prefer to view the attractiveness of members as only one of several possible sources of attraction to group membership. Thus, for example, a man may maintain his membership in a golf club primarily because it affords the best available opportunity to play golf while he may have neutral or even negative feelings about most of the habitués of the place.

A clear specification of the conditions under which interpersonal attraction does have incentive value for group membership is yet to be achieved. It appears, however, that if group membership puts a person in close association and frequent interaction with other members, his evaluation of these members will influence his attraction to membership in the group. Evidence for this proposition is provided by Festinger and Kelley (8) from a study of a housing project in which the residents perceived one another as "low class." In this small community it was extremely difficult to develop a tenants' organization, even with the aid of professional community organizers, since participation in its programs forced people to associate with others they regarded as undesirable.

If conditions are such that the members of a group do engage in frequent interaction, this interaction may affect their evaluations of one another and hence of group membership itself. Homans (15, 112) has proposed the following general hypothesis: "If the frequency of interaction between two or more persons increases, the degree of their liking for one another will increase, and vice versa." Thus, one might expect the attractiveness of a group to increase if the group initiates programs requiring interaction among members, and there is considerable evidence in support of this expectation. It appears, however, from data obtained by Festinger and Kelley that if people who dislike one another are induced to engage in interaction, the result may be an intensification of their antipathies. Further research is clearly required to elucidate the relation between interpersonal attraction and attraction to group membership.

SIMILARITIES AMONG MEMBERS

The theory of cognitive balance advanced by Heider (13) and elaborated by Newcomb (26, 27) holds that two people will be more attracted to each other the more similar their evaluations of objects in their common environment. A great deal of evidence in support of this assertion has been accumulated. Thus, for example, Newcomb obtained a wide variety of attitude measurements on a group of college students who were later to live together in a small dormitory. He found that over the course of several weeks high interpersonal attractions tended to develop among those who initially agreed most in their attitudes. He also found a striking correlation between initial similarity in values, as measured by the Allport-Vernon Study of Values, and interpersonal attraction after fourteen weeks of interaction. Results like these suggest that attraction to a group will increase with increasing similarity among members.

A somewhat different line of reasoning leads to the same conclusion. Festinger (7) argues that each individual has a need to evaluate his opinions and abilities, that in making such a self-evaluation he tends to compare himself with others, and that given a range of possible persons for comparison he will tend to choose someone similar to himself. Thus a person will be more attracted to situations in which others are similar to him with respect to abilities and

opinions than to ones in which others are divergent. Festinger cites a variety of studies that support this prediction, and additional confirmation has been provided by an experiment conducted by Zander and Havelin (47).

Research has made it clear, however, that similarity does not always generate attraction. Thus, in a study of industrial work groups Seashore (39) found no relation between a group's cohesiveness and its homogeneity with respect to the educational level or age of members. The degree of similarity regarding matters that are irrelevant to the group's functioning appears to have little consequence for interpersonal liking. There is evidence, moreover, that sometimes dissimilarity rather than similarity enhances attraction. A study of informal groups within the Air Force led Gross (10) to distinguish two types of groups: a *symbiotic* group, composed of men with dissimilar characteristics, where attraction is based upon different contributions that one member can make to another, and a *consensual* group made up of men with similar characteristics. He concludes that symbiotic relationships provide a more stable basis for attraction than do consensual ones.

The total body of evidence indicates that similarity with respect to values, interests, attitudes, and beliefs that are important to the members of a group usually heightens attraction but that dissimilarity may sometimes be a source of attraction. Further research is required to clarify the essential differences between these two types of situation.

GROUP GOALS

The goals of a group constitute another possible source of its attractiveness. Different groups may have, of course, widely different goals that may vary considerably in their explicitness and specificity. Having a distinctive goal or purpose serves to attract to the group people with a particular motive base. The members of such a group, being similar to one another with respect to relevant values and interests, may be expected to develop interpersonal bonds and to be attracted to group membership. Scott (38) has provided careful documentation of the ways in which the basic objectives of sororities and fraternities affect the kinds of students who are recruited to membership and who remain members.

Results of a laboratory experiment by Raven and Rietsema (32) indicate that the incentive value of a particular group goal for a particular person will depend not only upon its content but also upon how explicitly the goal is formulated, how clear the paths for goal attainment are, and the likelihood of successful achievement of the goal. When the best procedure for reaching a goal is not clearly evident to all members, disruptive disagreements may reduce the members' attraction to the group. In a study of problem-solving by groups, French (9) found that some members withdrew from participation when disagreements arose among members. He noted that withdrawal was most likely to occur when members were disagreeing over the method they should use in solving the problem.

If a member is highly identified with a group goal, one would expect him to gain satisfaction from group success and dissatisfaction from group failure. On the whole, research findings confirm this expectation, but as noted by Lott and Lott (22) the failure of a group to reach its goal may result, under certain conditions, in an increase in attraction to the group. Such an outcome appears to be most likely where the failure is perceived by the members as arbitrarily imposed by an external source.

TYPE OF INTERDEPENDENCE AMONG MEMBERS

When the members of a group accept a common goal and agree on actions required to reach it, they become cooperatively interdependent. Each member gains satisfaction from contributions made by others toward attainment of their common goal. In a theory of interpersonal cooperation, Deutsch (Chap. 35) advances the hypothesis that when people are cooperatively interdependent they will develop attraction to one another. He obtained empirical support for this in an experiment comparing cooperative and competitive classroom groups. In the cooperative groups the students were told that all would be given the same grade depending upon the quality of the group's product. The competitive groups were informed that each member would be graded on his merits relative to the others in his own class. The cooperative groups displayed more symptoms of high cohesiveness. Compared to the competitive groups, the members liked one another more, made more attempts to influence one another, accepted influence attempts

more readily, and were more friendly in their behavior. Other investigations have also produced results supporting the view that group attractiveness is greater when members are cooperatively interdependent than when they are in competition.

In Deutsch's experiment intragroup cooperation was accompanied by intergroup competition. Other studies by Sherif and Sherif (41), Myers (25), and Julian, Bishop, and Fiedler (18) have focused more directly upon the effects of competition between groups and have found that such competition promotes close interpersonal relations within groups. An interpretation of these results, different from that of Deutsch, holds that it is the common threat to the members, posed by a common enemy or opponent, that draws members together. These two interpretations, though different, are not incompatible; both cooperative interdependence and common threat may serve to heighten the attractiveness of a group. It should be added, however, that some investigators have found that threat serves to decrease attraction. The conditions producing these different effects of threat have not been thoroughly studied, but a review of the literature by Lott and Lott (22) led them to propose that

attraction among individuals will be found to increase when their common threat stems from an external source (i.e., is not a function of their own lack of skill), when there exists the possibility that cooperative behavior may reduce or eliminate the threat, and when single individuals cannot escape from either the group or the threat.

GROUP ACTIVITIES

To the extent that membership in a group involves a person in certain activities, his evaluation of these activities should affect his attraction to the group. Indeed, the attractiveness of some groups, such as social or recreational clubs, depends primarily upon the nature of the activities they provide members. Research conducted in business and industrial organizations reveals a general tendency for satisfaction with one's job to be negatively correlated with frequency of absence from work and the probability of voluntarily leaving the organization (46). In much of this research "job satisfaction" is loosely defined and represents many factors other than involvement in the task itself. Nevertheless, there is evidence that satisfaction with one's work activities is often a major component of total job satisfaction, and efforts to make work more satisfying through programs of "job enlargement" have generally resulted in an increase in total satisfaction (19).

One of the natural resultants of group life is that a member will be asked to assume responsibilities. Some of these, perhaps speechmaking, letter-writing, bookkeeping, or leading a discussion, are duties for which he feels he is not adequately prepared. The attractiveness of the group might well be reduced, then, when it is the source of such embarrassment. Horwitz (Chap. 34) reports from a laboratory experiment some incidental observations that illustrate this phenomenon. In this experiment the members of each group were girls from the same sorority. A group task was assigned and the girls were highly motivated to do well. In the course of this task it became apparent to some of the girls that their own inability to contribute to the group task might prevent the group from doing well. This realization was quite disturbing and made the whole group activity less attractive. If a group has standards of performance that members cannot meet, the prospect of repeated personal failure should adversely affect the attractiveness of the group. Consistent with this expectation are the findings from a study of industrial workers reported by Coch and French (Chap. 26). Here it was found that workers whose rate of production fell just below the group standard, so that feelings of failure were most intense, had an extremely high rate of leaving the company.

LEADERSHIP AND DECISION-MAKING

The classical experiments by Lewin, Lippitt, and White (Chap. 25) on styles of leadership provide several indications that children are more attracted to a group with democratic leadership than to one with autocratic or laissez faire leadership. Research conducted in quite different settings leads to similar conclusions. A study comparing two styles of leadership, reported by Preston and Heintz (30), showed that members of groups having participatory leaders, as compared with those having supervisory leaders, expressed more

satisfaction with the group's product, felt the group's task to be more interesting, believed the group to be more efficient, and gave more weight to the attitudes of other members in forming their own opinions. And, as noted above, Bovard (2) found that college students rate their class more favorably when the teacher is group centered than when he is leader centered.

Further evidence is provided by a field experiment, reported by Morse and Reimer (24), conducted in a large business organization employing female clerical workers. In two divisions decision-making among rank-and-file workers was increased while in another pair of divisions it was moved to higher levels of management. After one and one-half years, significant changes were found in the employees' satisfaction with the company; an increase in satisfaction occurred among the employees in the divisions affording increased opportunities for decision-making while a decrease occurred among those in the other two divisions. It should be noted, however, that additional analyses undertaken by Tannenbaum and Allport (44) show that people with different personality structures react to these two types of social organization in rather different ways.

These and other studies indicate that a group's attractiveness is influenced by the nature of its leadership. A democratic form of organization that encourages widespread participation in decision-making appears generally to induce more attraction to the group than does one in which decisions are centralized. This conclusion must be tempered, however, by the finding that people with different values and attitudes may react quite differently to the same type of leadership.

STRUCTURAL PROPERTIES

Although the effects of a group's structure upon its attractiveness have not been systematically investigated, there is evidence to suggest that such effects may be substantial. Research initiated by Bavelas (Chap. 37) shows that the communication structure of a group can affect members' satisfaction with participation in the group. Bavelas created groups in the laboratory that were to work on a problem requiring the exchange of information among members, and he specified for each group the communication network that it could use. He found that the average level of satisfaction was higher among members of groups with a decentralized network than among those with a centralized one. In a review of nineteen subsequent experiments, Shaw (40) reports that the results of seventeen confirm this finding. It would seem likely that research on other structural properties would show similar effects upon the attractiveness of groups.

If a group has a definite structure, a member's location within it may be expected to affect his attraction to the group. Bavelas found that members occupying the most central positions in a communication network were more satisfied with their jobs and with the group's performance than were those in the most peripheral positions. Porter and Lawler (29) in summarizing research on the effects of a person's position in the supervisory hierarchy of organizations assert "it can be stated with some degree of assurance that the available literature on job satisfaction across different levels of organizations shows increasing job satisfaction at each higher level."

Additional information about the effects of group structure upon attractiveness comes from a laboratory experiment in which Kelley (20) created a prestige hierarchy by giving some members the authority to tell others what to do and how to do it. He informed some of the higher-status persons that they were secure in their jobs and others that they might be changed to a lower status later in the experiment. Similarly, some of the lows were told that they would not be allowed to rise above their low positions, and other lows were informed that they might be promoted. Kelley found that the high-status job with the implied threat of demotion, and the low-status post with the impossibility of promotion, were clearly the most undesirable positions. He also noted that persons who were secure in their high status and those who felt that they might rise in status were most attracted to the rest of the members of the group.

GROUP ATMOSPHERE

Everyday experience makes it clear that a group often develops a general atmosphere that determines members' reactions to the group as a whole. Some groups are businesslike, impersonal, and efficient. Others are warm, relaxed, and friendly. And still others are full of tension and suspicion. The term "atmosphere," while clearly referring to impor-

tant features of a group, has remained conceptually unclear. As a result, little research has been directed toward elucidating its effects. Despite the lack of systematic evidence, we would expect a group's atmosphere to have pronounced effects upon its attractiveness.

It seems likely, for instance, that a group whose atmosphere is such that members feel accepted and valued will have attraction for its members. Dittes (4) found in a laboratory experiment that members who were made to feel well-accepted in a group were more attracted to it than were those made to feel poorly accepted. This difference, however, was much larger among persons with lower self-esteem than among those with higher self-esteem, presumably because members with lower self-esteem had a stronger need for acceptance by others. Similar findings have been reported by Jackson (17); in a study of professional workers in a child welfare agency, he obtained a significant correlation between a person's attraction to his work group and the evaluations of him made by the members of the group.

Although it may seem obvious that a warm and friendly atmosphere will contribute to the attractiveness of a group, there is evidence to indicate that under certain conditions such an atmosphere may generate processes leading to dissatisfaction. Riecken (33) has studied a work camp whose prevailing atmosphere placed a high value on friendly and gentle interactions. In the course of performing daily duties, however, minor antagonisms were bound to arise. Since the campers were members of an association that disapproves of both physical and verbal aggression, they found it difficult to raise problems in which some person or a subgroup was at fault. These problems, when discussed in staff meetings, were usually handled in an abstract and intellectual fashion and few of the resulting decisions were carried through. Typically, a member apologized for bringing up the problem and stated that he did not mean to blame anyone for the state of affairs. The resulting condition amounted, consequently, to a failure of communication on important matters, and antagonisms continued, much to the unhappiness of all.

GROUP SIZE

The effects of the size of a group upon its attractiveness have interested a number of investigators. Much of the research has focused on units, such as work groups, departments, or factories, within large organizations. The results, as reviewed by Porter and Lawler (29), are remarkably consistent in showing that as the size of these units increases there is a decrease in job satisfaction and a concomitant increase in absence rates, turnover rates, and the incidence of labor disputes.

In an attempt to explain the negative relationship between the size of a group and the satisfaction of its members, Indik (16) made an intensive study of groups in three organizations. He wished to ascertain whether larger groups show the following characteristics, each of which might be expected to reduce member satisfaction: (a) more difficulty in achieving adequate communication among members, (b) a higher degree of task specialization, (c) greater reliance upon impersonal forms of control, and (d) more severe problems of coordination that tend to be handled by inflexible bureaucratic rules and regulations. His results clearly indicate that larger groups do have more difficulties of communication and less satisfaction from work. The findings concerning the effects of size upon forms of control and problems of coordination are not entirely consistent across the three organizations.

It appears, then, that the size of a group affects its attractiveness by means of its effect on other properties of the group. If these properties become less satisfying as size increases, there will be a negative correlation between size and attractiveness. It is conceivable, however, that under certain conditions (for example, where goal achievement requires a large number of people), larger groups will possess more satisfying properties than will smaller ones. As a particular group changes in size, one would expect some of its properties to become less satisfying and some to become more so. The net effect on group attractiveness would then depend upon the balance of these two types of effect.

CONSEQUENCES OF GROUP COHESIVENESS

In the preceding discussion we have implicitly assumed that certain phenomena can be conceived as consequences of group cohesiveness. Thus, for example, we used such criteria as a group's rate of turnover or its ability to influence members in our evaluation of various indexes of cohesiveness and in our search for the determinants of group attractiveness. We turn now to a more systematic consideration of the consequences of cohesiveness. Since most of the relevant findings have already been cited, they will not be repeated here in any detail.

MAINTENANCE OF MEMBERSHIP

We asserted at the beginning of the chapter that the resultant force acting on a member to remain in a group is composed of forces arising from two sources: the attractiveness of the group and the attractiveness of alternative memberships. We would expect, then, that if the restraints against leaving are sufficiently weak, the rate of turnover of membership for a group will be negatively correlated with the group's attractiveness and positively correlated with the attractiveness of alternative memberships. As we have seen, there is considerable evidence in support of the first of these predictions—various indicators of group attractiveness correlate negatively with turnover of membership. It seems highly probable that research designed to test the second prediction would support it also.

In their treatment of the factors affecting the maintenance of group membership, Thibaut and Kelley (45) employ different concepts but arrive at conclusions essentially similar to ours. For them, it will be recalled, a person's attraction to a group depends upon how the level of expected outcomes from membership relates to his comparison level. They argue, however, that this attractiveness has no necessary relation to a person's tendency to maintain membership in a group. In order to account for this tendency, they introduce another concept, the *comparison level for alternatives,* which is the level of outcomes the person believes he can receive from the best available alternative membership. A person will remain in a group if and only if his level of outcomes lies above his comparison level for alternatives. According to this formulation, then, given a particular level of outcomes a person's attraction to a group depends upon his comparison level, but his tendency to remain in the group depends upon his comparison level for alternatives. It can be seen, however, that if the comparison levels and the comparison levels for alternatives remain constant for a particular population, then differences among groups in their levels of expected outcomes will result in corresponding differences both in their attractiveness and in their ability to retain members. Under these conditions, we should find a negative correlation between group attractiveness and turnover.

POWER OF A GROUP OVER MEMBERS

The consequence of cohesiveness most thoroughly investigated is the power that cohesiveness gives a group to influence its members. We have reviewed several studies showing that members conform more to the norms of a group the greater the group's cohesiveness. The evidence for this conclusion is presented more fully in Part Three. There can be little doubt that members of a more cohesive group more readily exert influence on one another and are more readily influenced by one another. Although the evidence is not so clear, we should also expect the members of a more cohesive group to accept more readily the group's goals, decisions, and assignment to tasks and roles.

Why should cohesiveness contribute to the power of a group over its members? Festinger (Chap. 14), who first postulated a relation between cohesiveness and power, asserts that the magnitude of force that a group can set up on a member counter to his own forces cannot exceed the resultant force acting on him to remain in the group, for the member would leave the group rather than submit to such pressure. Thus, the cohesiveness of a group sets an upper limit upon the group's capacity to influence its members. The treatment of this problem by Thibaut and Kelley (45), although essentially similar, takes on a slightly different form. They assert that a person's dependence on a group is greater the more his level of expected outcomes from membership exceeds his comparison level for alternatives and that the power of the group over a member is directly related to his dependence upon the group. Thus, according to Thibaut and Kelley, the power of a group over a member depends upon the level of outcomes he expects to receive from the group in contrast to the level he believes he can receive from his best available alternative membership. Which of these two theories is superior can be determined only by research specifically designed to provide measurements of their respective concepts.

PARTICIPATION AND LOYALTY

Since cohesiveness contributes to a group's capacity to retain members and to exert influence over them, we might expect it also to result in a heightening of participation in group activities. Several studies have shown that as cohesiveness increases there is more frequent communication among members, a greater degree of participation in group activities, and a lower rate of absences. The findings, however, are not always striking nor consistent; factors other than cohesiveness appear to enter into the determinants of participation. And as noted by Hill and Trist (14), the temporary withdrawal from participation, perhaps through absence from work, is not the same as withdrawal from group membership. A member who is highly attracted to the group may nevertheless fail to participate fully because of illness, competing obligations, or the need to avoid tensions arising from participation. Thus, we should expect to find a correlation between cohesiveness and the rate of participation only when these other factors are held constant or when the group exercises its power over members in order to induce participation.

PERSONAL CONSEQUENCES

There is some evidence concerning the effects of group cohesiveness on the personal adjustment of members. Thus, for example, Seashore (39) obtained a negative correlation between the cohesiveness of industrial work groups and the tendency for members to report that they often felt "jumpy" or nervous on the job. From a program of research on "quasi-therapeutic" effects of intergroup competition, Myers (25) and Julian, Bishop, and Fiedler (18) report results supporting the thesis that intergroup competition produces an increase in group cohesiveness that, in turn, leads to a heightening of self-esteem and a lowering of anxiety among the members of a group. These investigators believe that the improved interpersonal relations involved in an increase in cohesiveness lead to more acceptance, trust, and confidence among members and that each member consequently develops a sense of security and personal worth.

The proposition that group cohesiveness

leads to a sense of security among members is supported by the results of an experiment conducted by Pepitone and Reichling (28). In this experiment, two levels of group cohesiveness were created and the reactions of members in each setting were observed following an "insult" delivered to the group by an outsider. It was found that members of the more cohesive groups freely engaged in hostile remarks against the insulter, whereas those in groups with low cohesiveness sat quietly or spoke of matters unrelated to their embarrassing experiences. This difference in the readiness of members to express hostility presumably resulted, in part at least, from a greater sense of security experienced by members of the cohesive groups.

In summary, we have found evidence for several consequences of group cohesiveness. Other things being equal, as cohesiveness increases there is an increase in a group's capacity to retain members and in the degree of participation by members in group activities. The greater a group's cohesiveness the more power it has to bring about conformity to its norms and to gain acceptance of its goals and assignment to tasks and roles. Finally, highly cohesive groups provide a source of security for members which serves to reduce anxiety and to heighten self-esteem. Further research will undoubtedly discover additional consequences of cohesiveness.

SOME UNSOLVED PROBLEMS

Our definition of group cohesiveness as the resultant of all forces acting on members to remain in the group has helped considerably to bring many discrete research findings into a meaningful conceptual scheme. There remain, however, several ambiguities in this theoretical formulation, which we now consider briefly.

HOW VARIOUS SOURCES OF ATTRACTION COMBINE

In discussing the determinants of attraction to a group, we observed that a person's motive base may contain several needs and values and that a group may have many incentive properties. Thus, the resultant force acting on a member to remain in the group will usually be made up of component forces having a variety of sources. Little is known about the ways in which these combine into a single resultant force. Can we assume, for example, that forces deriving from different sources combine additively? Does the magnitude of the resultant force equal the sum of the component forces? To put the question in more concrete terms: If the attraction to the group's activities is the same in two groups, will one of them have greater attraction if in addition the members like one another better? We should expect that the addition of attractions from different sources would actually increase the total attractiveness of the group for an individual, but systematic research has yet to establish the fact.

IMPORTANCE OF SOURCE OF ATTRACTION

In our theoretical formulation, a variety of factors are conceived as determinants of a single variable, group cohesiveness, which in turn produces certain consequences. If any two of these determinants have equivalent effects on cohesiveness, they should have equivalent effects, mediated by cohesiveness, upon phenomena treated as consequences of cohesiveness. Is there, in fact, some common denominator among the various sources of attraction by which one can obtain consistent relations between a given degree of cohesiveness regardless of its specific source and other properties of a group?

To answer this question with finality, further research is needed. The best evidence bearing directly on this problem is provided by Back (1). In his experiment, three sources of attraction were compared: personal attraction, task attraction, and possible prestige gains from membership. The strength of attraction for each source was varied. It was found that for any two of these sources a similar increase in attraction led to a similar increase in the power of the group to influence its members. With respect to power to influence, then, there is some justification for assuming that different sources of attraction have the same effect. We should add, however, that more recent theorizing by French and Raven (Chap. 20) suggests that different bases of power affect the nature of power in certain ways. It seems likely, then, that if different sources of attraction serve as different bases of the group's power, the nature of this power will differ depending upon the source of attraction to the group. Further research on this problem would appear to hold considerable promise.

If it turns out that different sources of attraction do have some common effects, it does not necessarily follow that all of their effects will be the same. Indeed, Back found that differences in the ways in which cohesiveness was produced led to different styles of communication. When cohesiveness was based on personal attractions among members, they made their discussion a long, pleasant conversation in which they expected to be able to persuade one another easily. When cohesiveness was based on effective performance of the task they were given to do, the members wanted to complete the activity quickly and efficiently and discussed only those matters which they thought were relevant to achieving their purposes. And when cohesiveness was based on the prestige obtainable from membership, the members acted cautiously, concentrated on their own actions, and in general were careful not to risk their status.

COMBINING SEVERAL INDIVIDUAL SCORES OF ATTRACTION TO FORM A SINGLE VALUE OF COHESIVENESS

Even after we achieve a satisfactory method for determining an individual's resultant attraction to the group, there remains the problem of combining individual scores into an index of group cohesiveness. The simplest formulation of group cohesiveness would be that it equals the sum, or average, of the resultant forces on members to remain in the group. Each member would be given equal weight. A formulation essentially of this type has been used in most of the research conducted up to the present, and on the whole it has proved satisfactory. There can hardly be any doubt, however, that the degree to which certain members are attracted to the group makes a critical difference, while the degree of attraction of other members is relatively inconsequential to the group. Only further research can determine the most satisfactory method for relating individual attraction scores to an index of group cohesiveness.

THE SPECIAL CASE OF INVOLUNTARY MEMBERSHIP

It is not uncommon to find a group where members retain their membership even though the resultant forces acting on them are directed away from the group. In such an instance of "negative cohesiveness," membership is involuntary; members remain in the group simply because the restraints against leaving are too great. What are the consequences of cohesiveness when it takes on a negative value?

Although the literature provides little in the way of a systematic answer to this question, Festinger (Chap. 14) has made some interesting suggestions concerning the nature of a group's power over its members under such conditions. He argues that a group has power to bring about genuine covert changes in the opinions and attitudes of its members only if its cohesiveness is greater than zero. If, however, a group has negative cohesiveness, it can resort to threats of punishment, whose severity is limited only by the magnitude of the restraining forces on members against leaving the group. Such threats may be successful in bringing about overt compliance to the demands of the group, but it cannot directly produce changes in the private beliefs and attitudes of members. Thus, if we compare groups having positive cohesiveness with ones having negative cohesiveness, we should expect to find in the latter that group-relevant behavior of members is more often governed by the fear of punishment and less often arises from the members' own needs.

For a discussion of other possible consequences of negative cohesiveness, the reader is referred to the stimulating treatment of non-voluntary relationships given by Thibaut and Kelley (**45**, 169–187).

NEED FOR A MODEL OF CIRCULAR CAUSATION

In our attempt to discover some theoretical order among the many findings related to group cohesiveness, we have identified certain factors as determinants and others as consequences of cohesiveness. Such an approach seems justified as a first step, but there is good reason to believe that some of the consequences serve also as determinants. Thus, a more adequate model is needed to represent circular processes involving group cohesiveness.

These processes may take various forms. In one of these, factors that increase cohesiveness lead to consequences that, in turn, lead to greater cohesiveness. Several examples of such a benign circular system come readily to mind. Similarities of beliefs and values tend to generate interpersonal attractions among members, and the resulting cohesiveness gives the group power to influence members toward greater similarity. As a group becomes more cohesive its ability to satisfy the needs of members increases, thereby raising the incentive value of the group. And cohesiveness tends to generate frequent interaction among members, which, under certain conditions at least, heightens interpersonal attraction and thus cohesiveness. It is apparent that such circular processes cannot go on indefinitely, which raises an interesting question concerning the nature of the limitations on the level of cohesiveness that a group can attain.

Cohesiveness may also be involved in a degenerating circular causal system. Here a reduction in cohesiveness produces consequences that then lead to a further decrease in cohesiveness. Thus, for example, if a group fails to reach an important goal, the members may become less attracted to the group. The resulting decline in cohesiveness may reduce the group's ability to succeed in the future and thereby further diminish its cohesiveness.

It is possible, of course, for circular causal systems to have a more complex form as, for example, when an increase in cohesiveness has consequences that lead to a subsequent decrease in cohesiveness. In this case, cohesiveness will oscillate around a particular level. An instance of this sort may arise when the additional power derived from an increase in group cohesiveness is used to induce members to engage in activities that are frustrating and that then reduce the incentive value of the group.

The development of concepts and related empirical findings appropriate to a model of circular causation should significantly improve our understanding of the nature of group cohesiveness.

SUMMARY

Group cohesiveness is the resultant of two sets of component forces acting on members to remain in the group—those arising from the attractiveness of the group and those deriving from the attractiveness of alternative memberships.

A person's attraction to a group is determined by four interacting sets of variables: (a) his motive base for attraction; (b) the incentive properties of the group; (c) his expectancy that membership will result in beneficial, or detrimental, consequences for him; and (d) his comparison level, or the quality of outcomes he believes he deserves.

Nine properties of groups have been identified which have potential incentive value, depending upon the motive bases of the individuals involved: (a) attractiveness of group members, (b) similarities among members, (c) nature of group goals, (d) type of interdependence among members, (e) activities of the group, (f) style of leadership and opportunity to participate in decisions, (g) various structural properties of the group, (h) the group's atmosphere, and (i) size of the group.

Among the many possible consequences of group cohesiveness, four principal ones have been documented by research: (a) ability of the group to retain its members, (b) power of the group to influence its members, (c) degree of participation and loyalty of members, and (d) feelings of security on the part of members.

Certain problems remain to be solved before a fully satisfactory theory of group cohesiveness can be achieved: (a) How do various sources of attraction combine for a given person? (b) What difference does the source of attraction make? (c) How should separate individuals' scores of attraction to the group be combined to form a single value of cohesiveness? (d) How can the restraining forces against leaving a group be incorporated into a systematic treatment of cohesiveness? (e) Can models of circular causation be developed to give a more adequate account of the development, maintenance, and decline of cohesiveness for a particular group? The solution of these problems will require both theoretical ingenuity and the invention of better methods of measurement.

References

1. Back, K. Influence through social communication. *Journal of Abnormal and Social Psychology*, 1951, **46**, 9–23.
2. Bovard, E. Group structure and perception. *Journal of Abnormal and Social Psychology*, 1951, **46**, 389–405.
3. Dimock, H. *Rediscovering the adolescent*. New York: Association Press, 1941.
4. Dittes, J. Attractiveness of group as function of self-esteem and acceptance by group. *Journal of Abnormal and Social Psychology*, 1959, **59**, 77–82.
5. Eisenstadt, S. The social conditions of the development of voluntary association. *Scripta Hierasolymitana*, 1955, **3**, 104–125.
6. Eisman, B. Some operational measures of cohesiveness and their correlations. *Human Relations*, 1959, **12**, 183–189.
7. Festinger, L. A theory of social comparison processes. *Human Relations*, 1954, **7**, 117–140.
8. Festinger, L., & Kelley, H. *Changing attitudes through social contact*. Ann Arbor, Mich.: Research Center for Group Dynamics, 1951.
9. French, J. R. P., Jr. The disruption and cohesion of groups. *Journal of Abnormal and Social Psychology*, 1941, **36**, 361–377.
10. Gross, E. Symbiosis and consensus in small groups. *American Sociological Review*, 1956, **21**, 174–179.
11. Gross, N., & Martin, W. On group cohesiveness. *American Journal of Sociology*, 1952, **57**, 533–546.
12. Hagstrom, W. O., & Selvin, H. C. The dimensions of cohesiveness in small groups. *Sociometry*, 1965, **28**, 30–43.
13. Heider, F. *The psychology of interpersonal relations*. New York: Wiley, 1958.
14. Hill, J., & Trist, E. Changes in accidents and other absences with length of service. *Human Relations*, 1955, **8**, 121–152.
15. Homans, G. *The human group*. New York: Harcourt, Brace, 1950.
16. Indik, B. P. Organization size and member participation: Some empirical tests of alternative explanations. *Human Relations*, 1965, **18**, 339–350.
17. Jackson, J. M. Reference group processes in a formal organization. *Sociometry*, 1959, **22**, 307–327.
18. Julian, J. W., Bishop, D. W., & Fiedler, F. E. Quasi-therapeutic effects of intergroup competition. *Journal of Personality and Social Psychology*, 1966, **3**, 321–327.
19. Katz, D., & Kahn, R. L. *The social psychology of organizations*. New York: Wiley, 1966.
20. Kelley, H. H. Communication in experimentally created hierarchies. *Human Relations*, 1951, **4**, 39–56.
21. Libo, L. *Measuring group cohesiveness*. Ann Arbor, Mich.: Institute for Social Research, 1953.
22. Lott, A. J., & Lott, B. E. Group cohesiveness as interpersonal attraction: A review of relationships with antecedent and consequent variables. *Psychological Bulletin*, 1965, **64**, 259–309.
23. Mann, F., & Baumgartel, H. *Absences and employee attitudes in an electric power company*. Ann Arbor, Mich.: Institute for Social Research, 1952.
24. Morse, N., & Reimer, E. The experimental change of a major organizational variable. *Journal of Abnormal and Social Psychology*, 1956, **52**, 120–129.
25. Myers, A. E. Team competition, success, and adjustment of group members. *Journal of Abnormal and Social Psychology*, 1962, **65**, 325–332.
26. Newcomb, T. M. An approach to the study of communicative acts. *Psychological Review*, 1953, **60**, 393–404.
27. Newcomb, T. M. Varieties of interpersonal attraction. In D. Cartwright & A. Zander (Eds.), *Group dynamics: Research and theory*. (2nd ed.) Evanston, Ill.: Row, Peterson, 1960. Pp. 104–119.
28. Pepitone, A., & Reichling, G. Group cohesiveness and the expression of hostility. *Human Relations*, 1955, **8**, 327–337.

29. Porter, L. W., & Lawler, E. E., III. Properties of organization structure in relation to job attitudes and job behavior. *Psychological Bulletin*, 1965, **64**, 23–51.

30. Preston, M. G., & Heintz, R. K. Effects of participatory vs. supervisory leadership on group judgment. *Journal of Abnormal and Social Psychology*, 1949, **44**, 345–355.

31. Ramuz-Nienhuis, W., & Van Bergen, A. Relations between some components of attraction-to-group: A replication. *Human Relations*, 1960, **13**, 271–277.

32. Raven, B. H., & Rietsema, J. The effect of varied clarity of group goal and group path upon the individual and his relation to his group. *Human Relations*, 1957, **10**, 29–44.

33. Riecken, H. Some problems of consensus development. *Rural Sociology*, 1952, **17**, 245–252.

34. Rose, A. *Union solidarity*. Minneapolis: Univ. of Minnesota Press, 1952.

35. Ross, I., & Zander, A. Need satisfaction and employee turnover. *Personnel Psychology*, 1957, **10**, 327–338.

36. Sagi, P. C., Olmsted, & Atelsek, F. Predicting maintenance of membership in small groups. *Journal of Abnormal and Social Psychology*, 1955, **51**, 308–311.

37. Schachter, S. *The psychology of affiliation*. Stanford: Stanford Univ. Press, 1959.

38. Scott, W. A. *Values and organizations*. Chicago: Rand McNally, 1965.

39. Seashore, S. *Group cohesiveness in the industrial work group*. Ann Arbor, Mich.: Institute for Social Research, 1954.

40. Shaw, M. E. Communication networks. In L. Berkowitz (Ed.), *Advances in experimental social psychology*. Vol. 1. New York: Academic Press, 1964. Pp. 111–149.

41. Sherif, M., & Sherif, C. *Groups in harmony and tension*. New York: Harper, 1953.

42. Simon, H. A., Smithburg, D. W., & Thompson, V. A. *Public administration*. New York: Knopf, 1950.

43. Stouffer, S. A., *et al*. *The American soldier*. Vol. I. *Adjustment during army life*. Princeton, N. J.: Princeton Univ. Press, 1949.

44. Tannenbaum, A. S., & Allport, F. H. Personality structure and group structure: An interpretive study of their relationship through an event-structure hypothesis. *Journal of Abnormal and Social Psychology*, 1956, **53**, 272–280.

45. Thibaut, J. W., & Kelley, H. H. *The social psychology of groups*. New York: Wiley, 1959.

46. Vroom, V. *Work and motivation*. New York: Wiley, 1964.

47. Zander, A., & Havelin, A. Social comparison and interpersonal attraction. *Human Relations*, 1960, **13**, 21–32.

8

Opinion Evaluation and Affiliation

ROLAND RADLOFF

The present study was designed to test the hypothesis that a person's needs for self-evaluation regarding the correctness of his opinions arouse affiliative tendencies in him. It stems directly from results and discussion presented by Schachter (12) and is related to Festinger's theory of social comparison processes (3).

Schachter found a positive relation between emotional arousal and affiliative tendencies; specifically, under conditions of experimentally manipulated anxiety, highly anxious subjects wanted to be with others more than did nonanxious subjects. From a series of experiments designed and executed to explore the determinants of this relationship, Schachter (12, 123) concluded that the affiliative tendencies he found were manifestation of "needs for anxiety reduction and needs for self-evaluation; that is, ambiguous situations or feelings lead to a desire to be with others as a means of socially evaluating and determining the 'appropriate' and proper reaction."

Festinger (3, 117) has postulated that "there exists, in the human organism, a drive to evaluate his opinions and abilities." Further, Festinger proposes that in the absence of objective or physical evaluative criteria, opinions are evaluated by comparing them with those of other people. The opinion is then taken as correct or incorrect in terms of agreement or disagreement with the opinions that the others hold. The drive for self-evaluation has been successfully employed to account for a variety of behaviors in a number of laboratory studies. Specifically, group members have been found to change their opinions (1), exert influence to change the opinions of others (5), and reject

From *The Journal of Abnormal and Social Psychology*, 1961, **62**, 578–585. Reprinted by permission of the author and the American Psychological Association. This study is part of the author's doctoral dissertation (10) submitted to the faculty of the Graduate School of the University of Minnesota. The research was supported by a grant from the National Institute of Mental Health, United States Public Health Service.

unchanging deviates in order to create uniformity of opinion within the group (11), thereby providing validity for opinions by consensus. In all of the studies just cited, opinion comparisons were made in existing groups. No experimental evidence is yet available that bears directly on the question of opinion evaluation and affiliation. The present study was therefore planned to demonstrate that needs for evaluation of opinions are important determinants of group formation in addition to their function as sources of pressure to uniformity within groups. The major hypothesis of the study is: A person who is uncertain about the correctness of one of his opinions, for which he finds no objective criteria available by which to evaluate its correctness, should seek affiliation with other people in order to evaluate his opinion via social comparison.

In an experimental test of this hypothesis, specific predictions regarding affiliative tendencies would follow from a manipulation of evaluative needs. With initial need arousal held constant, if for some subjects information that satisfies evaluative needs is provided while for others it is not, affiliative tendencies should be stronger in the latter group than in the former. Since people are assumed to satisfy evaluative needs by comparing their opinions with those of others, one method of manipulating evaluative information would be to provide subjects in different conditions with information about the opinions of various groups of other people. Such information can be ordered on a continuum of adequacy for purposes of comparison and evaluation. Points ranging from inadequate to adequate could be represented by giving the subjects information about the opinions of: (*a*) no others, (*b*) irrelevant others or inferiors, (*c*) peers, (*d*) experts. (Inferiors are defined as people who have less education, information, and experience than the subjects, and whose inferiorities are relevant to the validity of their opinions on the issue in question. Experts are defined as people who have greater education, information, and experience than the subjects, and whose superiorities are relevant to the issue in question.)

The magnitude of evaluative needs (and therefore of affiliative tendencies) are predicted to vary in the following manner according to the conditions just specified $a > b > c > d$. These predictions depend in part on the

degrees of inferiority and expertness that the subjects attribute to groups *b* and *d*. According to the strength of the manipulation and the subject's perception, *b* could be closer to *a* or to *c*, and *d* could be close to or distant from *c* in terms of adequacy as comparison groups. In the absence of prior knowledge regarding the strength of the manipulations, predictions can be made only for the rank order of the groups and not for the magnitude of the differences.

The manipulations just considered assume that the subjects' commitment to an opinion is held constant. If commitment is allowed to vary, a person committed to an opinion may be expected to have greater evaluative needs than someone who is not so committed.

Differences can be predicted within the groups according to the subjects' agreement or disagreement with the opinions of the others provided him. According to Festinger (3), opinion evaluation is impaired when the only comparison available is a very divergent one. Therefore, subjects in the peer comparison condition who disagree with the opinions of a large majority of the comparison group should have evaluative needs that are relatively unsatisfied as compared with those who agree with the opinions of the large majority of the comparison group. Evaluative needs should be less affected by agreement or disagreement with a large majority of the members of inferior or expert comparison groups than they are by agreement or disagreement with peers. The magnitude of such differential effects is again dependent upon the extent to which these groups are perceived to be different from the peer group. Information about the opinions of inferiors should be irrelevant for both those who agree and those who disagree if the inferiors are sufficiently low in status. Receipt of information regarding the opinions of experts provides adequate evaluative information for both those who agree and those who disagree if the experts are sufficiently high in status.

Further within-group differences may be predicted on the basis of individual differences. Schachter (12) found an interaction between birth order, anxiety, and affiliation. Specifically, he found that affiliation tendencies of early born subjects were more strongly effected by the manipulation of anxiety than were those of later born subjects. Schachter attributed these differences to the greater dependency needs of first born and only children. Relevant to the present study the question may be asked, is this effect specific to anxiety or does it apply to a variety of situations in which the need for social evaluation is a motive? A partial answer to this question can emerge from a test of the following hypothesis in the present study: First born and only subjects, who are presumably more dependent on other people for the evaluation of their opinions than are later born subjects, should manifest greater differences in affiliative tendencies as a result of varying needs for social evaluation.

METHOD

The experiment designed to test these hypotheses was conducted as a combined survey of student opinion and a recruiting session for participants in discussion groups. Subjects were first asked to give their opinions on an issue in writing. Opportunities for evaluation were manipulated by telling them the opinions of groups of other people. Affiliation tendencies were measured by asking the subjects to volunteer for discussion groups that were to talk about the issue on which they had just given their opinions.

Procedure

Subjects were 480 females from introductory psychology classes at the University of Minnesota who were randomly assigned to experimental groups within the time limits their schedules would permit.

Subjects were assembled in groups of 25–30. After they had filled out a short questionnaire giving data on birth order, the experimenter read to all groups a statement designed to arouse interest in the topic, impress upon subjects the importance of the opinion they were asked to give, and provide a rationale for the procedure to follow. The gist of the remarks was that the number of potential students and costs of college education would present serious problems by 1970. Data were given to emphasize the gravity of the situation. The specific aspect of the problem the subjects were asked to consider was, who shall pay these increased costs, students or governmental units? Their stake in the problem as future parents and taxpayers was emphasized, and they were told that their special information on and concern for the problem would add weight to their opinions.

After hearing the statement, each subject received an opinion survey form asking her to "Please indicate by a check mark on the following scale what per cent of the cost of their education you feel college students or their parents should pay." The scale ranged from 0% to 100% with intervals of 5%. Subjects were also asked to indicate how certain they were of their opinions on a seven-point scale with categories ranging from "absolutely certain" to "completely uncertain."

Manipulation of Evaluative Information

At this point subjects were provided with differential opportunities to evaluate the correctness of their opinions by giving them information about the opinions of others, in the form of a frequency distribution that was drawn on the blackboard and explained in detail to the subjects. The abscissa of the distribution was the same scale on which subjects had made a check of their opinions; the ordinate represented frequency of response in the particular comparison group. For all groups given information the curves were identical in shape, skewed with a highly peaked mode. As a control for possible interaction between the subject's position on the opinion scale and agreement or disagreement with others, half the groups in each condition were shown a distribution with the mode between 20% and 40%, while the other half were shown a distribution with the mode between 60% and 80%. Seventy-five percent of the responses of the comparison group were ostensibly in this 20% range, with 12% in the long tail and 13% in the short tail of the distribution. By means of this graph each subject could see that either an overwhelming proportion of the comparison group (75%) agreed with her, or that an even larger proportion (87% or 88%) disagreed with her, according to the position she had checked on the opinion survey form.

These manipulations produced the following conditions:

No Information. Subjects in this condition were not given any information about the opinions of other people. That is, no frequency distribution was shown.

Inferior. Subjects in this condition were shown a distribution purportedly summarizing the opinions of high school sophomores.

Peer. Subjects in this condition were shown a distribution purportedly summarizing the opinions of college sophomores at their university.

Expert. Subjects in this condition were shown a distribution purportedly summarizing the opinions of leading economists, university presidents, and state legislators concerned with financing higher education.

No Decision. In a fifth condition, the extent to which the subjects held an opinion on the issue was manipulated by omitting administration of the survey form. Subjects in this condition were not given any information about the opinions of other people. Their interest in joining a discussion group was solicited immediately after the interest arousing statement had been read.

TABLE 1.   *Means of Interest in Joining a Discussion Group and Percentage in Each Group Indicating Maximum Interest*

Condition	N	Mean Interest in Joining a Discussion Group[a]	Percentage Indicating Maximum Interest
No information	114	2.02	40%
Inferior	93	2.30	30%
Peer	107	2.47	19%
Expert	87	2.63	14%
$F = 6.98$; $df = 396,3$; $p < .001$			
No decision	79	2.53	12%

[a] Lower scores indicate greater interest in joining discussion groups.

Measuring Affiliation Tendencies

Affiliation tendencies were measured by asking subjects to volunteer to take part in discussion groups that were to talk about the problem of financing higher education. The experimenter stated that the discussion groups would be composed of six to eight "students like yourselves." The ostensible purpose of the discussion groups was to "generate some original ideas that can be put to use." An information form was distributed on which the subject was asked to give her name and address and to indicate the amount of interest she had in volunteering for a discussion group. The four choices available were:

1. I would like very much to take part in a discussion group.
2. I wouldn't mind taking part in a discussion group.
3. I could take part in a discussion group if necessary.
4. I have no interest in taking part in a discussion group.

This instrument provided the measure of the dependent variable.

Independent Measure of Need for Social Evaluation

Subjects were asked their reasons for volunteering to join discussion groups as a check on the need for social evaluation. An open-ended questionnaire was distributed with the explanation that the Student Opinion Research Center, sponsors of the study, conducted many such discussion groups and was interested in the problem of why people do and do not take part in such groups in order that more effective recruitment techniques might be employed. Since this questionnaire was not introduced until the experiment had been in progress for some time, data are available for only a portion of the subjects.

At the conclusion of the experiment subjects were asked not to discuss the issue with other psychology students since the experimenter wanted to have a true expression of student opinion, uncontaminated by information about how others felt. A questionnaire labeled "Previous Interest" revealed that subjects in later groups had had no discussions with those in previous groups, and that they did not suspect the true nature of the experiment.

RESULTS

DIFFERENCES IN AFFILIATION TENDENCIES BETWEEN CONDITIONS

The major hypothesis of a positive relation between need for opinion evaluation and affiliation tendencies is strongly supported by the data reported in Table 1. Means indicating the strength of affiliation tendencies are in the predicted order of magnitude for the four conditions and the variance of the condition means around the grand mean is highly significant. The exact probability of the four means being ranked in the predicted order is .042 since there are 24 possible ways in which they could have been ordered by chance. Thus it can be concluded that providing subjects with differential opportunities to evaluate their opinions strongly affected affiliative tendencies.

A comparison of the No information and No decision condition affiliation means reveals that holding an opinion also affects affiliative tendencies. Subjects who were asked to form and record their opinions exhibited significant-

TABLE 2.   *Mean Affiliation Scores for Conformers and Deviates*

Condition	Conformers	N	Deviates	N
Inferior	2.19	27	2.35	66
Peer	2.53	34	2.44	73
Expert	2.70	23	2.61	64

ly stronger affiliative tendencies than those who were not asked to do so.

EFFECTS OF AGREEING OR DISAGREEING WITH OTHERS

According to the point they had checked in recording their opinions, subjects were divided into two groups for the purpose of an analysis of differences within conditions. If the check mark indicating the subject's opinion lay within the 20-point modal range of the comparison distribution that she had been shown, the subject was classified as a "conformer"; if it lay outside this range, she was classified a "deviate."

Results presented in Table 2 show no significant differences between the affiliation tendencies in any of the three conditions in which information was provided. However, a straight "conformer-deviate" division assumes that the subjects who were deviates at the time their opinions were measured were also deviates at the time affiliation tendencies were measured. Festinger's (3) theory of social comparison processes holds, and numerous experimental studies (1, 5, 8, 9) have found that one manifestation of pressures toward uniformity is a change of opinion toward the group norm by deviates. It may therefore be presumed that in the present study, many subjects who were deviates according to their opinion statements may no longer have been deviates at the time their affiliation tendencies were measured, having changed their opinions

to conform to the norm of the comparison group. Since it was not feasible to include a direct measure of opinion change in the study, the measure of certainty of opinion was employed to separate those who presumedly changed their opinions from those who did not. In previous studies in which opinion change has been measured, Hochbaum (9) and Ehrlich (2) found that subjects who were uncertain of their opinions changed to conform to a normative opinion significantly more than did those who were certain. Therefore, in the present study, subjects were dichotomized near the median according to their responses to the scale measuring certainty of opinion. Subjects who indicated that they were "absolutely," "very," or "quite" certain were called *certain;* while subjects checking "fairly" and "not at all" certain and "very" and "completely" uncertain were designated *uncertain* for purposes of analysis.

Comparisons of the affiliation means reported in Table 3 give strong support to the hypothesis that deviates in the Peer condition who were certain of their opinions have unsatisfied evaluative needs. The affiliation tendencies of subjects in this group were nearly equal to the affiliation tendencies of subjects in the No information group. Peer deviates who were certain of their opinions manifested stronger affiliative tendencies than did Peer conformers ($p < .10$) or Peer deviates who were uncertain of their opinions ($p < .01$). Also, as predicted, there were no differences within either the Inferior or Expert conditions between de-

TABLE 3.   *Mean Affiliation Scores for Certain and Uncertain Deviates*

Condition	Deviates Who Were Certain of Their Opinions	N	Deviates Who Were Uncertain of Their Opinions	N
Inferior	2.24	34	2.47	32
Peer	2.09	32	2.71	41
Expert	2.54	35	2.69	29

TABLE 4. *Social Evaluation Reasons Versus Other Reasons for Wanting to Join Discussion Groups*[a]

Group	Social Evaluation Seeking Reasons	Other Reasons	Total
High need	20	39	59
Low need	3	21	24
Total	23	60	83

$$X^2 = 3.89, df = 1, p < .05$$

[a] Two coders agreed on the assignment of reasons to categories in 100% of the cases.

viates who were certain of their opinions and deviates who were uncertain of their opinions and conformers.

ANALYSIS OF SUBJECTS' REASONS FOR JOINING GROUPS

Data presented in Table 4 provide a direct measure of the inferred construct "need for social evaluation." To simplify the analysis for "reasons" and birth order, subjects were divided into two groups—one group predicted to have *high needs* for opinion evaluation and the other to have *low needs,* according to the theory of social comparison processes. Needs for evaluation were expected to remain high for subjects in the No information and Inferior conditions and for deviates in the Peer condition who were certain of their opinions; they should be low for subjects in the Expert condition, for deviates who were uncertain of their opinions and conformers in the Peer condition. Affiliation means for the High need and Low need groups, respectively, were 2.14 and 2.63 ($p < .001$). The Ns in Table 4 are quite small compared to these in previous tables, since these data were gathered on only a portion of the subjects in each condition and very few subjects expressed interest in joining discussion groups in the Low need group. Reasons were given in response to the open-ended request: "Please indicate why you are or are not interested in joining a discussion group to talk about this issue." Each subject was free to give as many reasons as she desired, but the mean number of reasons given by the High need and Low need groups and the proportional frequencies of subjects stating a specific number of reasons were identical. A reason was coded as expressing a need for social evaluation only if the subject mentioned wanting to hear the views of other people or wanting to compare her views with those of others. Other categories of reasons for wanting to join discussion groups were: social or "fun" aspects of groups, interesting nature of discussion groups, information seeking (no mention of getting ideas from other participants), egocentric—wanting to make certain their opinion was heard, wanting to help own financial position, wanting to help younger sibs or their own children, performing a duty for society.

The data support the hypothesis that needs for social evaluation account for differences in affiliation tendencies between the two groups. Among subjects who desired to join discussion groups, those in the High need group gave reasons indicating needs for social evaluation significantly more often than did those in the Low need group ($p < .05$). In other words, the greater affiliative tendencies of subjects in the High need group may be directly attributed to greater needs for social evaluation.

The classification in terms of High need and Low need divides subjects from the Peer condition on theoretical grounds. While this internal analysis was necessary in order to provide an N of sufficient magnitude to permit a reliable measure of the "reasons" index, similar differences with respect to "reasons" apply as well for the treatment groups that could be classified in their entirety as High or Low in need. Thus subjects from the No information and Inferior conditions who desired to join groups gave reasons indicating needs for social evaluation more frequently than did their affiliatively inclined counterparts from the Expert condition ($.10 > p > .05$).

INDIVIDUAL DIFFERENCES: THE EFFECTS OF BIRTH ORDER

Data presented in Table 5 indicate that, in support of the hypothesis concerned with birth

TABLE 5. *Affiliation Means by Birth Order and Condition*

Birth Order Condition	Only and First	N	Later	N	Row Means
High need	2.03	118	2.26	116	2.14
Low need	2.81	74	2.50	82	2.65
Column means	2.33		2.36		

order, manipulation of evaluative needs produced a large and significant difference in affiliation tendencies for early borns ($p < .001$) and a smaller, nonsignificant difference for later borns. The interaction between birth order and needs is significant ($p < .01$). The results of the present experiment complement Schachter's (**12**) findings that early and later borns do not differ in overall affiliative tendencies; they only differ when dependency-related needs are aroused.

Again, it should be noted that while the analysis according to birth order includes subjects from the Peer condition, differences of similar magnitude are obtained when only the conditions that could be assigned entirely to High or Low need are considered (Table 6). Although the interaction of birth order with need is less reliable ($.05 > p > .01$) in Table 6 than it is in Table 5, the mean affiliation scores are virtually identical in the two tables.

An examination of the reasons for joining discussion groups provides evidence that the greater affiliative tendencies of early borns in the High need conditions were motivated by needs for social evaluation. Among subjects from whom reasons were solicited, there were 17 early borns and 14 later borns who showed maximum interest in joining groups in the High need conditions. Of these subjects, 9 early borns and 3 later borns gave reasons indicating need for social evaluation. The exact probability of a distribution this extreme or more so occurring by chance, given fixed marginals, is .075.

DISCUSSION

The results of the present experiment support the hypothesis that the drive for self-evaluation with respect to opinions can be an important determinant of affiliation.

As is generally the case in experimental social psychology, the manipulations in the present study were relatively weak. One could therefore not expect to arouse affiliative tendencies in all subjects in the High need group. The contention is plausible, however, that most people at some time experience evaluative needs, which can be satisfied only by social comparison, of sufficient strength to motivate them to seek out others. The relationship established would thus seem to have wide generality.

A theoretically significant contribution of the present study is the demonstration that the affiliative consequences of evaluative needs, first employed by Schachter (**12**) to account for affiliative responses under conditions of emotional arousal, are apparently applicable in a variety of seemingly disparate contexts. That is, whenever evaluative needs capable of being satisfied by social comparison are aroused, the arousal of affiliative tendencies is a potential

TABLE 6. *Affiliation Means by Birth Order and Condition*

Birth Order Condition	Only and First	N	Later	N	Row Means
No information and inferiors	2.00	99	2.28	108	2.14
Experts	2.83	35	2.50	52	2.63
Column means	2.22		2.35		

consequence. The arousal of evaluative needs concerning abilities, for example, should also produce affiliative tendencies in the absence of adequate nonsocial means of evaluation.

NO DECISION VERSUS NO INFORMATION

The large difference in affiliation tendencies between subjects in the No information and No decision conditions raises the question, what are the consequences of stating an opinion? One probable consequence is an increase in the salience of the issue; thus subjects in the No information condition may have a greater desire to discuss an issue which is more important or interesting to them. Another possible consequence is the generation of cognitive dissonance (4) which may arise when an individual commits himself to a position on a complicated, multisided issue. In the present experiment, dissonance may have been created in the following ways. First, the person may be aware that he could have taken a position other than the one he has assumed; second, he may feel that other people will not agree with his stand. There is evidence (6) that dissonance arising from these sources can produce affiliative behavior.

A CONTRADICTION (?)

The hypothesis that unchanging (certain) deviates in the Peer condition would want to join a discussion group composed of other people from their psychology classes contains a possible logical contradiction if it is presumed that the subjects were perceptive and logical. The distribution of opinions that these subjects, Peer deviates, had seen told them that nearly 90% of the potential discussants would disagree with them. Festinger (3) states that for social comparison to produce stable evaluation of opinions, the opinions of others must be close to one's own. Clearly there would be few if any people in a discussion group composed of six to eight people with opinions close to those of the deviate, given the distribution shown. Why, then, did the subject's behavior conform to the predictions of this apparently contradictory hypothesis?

Several explanations are possible. One is

that the subjects may simply not have made the logical inference necessary for them to have predicted the probable composition of the discussion groups. At the other extreme of the subjects' perceptive ability, it would probably be implausible to assume that subjects would hypothesize that groups would be composed largely of deviates; that subjects would realize that conformers would not want to join discussion groups because their opinions had already been evaluated.

A theoretically more interesting and experimentally testable hypothesis is that unchanging deviates considered but disregarded the probable composition of the discussion groups. They may have had such strong needs for more evaluative information that a potential comparison even with quite divergent views was sufficiently attractive to arouse affiliative tendencies. According to this reasoning, it would be expected that, given a choice, unchanging deviates would rather join a discussion group composed of people whose opinions were similar to their own.

BIRTH ORDER

As mentioned in the introduction, the hypothesis concerning the effects of ordinal position stemmed from Schachter's (12) experiments on anxiety and affiliation. He invoked dependency as a construct to account for the greater affiliative tendencies of early borns under conditions of high anxiety.

With reference to birth order and dependency, the present study fills in the missing cell in a 2 × 2 table summarizing the results of four experiments in which emotions and opinions were in need of evaluation, and changes as a result of social comparison and affiliative tendencies were measured. Compared with later borns: early born subjects showed greater changes in (a) emotional reactions (13) and (b) opinions (2) as a result of social comparison; early borns also manifested greater affiliative tendencies when in need of (a) emotional comparison (3) and (b) opinion comparison (present study). The complementary results of these four studies strongly suggest that the static variable of birth order is related to the more dynamic concept of dependency.

SUMMARY

The hypothesis that self-evaluative needs concerning opinions are an important determinant of group formation was tested experimentally.

Subjects were presented with a problem and asked to state their opinions. Adequacy of opinion evaluation was varied at four levels along a continuum by telling subjects in different conditions the opinions of various groups of other people. Affiliation tendencies were measured by assessing the level of interest the subjects had in joining discussion groups to talk about the opinion in need of evaluation.

Results gave strong support to the hypothesis. Affiliation tendencies varied according to strength of evaluative needs.

Consonant with Schachter's findings regarding emotional evaluation and affiliation, the affiliative responses of first born and only subjects were more strongly affected by varying evaluative needs than were those of the later borns.

References

1. Back, K. Influence through social communication. *Journal of Abnormal and Social Psychology*, 1951, **46**, 9–23.
2. Ehrlich, D. Determinants of verbal commonality and influencibility. Unpublished doctoral dissertation, Univ. of Minnesota, 1958.
3. Festinger, L. A theory of social comparison processes. *Human Relations,* 1954, **7**, 117–140.
4. Festinger, L. *A theory of cognitive dissonance.* Evanston, Ill.: Row, Peterson, 1957.
5. Festinger, L., *et al.* The influence process in the presence of extreme deviates. *Human Relations,* 1952, **5**, 327–346.
6. Festinger, L., Riecken, H., & Schachter, S. *When prophecy fails.* Minneapolis: Univ. of Minnesota Press, 1956.
7. Festinger, L., & Thibaut, J. Interpersonal communication in small groups. *Journal of Abnormal and Social Psychology*, 1951, **46**, 92–99.
8. Gerard, H. The effect of different dimensions of disagreement on the communication process in small groups. *Human Relations*, 1953, **6**, 249–272.
9. Hochbaum, G. The relation between group members' self-confidence and their reactions to group pressures to uniformity. *American Sociological Review*, 1954, **6**, 678–687.
10. Radloff, R. Opinion and affiliation. Unpublished doctoral dissertation, Univ. of Minnesota, 1959.
11. Schachter, S. Deviation, rejection, and communication. *Journal of Abnormal and Social Psychology*, 1951, **46**, 190–207.
12. Schachter, S. *The psychology of affiliation.* Stanford: Stanford Univ. Press, 1959.
13. Wrightsman, L. S. The effects of small-group membership on level of concern. Unpublished doctoral dissertation, Univ. of Minnesota, 1959.

9

Effect of Severity of Initiation on Liking for a Group

ELLIOT ARONSON AND JUDSON MILLS

It is a frequent observation that persons who go through a great deal of trouble or pain to attain something tend to value it more highly than persons who attain the same thing with a minimum of effort. For example, one would expect persons who travel a great distance to see a motion picture to be more impressed with it than those who see the same picture at a neighborhood theater. By the same token, individuals who go through a severe initiation to gain admission to a club or organization should tend to think more highly of that organization than those who do not go through the severe initiation to gain admission.

Two questions are relevant here: (*a*) Is this "common observation" valid, that is, does it hold true when tested under controlled conditions? (*b*) If the observation is valid, how can it be accounted for? The relationship might be simply a result of differences in initial motivation. To take the case of initiations, persons who initially have a strong desire to join a particular club should be more willing to undergo unpleasantness to gain admission to it than persons who are low in initial interest. Therefore, a club that requires a severe initiation for admission should be joined only by those people with a strong desire to become members. On the other hand, a club that does not require a severe initiation should be joined by some individuals who like it very much and by others who are relatively uninterested. Because of this self-selection, one would expect persons who are members of clubs with severe initiations to think more highly of their club, on the average, than members of clubs without severe initiations.

But is there something in the initiation itself that might account for this relationship? Is severity of initiation positively related to group preference when motivation for

From *The Journal of Abnormal and Social Psychology*, 1959, **59**, 177–181. Reprinted by permission of the authors and the American Psychological Association. This research was supported by a grant from the National Science Foundation.

admission is held constant? Such a relationship is strongly implied by Festinger's (1) theory of cognitive dissonance. The theory of cognitive dissonance predicts this relationship in the following manner. No matter how attractive a group is to a person it is rarely completely positive, i.e., usually there are some aspects of the group that the individual does not like. If he has undergone an unpleasant initiation to gain admission to the group, his cognition that he has gone through an unpleasant experience for the sake of membership is dissonant with his cognition that there are things about the group that he does not like. He can reduce this dissonance in two ways. He can convince himself that the initiation was not very unpleasant, or he can exaggerate the positive characteristics of the group and minimize its negative aspects. With increasing severity of initiation it becomes more and more difficult to believe that the initiation was not very bad. Thus, a person who has gone through a painful initiation to become a member of a group should tend to reduce his dissonance by over estimating the attractiveness of the group. The specific hypothesis tested in the present study is that individuals who undergo an unpleasant initiation to become members of a group increase their liking for the group; that is, they find the group more attractive than do persons who become members without going through a severe initiation.

METHOD

In designing the experiment it was necessary to have people join groups that were similar in every respect except for the severity of the initiation required for admission—and then to measure each individual's evaluation of the group. It was also necessary to randomize the initial motivation of subjects to gain admission to the various groups in order to eliminate systematic effects of differences in motivation. These requirements were met in the following manner: Volunteers were obtained to participate in group discussions. They were assigned randomly to one of three experimental conditions: A *Severe* initiation condition, a *Mild* initiation condition, and a *Control* condition. In the Severe condition, subjects were required to read some embarrassing material before joining the group; in the Mild condition the

material they read in order to join the group was not very embarrassing; in the Control condition, subjects were not required to read any material before becoming group members. Each participant listened to the same tape recording, which was ostensibly an ongoing discussion by the members of the group that he had just joined. Subjects then evaluated the discussion.

The subjects were 63 college women. Thirty-three of them volunteered to participate in a series of group discussions on the psychology of sex. The remaining 30, tested at a somewhat later date, were "captive volunteers" from a psychology course who elected to participate in the group discussions on the psychology of sex in preference to several other experiments. Since the results obtained from these two samples were very similar, they were combined in the analysis presented here.

Each participant was individually scheduled to "meet with a group." When she arrived at the experimental room, she was told by the experimenter that he was conducting several group discussions on the psychology of sex. The experimenter informed her that she was joining a group that had been meeting for several weeks and that she was taking the place of a girl who had to leave the group because of scheduling difficulties. He stated that the discussion had just begun and that she would join the other members of the group after he had explained the nature of the experiment to her. The purpose of the foregoing instructions was to confront the subject with an ongoing group and thus make plausible the recorded discussion to which she was to be exposed.

The experimenter then "explained" the purpose of the experiment. He said that he was interested in investigating the "dynamics of the group discussion process." Sex was chosen as the topic for the groups to discuss in order to provide interesting subject matter so that volunteers for the discussion groups could be obtained without much difficulty. He continued as follows:

But the fact that the discussions are concerned with sex has one major drawback. Although most people are interested in sex, they tend to be a little shy when it comes to discussing it. This is very bad from the point of view of the experiment; if one or two people in a group do not participate as much as they usually do in group discussions because they are embarrassed about sex, the picture we get of the group discussion process is distorted. Therefore, it is extremely important to arrange things so that the members of the discussion group can talk as freely and frankly as possible. We found that the major inhibiting factor in the discussions was the presence of the other people in the room. Somehow, it's easier to talk about embarrassing things if other people aren't staring at you. To get around this, we hit upon an idea which has proved very successful. Each member of the group is placed in a separate room, and the participants communicate through an intercom system using headphones and a microphone. In this way, we've helped people relax, and have succeeded in bringing about an increase in individual participation.

The foregoing explanation set the stage for the tape recording, which could now be presented to the participant as a live discussion conducted by three people in separate rooms.

The experimenter then mentioned that, in spite of this precaution, occasionally some persons were still too embarrassed to engage in the discussions and had to be asked to withdraw from the discussion group. The subject was asked if she thought she could discuss sex freely. She invariably answered affirmatively. In the Control condition the subject was told, at this point, that she would be a member of the group.

In the other two conditions, he went on to say that it was difficult for him to ask people to leave the group once they had become members. Therefore, he had recently decided to screen new people before admitting them to the discussion groups. The screening device was described as an "embarrassment test" which consists of reading aloud some sexually oriented material in his presence. The subject was told that the experimenter would make a clinical judgment of her degree of embarrassment, based upon hesitation, blushing, etc., and would determine whether or not she would be capable of participating in the discussion group. He stressed that she was not obligated to take this test, but that she could not become a member unless she did. Only one woman declined to take the test. She was excluded from the experiment. It was also emphasized, at this point, that the "embarrassment test" was a recent innovation and that

the other members had joined the group before it was required for admission. These instructions were included in order to counteract any tendency to identify more strongly with the group as a result of feelings of having shared a common unpleasant experience. Such a process could conceivably bring about a greater preference for the discussion group on the part of those persons in the Severe condition, introducing ambiguity in the interpretation of the results.

In the Severe condition, the "embarrassment test" consisted of having the subjects read aloud, from 3×5 cards, 12 obscene words. Subjects also read aloud two vivid descriptions of sexual activity from contemporary novels. In the Mild condition, they read about five words that were related to sex but not obscene. In both the Severe and the Mild conditions, after each person finished reading the material, she was told that she had performed satisfactorily and was, therefore, a member of the group and could join the meeting that was now in progress.

It was of the utmost importance to prevent the new member from attempting to participate in the discussion, for if she did, she would soon find that no one was responding to her statements and she would probably infer that the discussion was recorded. To insure their silence, all participants were told that, in preparation for each meeting, the group reads an assignment which serves as the focal point of the discussion; for this meeting, the group read parts of the book, *Sexual Behavior in Animals*. After the subject had indicated that she had never read this book, the experimenter told her that she would be at a disadvantage and would, consequently, not be able to participate as fully in this discussion as she would had she done the reading. He continued, "Because the presence of a participant who isn't contributing optimally would result in an inaccurate picture of the dynamics of the group discussion process, it would be best if you wouldn't participate at all today, so that we may get an undistorted picture of the dynamics of the other three members of this group. Meanwhile, you can simply listen to the discussion, and get an idea of how the group operates. For the next meeting, you can do the reading and join in the discussion." The subjects were invariably more than willing to comply with this suggestion. The above instructions not only prevented them from attempting to participate in the discussion but also served to orient her toward the actual content of discussion.

Under the guise of connecting the subject's headphones and microphone, the experimenter went into the next room and turned on the tape recorder. He then returned to the experimental room, put on the headphones, picked up the microphone, and pretended to break into the discussion which supposedly was in progress. After holding a brief conversation with the "members of the group," he introduced the new member to them. Then he handed the headphones to her. The tape was timed so that at the precise moment that she donned her headphones, the "group members" introduced themselves and then continued their discussion.

The use of a tape recording presented all participants with an identical group experience. The recording was a discussion by three female undergraduates. It was deliberately designed to be as dull and banal as possible in order to maximize the dissonance of the subjects in the Severe condition. The participants spoke dryly and haltingly on secondary sex behavior in the lower animals, "inadvertently" contradicted themselves and one another, mumbled several *non sequiturs,* started sentences that they never finished, hemmed, hawed, and in general conducted one of the most worthless and uninteresting discussions imaginable.

At the conclusion of the recording, the experimenter returned and explained that after each meeting every member of the group fills out a questionnaire expressing her reactions to the discussion. The questionnaire asked the new member to rate the discussion and the group members on 14 different evaluative scales, e.g., dull-interesting, intelligent-unintelligent, by circling a number from 0 to 15. After completing the questionnaire, she made three additional ratings, orally, in response to questions from the experimenter. Nine of the scales concerned the subject's reactions to the discussion, while the other eight concerned her reactions to the participants.

At the close of the experiment, he engaged each subject in conversation to determine whether or not she was suspicious of the procedure. Only one entertained definite suspicions; her results were discarded.

Finally, the true nature of the experiment was explained in detail. None of the partici-
pants expressed any resentment or annoyance at having been misled. In fact, the majority were intrigued by the experiment and several returned at the end of the academic quarter to ascertain the results.

RESULTS AND DISCUSSION

The sum of the ratings for the 17 different scales provides an index of each member's liking for the discussion group. The means and SDs for the three experimental conditions for this measure are presented in Table 1. Means and SDs are also presented in Table 1 separately for the eight scales which tapped the subjects' attitudes toward the discussion and the seven scales which tapped their attitudes toward the participants. The significance of the differences between the means for the different conditions were determined by *t* tests. The *t* values and significance levels are presented in Table 2.

Examination of Table 1 shows that persons in the Severe condition rated both the discussion and the participants higher than did those in the Control and Mild conditions. The overall difference between the ratings by subjects in the Severe condition and those in the Control condition reaches the .01 level of significance. The over-all difference between the ratings by subjects in the Severe initiation condition and those in the Mild initiation condition reaches the .05 level.

These differences cannot be explained by differences in initial motivation to become members of the group, since women (with varying degrees of motivation) were randomly assigned to the three experimental conditions. The differences in liking for the group must be considered a consequence of the unpleasant experience. The results clearly substantiate the hypothesis: persons who undergo a severe initiation to attain membership in a group increase their liking for the group. This hypothesis follows directly from Festinger's theory of cognitive dissonance. According to the theory, subjects in the Severe initiation condition held the cognition that they had undergone a painful experience to become members of the discussion group. Then they listened to a dull, banal discussion. Negative cognitions about the discussion which they formed from listening to it were dissonant with the cognition that they had undergone a painful experi-

TABLE 1.   *Means of the Sum of Ratings for the Different Experimental Conditions*

Rating Scales	Experimental Conditions		
	Control (N = 21)	Mild (N = 21)	Severe (N = 21)
Discussion (9)			
M	80.2	81.8	97.6
SD	13.2	21.0	16.6
Participants (8)			
M	89.9	89.3	97.7
SD	10.9	14.1	13.2
Total (17)			
M	170.1	171.1	195.3
SD	21.6	34.0	31.9

ence to gain membership in this group. The presence of dissonance leads to pressures to reduce it. Persons in this condition could reduce their dissonance either by denying the severity of the initiation or by distorting their cognitions concerning the group discussion in a positive direction. The initiation of the subjects in the Severe condition was apparently too painful for them to deny—hence, they reduced their dissonance by overestimating the attractiveness of the group.

There was no appreciable difference between the ratings made by subjects in the Control condition and those made by subjects in the Mild condition. It would seem that the Mild condition was so devoid of unpleasantness as to constitute little investment in the group. Hence, little dissonance was created. If any dissonance did occur in this situation it would be more realistic for the subject to reduce it by minimizing the pain of the initiation than by distorting her cognitions concerning the discussion. Thus, it is not an initiation per se that leads to increase in liking for a group. The initiation must be severe enough to con-

stitute a genuine investment and to render it difficult to reduce dissonance by playing down the extent of the pain involved.

An examination of Table 1 shows that the rating scales concerning the discussion show greater differences between the conditions than the scales dealing with the evaluations of the participants in the discussion. There are at least two possible explanations for this result: (a) It may be easier for people to express negative criticism about an impersonal discussion than about the people involved. Thus, persons in the Control and Mild conditions may have inflated their ratings of the participants to avoid making negative statements about fellow college students. (b) It is possible that those in the Severe condition had less need to distort their perception of the participants than of the discussion itself. The dissonance of the subjects in the Severe condition resulted from the actual discussion: they experienced dissonance between going through an unpleasant experience and taking part in worthless uninteresting discussions. The most direct way for them to reduce this dissonance

TABLE 2.   *Significance Levels of the Differences Between Experimental Conditions*

Rating Scales	Differences Between Conditions		
	Control-Severe	Mild-Severe	Control-Mild
Discussion (9)	$t = 3.66$ $P < .001$[a]	$t = 2.62$ $P < .02$	$t = .29$ N.S.
Participants (8)	$t = 2.03$ $P < .05$	$t = 1.97$ $P < .10$	$t = .15$ N.S.
Total (17)	$t = 2.92$ $P < .01$	$t = 2.33$ $P < .05$	$t = .49$ N.S.

[a] The P values given are based on both tails of the t distribution.

would be to change their perceptions of the discussion in a positive direction. The participants in the discussion were peripheral to the cause of dissonance. If persons in the Severe condition had less need to distort their perception of the participants than their perception of the discussion, their evaluations of the participants could be expected to be closer to the evaluations of the participants made by subjects in the Control and Mild conditions.

SUMMARY AND CONCLUSION

An experiment was conducted to test the hypothesis that persons who undergo an unpleasant initiation to become members of a group increase their liking for the group; that is, they find the group more attractive than do persons who become members without going through a severe initiation. This hypothesis was derived from Festinger's theory of cognitive dissonance.

College women who volunteered to participate in discussion groups were randomly assigned to one of three experimental conditions: A *Severe* initiation condition, a *Mild* initiation condition, and a *Control* condition. In the Severe condition, subjects were required to read some embarrassing material before joining the group; in the Mild condition the material they read in order to join the group was not very embarrassing; in the Control condition, subjects were not required to read any material before becoming group members. Each subject listened to a recording that appeared to be an ongoing discussion being conducted by the group which she had just joined. Afterwards, subjects filled out a questionnaire evaluating the discussion and the participants. The results clearly verified the hypothesis. The subjects who underwent a severe initiation perceived the group as being significantly more attractive than did those who underwent a mild initiation or no initiation. There was no appreciable difference between ratings by subjects who underwent a Mild initiation and those by subjects who underwent no initiation.

Reference

1. Festinger, L. A *theory of cognitive dissonance.* Evanston, Ill.: Row, Peterson, 1957.

10

Arousal and Reduction of Dissonance in Social Contexts

LEON FESTINGER AND ELLIOT ARONSON

The theory of dissonance is a theory concerning psychological processes which go on, somehow, inside of the individual organism. The core notions of the theory are extremely simple. These notions are that the simultaneous existence of cognitions which in one way or another do not fit together (dissonance) leads to effort on the part of the person to somehow make them fit better (dissonance reduction).

Of course, in order to make these notions amenable to empirical test and to give them predictive power, one must specify the conditions under which dissonance exists, the ways in which dissonance may be reduced, and the observable manifestations of attempts at dissonance reduction.

We cannot, in this chapter, take the space to spell these things out. A detailed and more formal account of the theory and related research may be found elsewhere (9). What we will concentrate on here is the explication of how this theory concerning individual psychological process has relevance for, and can help us make predictions about, social behavior and group behavior. The chapter will consist of three parts: (a) some introductory material to give the reader some impression of the scope of the theory and the kinds of behavior involved in dissonance reduction, and (b) consideration of the group as a source of dissonance arousal and (c) as an aid in the reduction of dissonance.

Throughout the chapter we will attempt to discuss the theory in connection with empirical data concentrating, for the most part, on recent material, that is, data which have been collected since the publication of the theory (9).

SOME DERIVATIONS FROM DISSONANCE THEORY

Although the theory is, in essence, a very simple one, it can be used to predict a wide range of human behavior. A few of the ramifications of the theory will be discussed below. It should be stressed that in the majority of the experiments to be discussed only one avenue of dissonance reduction has been examined. This is not meant to imply,

This chapter was prepared especially for this volume.

however, that only one means of dissonance reduction is possible in a particular situation. On the contrary, in uncontrolled situations many avenues for dissonance reduction are usually available.

Suppose, for example, that a person believes that the Democratic presidential candidate is the most qualified candidate for the position. For some reason, however, he votes for the Republican candidate. His cognition that the Democratic candidate is more qualified is dissonant with his cognition that he voted for the Republican candidate. This person might attempt to reduce dissonance by convincing himself that the Republican candidate is better than he had at first believed or that the Democratic candidate is less good. Such a change in his opinions would bring them more into line with his knowledge that he had voted for the Republican candidate.

His specific behaviors might involve: (*a*) subscribing to a Republican newspaper (where he'd be sure to read complimentary statements about the Republican candidate and derogatory statements about the Democratic candidate); (*b*) trying to associate with Republicans and trying to avoid Democrats; (*c*) trying to find subtle wisdom in the speeches of the Republican candidate which he hadn't noticed before, and the like. We have selected experiments for discussion below in an attempt to illustrate not only the variety of situations which produce dissonance but also the variety of ways in which dissonance reduction proceeds.

DISSONANCE AS A CONSEQUENCE OF DECISIONS

If an individual chooses one from among several possible courses of action, he is almost certain to experience dissonance because the chosen alternative is seldom entirely positive and the unchosen alternatives are seldom entirely negative. His cognitions concerning any negative aspects of the chosen alternative are dissonant with his cognition that he chose it. Similarly, his cognitions concerning any positive aspects of the unchosen alternatives are dissonant with his cognition that he rejected these alternatives. Consequently, the greater the attractiveness of the rejected alternative relative to the chosen alternative, the greater will be the dissonance.

The theory of dissonance predicts that, following a decision, a person will attempt to convince himself that the chosen alternative is even more attractive (relative to the unchosen one) than he had previously thought.

Brehm (4) demonstrated that, following a decision between two alternatives, there was a general tendency for people to rate the chosen alternative as being slightly more attractive than they had previously rated it, and to rate the rejected alternative as being slightly less attractive than they had previously rated it. Furthermore, Brehm found that the more nearly equal the initial attractiveness of the alternatives had been, the stronger was the effect obtained. In other words, dissonance reduction did ensue following a decision and the amount of dissonance reduction was related to the magnitude of dissonance created by the decision.

A subsequent experiment by Brehm and Cohen (6) tested two more implications concerning post-decision dissonance:

1. The greater the number of alternatives among which a person must choose, the greater would be the dissonance following the choice. The more alternatives which were rejected, the more knowledge there would be concerning favorable characteristics of these rejected alternatives. These cognitions would all be dissonant with the cognition concerning the alternative which the person actually chose.

2. The greater the qualitative dissimilarity between the alternatives among which the person must choose the greater would be the post-decision dissonance (assuming that the relative attractiveness of the alternatives is held constant). This follows from the fact that similar alternatives have many characteristics in common. Thus, some of the favorable aspects of the rejected alternatives are also favorable aspects of the chosen alternative. Cognitions concerning these aspects of similarity would not, hence, contribute to dissonance following the choice.

Brehm and Cohen asked children to rate how much they liked various toys. The experimenters explained that they were employed by toy manufacturers to find out what kind of toys people like. One week later they returned and offered the children a choice of one of the toys as a gift for having participated in the research. The children were then asked once more to rate how much they liked each of the toys. In this experiment, two variables were manipulated: (*a*) The number of alternatives. Some children were allowed to choose from among four toys; some children were given a choice between two toys. (*b*) The qualitative similarity of the alternatives. Some children had to choose from among toys which were qualitatively similar; for example, swimming fins *vs.* swimming masks. Other children had to choose from among toys which were qualitatively dissimilar; for example, swimming fins *vs.* archery sets.

The results supported both hypotheses. Regardless of the qualitative similarity of the toys, the greater the number of alternatives, the more the liking for the chosen toy increased and the more the liking for the unchosen toy decreased. Likewise, regardless of the number of alternatives, the greater the qualitative dissimilarity among the alternatives, the greater was the observed change in the attractiveness of the toys in the direction of dissonance reduction.

DISSONANCE ARISING FROM TEMPTATION

If an individual commits an act which he regards as immoral in order to obtain a reward, his cognition that the act is immoral is dissonant with his cognition that he committed it. One way in which he could reduce this dissonance would be by changing his attitudes concerning the morality of the act, that is, by convincing himself that the act is not very immoral. Thus, dissonance theory predicts that after a person has committed an immoral act, his attitudes concerning that act will be more lenient than they previously were.

On the other hand, if a person resists temptation and does not commit the act, his cognitions about the rewards he gave up are dissonant with his cognition concerning his behavior. Once again, he could reduce dissonance by changing his attitudes concerning the morality of the act. In this instance, the theory predicts that, after a person has resisted the temptation to commit an immoral act, his attitudes concerning the morality of the act will be more severe than they previously were. This would reduce dissonance by helping to justify the fact that he forsook the reward. The magnitude of the dissonance experienced by a person who commits an immoral act will, of course, be greater if the rewards he obtained by committing the act are small. Conversely,

the magnitude of dissonance in the person who refrains from committing the immoral act will be greater if the reward he gave up by not engaging in the act is large.

These hypotheses were tested by Mills (15) in an experiment involving sixth-grade students. After measuring his subjects' attitudes toward cheating, the experimenter had them participate in a contest with prizes offered. In some classes a small prize was offered, in others a large prize. During the contest it was possible for the subjects to cheat. As may be expected, some of the students cheated while others did not.

One day later the subjects were again asked to indicate their attitudes toward cheating. The results confirmed the hypothesis. In general, those children who cheated became more lenient toward cheating, while those who did not cheat became more severe toward cheating. Again, the magnitude of this effect was a function of how much dissonance was introduced experimentally. Those children who cheated for a small prize changed more in feeling lenient about cheating than those who cheated for a large prize. Among those who did not cheat, the changes in the direction of greater severity toward cheating were larger for those who gave up a large prize by not cheating than for those who gave up only a small prize.

DISSONANCE RESULTING FROM EFFORT

If an individual is in a situation in which he continues to expend effort in order to reach some goal, yet does not reach it, he will experience dissonance. His cognition that he is expending effort would be dissonant with his cognition that he is unrewarded. One way in which he could reduce dissonance would be by finding something about the situation to which he could attach value. Thus, an unsuccessful prospector might reduce dissonance by marveling at the magnificent beauty of the surrounding terrain; an unsuccessful fisherman might do so by boasting of the beautiful tan he received while wading through the streams or by becoming enamored of the skill involved in casting.

Aronson (2) tested these implications of the theory of dissonance in the laboratory. His subjects were given a task to perform in order to obtain rewards. Each subject was rewarded on about one-third of the trials. For some sub-jects the task was almost effortless while for others it involved considerable expenditures of effort and energy. For all subjects, the stimuli terminating a trial were different on rewarded trials from what they were on unrewarded trials. Specifically, on each trial the subject obtained a container. On rewarded trials the containers were red and contained money. On unrewarded trials the containers were green and empty. The subjects were asked to rate the relative attractiveness of the two colors both before and after the experiment.

The prediction was that, in the *Effortful* condition, the unrewarded color would be-come relatively more attractive than in the *Easy* condition. According to the theory, in the *Effortful* condition, each time the subject pulled out an unrewarded container, his cogni-tion that the container was empty would be dissonant with his cognition that he exerted effort to obtain it. It was predicted that in order to reduce dissonance, the subject would attach value to the unrewarded color. In this way, he could justify the expenditure of effort by convincing himself that the sight of the color was worth working for even though it contained no money. In the *Easy* condition, since very little effort was expended, very little dissonance was created. Hence, one would ex-pect no tendency to attach positive value to the unrewarded color.

The results are in line with the theoretical expectations. The *Easy* condition, where little or no dissonance was introduced on unre-warded trials, provides a baseline from which shifts in color preference may be evaluated. It happens that in the *Easy* condition there is a marked shift of preference toward the *re-warded* color. In the *Effortful* condition, where dissonance was present on nonre-warded trials, the effects of dissonance reduc-tion counterbalance this other effect. A large and clear difference is obtained between the dissonance (effortful) condition and the no dis-sonance (easy) condition in the relative prefer-ence of the two colors.

DISSONANCE INTRODUCED BY A FAIT ACCOMPLI

Very often persons find themselves in a posi-tion where they must endure some unpleasant situation. The cognition a person has that the situation is or will be unpleasant is dissonant

with his cognition that he must endure it. One way in which he can reduce this dissonance is by convincing himself that the situation is not as unpleasant as it first appeared. Brehm (5) induced eighth-grade children to eat a disliked vegetable in school by offering them a small reward. While eating, the children in the *experimental* condition were told that their parents would be informed which vegetable they had eaten; this strongly implied that they would be expected to eat more of this vege-table at home. The children in the *control* condition were told nothing. All of the subjects were asked to rate their liking for the vegeta-ble both before and after the experiment. Those subjects who were led to anticipate that they would be eating more of the vegetable at home showed a significantly greater increase in their rated fondness for the vegetable than did the subjects in the *control* condition.

In the preceding several pages we have pre-sented an extremely brief statement concern-ing the theory of dissonance and a few scat-tered illustrations of experimental studies on the reduction of dissonance in a variety of con-texts. The theoretical statement is not in-tended as a complete, formal presentation nor are the studies discussed intended to be an adequate coverage of the relevant empirical data. The purpose was, rather, to present as briefly as possible some overall understanding of the theory of dissonance, the kinds of situa-tions which arouse dissonance, and the kinds of effects one may anticipate as a result of dissonance reduction.

It has been illustrated by our previous dis-cussion that an individual can experience and reduce dissonance strictly as a result of his own actions. Other people need not be in-volved in the process. But an individual's in-teractions with other people may, in itself, be a source of dissonance. Moreover, an individ-ual may utilize his interactions with other people as a means of reducing dissonance. In the following two sections we will discuss and introduce more empirical data concerning the arousal and reduction of dissonance in situa-tions which are primarily social. It should be emphasized, however, that the social context does not introduce anything qualitatively dif-ferent into the processes of arousal and reduc-tion of dissonance. Sometimes a social context introduces greater complexities; sometimes a social context makes it more difficult or even impossible for a person to avoid the introduction of dissonance into his cognitions; and sometimes a social context can make it spectacularly easy to reduce dissonance.

These latter aspects of dissonance arousal and reduction in social contexts are, of course, the ones that will be stressed in the following pages. The reader will, however, note the conceptual similarity between the experiments we have discussed in the preceding pages and the ones we will discuss in the remainder of this chapter.

GROUP INTERACTION AS A SOURCE OF DISSONANCE

DISSONANCE ARISING FROM FAULTY ANTICIPATION OF SOCIAL ENVIRONMENT

An individual does not usually have good control over his social environment. One way in which this manifests itself is in his partial inability to predict the nature of the groups to which he exposes himself. For example, a person might go out on a blind date, join a club, or accept an invitation to a cocktail party, only to find the people to be less pleasant than he had anticipated. If he had not expended any time or effort in exposing himself to the group, he would experience little or no dissonance. But if he had invested a great deal in order to interact with these people—for example, if he had driven fifty miles to pick up his date, or paid a huge admission fee to join the club, or neglected preparing for an exam to go to the cocktail party—he would experience dissonance. His cognitions concerning his investment of time and effort would be dissonant with his cognitions concerning the negative aspects of the group.

There are at least two ways that a person could reduce dissonance in such a situation: (*a*) He could undervalue the amount of his investment, that is, convince himself that the effort or expense was really negligible, or (*b*) he could overvalue the group by emphasizing its positive aspects and blinding himself to its negative aspects.

This kind of situation was simulated in a laboratory experiment by Aronson and Mills (Chap. 9). In this experiment, college women volunteered to join a group for the purpose of participating in a series of discussions on the psychology of sex. The subjects were randomly assigned to one of three experimental conditions: a *severe initiation* condition, a *mild initiation* condition, and a *no initiation* condition. In the *severe* and *mild initiation* conditions each subject was told that, in order to gain admission to the group, she would be required to demonstrate that she was sophisticated enough to participate freely and frankly in a sexually oriented discussion. An "embarrassment test" was then administered in which the subject read aloud some sexually oriented material in the presence of the male experimenter. The experimenter explained that he would judge from her performance whether or not she qualified for admission to the group. In the *severe initiation* condition the "embarrassment test" consisted of the reciting of a number of obscene words plus some lurid sexual passages from contemporary novels. In the *mild initiation* condition the subjects were simply required to recite a short list of rather genteel sexually oriented words. In the *no initiation* condition the subject was allowed to enter the group without going through any initiation.

Each of the subjects then listened to the same tape recording of a group discussion which she believed was a live discussion being conducted by the group she had just joined. The recording was a rather dull, banal, and irrelevant discussion of the secondary sex behavior of lower animals. The participants spoke haltingly, inarticulately, and unenthusiastically. Immediately after listening to the tape recording, each subject was asked to rate the discussion and the group members on several evaluative scales; for example, dull-interesting, intelligent-unintelligent, etc.

The experimenters reasoned that, in the *severe initiation* condition, the subjects would experience dissonance; their cognition that they had undergone an extremely embarrassing experience to become a member of a group would be dissonant with their cognitions concerning the negative aspects of the group. They could reduce the dissonance by distorting their perceptions of the discussion in a positive direction. In the *no initiation* and *mild initiation* conditions, however, the subjects made relatively little investment in order to enter the group and hence would not be expected to experience much dissonance. It was expected, then, that the subjects in the *severe initiation* condition would rate the group as being more attractive than the subjects in either the *mild* or *no initiation* conditions. The results strongly supported the prediction. The subjects in the *no initiation* and *mild initiation* conditions were generally unimpressed by the discussion. Those in the *severe initiation* condition, however, felt that the discussion was quite interesting and intelligent. They also liked the other group members better.

DISSONANCE AROUSED BY DISAGREEMENT WITH OTHERS

When a person is confronted with an opinion contrary to his own which is held by people like himself, he experiences dissonance. The cognitions corresponding to his own opinions are dissonant with the cognition that these other persons hold differing opinions. It is almost impossible to avoid the introduction of such dissonance unless one altogether avoids any social interaction. One may be very attracted to a person or group of people because of shared interests and even shared opinions. But inevitably there will be some disagreement on matters of concern to the person.

There is considerable evidence from laboratory experimentation that the magnitude of the dissonance thus introduced will depend upon: (*a*) the importance of the person or group that voices the disagreement (3, 8) and (*b*) the importance and relevance to the individual of the issue concerning which the disagreement exists (16). There is also considerable evidence concerning the ways in which a person will attempt to reduce such dissonance. In general, he may attempt to convince himself that the content area in which the disagreement exists is relatively unimportant; he may attempt to derogate the person or group that disagrees with him; he may attempt to eliminate the disagreement either by changing his own opinion or attempting to influence the disagreeing persons to change theirs; or he may seek additional social support for the opinion he holds, thus, in essence, adding new cognitions which are consonant with his own opinions.

There are two major theoretical questions in this area about which there has not been much experimental evidence until recently. One question concerns the relation between the extent of disagreement and the magnitude of dissonance resulting from the disagreement. The other question concerns the conditions under which the dissonance will be reduced primarily by derogating the person who disagrees or primarily by attempting to lessen or eliminate the disagreement. We will discuss these two questions together, because, as will be seen, they are intertwined.

On purely theoretical grounds one would expect the magnitude of dissonance to increase as the extent of disagreement from someone else increases. Let us, for example, consider a person who believes that milk is very good for adults and everyone should drink at least one quart of milk a day. Let us suppose that he discovered that a friend of his believed that milk is poisonously harmful to adults and they should never drink milk. This would introduce more dissonance than if this friend only believed that one quart a day was too much and might be harmful and that, hence, adults should only drink one or two glasses of milk a day. If greater extent of disagreement implies greater magnitude of dissonance, then one should observe more attempts at dissonance reduction as extent of disagreement increases. Since opinion change is one means of reducing dissonance, one would expect that the more the extent of disagreement, the greater would be the ensuing opinion change.

Experimental work on the relation between extent of disagreement and amount of opinion change has not, however, yielded very consistent results (13, 14). Sometimes greater disagreement seems to result in more opinion change and sometimes in less opinion change. There are two possible explanations for these variable findings. It is possible that, if the disagreement is too extreme, that is, outside of the range that the person regards as a reasonable position, the dissonance introduced is rather negligible. Another possible explanation is that, as the extent of disagreement increases, the tendency to reduce dissonance primarily by derogating the disagreeing person also increases. If this were true, then an experiment which only measured opinion change and did not control the ease with which the disagreeing person could be derogated, might indeed be expected to show variable effects since these two are alternative methods of reducing dissonance.

Zimbardo (17) performed an experiment designed to yield results which would help choose between these two possible interpretations. In his study he attempted to minimize the possible use of derogation of the disagreeing person to reduce dissonance by always having the disagreement come from a very close friend. Eighty college women privately gave their opinion regarding the locus of blame in a hypothetical juvenile delinquency problem. Each of the subjects was then confronted with the alleged opinion of a close friend with whom she had been simultaneously exposed to the problem. After a short lapse of time, each subject was asked to state her opinion again.

Two variables were manipulated—the degree of involvement in the problem and the degree of the discrepancy of opinion. One-half of the subjects were told that their opinion in the case was extremely important since it provided a good index of their personality, etc. (high involvement). The other half of the subjects were told that their opinion in the case was inconsequential (low involvement). At the same time, one-half of the subjects were led to believe that the opinion of their friend was extremely discrepant from their own while one-half of the subjects were led to believe that it was only slightly discrepant from their own. "Extremely discrepant" in this study was defined as being in a range which the subject had previously indicated was unreasonable and indefensible.

On the assumption that derogation of a close friend would not occur, change in opinion was used as an index of dissonance reduction. The results showed that (*a*) the more involved a subject was, the more she tended to shift her opinion in the direction of that of her friend; (*b*) the greater the discrepancy between a subject's opinion and her friend's opinion, the more she tended to shift her opinion in the direction of that of her friend.

In short, the experiment by Zimbardo presents clear evidence that the magnitude of dissonance introduced by disagreement from another person does increase as the extent of the disagreement increases, even where the disagreeing person voices an opinion outside of the range that the person considers acceptable and reasonable. If alternative methods of dissonance reduction such as derogating the source of the disagreement are ruled out, then the effects of the greater magnitude of dissonance can be measured by opinion change.

One more point remains to be demonstrated in order to strengthen this interpretation. It is necessary to show that, if derogation of the source of the disagreement is not ruled out as

a possibility, then such derogation becomes increasingly preferred as a means of dissonance reduction as the extent of disagreement increases. Unfortunately, no controlled experimental studies exist on this point. There is relevant evidence, however, from a field study by Adams *et al.* (1) in which the tendency to derogate the disagreer and the tendency to change one's attitudes in the direction of the disagreer were studied simultaneously as alternative manifestations of increased dissonance. In this study, married women were interviewed regarding their attitudes on the proper time to begin toilet training. Two weeks later, the interviewers returned and asked each subject to read a short and rather credible booklet which strongly advocated that training should not begin until the child is twenty-four months old. The subjects were then immediately reinterviewed regarding their attitudes toward toilet training and their opinion of the booklet. The experimenters compared the responses of subjects whose views were widely discrepant from those advocated in the pamphlet with the responses of subjects whose views were close to those advocated by the pamphlet.

The results show rather clearly the simultaneous operation of the two avenues of dissonance reduction. Those for whom the pamphlet did not introduce much dissonance tend not to derogate it. Only 19 percent of these people say that it was unfair, biased, or the like. The comparable figure for those in whom the pamphlet introduced considerable dissonance is 59 percent. Certainly, the tendency to derogate the communication increased as the magnitude of dissonance increased. Furthermore, there are relatively few instances of opinion change among those who derogate the pamphlet. Among those who do not derogate the pamphlet, however, there is considerable opinion change and the amount of opinion change increases as the magnitude of dissonance increases. This latter point, of course, confirms the finding from the Zimbardo experiment.

DISSONANCE RESULTING FROM FORCED PUBLIC COMPLIANCE

There are many circumstances under which a group will force a person to behave overtly in a manner contrary to his beliefs. When this occurs, the person experiences dissonance. His cognition that he performed the overt act would be dissonant with his opinions and beliefs. One way in which a person could reduce dissonance would be by changing his beliefs to bring them more in line with his overt behavior.

Under what conditions will such dissonance be maximal? Suppose a great deal of force is brought to bear in order to induce a person to make a public statement which is contrary to his private opinion; for example, suppose he is offered a great reward if he makes the statement. The size of the reward serves as a justification for making the statement. That is, his cognition that he will receive a great reward for making the public statement is consonant with his cognition that he made the statement. The greater the reward the greater the consonance and hence the less the over-all dissonance. Conversely, if a person makes a public statement which is dissonant with his beliefs in order to receive a small reward, there is little justification for having made the statement. Since there is little consonance between making the statement and receiving a small reward, the over-all dissonance will be greater. Thus, dissonance theory leads to the following prediction: if a person makes a public statement which he does not believe to be true, in order to receive a small reward, he will change his private belief in the direction of the public statement; increasing the size of the reward will decrease the degree to which he will change his private opinion.

This prediction was tested in a study by Festinger and Carlsmith (10). In this experiment, subjects performed a series of extremely boring and tedious tasks for one hour. After they had finished the tasks, the experimenter falsely "explained the purpose of the experiment." The subjects were told that the purpose of the experiment was to see whether people perform better if they are told beforehand that the tasks are interesting and enjoyable than if they are not told anything. Each subject was told that he was in the control condition; that is, he had not been told anything ahead of time about the tasks. The experimenter explained that in the experimental condition, an accomplice poses as a subject who has just finished the experiment and tells the waiting subject that the task was a lot of fun. The experimenter then appeared very uncomfortable and explained to the subject that a girl was now waiting to be tested and the

accomplice had not shown up yet. He then asked the subject if he would do him a favor and substitute for the accomplice and tell the waiting subject that the tasks are interesting and fun. He offered to pay the subject for doing this and for serving as a substitute accomplice in case of future emergencies.

The subjects were run in one of three conditions: (a) a $1 condition, in which the subjects were paid $1 for serving as an accomplice; (b) a $20 condition, in which the subjects were paid $20 for the same job; and (c) a control condition in which the subjects were not asked to lie to the waiting subject.

Each subject was then interviewed (by a different experimenter) and was asked to rate how enjoyable the tasks were. The results supported the predictions made from the theory. In the control condition and the $20 condition, the subjects felt the tasks were rather unenjoyable; there was no difference between the ratings made by the subjects in these two conditions. In the $1 condition, however, the subjects rated the tasks as rather enjoyable. The ratings of the tasks by the subjects in the $1 condition were significantly more positive than those in either the $20 condition or the control condition. In short, forcing a person to make a public statement which was contrary to his private belief introduced considerable dissonance when the reward offered for making the public statement was small. Under these circumstances the person reduces dissonance by changing his private opinion so as to lessen the discrepancy between what he privately believes and what he has publicly said. If too much force is applied to elicit the overt behavior, the dissonance aroused is correspondingly less and private change of opinion does not occur.

We have tried to illustrate in the preceding section some of the variety of ways in which groups and other persons arouse dissonance in an individual and the ways in which such dissonance tends to be reduced. We have given three examples; namely, (a) dissonance introduced by the behavior of others in providing or not providing satisfactions for the individual, (b) dissonance introduced by the expression of disagreement, and (c) dissonance introduced when others force an individual to behave in manners contrary to his private beliefs. Interaction with other people and membership in groups are not, however, only potentially dissonance arousing. There is also another side to the coin. Other people and groups can be and are used as a very effective means of reducing dissonance which has been introduced in some way. We will proceed, in the next section, to a discussion of this aspect of interaction with other people.

GROUP INTERACTION AS A MEANS OF REDUCING DISSONANCE

When a person experiences dissonance, he can use his interactions with other people as a means of reducing the dissonance. In general, there are two processes involved here:

1. He can reduce dissonance by obtaining support from people who already believe what he wants to persuade himself about.
2. He can reduce dissonance by persuading others that they too should believe what he wants to persuade himself about.

Individuals can and do employ both of these methods simultaneously. But something can also be said concerning the conditions under which one or the other will be used primarily. If a person's cognitions regarding an opinion are largely consonant before he is confronted with someone who disagrees with him, this disagreer is the main source of dissonance. In this situation, one would expect that an individual would attempt to reduce the dissonance by trying to convince the other person to change his opinion. On the other hand, if a person has been exposed to a great deal of evidence contrary to an opinion he holds and he is then confronted with someone who disagrees, his cognition that the other person disagrees with him adds relatively little to his total dissonance. He might attempt to induce the disagreer to change his mind; but since the disagreer is not the major source of dissonance, influencing him would accomplish relatively little. This person is more likely to seek social support from persons who hold the same opinion he does. Persons who agree with him will very likely help reduce his dissonance by providing new information and new arguments consonant with his opinion and by discrediting arguments which are dissonant with the opinion.

This distinction can be illustrated by comparing two experiments. In an experiment by Festinger and Thibaut (12) small groups of college students were presented with a problem to discuss. The problem was especially selected so as to elicit a wide range of opinions. Each of the members of the group was asked to state his opinion regarding the best solution to the problem. This was done by marking a point on a seven-point scale which represented the range of possible solutions. The scale rating of each person's opinion was placed on a white card in front of him in plain view of all of the other members of the group. The subjects were then allowed to discuss the problem by writing notes to one another for twenty minutes. Each note that a subject wrote could be sent to only one person.

What would one expect concerning the pattern of communication in such a situation? After having formed an opinion, each person of course discovered that several people in the group disagreed with him. This introduced dissonance regarding his opinion; the more extreme the disagreement the greater was the dissonance. One would expect that each person should direct the majority of his communications to the group members who disagree with him most. Furthermore, one would expect these communications to be mainly attempts to persuade the other person to change his opinion. The results are quite consistent with this line of reasoning. The notes that were written were almost exclusively attempts to persuade others and from 70 percent to 90 percent of all notes were addressed to members who held extreme opinions.

In contrast, let us examine the situation which was created in an experiment by Brodbeck (7). Groups of subjects were brought together and each subject was asked to indicate his opinion, privately, regarding the use of wire tapping by law enforcement officers. This issue was used because there was considerable spread of opinion concerning it. They were also asked to rate how confident they were of their opinion. The subjects then listened to an authoritative speech on the issue. For one half of the groups, the speech was a strong argument in favor of wire tapping while for the other half of the groups the speech was a strong argument against wire tapping. Thus, some subjects in each group were exposed to a persuasive communication which was in disagreement with their previously stated belief while other subjects in each group were exposed to a persuasive communication which supported their previously stated belief. After listening to the speech, each subject was asked, once again, to indicate whether he was for or against wire tapping and how confident he was of his opinion.

On the basis of the procedure thus far, the subjects could be divided into three classes: (a) *Consonant subjects*, those subjects whose initial opinions were supported by the communication. (b) *Strongly dissonant subjects*, those for whom the disagreeing speech had sufficient impact so that they lowered the confidence they had in their initial opinion. (c) *Mildly dissonant subjects*, those whose opinions disagree with the communication but who did *not* lower the confidence they had in their initial opinions.

In the second session of the experiment, four *consonant* subjects and four *dissonant* subjects were selected from each group so that in each of these second session groups there were four persons in favor of and four opposed to wire tapping. They were placed in a room, each sitting behind a clearly visible placard which stated his opinion. The experimenter then informed them that the group was going to split up into pairs to discuss the issue and asked them to list the two persons with whom they would most like to discuss the issue. The *strongly dissonant* subjects more frequently wanted to discuss the matter with persons who agreed with them than did the *consonant* subjects. These results can be interpreted as indicating that the *consonant* subjects wanted to reduce what little dissonance they felt by converting those people who introduced the dissonance; that is, those people who disagreed with them. They had little need to discuss the issue with individuals who held the same opinion. For the *strongly dissonant* subjects, however, the presence of people who disagreed with them was a relatively minor source of dissonance. Their primary source of dissonance was introduced by the communication. By discussing their opinions with persons who agreed with them they were more likely to gain the information and support needed to reduce this dissonance. The *mildly dissonant* subjects yielded results between the other two classes of subjects.

There are additional data from the Brodbeck experiment to support the interpretation offered above; namely, the *strongly dissonant* subjects wanted social support from those who agreed with them in order to reduce the dissonance introduced by the persuasive communication. The second session group of eight subjects did not split up into pairs but actually proceeded to discuss the issue in the total group. After this discussion, they were once more asked to state their opinion on the issue and the confidence they had in this opinion.

It should be stressed again that in the group which carried on the discussion there were four persons on each side of the issue. It is interesting to note, therefore that, following this discussion, the *strongly dissonant* subjects had, on the average, completely regained the confidence in their initial opinion which they had before having listened to the dissonance introducing speech. In other words, these subjects indicated, by their choice of the persons with whom they wanted to discuss the issue, that they wanted support for their shaken opinions. They then proceeded to obtain such support and regained their confidence even in a situation where half the members of the group disagreed with them. Clearly, they either listened more carefully or gave more weight to the arguments advanced in the discussion by those that agreed with them.

This kind of phenomenon can be seen more clearly and dramatically, as one might expect, in real life situations. An example of this may be taken from a study by Festinger, Riecken, and Schachter (11). The study involved the systematic observation of the behavior of a group of people who firmly believed that the world would end by a cataclysm on a certain date and, in many ways, had committed themselves heavily to this belief.

The investigators were concerned with the effects on these people when their prophecy failed to be confirmed. The cognitions concerning the tremendous sacrifices they had made for their beliefs would be dissonant with their cognition that their beliefs were wrong. They could reduce this dissonance by convincing themselves that their beliefs were correct in spite of the fact that their specific prophecy was disconfirmed. They might accomplish this in at least two ways:

1. *By receiving social support from one another.* That is, by finding an explanation for the disconfirmation and convincing one another that it is a valid one.

2. *By proselyting other people.* By convincing outsiders that their beliefs are valid,

they could add cognitions consonant with maintaining their beliefs and remaining in the movement.

On the night of the expected cataclysm, most of the believers gathered at a member's home where they were to await a flying saucer which was to rescue them at midnight. Several of the members, however, were instructed to wait by themselves at their own homes. When midnight came and passed, the group was overwhelmingly disappointed. They could not at first believe that their prophecy had not been fulfilled. When they finally grew to realize that the cataclysm would not be forthcoming they struggled to find a reason why. For several hours the believers kept assuring one another of the validity of their movement and they kept insisting to one another that an explanation would be forthcoming. Finally, they put forth the explanation that the earth was not destroyed precisely because of their belief and their faith. The group was able to accept and believe this explanation because they could support one another and convince each other that this was, in fact, a valid explanation. Although their belief was momentarily shaken by the disconfirmation, the members were able to maintain their membership in the movement because of the mutual social support which they received. Furthermore, the conviction of the members who had waited together did not show any signs of faltering several weeks after the disconfirmation (when the study was concluded). In fact, so powerful was the increased social support that two of the members who had occasionally expressed mild skepticism about a few tenets of the movement now firmly believed all of them. The importance of the social support in reducing dissonance, moreover, is shown by the contrast provided by those members of the movement who had waited for the fulfillment of the prophecy alone in their own homes. These persons did not maintain their beliefs. Without the continuous social support of their fellow members, the dissonance created by the disconfirmation was sufficient to cause them to renounce their belief in the movement in spite of their heavy commitment to it.

Perhaps even a more striking aspect of the effects of disconfirmation involved the proselyting behavior of the believers who remained believers. Prior to the disconfirmation, attempts on the part of the believers at convincing people of the validity of their movement were rather mild. For months before the disconfirmation they seemed to have little desire to attract new believers. They felt that those who had been chosen to be saved would join the group of their own accord. Hence, all visitors who expressed interest in the movement were treated casually; no attempt was made to sell the movement to them and very little information about the movement was given to them. There were even periods when the members were specifically instructed not to speak to outsiders. No attempt was made to attract publicity. On the contrary, all attempts on the part of the press to obtain interviews were rebuffed.

Immediately after the disconfirmation, the behavior of the believers changed dramatically. On four successive days they called press conferences, gave lengthy interviews, and posed for pictures. They also attempted to attract new members. They invited the public and press to attend a meeting at which they sang songs while awaiting the appearance of a spaceman "who might come."

In summary, the believers, by engaging in mutual social support and proselyting new members, were able to reduce dissonance sufficiently to enable themselves to maintain their beliefs. Those members of the group who had been cut off from social support at the crucial time were unable to maintain these beliefs following the failure of the prophecy.

References

1. Adams, J. S., *et al.* The effects of a persuasive communication on opinion change and rejection of the communication. Unpublished study, Stanford Univ.
2. Aronson, E. The effect of effort on the attractiveness of rewarded and unrewarded stimuli. *Journal of Abnormal and Social Psychology*, 1961, **63**, 375–380.
3. Back, K. The exertion of influence through social communication. *Journal of Abnormal and Social Psychology*, 1951, **46**, 9–24.

4. Brehm, J. Post-decision changes in desirability of alternatives. *Journal of Abnormal and Social Psychology*, 1956, **52**, 384–389.
5. Brehm, J. Increasing cognitive dissonance by a *fait accompli*. *Journal of Abnormal and Social Psychology*, 1959, **58**, 379–382.
6. Brehm, J., & Cohen, A. R. Re-evaluation of choice alternatives as a function of their number and qualitative similarity. *Journal of Abnormal and Social Psychology*, 1959, **58**, 373–378.
7. Brodbeck, M. The role of small groups in mediating the effects of propaganda. *Journal of Abnormal and Social Psychology*, 1956, **52**, 166–170.
8. Festinger, L. Informal social communication. *Psychological Review*, 1950, **57**, 271–282.
9. Festinger, L. *Theory of cognitive dissonance.* Evanston, Ill.: Row, Peterson, 1957.
10. Festinger, L., & Carlsmith, J. Cognitive consequences of forced compliance. *Journal of Abnormal and Social Psychology*, 1959, **58**, 203–210.
11. Festinger, L., Riecken, H., & Schachter, S. *When prophecy fails.* Minneapolis: Univ. of Minnesota Press, 1956.
12. Festinger, L., & Thibaut, J. Interpersonal communication in small groups. *Journal of Abnormal and Social Psychology*, 1951, **46**, 92–100.
13. Hovland, C. Reconciling conflicting results derived from experimental and survey studies of attitude change. *The American Psychologist*, 1959, **14**, 8–17.
14. Hovland, C., & Pritzker, H. Extent of opinion change as a function of amount of change advocated. *Journal of Abnormal and Social Psychology*, 1957, **54**, 257–261.
15. Mills, J. Changes in moral attitudes following temptation. *Journal of Personality*, 1958, **26**, 517–531.
16. Schachter, S. Deviation, rejection and communication. *Journal of Abnormal and Social Psychology*, 1951, **46**, 190–208.
17. Zimbardo, P. Involvement and communication discrepancy as determinants of opinion change. *Journal of Abnormal and Social Psychology*, 1960, **60**, 86–94.

PART THREE

PRESSURES TO UNIFORMITY IN GROUPS

11

Pressures to Uniformity in Groups: Introduction

It is a commonplace observation that the members of an enduring group are likely to display a striking homogeneity of beliefs, attitudes, values, and behavior. The members of an adolescent gang are readily identified by their distinctive style of dress. Work groups engaged in some specialized task develop a jargon that seems esoteric to outsiders. Marital partners tend to become more alike over the course of their marriage. And participants of a group engaged in social reform come to share an ideology about the nature of the social world that they aspire to change. Even among dedicated nonconformists one finds a monotonous similarity of hair styles.

Social scientists have devoted much energy and ingenuity toward attaining a better understanding of the homogenizing effects of groups. A program of research conducted by Asch (1) provides a dramatic demonstration of some of these effects. In a typical experiment, Asch brings several college students into a laboratory to participate in a study of visual perception. Their task is to make a series of judgments in which they compare the length of a given vertical line with three other lines. Each subject is asked to state in his turn which of the three lines best matches the given one. In actuality only one person is a naive subject, the other participants having been instructed beforehand to give markedly incorrect but unanimous answers on certain of the trials before the critical subject states his judgment. The subject thus finds himself among persons whose stated views frequently contradict the evidence of his own senses.

Asch reports that approximately three-quarters of the subjects yield to the unanimous judgment of others on at least one trial and that one-third yield on at least half of the trials. It should be noted that in this experiment the critical subject is unacquainted with the other participants and that they make no overt effort to influence his behavior. His judgments, moreover, concern matters having little intrinsic importance to him, to his future relations with the others, and to the fate of those in the room. Nevertheless, there are clearly strong pressures on him to conform. One would surely expect these

139

pressures to be even stronger in more natural settings and with respect to matters having greater significance for the participants.

Similarities among the members of a group may arise for a number of reasons. We will enumerate some of the more important of these and then turn to a fuller discussion of the ways in which members actively exert pressures toward uniformity upon one another.

SOME REASONS FOR SIMILARITY

COGNITIVE CONFLICT

Whenever a collection of people are exposed to the same environment, they will be inclined to assume that there is only one "correct" description of the situation. If a person finds that he sees this environment differently from the others, he is faced with a cognitive conflict: Should he believe his own perceptions, or should he trust the views expressed by others? Although individuals respond differently to this conflict, the demand for uniformity of opinion generated by such a situation would seem to be inevitable. Asch (**2**, 484) describes this cognitive conflict succinctly in accounting for his experimental findings:

The individual comes to experience a world that he shares with others. He perceives that the surroundings include him, as well as the others, and that he is in the same relations to the surroundings as the others. He notes that he, as well as the others, is converging upon the same object and responding to its identical properties. Joint action and mutual understanding require the relations of intelligibility and structural simplicity. In these terms the "pull" toward the group becomes understandable.

In keeping with this account of tendencies for uniformity, we should expect no cognitive conflict to arise when the subject does not assume that everyone is converging upon a single object in their common environment. Crutchfield (9) has provided support for this conclusion from an experiment, similar to that of Asch, in which subjects were asked to consider aesthetic matters and to announce their personal preferences. Under these conditions he found that virtually no subject abandoned his own judgment in favor of those expressed by others.

Research such as that by Asch suggests that the tendency for a person to accept others' opinions when these contradict the testimony of his own senses is stronger the more closely certain conditions are met: (*a*) The quality of the evidence presented by others is compelling. The existence of unanimity among the others is of crucial importance, but the absolute size of the group appears to make little difference beyond three or four. If the subject finds even one other person who agrees with him, he is much less likely to yield to the majority. (*b*) The stimulus being judged is ambiguous. (*c*) The subject's confidence in the correctness of his own perception is low. (*d*) The discrepancy between his own opinion and the opinions of others is large but not too large. (*e*) The subject knows that others are aware that his opinion differs from theirs. Finally, there is considerable evidence that certain personality characteristics predispose an individual to accept the opinions of others in such a conflictful situation (**9**).

Belonging to a group makes a person sensitive to his relations with others. Thus, if a person experiences such a cognitive conflict when he is a member of a group, we should expect him to be especially responsive to the judgments expressed by other members. Deutsch and Gerard (**11**) have repeated the Asch experiment with individuals who were led to perceive themselves as members of a group and obtained more conforming behavior than that reported by Asch.

SIMILARITY AMONG MEMBERS' ENVIRONMENTS

Membership in a group determines for an individual many of the things he will see, hear, think about, learn, and do. The nature of the stimuli in the environment of a person is in large part affected by his group membership. A member of a labor union, for example, is exposed to different facts and interpretations of these facts than is a member of the Chamber of Commerce. Because of the relatively restricted range of events encountered by the members of a group, they come to know, perceive, and do things in a similar fashion.

SELECTIVE MEMBERSHIP

It was noted in Chapter 7 that groups may differ significantly in their bases of attraction. Distinctive kinds of people may, therefore, be attracted to, or recruited by, a particular group, and a person who finds himself in a group whose members are too different from him may withdraw. As a result of such selective processes in the recruitment and maintenance of personnel, the members of a group will display certain similarities. Scott (27) found in a study of fraternities and sororities that most of the similarities among members could be attributed to processes of this sort.

COMMON SOCIETAL NORMS

The members of a particular group are also members of a larger society. To the extent that the norms of this society affect all members of the group in a similar way, they will exhibit similarities that do not derive from influences arising distinctively within the group. If societal norms affect two groups equally, there will be similarities among the members within each group but these will be no greater than the similarities between groups.

GROUP PRESSURES TO UNIFORMITY

The sources of similarity considered thus far do not require active processes of interpersonal influence among the members of a group. But it is clear that groups can, and often do, apply pressures on their members so as to bring about a uniformity of beliefs, attitudes, values, and behavior. For some groups it is recognized by all that the exertion of such pressures is a legitimate function of the group. Thus, churches, political parties, professional societies, character-building agencies, families, and other instrumentalities of socialization are expected to influence their members to behave in accordance with specific standards. Groups do not require, however, an explicit justification of this sort to demand conformity of their members. Quite informal groups, such as bridge clubs, fishing companions, or friendship cliques, develop informal group standards, often quite unconsciously, and thereby exert homogenizing influences on their members.

If a cohesive group has developed a standard or a norm, it may exert strong pressures on any member who attempts to deviate. Thus, for example, it is commonly observed that members of a work group agree, perhaps implicitly, on an acceptable rate of production and apply strong pressures on anyone who dares to deviate from this standard. The nature of these pressures was vividly described by a clerical worker in the following terms:

First we would talk about her unfairness among ourselves. If that did not reach her, we talked about her where she could overhear us. If she still did not change, one of us would approach her in the lounge and ask her if she was trying to kill our jobs. That usually did the trick.

An especially vivid example of the operation of group pressures is provided by the U.S. Senate's hearing into charges that Senator Joseph McCarthy had engaged in conduct unbecoming a senator. William S. White (31) commented on the sessions:

It was not a trial in the commonly understood meaning of the term at all; the judges clearly and inevitably had prior opinions, for day after day they had all sat with McCarthy. They were not hearing an action at law; they were determining simply the *degree* that a member had transgressed the rules, written or not, and the spirit of the club to which he belonged.

After the examining committee reported an unfavorable judgment concerning McCarthy, White says: "Again and again when McCarthy rose to speak there was in the chamber that rarest of all demonstrations, a demonstration of conscious disorder and inattention. Tolerance is a long rope here, a very long one. But give a man enough rope . . . ."

In thinking about group pressures to uniformity there is danger that value judgments may color our views. The standards and norms of a group may operate to impose severe restrictions on the freedom of members, but they may also have beneficial, even necessary, consequences for both the group and its members. The basic problem for social policy is how to design social arrangements so as to strike an optimal balance between the benefits and costs resulting from pressures to uniformity. The problem is not new, for John Stuart Mill stated it well in his essay *On Liberty:* "There is a limit to the legitimate interference of collective opinion with individual independence: and to find that limit, and maintain it against encroachment, is as indispensable to a good condition of human affairs, as protection against political despotism."

In the remainder of this chapter, we examine some of the current theories and findings concerning the ways in which pressures toward uniformity operate. What functions do they serve? What is it that increases or decreases the strength of their influence? What are the consequences of deviation? Under what conditions does heterogeneity arise within groups? And how do group standards change?

FUNCTIONS OF GROUP PRESSURES TO UNIFORMITY

Theoretical explanations of why groups set up pressures to uniformity have stressed four functions served by the uniformity resulting from such pressures: (*a*) to help the group accomplish its goals, (*b*) to help the group maintain itself as a group, (*c*) to help the members develop validity or "reality" for their opinions, and (*d*) to help members define their relations to their social surroundings.

GROUP LOCOMOTION

Festinger (Chap. 14) has proposed that the pressures toward uniformity among members of a group may occur because uniformity is considered desirable or necessary in order for the group to achieve its goal. If a basketball team is to win games, for example, it is important that all players conscientiously practice in improving their skills. If an executive committee is to make workable plans, it is necessary that the committee's members believe in the same policies for the organization. If a library is to keep track of its books, it is mandatory that uniform methods be followed in lending volumes and in returning them to the shelves. Approved procedures for movement toward an agreed upon goal, then, often are the sources of pressures toward uniformity. Members view these procedures as the proper way to behave since the methods are seen as assuring progress toward the goal.

GROUP MAINTENANCE

Some group standards serve as a means for helping the group to maintain itself. For example, the requirements that members regularly attend meetings or wholeheartedly support the party platform serve to assure that the

group will continue to exist as an entity. Similarly, pressures against behavior that may bring disgrace to the group or divide the group and threaten its existence or make members uncomfortable and ready to resign also serve to ensure that the group survives.

The development of pressures toward uniformity during meetings of psychotherapy groups is described by Stock, Whitman, and Lieberman (**29**), who propose that a standard in such a group develops as a "solution" for potential interpersonal conflicts that might become disruptive in the group. Members may wish to discuss their interpersonal relations among themselves, for example, but may at the same time be wary of this topic because of the fear that some members may be hurt or that strained relations may develop. The conflict demands a solution that adequately satisfies the two conflicting motives and also is consistent with external reality. In this case the group might agree to hold impersonal discussions of relations that "often develop among persons like ourselves." Stock, Whitman, and Lieberman suggest that members are then pressed to conform to this solution as long as it adequately deals with the conflicting motives; if the conflict changes in character, the solution may be changed.

SOCIAL REALITY

Interpersonal pressures may arise to provide and maintain an acceptable belief by creating, through consensus, a social reality. Often there are no bases in logic, objective reality, or evidence of the senses that enable a person to arrive at a judgment or opinion that is clearly correct. With respect to a matter where no direct evidence is available, the subjective validity of an opinion comes to be established simply by the fact that members of the group agree. Forces then arise among relevant persons to maintain this uniformity of belief.

A curriculum committee in a high school must decide upon minimum requirements for graduation by answering questions like: What kind of world will our graduates face? What skills will they need in order to gain employment ten or twenty years hence? Is education in the humanities more important than training in the sciences? Shared agreement on any of these questions has a greater reality for each member than his previous private beliefs. Discussion groups, policy-making committees, and persons engaged in conversation at the dinner table are in large part concerned with establishing social reality for the participants.

A group can also provide members with a reality that helps them to understand themselves when there are no other criteria to help them do so. Persons who have a desire to accurately evaluate their abilities, for instance, can do so by comparing themselves with others. Festinger (13) assumes that such persons make more reliable self-evaluations when they compare themselves with others close to them in ability than when they compare themselves with others who are greatly different. They are therefore attracted to groups containing persons similar to themselves, and pressures arise among the members to keep all participants similar in ability so that valid social comparisons can be made. As a result of these tendencies, members of groups tend to increase in similarity and in dependence on one another.

Schachter (25) has proposed that tendencies to create a social reality also come into existence whenever people confront an unfamiliar social situation that arouses the emotions. Under such circumstances the person may not know whether his emotional disturbance should be viewed as fear, anger, chagrin, or excitement. He says (25, 128):

Just as there are pressures to establish the "correctness" of an opinion and the "goodness" of an ability, there are pressures to establish the "appropriateness" of an emotion or bodily state. In the case of opinions or abilities, when there is no possibility of a physical check or a check against authoritative sources, pressures arise to establish a social reality. In the case of an emotion, when the precipitating situation is ambiguous or uninterpretable in terms of past experience, again pressures arise to establish a social reality. And since emotion-producing situations are often novel and outside the realm of our past experience, it could be expected that the emotions would be particularly vulnerable to social influence. It may be this presumed vulnerability that will eventually help us to understand phenomena of emotional contagion such as panics or riots.

This possibility is given support by the finding of French (14) that members in groups with a long history, in contrast to those in newly formed groups, tended to react uniformly when smoke seeped unexpectedly under the locked door of the laboratory room either with fear or with derision toward the experimenter for perpetrating a "hoax." Darley (10) has shown that members more often imitate the behavior of others when they are frightened and presume that the others are too.

DEFINING RELATIONS TO SOCIAL SURROUNDINGS

Every group exists in a social environment consisting of groups, organizations, institutions, and other components of society. It is often important to the members of a group that they achieve a consensus concerning the relations between their group and its social surroundings—which groups can be considered as allies, which as enemies, how the group compares with others, or how membership in the group affects a person's opportunities in society at large. The construction of social reality on such matters permits the group to develop coordinated action in its social environment and gives members a firm basis for self-evaluation.

Sometimes groups form because the participants share similar problems of relating to their social surroundings. Such groups then develop a uniform set of beliefs and values that aid them in solving these problems. A sensitive and insightful description of a situation of this sort has been given by Burns (7) in a report of observations made of management personnel in a factory where he discovered certain informal groupings consisting of "intimates who—in the canteen, in the corridors after lunch, and after the factory stopped at night—constantly gravitated together in collusive-looking conversations." From an analysis of their composition and topics of conversation, Burns identified one type of group, labeled "cliques," that was composed of older men who had come to believe that the odds were great against further advancement in the firm. For these men the clique appeared to serve as a system of mutual defense that provided social support around new standards of reference by which the organization's norms of success could be discounted. Thus, "features of the organization—the bonus system, rate-fixing, progress meetings, the formal communication system—were mentioned depreciatingly as 'the way the firm does things.'" And leadership was often assumed by a comic who could make fun of the firm's procedures or by the man who had most clearly rejected his occupational role and was thereby most free to criticize the firm and successful people in it. Burns concludes (7, 476): "The clique thus appears as a form of counter-system, a characteristic element in our society in which patterns of behavior appropriate to dominant positions find their response in the countervailing patterns of conduct developed among the less privileged or less powerful positions."

A similar line of reasoning has been advanced by Cohen (8) to account for the norms developed by delinquent gangs of lower-class boys. He noted that these groups arise because society's expectations in school and work cannot be met by potential gang members. Those sharing common feelings of frustration and defeat provide support for one another by establishing a code they can fulfill— characterized by Cohen as nonutilitarian, malicious, and negativistic—that is the opposite of the demands placed on them by society.

Yinger (32) has proposed that such a "contraculture" can be found among many groups in society, including religious sects, the Black Muslims, and youth groups of various sorts. According to Yinger, ambivalence is the key to the appearance of contracultural norms. The individual accepts at some level the very standards of society that he cannot meet, but to avoid feelings of perpetual failure, "he represses his sense of identity with the legitimate community." In order to stabilize this repression he does not merely repress these values; he reverses them and seeks out other people who employ the same mechanism of defense. By establishing new relationships to society, the resulting group with its contracultural norms provides its members with a tolerable resolution of their ambivalences.

DETERMINANTS OF STRENGTH OF PRESSURES

The list of functions served by group pressures to uniformity suggests several hypotheses concerning the determinants of their strength. We may assume that the magnitude of pressure will be greater the more important is the function to be served by uniformity and the more that members believe that such uniformity will in fact lead to the fulfillment of the function.

We should expect, for example, that if a group has agreed upon certain procedures for achieving a goal, pressures for conformity will be stronger the more important the goal is and the more clearly the procedures are seen as instrumental to its attainment. If a particular group standard serves as a means for helping the group maintain itself, then enforcement of the standard should be more vigorous the more important the group's survival is for its members. If consensus regarding a certain belief helps to establish its social reality, pressures to uniformity should be greater the more significant the belief is for the participants. And if a group's norms serve to define the members' relationships to their social surroundings, there should be more insistence on adherence to them the more that members need to have these relationships defined.

When uniformity of beliefs, attitudes, values, or behavior is felt to be in the group's interest, the group may be expected to use its available means to bring about such uniformity. But groups differ considerably in their capacity to exert influence on their members. In Chapter 7 it was shown that cohesiveness gives a group power to influence its members and heightens their readiness to attempt to influence and be influenced by others. We should expect to find, then, that the greater the cohesiveness of a group is the stronger its pressures to uniformity will be whenever this uniformity serves a group function. There is considerable evidence in support of this expectation.

Most groups have a variety of rewards they can give to members for conforming. Perhaps the most important of these are indications of esteem and acceptance. Since the members of a cohesive group value their membership, they are likely to be sensitive to evidence of acceptance by other members. Some groups attempt to increase the strength of their pressures to uniformity by more formal systems of rewards. Examples are school honor rolls, bonus payments for high production in industry, and awards for good citizenship in the community. Although such systems are not always effective, an awareness that rewards will follow approved behavior ordinarily reduces resistance to group pressures to uniformity.

Groups also possess punishments they can employ to inhibit deviance. Members are likely to know the costs of deviation, and if they want to remain in the group or cannot leave, they may be expected to try to avoid these costs by conforming to the group's demands or by acting as if they are doing so. The greater is a member's subjective probability that punishments will result from nonconformity, the more likely is he to try to avoid the appearance of deviating. In a study (30) of 700 members of committees concerned with "educating" the public to appreciate the products of a nationwide industry, the observation was made that members more actively followed the practices approved by their groups if negative sanctions were often used than if they were not. Thus, members behaved as expected by their colleagues because they knew that unpleasant consequences were likely to follow if they did not. In Chapter 20, French and Raven suggest, however, that when based on coercion the power of the group is more effective if members perceive such threats as legitimate—that is, in accord with the values of members—than if they view them as nonlegitimate.

Because the likelihood that punishments will be administered is greater if others know that a member is a deviant than if he is successful in concealing his nonconformity, it follows that public behavior is more likely to be conforming than private behavior and that overt acts are more likely to conform to the group's expectations than are covert beliefs, when punishments are primarily used in their enforcement.

Everyone is simultaneously a member of several groups, and the influence of a particular group upon a member at a given time may be expected to depend upon the momentary salience of that membership for the individual. A member of a group often receives cues that remind him that he is "one of us," that he is a Methodist, an Elk, a Rotarian, a member of his profession, or the like. Because they make his membership prominent and present for him, these cues heighten the salience of the group. Furthermore, they are reminders that the group has standards he is expected to abide by. In an experiment on attitude change, Kelley (20) exposed Catholic students to persuasive communications that opposed certain views taken by the Church. Prior to receiving these communications, some students were reminded of their membership in the Catholic Church but others were not. Kelley found that heightening the salience of membership resulted in a greater resistance to a change of the group-anchored attitudes. For some reason, the effects were more pro-nounced for high school students than for college students.

CONSEQUENCES OF DEVIATION

When someone deviates from the standards of a group, other members exert pressures on him, urging him to mend his ways. In observing the process of a group meeting, we find a quickening of interest when a deviant remark is made, a concentration of communication toward the deviant, and sometimes an unreasonableness in reacting to the content of the deviant's remarks. The frequency of such communication, we might expect, will be greater the more serious the deviation is taken to be. In accordance with this assumption, investigators have noted that members communicate to a colleague more often the more his actions deviate from the group's standard (5) and the more important the standard is to the group (24). Communications are more often directed to a deviant person if the senders perceive there is a reasonable probability of changing him. Should it become evident that the deviant is persistently unwilling or unable to change, the amount of communication directed to him markedly declines (24).

A group has a potent punishment for a member who persists in his deviancy despite pressures on him to shift: it may redefine its boundaries so as to exclude the deviant, thereby protecting uniformity among members. Rejection of a deviant can be accomplished in various ways. He may be set apart so that no one talks or listens to him, he may be dropped from activities of the group, or he may be expelled. Obviously, the more attractive the group is to a member, the more he wishes to avoid such extreme sanction. Paradoxically, the greater the cohesiveness of the group is, the more likely the members are to reject the persistently deviant member.

In Chapter 13 Schachter describes the results of a laboratory experiment in which college students were given an opportunity to accept or reject their companions in anticipation of further meetings. Three paid participants took different positions with respect to the opinions that developed in group discussions. One began as a deviant from the predominant opinion in the group but changed his position to conform with that of the group (the slider), one remained a nonconformist throughout the experimental meeting (the deviant), and the third adopted attitudes that closely resembled the mode of the group (the conformer). The results show that the deviant was strongly rejected but neither the conformer nor the slider was. It was found, furthermore, that the inclination of the members to reject the deviant was greater the higher the cohesiveness of the group became and the more the deviation was relevant to the purposes of the group. This experiment has been repeated on different populations of subjects. Emerson (12) found among high school students a somewhat smaller tendency to reject deviants than Schachter found among college students. He suggests that these younger students were not as sure of themselves on the issues discussed and often changed their minds to suit the arguments of the deviants. Replications of this study in seven European nations also produced results generally in accord with Schachter's earlier work (26); apparently the tendency to reject deviants is not a phenomenon limited to the United States alone.

A member who is able to live up to the group's standards wins the approval of others and derives a sense of satisfaction from doing what is right. Social pressures make great demands on his courage when he prefers to stand by personal principles that contradict the group's standards (21). Worse, if he cannot achieve as well as others expect him to, he may have feelings of failure, reducible only by getting the group to lower its demands or by departing from the group. Gross, Mason, and McEachern (16) have shown in an analysis of the school superintendent's role that the mental health and efficiency of a superintendent is directly related to the degree that he and his school board have similar values about education.

A deviant person develops uneasiness, then, when interacting with his colleagues. If he is rejected for maintaining his unpopular position, his anxiety is likely to increase. In an experimental study, Pepitone and Wilpizeski (23) demonstrated that members who were ignored by their group mates because of unacceptable beliefs depreciated themselves and became angry toward the persons who were responsible for their dilemma. It seems probable too, although these researchers did not examine the point, that a rejected person may be likely to withdraw and say little to others, thereby increasing his isolation.

From practical experience we know that members are not always vulnerable to group pressures even when their confidence in a belief has been shaken. They may find ways of protecting themselves. Brodbeck (6) and Berkowitz (4) have observed that persons whose confidence in a belief has been reduced by exposure to counter pressures prefer to hear arguments from their own side rather than from the other side. As a result of listening preferentially to those who agree with them and ignoring arguments of their opponents, their confidence in their own opinions is bolstered.

A deviant can adopt other means of protecting himself from social pressures and from the implied possibility of rejection. He may avoid surveillance by those who would monitor his behavior, knowing that they cannot control him if his behavior is not visible. He may oppose the spirit, if not the letter, of a standard by making minimally acceptable behavior the maximum for himself. Or he may conform so strictly that his actions are destructive even though they cannot be called deviations. A deviant who has sufficient social power may make it difficult for others to enforce their corrective actions or may attempt to change the standard in ways that allow him more freedom. And if there is more than one deviant in the group, they may band together in an effort to attain more tolerable standards for the group (32).

Even when an individual decides to conform he is likely to retain some reservations about his decision, since the chosen alternative is seldom entirely positive. He thus experiences a state of cognitive dissonance: awareness of any negative aspect of the chosen alternative is dissonant with his cognition that he has rejected the belief. Thus, the greater the attractiveness of the belief he gave up in order to conform, the greater is the dissonance following his decision. In Chapter 10, Festinger and Aronson showed that efforts are made to reduce a dissonant state. One way is for the person to convince himself that the belief of others is even more attractive, relative to his own original belief, than he had previously thought. It follows from this view that persons who conform may seek to convince themselves and others that there is high value in their changed belief. Such persons may actually heighten the pressures to conformity within a group.

The literature provides ample evidence that when a person deviates from a group standard that is viewed as applicable to him, pressures of various sorts are brought to bear upon him to bring about his conformity. One may ask, however, whether there are not conditions under which a group will tolerate an individual's deviancy. This interesting issue has not received the study it deserves, but Hollander (18) has made useful and testable suggestions. He proposes that a member may be excused for deviant behavior if he has proven himself in some fashion. If he makes a useful contribution to the group, for example, he stores up what may be called *idiosyncrasy credits*, which provide him the right to deviate from established customs to some degree. A high-status person usually will have collected a store of credits and, according to the approach offered by Hollander, may therefore deviate from his group's standards without invoking the corrective reactions a regular member receives. It follows that higher status members may deviate from group standards more often than low-status members.

But a high-status person is ordinarily in a better position to affect the group's outcomes than is a regular member. Would not the members expect him to use this ability toward attaining their outcomes? If so, members might be especially ready to disapprove deviations by a high-status member. In Chapter 40 Wiggins, Dill, and Schwartz examine the reactions of members to deviants who differ in status. They report that a high-status person will be allowed to transgress against a standard as long as his behavior is not detrimental to the group. If, however, his actions hurt the group, the members respond with greater hostility than when a lower status person does the same thing.

SOURCES OF HETEROGENEITY AMONG MEMBERS

Thus far we have discussed group standards as though social pressures are always toward uniform behavior for all members. In reality, a group may require different standards of different people. Many groups create specialized positions, each with its own set of responsibilities and procedures, and members assigned to these roles are expected to act in the manner prescribed for each role, as, for example, in a hospital group consisting of a nurses' aide, a nurse, an intern, and a resident doctor. The role prescriptions are pressures toward uniformity among those occupying a certain position in the group. We should expect that the greater the cohesiveness of a group is, the stronger will be the pressures on the role-occupant to act as he is expected to do. This proposition was examined by Hall (17) in a study of the cohesiveness of bomber crews. He found that greater cohesiveness was associated with stronger agreement among crew members as to how the aircraft commander should act toward them and with greater adaptation of the commander's behavior to the pressures from his crew.

Heterogeneity of beliefs, attitudes, values, or behavior may arise in a group because the members belong also to other groups whose standards differ from one another. The development of a uniform standard in such a group would place some of the members in a conflict of loyalty: Which group standard should they follow? This type of conflict was generated in a laboratory experiment conducted by Gerard (15). He formed discussion groups and assigned them the task of arriving at a unanimous decision concerning the best solution to a social problem. A week later he placed the members in different groups, where they found the decision of their previous groups opposed by their new colleagues (who were paid participants assigned the task of disagreeing with the subjects). Pressures to change were resisted in the latter groups to the degree that the former groups were attractive to the subjects. The study by Kelley described earlier concerning the beliefs of Catholics indicates that a person is most likely to adhere at any moment to the beliefs of the group that is salient. When heterogeneity arises in a group because its members belong also to other groups, the group may find it difficult to establish standards required for its effective functioning.

Groups sometimes agree that pressures to uniformity will not be permitted to develop in certain areas of the group's life so that creativeness can be encouraged, for example, or so that freedom of thought can be respected. The importance placed by professors on academic freedom is an example of an agreement to allow disagreement. But heterogeneity is probably most often tolerated because no need for uniformity exists; practices and beliefs disparate with respect to certain matters pose no threat to the group's purposes or processes. It would seem, for example, that no useful function would be served in a poker club by insisting on uniform opinions concerning the age of the universe, although such uniformity might be viewed as essential by the members of a religious group. Further research is needed to elucidate the conditions that foster a broad tolerance for differences within a group.

HOW GROUP STANDARDS CHANGE

Once group standards have been established they appear to be remarkably resistant to change, as full testimony provides in health habits, farming practices, production methods, religious customs, and many other ways of life. Yet there is evidence that they do change and can be changed.

One might expect, for example, that in a group with a substantial turnover in membership new arrivals will be likely to bring to the group fresh points of view and an impetus to change established standards. Jacobs and Campbell (19) examined this possibility. They created a group standard, by means of a technique first employed by Sherif (28), in which a group of subjects sat in a dark room and observed a tiny spot of light which, though physically stationary, appeared to move (the autokinetic phenomenon). Each subject was instructed to announce, in turn, the distance the light moved during a certain interval of time. The group consisted, in fact, of one critical subject and several other "members" who had been instructed in advance to announce that they had observed a much larger movement than most naive subjects reported. After several such trials, the critical subject came to report judgments conforming to those of the other "members."

At this point, one of the collaborating "members" left the group and a naive subject took his place. With repeated trials this new subject came also to make judgments consistent with the group standard. The procedure was continued until one by one all experimental assistants had been removed from the group, at which point the group consisted entirely of naive subjects whose behavior was guided by the group's standard. Jacobs and Campbell then continued the experiment by substituting, one at a time, a new naive subject for each old member. How long did the original uniform belief persist? The results show that by the time the sixth "generation" of subjects had arrived, the influence of the original group of instructed "members" had completely disappeared. At each intervening stage the group gave relatively uniform judgments but as membership changed these gradually shifted to the level that individuals gave when making judgments alone. It appears, then, that new members, when added to the group, tended to conform to the group's present standard but also exerted a small influence on the standard itself.

Some of the conditions affecting the reactions of a group to the arrival of newcomers have been examined by Ziller and his associates (33). If one individual comes into a group where the members do not expect additional newcomers, he is likely to be ignored. If, however, the members expect others to be added to the group, they are likely to respond to him more actively and to pay some attention to his opinions. The first type of group is described as "closed" and the second as "open." It is interesting to note that the groups studied by Jacobs and Campbell were "open" according to this distinction. If, then, their experiment were repeated on "closed" groups, one would expect to find a much smaller influence of newcomers on the group's standard.

Coch and French (Chap. 26) have reported results from a field experiment in which groups made striking changes in their standards. Following the introduction of a new work method no more difficult than the former one, the workers in one group lowered their production rate and exerted strong pressures for conformity to this new standard. Other groups of workers changed their group standards also, but in the opposite direction: they demanded greater speed of production. The major variable determining the amount of production in the two kinds of groups was the amount of opportunity they had to participate in making decisions about how the work transfer should be carried out. Those workers who participated in group discussion about the transfer raised their production rate after the transfer; those who were simply notified about it lowered their production rate. Apparently the standards changed in response to the changes in the relation of the group to its environment.

Although group standards can be changed,

the more striking characteristic about them is their enduring quality and the fact that they may be the sources of resistance to change in group practices. This has led to a number of experimental demonstrations in which it has been shown that if an entire group makes a decision about some change in behavior which the members will make, the agreed-upon behavior will occur even when the members are away from the group. Group decisions have been shown to be more effective than other methods in stimulating behavior changes to such things as feeding babies orange juice, increasing the production of pajamas, improving the reliability of merit ratings, examining breasts for cancer, serving liver, kidneys, and brains or whole wheat bread. Lewin (22) has described the results from a number of such demonstrations, showing that change is more likely to occur when a group takes "the pledge" as a group than when individuals make promises to themselves alone.

It appears, then, that group decisions are more effective in changing behavior than lectures or group discussion without any decision, but it is not entirely clear what it is that makes them work. It has been assumed by some that public commitment to carry through the behavior decided upon by the group creates an awareness of the expectations that the members had for one another, thus creating forces on each member to comply with these widely felt sentiments. The pressures for uniformity thus serve to develop a group standard. In line with Festinger's theory briefly described in Chapter 14, one would assume that more cohesive groups would develop stronger standards as a result of a group decision. This notion, however, has never been adequately tested. Other conditions, described earlier, serving to strengthen pressures to uniformity would also heighten the impact of the group decisions.

A study by Bennett (3) casts doubt on the importance of public commitment in group decisions. She used small groups that met for a brief period. Comparing the results of several methods of influence, she finds that the group discussion and the public commitment aspects of group decisions do not significantly increase the probability that the behavior agreed upon by the group will be carried out. The more important features are the fact that a decision has been made and the degree to which group consensus is obtained. These two variables account for most of the change brought about

by group decision. The finding concerning the importance of group consensus supports the notion that group pressures toward uniformity may be stronger when there is unanimity on a proposal.

In a theoretical analysis of pressures to uniformity, Lewin (22) employed the concept of "quasi-stationary equilibrium." He proposed that a group standard consists of a field of forces whose distribution is such that any deviation from the level of the standard encounters forces whose effect is to bring about a return to that level. He concludes that a successful change of behavior governed by a group standard includes three aspects: "unfreezing" the existing field of forces, moving to a new level of equilibrium, and "freezing" group life on the new level. Although Lewin did not give a detailed description of the processes involved in each of these phases, his general approach serves to identify certain critical aspects of the process by which group standards change.

OVERVIEW OF RESEARCH REPORTED IN PART THREE

The research on uniformity in groups has been conducted in a wide variety of ways and places. The work reported in this section illustrates the approach, given emphasis in earlier pages, in which standards have instrumental value for group members and are supported by interpersonal pressures toward uniformity.

A field study of standards in informal groups, which provided the impetus for several of the investigations included in later chapters, is reported by Festinger, Schachter, and Back (Chap. 12). By means of interviews, they determined the cohesiveness of the various courts and buildings in two housing projects and the attitudes of the residents toward a tenant's organization. They show that the cohesive courts are likely to have more uniformity of attitude toward the organization and more uniformity of behavior in the degree to which they participate in the organization. One of the important findings is that persons who are deviant from the standards within the court are less likely to be accepted as friends by the rest of the persons living there.

The latter finding was subject to more rigorous study in a laboratory experiment by Schachter (Chap. 13). He invited students to join a club organized to discuss topics of lively interest. Three paid participants attended each meeting, of whom two conformed to the beliefs of the group and one took a clearly deviant position. We noted earlier in the present chapter that the deviant was rejected while the other two participants were accepted. Rejection of the deviant was stronger in groups with high cohesiveness and where his deviancy concerned matters highly relevant to the purposes of the group.

In Chapter 14, Festinger develops the theory on which the two studies described previously were based and explains how cohesiveness of a group will determine the power that a group has in requiring uniformity among the members.

In Chapter 15, Schachter, Ellertson, McBride, and Gregory examine the way in which cohesiveness affects group productivity. They maintain that cohesiveness as such does not necessarily increase or decrease the productivity of a group. Rather, cohesiveness serves to heighten group members' susceptibility to influence from one another. Thus, if the predominant influences are to restrict production, cohesiveness will tend to heighten these influences and will lower productivity. If, on the other hand, the group influences are in the opposite direction, cohesiveness will heighten productivity.

Converse and Campbell demonstrate in Chapter 16 that the theory proposed by the preceding writers can be usefully employed in explaining voting behavior and identification in political parties. Using data obtained in a national sample survey of voting preferences, they report that persons who are most identified with their party are most likely to vote in accordance with the party's plans, and they further observe that the impact of political matters upon the standards of nonpolitical groups depends upon the degree to which political issues are relevant for these groups.

References

1. Asch, S. Effects of group pressure upon the modification and distortion of judgments. In H. Guetzkow (Ed.), *Groups, leadership, and men.* Pittsburgh: Carnegie Press, 1951.
2. Asch, S. *Social psychology.* New York: Prentice-Hall, 1952.
3. Bennett, E. Discussion, decision, commitment, and consensus in "group decision." *Human Relations,* 1955, **21,** 251–273.
4. Berkowitz, L. Cognitive dissonance and communication preferences. *Human Relations,* 1965, **18,** 361–372.
5. Berkowitz, L., & Howard, R. Reactions to opinion deviates as affected by affiliation need and group member interdependence, *Sociometry,* 1959, **22,** 81–91.
6. Brodbeck, M. Role of the small group in mediating the effects of propaganda. *Journal of Abnormal and Social Psychology,* 1956, **52,** 166–170.
7. Burns, T. The reference of conduct in small groups: Cliques and cabals in occupational milieux. *Human Relations,* 1955, **8,** 467–486.
8. Cohen, A. K. *Delinquent boys.* Glencoe, Ill.: Free Press, 1955.
9. Crutchfield, R. Conformity and character. *The American Psychologist,* 1955, **10,** 191–198.
10. Darley, J. Fear and social comparison as determinants of conformity behavior. *Journal of Personality and Social Psychology,* 1966, **4,** 73–78.
11. Deutsch, M., & Gerard, H. A study of normative and informational social influences upon individual judgment. *Journal of Abnormal and Social Psychology,* 1955, **51,** 629–636.
12. Emerson, R. Deviation and rejection: An experimental replication. *American Sociological Review,* 1954, **19,** 688–693.
13. Festinger, L. A theory of social comparison processes. *Human Relations,* 1954, **7,** 117–140.
14. French, J. R. P., Jr. Organized and unorganized groups under fear and frustration. *Univ. of Iowa Studies in Child Welfare,* 1944, **20,** 231–308.
15. Gerard, H. The anchorage of opinions in face-to-face groups. *Human Relations,* 1954, **7,** 313–325.
16. Gross, N., Mason, W., & McEachern, A. *Explorations in role analysis.* New York: Wiley, 1958.

17. Hall, R. Social influence in the aircraft commander's role. *American Sociological Review,* 1955, **20,** 292–299.

18. Hollander, E. Conformity, status, and idiosyncrasy credit. *Psychological Review,* 1958, **65,** 117–127.

19. Jacobs, R., & Campbell, D. The perpetuation of an arbitrary tradition through several generations of a laboratory microculture. *Journal of Abnormal and Social Psychology,* 1961, **62,** 649–659.

20. Kelley, H. Salience of membership and resistance to change of group anchored attitudes. *Human Relations,* 1955, **8,** 275–289.

21. Kennedy, John F. *Profiles in courage.* New York: Harper, 1955.

22. Lewin, K. Frontiers in group dynamics. *Human Relations,* 1947, **1,** 5–42.

23. Pepitone, A., & Wilpizeski, C. Some consequences of experimental rejection. *Journal of Abnormal and Social Psychology,* 1960, **60,** 359–364.

24. Sampson, E. E., & Brandon, A. The effects of role and opinion deviation on small group behavior. *Sociometry,* 1964, **27,** 261–281.

25. Schachter, S. *The psychology of affiliation.* Stanford: Stanford Univ. Press, 1959.

26. Schachter, S., *et al.* Cross-cultural experiments on threat and rejection. *Human Relations,* 1954, **7,** 403–439.

27. Scott, W. A. *Values and organizations.* Chicago: Rand McNally, 1965.

28. Sherif, M. *The psychology of social norms.* New York: Harper, 1936.

29. Stock, D., Whitman, R., & Lieberman, M. The deviant member in therapy groups. *Human Relations,* 1958, **11,** 341–371.

30. Survey Research Center. *Participation in voluntary committees.* Ann Arbor, Mich.: Institute for Social Research, 1956.

31. White, W. S. Who really runs the senate? *Harper's Magazine,* 1956, **213,** 35–40.

32. Yinger, J. M. Contraculture and subculture. *American Sociological Review,* 1960, **25,** 625–635.

33. Ziller, R., Behringer, R., & Jansen, M. The newcomer in open and closed groups. *Journal of Applied Psychology,* 1961, **45,** 55–58.

12

Operation of Group Standards

LEON FESTINGER, STANLEY SCHACHTER, AND KURT BACK

The term *group standard,* or *group norm,* has been used freely either to describe or to explain the rather well substantiated finding that members of the same face-to-face group exhibit relative uniformity with respect to specified opinions and modes of behavior. The use of the term, whether in a descriptive or an explanatory manner, has generally carried with it the meaning that this observed uniformity derives in some manner from influences which the group is able to exert over its members. The fact that members of some social set all have relatively similar tastes in, for example, selecting recreational activities, has generally been explained on the basis of interindividual or group influences rather than on the basis of similar circumstances producing similar but independent reactions in a number of people.

There is no question any longer that individuals and groups do exert influences on others which can and do result in uniform opinions and behavior patterns. There have been many studies which have demonstrated the existence and importance of this phenomenon. The classic experiment by Sherif (3) clearly demonstrated that, at least in a situation which was almost completely unstructured, the individual was virtually entirely dependent upon the group for forming a stable mode of response. The strength of the group influence was plainly sufficient to override most individual factors.

It has also been shown, by a series of independent studies (1), that people's aspirations and goal-setting behavior are strongly influenced by information they possess about how others behave and their relationship to these others. All of these influences produce changes in the individual's behavior which result in his being more similar to other members of the group to which he feels he belongs.

Condensed from Chapters 5 and 6 of the book by the same authors, entitled *Social pressures in informal groups.* New York: Harper, 1950. Reprinted by permission of the authors and Harper & Row.

Once we depart from the well-controlled laboratory situation it is no longer easy to claim unequivocally that observed uniformity is due to group influence. Newcomb (2), for example, in his study of a college community which had a reputation for being liberal found that students consistently became more liberal with increasing length of attendance at the college. It is possible plausibly to maintain that these changing attitudes resulted from group pressures and influences once the student became a member of the community. It would also, however, be possible to maintain that these changes occurred in different people independently as a result of the similar experiences, curricular and otherwise, to which they were all subjected in the rather unique college. The demonstration that a group standard existed would indeed be difficult. Such demonstration would have to rest upon a series of empirical facts concerning the means by which the group enforces the standard, the relation between the pattern of conformity and the group structure, and the relationship to the group of members who deviate from the standard.

The study to be reported here undertook to investigate the nature and operation of group standards in two housing projects. These two projects, Westgate and Westgate West, were occupied by families of students of the Massachusetts Institute of Technology. The homes in Westgate were houses arranged in U-shaped courts. Those in Westgate West were apartments in rows of two-story barracklike structures. The same tenants' organization served both projects. The court in Westgate, and the building in Westgate West, had become the unit of social life in these projects by the time of the study. Friendship groups formed mainly within the court and within the building. The backgrounds and interests of the residents were relatively homogeneous throughout both projects and the assignment of houses or apartments to particular people had not been made on any kind of selective basis. It was also clear that there had been no differential treatment of courts or of buildings. The study of group standards might consequently be pursued fruitfully by carefully examining the reasons for differences in behavior among these social units where such differences emerged.

It was found that differences between courts did exist to a rather marked extent on matters concerning the Westgate tenants' organization. This organization was, at least potentially, of equal relevance and importance to all residents of Westgate and of Westgate West, and all residents were urged to support it. Representation in the Westgate Council was on the basis of courts and buildings and consequently called for action from each court and each building. Yet, in spite of this equality of relevance, some courts and buildings supported the organization, others were overtly hostile, while still others were indifferent. We shall proceed to examine the determinants of these differences among courts and among buildings to see whether group standards were or were not operating and, if they were, how they made themselves effective.

ATTITUDES TOWARD THE WESTGATE COUNCIL

By May of 1947, when interview data concerning the attitudes of residents toward the Westgate organization were collected, the Council had almost completed the first semester of active existence. Since the turnover in residents occurred mainly at the break between semesters, practically all residents who were living there at the time of the interview had been living in the project when the Council started its active program.

All of the 100 Westgate families and 166 of the 170 Westgate West families were asked, as part of a larger interview, "We understand there is a tenants' organization here. What do you think of it? Are you active in it?" The interviewers were instructed to follow these questions with nondirective probes until they were satisfied that they had obtained an adequate picture of the attitude toward the organization and the degree and kind of participation in its activities. These data were then categorized in the following way:

ATTITUDES TOWARD THE ORGANIZATION

Favorable. People who considered the organization primarily a good thing. Usually they endorsed both the idea of organization as such and some aims of the Council. Statements ranged from warm approval, "I am definitely in favor of it. It's a worth-while project. It's functioning well," to a vaguely approving, "It's all right."

Neutral. People who mentioned specific good and bad points about the organization so that no definitely favorable or unfavorable attitude could be assigned. In effect, this category included border-line people who had some basic attitude, but saw many points contrary to it. Examples are "I guess it's all right if they accomplish something—I don't think they have as yet." "It's a good idea, but there are not too many problems for the community to deal with."

Apathetic. People who said they had not been interested enough to find out anything about the organization. In a sense this is a mildly unfavorable attitude—the organization did not concern them. On the other hand, they did not express any directly unfavorable opinion: "Don't know anything about it. Haven't been to any of the meetings or anything. Not knowing, I wouldn't want to say anything."

Unfavorable. People who expressed a definitely unfavorable opinion about the organization, saying that it was a waste of time, that the people in it were objectionable, that they never would achieve anything. "A large majority of the members are reactionary. They give no attention to wider aspects." "It's unnecessary and highschoolish."

ACTIVITIES IN THE ORGANIZATION

Active Leader. People who took a definite part in the activities of the Council as a whole, as representatives, committee members, or doing volunteer work. "We've been to meetings as delegates two or three times. I volunteered as bartender for the block party." "I am one of the court representatives. I'm a member of the welcoming committee greeting new residents."

Active Follower. People who, though not active in the sense of the previous category, had attended more than one court meeting. They cooperated with the Council as it was set up on the court level. They went to the meetings in which the representatives were elected. They listened to the representatives' reports of the Council's actions and gave their suggestions and complaints to be taken up in the next meeting. They were, therefore, a necessary working part of the organization, although they took no part in the workings of the Council as such. "We have been to the building meetings; that's as far as it goes." "We go to the meetings. Everybody goes to them."

Inactive. People who did not make any effort to keep in contact with the organization. This included both the people who belonged (that is, they considered themselves represented by the Council) and those who did not feel even a formal connection with the Council. From the point of view of actual behavior, these two groups are indistinguishable. "To be truthful, I'm not active. Splendid idea, but I'm too busy." The principal answer from this group was a curt "No." These people did not even attend court meetings.

The questions about attitudes and activity measure two different aspects of a person's relation to the organization. His attitude may stem from a variety of interests and beliefs. He may view the Council as a way of having certain needs satisfied, as a way to meet his fellow tenants, as unrelated to his needs, or as a childish pastime. It is clear that some of these ways of looking at the Council will lead more readily to activity than others. But a resident's actual activity will also depend on other factors—whether he has time, whether a neighbor draws him into some work, whether he sees something that he personally can do. It is therefore possible that attitude and activity may occur together in all combinations, although some are more likely than others. They are distinct, though correlated, variables.

PATTERNS OF ATTITUDE AND ACTIVITY

There were differences from one court to another in attitude toward and activity in the tenants' organization. This implies that within any one court there was relative homogeneity with respect to both of these factors. In the extreme case, where all members of a court coincided exactly on both of these dimensions, the demonstration of homogeneity would be a simple matter. This extreme case does not occur, of course, and some method must be devised for describing the pattern within any court both with respect to the content of the pattern and the degree of homogeneity. That is, is it a favorable and active court or is it an unfavorable and inactive court? Do 80% of the court members show this behavior and attitude combination, or do only 60% of the court members show it?

It seemed feasible, from the nature of the data, to distinguish four possible types of court patterns: namely, favorable-active, favorable-inactive, unfavorable-active, and unfavorable-inactive. Once it was determined in which of these categories a court was located, the number of people in the court who conformed to or deviated from the court pattern could then be easily computed. When this was done it would be possible to proceed to a careful examination of whether or not the observed degree of homogeneity within courts was worthy of note and whether or not it could be attributed to the existence of group standards.

If only these four types of patterns are to be distinguished we must, for this purpose, do some additional combining of the original categories into which the data were classified. This presents no problem for the activity dimension. Clearly the active leader and active follower categories should both be called active, but the combination of the attitude categories presents somewhat more of a problem. The extreme categories, favorable and unfavorable, clearly fall into their proper place. The categories of apathetic and neutral are not quite so clear. It was reasoned that the apathetic people were at least mildly unfavorable to the organization, since they either did not care to know about it or else had simply remained sufficiently out of things not to have heard about what was going on. On the basis of this reasoning, the apathetic people were classed as unfavorable.

The few residents who were classified as neutral were really borderline cases. To some extent they were favorable and to some extent unfavorable. Whatever the court pattern happens to be, in this sense they both conform to and deviate from it on the attitude dimension. In accordance with this view, the neutral people were not considered in determining the court pattern. In any event there were too few people thus categorized to have affected this determination much. Once the court pattern was determined, these neutrals were regarded as conformers if they fell into the proper activity category and were, of course, considered deviates if they did not.

We shall describe the method used for determining the court pattern by using Tolman Court as an example. Looking first at the activity dimension, we found that twelve residents were active and only one was not. On the attitude dimension, nine residents were favorable and two were unfavorable. The classification of this court, then, is "favorable-active." In this case, following our procedure for neutrals, we shall consider anybody who

was neutral and active as conforming to the group standard. Of the two neutrals in the court, one followed the group standard and the other did not. The conformers include everybody who was favorable or neutral and active. There were ten conformers and three deviates from the pattern.

A different type of pattern is shown in Main Court. Here six of the seven residents were inactive, while five were either apathetic or unfavorable. The pattern is therefore "unfavorable-inactive." As the only neutral resident was active, he cannot be considered as conforming to the pattern; he and the favorable inactive resident were deviates. The five inactive residents, who were either apathetic or unfavorable, conformed to the pattern.

This procedure was carried out for each of the nine Westgate courts and for each of the seventeen Westgate West buildings. In Westgate, five of the courts showed a favorable-active pattern, one court showed a favorable-inactive pattern, and three courts showed an unfavorable-inactive pattern. Wide differences did exist among the courts. Also, within each court there was relative homogeneity. Five of the nine courts had a small proportion of deviates. In all but one of the courts the majority conformed to the court pattern.

In Westgate West the degree of homogeneity within the building was perhaps even more striking. Only four of the seventeen buildings had as many as 40% deviates from the building pattern, and nine of the buildings had only one or two such deviates. In contrast to Westgate, however, there were no marked differences among the patterns in different buildings. Thirteen of the buildings had favorable-active patterns and four of them had favorable-inactive patterns. There were no buildings with an unfavorable pattern. While in Westgate there was evidence for homogeneity within the court, and heterogeneity among the courts, in Westgate West there seems to have been the same amount of homogeneity among buildings as was found within the building.

If we combine all courts into an over-all Westgate pattern, and all buildings into an over-all Westgate West pattern, this difference between the projects emerges even more clearly. These over-all patterns for the two projects are shown in Table 1. In Westgate, no homogeneous over-all pattern exists. Favorable attitudes were displayed by 54% of the residents, unfavorable or apathetic attitudes by 33%, while 49% were active and 51% inactive.

TABLE 1.   *Attitude-Activity Distribution (Percentages)*[a]

		Active Leaders	Active Followers	Inactive	Unclassified	Total
		Westgate ($N = 100$)				
Favorable		22	14	18		54
Neutral		2	6	4		12
Apathetic			1	15		16
Unfavorable		2	2	13		17
Unclassified				1		1
	Total	26	23	51		100
		Westgate West ($N = 166$)				
Favorable		16	38	24	1	79
Neutral			2	1		3
Apathetic		1	2	8		11
Unfavorable		1		3		4
Unclassified			2	1		3
	Total	18	44	37	1	100

[a] Significance of difference between Westgate and Westgate West: Attitude $x^2 = 37.86$; $p = .01$ Activity $x^2 = 12.42$; $p = .01$.

If we use the same criteria for determining the over-all pattern here as was used for the individual courts, we would conclude that Westgate had a favorable-inactive pattern from which 78% of the residents deviated. Clearly, the greatest concentrations were in the favorable-active and the unfavorable-inactive quadrants. Even if we depart from our rigorous method of determining patterns and regard the pattern in Westgate as favorable-active, we still find that a majority (56%) of the residents were deviates.

The situation in Westgate West is clearly different. Here 79% of the residents were favorable and only 15% were unfavorable or apathetic, while 62% of the residents were active and 37% were inactive. The over-all pattern is favorable-active. Most of the deviation that did occur from this pattern was on the activity dimension, with little deviation on the attitude dimension.

What may we conclude from this analysis of the patterns within Westgate and within Westgate West? Do we as yet have any evidence for asserting the existence or nonexistence of group standards? With regard to Westgate we can clearly say that there was no group standard for the project as a whole. There were obviously opposing subgroups within Westgate with regard to both attitude and activity. Can one, however, maintain that there were group standards within each court? At this point this conclusion would seem plausible, although it is by no means unequivocally demonstrated. We must, however, find some explanation why different courts, each composed of the same kinds of people in similar circumstances, reacted so differently from each other toward the organization and why, in spite of different reactions from different courts, there was relatively homogeneous behavior within each court. We at least are led to suspect that group standards or group norms were operating.

In Westgate West, however, we cannot come to the same conclusions. Here it is possible that a group standard existed for the project as a whole; it is possible that group standards existed within each building; and it is possible that no group standards or norms existed at all, but that the obtained high degree of uniformity was due to similar independent reactions of the residents to the same state of affairs. As we have pointed out before, the hypothesis that the uniformity in Westgate West resulted from similar independent reactions of the residents seems probable on the basis of several considerations: unlike the residents of Westgate, who had been living there up to fifteen months and had had four months' actual experience with the organization, the residents of Westgate West were all relative newcomers. The oldest residents of Westgate West had only been living there about five months, and their contact with the Westgate organization had been limited. It was only about one month prior to the collection of these data that Westgate West actually joined the organization. We might expect, then, that in Westgate West, where the social groupings had not had time to form into cohesive units, and where the contact with the tenants' organization was only recent, group norms would not have developed to any considerable degree. The tenants, however, all in the same situation and pretty much the same kinds of people, tended individually to react favorably to the organization.

THE EVIDENCE FOR GROUP STANDARDS

On the basis of an examination of the actual distribution of conformity to and deviation from patterns of majority behavior, we have arrived at hypotheses concerning the reasons behind the observed degree of uniformity. It has seemed reasonable to suppose that group standards existed in the Westgate courts but that none existed in Westgate West. If this is true, there should be other differences between these two projects which would support these hypotheses. One derivation may immediately be made. If the behavior in Westgate was determined largely by group influences while the behavior in Westgate West was determined largely by individual reactions, then individual differences on relevant factors should show more relationship to attitude and activity in Westgate West than in Westgate.

The personal reasons which residents of the two projects gave for their attitudes, and for whether or not they participated in the activities of the organization, were numerous and varied. Some people had special interests which were aided by the organization; some did not believe in organized activities in general; some said they had no time; some felt that their efforts would be fruitless for the short time that remained for them to stay in the project. All these factors, and others of the same kind, were influences acting on the individual, independently of the group to which he belonged. It would have been desirable, but almost impossible, to obtain reliable indi-

cations as to whether or not each of these factors was operating on a particular individual.

Reliable data are at hand, however, concerning the length of time they expected to remain in the project. This, of course, coincided with the length of time they expected to remain in school and was fairly frequently mentioned as a reason for not participating in the activities of the tenants' organization. These data reveal that there was hardly any difference in attitude between long-term and short-term residents in either Westgate or Westgate West.

The breakdown by activity tells a different story. In Westgate, again, little difference was found. The shortest time group—those moving out in June—could not be affected by any medium or long-range program of the Council. In spite of this, 9 out of 16 cooperated with the Council. The group expecting the longest residence—those who intended to stay at least for a year and were frequently indefinite about how much longer—cooperated even a little less with the Council; only 14 out of 29 fell into these categories. The differences are not statistically significant.

In the activity ratings of the Westgate West residents, however, we find that length of expected residence made a difference. Among the short-term residents, 50% were actively cooperating with the Council, while 72% of the long-term residents were. The median expected residence for the active leaders was 17 months; for the inactive residents 12 months. These differences are significant at the 5% level.

We thus find our derivation borne out. The data support our hypotheses concerning the difference between Westgate and Westgate West. In Westgate West, where individuals were reacting more or less independently in terms of their own needs and preferences, we find a significant and appreciable degree of relationship between how much longer they expected to stay in the project and whether or not they became active in the affairs of the tenants' organization. In Westgate, group influences were important. A major determinant of an individual's activity was whether or not others in his group were active. There was, consequently, no relationship at all between how long one expected to stay there, or how much benefit one would derive from the organizational activities, and whether or not one

TABLE 2.   *Cohesiveness of Court and Strength of Group Standard (Westgate)*

Court	N of Residents	% Deviates	Choices in Court $\frac{\text{Choices in Court}}{\text{Total Choices}}$	Choices in Court $-\frac{1}{2}$ Pairs $\frac{\text{Choices in Court} - \frac{1}{2}\text{ Pairs}}{\text{Total Choices}}$
Tolman	13	23	.62	.529
Howe	13	23	.63	.500
Rotch	8	25	.55	.523
Richards	7	29	.47	.433
Main	7	29	.67	.527
Freeman	13	38	.48	.419
Williams	13	46	.53	.447
Miller	13	46	.56	.485
Carson	13	54	.48	.403
	R.O. correlation with % deviates		−.53	−.74
	t [a]		1.65	2.92
	p		.15	.02

[a] Testing significance of file and rank order correlation as suggested by M. G. Kendall, *The advanced theory of statistics.* Vol. I. London: Charles Griffin and Co., 1943, p. 401.

became active. We may reaffirm our hypotheses with somewhat more confidence now and look for the next testable derivation which we can make.

To be able to create and maintain group standards, a group must have power over its members. This power, the ability to induce forces on its members, has been called cohesiveness. If the group uses this power to make the members think and act in the same way, that is, if there are group standards, the homogeneity of the attitude and activity patterns should be related to the cohesiveness of the group. Correspondingly, if no relation exists between cohesiveness and homogeneity of the pattern, the group does not use its power to induce the members to conform, and we may take it as indicative of the absence of group standards.

The power of a group may be measured by the attractiveness of the group for the members. If a person wants to stay in a group, he will be susceptible to influences coming from the group, and he will be willing to conform to the rules which the group sets up.

The courts and buildings in Westgate and Westgate West were mainly social groups. The attractiveness of the group may, therefore, be measured by the friendships formed within the group. If residents had most of their friends within the court, the group was more attractive to them than if they had few friends within the court. The former situation will imply a more cohesive court, which should be

able to induce stronger forces on its members. This should result in greater homogeneity within the more cohesive court than within the less cohesive one.

The necessary measures for determining the relationship between the cohesiveness of the court and the effectiveness of the group standard are easily obtained. Sociometric data from a question regarding who the residents saw most of socially may be used here. Thus, if the members of one court give a total of 30 choices, 18 of which are given to others in their own court, the percentage of "in-court" choices is 60. This court is then considered more cohesive than some other court which gives a total of 32 choices, only 16 of which are to others in the same court. The homogeneity of the court, or how effective the group standard is, may be measured simply by the percentage of members of the court who deviate from the court pattern. The more effective the group standard and the more homogeneous the court, the lower will be the percentage of members who deviate. The second and third columns of Tables 2 and 3 show the percentage of deviates and the proportion of "in-court" choices for each court in Westgate and for each building in Westgate West.

From our hypotheses concerning the existence of group standards in the Westgate courts and the absence of group standards in the Westgate West buildings, we would expect to find an appreciable negative correlation in Westgate and no correlation in West-

TABLE 3. *Cohesiveness of Building and Strength of Group Standard (Westgate West)*

Building	% Deviates	Choices in Building Total Choices	Choices in Building − ½ Pairs Total Choices
211–20	10	.58	.50
221–30	10	.66	.59
201–10	11	.60	.54
231–40	20	.80	.64
241–50	20	.70	.61
251–60	20	.74	.63
281–90	20	.80	.68
311–20	20	.66	.53
261–70	25	.57	.46
271–80	30	.47	.38
341–50	30	.62	.50
351–60	30	.85	.76
321–30	33	.62	.52
361–70	40	.67	.56
291–300	50	.59	.50
301–10	50	.72	.64
331–40	70	.42	.35
R.O. correlation with % deviates		− .20	− .27
t		.79	1.09
p		not significant	

gate West between the percentage of deviates and the proportion of "in-court" choices. In Table 2 it may be seen that the correlation is − .53 in Westgate. Here, the more cohesive the court (that is, the greater the proportion of "in-court" choices) the smaller the proportion of people who deviated from the court standard. As we expected, this correlation is virtually zero in Westgate West (Table 3). Here the proportion of people who deviated from the building pattern had little or nothing to do with the cohesiveness of the building group.

The measure of cohesiveness which we have used may, however, be considerably improved. The major uncertainty in the measure, as it stands, lies in our inability to distinguish between the cohesiveness of the whole group and the cohesiveness of subgroups. For example, a group of eight people all making choices within the group might or might not have high cohesiveness as a total group. As an extreme illustration, there conceivably might be two subgroups of four people each, every member within each subgroup choosing every other member, but without any choices at all between the subgroups. In this case each of the subgroups may have great cohesiveness, but the cohesiveness of the group as a whole would be low. Similarly, if in a group of eight or ten people there is a subgroup of three, the total group would be less cohesive than if no subgroup existed. It appears that if a strongly knit subgroup includes a large majority of the group, the cohesiveness of the whole group may still be high.

This effect of tendencies toward subgroup formation may be taken into account in our measure by correcting for the number of mutual choices which occurred. If there were no tendencies at all toward subgroup formation within a group, then the number of mutual choices which we would expect to occur would be quite low. In a group of ten people with each person giving, say, two choices within the group, we would only expect to obtain two mutual choices in the complete absence of tendencies toward subgroup or pair formation. As the tendencies toward subgroup formation increase, we shall expect to find more and more mutual choices. Thus, the existence of mutual choices to some extent decreases the cohesiveness of the group as a whole.

We may check further on whether or not this relationship was a property of the group as a whole. A corrected measure of cohesiveness, obtained by subtracting half of the number of mutual pairs of choices, is certainly meaningful only as a measure of the group as a whole. The fact that mutual choices occurred certainly does not detract from the personal attractiveness of the individuals involved in these mutual choices. We should then expect the correlation with the measure of prestige of the subgroup to increase when the corrected measure of cohesiveness is used. This correlation in Westgate is − .74, representing an appreciable increase in relationship. In Westgate West, where the buildings did not constitute really functional social units, the correlation remains unchanged—still very close to zero.

THE SOCIAL STATUS OF THE DEVIATE

What are the conditions which produce deviates? When pressures and influences are being exerted on people to adopt a certain way of thinking or a certain pattern of behavior, some people conform quite readily while others are able entirely to resist these influences. The mere knowledge that these "individual differences" exist does not explain the reasons for them or the factors which are responsible for producing deviates. To learn this, we must examine the means by which group influences may be resisted.

The pressure which a group exerts on its members may be overt and sometimes even formalized. Laws, rules, mores, etiquette, and so on exemplify some of these overt pressures. The pressures which induce men to open doors for women, to dress in certain special ways on certain special occasions, or to enter their fathers' businesses are all overt and recognized. It is likely, of course, that before a group norm or standard can become thus openly formalized it must be in existence for a long time, or else must be of such a nature that deviation from the standard is harmful to the group. Such open pressures are generally also accompanied by open punishment for deviation in the form of censure, overt disapproval, or even rejection from the group.

On the other hand, the pressures which a group exerts on its members may be subtle and difficult to locate. The weight of others' opinions, the gradual change in one's ideas of what is the "normal" thing to do simply because everyone else does it, the mutual influences of people who share their ideas and

their attitudes, also serve effectively as pressures toward conformity with the behavior pattern of the group. Under these circumstances the consequences of nonconformity are also more subtle. These consequences may merely be a tendency to prefer those people who are not "different."

There is no indication that in Westgate there was any overt or formalized pressure on court members to conform to the court standard. Many of the residents realized that the people in their court were different from the people in some other court, but the influences which created and maintained these differences among courts were indirect and nonovert. Members of the courts were being influenced in their opinions and behavior merely by virtue of their association with others in their courts, without any formalized "group intent" to influence.

The strength of the influence which the group can exert in this manner depends partly upon the attractiveness of the group for the member and partly on the degree to which the member is in communication with others in the group. No matter how attractive the group is to a particular person, it will be impossible for the group to exert any influence on him if he is never in communication with the group. We may now examine some of the conditions under which individuals will be able to resist these influences.

1. *The group may not be sufficiently attractive to the member.* Under these circumstances, the relatively weak influence which the group exerts cannot overcome personal considerations which may happen to be contrary to the group standard. An example will illustrate this phenomenon:

(*Mr. and Mrs. C, in Williams Court.*) We don't have any opinion at all about the organization. We're bad ones for you to interview. We have no need for an organization because we're pretty happy at home. We're socially self-sufficient. Others in the court feel it is wonderful and we discovered many that felt that way. We have friends in this and other courts but our main interests are in the home.

2. *There may not be sufficient communication between the member and others in the group.* Under these conditions the pressures from the group are simply not brought to bear on the member although, if they had been

exerted, they might have been very effective. In such instances the deviate may not even be aware of the fact that he is different from most of the others in his group. An example of this type of deviate follows:

(*Mr. and Mrs. S, in Freeman Court.*) The organization is a good idea, but the trouble with people like us is that we don't have time. That's why we haven't had anything to do with it. I think it's the consensus of opinion that people don't have the time. [Actually the majority of the people in the court were active.] There are wonderful people living here, but it seems peculiar to Westgate that people are hard to get to know. A lot of people come here expecting to make friends without any trouble, and then find it isn't so easy. It would be a good thing if the organization helped people to get acquainted.

3. *The influence of some other group to which the people belong may be stronger than the influence which the court group is able to exert on them.* Under these conditions the person who appears as a deviate is a deviate only because we have chosen, somewhat arbitrarily, to call him a member of the court group. He does deviate from his own court, but he conforms to some other group to which he actually feels he belongs. Such a group may, of course, be outside of Westgate altogether. There are instances, however, of people belonging to groups other than their own court, but still within the limits of Westgate:

(*Mr. and Mrs. M, in Carson Court.*) We think the organization is fine and Mrs. M is the chairman of the social committee which is holding its first big event tomorrow night. I don't see much of the others in this court. My real friends are in the next court over there, in Tolman Court. There are only two people living in this court that do anything for the organization, myself and one other person. It's generally understood that the others have different interests. The people in Tolman Court are more active. Carson Court people aren't as sociable as people in Tolman Court.

THE DEVIATE IN WESTGATE

These three types of conditions do, then, appear to produce deviates; at least we were able to locate deviates who seemed to exhibit such patterns of relationship between them-

selves and the group. If these are the major factors which make for nonconformity, we should also be able to demonstrate their relevance for all of the deviates rather than for a few selected examples. The two variables, attractiveness of the group for the member and amount of communication between the member and the group, should be reflected in the sociometric choices which people gave and received. We should expect that deviates would give fewer choices to others in their court and would receive fewer choices from them. Whether this happened because they were not in full communication with the group or because the group was not attractive to them, the result in the sociometric choices should be essentially the same—the deviates should be sociometric isolates in their court.

TABLE 4. *Average Number of "In-Court" Choices of Deviates and Conformers in Westgate*

	N	Choices Given	Choices Received
Deviates	36	1.25	1.11
Conformers	64	1.53	1.61

Table 4 shows the average number of "in court" choices given and received by the 36 deviates and the 64 conformers in Westgate. It is readily apparent that the deviates were more isolated sociometrically than were the conformers. They both gave and received fewer choices than did the conformers.[1] Moreover, the conformers tended to receive more choices than they gave, while the deviates tended to receive fewer choices than they gave. Deviates tended to choose conformers more than conformers chose deviates. This might be called relative rejection by the conformers.

Deviate status, then, was accompanied by a smaller degree of association with others in the court. It is still possible, however, that these deviates were not true isolates, but merely members of groups other than the court group.

---

[1] The significance of the differences in this and the following tables was computed by taking the means for each court and comparing the distributions of these means. This was done because the effects of group standards made the group, not the individual, the unit of sampling. This difference is significant at the 7% level of confidence for choices given. Significance is at the 17% level of confidence for choices received.

In our case studies we saw two examples of this sort. An examination of all sociometric choices exchanged with people outside the court, however, reveals that this was not true of the deviates as a whole. Table 5 shows the average number of "out-court" choices given and received by the deviates and conformers. It is clear that the deviates, in the main, were not members of groups other than those of their own court. They gave only as many choices to people outside their own court as did the conformers, but received considerably fewer choices from outside than the conformers.[2] We must conclude that these deviates, who had fewer associations within their own court, also had fewer associations with others in Westgate—at least, insofar as this is reflected by the number of choices they received.

TABLE 5.   *Average Number of "Out-Court" Choices of Deviates and Conformers in Westgate*

	N	Choices Given	Choices Received
Deviates	36	1.14	.89
Conformers	64	1.16	1.55

Choices given by deviates to people outside their own court tended to be given to the conformers in other courts. These conformers tended not to reciprocate the choices. The deviate, who was perceived as being different from the others in his court, was not as often chosen by outsiders. This is consistent with our knowledge that the court is perceived as the basis for social grouping in Westgate. People who were on the fringes of their own group were also on the fringe of social life between courts. While conformers in Westgate received an average of 3.16 choices from others, the deviates received an average of only 2.00 such choices. The deviates were relative isolates. It is clear that this isolation was not wholly voluntary on the part of the deviates, since they gave only slightly fewer choices than the conformers.

It is possible to examine the situation of the deviate more closely if we restrict ourselves to the six full-size courts in Westgate. Ten of the houses in these six courts faced onto the street rather than into the courtyard area, so that the

people living in these houses had fewer contacts with others in the court. Of the other 68 people living in these courts only 34% were deviates, while 7 of the 10 corner-house residents were deviates. It appears that the isolated geographical position in which these 10 found themselves, and the resultant lack of contact between them and the rest of the court, made it difficult for the court to exert influence on them. The lack of contact suggests that mainly chance factors would determine whether they would show the pattern of attitude and behavior that had become the standard in the court.

Table 6 shows the "in-court" choices for these six full-size courts with the corner-house deviates separated from the others. The lack of contact between the court and the deviates in these corner houses is readily apparent. They both gave and received only about one-third as many choices as did the others in the court.[3] It is not surprising that they had remained uninfluenced by the group standard in their particular court.

TABLE 6.   *Average Number of "In-Court" Choices of Deviates and Conformers for the Six Large Courts in Westgate*

	N	Choices Given	Choices Received
Deviates in corner houses	7	.57	.43
Deviates in inner houses	23	1.52	1.39
Conformers	48	1.52	1.60

The other deviates in the court did not suffer from such lack of contact. They gave as many choices to the others in the court as did the conformers. As was true for all the deviates in Westgate, however, they tended to receive fewer than they gave, while the conformers tended to receive more choices than they gave.[4]

Table 7, again, shows that these inner-house deviates were not members of groups other than the court group. They gave only as many choices to people outside their own court as did the conformers and, again, received many fewer.

The deviates stood out as relative isolates,

---

[2] Significant at the 2% level of confidence.

[3] For all comparisons this is significant, at least at the 3% level of confidence.

[4] Not statistically significant.

TABLE 7. *Average Number of "Out-Court" Choices of Deviates and Conformers for the Six Large Westgate Courts*

	N	Choices Given	Choices Received
Deviates in corner houses	7	1.29	1.14
Deviates in inner houses	23	1.13	.87
Conformers	48	1.17	1.58

not only within their own court, but in Westgate as a whole. The corner-house deviates received, from all sources, an average of only 1.57 choices, the other deviates received an average of 2.26 choices, while the conformers received an average of 3.18 choices. The conformers were more closely involved with the social life in Westgate than were the deviates. Whether relative isolation brings about deviate status (as seems to be the case for those living in corner houses), or whether deviate status tends to bring about isolation through "rejection by others" (as might be the case with the deviates living in inner houses), the two things seem to go hand in hand.

THE DEVIATE IN WESTGATE WEST

We concluded above that there was no relation in Westgate West between the uniformity of behavior within a building and the cohesiveness of the building, and that group standards were not operating in Westgate West. The opinions of the people about the tenants' organization and their degree of activity in it would, consequently, not be determined by pressures or influences from the group. The behavior of the individual would be more a matter of individual reaction and influence from other individuals than of group pressures.

We may well examine the sociometric status of those people who were different from the majority in their building, although we should not expect the isolation which we found among the deviates in Westgate. These people were deviates only in the sense that they reacted differently from most of the residents, and not in the sense of having successfully resisted group pressures to conform.

Few people in Westgate West expressed unfavorable attitudes toward the organization. Consequently, few people differed from the pattern of their building on the attitude dimension. The great majority of the deviates differed only on the activity dimension from the others in their building. Thirteen of the seventeen buildings had "favorable-active" patterns, and most of the deviates were people who felt favorably inclined but had merely not attended the meetings of their building. It is plausible to expect, then, that we would find these deviates not to be isolates in the community despite their absence from building meetings. The data corroborate these expectations. Altogether, deviates and conformers both gave an average of about two and one-half choices, and both received an average of about two and one-half choices. We may thus conclude that in the absence of strong group formation, and in the absence of group standards, being different from the people in the group did not result in isolation.

SUMMARY

In order to conclude that observed uniformity in behavior of a number of individuals is the result of the operation of group standards or the existence of "social norms," we must be able to show the existence of psychological groups which are enforcing such standards. A collection of individuals with a relatively high number of sociometric linkages among them may constitute such a psychological group, or may merely constitute a series of friendship relationships with no real unification of the group as a whole. It is highly likely, of course, that such a series of friendship relationships among a number of people will in time make for the development of a cohesive group. In Westgate West, where there had not been time for this process really to develop, evidence indicating the absence of group standards was found.

When a cohesive group does exist, and when its realm of concern extends over the area of behavior in which we have discovered uniformity among the members of the group, then the degree of uniformity must be related to the degree of cohesiveness of the group, if a group standard is operative. The more cohesive the group, the more effectively it can influence its members. Thus we have found that in the more cohesive groups in Westgate there were fewer deviates from the group pattern of behavior. The cohesiveness of the court group as a whole was the important determinant of the number of deviates. Subgroup formation within the larger group, no matter how cohesive these subgroups may have been, tended to disrupt the cohesiveness of the larger unit.

Although, on the basis of the data available to us, we have not been able to separate clearly the different means by which people can resist group influences and thus become deviates, there is abundant evidence that the attractiveness of the group and the amount of communication between the member and the group are major determinants. It also would seem likely that these two factors would generally not occur separately but would operate together in most situations. The sociometric status of the deviate is clearly different from that of the conformer—isolation seems to be both a cause and an effect of being a deviate.

References

1. Lewin, K., *et al.* Level of aspiration. In J. McV. Hunt (Ed.), *Personality and the behavior disorders.* Vol. I. New York: Ronald Press, 1944.
2. Newcomb, T. *Personality and social change.* New York: Dryden, 1943.
3. Sherif, M. *The psychology of social norms.* New York: Harper, 1936.

13

Deviation, Rejection, and Communication

STANLEY SCHACHTER

The present study is concerned with the consequences of deviation from a group standard. Its immediate background is a study by Festinger, Schachter, and Back (3) of the relationships between group structure and group standards. Findings pertinent to the present study will be briefly reviewed.

1. Within each social group in a housing community there was homogeneity of attitude toward a community-wide problem. Among these groups, however, there was marked heterogeneity of attitude.

2. There was a high positive correlation between cohesiveness of the social group (measured by per cent of in-group sociometric choices) and strength of the group standard (measured by per cent of conformers to the standard).

3. Within a social group, deviates from the group standard received far fewer sociometric choices than did conformers.

The theory developed to explain these findings is as follows: Within any social group, pressures operate toward uniformity of attitude. The origins of such pressures are at least twofold: social reality and group locomotion.

1. Social reality. On any issue for which there is no empirical referent, the reality of one's own opinion is established by the fact that other people hold similar opinions. Forces exist to establish uniformity and thus to create "reality" for the opinion.

2. Group locomotion. Uniformity may be necessary or desirable for the group to locomote toward its goal. Locomotion will be facilitated if all members agree on a particular path to the goal.

The strength of the pressures toward uniformity that a group can exercise on its members will vary with the *cohesiveness* of the group and the *relevance* of the issue to

From *Journal of Abnormal and Social Psychology*, 1951, **46**, 190–207. Reprinted by permission of the author and the American Psychological Association.

the group. *Cohesiveness* is defined as the total field of forces acting on members to remain in the group. Stemming from cohesiveness is the property called the *internal power of the group,* which is defined as the magnitude of change the group can induce on its members. The degree of internal power will be equal to the magnitude of the force on the member to remain in the group. If we assume that all groups are attempting to induce the same amount, we can derive that there will be fewer deviates from a group standard in highly cohesive groups than in less cohesive groups.

Relevance refers to the ordering, in terms of importance to the group, of the activities over which the internal power of the group extends. The conceptual dimension along which we can order particular activities as relevant or irrelevant to a particular group still remains unclear. There appear to be three possible bases for such ordering: the importance of the activity for group locomotion, the value which the group places upon the activity, and some hierarchy of needs common to group members in their roles as group members. Whatever the basis for ordering, we may anticipate that a group will exercise greater influence over relevant than over irrelevant activities.

It is assumed that there is a parallel between the process of induction and actual communication; that is, communication is the mechanism by which power is exerted. Therefore, one method by which deviation from a group standard may be maintained is to cut off the deviate from communication with the group. Lack of communication may result from little initial contact between the individual and the group or rejection from the group. In the latter case, if the magnitude of the change that the group attempts to induce is greater than the force on the individual to stay in the group, the deviate will want to leave the group, or the group will tend to push the deviate out of the group, or both.

The present study is specifically concerned with the rejection of a deviate by the group. It is probable that not all groups reject to the same degree and that rejection is a consequence of deviation on only certain kinds of issues. To delineate more carefully some of the conditions affecting rejection, this experiment examines the effect of degrees of cohesiveness of the group and relevance of the issue on the degree of rejection of a deviate. The effects of these variables on communication and induction within the groups are also studied.

THE EXPERIMENT

The experiment was conducted as the first meeting of a club. Four types of clubs were set up, each representing a different degree and combination of cohesiveness and relevance. In each club, paid participants deviated from and conformed to an experimentally created group standard. Discussion in each club was systematically observed. At the end of each meeting members were nominated for committees and sociometric questionnaires were filled out. These served as measures of rejection.

The four types of clubs set up were case-study, editorial, movie, and radio clubs. There was a total of 32 clubs, eight of each type. Each club had from five to seven members and three paid participants who were perceived as fellow club members. All of the subjects (Ss) in the clubs were male college students.

In a typical meeting, after preliminary introductions, each club member read a short version of the "Johnny Rocco" case (2), the life history of a juvenile delinquent, which ended as Johnny was awaiting sentence for a minor crime. The case was presented as that of a real person. The leader of the club, in all instances the experimenter, asked the members to discuss and decide the question, "What should be done with this kid?" The discussion was guided by a 7-point scale made up of alternative suggestions ordered along a love-punishment dimension. Point 1 presented the "all love" viewpoint, point 7 the "all-punishment" viewpoint. Between these extremes were graded variations of the two points of view.[1] This scale was used to point up the differences of opinion within the group. It was introduced to the club members as a convenient device for learning everyone's position and for channelizing discussion.

After reading the case, each club member announced the position on the scale that he had chosen. Then the three paid participants in each club announced their positions. One paid participant, the "deviate," chose a position of extreme deviation and maintained it throughout the discussion; the second, the "mode," chose and maintained the modal position of group opinion; and

[1] For example, point 3 read: "He should be sent into an environment where providing Johnny with warmth and affection will be emphasized slightly more than punishing him, but discipline and punishment will be frequent if his behavior warrants it." For purposes of brevity the revised case study and the complete love-punishment scale are omitted from this paper. Interested readers may obtain copies by writing to the author.

the third, the "slider," chose the position of extreme deviation but allowed himself to be gradually influenced, so that at the end of the discussion he was at the modal position.

The case was written sympathetically to ensure that the deviate paid participant would be a deviate. In all clubs almost all members chose positions on the scale emphasizing love and kindness (positions 2–4), and the deviate chose the position of extreme discipline (position 7).

The discussion, limited to 45 minutes, was largely a matter of thrashing out differences of opinion among club members. After 20 minutes the leader took a census to ensure that everyone was fully aware of everyone else's position. He took no part in the discussion except to answer the few questions directed to him. At the end of the discussion a final census was taken. Then the leader turned the discussion to the future of the club. At this time the committee nomination blanks and sociometric questionnaires were filled out.

After each meeting the Ss were told that this had been an experiment and not a club, and the purposes of the experiment and the various devices used were fully explained. The Ss were asked not to disclose the true nature of these "clubs." There was no indication that anyone gave away the experiment.

How the Variables, Cohesiveness and Relevance, Were Produced

Cohesiveness has been defined as the total field of forces acting on members to remain in the group. The greater the valence of the group for its members, the greater the cohesiveness. Valence of the group derives from at least two sources, the attractiveness of the activities the group mediates and the attractiveness of the members of the group. In this experiment, two degrees of cohesiveness were produced by manipulating the attractiveness of the activities mediated by the groups.

Subjects were recruited for club membership from economics classes at the University of Michigan. The case-study and editorial clubs were described to half of these classes. The case-study clubs were purportedly being set up at the request of a group of lawyers, judges, and social workers to advise on the treatment and disposition of delinquents, sex offenders, etc. The editorial clubs were supposedly being organized at the request of a new national magazine to advise on feature articles, format, policy, etc. Interested students filled out a blank indicating which club they were interested in joining, and checked two rating scales noting the extent of their interest in each club. These were 4-point scales: "not interested at all," "only mildly interested," "moderately interested," and "extremely interested."

The movie and radio clubs were described to the other half of these classes. The movie clubs were purportedly being set up for a local theatre. The club members were to see films and decide which ones the theatre could successfully program. Radio clubs were supposedly being formed to serve a similar market research function for a local radio station. Students indicated their interest in these two clubs in the manner described above.

The case-study and movie clubs were high cohesive groups, made up of students who had checked between "moderately interested" and "extremely interested" on the scales for these clubs. The editorial and radio clubs were low cohesive groups, made up of students who indicated high interest in joining the case-study or movie clubs and little or no interest in joining the editorial or radio clubs.[2] Students becoming members of clubs they were interested in joining made up the high cohesive groups. Those becoming members of clubs they were not interested in joining made up the low cohesive groups. In short, *cohesiveness* is defined here in terms of the valence of the activity.[3]

Relevance has been defined as an ordering of group activities along a dimension of "importance" to the group. Two degrees of relevance were produced experimentally. In one case, Ss were concerned with an activity corresponding to the purpose of the club. In the other case, Ss were concerned with an activity which had nothing to do with the purpose of the club.

Case-study and editorial clubs discussed a case study and a feature article, respectively. Movie and radio clubs discussed issues foreign to the purpose of the clubs; each began with an appropriate subject but was diverted to a side issue. The movie clubs saw a 15-minute film, and the radio clubs listened to a 15-minute recording. Then the leader introduced the observer as someone who had written up the "Johnny Rocco" case and wanted the help of the group to discuss what should be done with him. The group was assured that this had nothing to do with the club and would never happen again. With some enthusiasm from the paid participants, the group always agreed to discuss the case.

To make constant the time of interaction among Ss, radio and movie clubs were chosen as a setting

[2] A subject did not know which of the two clubs he had come to until the meeting was under way.

[3] This may seem a rather restricted definition of cohesiveness. Back (1), however, has demonstrated that cohesiveness, no matter what its source, can be considered a unitary concept. Whether cohesiveness is based on friendship, the valence of the activity mediated by the group, or group prestige, the consequences of increasing cohesiveness are identical.

for the irrelevant issue. The Ss were unable to interact while looking at a movie or listening to a recording. Therefore, their discussion time was the same as that of Ss discussing relevant issues.

To compare data obtained in the four types of clubs, it was necessary that the content be constant. This was done by using the "Johnny Rocco" case and the love-punishment scale in all the clubs. In case-study clubs, "Johnny Rocco" was the case for the day. In editorial clubs, "Johnny Rocco" was part of a feature article on juvenile delinquency. In movie and radio clubs, "Johnny Rocco" was the irrelevant issue. In all clubs the scale was the basis for discussing, "What should be done with the kid?"

In summary, there were four kinds of clubs, each reproducing a different combination of the experimental variables, as follows:

1. High cohesiveness—relevant issue (Hi Co Rel): Case-Study Club
2. Low cohesiveness—relevant issue (Lo Co Rel): Editorial Club
3. High cohesiveness—irrelevant issue (Hi Co Irrel): Movie Club
4. Low cohesiveness—irrelevant issue (Lo Co Irrel): Radio Club

In the procedure used there are two possible sources of selective error: (*a*) Possibly students interested in the case-study and editorial clubs were selectively different from those attracted to the movie and radio clubs. However, more than 80% of the students addressed asked to join one of the clubs. More than 90% of these expressed preferences for case-study or movie clubs. (*b*) Students assigned to case-study and movie clubs rated editorial and radio clubs slightly more favorably than students assigned to editorial and radio clubs. Possibly students in case-study and movie clubs were more attracted to the idea of a club, any kind of club. This factor, however, probably had little effect on experimental results. In the degree of rejection of the deviate, no difference was found in high cohesive groups between students who rated the nonpreferred activity high and those who rated it low.

The Validity of the Manipulation of Cohesiveness

The manipulation of cohesiveness began with the canvassing for Ss and their assignment to clubs on the basis of preliminary interest ratings. This method of assignment is summarized in Table 1, where figures were obtained by assigning numerical values to the four points of the rating scale. "Not interested at all" has the value 1; "extremely interested" has the value 4; and the two intermediate points, the values 2 and 3. The figures are the mean ratings of each club made by all Ss assigned to a particular experimental condition. There is a marked difference between Ss in high

TABLE 1.   *Mean Ratings on Sign-up Sheets*

Group	Case-Study	Editorial
Hi Co Rel	3.27	2.20
Lo Co Rel	3.33	1.71
	Movie	*Radio*
Hi Co Irrel	3.53	2.24
Lo Co Irrel	3.34	1.59

and low cohesive groups in their ratings of the clubs to which they were assigned. In the low cohesive conditions, all but two Ss rated the clubs in which they were placed between "not interested at all" and "only mildly interested." In the high cohesive conditions, all but two Ss rated the clubs in which they were placed between "extremely interested" and "moderately interested."

How successful was this method in manipulating cohesiveness? At the end of each meeting, each S filled out a cohesiveness questionnaire designed to determine his intentions toward the club. There were three questions:

1. Do you want to remain a member of this group?
2. How often do you think this group should meet?
3. If enough members decide not to stay so that it seems this group might discontinue, would you like the chance to persuade others to stay?

Table 2 summarizes the data from this questionnaire and shows marked differences between high and low cohesive groups. In high cohesive groups 101 of the 102 Ss wanted to continue their memberships; in low cohesive groups only 62 of 96 Ss wanted to do so. There are differences, too, between Ss in the two conditions who wanted to remain in their clubs. Such Ss in low cohesive groups wanted to meet less often and were less willing to persuade others to stay in the club than were Ss in high cohesive groups. The manipulation was clearly successful in producing groups with different degrees of cohesiveness.

The Paid Participants

The three paid participants in each group were perceived as fellow club members. Like the Ss, they were male undergraduates. In each meeting, in each condition, they played three roles, deviate, mode, and slider. The deviate adopted the position of extreme discipline and maintained it throughout the discussion. The mode championed that position which the modal number of members supported. If during the meeting the modal position shifted, he shifted. The slider began as an extreme deviate (position 7) and during the meeting moved step by step to the modal position.

TABLE 2.   *Breakdown of Answers to the Cohesiveness Questionnaire*

Group	N	Question 1 Want to remain member?		Question 2 Frequency of meetings?		Question 3 Want to induce others to stay in club?	
		Yes	No	Once or Twice a Week	Once Every 2, 3, or 4 Weeks	Yes	No
Hi Co Rel	53	98%	2%	61%	39%	73%	10%
Lo Co Rel	50	68	32	54	46	51	34
Hi Co Irrel	49	100	0	73	27	61	35
Lo Co Irrel	46	61	39	36	64	21	71

The mode and slider roles were controls. The deviate and the mode provided evidence of the effect of deviation as contrasted to conformity. Comparison of the slider and the deviate tested whether rejection was a result of having at one time, but no longer, championed a deviate position, or of simply maintaining deviancy against all attempted influence.

The three roles were systematically rotated among four paid participants so that each played each role twice in each experimental condition. To assure constancy from meeting to meeting, rules of behavior guiding the paid participants in any role were carefully defined: (*a*) Each paid participant had to speak once every five minutes. If during any five-minute interval no one addressed a remark to him, he initiated a communication. (*b*) Where possible, all communications made by the paid participants, whether initiated or in response to someone, were rephrasings of the position he was maintaining at the time. (*c*) When it was impossible simply to rephrase the position, the paid participants at the deviate position were permitted two standard arguments:

1. Despite the fact that Johnny was shown love and affection, he went back to stealing.

2. It could not be said that discipline would not work, since it had not consistently been applied to Johnny.

Measures of Rejection

After the discussion the leader introduced the subject of the club's future and proposed a plan by which a functioning group could be organized. To expedite such organization, each member filled out three mimeographed sheets: a committee nomination blank, a sociometric test, and the cohesiveness questionnaire described earlier.

Committee Nominations. Three committees were set up, differing with respect to interest of the work, importance of the assigned functions, and delegated responsibility for club activities. They were called the Executive, Steering, and Correspondence Committees. In each club, the job of each committee was defined in much the same way, but with slightly different content. The Ex-

ecutive Committee was to decide what the group should discuss, to act as liaison agent between the club and its sponsoring agency, and to determine club policy. The Steering Committee was to prepare and present discussion materials and determine discussion procedure. The Correspondence Committee was to perform secretarial functions.[4]

The Ss were instructed to nominate persons whom they considered most capable of handling the work of each committee. They were not to nominate themselves or the same person for more than one committee. The number of members on each committee was manipulated so that no matter what number were present in any particular group, everyone had to nominate everyone else present for some committee. When ten people were present, each member nominated three people for each committee; when nine people were present, only two people were nominated for the Correspondence Committee; and, when eight people were present, two people were nominated for the Steering Committee and two for the Correspondence Committee. The importance or unimportance of the committees to which the paid participants were nominated serves as an index of acceptance or rejection.

The Sociometric Test. Subjects were informed that it might become necessary to reduce the number of club members or to break up the group and portion out its members to one of the other clubs, and that therefore it would be helpful to know which people would like to remain together. They were asked to rank everyone present in order of preference for remaining in the same group with themselves. In contrast to committee nomination instructions, the emphasis here was on congeniality. These data provide a sociometric index of rejection.

---

[4] To check on whether or not jobs on these committees actually did vary in attractiveness, in several of the groups the members were asked to write their own names next to those committees in which they were most interested. Most requested the Executive Committee, a few the Steering, and none the Correspondence Committee.

The Observation Schedule

An observer, introduced as a friend interested in what the club was doing and who could be imposed upon to take notes, recorded the following aspects of the group process: (*a*) who spoke to whom; (*b*) the length, in time, of the communication; (*c*) whether the speaker attacked or supported the position of the person to whom he spoke; (*d*) whether a communication, even if not addressed to a person at a specific position, implied approval or disapproval of this position; and (*e*) whether the speaker talked about experiences from his own or his friends' personal histories.

Rationale

The setup described, while constituting a reasonably well controlled experimental situation, represented for the Ss a real-life situation. What was for the experimenter a method of manipulating a variable was for S a club he was interested in joining. The measuring instruments were conventional methods of electing officers, and so on. In short, the experiment was fitted within a social framework completely consistent with the idea and operation of a club, with no sacrifice of experimental control. The rationale for this procedure was the assumption that it would be possible to reproduce the variables and phenomena under study with greater intensity in a purportedly "real-life situation" than in a laboratory setup that was identified as such. It is possible to produce complex social phenomena in laboratory experiments. Which procedure is more "effective" in the study of particular social phenomena can only be determined by additional investigation.

THE THEORETICAL RELATIONSHIPS AMONG COHESIVENESS, RELEVANCE, AND REJECTION

The theory presented in the introduction can now be expanded to make specific derivations as to the degree of rejection anticipated in each experimental condition. The theory states that there are pressures toward uniformity of behavior and attitude among members of most social groups. If differences of opinion exist within a group, forces will arise on the members to restore uniformity. A number of corrective tendencies will develop: for example, pressures develop to change the opinions of members of the group holding opinions different from one's own; pressures arise to change one's own opinion to coincide more closely with those of other group members; a ten-dency develops to decrease one's dependence on deviant members as appropriate reference points in establishing the reality of one's own opinion. In any group where differences of opinion exist probably all of these tendencies exist and are, we shall say, simultaneously a function of the total pressures toward uniformity. In the present experimental situation where almost all group members were of similar opinions and there was only one deviate, it seems reasonable to suggest that the predominant tendencies acting on them were the pressures to change the opinion of the deviate, and the tendency to decrease dependence on the deviate as a point of reference for establishing social reality.

A. *Pressures to change* (Pch) refer to the magnitude of pressures acting on group members to change a deviant opinion to conform more closely with their own. We make these assumptions about the relationship of Pch with the variables cohesiveness, relevance, and state of opinion:

1. *With increasing difference of opinion the magnitude of Pch should increase.* If uniformity exists, Pch should have zero magnitude. As group opinion departs more and more from uniformity, Pch should correspondingly increase.

2. *With increasing cohesiveness, the magnitude of Pch should increase. At any point along a scale of difference of opinion, Pch should be greater for high than for low cohesive groups.*

   Pressures to uniformity arise in part from a need for social reality within an appropriate reference group. A cohesive group, in which membership is valued, can be considered a more important reference group than a low cohesive group in which membership is not particularly cherished. Therefore, we can anticipate that pressures to uniformity will be greater in high than in low cohesive groups.

3. *With increasing relevance of issue, the magnitude of Pch should increase.*

   Any set of activities can be ordered along some dimension of "importance" (relevance) for a particular reference group. It is plausible to assume

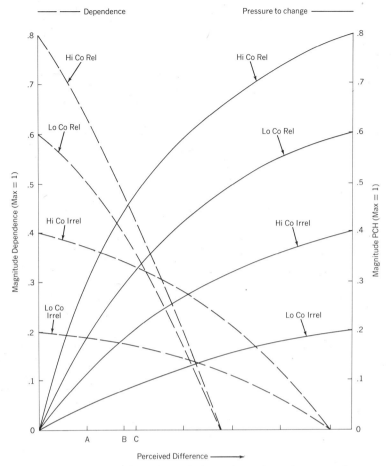

FIGURE 1. Theoretical curves of the relationships between dependence, pressures to change, and cohesiveness, relevance, and perceived difference of opinion.

that for activities which are of importance to the group, greater pressures to change will exist than for activities which are unimportant.

B. *Dependence* (Dep) refers to the extent to which members of a group rely on one another as reference points in establishing social reality. We make these assumptions about the relationships of dependence with the variables cohesiveness, relevance, and state of opinion:

1. *With increasing difference of opinion the magnitude of Dep will decrease.*

 If opinions are identical, dependence will be high. When persons have different opinions, it is unlikely that they will depend on one another to establish the reality of their opinions.

2. *With increasing cohesiveness, the magnitude of Dep will increase.*

 Members of a high cohesive group (a valued and important reference group) will be more dependent on one another than will members of a low cohesive group.

3. *With relatively small difference of opinion, the magnitude of Dep will increase with increasing relevance of issue. As difference of opinion increases, Dep for relevant issues decreases more rapidly than Dep for irrelevant issues, and a point of zero Dep will be reached with less difference of opinion for relevant than for irrelevant issues.*

The more "important" an issue to a particular group, the greater the extent to which group members depend on one another for social reality. On relevant issues, it will be more important that the reference group which establishes social reality have similar opinions than on less relevant issues. Therefore, dependence should decrease more rapidly with increasing perceived difference, and should reach the point of zero dependence earlier for highly relevant issues than for irrelevant issues.

These relationships are presented graphically in Figure 1. The rising Pch curves and falling Dep curves with increasing difference of opinion express assumptions A1 and B1, above. The greater magnitude of high cohesive than of low cohesive curves (relevance held constant), and of relevant than of irrelevant Pch curves (cohesiveness held constant), expresses assumptions A2, A3, and B2. At low levels of perceived difference with cohesiveness held constant, the magnitude of relevant Dep curves is greater than that of irrelevant Dep curves. Curves for relevant conditions drop at a faster rate and reach the point of zero dependence with far less perceived difference than do curves for irrelevant conditions. This is an expression of assumption B3.

For each condition, the maxima of the Pch and Dep curves are of the same magnitude. We assume that the maxima of both factors are similarly a function of total pressures to uniformity. The scale of magnitude along the ordinate of this graph has maximum = 1. The values assigned are, of course, arbitrary and purely illustrative.

From these curves we can make predictions concerning the interrelationships among cohesiveness, relevance, and degree of rejection.

We shall coordinate rejection to the amount of pressures to change that do not find public expression. The amount of pressures that do find public expression we call *communication*. Dependence defines the proportion of pressures to change that can be expressed. Multiplying these two factors, therefore, gives the amount of pressures that will actually be exerted.[5]

$$\text{Comm} = \text{Pch} \times \text{Dep}$$

Rejection, then, which is defined as the amount of pressures not exerted, is computed by multiplying Pch by the quantity (1 − Dep).

[5] This theory of communication will be developed and expanded in the following section.

$$\text{Rej} = \text{Pch} \times (1 - \text{Dep})$$

The number 1 represents maximum dependence, the point at which all Pch will be communicated. The greater the pressures and the smaller the dependence, the greater the rejection. In effect, this formula suggests that rejection requires relatively little dependence on a person and, at the same time, relatively high pressures to change him. If pressures to change are high but dependence is high, rejection will be relatively slight. If dependence is low but there are no pressures to change, rejection will not occur.

Applying this formula to the postulated curves in Figure 1, we find these relationships. At point *A* in this figure:

$$\text{Pch} \times (1 - \text{Dep}) = \text{Rej}$$

Hi Co Rel	.300 × (1 − .650)	=	.105
Lo Co Rel	.185 × (1 − .513)	=	.090
Hi Co Irrel	.110 × (1 − .375)	=	.069
Lo Co Irrel	.050 × (1 − .185)	=	.041

At point *B* where the perceived difference is somewhat greater:

$$\text{Pch} \times (1 - \text{Dep}) = \text{Rej}$$

Hi Co Rel	.437 × (1 − .487)	=	.224
Lo Co Rel	.295 × (1 − .409)	=	.174
Hi Co Irrel	.175 × (1 − .341)	=	.115
Lo Co Irrel	.075 × (1 − .175)	=	.062

These trends become clear: (*a*) As perceived difference increases, the degree of rejection in each of these conditions will increase. (*b*) At any point beyond zero, along the axis of perceived difference:

Rej in Hi Co Rel   > Rej in Lo Co Rel
Rej in Hi Co Irrel > Rej in Lo Co Irrel
Rej in Hi Co Rel   > Rej in Hi Co Irrel
Rej in Lo Co Rel   > Rej in Lo Co Irrel [6]

Thus, the set of assumptions determining the shapes of these curves leads to these experimental predictions:

1. Persons in the mode and slider roles (who at the end of a meeting are close to zero perceived difference) will be rejected less (if at all) than will persons in the deviate role.

[6] It is impossible to make an exact prediction about relative rejection between the Lo Co Rel and Hi Co Irrel conditions. Though the curves imply Rej in Lo Co Rel > Rej in Hi Co Irrel, this was done purely for illustrative simplicity. We have, of course, no way of determining the relative contributions of cohesiveness and relevance in a comparison of Lo Co Rel and Hi Co Irrel conditions.

2. From experimental condition to condition, the degree of rejection of persons in the deviate role will vary in the order noted in trend (*b*) above. With cohesiveness constant, rejection will be greater in relevant than in irrelevant groups. With relevance constant, rejection will be greater in high than in low cohesive groups.

RESULTS

The post-meeting nominations for committees and the sociometric rankings of all club members provide two indices of rejection, i.e., nominations to the less important committees and relatively low sociometric rankings.

SOCIOMETRIC RANKINGS

At the end of each meeting the members of each club ranked everyone in the order of his desirability as a fellow club member. The instructions emphasized congeniality and compatibility as the basis for ranking. The lower the ranking, the greater the rejection.

Table 3 presents mean sociometric rankings of each paid participant in each condition. Each figure in the table is the mean of the mean sociometric rankings in each group. The N for each figure is eight, the number of groups in each condition. Since the groups varied in size from eight to ten members, all rankings were corrected to equivalent scores by adopting the nine possible rankings in a group of ten people as a basic scale and correcting rankings in smaller groups to equivalent scores. The mean rank in every group is five.

These relationships emerge from Table 3: (*a*) In any condition, mean rankings of either mode or slider are considerably below mean rankings of the deviate. All mode-deviate differences are significant by a *t*-test at the 7% level of confidence or better. Clearly, a penalty of relative rejection is imposed on a deviate. (*b*) There are no significant differences in rankings of either the mode or slider when comparisons are made between conditions.[7] The variables of cohesiveness and relevance have no effects on group evaluation of individuals who are at, or who adopt, the

group norms. (*c*) The deviate is rejected more strongly in high than in low cohesive groups. Between rankings in high and low cohesive groups, the *t* is significant at the 12% level for the difference between Hi Co Rel and Lo Co Rel, and at the 1% level for the difference between Hi Co Irrel and Lo Co Irrel.[8] As predicted, greater cohesiveness produces greater rejection.

TABLE 3. *Mean Sociometric Rankings of the Paid Participants*

Group	Deviate	Mode	Slider
Hi Co Rel	6.44	4.65	5.02
Lo Co Rel	5.83	4.70	4.56
Hi Co Irrel	6.51	4.68	4.44
Lo Co Irrel	5.67	3.83	5.03

There is, however, no immediate evidence that the variable, relevance, affects the degree of rejection. The mean sociometric rankings of the deviate in the relevant and irrelevant condition, with cohesiveness constant, are about the same. This may be attributed in part to the fact that the measurement is a relative one, indicating only an individual's relative preference for one person over another, with no indication of the absolute intensity of like or dislike. There is, however, some indication of the relative intensities of the ratings in each condition. Occasionally an individual refused to fill in the sociometric sheet, or simply put in numbers in sequence, explaining that he was unable to discriminate among the people present. Random ranking implies that there was no genuine basis on which to express preference. If, therefore, any one experimental condition has a significantly greater number of random rankings than do the others, it may be inferred that, in general, all rankings in this condition were made with less basis for expressing preference and imply less intensity of like or dislike than in a condition where random responses are rare. More than twice as many random rankings were made in irrelevant conditions as in relevant. Of all group members, 16% ranked randomly in the irrelevant conditions and 6.8% in the relevant conditions. This difference is significant by chi-square with 1 *d.f.* at the 2% level. There were no significant differences between Hi Co Rel and Lo Co Rel or between Hi Co Irrel

---

[7] The largest difference, that between the Hi Co Irrel and Lo Co Irrel conditions for the mode, is significant by *t*-test at only the 28% level.

[8] In all tests of significance mentioned in this section, the group rather than the individual was considered the unit.

and Lo Co Irrel. Though mean rankings are about the same for relevant and irrelevant conditions, random rankings of the deviate seem to imply less strong feelings of rejection in the irrelevant groups.

These sociometric data are in the directions predicted: (*a*) Paid participants in the mode and slider roles· were not rejected; as deviates they were definitely rejected. (*b*) There is greater rejection of the deviate in high than in low cohesive groups. (*c*) Though sociometric rankings of the deviate are about the same for relevant and irrelevant conditions, random sociometric rankings indicate that the intensity of rejection in irrelevant conditions was less than in relevant conditions.

ASSIGNMENT TO COMMITTEES

With instructions emphasizing competence for the job, the members of each club nominated people for membership on the Executive, Steering, and Correspondence Committees. Rejection is coordinated to assignment to the least desirable committee. The Executive was the most attractive committee and the Correspondence the least attractive.

Tables 4, 5, and 6 present the data on the assignment of paid participants in the mode, slider, and deviate roles to the three committees. All figures in each table represent the

TABLE 4. *Percentage of Subjects Above Chance Assigning "Mode" to Committees*

Group	Executive	Steering	Correspondence
Hi Co Rel	−4.56	+6.76	−2.22
Lo Co Rel	−9.83	+20.15	−10.44
Hi Co Irrel	−0.08	+6.85	−6.93
Lo Co Irrel	+3.70	+3.70	−8.07

percentage, above or below chance expectancy, of all persons in each condition who assigned the various roles to the different committees. In Table 4, the mode was nominated for the Executive Committee by 4.56% less than we would expect if nominations in the Hi Co Rel condition had been made on some randomly determined basis. Varying group sizes, affecting the probability of any one person being assigned to a particular committee, necessitated computation of chance expectancies.

The standard errors of all chance percent-

TABLE 5. *Percentage of Subjects Above Chance Assigning "Slider" to Committees*

Group	Executive	Steering	Correspondence
Hi Co Rel	+1.76	−5.93	+4.16
Lo Co Rel	+7.32	−7.86	+0.50
Hi Co Irrel	−4.97	+4.38	+0.39
Lo Co Irrel	+2.69	−3.52	+0.16

ages are close to 6.20.[9] Any score greater than 10.23 is significant at the 10% level, greater than 12.09 is significant at the 5% level, and greater than 15.93 is significant at the 1% level. If the 5% level is accepted, Table 5 reveals no significant fluctuations from chance in assigning the slider to any one particular committee. Similarly, for the mode, in Table 4, we find only one score that departs significantly from chance, assignment of the mode to the Steering Committee in the Lo Co Rel condition. With the large number of scores obtained, this may be interpreted as a chance fluctuation. There is no indication of systematic rejection for the mode or slider roles.

Table 6 for the deviate presents a completely different picture. In all conditions, except Lo Co Irrel, the deviate is overnominated for the Correspondence Committee and undernominated for the Executive Committee. Deviation results in assignment to a relatively peripheral position in the role structure of the group. Not only is the deviate considered relatively undesirable as a fellow club member, but also least capable of handling the important jobs in the club.

The degree of rejection, however, is af-

TABLE 6. *Percentage of Subjects Above Chance Assigning "Deviate" to Committees*

Group	Executive	Steering	Correspondence
Hi Co Rel	−14.00	−8.34	+22.31
Lo Co Rel	−17.58	−7.81	+25.26
Hi Co Irrel	−16.41	+4.83	+11.44
Lo Co Irrel	+10.16	−9.40	−1.30

[9] This score was computed using $\sqrt{\frac{pq}{n}}$, the customary formula for computing the standard error of a percentage. Since the number of cases varied slightly from condition to condition, and p varied slightly with the number of people in each group, the standard error 6.20 is a convenient approximation. The obtained standard errors for each committee in each condition are all quite close to this figure.

fected by the experimental variables. Rejection is greater in both relevant conditions than in the irrelevant conditions. A *t*-test with 30 *d.f.* yields significance at the 2% level of confidence for this difference. Differences between the degree of rejection in high cohesive groups and low cohesive groups, however, are less clear cut. Although there is a difference between high and low cohesive irrelevant conditions significant by *t*-test at the 10% level, there is no difference between the two relevant conditions. This is clearly inconsistent with theoretical expectations. Possibly the committee assignment measure should also be considered a relative measure that gives no indication of intensity of feeling. It is plausible that though there is no difference between high and low cohesive relevant groups in the percentage of people assigning the deviate to the Correspondence Committee, the intensity of rejection is greater in high than in low cohesive groups. In contrast to the sociometric ranking, however, no individual had difficulty in making these judgments, and there is no evidence of random assignment to committees. This may possibly be attributed to the different natures of the measures. A judgment of fitness for a particular job is a fairly everyday matter. Decisions about which people should be in or out of a group appear to be a more unusual sort of judgment to make.

Except for this single inconsistency, the data support the predictions. Neither the mode nor the slider was rejected. In all conditions except Lo Co Irrel, where we anticipated very little rejection, the deviate was overnominated for the Correspondence Committee. Rejection of the deviate was greater in the relevant than in the irrelevant conditions, and greater in the Hi Co Irrel than in the Lo Co Irrel condition.

THE PROCESS OF COMMUNICATION

The previous section has treated the relationships between experimental manipulations and post-meeting measurements. This section relates the processes of induction and communication, as they occurred during the meetings, to the experimental variables, cohesiveness and relevance, and to the post-meeting measurements.

We shall consider communication, the process of one person talking to another, as the mechanism of induction, i.e., the means by which influence is exerted. There are, of course, other reasons why people communicate, but within the confines of this experiment and theory we shall largely limit ourselves to communication as influence.

From the theoretical elaboration of "pressures to uniformity," specific derivations may be made about certain aspects of the patterns of communication that occurred in these meetings. Let us first relate the constructs, Pch and Dep, to the occurrence of communication.

1. Pressures to change others mean pressures to influence others, which we will consider identical with pressures to communicate. Our earlier assumptions may, therefore, be extended to communication pressures. The pressures to communicate to a deviate will rise with increasing perceived difference, increasing cohesiveness, and increasing relevance.

2. Dependence refers to the extent to which a person relies on another person or group of persons to establish social reality. It defines the proportion of pressure to change that can actually find public expression. Actual communication, then, is a function of both Dep and Pch, with dependence modifying the proportion of pressures to change that will be expressed publicly. Actual communication is formulated as

$$Comm = Pch \times Dep.$$

In Figure 2, the dotted lines, constructed by making the proper multiplications at each point, represent the magnitude or frequency of actual communication that should be directed at positions with different degrees of perceived difference in the four experimental conditions.[10] This figure is the same as Figure 1, with the curves for predicted communication added.

Let us examine more closely the meaning of "perceived difference." It refers to the phe-

[10] The coordination of rejection to the amount of pressures that are not publicly expressed can be demonstrated graphically in Figure 2. At any point along the axis of perceived difference, rejection is equal to the difference between the height of the appropriate derived curve of actual communication and the height of the corresponding curve for Pch.

This relationship is simply stated algebraically:

$$Rej = Pch \times (1 - Dep)$$
$$= Pch - Pch \times Dep$$
$$Comm = Pch \times Dep$$
$$\therefore Rej = Pch - Comm$$

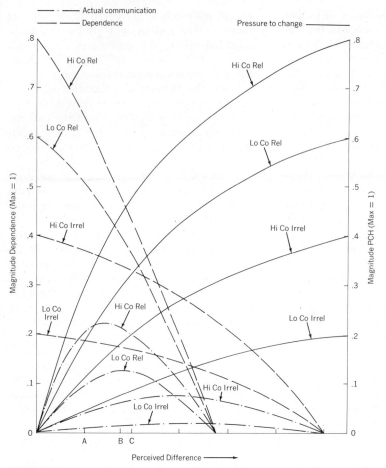

FIGURE 2. Derived curves of actual communication in the four experimental conditions.

nomenological difference between two people rather than to the absolute difference between two points on the love-punishment scale. Two people may be at position 4 on the scale and perceive the difference between themselves and someone at position 7 as of very different orders of magnitude. We shall postulate that in this experiment perceived differences increased with discussion. In all club meetings the question, "How much do we really differ?" was frequently discussed, and attempts were made to reduce the distance between points on the scale. The deviates, however, were specifically instructed to resist attempts to minimize differences between themselves and people at other positions. The assumption that perceived difference increases with discussion seems reasonable, therefore, in this situation.

Accepting this assumption, we may say that the dotted curve of communication in Figure 2 represents the actual pattern of communica-

tion during the course of the meeting. From these considerations a number of testable derivations may be made about the frequency and pattern of communication to each paid participant in each condition.

COMMUNICATION PATTERNS TO THE DEVIATE

A prediction previously developed was that rejection will increase with increasing perceived difference. Therefore, people who strongly reject the deviate perceive a greater difference between themselves and the deviate than do people who do not reject. In Figure 2, point *C* represents the position of a rejector at the end of a meeting, point *B* the position of a mild rejector, and point *A* the position of a non-rejector. If perpendiculars are projected from these points, they intercept the communication curves at different relative positions.

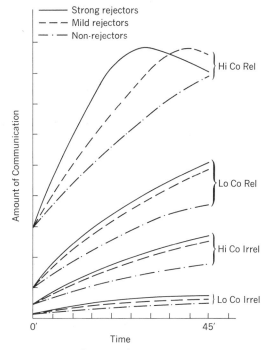

FIGURE 3. Theoretical curves of communications from strong rejectors, mild rejectors, and non-rejectors to the deviate in the four experimental conditions.

If we accept the assumption that perceived difference increases with discussion time, and postulate that points *C, B,* and *A* in Figure 2 represent, respectively, the end-of-the-meeting perceptions of people who reject the deviate strongly, reject mildly, and do not reject, then we must say that the curves of actual communication up to points *C, B,* and *A* represent the patterns of communication from these three kinds of people to the deviate during the course of the meeting. In Figure 3 these predicted curves of communication, projected from Figure 2, are drawn for these three kinds of people for each experimental condition. These curves are specific predictions about the pattern and magnitude of communication to the deviate.

In Figure 3 the ordinate represents the amount of communication during the meeting, and the abscissa represents the flow of time from zero to 45 minutes. A point on these curves represents the amount of communication that will be addressed to the deviate at a particular time in the course of the meeting by either the people who reject him strongly, reject mildly, or do not reject. All curves start

slightly above the zero point, for it seems likely that even at the beginning of a meeting there is some perception of difference.

In the Hi Co Rel condition, the communication curve of non-rejectors increases continuously throughout the meeting. The curve of strong rejectors reaches a peak during the meeting and then declines continuously, and the mild rejectors' curve reaches a peak somewhat later and then declines. In all other conditions, all communication curves to the deviate rise continuously throughout the meeting.

The data testing these derivations are presented in Table 7. The meeting is here divided into 10-minute intervals and communications to the deviate during each interval tallied. The three categories of rejectors are determined by sociometric rankings of the deviate. Non-rejectors ranked the deviate from 1.0–3.72, mild rejectors from 4.0–7.92, and strong rejectors between 8 and 9. The figures in the table represent the total number of communications in each time interval made by all people in each rejector category, divided by the number of people in this category.

Let us examine first the data for the Hi Co Rel groups in Table 7. The strong rejectors reach their peak of communication to the deviate in the 15–25 minute interval and then decline steadily. The difference between the peak interval and the final time interval is significant at better than the 1% level.[11] Mild rejectors reach their peak somewhat later, in the 25–35 minute interval, and then decline. The difference between this peak and the final time interval is significant at the 3% level. Non-rejectors seem to reach a peak and then decline, but this difference is due entirely to one case and is significant at exactly the 50% level of confidence. The data, then, essentially parallel theoretical expectations.

In the other experimental conditions, the theory anticipates a steady rise in the number of communications addressed to the deviate by either mild, strong, or non-rejectors. The remaining data in Table 7 indicate that this is

[11] All of the levels of significance reported with this set of data were obtained by tabulating for each individual in each category whether or not the number of communications he had addressed to the deviate was higher in one time interval than in the interval with which it was being compared. Probabilities were then computed by means of binomial expansion.

TABLE 7. *Mean Number of Communications Addressed to Deviate During the Course of the Meeting by Subjects with Different Post-Meeting Reactions to Him*

Group	N	5–15[a]	15–25	25–35	35–45
		Time Interval in Minutes			
Hi Co Rel					
Non-rejectors	13	1.15	0.92	2.15	1.54
Mild rejectors	15	0.40	1.27	1.87	0.86
Strong rejectors	25	0.68	1.60	1.52	0.76
Lo Co Rel					
Non-rejectors	13	0.38	0.54	0.84	0.46
Mild rejectors	22	0.58	0.50	1.23	1.73
Strong rejectors	15	0.26	0.47	1.27	2.99
Hi Co Irrel					
Non-rejectors	9	1.32	1.44	0.99	2.44
Mild rejectors	20	1.15	1.35	1.55	1.20
Strong rejectors	20	0.75	1.15	1.60	3.42
Lo Co Irrel					
Non-rejectors	16	1.69	1.69	2.34	2.12
Mild rejectors	15	1.47	0.94	2.20	3.74
Strong rejectors	15	1.20	0.74	2.47	2.87

[a] Because the first few minutes of many meetings were concerned with technical problems and deciding just what was to be done, data from the 0–5 time interval are not reported.

essentially correct. In six of these nine breakdowns, the number of communications to the deviate rises continuously, and differences between the last two time intervals are significant at the 12% level or better for all but the rising Lo Co Irrel curves. In three cases (non-rejectors in Lo Co Rel and Lo Co Irrel, mild rejectors in the Hi Co Irrel) there is a slight drop in the final interval. None of these drops is significant.

The theoretical derivations seem as well corroborated as can be anticipated with the relatively small number of cases involved. Most of the curves rise, and the only significant declines are the predicted ones.

COMMUNICATION PATTERNS TO THE MODE AND SLIDER

The position of the mode on the scale of perceived difference in Figure 2 should be at zero, the point of no perceived difference between himself and most of the others in the group. At this point $Pch = 0$, and dependence is at a maximum. There should therefore be no communications to the mode during any meeting in any experimental condition. This conclusion, however, must be qualified by two considerations: (a) As a rule, most, but not all, of the members of any one club were at the modal position. There were slight differences, therefore, between the mode and a few members of the group. (b) A paid participant in the modal role was required to speak once every five minutes. Courtesy would probably demand an occasional response.

We may anticipate, then, that the curve of communication to the mode in all experimental conditions should be a low straight line, parallel to the horizontal time axis. In Table 8, we see that this is the case. The figures in this table are computed on the same basis as those in the previous table. In all conditions only a very small number of communications were addressed to the mode at any time. Fluctuations from a straight line are all within the range of chance expectancy.

Theoretically, communications to the slider present a more complicated picture, for it is impossible to predict exactly the interaction between perceived difference and decreasing absolute difference. But it is reasonable to suggest that communications to the slider should be at about the same level as to the deviate until the slider makes his first shift, and then communications should gradually decrease until by the end of the meeting they

TABLE 8. *Mean Number of Communications Addressed to the Mode and Slider During the Course of the Meeting*

Group	N	Time Interval in Minutes			
		5–15	15–25	25–35	35–45
Hi Co Rel					
Mode	53	0.13	0.06	0.06	0.10
Slider	53	0.53	0.55	0.21	0.17
Lo Co Rel					
Mode	50	0.06	0.10	0.14	0.22
Slider	50	0.30	0.20	0.20	0.20
Hi Co Irrel					
Mode	49	0.18	0.16	0.37	0.12
Slider	49	0.79	0.47	0.20	0.04
Lo Co Irrel					
Mode	46	0.14	0.15	0.13	0.45
Slider	46	0.72	0.63	0.41	0.30

are at about the same level for both the slider and the mode. The data presented in Table 8 essentially substantiate these expectations. About 15 minutes after the meeting started the slider shifted from position 7 to 5, and finally adopted the modal position between the 35- and 40-minute marks. In all experimental conditions, communications to the slider are at first considerably above the level of communication to the mode and then decline steadily to the level of the mode in the final time interval.[12]

THE FREQUENCY OF COMMUNICATION

From the theoretical considerations previously formulated, additional derivations can be made about the magnitude or absolute amounts of communication in each experimental condition. It may be predicted, from the curves of communication in Figure 3, that the amount of communication to the deviate will decrease from Hi Co Rel condition to Lo Co Rel to Hi Co Irrel to Lo Co Irrel. And, since the distribution of positions on the love-punishment scale is the same from condition to

condition, it may also be anticipated that the mean amounts of communication for meetings, within each condition, will vary in the same order. The data collected with the present observation schedule are, however, inadequate to substantiate or disprove these derivations. It has been postulated that the magnitude of pressures to uniformity is greater on relevant than on irrelevant issues, in high than in low cohesive groups. These derivations will hold *only* for communications that arise from pressures to uniformity, and we can say nothing about communications that arise from other sources. However, people communicate for numberless reasons beyond that of restoring uniformity of opinion. It seems a reasonable assumption that the more irrelevant an issue, the greater will be the number of communications that have sources other than pressures to uniformity. If this analysis of the differences between the discussions of relevant and irrelevant issues is correct, supporting evidence must be found in areas other than the directions and amounts of communication.

Differences between the communication process in relevant and irrelevant conditions are shown in Table 9. Communications in the relevant groups tended to be longer. Slightly more than 30% of all communications in the relevant groups were long communications (more than 30 seconds), and only 21% were long in the irrelevant condition.[13] In addition, discussion in these two conditions went at a different clip. There were far more interruptions

---

[12] In the first time interval, though the number of communications to the slider is considerably higher than that to the mode, comparison with Table 7 reveals that the number of slider-directed communications is consistently lower than that to the deviate. Probably this is an artifact of the slider role. In preparing to shift position, the slider probably tended to be somewhat less extreme and emphatic in his defense of position 7.

[13] This difference has a $t = 2.06$, which with 30 *d.f.* is significant at the 5% level.

TABLE 9. *Interruptions, Pauses, Personal References, and Long Communications in All Conditions*

	Hi Co Rel	*Lo Co Rel*	*Hi Co Irrel*	*Lo Co Irrel*
Per cent long communications	28	33	25	17
Mean interruptions per meeting	67.71	29.86	78.71	82.00
Total pauses	1	1	3	7
Personal history references	18	14	5	8

in irrelevant than in relevant groups.[14] An interruption is defined as any attempt to break into a speech before it is completed. Oddly enough, in the face of the greater number of communications and the more rapid clip in irrelevant groups, there was a greater number of pauses in the discussions of the irrelevant groups. Though there was no systematic notation of pauses, the observer noted all particularly long, uncomfortable intervals when no one had anything to say. In short, there were marked differences in the character of discussion in the two conditions. Discussion in irrelevant groups might be characterized as cocktail party conversation— fast, brief, clipped, and in bursts; discussion in the relevant groups resembled the board meeting—slow, even-paced, long, and well-considered.

Consistent with these characterizations of the meeting are the additional data presented in Table 9 on the relative frequency of personal history references. Reference to personal history may be considered evidence of real involvement in the discussion. In relevant groups, there were more than two and a half times as many personal references as there were in irrelevant groups.[15] Not only were the discussions of the irrelevant groups more glib but also apparently more superficial.

The marked differences in the manner of relevant and irrelevant groups indicate that communications in irrelevant groups resulted in good part from sources other than pressures to uniformity. The data, therefore, do not serve as an adequate test of the derivations concerning the relative amounts of communication in the various conditions.

SUMMARY

A set of assumptions has been developed which defines the relationships of the constructs dependence and pressures to change, to cohesiveness, relevance, and state of opinion. Both communication and rejection have been coordinated to these constructs. Dependence defines the proportion of the pressures to change that can find public expression, and communication is defined as $Comm = Pch \times Dep$.

Rejection is coordinated to the amount of pressures to change which are not exerted and is defined as $Rej = Pch \times (1 - Dep)$.

These coordinations and the assumptions defining Pch and Dep allow us to make a number of predictions as to the results of the experiment. Predictions about rejection and the evidence supporting them will be reviewed briefly.

1. *Persons in the mode and slider roles will be rejected less (if at all) than will persons in the deviate role.* On both the sociometric and committee assignment measures there was no evidence that either the mode or slider was rejected. The deviate, on the other hand, was rejected in all experimental conditions except Lo Co Irrel. Where the magnitudes of both Dep and Pch are low, we anticipate relatively little rejection. Thus, in the Lo Co Irrel condition, the sociometric ranking of the deviate was only slightly above the mean, and he was not overnominated for the correspondence committee.

[14] The difference between mean number of interruptions in relevant and irrelevant groups is significant at better than the .001 level of significance, with $t = 5.74$ for 30 d.f. These measures of interruption and length of communication are relatively independent. Rank order correlations between the two are only $+.39$ in the irrelevant condition and $+.45$ in the relevant condition.

[15] The difference yields a t of 1.89, which with 30 d.f. is significant at the 8% level.

2. *With cohesiveness held constant, rejection will be greater in relevant groups than in irrelevant groups.* On the committee assignment measure, the deviate was assigned to the Correspondence Committee to a far greater extent in the relevant groups than in the irrelevant groups.

Though sociometric rankings of the deviate are about the same for the relevant and irrelevant conditions, there is evidence from random sociometric rankings that the intensity of rejection is greater in the relevant than in the irrelevant conditions.

3. *With relevance held constant, rejection will be greater in high cohesive than in low cohesive groups.* The mean sociometric ranking of the deviate was considerably higher in both high cohesive conditions than in the corresponding low cohesive conditions.

On the committee assignment measure the deviate was nominated to the Correspondence Committee to a greater extent in the Hi Co Irrel than in the Lo Co Irrel condition. There is no difference, however, between the Hi Co Rel and the Lo Co Rel conditions. This inconsistency may be explained in terms of the relative nature of the measure. Here, too, the intensity of rejection may be stronger in Hi Co Rel than in Lo Co Rel groups. There is no immediate evidence, however, to support this argument.

Predictions about patterns of communication follow:

1. In the Hi Co Rel condition, the amount of communication addressed to the deviate by non-rejectors should increase continuously throughout the meeting. Strong rejectors should reach a peak of communication during the meeting and then decline continuously, and mild rejectors should reach a peak somewhat later and then decline.

2. In all other experimental conditions, communications to the deviate from strong, mild, or non-rejectors should increase continuously throughout the meeting.

3. In all experimental conditions, there should be relatively few communications addressed to persons in the modal role and no increase in communications during the meeting.

4. In all conditions, communications to the slider should decrease during the meeting as the slider shifts from a deviate to a modal position.

The data essentially substantiated all of these predictions. The theory leads to other predictions about the relative magnitudes of communication in each experimental condition. These derivations, however, hold only for communications arising from pressures to uniformity. Since in irrelevant conditions many communications arose from other sources, it is impossible to test these derivations.

References

1. Back, K. W. The exertion of influence through social communication. *Journal of Abnormal and Social Psychology*, 1951, **46**, 9–23.
2. Evans, J. Johnny Rocco. *Journal of Abnormal and Social Psychology*, 1948, **43**, 357–383.
3. Festinger, L., Schachter, S., & Back, K. *Social pressures in informal groups: A study of a housing community.* New York: Harper, 1950.

14

Informal Social Communication

LEON FESTINGER

This article is a statement of the theoretical formulations which have been developed in the process of conducting a program of empirical and experimental research in informal social communication. It has grown out of our findings thus far and is, in turn, guiding the future course of the research program. This program of research concerns itself with finding and explaining the facts concerning informal, spontaneous communication among persons and the consequences of the process of communication. It would seem that a better understanding of the dynamics of such communication would in turn lead to a better understanding of various kinds of group functioning. The theories and hypotheses presented below vary considerably in precision, specificity, and the degree to which corroborating data exist. Whatever the state of precision, however, the theories are empirically oriented and capable of being tested.

Since we are concerned with the spontaneous process of communication which goes on during the functioning of groups we must first differentiate the variety of types of communication which occur according to the theoretical conditions which give rise to tendencies to communicate. It is plausible to assume that separating the sources or origins of pressures to communicate that may act on a member of a group will give us fruitful areas to study. This type of differentiation or classification is, of course, adequate only if it leads to the separation of conceptually clear areas of investigation within which communication can be organized into statable theoretical and empirical laws.

We shall here deal with those few of the many possible sources of pressures to communicate in which we have thus far been able to make theoretical and empirical progress. We shall elaborate on the theory for regarding them as giving rise to pres-

From *Psychological Review*, 1950, 57, 271–282. The research was conducted under contract with the Office of Naval Research. Reprinted by permission of the author and the American Psychological Association.

sures to communicate and on specific hypotheses concerning the laws of communication which stem from these sources.

PRESSURES TOWARD UNIFORMITY IN A GROUP

One major source of forces to communicate is the pressure toward uniformity which may exist within a group. These are pressures which, for one reason or another, act toward making members of a group agree concerning some issue or conform with respect to some behavior pattern. It is stating the obvious, of course, to say that these pressures must be exerted by means of a process of communication among the members of the group. One must also specify the conditions under which such pressures toward uniformity arise, both on a conceptual and an operational level, so that in any specific situation it is possible to say whether or not such pressures exist. We shall, in the following discussion, elaborate on two major sources of pressures toward uniformity among people, namely, social reality and group locomotion.

SOCIAL REALITY

Opinions, attitudes, and beliefs which people hold must have some basis upon which they rest for their validity. Let us, as a start, abstract from the many kinds of bases for the subjective validity of such opinions, attitudes, and beliefs one continuum along which they may be said to lie. This continuum we may call a scale of degree of physical reality. At one end of this continuum, namely, complete dependence upon physical reality, we might have an example such as this: a person looking at a surface might think that the surface is fragile or he might think that the surface is unbreakable. He can very easily take a hammer, hit the surface, and quickly be convinced as to whether the opinion he holds is correct or incorrect. After he has broken the surface with a hammer, it will probably make little dent upon his opinion if another person should tell him that the surface is unbreakable. It would thus seem that where there is a high degree of dependence upon physical reality for the

subjective validity of one's beliefs or opinions, the dependence upon other people for the confidence one has in these opinions or beliefs is very low.

At the other end of the continuum where the dependence upon physical reality is low or zero, we might have an example such as this: a person looking at the results of a national election feels that if the loser had won, things would be in some ways much better than they are. Upon what does the subjective validity of this belief depend? It depends to a large degree on whether or not other people share his opinion and feel the same way he does. If there are other people around him who believe the same thing, then his opinion is, to him, valid. If there are not others who believe the same thing, then his opinion is, in the same sense, not valid. Thus where the dependence upon physical reality is low, the dependence upon social reality is correspondingly high. An opinion, a belief, an attitude is "correct," "valid," and "proper" to the extent that it is anchored in a group of people with similar beliefs, opinions, and attitudes.

This statement, however, cannot be generalized completely. It is clearly not necessary for the validity of someone's opinion that everyone else in the world think the way he does. It is only necessary that the members of that group to which he refers this opinion or attitude think the way he does. It is not necessary for a Ku Klux Klanner that some northern liberal agree with him in his attitude toward Negroes, but it is eminently necessary that there be other people who also are Ku Klux Klanners and who do agree with him. The person who does not agree with him is seen as different from him and not an adequate referent for his opinion. The problem of independently defining which groups are and which groups are not appropriate reference groups for a particular individual, and for a particular opinion or attitude, is a difficult one. It is to some extent inherently circular since an appropriate reference group tends to be a group which does share a person's opinions and attitudes, and people tend to locomote *into* such groups—and *out of* groups which do not agree with them.

From the preceding discussion it would seem that if a discrepancy in opinion, attitude, or belief exists among persons who are members of an appropriate reference group, forces to communicate will arise. It also follows that the less "physical reality" there is to validate the opinion or belief, the greater will be the importance of the social referent, the group, and the greater will be the forces to communicate.

GROUP LOCOMOTION

Pressures toward uniformity among members of a group may arise because such uniformity is desirable or necessary in order for the group to move toward some goal. Under such circumstances there are a number of things one can say about the magnitude of pressures toward uniformity.

They will be greater to the extent that the members perceive that group movement would be facilitated by uniformity.

The pressures toward uniformity will also be greater the more dependent the various members are on the group in order to reach their goals. The degree to which other groups are substitutable as a means toward individual or group goals would be one of the determinants of the dependence of the member on the group.

We have elaborated on two sources of pressure toward uniformity among members of groups. The same empirical laws should apply to communications which result from pressures toward uniformity irrespective of the particular reasons for the existence of the pressures. We shall now proceed to enumerate a set of hypotheses concerning communication which results from pressures toward uniformity.

HYPOTHESES ABOUT COMMUNICATION RESULTING FROM PRESSURES TOWARD UNIFORMITY

Communications which arise from pressures toward uniformity in a group may be seen as "instrumental" communications. That is, the communication is not an end in itself but rather is a means by which the communicator hopes to influence the person he addresses in such a way as to reduce the discrepancy that exists between them. Thus we should examine the determinants of: (*a*) when a member communicates, (*b*) to whom he communicates and

(*c*) the reactions of the recipient of the communication.

1. Determinants of the magnitude of pressure to communicate:

Hypothesis 1a. The pressure on members to communicate to others in the group concerning "item x" increases monotonically with increase in the perceived discrepancy in opinion concerning "item x" among members of the group.

Remembering that we are considering only communication that results from pressures toward uniformity, it is clear that if there are no discrepancies in opinion—uniformity already exists in the group—there will be no forces to communicate. It would be plausible to expect the force to communicate to increase rapidly from zero as the state of affairs departs from uniformity.

Hypothesis 1b. The pressure on a member to communicate to others in the group concerning "item x" increases monotonically with increase in the degree of relevance of "item x" to the functioning of the group.

If "item x" is unimportant to the group in the sense of not being associated with any of the values or activities which are the basis for the existence of the group, or if it is more or less inconsequential for group locomotion, then there should be few or no forces to communicate even when there are perceived discrepancies in opinion. As "item x" becomes more important for the group (more relevant), the forces to communicate when any given magnitude of perceived discrepancy exists should increase.

Corroborative evidence for this hypothesis is found in an experiment by Schachter (8) where discussion of the same issue was experimentally made relevant for some groups and largely irrelevant for others. It is clear from the data that where the discussion was relevant to the functioning of the group there existed stronger forces to communicate and to influence the other members. Where the issue is a relevant one, the members make longer individual contributions to the discussion and there are many fewer prolonged pauses in the discussion.

Hypothesis 1c. The pressure on members to communicate to others in the group concerning "item x" increases monotonically with increase in the cohesiveness of the group.

Cohesiveness of a group is here defined as the resultant of all the forces acting on the members to remain in the group. These forces may depend on the attractiveness or unattractiveness of either the prestige of the group, members in the group, or the activities in which the group engages. If the total attraction toward the group is zero, no forces to communicate should arise; the members may as easily leave the group as stay in it. As the forces to remain in the group increase (given perceived discrepancies in opinion and given a certain relevance of the item to the functioning of the group), the pressures to communicate will increase.

Data from an experiment by Back (1) support this hypothesis. In this experiment, groups of high and low cohesiveness were experimentally created using three different sources of attraction to the group; namely, liking the members, prestige attached to belonging, and possibility of getting a reward for performance in the group activity. For each of the three types of attraction to the group, the more cohesive groups were rated as proceeding at a more intense rate in the discussion than the corresponding less cohesive groups. In addition, except for the groups where the attraction was the possibility of reward (perhaps due to wanting to finish and get the reward), there was more total amount of attempted exertion of influence in the highly cohesive groups than in the less cohesive groups. In short, highly cohesive groups, having stronger pressures to communicate, discussed the issue at a more rapid pace and attempted to exert more influence.

2. Determinants of choice of recipient for communications:

Hypothesis 2a. The force to communicate about "item x" to *a particular member* of the group will increase as the discrepancy in opinion between that member and the communicator increases.

We have already stated in Hypothesis 1a that the pressure to communicate in general will increase as the perceived nonuniformity in the group increases. In addition, the force to communicate will be strongest toward those whose opinions are most different from one's own and will, of course, be zero toward those in the group who at the time hold the same opinion as the communicator. In other words, people will tend to communicate to those within the group whose opinions are most different from their own.

There is a clear corroboration of this hypothesis from a number of studies. In the previously mentioned experiment by Schachter (8), the distribution of opinions expressed in the group was always as follows: Most of the members' opinions clustered within a narrow range of each other while one member, the deviate, held and maintained an extremely divergent point of view. About five times as many communications were addressed to the holder of the divergent point of view as were addressed to the others.

In an experiment by Festinger and Thibaut (5) the discussion situation was set up so that members' opinions on the issue spread over a considerable range. Invariably 70%–90% of the communications were addressed to those who held opinions at the extremes of the distribution. The curve of number of communications received falls off very rapidly as the opinion of the recipient moves away from the extreme of the distribution. The hypothesis would seem to be well-substantiated.

Hypothesis 2b. The force to communicate about "item x" to *a particular person* will decrease to the extent that he is perceived as not a member of the group or to the extent that he is not wanted as a member of the group.

From the previous hypothesis, it follows that communications will tend to be addressed mainly toward those with extreme opinions within the group. This does not hold, however, for any arbitrarily defined group. The present hypothesis, in effect, states that such relationships will apply only within *psychological* groups; that is, collections of people that exist as groups psychologically for the members. Communications will tend not to be addressed toward those who are not members of the group.

The study by Schachter (8) and the study by Festinger and Thibaut (5) both substantiate this hypothesis. In Schachter's experiment, those group members who do not want the person holding the extremely divergent point of view to remain in the group tend to stop communicating to him toward the end of the discussion. In the experiment by Festinger and Thibaut, when the subjects have the perception that the persons present include different kinds of people with a great variety of interests, there tends to be less communication toward the extremes in the last half of the discussion after the rejection process has had time to develop. In short, communication toward those with different opinions decreases if they are seen as not members of the *psychological* group.

Hypothesis 2c. The force to communicate "item x" to a particular member will increase the more it is perceived that the communication will change that member's opinion in the desired direction.

A communication which arises because of the existence of pressures toward uniformity is made in order to exert a force on the recipient in a particular direction; that is, to push him to change his opinion so that he will agree more closely with the communicator. If a member is perceived as very resistant to changing his opinion, the force to communicate to him decreases. If it seems that a particular member will be changed as the result of a communication so as to increase the discrepancy between him and the communicator, there will exist a force not to communicate to him. Thus under such conditions there will be tendencies *not* to communicate this particular item to that member.

There is some corroboration for this hypothesis. In a face-to-face verbal discussion where a range of opinion exists, the factors which this hypothesis points to would be particularly important for those members whose opinions were near the middle of the range. A communication which might influence the member at one extreme to come closer to the middle might at the same time influence the member at the other extreme to move farther away from the middle. We might then expect from this hypothesis that those holding opinions in the middle of the existing range would communicate less (because of the conflict) and would address fewer communications to the whole group, attempting to influence only one person at a time.

A number of observations were conducted to check these derivations. Existing groups of clinical psychologists, who were engaging in discussions to reconcile their differences in ratings of applicants, were observed. Altogether, 147 such discussions were observed in which at least one member's opinion was in the middle of the existing range. While those with extreme opinions made an average of 3.16 units of communication (number of communications weighted by length of the communication), those with middle opinions made an average of only 2.6 units of communication. While those with extreme opinions addressed 38% of their communications to the whole group, those with middle opinions addressed only 29% of their communications to everyone.

3. Determinants of change in the recipient of a communication:

Hypothesis 3a. The amount of change in opinion resulting from receiving a communication will increase as the pressure towards uniformity in the group increases.

There are two separate factors which contribute to the effect stated in the hypothesis. The greater the pressure toward uniformity, the greater will be the amount of influence exerted by the communications and, consequently, the greater the magnitude of change that may be expected. But the existence of pressures toward uniformity will not only show itself in increased attempts to change the opinions of others. Pressures toward uniformity will also produce greater readiness to change in the members of the group. In other words, uniformity may be achieved by changing the opinions of others or by changing one's own opinions or both. Thus we may expect that with increasing pressure toward uniformity there will be less resistance to change on the part of the members. Both of these factors will contribute to produce greater change in opinion when the pressure toward uniformity is greater.

There is evidence corroborating this hypothesis from the experiment by Festinger and Thibaut (5). In this experiment three degrees of pressure toward uniformity were experimentally induced in different groups. Irrespective of which of two problems were discussed by the group, and irrespective of whether they perceived the group to be homogeneously or heterogeneously composed, the results consistently show that high pressure groups change most, medium pressure groups change next most, and low pressure groups change least in the direction of uniformity. While the two factors which contribute to this effect cannot be separated in the data, their joint effect is clear and unmistakable.

Hypothesis 3b. The amount of change in opinion resulting from receiving a communication will increase as the strength of the resultant force to remain in the group increases for the recipient.

To the extent that a member wishes to remain in the group, the group has power over that member. By power we mean here the ability to produce real change in opinions and attitudes, and not simply change in overt behavior which can also be produced by means of overt threat. If a person is unable to leave a group because of restraints from the outside, the group can then use threats to change overt behavior. Covert changes in opinions and attitudes, however, can only be produced by a group by virtue of forces acting on the member to remain in the group. Clearly, the maximum force which the group can successfully induce on a member counter to his own forces cannot be greater than the sum of the forces acting on that member to remain in the group. The greater the resultant force to remain in the group, the more effective will be the attempts to influence the member.

This hypothesis is corroborated by two separate studies. Festinger, Schach-ter, and Back (4) investigated the relationship between the cohesiveness of social groups in a housing project (how attractive the group was for its members), and how effectively a group standard relevant to the functioning of the group was maintained. A correlation of .72 was obtained between these two variables. In other words, the greater the attractiveness of the group for the members, the greater was the amount of influence which the group could successfully exert on its members, with the result that there existed greater conformity in attitudes and behavior in the more cohesive groups.

Back (1) did a laboratory experiment specifically designed to test this hypothesis. By means of plausible instructions to the subjects, he experimentally created groups of high and low cohesiveness; that is, conditions in which the members were strongly attracted to the group and those in which the attraction to the group was relatively weak. The subjects, starting with different interpretations of the same material, were given an opportunity to discuss the matter. Irrespective of the source of the attraction to the group (Back used three different types of attraction in both high and low cohesive conditions), the subjects in the high cohesive groups influenced one another's opinions more than the subjects in the low cohesive groups. In short, the greater the degree of attraction to the group, the greater the amount of influence actually accomplished.

Hypothesis 3c. The amount of change in opinion resulting from receiving a communication concerning "item x" will decrease with increase in the degree to which the opinions and attitudes involved are anchored in other group memberships or serve important need satisfying functions for the person.

If the opinion that a person has formed on some issue is supported in some other group than the one which is at present attempting to influence him, he will be more resistant to the attempted influence. Other sources of resistance to being influenced undoubtedly come from personality factors, ego needs, and the like.

Specific evidence supporting this hypothesis is rather fragmentary. In the study of social groups in a housing project by Festinger, Schachter, and Back (4), the residents were asked whether their social life was mainly outside the project or not.* Of those who conformed to the standards of their social groups within the project, about 85% reported that their social life was centered mainly within the project. Less than 50% of those who did not conform to the standards of the project social group, however, reported that their social life was centered mainly in the project. It is likely that they were able to resist the influences from within the project when their opinions and attitudes were supported in outside groups.

The experiments by Schachter (8) and by Festinger and Thibaut (5) used the same discussion problem in slightly different situations. In the former experiment, subjects identified themselves and verbally supported their opinions in face-to-face discussion. In the latter experiment, the subjects were anonymous, communicating only by written messages on which the sender of the message was not identified. Under these latter conditions many more changes in opinion were observed than under the open verbal discussion situation, even though less time was spent in discussion when they wrote notes. This difference in amount of change in opinion is probably due to the ego defensive reactions aroused by openly committing oneself and supporting one's opinions in a face-to-face group.

4. Determinants of change in relationship among members:

Hypothesis 4a. The tendency to change the composition of the psychological group (pushing members out of the group) increases as the perceived discrepancy in opinion increases.

We have already discussed two of the responses which members of groups make to pressures toward uniformity; namely, attempting to influence others and being more ready to be influenced. There is still a third response which serves to move toward uniformity. By rejecting those whose opinions diverge from the group, and thus redefining who is and who is not in the psychological group, uniformity can be accomplished. The greater the discrepancy between a person's opinion and the opinion of another, the stronger are the tendencies to exclude the other person from the psychological group.

There is evidence that members of groups do tend to reject those whose opinions are divergent. In the study of social groups within a housing project, Festinger, Schachter, and Back (8) found that those who did not conform to the standards of their social group were underchosen on a sociometric test; that is, they mentioned more persons as friends of theirs than they received in return. Schachter (8) did an experiment specifically to test whether or not members of groups would be rejected simply for disagreeing on an issue. Paid participants in the groups voiced divergent or agreeing opinions as instructed. In all groups the paid participant who voiced divergent opinion on an issue was rejected on a postmeeting questionnaire concerning whom they wanted to have remain in the group. The same paid participants, when voicing conforming opinions in other groups, were not rejected.

Hypothesis 4b. When nonconformity exists, the tendency to change the composition of the psychological group increases as the cohesiveness of the group increases and as the relevance of the issue to the group increases.

We have previously discussed the increase in forces to communicate with increase in cohesiveness and relevance of issue. Similarly, these two variables affect the tendency to reject persons from the group for nonconformity. Theoretically, we should expect any variable which affected the force to communicate (which stems from pressures toward uniformity) to affect also the tendency to reject nonconformers in a similar manner. In other words, increases in the force to communicate concerning an item will go along with increased tendency to reject persons who disagree concerning that item.

The previously mentioned experiment

by Schachter (8) was designed to test this hypothesis by experimentally varying cohesiveness and relevance in club groups. In this experiment the more cohesive groups do reject the nonconformer more than the less cohesive groups, and the groups where the issue is relevant reject the nonconformer more than groups where the issue is not very relevant to the group functioning. Those groups where cohesiveness was low and the issue was not very relevant show little, if any, tendency to reject the deviate.

FORCES TO CHANGE ONE'S POSITION IN A GROUP

Another important source of forces to communicate are the forces which act on members of groups to locomote (change their position) in the group or to move from one group to another. Such forces to locomote may stem from the attractiveness of activities associated with a different position in the group or from the status of that position, or the like. Thus a new member of a group may wish to become more central in the group, a member of an organization may wish to rise in the status hierarchy, a member of a business firm may want to be promoted, or a member of a minority group may desire acceptance by the majority group. These are all instances of forces to locomote in a social structure.

It is plausible that the existence of a force acting on a person in a specific direction produces behavior in that direction. Where locomotion in the desired direction is not possible, at least temporarily, there will exist a force to communicate in that direction. The existence of a force in a specific direction will produce behavior in that direction. One such kind of behavior is communication. This hypothesis is not very different from the hypothesis advanced by Lewin (6) to account for the superior recall of interrupted activities.

An experiment by Thibaut (9) tends to corroborate this theoretical analysis. In his experiment he created two groups—one of high status and privileged, the other of low status and underprivileged. These two groups, equated in other respects, functioned together so that the members of the high status group could play an attractive game. The low status

group functioned merely as servants. It was clear that forces were acting on the members of the low status group to move into the other group. As the privileged position of the high status group became clearer and clearer, the amount of communication from the low status team to the high status group increased. The number of communications from members of the high status group to the low status group correspondingly decreased. When, in some groups, the status and privilege relationship between the two teams was reversed toward the end of the experimental session, thus reducing the forces to locomote into the other group, the number of communications to that other group correspondingly decreased.

Further corroboration is found in a preliminary experiment, mainly methodologically oriented, conducted by Back *et al.* (2). In this experiment new items of information were planted with persons at various levels in the hierarchy of a functioning organization. Data on transmission of each of the items of information were obtained through cooperators within the organization who were chosen so as to give adequate coverage of all levels and all sections within it. These cooperators recorded all instances of communication that came to their attention. Of seventeen acts of communication recorded in this manner, eleven were directed upward in the hierarchy, four toward someone on the same level and only two were directed downward. The existence of forces to move upward in such a hierarchical organization may be taken for granted. The great bulk of the communications recorded went in the same direction as these forces to locomote.

In considering communication among members of differentiated social structures, it is important also to take into account restraints against communication.

Infrequent contact in the ordinary course of events tends to erect restraints against communication. It is undoubtedly easier to communicate a given item to a person whom one sees frequently, or to a person to whom one has communicated similar items in the past. The structuring of groups into hierarchies, social clusters, or the like undoubtedly tends to restrict the amount and type of contact between members of certain different parts or levels of the group, and also undoubtedly restricts the content of the communication that goes on between such levels in the ordinary course of events. These restrictions erect restraints against certain types of communication.

There are some data which tend to specify some of the restraints against communication which do exist. In the study of the communication of a spontaneous rumor in a community by Festinger, Cartwright *et al.* (3), it was found that intimacy of friendship tended to increase ease of communication. Persons with more friends in the project heard the rumor more often than those with only acquaintances. Those who had few friends or acquaintances heard the rumor least often. At the same time, this factor of intimacy of friendship was not related to how frequently they relayed the rumor to others. In other words, it was not related to forces to communicate but seemed to function only as a restraint against communicating where friendship did not exist.

There is also some evidence that the mere perception of the existence of a hierarchy sets up restraints against communication between levels. Kelley (7) experimentally created a two-level hierarchy engaging in a problem-solving task during which they could and did communicate within levels and between levels. Control groups were also run with the same task situation but with no status differential involved between the two subgroups. There was more communication between subgroups under these control conditions than where there was a status differential involved.

It seems that, in a hierarchy, there are also restraints against communicating hostility upward when the hostility is about those on upper levels. In the same experiment by Kelley there was much criticism of the *other group* expressed by both high status and low status members. The proportion of these critical expressions which are directed upward by the low status group is much less, however, than the proportion directed downward by the high status groups.

EMOTIONAL EXPRESSION

An important variety of communications undoubtedly results from the existence of an emotional state in the communicator. The existence of joy, anger, hostility, and the like seems to produce forces to communicate. It seems that communications resulting from the existence of an emotional state are consummatory rather than instrumental.

By an instrumental communication, we mean one in which the reduction of the force to communicate depends upon the effect of the communication on the recipient. Thus in communication resulting from pressures toward uniformity in a group, the mere fact that a communication is made does not affect the force to communicate. If the effect has been to change the recipient so that he now agrees more closely with the communicator, the force to communicate will be reduced. If the recipient changes in the opposite direction, the force to communicate to him will be increased.

By a consummatory communication, we mean one in which the reduction of the force to communicate occurs as a result of the expression and does not depend upon the effect it has on the recipient. Certainly in the case of such communications the reaction of the recipient may introduce new elements into the situation which will affect the force to communicate, but the essence of a consummatory communication is that the simple expression does reduce the force.

Specifically with regard to the communication of hostility and aggression, much has been said regarding its consummatory nature. The psychoanalytic theories of catharsis, in particular, develop the notion that the expression of hostility reduces the emotional state of the person. There has, however, been very little experimental work done on the problem. The previously mentioned experiment by Thibaut in which he created a "privileged-underprivileged" relationship between two equated groups has some data on the point. There is evidence that those members of the "underprivileged" groups who expressed their hostility toward the "privileged" groups showed less residual hostility toward them in post-experimental questionnaires. There is, however, no control over the reactions of the recipients of the hostile communications nor over the perceptions of the communicators of what these reactions were. An experiment is now in progress which will attempt to clarify some of these relationships with both negative and positive emotional states.

SUMMARY

A series of interrelated hypotheses has been presented to account for data on informal social communication collected in the course of a number of studies. The data come from field studies and from laboratory experiments specifically designed to test the hypotheses.

Three sources of pressures to communicate have been considered:

1. Communication arising from pressures toward uniformity in a group. Here we considered determinants of magnitude of the force to communicate, choice of recipient for the communication, magnitude of change in recipient, and magnitude of tendencies to reject nonconformers.

2. Communications arising from forces to locomote in a social structure. Here we considered communications in the direction of a blocked locomotion, and restraints against communication arising in differentiated social structures.

3. Communications arising from the existence of emotional states. In this area data are almost completely lacking. Some theoretical distinctions were made, and an experiment which is now in progress in this area was outlined.

References

1. Back, K. Influence through social communication. *Journal of Abnormal and Social Psychology,* 1951, **46,** 9–23.
2. Back, K., *et al.* The methodology of studying rumor transmission. *Human Relations,* 1950, **3,** 307–313.
3. Festinger, L., *et al.* A study of rumor: Its origin and spread. *Human Relations,* 1948, **1,** 464–486.
4. Festinger, L., Schachter, S., & Back, K. *Social pressures in informal groups: A study of a housing project.* New York: Harper, 1950.
5. Festinger, L., & Thibaut, J. Interpersonal communication in small groups. *Journal of Abnormal and Social Psychology,* 1951, **46,** 92–99.
6. Lewin, K. Formalization and progress in psychology. *Univ. of Iowa Studies in Child Welfare,* 1940, **16** (3).
7. Kelley, H. H. Communication in experimentally created hierarchies. *Human Relations,* 1951, **4,** 39–56.
8. Schachter, S. Deviation, rejection, and communication. *Journal of Abnormal and Social Psychology,* 1951, **46,** 190–207.
9. Thibaut, J. An experimental study of the cohesiveness of underprivileged groups. *Human Relations,* 1950, **3,** 251–278.

15

An Experimental Study of Cohesiveness and Productivity

STANLEY SCHACHTER, NORRIS ELLERTSON, DOROTHY McBRIDE, AND DORIS GREGORY

The once modest concept of cohesiveness has in recent years become distinguished by the proliferation of meaning attached to it. With the growing interest in group psychology, cohesiveness as a concept has assumed some importance, for it represents an attempt to formalize or simply to verbalize the key group phenomena of membership continuity—the "cement" binding together group members and maintaining their relationships to one another. Discussions of this group property have been notably loose and *cohesiveness* has been defined variously as referring to morale, "sticking togetherness," productivity, power, task involvement, feelings of belongingness, shared understanding of roles, and good teamwork.

It is possible roughly to categorize these assorted meanings into two classes. One class of definitions centers chiefly around particular aspects of group behavior or process and the word *cohesiveness* refers to such things as the morale, efficiency, or "spirit" of the group. The attractiveness of the group for its members may be implicit in such formulations but is usually of secondary importance. The second class of definitions is concerned exclusively with the attractiveness of the group for its members. Thus, Festinger, Schachter, and Back (3) define *cohesiveness* as the average resultant force acting on members with direction toward the group. No assumptions are made about the behavior or "atmosphere" of cohesive groups.

The distinction between these two formulations becomes clear in their treatments of the relationship of cohesiveness to group productivity. The cohesiveness-morale formulation suggests that since a cohesive group is marked by good morale and since the members of such a group like one another and get on well together, it should follow

From *Human Relations*, 1951, **4**, 229–238. The research was conducted in the Laboratory for Research in Social Relations, University of Minnesota, under a grant from the Carnegie Corporation. The article is reprinted by permission of the authors and *Human Relations*.

that the more cohesive the group the greater should be its productivity. At least two studies have tested this hypothesis. R. L. French (4) in a study of a military camp has attempted to relate a sociometric index of cohesiveness of the company to a variety of measures of performance in drill and athletic competition, academic work, participation in community activities, etc. Darley, Gross, and Martin (2) have investigated the relationship of sociometric indices of cohesiveness to judges' ratings of the excellence of group written essays. Neither study has supported the anticipated relationship.

The cohesiveness-attraction theory leads to a very different set of derivations [see Chapter 14]. From this theory the derivation has been made (1, 3) that the greater the cohesiveness the greater the power of the group to influence its members. The power of the group will be equal to the magnitude of the force on the member to remain in the group. If the magnitude of change which the group attempts to induce is greater than the force on the member to stay in the group, the member will leave the group. The greater the force to remain in the group, the more successful will be the attempts of the group to influence the member.

If we conceive of group productivity as in part a function of the success of the group at influencing its members, it becomes clear that cohesiveness should be one of the determinants of productivity. Whether cohesiveness will increase or decrease productivity, however, is determined largely by the direction of group induction. If the group attempts to influence its members to increase production, high cohesive groups should be more productive than low cohesive groups. If the group attempts to decrease production, low cohesive groups should be more productive than high. In both cases, the more cohesive groups are more successful at influencing their members. The present study was designed to test these implications of the cohesiveness-attraction theory for productivity. .

THE EXPERIMENT

There were four combinations of the variables, cohesiveness and direction of induction:

1. High cohesive, positive or speed-up induction (abbreviated Hi Co + Ind).

2. Low cohesive, positive induction (Lo Co + Ind).
3. High cohesive, negative or slow-down induction (Hi Co − Ind).
4. Low cohesive, negative induction (Lo Co − Ind).

Except for variations introduced in order to manipulate the two variables, the procedure described below was followed in all experimental conditions. Each experimental group was made up of three people. When possible, the three people were all subjects. If because of scheduling difficulties it was possible to obtain only one or two subjects at a particular time, paid confederates posing as subjects were introduced to complete the group.

All subjects were female student volunteers from undergraduate education and psychology classes. The confederates, too, were female students. The subjects for any particular group were taken from different classes so that they would not know one another. There were thirteen subjects in each of the high cohesive conditions, and twelve in each of the low cohesive conditions.

The members of each group were first introduced to one another. The experimenter explained that this was a study of group psychology, elaborated briefly, and then went on to a description of the specific task of the group— the cooperative production of cardboard checkerboards. There were supposedly three jobs to be done: cutting the cardboard, mounting and pasting it on heavier stock, and painting the boards through a stencil. One group member was to be assigned to each of the jobs. In explaining the task, the experimenter implied that speed and quantity of production were desirable.

After these preliminaries, each member of the group was assigned to a different workroom. Here, although all subjects were assigned the job of cutting, each girl was given the impression that the other two members were painting or pasting. The members of the group were allowed to communicate with one another only by notes delivered by a messenger. A subject was allowed to write as many notes as she pleased to either of the other two group members. Actually, all notes were intercepted by the messenger, who substituted notes from a standard prewritten set. The subject, however, believed the notes that she received were written by the other members of the group. These notes furnished the means by which direction of induction was manipulated.

Every four minutes the messenger delivered prewritten notes to the subject and collected both any notes the subject had written and the cardboard she had cut during the preceding four minutes. The subject cut cardboard for 32 minutes. Then, after filling out a questionnaire, she was brought together again with her group. The purpose of the experiment was discussed and the various deceptions were explained in detail.

THE MANIPULATION OF THE VARIABLES

1. Cohesiveness has been defined as the average resultant force acting on members to remain in the group. The valence of the group derives from at least two sources: the attractiveness of the activities mediated by the group and the attractiveness of other group members. High and low cohesiveness were produced here by manipulating the attractiveness of the group members.

In the speeches recruiting subjects, the experiment was described as a study concerned with "people who really like one another." It was emphasized that on the basis of recent and striking research, it was now possible to select people who would be genuinely fond of one another. This research would determine the selection of work groups. Volunteers filled out questionnaires designed ostensibly to get detailed personality information. Examples of the questions asked are, "If your worst enemy were to describe you, what do you think he would say?" "Which people in history do you most admire?" "Would you have any objection to our looking over the test data available on you at the records office?"

In the experiment proper, as soon as a subject arrived and before she had met the other members of her group, she was privately interviewed by one of the experimenters. During this interview, apparently designed simply to collect routine information, the interviewer informed the subject in the high cohesive conditions that she was a member of an extremely congenial group and that "there is every reason to expect that the other members of the group will like you and you will like them." In the low cohesive conditions, subjects were told that due to scheduling difficulties it had been impossible to bring together a congenial group and that "there is no particular reason to think that you will like them or that they will care for you."

At the end of the experiment, the subject filled out a cohesiveness questionnaire designed to test the success of the manipulation. The following questions were asked:

A. How did you like your team?
B. If you were taking part in another experiment, how much would you like to work with these same girls?
C. How much do you think you would like to see your teammates?

Questions *A* and *B* were answered on 5-point rating scales designed to determine how much the subject liked her group and how much she would like to work with them again. Question *C* is a 7-point scale devised by Back (1) using an abbreviated Thurstone technique to measure the "intensity of attraction."

Table 1 presents the data from this questionnaire. All scores represent the mean position of all subjects in each of the four conditions. The higher the score, the greater the cohesiveness. For question *C* the score was the highest point checked on the scale. With the direction of induction held constant, the scores on each question are higher for the high cohesive than for the low cohesive groups.

TABLE 1. *Responses to Cohesiveness Questionnaire*

	N	*Question A:* "Like Team"	*Question B:* "Work with Same Girls"	*Question C:* "Intensity of Attraction" Scale
Hi Co + Ind	13	3.62	3.77	3.77
Lo Co + Ind	12	2.92	2.92	2.50
Hi Co − Ind	13	3.85	4.31	3.69
Lo Co − Ind	12	3.50	3.25	2.75

Experimental time elapsed before delivery	*All subjects received these notes:*
4 min.	"I wonder who will use these boards." (signed) Paster.
	"I wish I had a coke right now." Painter.
8 min.	"Gee, but my fingers are getting sticky." Paster.
12 min.	"I wish I had a radio in here." Paster.
	"Don't you think this will make awfully loud checker-boards?" (smear of red paint). Painter

Positive induction subjects received these notes:	*Negative induction subjects received these notes:*
16 min. "Can you hurry things up a bit?" Painter.	"Let's try to set a record—the slowest subjects they ever had." Painter.
	"You're getting way ahead of me—relax." Paster.
20 min. "The painter is hounding me for more boards—can you cut them out a little faster?" Paster.	
"Hate to bother you, but I'm twiddling my thumbs. Couldn't you speed it up?" Painter.	"Please work a little slower. I'm flooded in cardboard and drowning in paint." Painter.
24 min. "I've only got one board left, can you step on it?" Paster.	"Take it easy, I'm tired." Paster.
28 min. "Time's running out, let's really make a spurt." Paster.	"Painting takes more time than you think—slow down." Painter.
"The messenger says we only have a few minutes—see how fast we can go." Painter.	"We've done a lot of these things. Let's take it easy now." Paster.

On questions B and C, all differences between high and low cohesive groups in either induction condition are significant by t test at the 1% level of confidence. On question A the difference between the Hi + and Lo + is significant at the 5% level and that between Hi − and Lo − at the 20% level of confidence. The manipulation seems to have been successful in producing high and low cohesiveness.

2. Direction of induction refers here to attempts by the group to influence a member to increase or decrease her rate of production. All attempts to influence the subject were via pre-written notes which the subject believed were from other members of her group. During the first 16 minutes of the experiment, all subjects received five notes which made no attempt to influence their rate of production. In the remaining 16 minutes, the subject received six notes all attempting either to increase or to decrease her rate of production. In the positive induction conditions, these notes requested that she work more rapidly; in the negative induction conditions, the notes requested that

she work more slowly. The specific notes and the time schedule governing their delivery are shown at the top of the page.

RESULTS

The difference in the number of cardboards cut during the intervals of neutral and of induction notes is taken as an indication of the extent of acceptance of induction.

Table 2 presents data on the effect of induction on the subject's productivity.

For purposes of analysis, the experiment is divided into four 8-minute periods. The 8—16 minute period is taken as a base line. During these 8-minute periods the subject receives only neutral notes and no attempt is made to influence her rate of production.[1] The figures

[1] During the first 8-minute period, the subject was growing accustomed to her job and the note writing procedure. In addition, she received only two notes during this time, whereas in each of the

TABLE 2. *Mean Deviation from Level of Production in the 8–16 Minute Pre-Induction Period*

	N	16–24 Minute Induction Period	24–32 Minute Induction Period
Hi Co + Ind	13	+ 2.92	+ 5.92
Lo Co + Ind	12	+ 2.92	+ 5.09
Hi Co − Ind	13	− 1.00	− 2.16
Lo Co − Ind	12	− .58	− .42

reported represent mean deviations from this base during the two later induction periods.

It is clear, first, that the direction of "group" induction, via the notes, had a major effect on the rate of production. In the positive induction conditions, production increases markedly. In the negative induction conditions, the rate of production decreases. During either of these two induction periods (16–24 minutes and 24–32 minutes), differences between production in positive and negative induction conditions are all significant by *t* test at the 1% level of confidence, at least.

The relations between cohesiveness and productivity are as follows: Communications calling for increased production result in no significant differences between the high and low cohesive groups. There are differences, however, when the notes urge a reduction in production. In this "slow-down" condition, subjects in high cohesive groups decrease continuously from induction period to induction period. Scores for both periods are significantly below the base line level of production at better than the 1% level of confidence. In the low cohesive groups, subjects decrease slightly in the 16–24 minute period and then increase their output. Neither of these scores is significantly below base line production. The difference between Hi Co − and Lo Co − subjects, in the 24–32 minute period, is significant by *t* test at better than the 2% level of confidence. In the 16–24 minute period, the difference is in the predicted direction but is not significant.

The effects of the cohesiveness variable stand out more clearly in Table 3. This table presents a breakdown, by condition, of subjects who accepted and who did not accept group induction. A *non-accepter* is defined as a subject who, during at least one of the last

_____

other 8-minute periods she received three notes. For these reasons, data for the first period are not comparable to the remaining periods and are not reported.

two periods, shifted her rate of production in a direction opposite to that of group induction. Thus, a negative induction subject who in at least one of these periods increased her rate of production over that of the immediately preceding period would be classed as a non-accepter. Similarly, a positive induction subject who decreased her rate of production would be so classified. Again there are no differences between Hi Co + and Lo Co + ; almost all subjects in both conditions accepted induction. Differences between Hi Co − and Lo Co − are marked. Seventy-five per cent of all Lo Co − subjects are non-accepters and only 15% of Hi Co − are non-accepters. This difference is significant at the 1% level of confidence using Fisher's exact treatment of a 2 × 2 table.

TABLE 3. *Accepters and Non-Accepters of Group Induction*

	Number of Accepters	Number of Non-Accepters
Hi Co + Ind	13	0
Lo Co + Ind	11	1
Hi Co − Ind	11	2
Lo Co − Ind	4	8

Table 4 presents gross production data for the last three periods. The figures represent the mean of the total number of cardboards cut by the subjects in each condition. The differences between high and low cohesive groups are similar to those presented in Table 2. In the negative induction conditions, low cohesive subjects are less acceptant of induction and more productive than high cohesive subjects. Though, again, there are no significant differences in the positive induction conditions, the small differences that do exist are in favor of the low cohesive subjects. This may be attributable to the lower initial level of cutting of the high cohesive subjects. Despite the

TABLE 4. *Mean Number of Cardboards Cut in Each Period*

	N	8–16 Minute Pre-Induction Period	16–24 Minute Induction Period	24–32 Minute Induction Period
Hi Co + Ind	13	5.31	8.23	11.23
Lo Co + Ind	12	6.16	9.08	11.25
Hi Co − Ind	13	6.31	5.31	4.15
Lo Co − Ind	12	6.42	5.84	6.00

random assignment of subjects to the various experimental conditions, for some reason subjects in the Hi Co + groups cut at a slower rate than subjects in any of the other conditions.

In summary, the data indicate no necessary relationship between cohesiveness and high productivity. Group members will accept induction either to increase or decrease production. Whether or not highly cohesive groups are more likely to develop standards of high production rather than low production is a separate question, but evidence from industrial studies (2), e.g., the slow down, indicates that this is not the case.

Cohesiveness appears to be a determining variable in the negative but not in the positive induction condition. In the latter, both high and low cohesive subjects accept group induction and increase their output markedly. In the negative induction condition, the high cohesive subjects are more accepting of group induction and, consequently, less productive than low cohesive subjects.

DISCUSSION

These experimental results indicate that it is necessary to study more carefully the relationships between the direction of induction and its acceptance. In an earlier study (3), induction has been formulated as the direction imposed on an own force. It is presumed that a relationship exists between inducer and inducee such that the inducer either controls or represents a goal object for the inducee. The desirability of the goal object is a determinant of the magnitude of the force on the inducee toward the goal. The specific activities necessary to achieve the goal determine the direction of this force. At various times, a number of very diverse activities may lead to any one goal. In order, for example, that a farm boy be able to please his father, it may be necessary

at one time to slop the hogs and at another time to mix chicken mash. Thus, the inducer can modify the direction of an inducee's own force by specifying the activities necessary to reach the goal. The inducer's success will depend on the direction and magnitude of other forces acting on the inducee. If the specified activity is negatively valent, or if other inducing agents are attempting to exert contrary influence, the inducer may be unsuccessful. Induction will be accepted up to the magnitude of the force toward the goal object. If other forces of greater magnitude and opposite direction are active, induction will be unsuccessful.

In the present experimental arrangement it is assumed that there are essentially two forces operating on the subject:

1. A force to be an accepted member of his particular group $(f_{p, gr})$.
2. A force to do a good job and win the praise of the experimenter $(f_{p, exp})$.

It is presumed that the magnitude of $f_{p, exp}$ is similar in all experimental variations and that the magnitude of $f_{p, gr}$ is greater in the high than in the low cohesive conditions. The direction of $f_{p, exp}$ is always the same, since the experimental instructions implied that speed and quantity of output were important. The direction of $f_{p, gr}$ is different in the positive and the negative induction situations. In the positive condition the group induces the subject to speed up and in the negative condition, to slow down.

It is apparent that the force constellations in the positive and the negative inductions situations are quite different. In the positive induction condition the two forces, $f_{p, gr}$ and $f_{p, exp}$, have precisely the same direction. In the negative induction condition they have opposite directions.[2] Our experimental results

[2] There are two bits of related evidence which support this analysis. Table 3 shows that 40% of all cases in the negative induction conditions did at

suggest that only when these two forces are opposite in direction does the magnitude of $f_{p, gr}$ determine the degree of acceptance of induction.

More generally, this relationship may be stated in this way: induction is formalized as the direction imposed on an own force. The success of induction will depend upon the magnitude and direction of other forces operating in the field. If other forces are opposite in direction to the induced direction, the acceptance of induction will depend upon the magnitude of the own force toward the goal controlled by the inducing agent. If all other forces are similar in direction to the induced direction, the acceptance of induction will be relatively independent of the magnitude of this own force.[3]

The application of this conceptualization to predictions of a differential acceptance of induction in high and low cohesive groups demands further specification of the magnitude of forces opposite in direction to the group forces. If the opposing force has a magnitude greater than that of the force toward the high cohesive group, or less than that of the force toward the low cohesive group, there should

be no differences between high and low cohesive groups. Between these limits, high cohesive groups should win greater acceptance of induction than low cohesive groups.[4] In the present experiment, then, it is presumed that in the positive induction condition any opposing forces that existed were of a lesser magnitude than the force toward the low cohesive group,[5] and that in the negative induction condition the magnitude of the opposing force was between the specified limits.

Though the term *group productivity*, as employed in this study, has a very limited and specific meaning (output per unit time), these elaborations of the cohesiveness-attraction theory do seem applicable to other formulations of productivity. *Group productivity* does commonly have a variety of other meanings: for example, the quality of a group product, or the speed and efficiency with which a group locomotes toward a given goal, or the degree of realization of group potential, etc. No matter what the criteria of productivity, or the structure of the particular task, high cohesive groups should (within the specified limits) be more successful at overcoming forces with direction opposite to group induced direction.

References

1. Back, K. W. Influence through social communication. *Journal of Abnormal and Social Psychology*, 1951, **46**, 9–23.
2. Darley, J., Gross, N., & Martin, W. Studies of group behavior: Factors associated with the productivity of groups. *Journal of Applied Psychology*, 1952, **36**, 396–403.
3. Festinger, L., Schachter, S., & Back, K. *Social pressures in informal groups.* New York: Harper, 1950.
4. French, R. L. Sociometric status and individual adjustment among naval recruits. *Journal of Abnormal and Social Psychology*, 1951, **46**, 64–71.

some time reject group induction, whereas only 4% of subjects in the positive induction conditions did so. Further, in Table 2 it can be seen that positive induction subjects accelerated their rate of production at a far more rapid rate than did negative induction subjects decrease their production rate.

[3] It would be possible to further test this formulation of the induction process by reversing the experimental design used in this study. If the experimenter were somehow to induce forces on the subjects to work slowly, we should predict the opposite of the results reported in this paper. There should be differences between high and low cohesive groups in the positive induction condition and no differences in the negative induction condition.

[4] Essentially, this is a theory of the occurrence or nonoccurrence of a specific induced act. Implicit is the assumption that if the resultant force towards a particular activity is greater than zero, the person will perform that activity whether the resultant force has a high or low magnitude. Quite possibly employing criteria such as "eagerness to perform an activity," or "effort expended attempting to overcome a barrier," will necessitate further refinement of the present theory to include the effects of varying magnitudes of resultant force.

[5] It is conceivable that if the induction period had been extended in time, restraining forces would have grown to such magnitude that a difference between high and low cohesive groups would have appeared.

16

Political Standards in Secondary Groups

PHILIP CONVERSE AND ANGUS CAMPBELL

The distinctive voting patterns of certain large-scale groupings in the population suggest the presence of group standards and group influence. It has generally been recognized, for example, that members of business and labor organizations and Catholics, Jews, Negroes, and other ethnic groupings tend to show a characteristic bias toward one party or another at the polls. Since the members of each of these groupings share many of the same life experiences, there has been some question as to whether this distinctiveness of political behavior reflects only parallel responses to parallel experience or is mediated by the group in a more active sense (2).

Current evidence concerning the more prominent of these secondary groups indicates that it is reasonable to treat them in terms of active group standards. This evidence is of two types. First, it may be shown that members of these groups remain distinctive in their partisanship when paired with nonmembers of similar background. For example, a union member is more likely to vote Democratic in the current era than the nonmember of equivalent occupation, education, income, religion, urban-rural residence, region, ethnic background, race, age, and the like. Except as some politically potent aspect of experience may escape our attention, we would conclude that, life situation aside, the fact of group membership itself leads to differences in behavior.

Where the first line of evidence pits member against nonmember, the second depends on intragroup differences. In the 1948 study of voting conducted by Berelson *et al.*, in Elmira, New York, members of ethnic and religious groups of distinctive political coloration were asked questions designed to reveal the importance or valence which the group held for the individual. Suchman and Menzel (5) have shown that members who deemed the group important were more likely to vote "with the group" than were more indifferent members.

This chapter was prepared especially for this volume.

In our national study of the 1956 presidential election we asked Catholics, Jews, Negroes, and members of labor unions to respond to the following questions in terms of their group: [1]

Would you say you feel pretty close to (for example, Negroes) in general or that you don't feel much closer to them than you do to other kinds of people?

How much interest would you say you have in how (for example, Negroes) as a whole are getting along in this country? Do you have a good deal of interest in it, some interest, or not much interest at all?

Responses to these items were combined to form a scale indicating the degree to which the member identified with the group in question. Each group had a putative Democratic voting norm. As hypothesized, highly identified members were more likely to vote Democratic than the less strongly identified.

In both the 1948 and 1956 instances, the only apparent difference between group members was the nature of the relationship with the group. Yet, in each case, this difference turned out to be associated with more or less distinctive partisan choice. The conclusion once again seems to be that the partisanship which characterizes these groups as aggregates are mediated in some manner by the group *qua* group.

There are further provocative aspects to the data. It is clear, for example, that some groupings are much more solidary in their support of a particular party than are other groupings likewise thought to have partisan voting norms. If comparable nonmembers are dividing their vote 50–50 between the two major parties, then the "Democratic" group which casts 85 percent of its votes for the Democratic party is more distinctive than the "Democratic" group which favors that party by only a 55–45 margin. We do in fact find wide differences of this sort in the degree to which groups vote distinctively.

[1] This study, supported by a grant from the Rockefeller Foundation, was carried out at the Survey Research Center, University of Michigan. It involved a cross-section sample of 1,772 respondents, chosen by strict probability methods from all adult citizens living in private households in the United States.

It is apparent, too, that the partisan division of the vote among the highly identified members of certain groups departs more strongly from the vote division of the less identified members than is the case within other groups. In other words, the strength of relationship between identification and vote varies substantially from group to group. Among Catholics, for example, it is relatively low; among union members it is notably higher.

Furthermore, these "within-group" and "between-group" contrasts are correlated. Where a group is more distinctive by comparison with nongroup voters, it is likely to be the case as well that its members are more differentiated one from another in their voting choice as a function of group identification. We may think of a continuum representing percentage Democratic of the two-party vote, on which we locate three or more points representing group members of varying strength of identification, along with some comparable set of nonmembers. If we compare continua of this sort constructed for several groups, the distances between the several points for one group will be small, while the analogous distances for another group will quite generally be larger. We may readily imagine forces emanating from the group which act to disperse these points along each continuum, and differences in distances from group to group may be taken to reflect differences in the strength of group forces operative on the membership.

It is our purpose in this paper to expand our view of the influence process to encompass these systematic differences. We may thereby cast further light on the familiar waxing and waning of partisan homogeneity within groups of this sort over time, while illuminating, at an individual level, the circumstances of deviation from group standards in this behavioral setting.

A MODEL FOR THE POLITICAL INFLUENCE SITUATION

We are interested in the effects of a membership group upon the response of an individual toward the world of politics. Thus three elements—individual, group, and political world—are involved in the situation. Between these elements lies a triangle of relationships. Two of these involve the actor directly; we may consider the third leg, the relationship between the group and the world of politics, as having the properties which the actor perceives to exist. Logically, a proper understanding of the character of these relationships from member to member should permit us to account for the final partisan behavior of each. Let us therefore consider some of the specific properties of these relationships which we might measure and combine to form a system of explanatory variables.

THE INDIVIDUAL AND
THE POLITICAL WORLD

We must recognize at the outset that, group considerations aside, the individual is engaged in a set of ongoing reactions to the political process. Hence if we wished to predict the full response made by the membership of any grouping at the polls, our characterization of the relationship between the individual and politics would become elaborate indeed, involving many terms that have nothing to do with the specific group membership. The member is exposed to much political information not mediated by the group. If the party favored by the group is enveloped in scandal, this fact will make inroads on the valence it holds for the member. Similarly, a very attractive candidate proffered by the opposition cannot be written off as lightly as an unattractive one. In short, the events of politics affect the member's reaction directly in some degree, independent of group standards. The group member does not make decisions in a psychological field limited to group forces any more than a nonmember makes decisions in a vacuum.

Our purpose here is not, therefore, to account for the total response of the individual member to current politics, but rather to account for the differences introduced in this response because the group impinges on his political evaluations. It is for this reason that we have referred above not simply to group voting, but to the "distinctiveness" of group voting. The difference is readily illustrated. Several national surveys conducted in 1956 showed that the Democratic vote for President among Catholics had dipped below a 50–50 split for the first time since relevant data had been collected. In one sense, Catholic voters had suddenly "turned" Republican. It was true that the distinctiveness of the Catholic vote had been waning, but it remained Democratic

relative to the vote among non-Catholics even in 1956, and this residual distinctiveness merely formed another point on a declining trend which we have had the opportunity to watch since 1948. In absolute terms the Catholic vote became sharply more Republican in 1952 and 1956, as did the vote among virtually all prominent groupings of this sort. But the degree of partisan bias *attributable to the group* did not shift violently.

It is to recognize the individual's independent access to politics as well that we wish to measure distinctiveness as a deviation from a base-line provided by a "control group" of nonmembers whose life situations are equivalent. Catholics have tended to vote Democratic in times past, but so have other individuals of lower status. Is the Democratic bias in the Catholic vote an effect of active group mediation, or would Catholics have responded to lower status with the same increase in Democratic voting independent of their religious ties? This question may best be answered by gauging their distinctiveness relative to other voters *of equivalent status*. And, since status is not the sole aspect of life situation which affects partisan response, the control groups that we have constructed to assess group distinctiveness of vote take into account a variety of other dimensions as well.[2]

[2] Control groups were formed for each secondary grouping in the following fashion. Two variables whose interaction terms were known to be potent vis-à-vis partisan behavior were controlled in a "precision" matching: region (South vs. non-South) and urban-rural residence (3 categories). For union members, occupation status (3 categories) was controlled in the precision sense as well. Within groups so defined looser "distribution" controls were used. Thus the control groups have the same distribution as the member groups on region of nativity (2 categories), urban-rural background (3), education (3), occupation (3), income (3), generations in the United States (2), and age (3). Finally, within each group the effect of other prominent secondary membership groups was equated: the Catholic control group had the same proportion of union members and Negroes as appeared among Catholics, etc. Disregarding redundant percent deviations, the differences between proportions of group and nongroup controls distributed in the several categories employed was 1.2 percent in the case of Catholics, 1.5 percent for Jews, 1.9 percent for union members, and for Negroes, where matching was difficult, 4.3 percent. It might be noted that after the first precision controls had been applied and occupation

The use of these control groups does not mean of course that life situations have no role in the group influence process. Quite to the contrary, the distinctive needs which arise because group members find themselves relegated to peculiar positions in the social structure may contribute substantially to the motive power of the group *qua* group. What is important for our purposes, however, is the fact that shared membership appears to lend a focus and direction to behavior that is less visible for nonmembers who exist under similar conditions and can be presumed to have similar needs. This focus and direction is an integral part of what we mean by "group influence."

If we estimate the distinctiveness of our several groups in this fashion, we find the largest deviation in a Democratic direction from a base line set by a control group to occur in the case of Jewish respondents (a difference of proportions of 45 percent). Union members (20 percent), non-Southern Negroes (12 percent), and Catholics (3 percent) follow in descending order.[3] While these are crude estimates at best, the range of variation presented is substantial. It is our assumption that this variation reflects differences in the strength of group forces in the psychological field as members evaluate the political world in reaching a vote decision. The strength of these forces is some function of (a) the relationship of the individual to the group and (b) the relationship of the group to the world of politics.

THE INDIVIDUAL AND THE GROUP

A variety of research undertakings have lent weight to the proposition that individuals attracted to a group are more likely to conform to its standards. The findings cited above from the 1948 and 1956 voting studies may be taken as a special case of such a phenomenon. The items that we used to measure strength of

member identification with the group clearly provide an assessment of the attractiveness or valence of the group for the member. While the term "identification" seems best suited for the groupings of interest here, any method of summarizing the valence that marks the individual-group relationship appears to help us in discriminating between group members who will follow or deviate from group standards.

By the same token, if "cohesiveness" refers to a summation of the attraction exerted by the group across its membership, then the relative cohesiveness of various groups can help to explain differences in their heterogeneity as voting "blocs." We chose items to measure group identification that might be applied to a variety of groups in order to facilitate such intergroup comparisons. The resulting distribution of member identifications which characterizes each group fits our intuitive preconceptions extremely well. Negroes, in a ferment over the problem of group advancement that was approaching the proportions of a nationalist movement, responded with almost unanimous warmth to our questions concerning group identification. Similarly, Jewish respondents, members of an ethnic community commonly considered to be "tightly knit," showed almost the same strong cohesiveness. Union members were, more often than not, positively disposed to their organizations, but there was a notable reduction in the proportion of favorable responses to the group here by comparison with Negroes or Jews. Catholics, presumed to be nearing the end of an assimilation process that has gone on in this country for many decades, registered as somewhat less cohesive still.

The ordering of these groups in terms of relative cohesiveness bears fair resemblance to their ordering in terms of partisan distinctiveness in 1956. Jews show high distinctiveness in their vote and are highly cohesive as well. Similarly, among our four groupings, Catholics are both least cohesive and least distinctive. Thus we get a sense that trends in the partisan solidarity of groups in the national electorate may be traced in some measure to the same mechanisms that have been subjected to examination in the laboratory with face-to-face groups.

However, the match between the two orderings is not perfect, suggesting that other variables are operative that deserve recognition in any full explanatory scheme. The distinctive-

---

was added, further variables created only trivial fluctuation in the vote division of the control group.

[3] The Negro and Jewish groups are considerably smaller (Ns of 63 and 56 respectively) than the Catholic and union contingents (Ns of 253 and 373, respectively). Hence estimates for these groups are subject to greater sampling error. For the same reason, much of our intragroup analyses will be restricted to the union and Catholic groups.

ness of the Negro vote, for example, is much lower than its group cohesiveness would lead us to expect, even when we restrict our focus to Negroes residing outside the South. On the basis of independent knowledge of events surrounding the 1956 election, we might well conclude that the missing term here has to do with the character of group standards that are propagated. We know, for example, that Negro leadership was badly split in its political endorsements in the 1956 campaign. Adam Clayton Powell, the foremost legislator of his race on the national scene, bolted from a Democratic affiliation to recommend the election of the Republican candidate. At the same time, the National Association for Advancement of Colored People, the major formal organization representing the group, adopted a posture of watchful waiting during the campaign, with vague intimations of a Republican endorsement from the executive secretary. Meanwhile, visible Negro political leaders in other non-Southern cities tended to hew to the traditional Democratic choice in their public pronouncements. Along similar lines, although case numbers are small, we find in our own trend data that the distinctiveness of the non-Southern Negro vote was cut almost in half between 1952 and 1956.

This case study instructs us to shift our attention from the relationship between member and group to that which the member perceives to exist between the group and the political world. Tentatively, we leave the individual-group leg of the triangle to be represented by the single estimate of member identification with the group. There are a number of directions in which the notion of a generalized group valence has been expanded (1), and such expansions might increase the explanatory significance of this portion of the system of variables. Nonetheless, it appears that we may enhance our understanding more rapidly by proceeding directly to the third leg of the triangular relationship.

THE GROUP AND THE WORLD OF POLITICS

In a general way, we may characterize the relationship between the group and the world of politics in terms of the proximity that the individual perceives to exist between the two entities. This sense of proximity may be difficult to specify, for in many ways the world of politics is a poorly defined region. Phenomenologically, however, it does seem to have some vague boundaries. It is in this spirit, for example, that a person may decide to "go into politics," a group should "stay out of politics," or a public problem is "made a political issue."

The notion of proximity is closely akin to what Schachter (4) has treated as the "relevance" of a topic for a group. Yet it subsumes a manifold process that we shall wish to examine in greater detail. It is of particular importance in this setting because the secondary groupings we are examining are not at core "political" groups. That is, the basic goals of these groups are not directly political. The labor union exists to force management to provide more liberally for the worker; the Catholic church exists for religious worship. Yet these groups are *more nearly* political than the American Bowling Congress, for example, because from time to time influential group members come to see political instruments as important for the attainment of certain group goals. How nearly political any given member perceives the group to be will affect the way in which he reacts to a particular political standard felt to emanate from the group.

Groups that take political positions frequently are likely to communicate a sense that they are more rather than less political groups. Similarly, the strength of the standards conveyed contributes to a perception of proximity between group and politics. Even where strong standards are frequently transmitted, however, there may be further barriers acting to compartmentalize the world of politics from the sphere of group activity. The member may perceive that political action is relevant for the accomplishment of group goals, yet he may have qualms about the legitimacy of group intrusion in politics. There are cultural values bound up with beliefs about democracy and the individual that inveigh against such activity. Values of this sort might prevent a sense of proximity from developing whatever other conditions obtained.

Thus we would expect some of the residual differences in vote homogeneity not explained by cohesiveness to depend on such factors as the strength and clarity of the standards that have been emitted in the name of the group, their successful transmission to the membership, and the values held by members concerning the appropriateness of political standards for the group concerned.

STRENGTH OF EMITTED STANDARDS

One of the anomalies evident as we compare the ordering of our groups on vote distinctiveness and cohesiveness has to do with the union vote. Union members do not appear greatly more cohesive than Catholics, yet they are much more distinctive in their voting. This difference is reflected in another manner as well. Within the set of union members, the degree of association between identification and vote is considerably higher than among Catholics.[4] Since this difference depends on contrasts in the behavior of more and less identified members within each group, it cannot be accounted for in terms of group identification itself but must depend on variation elsewhere in the influence process.

There are quite obvious differences between Catholic and union groups in the clarity with which political standards are emitted. In the current era, partisan voting norms among Catholics are probably maintained by diffuse primary-group mechanisms at a mass level. Such mechanisms for influence may not be intrinsically weak, but they probably are rendered rather impotent as group cohesiveness decreases. In the union case, however, political standards are often vigorously propagated by leadership, both through public endorsements in the name of the group and through more elaborate communication to the rank and file.

The very diffuseness of norm emission among Catholics makes empirical test of these surmises difficult. Within the set of union members, however, communication channels are more readily tapped, and we know that there is a good deal of variation in the vigor with which clear political standards are disseminated.

In the degree that union political standards are propagated in published form, they tend to flow from one of three levels of a hierarchy: the local, the international, or the remains of the massive federations which were, in 1956, still visible despite the AFL-CIO merger. The federations permit a first gross comparison. We would not hesitate long in labelling the

CIO as the "more political" of the two federations, in terms of differences apparent during the period of schism. While these differences were declining in later years, the CIO leadership generally had emitted many more political standards more clearly and had challenged directly the older norms against extension of union activities into political areas. National surveys during the 1940's and 1950's showed quite regularly that CIO members were 5–10 percent more Democratic in their vote than were AFL members. In 1956, at least, a contrast of the same magnitude remained even after differences in occupation status were controlled. At the level of the great federation, then, it seems to be true that the "more political" group shapes a more distinctive political response across its membership.

We know further that there are radically different approaches to the problem of politics from one international union to another. These contrasts tend to cut across the old AFL and CIO distinction in some degree, since there is a scattering of AFL unions that expend much effort in political activity, while some CIO internationals attempt relatively little.

To capture this variation in 1956 we analyzed the political content of the pre-election editions of the official journals from several dozen of the large internationals whose members fell into our sample. The differences from journal to journal were sharp, making classification quite simple. At one extreme, large portions of the journal were given over to the elections, with fervently partisan pro-Democratic materials in abundance. As the proportion of content devoted to the campaign decreased, the tone became less strident. Short factual accounts of the AFL-CIO endorsement of the Democratic ticket, with mild-mannered editorials indicating the importance of voting for "candidates favorable to labor," became typical fare. A number of other journals made no partisan comment at all, nor did they report endorsements by other related groups. Finally, the journal of one giant union, while making no endorsement, included a picture of the international president in a friendly moment with President Eisenhower.

We have no evidence that the union members involved drew their perceptions of group standards from these particular journals. But we assumed that these journals were representative of the political efforts of the internationals more generally. Whatever the actual

---

[4] A Kendall tau-beta rank-order correlation between identification and vote is .10 for Catholics, .24 for union members.

TABLE 1. *The Relationship of Union Identification and Presidential Vote for Union Members, by Strength of Group Standards* [a]

| | *Nature of International Union's Political Standard* | | | | |
	I Strong, Democratic	II Weak, Democratic	III None	IV Weak, Republican	Total N
High identification	81% (21)	66% (56)	59% (37)	43% (14)	128
Low identification	50% (18)	42% (50)	41% (32)	45% (11)	111
Number of cases	39	106	69	25	239
$T\beta$, identification × vote	+.33	+.25	+.18	−.02	

[a] The entry in each cell indicates the percent Democratic of the two-party vote for President in the 1956 election for the designated group. Numbers of cases involved in each proportion are indicated in parentheses below each entry. Rank-order correlation coefficients (tau-beta) between union identification and vote have been calculated for each category of political standard and are entered in the bottom row.

channels of communication, it was found that members faithfully reflected differences in clarity of standard from international to international by their reports of how they thought leaders of their union would vote. Where standards were clear in the group publications, member perceptions of leader behavior were clear and unidirectional. Where no standards were communicated, a much smaller proportion felt they knew how leaders would vote, and their guesses were less unanimously in a Democratic direction.

Within internationals where standards were most clear according to the content analysis of the journals, the vote division was 67 percent Democratic. This fell to 55 percent where standards were weaker and then to 51 percent in the category where no standards were visible at all in the analysis of journals. In the final category, where there appeared to be a slight Republican standard, the vote was only 44 percent Democratic. Since the proportion of high identifiers across each of these categories varies within a range of nearly 3 percent, it cannot be argued that these differences result from stronger identifications held by members of more militant unions.

However, group identification does play an interesting role in the situation. Table 1 gives some suggestion of the way in which these parts of the model—identification and strength of standards—combine as factors in the influence situation. As we see, there is little sys-

tematic variation in the behavior of the weakly identified in internationals of differing standards. It is among the highly identified that the character of group standards that are disseminated affects behavior. In other words, influence only appears with clarity when both identification and unequivocal standards are present in combination. If either is missing, the evidence for influence is weak indeed.

Table 1 is informative in other directions as well. We note, for example, that there is no sign here of any substantial negative influence or "boomerang" effect. If such effect were to occur, we would expect it to attain a maximum among the least identified where standards have greatest strength. However, the division of the vote in this cell is actually higher than among low identifiers under other conditions.

It is true furthermore that while there is little evidence of the effects of standards among low identifiers in terms of Table 1, these persons are more likely to vote Democratic than nonunion people of similar life situation. We must remember that, in examining the strength of standards emitted by organs at the level of the international union, we are capturing only a portion of the group standards to which union members are exposed. A Democratic endorsement by the newly merged AFL–CIO could be conceived as adding a broad force in the Democratic direction for members of all unions under its jurisdiction. Further effects of this sort may occur at the level of the local even within internationals that tend to avoid partisan commitment. And finally, we must suppose that there is influence as well at the primary-group level. Pressures here would produce a visible partisan bias in the vote of union people weakly identified with the union or members of neutral internationals to the degree that such persons were influenced by companions who happened to be more strongly identified or members of more militant unions.

Festinger, Schachter, and Back (3), in their study of college housing units, were forced to assume that a relationship between the cohesiveness and behavioral homogeneity of subunits guaranteed the presence of group norms, which could not be measured directly. Although the units in Table 1 are somewhat different, the coefficients entered at the bottom of the table lend weight to this assumption. The strength of the relationship between identification and vote varies with the strength of emitted standards that we have measured. This statistic is convenient for our further use, as it reveals variation in behavior which is, on the one hand, group-based, yet which is relatively independent of variation in identification on the other. While we cannot be sure that the differences it captures are due only to the *strength* of emitted standards, we do see that variation in strength of standard produces a gradient in the identification-vote relationship.

In these terms, it seems reasonable to assume that the weaker association between identification and vote that we have noted in the Catholic case does spring from standards that are less clear and strong than they are for many union members. The same chain of reasoning accounts for the much lower distinctiveness of the Catholic vote, despite a cohesiveness not unlike that of union groupings.

OTHER SIMPLE GROUP CUES AS POLITICAL STANDARDS

We may approach the matter of the Catholic vote from another point of view. For if Catholic standards are weak in terms of partisan loyalty toward a presidential candidacy, we can find cases in which group standards for Catholics could be expected to be much clearer.

Thus far we have considered only cases in which successful transmission of standards requires some relatively elaborate communication: at least a verbal endorsement and normally some further persuasion. When one of the candidates is cognized as a group member, however, the behavior appropriate for loyal members is apparent without further need for communication. We can examine the effects of this classic gambit of nominating conventions in the vote of Catholics for legislative seats involving contests between a Catholic and a non-Catholic.

These split-religion races do reveal a more distinctive Catholic vote than has been apparent at the presidential level, despite the fact that support of a Catholic nominee at times requires the loyal member to depart from the "normal" Democratic preference to vote for a Republican.[5] Of course no group effect would be expected save where there is actual recognition of the group affiliation of the candidate. We know that as a general rule voters are rather uninformed about the senatorial and congressional candidates for whom they vote. Of course in the case of ethnic groupings, the name of the candidate on the ballot may in itself be sufficient to indicate group membership. But if we restrict our comparisons to the set of respondents able to recall the name of the candidate for whom they have voted, we should be focusing upon individuals most likely to be aware of the group affiliation of the candidate. And indeed, the group effect, quite visible without this intensifying device, is thereby dramatized considerably (Table 2).

If the distinctiveness of the Catholic vote *for President* is so small as to create the impression of a politically impotent group, differences in Table 2, although based on fewer cases than we would like, are large enough to challenge any sweeping conclusion of this order. Therefore it is worthwhile to reflect upon some of the generic differences between the two situations.

The most obvious distinction springs from the fact that the 1956 presidential race studied did not pit group member against nonmember, while the congressional races were chosen precisely on this basis. We would expect a much firmer equation of political object with group interest where the object is part of

[5] The fact that "good" Catholics appear as candidates under a Republican label in itself helps to break down the sense of a unique group tie with the Democratic party.

TABLE 2. *The Vote of Catholics for Catholic Candidates Whose Names Can Be Recalled, in Races Involving Non-Catholics* [a]

	Catholic Identification		
	High	Low	Total Group
U. S. House of Representatives			
Catholic voters	85%	69%	77%
	(13)	(13)	(26)
Catholic control			51%
			(25)
U. S. Senate			
Catholic voters	86%	57%	70%
	(22)	(28)	(50)
Catholic control			49%
			(47)

[a] The percent entries refer to the proportion of the indicated groups who voted for the Catholic candidate in the split-religion congressional or senatorial race. The figures in parentheses indicate the number of cases involved in each proportion.

the group than where the group merely extends some kind of endorsement to a party or a nonmember candidate. Secondly, the pairing of member and nonmember in the competition for office in itself makes the group basis for choice more salient. This fact becomes more critical in view of the extremely limited information that appears to underlie most political decisions in the mass electorate. Lack of knowledge about legislative candidates is simply a case in point. Where ethnic background or religion is suggested by the surname of the candidate, this datum, along with the candidate's party affiliation, may exhaust the information brought to bear on partisan choice by substantial proportions of the public. In these cases, the question posed by the ballot is in effect: "Other things equal, would you prefer a member of your own group to a nonmember?" In the degree that such a situation obtains, it is likely that the group effects which we observe in these instances are virtually maximized.

It should be recognized also that Table 2 is restricted to those voters most likely to cognize the candidate's group affiliation. A parallel table including all Catholic voters shows group candidates favored by a 12 percent increment over the proper control group, as opposed to the increment of 20–25 percent in Table 2. We take this to mean that group effects are muted in this voting situation simply because some members lack the information necessary to recognize the relevance of group standards. As might be expected, this problem is at least equally acute where standards are

less self-evident. The fact that strong standards are emitted certainly raises the probability that some standard will be perceived; but it does not ensure reception, and failures at this point further limit the operation of influence in the political setting.

RECEPTION OF EMITTED STANDARDS

In the social groupings under consideration, the transmission of uniform political standards to a far-flung membership is a precarious process. This is bound to be true if leadership is decentralized or if propagation depends upon primary-group diffusion. But even in the union case, where channels of communication for political materials are clear-cut and much effort is devoted in some quarters to the problem of communicating political standards, there is good evidence that influence is circumscribed because portions of the membership simply fail to absorb information concerning group political standards.

Unfortunately, it is difficult to measure the cognizance of norms on the part of the member directly. In times past we have asked group members before the election whether they would predict any predominant direction in the vote of their leadership or of other members. For some uses responses to these items are illuminating. But there is internal evidence that such reports are clouded by various types of distortion. The identified member who for other reasons wishes to cast a vote

TABLE 3.   *Recognition of Union Political Standards as a Function of Education and Length of Union Membership*[a]

Length of Union Membership	Grade School	Education High School	College[b]	$T\beta$, Union Identification × Vote
4 Years or less	40% (20)	49% (35)	64% (22)	+.01
5–9 Years	56% (16)	69% (36)		+.09
10 Years or over	60% (48)	80% (60)		+.34
$\overline{T\beta}$, Union identification × vote	+.15	+.22	+.35	

[a] The percent entry in each cell refers to the proportion of the indicated group which perceives the union leadership as behaving in some predominant partisan direction. The remaining respondents indicated either that they did not know how the leadership stood in partisan terms for the 1956 election or thought that leadership would be "about evenly split" between the parties. Figures in parentheses indicate the number of cases involved in each proportion. The rank-order correlation coefficients are comparable to those employed in connection with Table 1.

[b] The number of college-educated people who are union members is too few for further subdivision. In a rough way, the college entry is placed appropriately on the continuum indicating length of union membership. That is, average length of membership is considerably lower here than is the case within the other education categories.

against the prevailing group standard may inhibit recognition that any standard exists; the poorly identified member who is unaware of any particular standard may simply project his own intentions on the group. Since it seems clear that such distortions will occur under certain critical combinations of identification and vote intention, we are not comfortable in using these responses to cast light on variations in identification and vote.

However, we feel more confident employing these reports to validate factors that we might suppose would affect reception of standards yet that should, by and large, cross-cut any effects due to distortion. We would hypothesize in the union case, for example, that group standards would be least evident for poorly educated members and for whose term of membership in a union had been most brief. We know that low education means relatively slight interest and involvement in politics, and general lack of information concerning prominent political issues of the day. It also means a higher dependence upon radio and television than upon the written word as a source of political information, if indeed any mass medium is monitored at all. If the reception of an

emitted standard is a probability matter, then the individual exposed to many emissions is more likely to have absorbed the message than one exposed to few emissions. The same rationale would lead to the prediction that long-term members would be more apt to cognize group standards than new arrivals.

We do in fact find sharp variation in the clarity with which standards are reported to be perceived, as a function of both education and length of membership (Table 3). Furthermore, the correlation between identification and vote, entered around both margins of the table, show precisely the type of covariation with each of these factors that we would demand as evidence of change in influence phenomena. These gradients of relationship associated with education and length of membership closely resemble the gradient that we discovered as a function of strength of emitted standards. However, it does not appear that they are merely derivatives or artifacts of the previous gradient, as might be the case if militant unions had memberships of longer standing and higher education. Actually, differences in mean education or length of membership across internationals of differing political stan-

TABLE 4. *The Role of Mass Media and Education in the Relationship Between Identification and Vote Among Union Members*[a]

Most Important Mass Media for Political News	Grade School	Education High School	College
Newspapers and magazines	.16 (21)	.37 (73)	.45 (18)
Radio and television	.19 (72)	.17 (112)	.41 (18)

[a]The entry in each cell is a coefficient of correlation (*Tβ*) between union identification and the presidential vote of the union member. The number of cases involved in the coefficient is indicated in parentheses.

dards are small at best. But to the degree that differences are present, they run in the opposing direction: internationals with stronger standards have more poorly educated members who are, on the average, of more recent vintage. Thus if we had sufficient cases to examine these several gradients within the same table, we would expect each to be more rather than less steep.

In predicting that perception of standards would increase as a function of education, we relied in part upon independent knowledge that more educated citizens are more apt to draw upon written communications for political information than audiovisual media such as radio or television. Aside from direct personal confrontation which may arise in some union situations, the transmission of political standards in the union case is likely to rest much more heavily upon the written word than upon radio or television presentation. Furthermore, people who depend primarily on newspapers and magazines for political information do tend to receive messages from radio and television as well, while persons depending on radio and television are much less likely to supplement their information from printed sources. Thus dependence upon newspapers and magazines is posited as an intervening mechanism whereby more educated people, if highly identified as well, become more apt to respond to group standards.

Data are arrayed in Table 4 to show that while education and type of media consumption are related for union members, each factor makes some independent contribution to an intensification of the identification-vote relationship. The independent role of the mass media appears trivial among grade school and college people but quite substantial within the high school category, where the bulk of the

cases are concentrated. The evidence that both factors make an independent contribution to variation in the identification-vote relationship raises our confidence that we properly interpret these patterns as steps in a process rather than spurious covariation arising from the other independent variable (education or media consumption) as a "third factor."

In short, then, a number of pieces of evidence suggest that the influence process is partially undermined in the union case by failure of identified members to recognize emitted political standards. We may suppose that if political messages were more carefully attended, newer union members would become aware of standards more rapidly, and poorly educated members would show a higher recognition of such standards. In such an event, we would expect the more identified persons within these categories to respond to standards with greater clarity than is now the case.

LEGITIMACY OF GROUP POLITICAL STANDARDS

Even where clear standards are successfully received by a membership, we have suggested that there may be resistance on value grounds against group intrusion upon political decision-making. Since the most obvious goals of these groups are not primarily political, a member may espouse these goals fervently without feeling that it is legitimate for political instrumentation to be sought.

In 1956 we asked the members of our several groups whether or not they felt it was "all right" for organizations representing the group to support relevant legislative proposals and candidates for office. The responses to these

TABLE 5. *Presidential Vote Across Four Secondary Membership Groups, by Strength of Group Identification and Belief in Legitimacy of Group Political Activity* [a]

Belief in Legitimacy of Group Political Activity	Group Identification			Total
	High	Medium	Low	
Strong	72%	64%	55%	65%
	(126)	(95)	(98)	(319)
Medium	62%	55%	45%	53%
	(52)	(55)	(56)	(163)
Weak	67%	45%	33%	41%
	(27)	(60)	(127)	(214)
Total	69%	56%	43%	
	(205)	(210)	(281)	

[a] Each cell entry represents the percent Democratic of the two-party vote for the appropriate combination of group identification and sense of legitimacy. The "Total" column shows the simple relationship between legitimacy and the vote, with no control on identification. The "Total" row shows the simple relationship between identification and the vote, without control on legitimacy.

questions showed a fairly strong relationship with the group identification variable in a direction that would seem to match theoretical expectations. That is, we would expect a person who is more absorbed in a group to accord it broader jurisdiction than one who is less enthusiastic about his membership.

With identification controlled, however, there remains a substantial relationship between beliefs concerning the legitimacy of group political standards and conformity to group norms across all of the groupings analyzed (Table 5). It is undoubtedly true that in some measure the beliefs of members as to the legitimacy of standards will be affected by perceived congruence of own and group political predispositions. In other words, a sense of legitimacy could be an effect, rather than a cause, of acceptance of the group position in politics.

Of course our data do not permit us to sort out these cases or estimate their contribution to the relationship portrayed in Table 5. Nevertheless, we feel that in some part at least we are tapping a set of beliefs that have independent causal status in the influence process. The pattern of correlates on the legitimacy responses are encouraging in this regard. For example, within each level of group identification, members of the two religious groups—Catholics and Jews—show much greater reluctance to accept the legitimacy statements than either of the two secular groupings. This suggests that our questions capture some appropriate underlying value structures, since taboos designed to insulate the political process from outside group pressures have been strongest where religious groupings have been concerned. Also, with identification controlled, there is somewhat less readiness to grant legitimacy among older people. This conforms with impressions that popular values opposing frank interest-group politics represent an older America.

Thus while Table 5 undoubtedly overstates the independent status of concern with legitimacy in inhibiting conformity, it seems that such concerns must be taken into account in any full assessment of the influence process in this setting.

SUMMARY

We have attempted to explore a variety of aspects of the group influence process, as it operates in the formation and erosion of voting blocks within secondary membership groupings in the national electorate. We cannot test elements of the model that has been sketched above against the observed behavior of our several groups in any rigorous fashion. But we have some sense that it increases our understanding of the reasons which underlie differences in the distinctiveness of vote across our several groups.

On many counts, the Negro community appears most ripe in the current period for political influence in the name of the group. Its cohesiveness is extremely high. The legitimacy of group activity in politics goes almost unquestioned. Its primary deficit lies in the impoverished education of group members, a fact which may in some degree disrupt the transmission of political standards despite high levels of group motivation. However, conflicting leadership standards appear to have reduced the efficiency of the group as a national voting bloc in the 1956 election.

Similar cohesiveness among Jewish people may permit high distinctiveness of the group vote when group standards are clear. In this case, the high level of education within the group facilitates the transmission of standards, although there are greater reservations felt by group members about the role of the group in politics than in the case for Negroes.

The union grouping is more cohesive than the Catholic, but the difference is slight. Nevertheless, the transmission of standards for union members is much more persistent and obvious, despite telling variation over the total labor movement. And there is a general willingness on the part of union members to accept group activity in politics that is clearly lacking among Catholics. The result is a much more distinctive group vote in the union case, although the evidence suggests that distinctiveness could be greater if stronger standards were expressed and their transmission rendered more effective.

We can expect that a number of these group characteristics which appear critical in terms of the model will shift over time. Continuing observation of the magnitude of group effects as they vary in response to such change should give us an increasingly firm understanding of the dynamics of the influence process, with its many potentialities and limitations, as it occurs in this field setting.

References

1. Back, K. Influence through social communication. *Journal of Abnormal and Social Psychology*, 1951, **46**, 9–23.
2. Campbell, A., & Cooper, H. C. *Group differences in attitudes and vote.* Ann Arbor, Mich.: Survey Research Center, 1956.
3. Festinger, L., Schachter, S., & Back, K. *Social pressures in informal groups: A study of a housing community.* New York: Harper, 1950.
4. Schachter, S. Deviation, rejection, and communication. *Journal of Abnormal and Social Psychology*, 1951, **46**, 190–207.
5. Suchman, E. A., & Menzel, H. The interplay of demographic and psychological variables in the analysis of voting surveys. In S. Lazarsfeld & M. Rosenburg (Eds.), *The language of social research.* Glencoe, Ill.: Free Press, 1955.

PART FOUR

POWER AND INFLUENCE IN GROUPS

17

Power and Influence in Groups: Introduction

In order to understand the functioning of groups, it is necessary to understand the nature of social influence. The pressures to uniformity, discussed in the preceding chapters, are exerted by means of social interaction in which members attempt to modify the beliefs, attitudes, and actions of one another. Similar processes arise whenever a group attempts to reach a decision as to what its goals will be or which means it will employ in pursuing them. The coordination of group activities requires that the behavior of each member be adjusted to that of others, and leadership is effected through the exercise of influence over followers. What are the sources of influence? What determines an individual's capacity to influence others? What consequences stem from different ways of exercising influence? What effects are generated when one person has power over another? In this and the following six chapters we consider some of the ways in which investigators have attempted to answer questions such as these.

The related topics of influence and power have long been of interest to social scientists, especially to social philosophers and political theorists (28, 39, 43, 57). In more recent years, empirical studies of influence and power have been conducted in communities, organizations, informal groups, and laboratories. Much of this work has been summarized by Cartwright (10) and Schopler (58). In recent years, too, several formal theories have been developed, representative examples being those of Cartwright (9), Dahl (15), Harsanyi (24), March (44, 45), Shapley and Shubik (59), Tannenbaum (63), and Thibaut and Kelley (64). They combine to form a useful framework for analyzing the nature of power and influence in groups.

Most theorists assume that influence should be viewed as a relationship between two social entities such as individuals, roles, groups, or nations. We shall refer to these as *agents* and denote them by O (the one viewed as exerting influence) and P (the one influenced). In examining specific instances of influence, we shall be concerned with *acts* performed by *O* and with changes in *states* of *P*. If *O* performs an act that results in a change in a particular state of *P*, we shall say that *O* *influences* *P* with respect to that state. And, if *O* is capable of influencing *P* with respect to a certain state, we shall say that *O* *has power over* *P* with respect to that state. By the *range of O's power over P* we shall mean the set of states of *P* with respect to which *O* can exert influence. The *domain of O's power* refers to the set of agents over whom *O* has power with respect to a specified range.

To illustrate how these terms can be given concrete meaning, let us suppose that we are interested in studying the influence processes among a group of people engaged in a discussion of political affairs. We observe that one member *O* expresses an opinion about capital punishment, and we note whether this act has any effect upon the attitudes toward capital punishment held by another member *P*. If we conclude that it has in fact brought about a change in the state of *P*'s attitude, then we may assert that *O* has influenced *P* with respect to this attitude. And if we know enough about the relationships between *O* and *P*, we may ascertain whether *O* is capable of influencing *P*—that is, whether *O* has power over *P* with respect to this attitude. And if we are sufficiently informed, we may specify the attitudes of *P* that *O* can influence—the range of *O*'s power over *P*. Finally, if we were to get similar information concerning relationships between *O* and each other member, we could state, for any particular attitude, which members *O* can influence—his domain of power in the group with respect to the attitude in question.

Certain features of this conception should be noted. First, one cannot meaningfully speak of influence or power without specifying, at least implicitly, its "content." The statement that a particular agent *O* has power over a particular agent *P* may be true with respect to certain states of *P* but false with respect to others. A foreman may be able to influence a worker's behavior on the job and yet be powerless when it comes to his political activities. Second, power is potential influence. *O* may be able to influence *P* in a certain way but still not exercise this power during a particular period of time. It should be clear, however, that a power relationship may produce important consequences even though it does not result in the actual exercise of influence. Third, the

definition of power does not require that the relation be asymmetric. Merely from knowing that one agent has power over another we may not conclude that the second has no power over the first. Given any two agents, we may find that each has power over the other, that only one has power over the other, or that neither has power over the other. It is an empirical problem to ascertain which of these patterns exists in any particular situation and, more generally, the conditions that give rise to each.

We shall limit our discussion here to the topic of *interpersonal* influence and power—that is, to relationships between agents conceived as individual people. It should be noted, however, that it is possible to speak of the power or influence of a person *O* over a group *P*, of a group *O* over a person *P*, or of a group *O* over another group *P*. In order to do so, it is only necessary to specify a suitable set of acts for each interpretation of *O* and a suitable set of states for each interpretation of *P*. We shall defer further discussion of the power of a person over a group until Chapter 24, where we consider phenomena of leadership, and of the power of a group over a member until Chapter 31, where we consider the influence of the goals of a group upon the behavior of its members.

In the remainder of this chapter, we examine in some detail the nature of interpersonal influence and power as these manifest themselves in group settings. We first inquire into the sources of an individual's power and his motivations for exercising power. We next examine the methods used in exerting influence. Then, we turn to the person subjected to influence and consider the conditions affecting his susceptibility to influence. We conclude with a consideration of some of the by-products arising from the existence of power relations.

AGENT EXERTING INFLUENCE

One person has power over another if he can perform an act that will result in a change in the other person. What determines whether a particular act of a person *O* will be influential with respect to another person *P*? To answer this question it is necessary to examine the situation both from the point of view of *O* and from that of *P*. The source of interpersonal power has at least two components: (*a*) certain "properties" of O, which we shall call the *resources of power*, and (*b*) certain needs or values of P, the *motive bases of power*. Suppose, for example, that O gets P to engage in a particular behavior by promising to pay him a certain sum of money. In order to be able to exert this influence, it is necessary that O have enough money to make the promised payment (or at least that P believe this to be so) and that P have a sufficiently strong interest in obtaining it. The effectiveness of this act of O depends upon O's possession of money—the resource of power—and upon P's need for money —the motive base of power. An influential act establishes a relationship between a resource of O and a motive base of P.

RESOURCES OF POWER

Lists of resources of interpersonal power usually contain such items as wealth, prestige, skill, information, physical strength, and the ability to gratify the "ego needs" that people have for such intangibles as recognition, affection, respect, and accomplishment. It is clear that such properties often do serve as resources and that a person possessing them often derives power from them. But it is also clear that one cannot construct a universally applicable list of resources, since any particular property of O can serve as a resource of power over P only if P has an appropriate need. An individual with a high IQ may be able to influence the members of a problem-solving group because they value his intelligence and need his intellectual skills, but the same individual may be totally incapable of influencing the members of a hockey team for whom intelligence is an irrelevant property. The property of intelligence, then, serves as a resource of interpersonal power in one group but not in the other.

In order to specify the properties of individuals that can serve as resources of power in any particular group, we need to ascertain the motive bases of its members. A study of power in the classroom, reported by Gold in Chapter 19, illustrates how such research might proceed. By means of interviews, he identified seventeen characteristics of children that other children viewed as valuable and important. These resources appeared to fall into five categories: (*a*) *expertness*—"is smart at school," "has good ideas about how to have fun," "is

good at making things"; (*b*) *coerciveness*— "knows how to fight," "is strong"; (*c*) *social emotion*—"acts friendly," "knows how to act so people will like him"; (*d*) *association*—"plays with you a lot," "likes to do the same things you like to do"; and (*e*) *other*—"is nice looking," "does things for you." Gold found that the importance of these resources varied with age and sex. He then showed that specific individuals who possessed many important resources were considered by their classmates as better able to influence them than individuals who possessed only a few.

In many groups one person is assigned responsibility for supervising or coordinating the activities of members. If this person is to be successful, he must have resources that enable him to influence the members of the group. For this reason, a supervisor is frequently given control over such matters as rates of pay, promotions, and job assignments, which it is assumed will serve as resources for his power in the group. We should expect, however, that a supervisor's actual ability to exert influence will depend upon whether the things he controls are in fact valued by the members. This expectation has been supported by the results of a study conducted by Bennis *et al.* (**5**). These investigators collected data from nurses and their supervisors, who were employed in the out-patient departments of several hospitals. They obtained measures from each nurse concerning the rewards she hoped to get from her job—things such as salary increases, praise, promotions, better jobs without promotions, and educational opportunities. To measure the amount of influence exerted by the supervisor, they determined the congruence between the amount of time each nurse spent on certain activities and the amount of time her supervisor wanted her to spend. The results of this study indicate two major limitations on the influence of supervisors: (*a*) an incorrect perception by the supervisor of what rewards the nurses desire and (*b*) an inability to increase or withhold these rewards. In hospitals where these limitations were less extreme, supervisors were found to exert greater influence over the activities of the nurses.

The way in which the possession of a resource gives a person power has been examined in some detail by Levinger (**40**). In an experimental study of the formation of power relationships, he brought together two previously unacquainted people to engage in a task requiring a series of joint decisions. At the outset of the experiment the critical subject was led to believe that his knowledge about the task was either superior or inferior to that of his partner. Careful observation of the ensuing interactions revealed that those subjects who believed they possessed superior knowledge made more influence attempts, more frequently resisted their partner's suggestions, and displayed a higher degree of assertiveness. The subjects who thought they had superior knowledge also rated themselves as having more influence over decisions. It appears, then, that the possession of resources not only gives an individual power but also affects his behavior in a variety of ways.

POWER MOTIVATION

A person with resources has the capacity to perform acts that will influence those who value these resources. If such a person wishes to accomplish some objective requiring changes in the behavior, beliefs, or attitudes of other people, he may be expected to perform acts that he believes will bring about these changes. On the other hand, a person with few resources is likely to realize that ordinarily there is little point in his attempting to influence others. If we assume that people frequently seek objectives whose attainment requires the exertion of influence, we should expect to find a close association between the possession of power and the exercise of influence.

Several investigations provide data in support of this expectation. In a study by Zander, Cohen, and Stotland (67) of role relations among psychiatrists, social workers, and clinical psychologists, each respondent was asked certain questions about the authority he possessed and about his use of this authority with respect to several activities. The correlations between amount of power possessed and the frequency of its use were all .80–.89 and above. Hurwitz, Zander, and Hymovitch (Chap. 23) found that professional mental health workers with high attributed power talked more frequently in group discussions than did those with less power. And Lippitt *et al.* (Chap. 18) found correlations ranging from .35 to .66 between the power attributed to each boy in a summer camp and the frequency of his attempts to influence other campers.

Results such as these indicate that more powerful people tend more frequently to attempt to influence others, but they also make it clear that the relation between possession and use of power is far from perfect. Some people use less power than they actually have, and some attempt to use more. What determines when a person will make an influence attempt?

Assessment of Gains and Costs to O. It has been proposed, especially by authors influenced by the theory of games, that a person, when deciding whether to make a particular influence attempt, "calculates" in some sense the net advantage to him of performing the act. Thus, for example, Thibaut and Kelley assume that any act a person might perform will have an "outcome" of significance to him and that an individual will tend to perform acts that he believes will result in the best possible outcome. They then observe that "power is not usable to the degree that its use penalizes the possessor," and they define *usable power* as "the power that it is convenient and practical for him to use" (64, 107). We should expect, then, that an individual will convert his power into influence only when he expects the gains from an act of influence to exceed its costs.

As an illustration of these rather abstract concepts, let us consider a boss who wants his secretary to stay after office hours to type a report. Even though he may be certain that she will comply if he asks, he may hesitate to exercise his power in this way because he knows that she would sulk for a week thereafter if he were to impose on her in this way. In deciding whether to perform this act of influence, he presumably compares the value of getting the report quickly with the costs of having a sulky secretary. Calculations of this sort are especially evident when the exercise of power involves the expenditure of resources of power, as for example when a person contemplates paying another to do something for him.

Assessment of Gains and Costs to the Group. A person who is a member of a group is likely to be concerned not only with his own welfare but with that of the group as well. We may expect, then, that in calculating the net advantage to be derived from a possible act of influence within the group, he will take into account gains and costs to the group as a whole. Consider, for example, a psychotherapist who knows that he can induce a particular patient to discuss his symptoms in a group therapy session. Before doing so, the therapist is likely to weigh the positive and negative consequences of this act for the progress of the group. And he is likely to make an intervention only if he believes that the group will thereby gain more than it will lose.

Subjective Probability of Success. Let us assume that an individual has engaged in a calculation of the net advantage entailed by some particular act. He cannot, of course, be absolutely certain that the act will actually have its intended effects. We should therefore expect him to weight the value associated with the act by his estimate of the probability that the act will succeed. In other words, his decision whether to perform the act will be based, in part at least, upon its expected value. Now if we make the reasonable assumption that the subjective probability of success increases with one's assessment of his power, we should expect to find a positive correlation between a person's view of his power and his readiness to exert influence. And we can account for the correlations, reported above, between attributed power and frequency of influence attempts by assuming that people tend to have an accurate assessment of their own power.

Role Expectations. A rather different set of determinants has been emphasized by authors writing in the tradition of role theory. Viewed in this perspective, a group is composed of "positions," each of which has an associated "role," and the occupant of a particular position is subjected to "role expectations" from others to engage in actions appropriate to this role. Some of these acts involve the influencing of other members. According to this view, which has been well stated by Stogdill (62), the occupant of a position engages in specific influence attempts because they conform to the expectations that others attach to his position. The occupant's motivation is not so much to derive benefits from the induced behavior as it is to gain rewards given for fulfilling role expectations. Thus, for example, when a mother uses her power to discipline a child, she may be motivated primarily to be viewed as a "good" mother by those who believe that it is the responsibility of a mother to instill moral values in her children and to see that they behave properly. If the mother finds that she does not have sufficient power to influence her children, she is likely to experience failure and frustration. Social settings that subject a person to role expectations that he is powerless to fulfill would seem to be especially damaging to his self-esteem.

Research on the motivation to perform acts of leadership (discussed more fully in Chapter 24) suggests that an individual's readiness to exercise power may be affected simultaneously by various combinations of the four determinants discussed above. Thus Hemphill (27, 213) concludes from a series of experiments that motivation to lead is heightened by

(*a*) large rewards promised by accomplishing the group's task, (*b*) reasonable expectancy that by working on the task it can be accomplished, (*c*) acceptance by other members of the group for attempting to lead, (*d*) a task which requires a high rate of group decisions, (*e*) possession of superior knowledge or competence relevant to the accomplishment of the task, and (*f*) previously acquired status as the group's leader.

In summary, it is evident that the decision whether to engage in an act of influence is complexly determined and is governed by at least four considerations: (*a*) the net advantage to the individual in performing the act, (*b*) the consequences of the act for the group, (*c*) the subjective probability that the act will be successful, which depends in part upon the individual's assessment of his own power, and (*d*) the prospect of being rewarded for fulfilling role expectations. Further research is needed to specify the conditions that determine the relative weight given to each of these considerations.

METHODS OF INFLUENCE

When one person has power over another, there are usually several ways in which he can exercise influence. Consider, for example, a parent who wants to prevent his teenage daughter from associating with certain other girls. What methods might he use? Clearly there are many possibilities. He might attempt by persuasion to get his daughter to recognize the undesirability of her companions. He might appeal to his authority as a parent and order her not to be seen with them. He might offer to increase her allowance for conforming with his wishes, or he might threaten some punishment if she does not. He might resort to manipulation by sending her to a finishing school in a foreign country. Or he might attempt to constrain her physically from leaving the house when the other girls are around.

This example makes it abundantly clear that influence can take many forms. A person with power may employ any of a variety of methods of influence, and when he wishes to exercise his power he must choose among those available to him. We turn now to a consideration of the nature of these methods and inquire into the conditions affecting their use.

CONTROL OVER GAINS AND COSTS TO *P*

A person *O* who controls resources having motivational significance for another person *P* can make these resources available to *P*, or withhold them from him, as he sees fit. In other words, *O* has the ability to control some of the outcomes available to *P*, and he may use this ability to influence *P*. He may, for example, offer to reward *P* for doing him a favor, or he may threaten to withhold something of value from *P* or to harm him unless *P* engages in a particular form of behavior. Acts of influence in situations of this sort typically convey, with varying degrees of explicitness, a direction ("do this," "believe this," or "favor this") and a motivational consequence ("you will be paid," "you will be wise," "you will be respected," or "you will be loved"). They are influential because *O* can affect the gains and costs experienced by *P*.

In order to be assured that his influence attempts will actually produce their intended effects, *O* may make his payoffs to *P* contingent upon *P*'s compliance with his wishes. He rewards *P* only after receiving information that *P* has met his conditions (or after getting trustworthy assurances from *P* that he will meet them), and he punishes *P* only after learning that *P* has failed to do so. This method of influence requires continuous monitoring of *P* and can be counted on to be effective only with respect to aspects of *P* that *O* can observe. Thus it is better suited for modifying overt behavior than covert attitudes or private beliefs. This and other implications of the need for monitoring have been described in some detail by Thibaut and Kelley (**64**).

In Chapter 21, Ring and Kelley report a study of two methods of influence that they call *augmentation* and *reduction*. Under augmentation, *O* provides rewards in order to induce *P* to perform some desired behavior; under reduction, *O* provides punishments whenever *P* performs a behavior other than the desired one. These authors reason that under augmentation *P* will tend to present evidence to *O* of his compliance in order to receive the reward, whereas under reduction he will tend to conceal his behavior, since his best outcomes will be derived through either compliance or concealment. They argue further that when augmentation is used *P* will come to value *O* and hence adopt his standards, but when reduction is used *P* will not privately adopt *O*'s standards even though he may conform publicly. Results obtained from this experiment and a subsequent one (**35**) support this line of reasoning. They suggest that if *O* wishes to train *P* to engage in a certain form of behavior his best over-all strategy would be one that provides punishment for detected instances of concealment on the part of *P*, very mild punishment for revealed errors, and strong reward for revealed correct behavior.

Discussions of influence tend to emphasize the contingency of *O*'s payoffs upon *P*'s compliance, but it is possible for *O* to influence *P* by giving him, "with no strings attached," something he needs to accomplish an objective. In this case, *O* gives *P* unconditional help, and such actions may be expected only when *O* believes that *P*'s objectives are congenial with his own or when he has some reason for being "altruistic." It is possible, of course, for *O* to give unconditional hindrance or harm by taking actions, regardless of what *P* does, that serve to make a particular behavior of *P* expensive or otherwise undesirable. We shall return in Chapter 31 to a fuller discussion of the conditions affecting an individual's readiness to help or hinder another.

PERSUASION

A rather different method of influence relies on *O*'s ability to affect *P*'s knowledge, beliefs, and attitudes. Just as with the other forms of influence, the use of persuasion requires that *O* have appropriate resources at his disposal. One of the most obvious of these is the possession of information. Thus a person whose location in a group gives him special access to relevant information is likely to be able to influence the beliefs and attitudes of others. Research on persuasion, which has been summarized by Klapper (**38**), makes it clear that the perceived nature of the "source" of a message affects its effectiveness. If, for example, a person has prestige in a group, his messages tend to carry weight among its members. Prestige is thus a resource of influence. Other resources are credibility, expertness, a reputation for objectivity, and personal charm. By acquiring or losing these intangible resources a person increases or decreases his capacity to exert influence.

It is commonly argued that the method of persuasion is an especially appropriate means of influence in "democratic" or "rational" social systems. This argument cites two features of persuasion. First, when a person O attempts to influence P solely by means of persuasion, he applies no extraneous inducements (rewards and punishments) for accepting his message. P is constrained only by his own evaluation of the merits of the message, even though this evaluation may be colored by his feelings toward O. Second, when O employs persuasion to control P's overt behavior, he still permits P to behave "voluntarily" or "freely." A successful act of persuasion affects P's behavior only indirectly by influencing the beliefs, attitudes, and values that guide his behavior, and P feels that his behavior is under his own control. Persuasion, then, respects the integrity of the individual.

The need for O to monitor P's behavior, which is essential in the contingent administration of gains and costs to P, takes a rather different form in persuasion. We may assume that when O attempts to persuade P he is motivated by a desire to bring about a change in P and that this motivation will persist until he has evidence that P has in fact changed or until he gives up hope of producing the change. (The data presented by Schachter in Chapter 13 are consistent with this assumption.) If O believes that he has successfully induced a change in P's opinions or attitudes, he is unlikely to feel the need to exert further influence unless he gets some indication of "backsliding" on the part of P. Monitoring, then, is involved in persuasion, but it serves to guide O's influence attempts rather than his administration of rewards and punishments.

USE OF P'S ATTITUDE TOWARD BEING INFLUENCED BY O

A third method of influence is often available to members of well-established groups. Relationships existing between members O and P may be such that P has a desire or a sense of obligation to accept influence attempts made by O. Under these circumstances, O does not have to administer rewards or punishments in order to exert influence, nor does he have to employ persuasion. He can influence P merely by indicating the changes in P that he desires. His resource of influence is P's attitude toward being influenced by him. A charismatic leader may bring about changes in the opinions or behavior of his devoted followers simply by making a suggestion or a request. He may even exert influence unintentionally, as for example when his followers attempt to anticipate his wishes or seek to model their behavior after his. A hero or someone who has undergone hardship for the group is especially likely to be able to exert influence in this way.

In many groups certain individuals have authority over designated others. It is expected that supervisors will supervise, that coordinators will coordinate, and that leaders will lead. Members of a group who accept its authority structure as legitimate feel that authority figures can properly tell them what to do, and they are likely to be influenced by authoritative acts such as directives or commands simply because they accept the system. When authority relations are established by group consensus, the person with authority exercises his authority by appealing, explicitly or implicitly, to the consensual decision giving him the right to influence. For a more detailed discussion of this aspect of authority, the reader is referred to an insightful analysis by Gilman (21).

It has frequently been observed that when a group of people interact with one another over an extended period of time there tends to emerge a system of interpersonal obligations. If at one point in time a person O does a favor for P or helps him in some way, then P is likely to incur an obligation to O which O can subsequently employ to influence P. When O does so, he makes use of P's attitude toward being influenced by him. Whyte (65), who has stressed the importance of obligation in the functioning of groups in street corner society, observes that when a person uses this method of influence he is unlikely to make explicit reference to the obligations involved and that "it is only when the relationship breaks down that the underlying obligations are brought into light." It appears that the feeling of obligation arises when the participants commonly hold a value, which Gouldner (22) has called the "norm of reciprocity." This norm is reflected in the attitude of P that serves as the resource for O's influence.

CONTROL OVER P'S ENVIRONMENT

The methods of influence considered thus far involve some direct interaction between O and P. In one way or another O acts directly on P in order to bring about a desired change in P, whether by administering rewards and punishments, by persuasion, or by exploiting P's readiness to be influenced by O. But there is another, more indirect, method of influence. This method relies on the fact that the beliefs, attitudes, values, and behavior of a person are determined in large measure by his immediate social and physical environment. It is possible, then, for a person O who wants to bring about a particular change in P to do so by taking actions that have effects not directly on P but upon his environment. If O has the ability to control critical aspects of P's environment, we say that O has *ecological control* over P. When O attempts to influence P by means of ecological control, he takes some action which he believes will modify P's social or physical environment in such a way that the new environment will bring about the desired change in P. Since this method of influence can be used without the knowledge or consent of those affected, it is sometimes labeled as "manipulation."

Influence by ecological control can be observed in virtually every kind of social setting. The teacher exerts such influence in forming work groups, designing projects, and making seating assignments. If, for example, she wants to curb a pupil's whispering in class, she may assign him a seat where he is surrounded by well-behaved and orderly children. Parents use their ability to control the environments of their children in a variety of ways in order to shape their interests and values. The manager of a research department who wishes to heighten the creativity of his scientists may periodically reorganize his research teams in the hope that each scientist, by being exposed to a variety of viewpoints, will consider a broader range of approaches in working on any particular problem. And a therapist in charge of groups of disturbed children may use findings—such as those reported by Gump and Sutton-Smith (23) that different types of games activate different psychodynamic processes in the participants—to design a therapeutic program of recreational activities.

Research in group dynamics has made it clear that many of the beliefs, attitudes, values, and behaviors of an individual are fundamentally shaped by the groups he belongs to. Cartwright, in a discussion of the implications of this research for those who want to bring about change in individuals, has made the following observation (8, 387):

To change the behavior of individuals it may be necessary to change the standards of the group, its style of leadership, its emotional atmosphere, or its stratification into cliques and hierarchies. Even though the goal may be to change the behavior of *individuals,* the target of change becomes the group.

We see, then, that anyone who can significantly affect the critical properties of groups has ecological control over its members. And if he has a correct understanding of how these properties determine the states of a particular member P, he can use his ecological control to bring about desired changes in P.

An important form of ecological control has been identified by Lewin (41, Chap. 8) in his discussion of "social gatekeepers." Lewin was led to this concept by an interest in the problem of changing people's food habits. He began by asking the question, "Why do people eat what they eat?" Noting that food tends to be eaten once it is on the table, he was stimulated to ask another question, "How does food get on the table?" In an attempt to answer this question, Lewin proposed that food can be conceived as moving through certain "channels" that are controlled by individuals who serve as "gatekeepers." Thus a housewife functions as a gatekeeper when she purchases food at the grocery store, and her decisions there influence the eating behavior of her family. And since there is a tendency for people to come to like what they regularly eat, these decisions eventually shape the food preferences of the members of her family. It is possible, of course, that the housewife is not aware of the power she derives from being a gatekeeper, but if she is, she can use it deliberately to influence the members of her family. Lewin suggested that the concept of gatekeeper can be applied to any social system in which material objects, information, or personnel "flow through channels" and that social change can often be most effectively induced by modifying the behavior of the relevant social gatekeepers.

If a person O is to influence another person P by means of ecological control, it is of course necessary that he have the ability to produce changes in P's environment. This ability, then, is a resource for such influence. But if O desires to bring about a particular change in P, it is also necessary that O have an understanding of how the relevant states of P are determined by his environment. In principle, O may successfully influence P by ecological control whenever particular changes in P are predictably related to some manipulable feature of P's environment. Since behavioral science provides knowledge about the environmental determinants of behavior, it increases the possibilities for using ecological control as an effective means of social influence.

REDISTRIBUTION OF RESOURCES

It has been proposed by several theorists that every method of influence involves an exchange of some sort between O and P. This thesis has been stated by Homans in the following way (**29**, 606):

Social behavior is an exchange of goods, material goods but also nonmaterial ones, such as symbols of approval or prestige. Persons that give much to others try to get much from them, and persons that get much from others are under pressure to give much to them. This process of influence tends to work out at an equilibrium to a balance of the exchanges.

Detailed descriptions of the nature of exchanges of this sort in social life have been presented by Homans (**30**) and Blau (**6**).

An example of the way in which exchange enters into influence processes is provided by the employment contract, as analyzed by Simon (**60**). In this treatment, an employee P enters into an employment contract with an employer O when P agrees to accept the authority of O and O agrees to pay P a stated wage. The critical exchange is wages for submission to authority. Although there are always limits, explicitly stated or implicitly understood, on the range of O's authority, P in effect signs a blank check. Once the contract is made, O or his delegates can use it to justify specific directives to P, and P is bound by the contract to comply. Something analogous to an employment contract would seem to be operative even in groups that do not pay wages to members. Here, the member agrees to do whatever is necessary to advance the welfare of the group in return for whatever benefits he derives from membership. Some mechanism of this sort might well account for the frequently reported correlation between a member's tendency to conform to group standards and his degree of attraction to the group.

The concept of exchange suggests that when a person "uses" a resource in order to exert influence he "uses it up" in some sense. What actually happens, however, deserves careful consideration. In some situations, the exercise of influence seems clearly to involve the relinquishing of ownership of a resource, as when O gives P some tangible reward for complying with his wishes, when O "cashes in" an obligation in order to influence P, or when the very nature of O's influence attempt destroys his prestige. This last example suggests, however, that the exercise of influence may result in an actual increase in the resources of O, since it is clearly possible to increase one's prestige through the effective use of influence. And many examples could be cited in which O gives up no obvious resource when he influences P. Influence by persuasion or by use of P's attitude toward being influenced by P frequently appears to have this characteristic.

These observations suggest four possible outcomes from an act of influence for the distribution between O and P of the resources in question: (*a*) *transfer*—O loses and P acquires the resource, (*b*) *consumption*—O loses but P does not acquire the resource, (*c*) *spread*—O keeps but P acquires possession, as in the spread of information, and (*d*) *no change* —O keeps and P does not acquire possession. It appears, then, that the attempt to conceptualize all influence as an exchange of resources encounters severe difficulties. These are especially pronounced in the use of noncontingent rewards and punishments, persuasion, and ecological control. And even when exchange may plausibly be said to occur, it is often most difficult to describe the exchange in commensurate units of value. Despite these difficulties, it is clear that the concept of exchange is useful in describing many instances of interpersonal influence.

CHOICE OF METHOD
OF INFLUENCE

Let us suppose that a person has the capacity to employ any method of influence he wishes. What determines which one he will actually use? In most general terms, we may assume that his choice will be guided by his appraisal of the consequences entailed by each: How likely is it to succeed? How much will it cost? How will others react? Is it consistent with his norms concerning interpersonal relations?

Remarkably little research has been conducted to ascertain the nature of the processes governing a person's choice of a method of influence, but a good example of how such research might proceed is provided by Rosenberg and Pearlin (56) in their study of types of influence used by nurses in a mental hospital. Employing questionnaires and interviews, they attempted to discover what criteria nurses consider in choosing a method for influencing the behavior of a patient. Each respondent was given a hypothetical situation calling for a change in a patient's behavior and five possible actions that might be taken. Each action was designed to represent one of five types of influence. The percentage of nurses who reported that they would first use each type are: persuasion (54 percent), manipulation (38 percent), legitimate authority (5 percent), coercion (2 percent), and contractual power (1 percent). Analysis of the reasons given for preferring a particular method reveals a number of factors: (*a*) the value system of the nursing profession, (*b*) the predicted effectiveness of the method, (*c*) immediate costs to the nurse, (*d*) delayed consequences that might be expected, (*e*) consequences for relationships with other patients, (*f*) the nurse's orientation to work, and (*g*) the nurse's status or position in the hospital structure.

In thinking about the determinants of a person's choice of method of influence, it is important to recognize that influence ordinarily takes place in an established social system that has norms concerning its exercise. Thus it is generally considered reprehensible in "enlightened" school systems for a teacher to discipline children by corporal punishment, and there are laws governing the techniques of influence that an employer may use with respect to employees. There appears to be a general tendency for social norms to distinguish among methods of influence according to their "harshness," with milder methods being preferred to harsher ones. Persuasion is "better" than coercion, and it is socially more desirable to use rewards than punishments. The bad connotations of the word "manipulation" reflect some of the social norms related to this method of influence. Since norms differ greatly from one group to another, we should expect to find corresponding differences among groups in their prevailing methods of influence.

Individuals undoubtedly differ, even within the same group, as to their preferred methods of influence. A particular person may typically rely upon coercion, bribes, "gentle" persuasion, manipulation, or an appeal to values. Although these stylistic differences are pronounced and easily recognized, there is little systematic evidence concerning their determinants. One hypothesis deserving further investigation has been proposed by McGregor (42) in his discussion of the management of formal organizations. He proposes that a manager's implicit "theory of human nature" basically affects the method of influence that he typically employs. Thus a manager who believes that people are "interested only in money" will tend to employ financial incentives; one who thinks that people "respond only to the big stick" will rely on coercion; and one who sees people as "basically reasonable" will tend to use persuasion. McGregor's hypothesis seems plausible since a person's philosophy of human nature is likely to affect his expectations concerning the probable success of various methods of influence and thereby his choice of method.

THE PERSON SUBJECTED TO INFLUENCE

At the beginning of the chapter we noted that influence is best conceived as a relationship between two agents *O* and *P*, but thus far we have viewed the process primarily from the perspective of *O*, the person exerting influence. To complete our analysis, then, we must look at these same phenomena from *P*'s point of view. What conditions affect a person's willingness to be influenced? What are the motive bases of power and influence?

MOTIVE BASES OF INFLUENCE

Let us consider the situation of a faculty member who is asked by his departmental chairman to serve on a certain committee. Clearly there are many reasons that might lead him to accept the assignment. He might accept because he believes that it would enhance his chances of being promoted or receiving an increase in salary. He might fear that if he did not he would acquire the reputation of being "uncooperative." He might take on the assignment because he admires the chairman and believes that the chairman would do so if he were in the member's shoes. He might accept because he feels that such service is the duty of any "good" member of the department. Or he might agree to serve simply because he thinks that he would enjoy it. His decision might, of course, be swayed by some combination of these considerations, and the weight given to each would undoubtedly be affected by the method of influence employed by the chairman.

It is reasonable to assume that an individual's reactions to any influence attempt will depend basically upon his view of the motivational consequences to him of accepting or rejecting it. He may be expected to adopt the advocated change only if he believes that in some sense it is in his best interest to do so. The motivations possibly affecting *P*'s decision may be grouped under the following six broad headings.

Desire to Receive Reward or Avoid Punishment.   The simplest instances of influence are those in which *P* accepts an influence attempt of *O* in order to obtain something he wants; *P*'s response is instrumental to receiving a reward from *O*. This sort of influence has been labeled by Kelman (**37**) as *compliance* and by French and Raven (Chap. 20) as *reward power*. We may assume that *P* will be more willing to comply with an influence attempt of *O* the more highly he values the rewards mediated by *O*. Thus, in a situation where a person can gain social approval by expressing agreement with the opinions of others, we should expect greater overt conformity among those with a high need for affiliation or approval than among those with a lower need. Results consistent with this expectation have been reported by Becker and Carroll (**4**) and by Crowne and Strickland (**14**). It is clear,

however, that the strength of *P*'s need is not the only determinant of his readiness to comply. Another determinant is his belief concerning the chances of actually satisfying the need through compliance. Other things being equal, we should expect *P*'s readiness to be greater the greater is his subjective probability that compliance will result in favorable outcomes. And if he does comply, we should expect him to make this fact evident to *O* in order to heighten the likelihood of reward.

A negative form of instrumental compliance arises when *P* modifies his behavior in order to avoid being punished by *O*, as when a person expresses agreement with another out of fear of rejection or ridicule. The base of this form of influence is called *coercive power* by French and Raven (Chap. 20). Here, *P*'s readiness to comply may be expected to increase with the severity of the anticipated punishment and with *P*'s assessment of the probability that he can avoid punishment if he complies. If *P* changes his behavior in response to a threat of punishment, he is likely to develop negative feelings toward *O* and to revert to his former behavior once the threat is withdrawn. Experimental studies by French, Morrison, and Levinger (**17**) and by Raven and French (**55**) lend general support to these hypotheses.

The immediate effect of influence based on the desire to receive rewards or to avoid punishments is a modification of *P*'s overt behavior, since this is the requirement for bringing about the desired effects. There is, however, no direct inducement for *P* to change his private beliefs. This form of influence therefore frequently produces a discrepancy between overt behavior and private beliefs, thereby creating a state of dissonance in *P* and activating dissonance-reducing behaviors of the sort described by Festinger and Aronson in Chapter 10. Under certain circumstances, *P* may ultimately change his beliefs so as to make them consonant with the induced behavior.

Desire to Be Like an Admired Person.   A rather different motive base underlies a second form of influence, called *identification* by Kelman (**37**) and *referent power* by French and Raven (Chap. 20). Such influence occurs when *O* is a person to whom *P* is attracted or one with whom he wishes, in the words of Kelman, "to establish or maintain a satisfying self-defining relationship." *P*'s desire to have a close unity with O leads him to model his beliefs, values, and behavior after those of O. When thus motivated, P will be sensitive to O's wishes and ready to accept influence attempts from him. Under these conditions O may exert influence on P even though he makes no deliberate attempt to do so. A study of such "behavioral contagion" in a group setting is reported by Lippitt *et al.* in Chapter 18. The related phenomenon of "imitation" has been subjected to intensive investigation by Miller and Dollard (49) and by Bandura (2, 3).

The psychological processes within P that make him susceptible to this kind of influence are undoubtedly complex. They would seem, however, to be based in part upon a general property of cognitive systems, identified by Heider (26) as "a tendency toward balance." According to Heider's analysis, if P has a positive affective attachment to O, then a state of cognitive balance will obtain when P's attitudes resemble O's. One consequence of the tendency toward balance is for P to modify his attitudes so as to make them similar to O's. Essentially the same conclusions are drawn by Osgood and Tannenbaum (52) from their "principle of congruity" and by Newcomb (51), who has made additional derivations concerning the effects of "the strain toward symmetry" on interpersonal communication. Cartwright and Harary (11, 12) have developed a formal model of cognitive balance and have shown its relevance to the Freudian concepts of "internalization" and "projection."

Influence based on P's desire to be like O, in contrast to that based on the desire to receive rewards or to avoid punishments, may be expected to affect both P's overt behavior and his private beliefs and attitudes. Results consistent with this expectation have been reported by Zander and Curtis (68), who compared social influence based on referent power with that based on coercive power. They constructed an experimental situation in which P was given a standard for his performance either by others whom P liked and admired (referent power) or by others who could punish him for not doing well (coercive power). They reasoned that under conditions of referent and not coercive power, P would "internalize" the proposed standard and adopt it as his personal level of aspiration. He would then be motivated to work toward its attainment and employ it in evaluating the quality of his performance. The experimental results bear out this line of reasoning: there was a stronger motivation to achieve the proposed standard and a more intense feeling of failure when not achieving it under referent power than under coercive power.

Desire to Abide by One's Values. Even a casual observation of interpersonal influence as it occurs in everyday life reveals how frequently an appeal is made to values such as fairness, rationality, generosity, honesty, and bravery. When P accepts this appeal by O as appropriate, there can be little doubt that it adds weight to O's influence attempt. Although it is true that the motive base for this type of influence is often P's desire to receive approval from others who share the invoked value, a rather different one is also commonly involved. A person may adopt the advocated change because he derives satisfaction from stating attitudes or otherwise engaging in actions that express his basic values. In the words of Katz (32), "the reward to the person in these instances is not so much a matter of gaining social recognition or monetary rewards as of establishing his self-identity and confirming his notion of the sort of person he sees himself to be."

The values of an individual may enter into the influence process in another way by serving as the motive base of what French and Raven (Chap. 20) call *legitimate power*. The values in this case apply to the relationship between O and P and indicate to P that he has an obligation to accept influence from O. Many social norms governing role relationships, as between a son and his father, specify that it is the duty of one party to comply with directives from the other. A person who accepts such a norm thereby accepts the legitimacy of O's influence. In a group setting, the election procedure is a common method for designating the legitimate power of that office. Raven and French (54) conducted an experiment in which two work situations were identical except that in one the supervisor was elected and in the other he took office without the benefit of an election. They found that a standard request made by the supervisor was more effective when he had been elected than when he had not. One might expect, in general, that the more a person accepts the authority structure of a group, the more readily will he conform to the wishes of its legitimate authority figures.

Desire to Be Correct.   When influence processes are aimed at changing beliefs or opinions of P, the most important motive base is P's desire to have an accurate view of reality. If P views O as having special knowledge or expertness, this desire gives O what French and Raven (Chap. 20) call *expert power.* P may have many reasons for attributing expertness to a particular other person—O's experience, training, intelligence, reputation for credibility, or special access to relevant information. Mausner (**46**) obtained more convergence in judgments toward partners who had previously succeeded on a related task than toward those who had failed. And French and Snyder (**18**) found that group leaders were able to exert more influence over the judgments of members the more highly they were rated on general intelligence. One might expect that O's expert power over P will extend only to those matters with respect to which P attributes superior knowledge to O, even though experts in one field often attempt to exert influence beyond their sphere of demonstrated competence.

Group-oriented Desires.   Much of the interpersonal influence that occurs among the members of a group has as its motive base the members' concern for the welfare of the group. A member P who is committed to a certain outcome for the group will be susceptible to influence attempts made by another member O when these are seen as instrumental to the attainment of this outcome. In discussing the nature of pressures to uniformity in groups (Chap. 11), we noted four functions that may be served by the uniformity resulting from such pressures: (a) to help the group accomplish its goals, (b) to help the group maintain itself as a group, (c) to help the members develop validity or "reality" for their opinions, and (d) to help members define their relations to their social environment. Pressures to uniformity give rise to a tendency for members both to exert influence on one another and to accept influence from one another. If under these conditions P views an influence attempt by O as motivated by a concern for the group's welfare, we should expect P to be more willing to accept this influence the more strongly he desires one or more of these functions to be served. This desire, then, is a motive base for influence within the group.

Intrinsic Gratification.   Finally, it should be noted that an influence attempt of O may be accepted by P simply because P comes to view the advocated change as intrinsically rewarding. Influence of this sort, which is labeled *internalization* by Kelman (**37**), may be expected to affect both private beliefs and overt behavior and to persist even when O is no longer physically present. Use of the methods of persuasion and ecological control relies upon the assumption that P will be led to appreciate the desirability of the change sought by O. It should be apparent, however, that the effectiveness of these methods will be limited by the nature of P's motives and values since these are the source of P's gratification.

OPPOSITION AND RESISTANCE

It is important when analyzing the nature of interpersonal influence to keep in mind that O's objective in making an influence attempt is to bring about some change in P. If an act of O is to be successful in modifying the beliefs, attitudes, or behavior of P, it must counteract the reasons P had for adhering to them prior to the influence attempt. It is for this reason that efforts to bring about change so often encounter opposition. Whenever P yields to an influence attempt of O he must "give up" something, even though he may ultimately decide that the benefits of yielding outweigh the costs.

The strength of opposition to an influence attempt would seem to depend, in general, upon (a) the degree of incompatibility between the state to be induced and the pre-existing state of P and (b) the strength of anchorage of the pre-existing state. Allen (**1**) has summarized a considerable body of literature that lends support to this generalization. Thus, it has been found repeatedly that a person conforms less to an influence attempt the more certain he is of his initial position, the more important this position is to him, and the more committed he is to it. Research conducted by Gerard (**20**), Kelley (**34**), and Kelley and Volkhart (**36**) indicates that an attempt to make a person's attitudes deviate from the norms of a reference group will encounter more opposition the more salient or important this group is for him.

In considering the factors that inhibit the acceptance of an influence attempt, it is useful to distinguish between the processes that Cartwright (**9**) and French and Raven (Chap. 20) have called "opposition" and "resistance."

This distinction may be illustrated by reference to our earlier example of the faculty member who is asked by his departmental chairman to serve on a certain committee. He may be reluctant to accept this assignment either because he would find such service disagreeable or because he resents the way in which the chairman asked him. In the former case, the influence attempt encounters opposition stemming from the faculty member's evaluation of the advocated behavior, whereas in the latter the chairman's act itself generates resistance. When P opposes an influence attempt of O, the critical element is P's negative evaluation of the content of the proposed change; when he resists, this content is secondary or irrelevant. Resistance in contrast to opposition often appears to be irrational, since it may lead a person to engage in behavior that appears to be contrary to his own best interests.

A beginning toward an understanding of the sources of resistance was made by Frank (16) in one of the earliest experimental investigations of interpersonal influence. He found that "resistance to an activity is readily aroused if doing it involves submitting to an arbitrary personal demand of someone else, and is thereby equivalent to a personal defeat" or if the situation becomes one of a "clash of wills." Several more recent studies, by French, Morrison, and Levinger (17), Raven and French (54, 55), and Zipf (69), indicate that P is likely to resist an influence attempt by O when the attempt is viewed by P as illegitimate, when it is coercive, or when P dislikes or mistrusts O. And Brehm (7) has reported results from a number of experiments supporting a theory of "psychological reactance" that predicts, among other things, that whenever an attempt reduces or threatens to reduce P's subjective sphere of freedom it will generate resistance and counteractive tendencies in P.

One of Frank's more striking findings was that when students agreed to be subjects in an experiment they gave such authority to the role of experimenter that he could not get them to resist his instructions to perform quite disagreeable tasks, and he drew the general conclusion that "resistance to an activity is strongly inhibited by making the activity appear to be implied by a previous agreement." That such an agreement can strongly inhibit

resistance has been dramatically demonstrated by Milgram (47, 48) in a series of experiments in which a critical subject is instructed by the experimenter to administer increasingly severe electric shocks to another subject in the context of a learning experiment. His results show a remarkably high incidence of "obedience" even when the critical subject is aware that his behavior is causing his victim extreme suffering. Milgram offers a number of interesting hypotheses to account for the low level of resistance in his experimental settings, but a fully satisfactory explanation of these phenomena is yet to be achieved.

One might expect that P's reactions to a particular influence attempt will depend in part upon the nature of his personality. Although this possibility has not been examined in detail, Zipf (69) reports a weak tendency for subjects with a stronger need for independence to display more resistance to coercive influence. And several studies have investigated the relationship between authoritarianism and conformity, but, as noted by Harvey (25), the effects of authoritarianism are complex and difficult to interpret. At present there is no comprehensive theory of personality from which one can predict an individual's reactions to influence attempts of various kinds.

Lewin (41, Chap. 9), on the basis of an analysis of the psychological forces acting on P when he is subjected to an influence attempt, concludes that there are three distinctively different ways in which influence can be accomplished: (a) by adding new forces on P, (b) by changing the direction of pre-existing forces, and (c) by reducing the magnitude of opposing forces. Lewin proposes that the first method is generally less desirable than the other two because it creates a stronger conflict of forces within P and thereby generates more emotional tension with its concomitants of hostility, rigidity, and regression. If an act of O also creates resisting forces, the conflict may be heightened further. An attempt to bring about changes in P through the use of rewards, punishments, or legitimate power leaves the pre-existing forces in operation, and P must deal with these even if he yields. Milgram's report (48) of an extremely high level of emotional tension among his "obedient" subjects would appear consistent with Lewin's analysis.

GROUP COHESIVENESS AND POWER

The preceding discussion of the motive bases of influence and of the sources of opposition and resistance permits a better understanding of the reasons for the frequently reported correlation between group cohesiveness and the power of a group over its members. In Chapter 7 we saw that the cohesiveness of a group increases with its capacity for satisfying the needs of its members. A person will be more attracted to a group the more he expects to satisfy his needs through membership and participation in the group's activities. Now it is clear that these needs, which constitute the motive bases of attraction to the group, will also serve as motive bases of interpersonal influence within the group. Thus, for example, if a person P is attracted to a group because he believes that membership will satisfy his need for social approval, he will be susceptible to influence by a member O who makes his approval of P contingent upon P's compliance. In other words, P's desire for social approval, which is the basis for his attraction to the group, serves as a motive base of reward power and coercive power for the other members of the group. The stronger is P's need the greater will be both his attraction to the group and the power of other members over him. Cohesiveness based on interpersonal attraction is related to referent power in a similar way. P's liking or admiration for the other members of the group leads him to want to model himself after them, and we should expect him to be more susceptible to influence from them the more strongly he is attracted to the group.

It would appear that group cohesiveness can lead to power in other, more indirect ways. A member of a highly cohesive group may be expected to be concerned with the group's welfare and therefore ready to accept influence attempts that appeal to these group-oriented desires. He is also likely to accept group decisions concerning the assignment of responsibilities among members and consequently to attribute legitimacy to influence attempts made by anyone assigned to supervise his activities. And he may even come to refer his judgments concerning the nature of reality to other members, thus giving them expert power over him. Each of these processes is more likely to become operative the greater the cohesiveness of the group.

Finally, there are reasons to expect opposition and resistance to be less strong in more cohesive groups. We have seen that, in the long run, members of highly cohesive groups tend to become similar in their beliefs, attitudes, and values, as a result either of pressures to uniformity or of selective processes of recruitment and attrition. For this reason it is not likely that members will attempt to induce changes in others that run counter to their basic motivations, nor will they be likely to employ methods of influence that would arouse resistance.

All of these processes would lead to a correlation between group cohesiveness and the magnitude of influence that the members of a group can exert on one another. It is apparent, however, that the exact nature of these processes will depend upon the nature of the motive bases of attraction and the state of the group's development.

BY-PRODUCTS OF POWER

Our discussion thus far has primarily focused upon the nature of the influence process itself, but we have noted at several points that the exercise of influence by O may have certain side effects on the relationship between O and P. Thus, for example, we have seen that if O attempts to influence P by the use of threats, P may come to dislike O even though he complies with O's wishes. If, on the other hand, O employs rewards to gain P's compliance, the effect may be to increase P's liking for O. We have also seen that certain methods of influence are likely to bring about a change in P's overt behavior while leaving his covert beliefs and attitudes unmodified. The resulting discrepancy between P's beliefs and behavior creates a situation in which P is motivated to hide his true feelings while O is motivated to watch P closely to be certain that he is complying. This combination of deviousness and close monitoring is bound to generate interpersonal stress and to color other relationships between O and P. Clearly an act of influence by O may bring about changes quite different from those motivating it, and the mere existence of a power relationship between O and P may have various consequences for both parties. We turn now to a brief consideration of these by-products of power.

EFFECTS ON THE PERSON HAVING POWER

The most obvious consequence of the possession of power is that it enhances a person's ability to achieve the outcomes he desires. *O*'s chances of being able to accomplish something that requires the help of *P* will increase with the magnitude of his power over *P*. And, in general, *O* will be better able to gratify his needs the larger is his domain of power. This fact accounts in part for the findings, reported in Chapter 7, that the job satisfaction of employees tends to be greater at successively higher levels in the supervisory hierarchy of an organization. And it helps to explain the findings from research on communication networks that those in more central locations experience greater satisfaction than do those in less central ones.

Thibaut and Kelley (64), in their analysis of dyadic interactions, have specified several advantages that accrue to the person with greater power. They point out that the high-power person is able to initiate activities, set the pace, and "call the changes" in the interaction. He can let his own motivations dominate the situation; when he has derived sufficient satisfaction from a particular joint activity, he can terminate it even though the other person may wish to continue. The possession of power enlarges what Lewin has termed "the space of free movement," increases one's sense of personal security, and permits the making of plans that extend farther into the future.

A person who can initiate activities and determine the tasks of others is likely to be treated deferentially—a finding reported by Lippitt *et al.* in Chapter 18—and be accorded prestige. Such reactions from others will tend to raise his self-esteem and add to the other satisfactions gained through the possession of power. An interesting demonstration of these effects has been reported by Zander and Cohen (66), who created a situation in which members of a group were privately instructed to behave toward one of their members as if he had high status and toward another as if he had low status. Subsequent ratings by the highs revealed greater satisfaction and enjoyment of the interaction than did those of the lows.

Since the possession of power is instrumental to the attainment of many satisfactions and produces such gratifying side effects, a person who has tasted the fruits of power is likely to be reluctant to relinquish his power. He may even be prepared to resort to extreme measures to preserve it. The possession of power may become an end in itself, for the powerful person may find, as Mulder claims (50), that "the exercise of power *per se* leads to satisfactions not only through such variables as increase of status, more pleasant activity, or other concomitant gains, but in itself." And, since powerful people can readily have their own way, they may tend to become insensitive to the needs of others.

These various features of the power relationship lend plausibility to the popular notion that "power corrupts." It would seem, however, that such characterization of the personal consequences of possessing power is too simple. The security afforded by power may free a person to be responsive to the needs of others. Perhaps it is this security which accounts for the results reported by Solomon (61), who found that in a game situation higher power persons more frequently engaged in "trusting behavior." Everyday experience indicates that power can be used responsibly and with compassion, that the burdens and responsibilities of power can be great, and that powerful people do sometimes voluntarily give up their power. More research is clearly needed before we can safely draw any general conclusions concerning the long-term effects on the personality and character of the person who possesses power.

EFFECTS ON THE PERSON SUBJECTED TO POWER

The subordinate member of a power relationship confronts a situation containing many potential inconveniences, disadvantages, and threats. If *O* has power over *P*, it follows by definition that *O* can bring about changes in *P*. And if this power extends over matters of importance to *P*, his welfare is dependent upon the behavior of *O; O* can use his power to help or to hinder *P*. When *P* interacts with *O*, it is *O*'s interests that control the interaction; he can initiate activities, set the pace, and change or terminate the activities as he sees fit. Interaction under these conditions is likely to produce frustrations for *P* and make him feel that his freedom of action is curtailed. We see, then, that the mere existence of a power relationship poses a threat to *P*, and we should expect him to seek ways of defending himself against it.

One method of defense that is essentially autistic is for P to bias his cognitions of O so as to see O as having benevolent feelings toward him. If P can lead himself to believe that O will use his power only in "safe" or helpful ways, the feeling of threat will be diminished. Pepitone (53) observed the operation of this sort of defensive cognitive process. He placed boys in a situation in which the achievement of an attractive object was under the control of a panel of three judges. After a standardized interaction between the boys and the panel, each boy was asked to rate the relative power and relative benevolence of each panel member. In this setting Pepitone found cognitive distortions designed, as it were, to minimize the threatening power of the panel members— if a member was rated as powerful, his benevolence was rated higher, and if he was rated as malevolent, his power was rated lower.

Several studies have demonstrated that O's power over P affects the frequency of communication between them in both directions as well as the content of this communication. Thus, for example, Hurwitz *et al.* (Chap. 23) and Kelley (33) found a general tendency for both low-power and high-power individuals to direct their communications more often to highs than to lows. They found, too, that lows tend to approach highs with deference and caution—their messages tend to flatter the highs and not to contain criticisms. Similar findings have been reported by Lippitt *et al.* (Chap. 18) and by Cohen (13). It would appear that the communications directed by P to O are designed, in part at least, to enhance the likelihood that O will think well of P and not use his power to harm him.

The variety of defensive actions that P may resort to in order to protect himself from the power of O has been documented by Zander, Cohen, and Stotland (67) in a study of role relations among psychiatrists, psychologists, and social workers. They report that psychologists and social workers who feel that they have relatively little power in their interactions with psychiatrists tend to desire many contacts with psychiatrists, seek advice from them, praise them, indicate that they value their help, and generally communicate in a way to protect good relations. These behaviors would appear to be motivated by a desire to induce the more powerful person to use his

power in a benevolent way. The use of ingratiation as a technique for reducing the threat inherent in power has been studied extensively by Jones (31), and an experiment growing out of this line of investigation is reported in Chapter 22.

Because of the disadvantages of being under the power of another, it might be expected that powerless people would take actions to change the power relation itself. There are, of course, many instances of revolution or rebellion against "the power structure," but there are also innumerable situations in which those disadvantaged by the lack of power make no efforts to improve their lot. Unfortunately, little systematic research has been directed toward increasing our understanding of the conditions that generate attempts to change the power relation in contrast to those that lead to accommodation.

It should be apparent from our analysis of the nature of power that there are a variety of ways in which people with little power may improve their situation. One of these is to restrict the range of legitimate power or to limit the methods by which power can be exercised. Thus, subordinates in an organization may seek to reduce the rights, prerogatives, or latitude of superiors by redefining, through legislation and collective bargaining, the acts a superior may legitimately perform. Another frequently employed technique is for the subordinate to avoid social situations in which the superior might perform a strong, disagreeable act. A third technique is based on the recognition that power arises from the possession of resources and that a redistribution of power can be accomplished by a redistribution of resources. The specific procedures required for a change in the control of resources will depend, of course, upon the particular resources involved; when they are of such nature that they can be "pooled" and used in a concerted way by several people, a person may enhance his power by forming coalitions with others. Research into the conditions governing the formation and operation of coalitions has been summarized by Gamson (19).

There are undoubtedly long-term effects on the person who is consistently subjected to power by others. The literature contains suggestions that he will tend to become apathetic, submissive, pessimistic, or generally alienated from the social system. But it also contains indications that he will tend to become hostile, angry, aggressive, or rebellious against authority. That both of these strikingly different kinds of reaction are possible is supported by the research of White and Lippitt (Chap. 25), who found two characteristic responses to autocratic leadership, which they labeled "apathetic" and "aggressive." Further research on this important problem is clearly needed.

OVERVIEW OF RESEARCH REPORTED IN PART FOUR

The material in the following six chapters contains findings from research into the nature of interpersonal power and influence. It explores the sources of power, some of the forms it may take, and its consequences for the relationships among the members of a group.

In Chapter 18, Lippitt *et al.* report results from a study of influence among participants in a summer camp. They distinguish between *behavioral contagion*, which is "the spontaneous pickup or imitation by other children of the behavior initiated by one member of the group where the initiator did not display any intention of getting the others to do what he did," and *direct influence*, "in which the actor initiates behavior which has the manifest objective of affecting the behavior of another member of the group." An important finding of this study is the demonstration that the resources that give a child the capacity to exert direct influence are essentially the same as those that give him the capacity to initiate behavioral contagion. The study also describes the different ways in which those with more and those with less power behave in interactions with others.

The next two chapters investigate more directly the motive bases of power. Chapter 19 presents a study by Gold of the personal properties of children that may serve as resources of influence. He shows that the properties valued by others differ with the age and sex of those making the evaluations and that

children who possess valued properties are viewed by their classmates as having power over them. In Chapter 20, French and Raven present a penetrating theoretical analysis of "the bases of power." They identify five different bases and present a number of hypotheses concerning the nature of the influence processes that rely on each.

In Chapter 21, Ring and Kelley report the results of an experiment investigating two methods of influence which they call "augmentation" and "reduction." When a person uses augmentation he provides rewards to induce another person to perform some desired behavior. When he uses reduction he administers punishments to bring about desired effects. These authors document a variety of effects of these two methods of influence on the subordinate's readiness to reveal his behavior and to adopt the standards of his superior.

The last two chapters of this section are concerned with the effects of power relations on the person subjected to power. Jones *et al.* describe, in Chapter 22, an experiment designed to study some of the conditions affecting the occurrence of ingratiation. They show that a person whose performance is to be evaluated by another will be more motivated to create an attractive impression when he believes that the evaluator's behavior can be influenced than when he sees it as fixed. In the final chapter, Hurwitz, Zander, and Hymovitch report findings from a conference attended by people with differing degrees of power. They report that those with less power participate less frequently but that when they do their communications are more frequently directed toward those with greater power. Furthermore, those with little power tend to perceive that they are liked more by those with greater power than the situation justifies. These results suggest that those with less power attempt to reduce the threat inherent in the situation both through their behavior and through distorting their perceptions of the more powerful people.

References

1. Allen, V. L. Situational factors in conformity. In L. Berkowitz (Ed.), *Advances in experimental social psychology*. Vol. 2. New York: Academic Press, 1965. Pp. 133–175.
2. Bandura, A. Social learning through imitation. In M. R. Jones (Ed.), *Nebraska symposium on motivation*, 1960. Lincoln: Univ. of Nebraska Press, 1962. Pp. 211–268.

3. Bandura, A. Vicarious processes: A case of no-trial learning. In L. Berkowitz (Ed.), *Advances in experimental social psychology.* Vol. 2. New York: Academic Press, 1965. Pp. 1–55.

4. Becker, S., & Carroll, J. Ordinal position and conformity. *Journal of Abnormal and Social Psychology,* 1962, **65**, 129–131.

5. Bennis, W. G., *et al.* Authority, power, and the ability to influence. *Human Relations,* 1958, **11**, 143–155.

6. Blau, P. M. *Exchange and power in social life.* New York: Wiley, 1964.

7. Brehm, J. W. *A theory of psychological reactance.* New York: Academic Press, 1966.

8. Cartwright, D. Achieving change in people: Some applications of group dynamics theory. *Human Relations,* 1951, **4**, 381–393.

9. Cartwright, D. A field theoretical conception of power. In D. Cartwright (Ed.), *Studies in social power.* Ann Arbor, Mich.: Institute for Social Research, 1959. Pp. 183–220.

10. Cartwright, D. Influence, leadership, control. In J. G. March (Ed.), *Handbook of organizations.* Chicago: Rand McNally, 1965. Pp. 1–47.

11. Cartwright, D., & Harary, F. Structural balance: A generalization of Heider's theory. *Psychological Review,* 1956, **63**, 277–293.

12. Cartwright, D., & Harary, F. A note on Freud's "Instincts and their vicissitudes." *International Journal of Psychoanalysis.* 1959, **60**, 1–4.

13. Cohen, A. R. Upward communication in experimentally created hierarchies. *Human Relations,* 1958, **11**, 41–53.

14. Crowne, D. P., & Strickland, B. R. The conditioning of verbal behavior as a function of the need for social approval. *Journal of Abnormal and Social Psychology,* 1961, **63**, 395–401.

15. Dahl, R. A. The concept of power. *Behavioral Science,* 1957, **2**, 201–215.

16. Frank, J. D. Experimental studies of personal pressure and resistance. I. Experimental production of resistance. *Journal of General Psychology,* 1944, **30**, 23–41.

17. French, J. R. P. Jr., Morrison, H. W., & Levinger, G. Coercive power and forces affecting conformity. *Journal of Abnormal and Social Psychology,* 1960, **61**, 93–101.

18. French, J. R. P. Jr., & Snyder, R. Leadership and interpersonal power. In D. Cartwright (Ed.), *Studies in social power.* Ann Arbor, Mich.: Institute for Social Research, 1959. Pp. 118–149.

19. Gamson, W. Experimental studies of coalition formation. In L. Berkowitz (Ed.), *Advances in experimental social psychology.* Vol. 1. New York: Academic Press, 1964. Pp. 81–110.

20. Gerard, H. The anchorage of opinions in face-to-face groups. *Human Relations,* 1954, **7**, 313–325.

21. Gilman, G. An inquiry into the nature and use of authority. In M. Haire (Ed.), *Organization theory in industrial practice.* New York: Wiley, 1962. Pp. 105–142.

22. Gouldner, A. W. The norm of reciprocity: A preliminary statement. *American Sociological Review,* 1960, **25**, 161–178.

23. Gump, P. V., & Sutton-Smith, B. Activity-setting and social interaction: A field study. *American Journal of Orthopsychiatry,* 1955, **25**, 755–760.

24. Harsanyi, J. C. Measurement of social power, opportunity costs, and the theory of two-person bargaining games. *Behavioral Science,* 1962, **7**, 67–80.

25. Harvey, O. J. Personality factors in resolution of conceptual incongruities. *Sociometry,* 1962, **25**, 336–352.

26. Heider, F. *The psychology of interpersonal relations.* New York: Wiley, 1958.

27. Hemphill, J. K. Why people attempt to lead. In L. Petrullo & B. Bass (Eds.), *Leadership and interpersonal behavior.* New York: Holt, Rinehart, and Winston, 1961. Pp. 201–215.

28. Hobbes, T. *Leviathan.* (First published, 1651.) Cambridge, Eng.: Cambridge Univ. Press, 1904.

29. Homans, G. C. Social behavior as exchange. *American Journal of Sociology,* 1958, **63**, 597–606.

30. Homans, G. C. *Social behavior.* New York: Harcourt, Brace, 1961.

31. Jones, E. E. *Ingratiation: A social psychological analysis.* New York: Appleton-Century-Crofts, 1964.

32. Katz, D. The functional approach to the study of attitudes. *Public Opinion Quarterly,* 1960, **24,** 163–204.

33. Kelley, H. H. Communication in experimentally created hierarchies. *Human Relations,* 1951, **4,** 39–56.

34. Kelley, H. H. Salience of membership and resistance to change of group-anchored attitudes. *Human Relations,* 1955, **8,** 275–290.

35. Kelley, H. H., & Ring, K. Some effects of "suspicious" versus "trusting" training schedules. *Journal of Abnormal and Social Psychology,* 1961, **63,** 294–301.

36. Kelley, H. H., & Volkhart, E. H. The resistance to change of group-anchored attitudes. *American Sociological Review,* 1952, **17,** 453–465.

37. Kelman, H. C. Compliance, identification, and internalization: Three processes of attitude change. *Journal of Conflict Resolution,* 1958, **2,** 51–60.

38. Klapper, J. T. *The effects of mass communication.* Glencoe, Ill.: Free Press, 1960.

39. Lasswell, H. D., & Kaplan, A. *Power and society.* New Haven, Conn.: Yale Univ. Press, 1950.

40. Levinger, G. The development of perceptions and behavior in newly formed social power relationships. In D. Cartwright (Ed.), *Studies in social power.* Ann Arbor, Mich.: Institute for Social Research, 1959. Pp. 83–98.

41. Lewin, K. *Field theory in social science.* New York: Harper, 1951.

42. McGregor, D. M. *The human side of enterprise.* New York: McGraw-Hill, 1960.

43. Machiavelli, N. *The prince.* (First published, 1513.) New York: Hendricks House, 1946.

44. March, J. G. An introduction to the theory and measurement of influence. *American Political Science Review,* 1955, **49,** 431–451.

45. March, J. G. Measurement concepts in the theory of influence. *Journal of Politics,* 1957, **19,** 202–226.

46. Mausner, B. The effect of one partner's success or failure in a relevant task on the interaction of observer pairs. *Journal of Abnormal and Social Psychology,* 1954, **49,** 557–560.

47. Milgram, S. Behavioral study of obedience. *Journal of Abnormal and Social Psychology,* 1963, **67,** 371–378.

48. Milgram, S. Some conditions of obedience and disobedience to authority. *Human Relations,* 1965, **18,** 57–76.

49. Miller, N. E., & Dollard, J. *Social learning and imitation.* New Haven, Conn.: Yale Univ. Press, 1941.

50. Mulder, M. The power variable in communication experiments. *Human Relations,* 1960, **13,** 241–256.

51. Newcomb, T. An approach to the study of communicative acts. *Psychological Review,* 1953, **60,** 393–404.

52. Osgood, C. E., & Tannenbaum, P. H. The principle of congruity in the prediction of attitude change. *Psychological Review,* 1955, **62,** 42–55.

53. Pepitone, A. Motivational effects in social perception. *Human Relations,* 1950, **3,** 57–76.

54. Raven, B. H., & French, J. R. P. Jr. Group support, legitimate power, and social influence. *Journal of Personality,* 1958, **26,** 400–409.

55. Raven, B. H., & French, J. R. P. Jr. Legitimate power, coercive power, and observability in social influence. *Sociometry,* 1958, **21,** 83–97.

56. Rosenberg, M., & Pearlin, L. I. Power-orientations in the mental hospital. *Human Relations,* 1962, **15,** 335–350.

57. Russell, B. *Power: A new social analysis.* London: Allen & Unwin, 1938.

58. Schopler, J. Social power. In L. Berkowitz (Ed.), *Advances in experimental social psychology.* Vol. 2. New York: Academic Press, 1965. Pp. 177–218.

59. Shapley, L. S., & Shubik, M. A method for evaluating the distribution of power in a committee system. *American Political Science Review,* 1954, **48,** 787–792.

60. Simon, H. A. *Models of man.* New York: Wiley, 1957.

61. Solomon, L. The influence of some types of power relations and game strategies upon the development of interpersonal trust. *Journal of Abnormal and Social Psychology,* 1960, **61,** 223–230.

62. Stogdill, R. M. *Individual behavior and group achievement.* London: Oxford Univ. Press, 1959.

63. Tannenbaum, A. S. An event-structure approach to social power and to the problem of power comparability. *Behavioral Science*, 1962, **7**, 315–331.
64. Thibaut, J. W., & Kelley, H. H. *The social psychology of groups.* New York: Wiley, 1959.
65. Whyte, W. F. *Street corner society.* Chicago: Univ. of Chicago Press, 1943.
66. Zander, A., & Cohen, A. R. Attributed social power and group acceptance: A classroom experimental demonstration. *Journal of Abnormal and Social Psychology*, 1955, **51**, 490–492.
67. Zander, A., Cohen, A. R., & Stotland, E. *Role relations in the mental health professions.* Ann Arbor, Mich.: Institute for Social Research, 1957.
68. Zander, A., & Curtis, T. Effects of social power on aspiration setting and striving. *Journal of Abnormal and Social Psychology*, 1962, **64**, 63–74.
69. Zipf, S. G. Resistance and conformity under reward and punishment. *Journal of Abnormal and Social Psychology*, 1960, **61**, 102–109.

18

The Dynamics of Power

RONALD LIPPITT, NORMAN POLANSKY,
FRITZ REDL, AND SIDNEY ROSEN

This is one in a series of reports on a program of research into the process of social influence in groups of children (5, 8, 9, 10). Our initial curiosity focused on the phenomenon of behavioral contagion described and clinically conceptualized by Redl (11) in an analysis of some of the operational problems of group therapy. We defined *behavioral contagion* as the spontaneous pickup or imitation by other children of a behavior initiated by one member of the group where the initiator did not display any intention of getting the others to do what he did. This is distinguished from *direct influence*, in which the actor initiates behavior which has the manifest objective of affecting the behavior of another member of the group. We decided to study the hypothesis that the initiation of, and receptivity to, such social influences was related to the position of the actor in the social structure of the group.

The first field study, in 1948, collected data in two camps for disturbed children. One was a boys' camp and the other was for girls. We decided it would be desirable to replicate the study in the boys' camp and were fortunate in again securing full collaboration from the same camp, the University of Michigan Fresh Air Camp [1] (hereafter referred to as M-camp). We selected the same age group as in the earlier study and again chose for investigation four cabins during each of the two camp sessions. The most significant measurements were duplicated as carefully as possible.

The first study was concerned with groups of disturbed children from a lower socio-economic background. We decided to find a contrasting population of middle-class

From *Human Relations*, 1952, **5**, 37–64. Reprinted by permission of the authors and *Human Relations*. The research reported here was supported by a grant from the National Institute of Mental Health of the U. S. Public Health Service.

[1] We wish to express deep appreciation to William Morse, Director of the Michigan Fresh Air Camp, and to Elmer Ott, Director of Camp Manito-wish of the North Central Area Council of the YMCA, for their understanding support, without which this project could not have been possible.

nondisturbed boys. It seemed important to try to find a camp with the same double four-week session, the same size group and adult-child ratio, and as nearly the same program philosophy as possible. After considerable exploration, we were fortunate in securing the wholehearted collaboration of Camp Manitowish in Wisconsin (hereafter referred to as W-camp). The two research teams of three each were trained together in the use of the same instruments and then spent the summer separated, collecting data in the two camps. One member of the W-camp team spent a final week in M-camp to get an estimate of the intercamp observation reliability.

This report summarizes the comparative findings on behavioral contagion and direct influence processes in the M- and W-camps, and also reports the 1948 data so that the replication of the findings in M-camp can be evaluated, as well as the degree of generalization of the findings to the new type of population in W-camp.

After a number of exploratory excursions, it has seemed to us most fruitful to reformulate our theorizing as contributing to a systematic theory of social power in the face-to-face group. Theorizing about the dynamics of power in larger social structures has proved stimulating in such contributions as those of Weber (3), Parsons (7), and Goldhammer and Shils (4). The latter have suggested that power may be measured by the number of successful power acts divided by the number of attempts made. This idea is very similar to one of the indices used in our two studies (percentage of success of direct influence attempts). Another springboard for us has been the work of Festinger and his co-workers (2). They have followed Lewin (6) in defining power as potentiality to exert influence. As we see it, the dimensions of the concept of social power can be differentiated as units in the following definition.

Social power is (*a*) the potentiality (*b*) for inducing forces (*c*) in other persons (*d*) toward acting or changing in a given direction.

Obviously, there can be no direct operational definition of this concept because so many situations and interactions would have to be explored to discover the exact boundaries of "potential" power. In our study we have made two attempts to approximate a measure of power.

By getting the judgments of all members on the degree of ability of each member to influence "the other fellow," we have computed an *index of attributed power*. This index is, of course, an inadequate direct measure of power for several reasons. For example, the power of one or several members may be untested by the events of group life. There may be a bias of being unwilling to recognize the power of a member to whom one does not willingly submit. But the stability of the index over time, the amount of intermember agreement in making the judgments, and the consistent predicted relationships to other variables suggest that this index represents a good approach to one aspect of the power syndrome.

The second measure is an index of the degree of behavioral success the member has in attempting to influence others. We might call this an *index of manifest power*. This also is only an indirect approximation of power, because a person with high power may not attempt to exert that power or may exercise it only in very limited degrees and situations.

It is within this general theoretical framework that we have attempted to organize our findings, and to which we shall return for interpretation in the final section.

METHODS OF DATA COLLECTION AND ANALYSIS

The variables we wanted to measure have been indicated by the theoretical interests outlined above. Because one important objective of the study was to replicate the previous one, we had to consider seriously whether to repeat a particular measurement procedure exactly or refine our measurement of the variable on the basis of what we had learned from experience.

MEASUREMENT OF ATTRIBUTED POWER

In the first study, the children sorted the pictures of the other members of the group into colored boxes on a number of dimensions which were combined into an attributed power index. This was an individual interview situation (10). On each dimension the child was only asked to select two children, the top one and the bottom one. The data from the five highly correlated dimensions of (*a*) ability in athletics, (*b*) independence of adults, (*c*) having ideas for fun, (d) sex sophistication, and (e) independence of social pressure, were combined into an attributed power index in order to get a stable measure which would differentiate the children. This combined index was highly related to the single criterion of projected group influence ("who is best at getting the others to do what he wants them to do"); but each child had only rated two children, so we did not feel the single measure was stable enough to use alone as the measurement of attributed power. In the current study, we refined the data from the single question of "who has influence" by asking each child to rank every other child by hanging the pictures in rank order on a row of nails on a board.

We decided to use this single "purer" measure of attributed power rather than the combined index because it seemed likely to us that, if the two camps were as widely different as we predicted, the various questions about physical strength, sex sophistication, etc., would have quite different meanings and relations to attributed power in the two camps. Therefore in our report of findings our improved direct measurement of perceived influence is compared with the combined attributed power index of the 1948 study. As in that study, these sociometric interviews were conducted during the first and last weeks of the four-week camp session.

MEASUREMENT OF LIKING AND IDENTIFICATION

In 1948 and in 1950, each child ranked the other members of his cabin group on the criterion of "like to be with." In the 1950 study, we added another question which asked each boy to select some other boy in the cabin he "would most like to be." We hoped this latter question would sharpen our understanding of the relationship between interpersonal feelings and the exerting of social influence.

MEASUREMENT OF PERCEIVED CHARACTERISTICS OF EACH MEMBER

Using the same picture-ranking technique, each child ranked the other group members on goodness in sports, fighting ability (added in second study), sex sophistication, and knowledge of campcraft.

Each counselor ranked each child in his group four times during the period on scales of adult relatedness, impulsiveness, group belongingness need, feeling of acceptance by the group, conformity to group pressures, warmth of relations with peers, social sensitivity, and activity level. The counselors also did the same rank ordering task as the boys on the items above (liking, attributed power, projected popularity, goodness in sports, fighting ability, sex sophistication, campcraft knowledge).

MEASUREMENT OF SELF-PERCEPTION

A significant addition to the measurement program of the second study was asking each child to place his own picture in the rank order for the dimensions of fighting ability, independence of adults, being liked, and influence in the group. A pilot study in the intervening summer had indicated that children were ready and able to do this without any discoverable problems of anxiety or other aftereffects in the group.

MEASUREMENT OF BEHAVIORAL CONTAGION AND DIRECT INFLUENCE

A precategorized observation schedule was used by a team of field observers to record behavior. As in the first study, an incident of *behavioral contagion* was defined as: "An event in which a person's behavior is changed to resemble that of another person. This change occurs in a social interaction situation in which the person acting as the 'initiator' has not communicated intent to evoke such a change in the other." Each child who picked up the behavior was recorded as a *recipient* of the particular contagion. A *direct influence attempt* was defined as: "a social interaction in which one child consciously and deliberately tries to get another child to do something, in such a way that the research observer is aware of the intent." The manner of the influence attempt was coded as directive (ordering, commanding) or nondirective (suggesting, requesting).

MEASUREMENT OF TOTAL ACTIVITY

On a periodic sampling basis, as indicated by the time schedule below, the observer

TABLE 1. *Interobserver Reliability on Relative Frequencies of Behavior in 1950 Study* [a]

	M-Camp Av. Rho	W-Camp Av. Rho
Contagion initiation	.79	.90
Contagion pickup	.76	.70
Direct attempt to influence	.91	.76
Recipient of influence attempt	.87	.59
Initiator of other behavior indicators	.89	.87
Recipient of other behavior indicators	.77	.82
Total activity level	.87	.87
Per cent social behavior	.77	.87

[a]Although all these figures were not computed in a comparable manner in the first study, the comparable average reliability correlation was .87 for contagion initiation and .76 for contagion pickup in the M-camp in 1948.

focused on a single child in the group and recorded all of his activity, coding it in the two categories of social activity and nonsocial activity. Social acts had as their target other persons and referred to the realm of social interaction. Nonsocial acts were directed toward objects or focused on individual activity and autistic verbalizations and expressive movements. This was an addition to the measurements used in the first study.

MEASUREMENT OF OTHER CHARACTERISTICS OF SOCIAL INTERACTION

In addition to the recording of influence and total activity, the observers coded a number of "other behavioral indicators" designed to test hypotheses about behavioral aspects of status. These categories were: (a) implies superior knowledge or skill in the other, (b) asks permission of the other, (c) demonstrates sympathetic or solicitous behavior, (d) shows affection-seeking behavior, and (e) displays negative or hostile behavior. All observations, in all categories, were recorded in terms of the initiator and the recipient of the act.

BEHAVIOR SAMPLING PROCEDURE

The observer, following the group throughout the day, recorded data whenever at least three children of the particular cabin group were together. The three observers were rotated systematically among the four cabins being studied. During the total camp period certain children were, of course, observed together more than others. This was an interesting item of data. But to compare the children on such measures as the amount of behavioral

influence, all the data were corrected to equate for amount of time together for each pair of children. Corrected indices were computed as frequencies per time under observation. The amount of observation time was roughly comparable in the first and second studies.

INTEROBSERVER AND INTERCAMP RELIABILITY OF OBSERVATIONS OF BEHAVIOR

Periodic interobserver reliability checks were made in each camp by having two observers record a sample of cabin behavior simultaneously. The observations of each observer were systematically paired with each other observer's records. Interobserver reliability on relative frequencies of behaviors was computed as a rank order correlation of the data of the two observers for each time sample. The results of this reliability analysis are indicated in Table 1. The correlations seem uniformly high enough to give us reasonable confidence in relating our various items of data, and in comparing data from the two camps.

SECURING OTHER OBJECTIVE INDICES ON EACH CAMPER

In addition to the observation data, counselor rating data, and camper rank-order judgments, we obtained the following information for each camper: (a) age, (b) height, (c) weight, (d) last school grade completed, (e) socio-economic status of parent as estimated by classification of father's occupation, and (f) IQ estimate from the vocabulary section of the Stanford-Binet (Form L, 1937).

TABLE 2. *Relationship of Attributed Power to Contagion Initiation*

Popula-tion	1948 Study			1950 Study			Av. Rho Corrected
	N	Av. Rho	Sig.	N	Av. Rho	Sig.	
M-camp	8 groups 64 boys	.52	.001	8 groups 63 boys	.58	.001	.52
Girls	8 groups 40 girls	.71	.001				
W-camp				8 groups 65 boys	.58	.001	.52

THE FINDINGS

The results of our two studies are summarized in four sections which focus on answering the following questions: (*a*) To what extent is behavior toward power figures consistent with verbalized attribution of power? (*b*) To what extent is there a self-perception of own power? Does it seem to "guide" behavior output? (*c*) How is the behavior of recipients of high attributed power different from that of recipients of low attributed power? (*d*) What evidence is there concerning the determinants of how power is acquired in the group?

THE ATTRIBUTOR'S BEHAVIOR TOWARD HIS HIGH POWER CHOICE

1. *The group member is more likely to "contage" from the behavior of a high power member.* This central hypothesis is confirmed by the data from the M-camp in 1948 and 1950, and the generalization is extended by the similar findings from the new population of normal middle class boys in W-camp. Table 2 indicates that the average correlation between frequency of contagion initiation and attributed power position was .58 as compared with .52 in the 1948 study in the M-camp. The average correlation for the new population is also .58. In all four populations studied, a total of 32 groups, it is clear that group members tend to imitate the behavior of those members to whom they have attributed power to influence the group.

An inadequacy of the 1948 study was our inability to give a precise answer to the question: Might the greater volume of behavioral contagion from children with high attributed power be due almost entirely to a generally higher behavioral output of such children? In the second study an independent measure of total behavior output was made. It will be recalled that the acts making up this total behavior sample were obtained independently from the observations of direct influence and behavioral contagion.

The frequency of contagion initiation for each child was divided by his total activity index, and this weighted frequency was correlated with the prestige ranking of each child. As indicated in the right-hand column of Table 2, there was no significant drop in the relationship between attributed power and contagion initiation when this correlation for total activity level was introduced. Our initial interpretation, that perception of power is a major determinant of contagion pickup, rather than sheer activity output, seems to be confirmed.

2. *The group member is more likely to accept direct attempts to influence him which are initiated by a high power figure.* The 1948 study demonstrated that there are important differences for the recipient between the behavioral contagion type of influence, where the imitation is a spontaneous voluntary act, and the direct influence situation where the actor is explicitly trying to influence the behavior of the recipient of his induction attempt. But, although these are two different types of influence situations, the previous study discovered a comparable relationship between success of direct induction attempts and attributed power position to that discovered between contagion initiation and

TABLE 3. *Relationship of Attributed Power to Frequency of Successful Influence Attempts*

Population	1948 Study			1950 Study			Av. *Rho* Corrected for Total Activity
	N	Av. *Rho*	Sig.	N	Av. *Rho*	Sig.	
M-camp	8 groups 64 boys	.56	.001	8 groups 63 boys	.61	.001	.60
Girls	8 groups 40 girls	.54	.001				
W-camp				8 groups 65 boys	.48	.001	.45

power. Table 3 indicates that this relationship is confirmed by the replication study and can be generalized to the new population. In the population of M-camp boys the second study found an average cabin correlation (*rho*) of .61, compared to a correlation of .56 in the first study. The new population of groups of W-camp boys yields an average correlation of .48. All of these relationships are statistically significant.

Again we were able to check in the second study the extent to which total behavior output might be a factor in determining the frequency of successful influence. The right-hand column of Table 3 indicates that a correction for total activity of each child does not change the relationship appreciably.

A second and even more important question may be asked. Is the member with high attributed power really more likely to succeed with each of his influence attempts, or does he just make more influence attempts? To check this question, we computed the percentage of induction attempts successful for each child and correlated the rank order of these percentages with rank order of attributed power in each cabin. The average correlation for the 16 groups is .42, which is statistically significant (.001). The average correlation is identical in both camps. In general, then, the higher a member's attributed power, the more likely it is that each of his influence attempts will be successful.

3. *A boy who attributes power to a specific other boy is more likely to "contage" and to accept influence from him.* The

statistical analyses reported above have shown that, in general, the boys who receive the most verbal choices as power figures in the group are the most frequent sources of behavioral contagion and are most successful in their influence attempts. But this does not actually demonstrate that the behavior of a particular actor is consistent with his particular attribution of power to others. Perhaps this relationship works in general but it is not a very consistent psychological phenomenon from member to member. To check on this possibility a more refined analysis was made in the second study. The data for each boy were analyzed to check the average amount of his contagion pickup and acceptance of influence from members whom he specifically ranked high (upper half of group) or low (lower half of group) on the dimension of group influence.

Because of our interest in the development of social stratification, we made separate analyses for the first and second half of the four-week camp sessions. With one interesting exception, these data, presented in Table 4, confirm the more general statistics reported above.

The table indicates that in both camps, during the early and later parts of the periods, the average camper picked up more behavioral contagion from the boys he specifically rated high on influence as compared to those he rated in the bottom half of the cabin group. In the early part of their life together, the average member did not accept a significantly larger proportion of the influence attempts directed toward him by his high

TABLE 4.   *Relation of Own Power Choices to Behavior*

A. Contagion Pickup from High as Compared to Low Power Choices

	W-groups			M-groups		
	N[a]	M. diff.[b]	Sig.[c]	N	M. diff.	Sig.
First half session	64	+.42	.001	61	+.60	.001
Second half session	65	+.76	.001	57	+.81	.001

B. Percentage of Direct Influence Attempts Accepted from High as Compared to Low Power Choices

	W-groups			M-groups		
	Number Showing Greater Per cent Acceptance From		Chi-Square Test Sig.	Number Showing Greater Per cent Acceptance From		Chi-Square Test Sig.
	High	Low		High	Low	
First half session	41	19	.01	31	30	not sig.
Second half session	40	25	.10	38	19	.02
Combined halves	45	19	.01	31	25	not sig.

[a] The number of campers changes slightly from first to second half of session because of new boys entering groups or insufficient data on several children.

[b] M. diff. equals mean pickup of contagion from high power choices minus mean pickup of contagion from low power choices.

[c] p-value was based on t-test of difference between related means.

power choices than by his low power choices. A more consistent relationship between perception of power and behavioral submission seems to have developed by the second half of the camp period. In the groups of W-camp boys behavior seems to be in line with perception more consistently from the very beginning.

4. *Attempts to influence high power figures are more likely to be nondirective in manner.* A third prediction of the 1948 study was that when the average group member attempted to influence high power members he would tend to be deferential in his manner of induction. The distinction made by the observers was between directive and nondirective

manner of attempted influence. As indicated in Table 5, this relationship was confirmed again in the groups of M-camp boys; but the same relationship did not hold in the groups of middle class W-camp boys, nor did it hold in the girls' camp in the 1948 study. Several hypotheses concerning the meanings of this camp difference seem possible. Perhaps the general style of influence is different in the two camps. Or perhaps attempting to influence a member with considerable power is not so dangerous, nor so difficult, in the groups of W-camp boys.

5. *The average member tends to initiate deferential, approval-seeking behavior toward high power figures.* It seems prob-

TABLE 5.   *Relationship of Attributed Power to Receipt of Nondirective Influence*

Population	1948 Study			1950 Study		
	N	Av. Rho	Sig.	N	Av. Rho	Sig.
M-camp	8 groups 64 boys	.43	.01	8 groups 63 boys	.28	.10
Girls	8 groups 40 girls	.19	not sig.			
W-camp				8 groups 65 boys	.10	not sig.

able that there are many behavioral cues by which one member of the group communicates to another that he "looks up to him" or "looks down on him." Some individuals and groups will be clearer in this communication than others. Some individuals will be more sensitive in reading the cues than others. As described in the section on methodology, the observers in this study systematically recorded behaviors which had the meaning of "implying superior skill," "implying superior knowledge," and "asking for permission." In the first study a sample of four groups in each camp was analyzed. It was found that the upper half of the power hierarchy received significantly more deferential behaviors than the lower half (by t-test $p = .01$ level in boys' camp, .10 in girls' camp). This finding was confirmed in the second study ($p = .001$ and .02 for the two camps).

THE PERCEPTION OF OWN POWER POSITION IN GROUP

On the basis of the 1948 study we inferred that, from the types of interaction reported above, each member would receive cues which would tell him that he was "being looked up to" or "down at" by his fellow members. We inferred that these behavioral messages would usually effect the self-perception of own power or lack of power in the group and that this self-perception would tend to steer one's influence attempts in the group. Certainly there would be many distortions in these self-perceptions arising from past experience in other groups and from wishful thinking in the present situation, but we postulated that a specific self-percept about position in the present group was being formed and was exercising some control over behavior output. In the first study we lacked the data to check directly on this inference. We had evidence that members behaved differentially toward those to whom they attributed various degrees of power, that the members behaved as though they were aware of this information in their attempts to exert influence. But we lacked a mea-

sure of the inferred intervening self-perception of power. In the second study each boy ranked himself on amount of power in the group.

6. *Self-perception of own power tends to be consistent with attribution of power by other members.* The strength and direction of this relationship has been tested by two statistics. All self-rankings of influence in the group were ordered in accordance with attributed rankings. For example, self-rankings of all children ranked highest by the group were tabulated together, those ranked next highest were put together. Means of these grouped self-rankings were then placed in rank order and compared with the attributed rank order. The degree of correspondence was computed as a rank order correlation (see Table 6) and shows nearly perfect correspondence. But this type of correlation may give a maximal statement of the degree of relationship. For example, if all self-rankings were distributed at random among attributed positions, mean self-rankings would be equal. The additions of the self-rankings of one set of accurate children would bring the means into perfect correlation with average attributed rankings. A more accurate index of degree of relationship might be one that determines the amount of variance in self-rankings which can be accounted for by attributed rankings. The values of *eta* for this relationship are reported in the right-hand part of Table 6. We can conclude that there is a rather strong positive relationship between the boys' self-rankings of their relative power positions in the group and the way they are ranked by the other members of the group.

7. *Self-perception of own power tends to be consistent with behavior directed toward other members.* Certainly the influence attempts of a given person toward another person or group at a particular moment, in a particular situation, are determined by other factors in addition to one's self-perception of relative power. The requiredness of the activity will be very important in many situations. The potency of the need which one is seeking to satisfy by influencing the other will

TABLE 6. *Relationship of Self-Rankings of Influence to Attributed Rankings*

Population	N	Rho	Sig.	Eta	Sig.
M-camp 1950 study	8 groups 63 boys	.99[a]	.001	.58	.001
W-camp 1950 study	8 groups 65 boys	.98	.001	.81	.001

[a] The N for the *rhos* is actually 8 averaged self-rankings and attributed rankings for M-camp and 9 for W-camp.

often be important, as will be who is present at the moment. Emotional relationships will also affect the selection of a particular child as a target. The need of the other child to be influenced may play a part. But over the wide range of camp situations, and over the wide range of opportunities to select one child rather than another as an influence target, we would expect self-perception of own power to be an important factor in determining the nature and amount of one's behavior toward others. Our findings are reported in Table 7.

We see that in both camps the boys who perceive themselves as being more influential tend to be more frequent initiators of direct influence attempts (combined *p* is .02). But only in the groups of M-camp children does this self-perception seem to relate to a more directive pattern of exerting influence. This is part of a consistent picture of camp differences in style of influence. It is interesting to note that in the groups of W-camp boys the members who perceive themselves to be in secure power positions are as ready to accept as to reject influence attempts from others and are generally more active in total behavior toward their social and physical

environment. This is not true of the boys in comparable positions in the M-camp where the boys who perceive themselves as high in power are more active rejectors of the influence of others.

THE BEHAVIOR OF RECIPIENT OF ATTRIBUTED POWER IN GROUP

Now we return to the data which replicate the first study, analyzing the relationship between actual attributed power and behavior by the recipient of the attribution.

8. *The recipient of attributed power makes more frequent attempts to influence the behavior of others and is more successful in these attempts.* As we have seen above, those members to whom high power has been attributed tend to be correct in perceiving this attribution. They tend to use this perceived status as a basis for making more influence attempts than less-powerful members. From this linkage, we would expect to find a positive relationship between attributed position and volume of influence attempts. Table 8 confirms this inference. We have already noted in Table 3 that

TABLE 7. *Relationship of Perception of Own Power to Behavior Toward Others*

Type of Behavior	M-camp (N = 8 Groups; 63 Boys) Chi-Square Test (p)	W-camp (N = 8 Groups; 65 Boys) Chi-Square Test (p)
Frequency of influence attempts	.10	.10
Per cent of influence attempts which are directive	.01	.70
Per cent of influence attempts from others which are accepted	(−).01[a]	.70
Total activity output	.70	.001

[a] This relationship was significantly negative, i.e., high power members are more resistant to influence attempts. All other relationships in this table are in the positive direction.

TABLE 8. *Relationship of Attributed Power to Frequency of Influence Attempts*

Popula-tion	1948 Study			1950 Study		
	N	Av. Rho	Sig.	N	Av. Rho	Sig.
M-camp	8 groups 64 boys	.43	.01	8 groups 63 boys	.49	.001
Girls	8 groups 40 girls	.66	.01			
W-camp				8 groups 65 boys	.35	.02

these influence attempts tend to be more successful when initiated by recipients of high power ratings. Although these relationships are all significant, they are low enough to remind us that important forces are not accounted for. As the 1948 study pointed out, some children who are not high in attributed power act as though they were, in terms of influence attempts, and other children who do have high power positions do not use their power to wield influence in the group.

9. *The recipient of attributed power is more directive in his influence attempts.* We have noted previously (Table 5) that the second study confirmed the first in showing that members with high attributed power in the groups of M-camp boys tend to be approached more non-directively in the influence attempts that are directed toward them. This did not seem to be the case in the groups of W-camp boys. Now we ask the question: "Do members with the power to make successful inductions tend to be more directive in their manner?" In Table 9, we see that this is the case in the M-camp. In these M-camp cabins those boys with high attributed power are more dominating in

behavior pattern, and those with less power are more submissive and deferential in behavior. This is not so clearly the case in W-camp or in the girls' camp.

CHARACTERISTICS ASSOCIATED WITH BEING A RECIPIENT OF ATTRIBUTED POWER

Although the focus of the study was on the process of influence rather than on the determinants of influence positions, we have a variety of clues which can be summarized at this point.

10. *High power boys tend to be different in the amount and pattern of their total activity output.* The reader will remember that independent samples of total activity were taken which were broken down into social or person-oriented behavior and nonsocial, i.e., object and activity-oriented behavior. A chi-square test of the upper half on power versus the lower half indicated positive relationships (M-camp, $p = .10$, W-camp, $p = .003$). The relationships with nonsocial activity were not significant. In making this analysis, it was noted that boys in the W-camp who were very low or very high in object-oriented

TABLE 9. *Relationship of Attributed Power to Proportion of Directive Influence Attempts*

Popula-tion	1948 Study			1950 Study		
	N	Av. Rho	Sig.	N	Av. Rho	Sig.
M-camp	8 groups 64 boys	.49	.001	8 groups 63 boys	.39	.01
Girls	8 groups 40 girls	.15	not sig.			
W-camp				8 groups 65 boys	.29	.10

TABLE 10.   *Relationship of Personal Liking to Attributed Power*

Ranked Characteristic of the Member	M-camp			W-camp		
	N	Av. Rho	Sig.	N	Av. Rho	Sig.
Being personally liked	8 groups	.63	.001	8 groups	.76	.001
Being identified with	7 groups	.68[a]	.001	8 groups	.82	.001

[a] One of the 8 cabin correlations was negative and significantly out of line with the rest as a population of correlations. It was omitted from this computation. With it included, the average *rho* is .48.

(nonsocial) behavior seemed to have less attributed power than those boys who showed an average amount. A chi-square test of the middle half against the combined upper and lower quarters on attributed power showed a significant relationship ($p = .05$). This suggests that the high power boy tends to be one who, among other characteristics, is high in his social relations output but also shows an average amount of object-related and program-activity-related behavior, while the boy who is lowest in power ranking is low in social activity and either very high or very low in nonsocial activity.

11. High power boys have physical superiority. On the basis of clinical observations, we postulated that the group standards of these cabin groups would place a positive value on physical prowess as a basis for attributing influence position in the group.

When we explore the meaning of this relationship further we find that neither height nor weight is significantly related to attributed power. In the W-camp height, weight, and age are significantly related to perceived fighting ability (by chi-square $p = .001$, .01, and .001, respectively). But in the M-camp none of these variables relate to perceived fighting ability. Observations in the two camps suggest that in the W-camp, where fighting hardly ever occurs, the perception of fighting ability is really a perception of potential fighting ability and is based on the most obvious clues of physical size. In the M-camp, where a good deal of fighting takes place, the perception is actually based on performance, which probably does not correlate very highly with physical size or age in a relatively homoge-

neous age population, such as in a cabin group.

12. High power boys are superior in campcraft. We also thought it was probable in these groups that some power value would be attached to skill in performing the variety of campcraft activities which the adult leadership provides as a part of camp life. This hypothesis is also confirmed. In the M-camp, the *rho* between skill in campcraft as perceived by cabinmates and ratings of power made by the same boys was .74; in the W-camp, the *rho* was .68. Both are significant at the .001 level.

We thought that the "old campers" who had attended camp before would have an advantage in campcraft skills as well as in other ways. But in neither camp did the "old campers" have significantly more attributed power. Evidently other characteristics outweighed this advantage before much time had elapsed in camp life.

13. High power boys are liked better and identified with more than other group members. Certainly we are not able, in this type of analysis, to demonstrate whether boys who achieve high power positions become liked because of their positions or whether boys who are liked have power attributed to them. Such an analysis calls for a developmental or experimental study. However, it will be recalled that each boy did rank all other members of the group on a dimension of personal liking, and also selected the boy in the group he would most like to be. The relationship of these choices to attributed power are reported in Table 10.

The intercorrelations between liking, perceived fighting ability, and perceived campcraft skills are appreciably lower than the correlation of each of these factors with attributed power. Probably the various perceived characteristics contribute to varying degrees in attributing influence to the power figures in the group.

14. *IQ and impulsiveness are unlikely determinants of attributed power.* We were able to compute an estimate of intelligence (IQ) in each camp from scores on a vocabulary test. As would be expected from the socio-economic differences, the mean IQ estimate was significantly higher in the W-camp (121 as compared to 103), but the total dispersion of scores was greater in the M-camp. In the M-camp there was no significant relationship of IQ level to attributed power, although the boys in the middle range on IQ tended to have more attributed power than those boys at the top or bottom of the scale. In the W-camp there was a significant positive relationship (by chi-square test $p = .01$) between IQ and attributed power.

Another measure which was of considerable theoretical interest to us, as the result of our findings in the first study, was the counselor ranking of impulse-control. In the 1948 study we found no relationship between ranked level of impulsiveness and influence in the *general run* of camp situations; but where frustration was high and need to attack authority was strong, we found that boys who were ranked high on impulsiveness tended to become the sources of contagion. In the second study the adult rankings of impulsiveness received indirect validation from relating these rankings to boys' judgments of which boys were most independent of adult control. Impulsiveness related to independence of adults (by chi-square test $p = .001$) in both camps. When we related the rankings of impulsiveness to influence position in the group we confirmed the findings of the first study. There was no relationship of impulsiveness to attributed power in either camp.

SUMMARY AND CONCLUSIONS

In our introduction we stated three objectives of the study reported in this paper. It seems appropriate to summarize in terms of these aims.

REPLICATION OF THE PREVIOUS FIELD STUDY

Our repetition of essentially the same study design in the same camp (of disturbed lower socio-economic class children) revealed the same relationship between the variables of attributed power, contagion initiation, successful direct influence, contagion pickup, and acceptance of influence. The following relationships were confirmed.

1. The group member is more likely to "contage" from the behavior of a high power member.
2. The group member is more likely to accept the induction attempts of members with high attributed power.
3. Attempts to influence members with high attributed power are more nondirective in manner than those attempts directed toward low power members.
4. Members with high attributed power receive more deference behavior from other members than do low power members.
5. Members with high attributed power initiate more social influence attempts than do low power members and are more successful.
6. Members with high attributed power are more directive in the manner of their influence attempts than the low power members.
7. It was again found that attributed power choices were highly related to child judgments of physical prowess and personal liking.
8. There was no relationship between ratings of behavioral impulsiveness and attributed power in the over-all camp situation.

This confirmation of the major findings of the first study seems to us to be a rather impressive check on the type of behavior sampling and categorization techniques used, as well as lending weight to the validity of the data as representing a true picture of the social influence dynamics of this type of population of groups.

CHECKING ADDITIONAL HYPOTHESES

In the theoretical interpretation of the findings of the first study, we postulated the existence of a self-perception of own power which we inferred would develop from the behavioral feedback of deferential behavior from fellow members. We inferred that this self-percept would act as one determinant of behavior output. By extending our methodology to the measurement of perception of own power in the second study, we were able to confirm the following.

9. Perception of own power position in the group is positively related to actual attributed position.
10. Perception of own power is related to social behavior produced. Those with a self-perception of high power make more frequent, more successful, and more directive influence attempts.

A second missing link in our first study was the lack of information on the variable of total activity level. It was impossible to check on the possible interpretations that high power children might be more frequent sources of contagion because of a higher total activity level than low power children. Our independent measurement of activity level in the second study makes it possible for us to draw additional conclusions.

11. Activity level is not an independent determinant of frequency of contagion initiation or of successful induction.
12. Members with high attributed power do tend to be more socially active than low power members. This is not true for frequency of nonsocial behavior.

In our attempt to explore further some of the determinants of attributed power in M-camp, we made two discoveries:

13. Old campers do not have significantly more attributed power.
14. Intelligence level is not significantly related to attributed power.

GENERALIZATION TO A DIFFERENT TYPE OF POPULATION

Our third objective was to explore the generalization of our findings to a very contrasting population of normal middle class boys in a different summer camp setting. As indicated in our presentation of results, most of the basic relations between attributed power, perception of own power, and behavioral influence were found to hold for this different population of groups. But differences were also discovered which have provided clues to further comparative analysis. Camp differences noted in the present paper are the following.

15. In W-camp low power members are not significantly more nondirective in attempting to influence high power members.

16. High power members are not more directive in their attempts to influence low power members.

17. In the W-camp boys who perceived themselves as having high power are not more directive than low power boys.

18. In the W-camp there is a significant relationship between intelligence and attributed prestige, and between height and weight and attributed fighting ability. None of these relationships hold in the M-camp.

These differences seem to suggest a difference in the style and reciprocity of social influence in the two camps, and also differences in certain sources of power, e.g., intelligence, physical size, and conformity.

TOWARD A THEORY OF THE DYNAMICS OF POWER

Our review of the data summarized above has led us to the following tentative theoretical formulation of the dynamics of power in interpersonal group situations of this type.

We hypothesize that achieving and maintaining a position of social power in the cabin group is a positive goal for the members of the cabin group. No doubt some members have stronger needs for social power than others. Some of the boys are probably primarily identified with other groups, so their position in the group under study is not a primary concern. The personality dynamics of other members provide internal restraints against utilizing the power attributed to them, or provide pressures to try to use more power than they have. But probably the acquiring and maintaining of some degree of social power has a positive valence for every member of the group.

We accept as demonstrated that the perceived possession of various combinations of physical, intellectual, and social-emotional resources results in each member being categorized by his fellow members as having more or less social power than others in the group. There is considerable agreement among the members in their judgments of "who is able to get the others to do what he wants them to." This rank ordered consensus we have called *attributed power*.

Our data lead us to believe that in these cabin groups, where group life approaches total 24-hour living, attributed power tends to be undifferentiated as to situation and activity. This is to say, the actor's power may have initially derived from preeminence in some particular type of activity or characteristic, e.g., fighting, sports, campcraft, disobeying adults, strength, or size, but fellow members tend to generalize this preeminence to the general range of group situations and activities.

The data have shown that members tend to behave toward a fellow member in a manner which is consistent with their attribution of power to that member, i.e., behavior toward those with high attributed power tends to be more deferential and less directive.

We accept as demonstrated that most group members perceive correctly the behavioral cues from fellow members which communicate to them their relative attributed power position in the group.

Also the data lead us to generalize that most members show a tendency to try to utilize (i.e., make manifest) the power which is attributed to them. These manifestations of power through successfully influencing the behavior of fellow members probably have several different psychological meanings at different times for different members, as a means to achieving individual goals calling for instrumental assistance from fellow members, and as a way of demonstrating one's power position in the group.

The findings demonstrate that behavior of a member with high attributed power is more likely to be contagious. We hypothesize that such imitative behavior frequently has the function of being an attempt at locomotion toward the goal of greater social power, in the following ways: (*a*) The behavior of a member in a high power position is sometimes perceived as representing group standards, and so his acts are spontaneously imitated as group approved or group desired acts. (*b*) The high power person is perceived (probably unconsciously) as having the kind of position in the group "I would like to have." Therefore, his actions may be perceived as "the kind of actions which help one to achieve a position like that," so his behavior is picked up by others who would like to be "looked up to as he is." (*c*) From clinical observations we have the hypothesis that in some incidents of contagion a third process may be operating. This is a form of magical thinking in which "acting like him" has the meaning that "I become him" and, therefore, "I am in the same position of influence as he when I act the way he does."

Our comparison of the two camps leads us to believe that, where there is a group atmosphere of competition for power, those in positions of social power tend to be more unwilling to contribute to the manifest power of others. They reject, rather than accept, the influence attempts directed toward them by others.

References

1. Allport, F. H., & Allport, G. W. Personality traits: Their classification and measurement. *Journal of Abnormal and Social Psychology,* 1921, **16,** 1–40.
2. Festinger, L., Schachter, S., & Back, K. *Social pressures in informal groups.* New York: Harper, 1950.
3. Gerth, H. H., & Mills, C. W. *From Max Weber: Essays in sociology.* New York: Harper, 1950.
4. Goldhammer, H., & Shils, E. Types of power and status. *American Journal of Sociology,* 1939, **45,** 171–182.
5. Grosser, D., Polansky, N., & Lippitt, R. A laboratory study of behavioral contagion. *Human Relations,* 1951, **4,** 115–142.
6. Lewin, K. *Field theory in social science.* New York: Harper, 1951.
7. Parsons, T. *The social system.* Glencoe, Ill.: The Free Press, 1951.
8. Polansky, N., *et al.* Problems of interpersonal relations in research on groups. *Human Relations,* 1949, **2,** 281–292.
9. Polansky, N., Lippitt, R., & Redl, F. An investigation of behavioral contagion in groups. *Human Relations,* 1950, **3,** 319–348.
10. Polansky, N., Lippitt, R., & Redl, F. The use of near-sociometric data in research on group treatment processes. *Sociometry,* 1950, **13,** 39–62.
11. Redl, F. The phenomenon of contagion and shock effect in group therapy. In W. Healy and A. Bronner (Eds.), *Searchlights on delinquency.* New York: International Universities Press, 1949.

19

Power in the Classroom

MARTIN GOLD

The stuff of leadership has been an elusive object for researchers. Because of the interest invested by laymen as well as by social psychologists, the qualities which distinguish the one whom others obey from those who obey him have often been the objects of speculation and scientific investigation. The lack of success of these investigations has been well-documented in reviews of the literature such as Stogdill's (7) and Gibb's (2). Gibb is forced to conclude that ". . . numerous studies of the personalities of leaders have failed to find any consistent pattern of traits which characterize leaders." Cartwright and Zander (1) write, "On the whole, the attempt to discover the traits that distinguish leaders from nonleaders has been disappointing."

In response to these failures, social psychologists have turned from what might be called "Great Man" theories of leadership, which are concerned with the traits of leaders, to *interactional* or *situational* theories; that is, theories which take into account not only the characteristics of the individual as they might equip him for leadership, but also the characteristics of the situation in which he might function as a leader, including the task to be accomplished, the characteristics of those who will function as followers, the structure of the group as a unit, and so on. But interactional theory poses a problem from the very first: How do we take into account *all* situational factors at once in order to distinguish leaders from followers? Do we consider each factor of equal importance or do we weight some factors more than others? What task-related variables should be considered? What about personality dimensions?

The research reported here is a first step toward the solution of this problem. It begins in an interactional theory of leadership and defines the "situation" broadly to

From *Sociometry*, 1958, **21**, 50–60. Reprinted by permission of the author and the American Sociological Association. This study was financed by a grant from the National Institute of Mental Health of the U. S. Public Health Service.

include the abilities and attitudes of the individuals, the goals and structures of their group, and the material environment. Further, it proceeds on the assumption that the *values* in the group which is being studied are results of and encompass the important aspects of the situation which must be considered in discovering the characteristics of its leadership.

THEORY AND CONCEPTS

The theoretical scheme which guided this study has three major concepts: *power, property*, and *resource.*

1. The conception of *power* follows that of Kurt Lewin. By power is meant the *potential* ability of one person to get another person to behave in a certain way (3). This does not necessarily mean that the first person actually gets the second to behave in this way; the power concept refers to the likelihood that the second will behave in a certain way *if* the first attempts to get him to do so. When we speak of actualized power, we use the concept *influence*. Power is therefore potential influence.

The definition of *leader* rests upon this concept of power. By "leader" we mean that person who has relatively greater power—greater influence potential—in a relationship. Just as power is something that one possesses in degrees and in comparison to others, so also leadership exists in degree, and where it resides depends upon the relative power of the individuals considered. We will not refer to leaders in this report; rather, we will refer to high power and low power children. The operations by which these two groups are identified are detailed below.

2. A *property* is any characteristic attributed to an individual. It is to be taken in a very broad sense, so that it may include something as concrete as being wealthy as well as something as ambiguous as being temperamental. It may include being able to manipulate people as well as being able to fashion a paper doll.

3. A *resource* is a form of property, distinguished by the fact that it is *valued*. But since different people and different groups value different things, a property of a person which is a resource in one social context may not be a resource in another. Similarly, as the same group of people face different situations, dif-

ferent properties of members may be valued; that is, different characteristics of people may become resources for themselves, for others, for the group. However, there is evidence that the overwhelming majority of our social relationships are stable, so that what may be considered resources do not change. It is the rare crisis which alters values to any extent.

The theory which links the concept of resource with the concept of power states that a resource has the function of inducing those who value it to be influenced by one who possesses it. This is an economic theory essentially. On the one hand we have someone who possesses something the other wants or wishes to avoid; on the other hand we have someone who wants or wishes to avoid it; and the coin of exchange is power.

But we find immediately that we must further qualify our concept of resource. For it is not enough in the economic scheme of things for a property to be valued that we consider it a resource; it must also be something that can be given. Even more, there must be the expectation that it might be given. For example, it is not enough that the property of money is valued in order that it be a resource. The person who has the money must be able and willing to give it away. Similarly, it is not enough for someone to be capable of being warm and friendly; he must be able to bestow this warmth and friendliness on another if it is to be considered a resource in the relationship.

METHOD

A broad investigation of the social relationships among children in classroom groups has been conducted at the Research Center for Group Dynamics at the University of Michigan. This study was a part of that research. The subjects were 152 boys and girls in the University Elementary School, the laboratory school supported by the University of Michigan. The children from kindergarten through the sixth grade—from about five to twelve years old—were included. These children are above average in intelligence and are exclusively from the middle class of a small city. There is little doubt that these characteristics of the children had some effect on the findings.

The study began with fairly lengthy inter-

TABLE 1.   *17 Properties Selected from Pre-Interviews*

1. Smart at school	10. Doesn't start fights and doesn't tease
2. Has good ideas about how to have fun	11. Knows how to act so people will like him
3. Good at making things	12. Plays with you a lot
4. Good at games with running and throwing	13. Likes to do the same things you like to do
5. Knows how to fight	14. Nice looking
6. Strong	15. Has things you'd like to have
7. Acts friendly	16. Gives you things
8. A good person to do things with	17. Does things for you
9. Asks you to do things in a nice way	

views with 21 of the children, 3 from each grade, in which we talked with them about their activities and their friends in and out of school. From these interviews we gleaned 17 characteristics of children which appeared as matters of concern in the children's conversations with us. We then made up simple statements of these 17 items and put each on a card.

Now, in our conceptual scheme, these 17 items represent possible properties of children. It is also true that since they all appeared in the responses of the children to broad questions, they must be of some importance to them, so to some extent they must be considered resources as well as properties.

We determined the power relations among the children by means of a near-sociometric technique, each child rating the others on how often he could get him to do something for

TABLE 2.   *Ranks of Items by Per Cent of Times They Were Rated "Very Important"*

	School Grade of Subject:	K—3rd				4th—6th			
	Sex of Subject:	Male		Female		Male		Female	
Items	Sex of Target Pair:	M	F	M	F	M	F	M	F
"Expertness" resources:									
1. Smart at school		13.5	13	17	15	16	17	17	16
2. Has good ideas about how to have fun		1	17	13	6	6	10	9	4
3. Good at making things		13.5	6.5	12	15	13	12.5	15	14
4. Good at games with running and throwing		16.5	3	14	17	17	11	13	13
"Coerciveness" resources:									
5. Knows how to fight		12	4	11	15	14	15	16	12
6. Strong		9.5	13	15	13	12	16	14	15
"Social-emotional" resources:									
7. Acts friendly		2	15.5	3	3	3	5	2	2
8. A good person to do things with		9.5	1	4	11	9	6	6	9
9. Asks you to do things in a nice way		5.5	5	1	4	4	2	1	5
10. Doesn't start fights and doesn't tease		5.5	11	7.5	1	7	1	4	7
11. Knows how to act so people will like him		15	13	5	2	2	8	5	3
"Associational" resources:									
12. Plays with you a lot		3	8.5	9	10	8	9	11	6
13. Likes to do the same things you like to do		5.5	6.5	10	5	1	7	8	1
Other:									
14. Nice looking		11	10	7.5	12	15	14	10	17
15. Has things you'd like to have		16.5	15.5	16	7	10	12.5	12	10
16. Gives you things		8	8.5	6	9	11	3	7	11
17. Does things for you		5.5	2	2	8	5	4	3	8

TABLE 3. *Significances of Differences in Ranks of Items by Resource Area Clusters: Importance* [a]

| | Resource Areas | | | |
Subjects	"Expertness" (4 Items)	"Coerciveness" (2 Items)	"Social-emotional" (5 Items)	"Associational" (2 Items)
Younger boys				
Boy target pairs	n.s.	n.s.	n.s.	n.s.
Girl target pairs	n.s.	n.s.	n.s.	n.s.
Younger girls				
Boy target pairs	>.05	n.s.	>.02	n.s.
Girl target pairs	.10	n.s.	>.02	n.s.
Older boys				
Boy target pairs	.10	n.s.	>.05	n.s.
Girl target pairs	n.s.	.10	>.02	n.s.
Older girls				
Boy target pairs	.05	.10	>.02	n.s.
Girl target pairs	n.s.	n.s.	>.05	n.s.

[a] By Mann-Whitney U-test: cell entries are probability levels.

him. There is a great deal of stability and consensus about the power structure of a classroom as measured in this way.

In order to find out, among other things, whether children who were seen by their peers as possessing certain types of resources would be higher in power than children who were not attributed such resources, we made up a pair of target children for each child in school. One member of each pair was somebody who could almost always get the child to do something for him, the other, a child who could hardly ever get him to do something for him. In reality, two target pairs were made up for each child: a pair of boys and a pair of girls, with the same procedure followed for both.

The interviewer presented the pictures of the children in the target pair to the child. Then he read the 17 item-cards and had the child say which child in the target pair each item best described. The child could assign an item to one member of the pair or the other, or he could put the item aside if he could not distinguish the members of the target pair in terms of it. When the child had disposed of the 17 items, those he had assigned to either child were read off to him again, but this time he was asked to say whether the item was *important, sometimes important,* or *not important* when he had to decide whether or not he would do something for the other child.

By this procedure we get two kinds of information. By ranking the items by the propor-

tion of times over all our subjects that they are assigned to the high power child, we can determine to what extent each is perceived as a characteristic of high power peers. By ranking them by the proportion of times they were considered important, we can determine their relative standings as resources, although, as has been pointed out, they must all be considered resources to some extent.

RESULTS

First, what properties do the children value most? It is important while asking this question and, in fact, while asking all the questions we ask of these data, that we control on the age of the children, their sex, and the sex of the target pair; we may expect that the values of older children differ from those of younger children, that boys have different values from girls, and that the values applied to boys and girls by either sex at any age differ. If we control on these three factors we generate eight experimental groups, younger boys with male target pairs, younger boys with female target pairs, younger girls with male target pairs, and so on. The smallest group contained 24 children; the largest, 42.

We can group our 17 items into resource areas so that we tap social-emotional resources such as friendliness and gentleness of manner; expertness resources, such as being smart or good at games; coerciveness resources such as being strong and knowing how to fight; and

TABLE 4. *Ranks of Items by Per Cent of Times They "Best Describe" High Power Children*

Items	School Grade of Subject:	K—3rd				4th—6th			
	Sex of Subject:	Male		Female		Male		Female	
	Sex of Target Pair:	M	F	M	F	M	F	M	F
"Expertness" resources:									
1. Smart at school		6	13	5.5	17	15.5	14	12.5	8
2. Has good ideas about how to have fun		3	10.5	13	1.5	1	4.5	9.5	4.5
3. Good at making things		6	4	7.5	14	14	17	11	16
4. Good at games with running and throwing		13.5	10.5	14	14	11	4.5	6.5	9.5
"Coerciveness" resources:									
5. Knows how to fight		10.5	4	17	14	13	15.5	17	17
6. Strong		15.5	6.5	16	14	17	15.5	12.5	12.5
"Social-emotional" resources:									
7. Acts friendly		1	13	10.5	5.5	4.5	7	4	9.5
8. A good person to do things with		8	1	3.5	9	11	4.5	2	7
9. Asks you to do things in a nice way		10.5	15.5	1.5	7	7	2	4	14
10. Doesn't start fights and doesn't tease		3	17	10.5	4	9	12	14.5	15
11. Knows how to act so people will like him		6	8.5	3.5	3	2	4.5	4	2
"Associational" resources:									
12. Plays with you a lot		3	2	7.5	1.5	4.5	10	8	2
13. Likes to do the same things you like to do		10.5	6.5	5.5	5.5	4.5	8.5	9.5	4.5
Other:									
14. Nice looking		17	4	1.5	14	8	1	1	2
15. Has things you'd like to have		13.5	15.5	15	11	15.5	12	14.5	6
16. Gives you things		15.5	13	10.5	9	11	12	16	11
17. Does things for you		10.5	8.5	10.5	9	4.5	8.5	6.5	12.5

associational resources such as playing with others a lot. Table 2 contains the rankings by proportion of times each item was considered important. Table 3 represents the results of Mann-Whitney U-tests (5), a statistical technique which enables us to test whether items in a resource area cluster at either end of the rankings.

Tables 2 and 3 reveal that the social-emotional resource area proves to be the most important to all the children but the younger boys. In the other groups the cluster of items in the area of social-emotional resources tended to rank higher in importance than the rest of the items; the higher ranking of this resource area could have occurred by chance five times out of a hundred or less.

Tables 4 and 5 present the data on the rankings of the items as properties of high power children. Younger girls attribute social-emo-

tional properties to high power children significantly more often than other properties. Older girls perceive older high power boys in the same way.

Coercive properties are attributed significantly *less* often than other properties to high power boys by younger and older girls. Older boys attribute coercive properties significantly less often to high power children of either sex.

If our theory which relates resources to power is to be supported, we should find that all the properties, which we have said represent resources to some extent, should be more characteristic of high power than of low power children. We find that this is in fact the case. No matter what the age group, no matter what the sex of the child or of the target pair, no matter what the item, it is more often said to characterize the high power child than the

TABLE 5. *Significance of Differences in Ranks of Items by Resource Area Clusters: Characteristic of High Power Children*[a]

Subjects	Resource Areas			
	"Expertness" (4 Items)	"Coerciveness" (2 Items)	"Social-emotional" (5 Items)	"Associational" (2 Items)
Younger boys				
Boy target pairs	n.s.	n.s.	n.s.	n.s.
Girl target pairs	n.s.	n.s.	n.s.	n.s.
Younger girls				
Boy target pairs	n.s.	>.02	>.10	n.s.
Girl target pairs	n.s.	n.s.	>.10	>.10
Older boys				
Boy target pairs	n.s.	>.10	n.s.	>.10
Girl target pairs	n.s.	>.05	n.s.	n.s.
Older girls				
Boy target pairs	n.s.	>.10	>.08	n.s.
Girl target pairs	n.s.	n.s.	n.s.	>.10

[a]By Mann-Whitney U-test: cell entries are probabilities.

low power child in the target pair. In *almost* every case, the item was said to characterize the high power child rather than the low power child more than 50 per cent of the time.[1]

The data allow us to explore even further the relationship between resources and the perceived properties of high power children. For, by means of the importance ratings of the items obtained from the children, we can rank our 17 properties by their importance, or, in the terms of our theory, by the extent to which they are resources. And we can similarly rank the properties by the percentage of children in each group who saw them as describing the high power child better than the low power child in the target pair. Our hypothesis must be that the more a property is considered a resource by the children, the more likely the

high power children will be perceived as possessing that property.

The data confirm the hypothesis. Using a Spearman rank order correlation coefficient to compare the items ranked by importance with their ranks as characteristic of high power children, we find that the relationships in seven out of eight groups could have happened by chance but once in ten times or less. In the eighth group where the relationship is not significant—where older girls judged their girl classmates—the relationship is in the predicted direction.

It seems clear that the more a property is considered a resource by the population studied the more it is associated with the higher power members of that population.

Now among the children in the University Elementary School, as is probably true in all

TABLE 6. *Spearman Rank Order Correlation Coefficients: Importance × Characteristic of High Power*

Subjects[a]	Rho	p[b]	Subjects[a]	Rho	p[b]
YBB	.46	.03	OBB	.74	>.001
YBG	.44	.04	OBG	.37	.08
YGB	.49	.02	OGB	.48	.03
YGG	.80	>.001	OGG	.26	.17

[a] YBB: *Younger Boys* judging *Boy* target pairs. YBG: *Younger Boys* judging *Girl* target pairs, etc.
[b] N = 17, the number of items. The probability level is for one tail of the distribution.

[1] A supplementary table indicating these data has been deposited with the American Documentation Institute, Auxiliary Publications Project, Library of Congress, Washington 25, D. C. Order Document No. 5357, remitting $1.25 for photoprints or $1.25 for 35-mm microfilm. Make checks or money orders payable to Chief, Photoduplication Service, Library of Congress.

sizeable groups of people, some children are about equal in power. That is, Donald reports that Gordy is no more likely to get him to do something for him than Pete is. We presented to a small proportion of the children in the study target pairs who were actually equal in power in their relations to them. Our hypothesis is that children will have more difficulty in assigning resources to one member of the target pair or the other under this condition. For, if it is true that power is generated by the possession of resources, equal power must indicate equal possession of resources.

You will remember that a child could say that an item was characteristic of one or the other child in the target pair, or he could put the item aside because he could not say which child the item best described. The number of times items were put aside was used as a measure of the difficulty of the task. We matched the children who judged an equal-power target pair on sex and grade with children who judged an unequal-power target pair. Using a Wilcoxen Signed-Ranks Test (6), we compared these two matched populations on this measure.

The data indicate that children who see the target pair as equal in power put items aside much more often than matched children who see a power differential in the target pair. Among the twenty children for whom the target pair is of the opposite sex, the difference in the likelihood that the one group would put more items aside than the other could have occurred by chance but three times out of a hundred. Among the seven children for whom the target pair is of the same sex, the difference is in the same direction, but largely because of the small number of children sampled here, the difference is not significant.

DISCUSSION

In several ways the data reveal a relationship between the values of the children in our study, the properties perceived to be possessed by the children and the power structure of the classroom group. What are the implications of these findings?

To begin with, it seems that we have really *two* classes of findings. On one hand we have the relationship between values and power; on the other, we have information about the values of this particular sample of children, who are not representative of all children certainly.

Only very limited statements can be made about the content of the values which the data reveal. We found that these children valued social-emotional properties. This may be characteristic of the middle class, bureaucratic culture which is socializing them. Although the same was found to be true in a lower class population, in a study by Lippitt, Polansky, and Rosen (4), a necessary next step would be to carry our technique to other samples. But the relationship found between values, properties, and power may be more generalizable.

At this point, it is necessary to focus on an issue which this study must face. It has been implied here that possession of resources leads to a higher power position. But the data in reality tell us nothing of the kind.

It is possible that the values of the children have nothing to do with the power structure of their peer groups at all, that power is based, for example, on the devaluated ability to apply brute force, but that once power is established, it is rationalized by projecting upon the power figures all the properties which *are* valued. In terms of a long-standing concept in psychology, our data may be shot through with *halo effect*.

While this is possible, other data we have collected lead us to doubt it. A vast amount of data has been gathered from observations of these children by their teachers over several years, by naive observers over several hours, and by members of the research project staff for shorter periods of time in standard behavioral situations. The data show that the higher power children are in fact more friendly as a group, more likely to be helpful to their peers, and more able in terms of their psychological adjustments to be outgoing in social relationships, while the low power children as a group are quite different, and are, for example, more likely to use physical force as a method of attempting to influence their peers and more likely to manifest behavior symptoms of deeper lying disturbances.

The results of this study suggest that the values of the children do reflect a great deal of the situation in which they interact. Further, these values seem to play an important role in transforming certain properties of the children into resources which in turn determine the relative power positions of the children in classroom groups.

References

1. Cartwright, D., & Zander, A. *Group dynamics research and theory.* Evanston, Ill.: Row, Peterson, 1953.
2. Gibb, C. A. Leadership. In G. Lindzey (Ed.), *Handbook of social psychology.* Cambridge, Mass.: Addison-Wesley, 1954.
3. Lewin, K. *Field theory in social science.* New York: Harper, 1951.
4. Lippitt, R., Polansky, N., & Rosen, S. Dynamics of power. *Human Relations,* 1952, **5,** 37–64.
5. Mann, H. B., & Whitney, D. R. On a test of whether one of two random variables is stochastically larger than the others. *Annals of Mathematical Statistics,* 1947, **18,** 50–60.
6. Siegel, S. *Nonparametric statistics.* New York: McGraw-Hill, 1956.
7. Stogdill, R. M. Personal factors associated with leadership. *Journal of Psychology,* 1948, **25,** 35–71.

20

The Bases of Social Power

JOHN R. P. FRENCH, JR., AND BERTRAM RAVEN

The processes of power are pervasive, complex, and often disguised in our society. Accordingly one finds in political science, in sociology, and in social psychology a variety of distinctions among different types of social power or among qualitatively different processes of social influence (1, 7, 14, 20, 23, 29, 30, 38, 40). Our main purpose is to identify the major types of power and to define them systematically so that we may compare them according to the changes which they produce and the other effects which accompany the use of power. The phenomena of power and influence involve a dyadic relation between two agents which may be viewed from two points of view: (*a*) What determines the behavior of the agent who exerts power? (*b*) What determines the reactions of the recipient of this behavior? We take this second point of view and formulate our theory in terms of the life space of P, the person upon whom the power is exerted. In this way we hope to define basic concepts of power which will be adequate to explain many of the phenomena of social influence, including some which have been described in other less genotypic terms.

Recent empirical work, especially on small groups, has demonstrated the necessity of distinguishing different types of power in order to account for the different effects found in studies of social influence. Yet there is no doubt that more empirical knowledge will be needed to make final decisions concerning the necessary differentiations, but this knowledge will be obtained only by research based on some preliminary theoretical distinctions. We present such preliminary concepts and some of the hypotheses they suggest.

From *Studies in Social Power*. D. Cartwright (Ed.), Ann Arbor, Mich.: Institute for Social Research, 1959. Reprinted by permission of the authors and the Institute for Social Research.

POWER, INFLUENCE AND CHANGE

PSYCHOLOGICAL CHANGE

Since we shall define power in terms of influence, and influence in terms of psychological change, we begin with a discussion of change. We want to define change at a level of generality which includes changes in behavior, opinions, attitudes, goals, needs, values, and all other aspects of the person's psychological field. We shall use the word "system" to refer to any such part of the life space.[1] Following Lewin (**26**, 305) the state of a system at time 1 will be denoted $s_1(a)$.

Psychological change is defined as any alteration of the state of some system a over time. The amount of change is measured by the size of the difference between the states of the system a at time 1 and at time 2:

$$ch(a) = s_2(a) - s_1(a).$$

Change in any psychological system may be conceptualized in terms of psychological forces. But it is important to note that the change must be coordinated to the resultant force of all the forces operating at the moment. Change in an opinion, for example, may be determined jointly by a driving force induced by another person, a restraining force corresponding to anchorage in a group opinion, and an own force stemming from the person's needs.

SOCIAL INFLUENCE

Our theory of social influence and power is limited to influence on the person, P, produced by a social agent, O, where O can be either another person, a role, a norm, a group, or a part of a group. We do not consider social influence exerted on a group.

The influence of O on system a in the life space of P is defined as the resultant force on system a which has its source in an act of O. This resultant force induced by O consists of two components: a force to change the system in the direction induced by O and an opposing resistance set up by the same act of O.

By this definition the influence of O does

[1] The word "system" is here used to refer to a whole or to a part of the whole.

not include P's own forces nor the forces induced by other social agents. Accordingly the "influence" of O must be clearly distinguished from O's "control" of P. O may be able to induce strong forces on P to carry out an activity (i.e., O exerts strong influence on P); but if the opposing forces induced by another person or by P's own needs are stronger, then P will locomote in an opposite direction (i.e., O does not have control over P). Thus psychological change in P can be taken as an operational definition of the social influence of O on P only when the effects of other forces have been eliminated.

It is assumed that any system is interdependent with other parts of the life space so that a change in one may produce changes in others. However, this theory focuses on the primary changes in a system which are produced directly by social influence; it is less concerned with secondary changes which are indirectly effected in the other systems or with primary changes produced by nonsocial influences.

Commonly social influence takes place through an intentional act on the part of O. However, we do not want to limit our definition of "act" to such conscious behavior. Indeed, influence might result from the passive presence of O, with no evidence of speech or overt movement. A policeman's standing on a corner may be considered an act of an agent for the speeding motorist. Such acts of the inducing agent will vary in strength, for O may not always utilize all of his power. The policeman, for example, may merely stand and watch or act more strongly by blowing his whistle at the motorist.

The influence exerted by an act need not be in the direction intended by O. The direction of the resultant force on P will depend on the relative magnitude of the induced force set up by the act of O and the resisting force in the opposite direction which is generated by that same act. In cases where O intends to influence P in a given direction, a resultant force in the same direction may be termed positive influence whereas a resultant force in the opposite direction may be termed negative influence.

If O produces the intended change, he has exerted positive control; but if he produces a change in the opposite direction, as for example in the negativism of young children or in the phenomena of negative reference groups, he has exerted negative control.

SOCIAL POWER

The *strength of power* of O/P in some system a is defined as the maximum potential ability of O to influence P in a.

By this definition influence is kinetic power, just as power is potential influence. It is assumed that O is capable of various acts which, because of some more or less enduring relation to P, are able to exert influence on P.[2] O's power is measured by his maximum possible influence, though he may often choose to exert less than his full power.

An equivalent definition of power may be stated in terms of the resultant of two forces set up by the act of O: one in the direction of O's influence attempt and another resisting force in the opposite direction. Power is the maximum resultant of these two forces:

$$\text{power of O/P } (a) = (f_{a,x} - f_{\overline{a,x}})^{\max}$$

where the source of both forces is an act of O.

Thus the power of O with respect to system a of P is equal to the maximum resultant force of two forces set up by any possible act of O: (a) the force which O can set up on the system a to change in the direction x, (b) the resisting force[3] in the opposite direction. Whenever the first component force is greater than the second, positive power exists; but if the second component force is greater than the first, then O has negative power over P.

It is necessary to define power with respect

---

[2] The concept of power has the conceptual property of *potentiality*, but it seems useful to restrict this potential influence to more or less enduring power relations between O and P by excluding from the definition of power those cases where the potential influence is so momentary or so changing that it cannot be predicted from the existing relationship. Power is a useful concept for describing social structure only if it has a certain stability over time; it is useless if every momentary social stimulus is viewed as actualizing social power.

[3] We define resistance to an attempted induction as a force in the opposite direction which is set up by the same act of O. It must be distinguished from opposition which is defined as existing opposing forces which do not have their source in the same act of O. For example, a boy might resist his mother's order to eat spinach because of the manner of the induction attempt, and at the same time he might oppose it because he didn't like spinach.

to a specified system because the power of O/P may vary greatly from one system to another. O may have great power to control the behavior of P but little power to control his opinions. Of course a high power of O/P does not imply a low power of P/O: the two variables are conceptually independent.

For certain purposes it is convenient to define the range of power as the set of all systems within which O has power of strength greater than zero. A husband may have a broad range of power over his wife but a narrow range of power over his employer. We shall use the term "magnitude of power" to denote the summation of O's power over P in all systems of his range.

THE DEPENDENCE OF S(A) ON O

Several investigators have been concerned with differences between superficial conformity and "deeper" changes produced by social influence (**1, 5, 7, 11, 12, 20, 21, 22, 23, 26, 36, 37**). The kinds of systems which are changed and the stability of these changes have been handled by distinctions such as "public versus private attitudes," "overt versus covert behavior," "compliance versus internalization," and "own versus induced forces." Though stated as dichotomies, all of these distinctions suggest an underlying dimension of the degree of dependence of the state of a system on O.

We assume that any change in the state of a system is produced by a change in some factor upon which it is functionally dependent. The state of an opinion, for example, may change because of a change either in some internal factor such as a need or in some external factor such as the arguments of O. Likewise the maintenance of the same state of a system is produced by the stability or lack of change in the internal and external factors. In general, then, psychological change and stability can be conceptualized in terms of dynamic dependence. Our interest is focused on the special case of dependence on an external agent, O (**31**).

In many cases the initial state of the system has the character of a quasi-stationary equilibrium with a central force field around s_1 (a) (**26**, 106). In such cases we may derive a tendency toward retrogression to the original state as soon as the force induced by O is removed.[4] Let us suppose that O exerts influence producing a new state of the system, $s_2 (a)$. Is $s_2 (a)$ now dependent on the continued presence of O? In principle we could answer this question by removing any traces of O from the life space of P and by observing the consequent state of the system at time 3. If $s_3 (a)$ retrogresses completely back to $s_1 (a)$, then we may conclude that maintenance of $s_2 (a)$ was completely dependent on O: but if $s_3 (a)$ equals $s_2 (a)$, this lack of change shows that $s_2 (a)$ has become completely independent of O. In general the degree of dependence of $s_2 (a)$ on O, following O's influence, may be defined as equal to the amount of retrogression following the removal of O from the life space of P:

$$\text{degree of dependence of } s_2 (a) \text{ on } O = s_2 (a) - s_3 (a)$$

A given degree of dependence at time 2 may later change, for example, through the gradual weakening of O's influence. At this later time, the degree of dependence of $s_4 (a)$ on O would still be equal to the amount of retrogression toward the initial state of equilibrium $s_1 (a)$. Operational measures of the degree of dependence on O will, of course, have to be taken under conditions where all other factors are held constant.

Consider the example of three separated employees who have been working at the same steady level of production despite normal, small fluctuations in the work environment. The supervisor orders each to increase his production, and the level of each goes up from 100 to 115 pieces per day. After a week of producing at the new rate of 115 pieces per day, the supervisor is removed for a week. The production of employee A immediately returns to 100 but B and C return to only 110 pieces per day. Other things being equal, we can infer that A's new rate was completely dependent on his supervisor whereas the new rate of B and C was dependent on the supervisor only to the extent of 5 pieces. Let us further assume that when the supervisor returned, the production of B and of C returned to 115 without further orders from the supervisor. Now another month goes by during which B and C maintain a steady 115 pieces

per day. However, there is a difference between them: B's level of production still depends on O to the extent of 5 pieces whereas C has come to rely on his own sense of obligation to obey the order of his legitimate supervisor rather than on the supervisor's external pressure for the maintenance of his 115 pieces per day. Accordingly, the next time the supervisor departs, B's production again drops to 110 but C's remains at 115 pieces per day. In cases like employee B, the degree of dependence is contingent on the perceived probability that O will observe the state of the system and note P's conformity (**5, 7, 11, 12, 23**). The level of observability will in turn depend on both the nature of the system (e.g., the difference between a covert opinion and overt behavior) and on the environmental barriers to observation (e.g., O is too far away from P). In other cases, for example that of employee C, the new behavior pattern is highly dependent on his supervisor, but the degree of dependence of the new state will be related not to the level of observability but rather to factors inside P, in this case a sense of duty to perform an act legitimately prescribed by O. The internalization of social norms is a related process of decreasing degree of dependence of behavior on an external O and increasing dependence on an internal value; it is usually assumed that internalization is accompanied by a decrease in the effects of level of observability (**37**).

The concepts "dependence of a system on O" and "observability as a basis for dependence" will be useful in understanding the stability of conformity. In the next section we shall discuss various types of power and the types of conformity which they are likely to produce.

THE BASES OF POWER

By the basis of power we mean the relationship between O and P which is the source of that power. It is rare that we can say with certainty that a given empirical case of power is limited to one source. Normally, the relation between O and P will be characterized by several qualitatively different variables which are bases of power (**30**). Although there are undoubtedly many possible bases of power which may be distinguished, we shall here define five which seem especially common and

---

[4] Miller (**32**) assumes that all living systems have this character. However, it may be that some systems in the life space do not have this elasticity.

important. These five bases of O's power are: (a) reward power, based on P's perception that O has the ability to mediate rewards for him; (b) coercive power, based on P's perception that O has the ability to mediate punishments for him; (c) legitimate power, based on the perception by P that O has a legitimate right to prescribe behavior for him; (d) referent power, based on P's identification with O; (e) expert power, based on the perception that O has some special knowledge or expertness.

Our first concern is to define the bases which give rise to a given type of power. Next, we describe each type of power according to its strength, range, and the degree of dependence of the new state of the system which is most likely to occur with each type of power. We shall also examine the other effects which the exercise of a given type of power may have upon P and his relationship to O. Finally, we shall point out the interrelationships between different types of power, and the effects of use of one type of power by O upon other bases of power which he might have over P. Thus we shall both define a set of concepts and propose a series of hypotheses. Most of these hypotheses have not been systematically tested, although there is a good deal of evidence in favor of several. No attempt will be made to summarize that evidence here.

REWARD POWER

Reward power is defined as power whose basis is the ability to reward. The strength of the reward power of O/P increases with the magnitude of the rewards which P perceives that O can mediate for him. Reward power depends on O's ability to administer positive valences and to remove or decrease negative valences. The strength of reward power also depends upon the probability that O can mediate the reward, as perceived by P. A common example of reward power is the addition of a piece-work rate in the factory as an incentive to increase production.

The new state of the system induced by a promise of reward (for example, the factory worker's increased level of production) will be highly dependent on O. Since O mediates the reward, he controls the probability that P will receive it. Thus P's new rate of production will be dependent on his subjective probability that O will reward him for conformity minus his subjective probability that O will reward

him even if he returns to his old level. Both probabilities will be greatly affected by the level of observability of P's behavior. Incidentally, a piece rate often seems to have more effect on production than a merit rating system because it yields a higher probability of reward for conformity and a much lower probability of reward for nonconformity.

The utilization of actual rewards (instead of promises) by O will tend over time to increase the attraction of P toward O and therefore the referent power of O over P. As we shall note later, such referent power will permit O to induce changes which are relatively independent. Neither rewards nor promises will arouse resistance in P, provided P considers it legitimate for O to offer rewards.

The range of reward power is specific to those regions within which O can reward P for conforming. The use of rewards to change systems within the range of reward power tends to increase reward power by increasing the probability attached to future promises. However, unsuccessful attempts to exert reward power outside the range of power would tend to decrease the power; for example, if O offers to reward P for performing an impossible act, this will reduce for P the probability of receiving future rewards promised by O.

COERCIVE POWER

Coercive power is similar to reward power in that it also involves O's ability to manipulate the attainment of valences. Coercive power of O/P stems from the expectation on the part of P that he will be punished by O if he fails to conform to the influence attempt. Thus negative valences will exist in given regions of P's life space, corresponding to the threatened punishment by O. The strength of coercive power depends on the magnitude of the negative valence of the threatened punishment multiplied by the perceived probability that P can avoid the punishment by conformity, i.e., the probability of punishment for nonconformity minus the probability of punishment for conformity (11). Just as an offer of a piece-rate bonus in a factory can serve as a basis for reward power, so the ability to fire a worker if he falls below a given level of production will result in coercive power.

Coercive power leads to dependent change also, and the degree of dependence varies with the level of observability of P's conformity. An excellent illustration of coercive power leading to dependent change is provided by a clothes presser in a factory observed by Coch and French (3). As her efficiency rating climbed above average for the group the other workers began to "scapegoat" her. That the resulting plateau in her production was not independent of the group was evident once she was removed from the presence of the other workers. Her production immediately climbed to new heights.[5]

At times, there is some difficulty in distinguishing between reward power and coercive power. Is the withholding of a reward really equivalent to a punishment? Is the withdrawal of punishment equivalent to a reward? The answer must be a psychological one—it depends upon the situation as it exists for P. But ordinarily we would answer these questions in the affirmative; for P, receiving a reward is a positive valence as is the relief of suffering. There is some evidence (5) that conformity to group norms in order to gain acceptance (reward power) should be distinguished from conformity as a means of forestalling rejection (coercive power).

The distinction between these two types of power is important because the dynamics are different. The concept of "sanctions" sometimes lumps the two together despite their opposite effects. While reward power may eventually result in an independent system, the effects of coercive power will continue to be dependent. Reward power will tend to increase the attraction of P toward O; coercive power will decrease this attraction (11, 12). The valence of the region of behavior will become more negative, acquiring some negative valence from the threatened punishment. The negative valence of punishment would also spread to other regions of the life space. Lewin (25) has pointed out this distinction between the effects of rewards and punishment. In the case of threatened punishment, there will be a resultant force on P to leave the field entirely. Thus, to achieve conformity, O must not only place a strong nega-

tive valence in certain regions through threat of punishment, but O must also introduce restraining forces, or other strong valences, so as to prevent P from withdrawing completely from O's range of coercive power. Otherwise the probability of receiving the punishment, if P does not conform, will be too low to be effective.

LEGITIMATE POWER

Legitimate power is probably the most complex of those treated here, embodying notions from the structural sociologist, the group-norm and role oriented social psychologist, and the clinical psychologist.

There has been considerable investigation and speculation about socially prescribed behavior, particularly that which is specific to a given role or position. Linton (29) distinguishes group norms according to whether they are universals for everyone in the culture, alternatives (the individual having a choice as to whether or not to accept them), or specialties (specific to given positions). Whether we speak of internalized norms, role prescriptions and expectations (34), or internalized pressures (15), the fact remains that each individual sees certain regions toward which he should locomote, some regions toward which he should not locomote, and some regions toward which he may locomote if they are generally attractive for him. This applies to specific behaviors in which he may, should, or should not engage; it applies to certain attitudes or beliefs which he may, should, or should not hold. The feeling of "oughtness" may be an internalization from his parents, from his teachers, from his religion, or may have been logically developed from some idiosyncratic system of ethics. He will speak of such behaviors with expressions like "should," "ought to," or "has a right to." In many cases, the original source of the requirement is not recalled.

Though we have oversimplified such evaluations of behavior with a positive-neutral-negative trichotomy, the evaluation of behaviors by the person is really more one of degree. This dimension of evaluation we shall call "legitimacy." Conceptually, we may think of legitimacy as a valence in a region which is induced by some internalized norm or value. This value has the same conceptual property as power, namely an ability to induce force fields

[5] Though the primary influence of coercive power is dependent, it often produces secondary changes which are independent. Brainwashing, for example, utilizes coercive power to produce many primary changes in the life space of the prisoner, but these dependent changes can lead to identification with the aggressor and hence to secondary changes in ideology which are independent.

(**26**, 40–41). It may or may not be correct that values (or the superego) are internalized parents, but at least they can set up force fields which have a phenomenal "oughtness" similar to a parent's prescription. Like a value, a need can also induce valences (i.e., force fields) in P's psychological environment, but these valences have more the phenomenal character of noxious or attractive properties of the object or activity. When a need induces a valence in P, for example, when a need makes an object attractive to P, this attraction applies to P but not to other persons. When a value induces a valence, on the other hand, it not only sets up forces on P to engage in the activity, but P may feel that all others ought to behave in the same way. Among other things, this evaluation applies to the legitimate right of some other individual or group to prescribe behavior or beliefs for a person even though the other cannot apply sanctions.

Legitimate power of O/P is here defined as that power which stems from internalized values in P which dictate that O has a legitimate right to influence P and that P has an obligation to accept this influence. We note that legitimate power is very similar to the notion of legitimacy of authority which has long been explored by sociologists, particularly by Weber (**41**), and more recently by Goldhammer and Shils (**14**). However, legitimate power is not always a role relation: P may accept an induction from O simply because he had previously promised to help O and he values his word too much to break the promise. In all cases, the notion of legitimacy involves some sort of code or standard, accepted by the individual, by virtue of which the external agent can assert his power. We shall attempt to describe a few of these values here.

Bases for Legitimate Power. Cultural values constitute one common basis for the legitimate power of one individual over another. O has characteristics which are specified by the culture as giving him the right to prescribe behavior for P, who may not have these characteristics. These bases, which Weber (**41**) has called the authority of the "eternal yesterday," include such things as age, intelligence, caste, and physical characteristics. In some cultures, the aged are granted the right to prescribe behavior for others in practically all behavior areas. In most cultures, there are certain areas of behavior in which a person of one

sex is granted the right to prescribe behavior for the other sex.

Acceptance of the social structure is another basis for legitimate power. If P accepts as right the social structure of his group, organization, or society, especially the social structure involving a hierarchy of authority, P will accept the legitimate authority of O, who occupies a superior office in the hierarchy. Thus legitimate power in a formal organization is largely a relationship between offices rather than between persons. And the acceptance of an office as *right* is a basis for legitimate power—a judge has a right to levy fines, a foreman should assign work, a priest is justified in prescribing religious beliefs, and it is the management's prerogative to make certain decisions (**10**). However, legitimate power also involves the perceived right of the person to hold the office.

Designation by a legitimizing agent is a third basis for legitimate power. An influencer O may be seen as legitimate in prescribing behavior for P because he has been granted such power by a legitimizing agent whom P accepts. Thus a department head may accept the authority of his vice-president in a certain area because that authority has been specifically delegated by the president. An election is perhaps the most common example of a group's serving to legitimize the authority of one individual or office for other individuals in the group. The success of such legitimizing depends upon the acceptance of the legitimizing agent and procedure. In this case it depends ultimately on certain democratic values concerning election procedures. The election process is one of legitimizing a person's right to an office which already has a legitimate range of power associated with it.

Range of Legitimate Power of O/P. The areas in which legitimate power may be exercised are generally specified along with the designation of that power. A job description, for example, usually specifies supervisory activities and also designates the person to whom the job-holder is responsible for the duties described. Some bases for legitimate authority carry with them a very broad range. Culturally derived bases for legitimate power are often especially broad. It is not uncommon to find cultures in which a member of a given caste can legitimately prescribe behavior for all members of lower castes in practically all regions. More common, however, are instances of legitimate power where the range is specifically and narrowly prescribed. A sergeant in the army is given a specific set of regions within which he can legitimately prescribe behavior for his men.

The attempted use of legitimate power which is outside of the range of legitimate power will decrease the legitimate power of the authority figure. Such use of power which is not legitimate will also decrease the attractiveness of O (11, 12, 36).

Legitimate Power and Influence. The new state of the system which results from legitimate power usually has high dependence on O though it may become independent. Here, however, the degree of dependence is not related to the level of observability. Since legitimate power is based on P's values, the source of the forces induced by O include both these internal values and O. O's induction serves to activate the values and to relate them to the system which is influenced, but thereafter the new state of the system may become directly dependent on the values with no mediation by O. Accordingly this new state will be relatively stable and consistent across varying environmental situations since P's values are more stable than his psychological environment.

We have used the term legitimate not only as a basis for the power of an agent, but also to describe the general behaviors of a person. Thus, the individual P may also consider the legitimacy of the attempts to use other types of power by O. In certain cases, P will consider that O has a legitimate right to threaten punishment for nonconformity; in other cases, such use of coercion would not be seen as legitimate. P might change in response to coercive power of O, but it will make a considerable difference in his attitude and conformity if O is not seen as having a legitimate right to use such coercion. In such cases, the attraction of P for O will be particularly diminished, and the influence attempt will arouse more resistance (11). Similarly the utilization of reward power may vary in legitimacy; the word "bribe," for example, denotes an illegitimate reward.

REFERENT POWER

The referent power of O/P has its basis in the identification of P with O. By identification, we mean a feeling of oneness of P with O, or a desire for such an identity. If O is a person toward whom P is highly attracted, P will have a desire to become closely associated with O. If O is an attractive group, P will have a feeling of membership or a desire to join. If P is already closely associated with O he will want to maintain this relationship (40). P's identification with O can be established or maintained if P behaves, believes, and perceives as O does. Accordingly O has the ability to influence P, even though P may be unaware of this referent power. A verbalization of such power by P might be, "I am like O, and therefore I shall behave or believe as O does," or "I want to be like O, and I will be more like O if I behave or believe as O does." The stronger the identification of P with O the greater the referent power of O/P.

Similar types of power have already been investigated under a number of different formulations. Festinger (6) points out that in an ambiguous situation the individual seeks some sort of "social reality" and may adopt the cognitive structure of the individual or group with which he identifies. In such a case, the lack of clear structure may be threatening to the individual and the agreement of his beliefs with those of a reference group will both satisfy his need for structure and give him added security through increased identification with his group (16, 19).

We must try to distinguish between referent power and other types of power which might be operative at the same time. If a member is attracted to a group and he conforms to its norms only because he fears ridicule or expulsion from the group for nonconformity, we would call this coercive power. On the other hand if he conforms in order to obtain praise for conformity, it is a case of reward power. The basic criterion for distinguishing referent power from both coercive and reward power is the mediation of the punishment and the reward by O: to the extent that O mediates the sanctions (i.e., has means control over P) we are dealing with coercive and reward power; but to the extent that P avoids discomfort or gains satisfaction by conformity based on identification, regardless of O's responses, we are dealing with referent power. Conformity with majority opinion is sometimes based on a respect for the collective wisdom of the group, in which case it is expert power. It is important to distinguish these phenomena, all grouped together elsewhere as "pressures toward uniformity," since the type of change which occurs will be different for different bases of power.

The concepts of "reference group" (39) and "prestige suggestion" may be treated as instances of referent power. In this case, O, the prestigeful person or group, is valued by P; because P desires to be associated or identified with O, he will assume attitudes or beliefs held by O. Similarly a negative reference group which O dislikes and evaluates negatively may exert negative influence on P as a result of negative referent power.

It has been demonstrated that the power which we designate as referent power is especially great when P is attracted to O (2, 6, 8, 9, 13, 23, 30). In our terms, this would mean that the greater the attraction, the greater the identification, and consequently the greater the referent power. In some cases, attraction or prestige may have a specific basis, and the range of referent power will be limited accordingly: a group of campers may have great referent power over a member regarding campcraft, but considerably less effect on other regions (30). However, we hypothesize that the greater the attraction of P toward O, the broader the range of referent power of O/P.

The new state of a system produced by referent power may be dependent on or independent of O; but the degree of dependence is not affected by the level of observability to O (7, 23). In fact, P is often not consciously aware of the referent power which O exerts over him. There is probably a tendency for some of these dependent changes to become independent of O quite rapidly.

EXPERT POWER

The strength of the expert power of O/P varies with the extent of the knowledge or perception which P attributes to O within a given area. Probably P evaluates O's expertness in relation to his own knowledge as well as against an absolute standard. In any case expert power results in primary social influence on P's cognitive structure and probably not on other types of systems. Of course changes in the cognitive structure can change the direction of forces and hence of locomotion, but such a change of behavior is secondary social influence. Expert power has been

demonstrated experimentally (9, 33). Accepting an attorney's advice in legal matters is a common example of expert influence; but there are many instances based on much less knowledge, such as the acceptance by a stranger of directions given by a native villager.

Expert power, where O need not be a member of P's group, is called "informational power" by Deutsch and Gerard (4). This type of expert power must be distinguished from influence based on the content of communication as described by Hovland *et al.* (17, 18, 23, 24). The influence of the content of a communication upon an opinion is presumably a secondary influence produced after the *primary* influence (i.e., the acceptance of the information). Since power is here defined in terms of the primary changes, the influence of the content on a related opinion is not a case of expert power as we have defined it, but the initial acceptance of the validity of the content does seem to be based on expert power or referent power. In other cases, however, so-called facts may be accepted as self-evident because they fit into P's cognitive structure; if this impersonal acceptance of the truth of the fact is independent of the more-or-less enduring relationship between O and P, then P's acceptance of the fact is not an actualization of expert power. Thus we distinguish between expert power based on the credibility of O and informational influence which is based on characteristics of the stimulus such as the logic of the argument or the "self-evident facts."

Wherever expert influence occurs it seems to be necessary both for P to think that O knows and for P to trust that O is telling the truth (rather than trying to deceive him).

Expert power will produce a new cognitive structure which is initially relatively dependent on O, but informational influence will produce a more independent structure. The former is likely to become more independent with the passage of time. In both cases the degree of dependence on O is not affected by the level of observability.

The "sleeper effect" (18, 24) is an interesting case of a change in the degree of dependence of an opinion on O. An unreliable O (who probably had negative referent power but some positive expert power) presented "facts" which were accepted by the subjects and which would normally produce secondary influence on their opinions and beliefs. However, the negative referent power aroused resistance and resulted in negative social influence on their beliefs (i.e., set up a force in the direction opposite to the influence attempt), so that there was little change in the subjects' opinions. With the passage of time, however, the subjects tended to forget the identity of the negative communicator faster than they forgot the contents of his communication, so there was a weakening of the negative referent influence and a consequent delayed positive change in the subjects' beliefs in the direction of the influence attempt ("sleeper effect"). Later, when the identity of the negative communicator was experimentally reinstated, these resisting forces were reinstated, and there was another negative change

in belief in a direction opposite to the influence attempt (24).

The range of expert power, we assume, is more delimited than that of referent power. Not only is it restricted to cognitive systems but the expert is seen as having superior knowledge or ability in very specific areas, and his power will be limited to these areas, though some "halo effect" might occur. Recently, some of our renowned physical scientists have found quite painfully that their expert power in physical sciences does not extend to regions involving international politics. Indeed, there is some evidence that the attempted exertion of expert power outside of the range of expert power will reduce that expert power. An undermining of confidence seems to take place.

SUMMARY

We have distinguished five types of power: referent power, expert power, reward power, coercive power, and legitimate power. These distinctions led to the following hypotheses.

1. For all five types, the stronger the basis of power the greater the power.
2. For any type of power the size of the range may vary greatly, but in general referent power will have the broadest range.
3. Any attempt to utilize power outside the range of power will tend to reduce the power.
4. A new state of a system produced by reward power or coercive power will be highly dependent on O, and the more observable P's conformity the more dependent the state. For the other three types of power, the new state is usually dependent, at least in the beginning, but in any case the level of observability has no effect on the degree of dependence.
5. Coercion results in decreased attraction of P toward O and high resistance; reward power results in increased attraction and low resistance.
6. The more legitimate the coercion the less it will produce resistance and decreased attraction.

References

1. Asch, S. E. *Social psychology.* New York: Prentice-Hall, 1952.
2. Back, K. Influence through social communication. *Journal of Abnormal and Social Psychology,* 1951, **46,** 9–23.
3. Coch, L., & French, J. R. P., Jr. Overcoming resistance to change. *Human Relations,* 1948, **1,** 512–532.
4. Deutsch, M., & Gerard, H. A study of normative and informational influences upon individual judgment. *Journal of Abnormal and Social Psychology,* 1955, **51,** 629–636.
5. Dittes, J., & Kelley, H. Effects of different conditions of acceptance upon conformity to group norms. *Journal of Abnormal and Social Psychology,* 1956, **53,** 629–636.
6. Festinger, L. Informal social communication. *Psychological Review,* 1950, **57,** 271–282.
7. Festinger, L. An analysis of compliant behavior. In M. Sherif & M. O. Wilson (Eds.), *Group relations at the crossroads.* New York: Harper, 1953. Pp. 232–256.
8. Festinger, L., Schachter, S., & Back, K. *Social pressures in informal groups.* New York: Harper, 1950, Chap. 5.

9. Festinger, L., *et al.* The influence process in the presence of extreme deviates. *Human Relations*, 1952, **5**, 327–346.

10. French, J. R. P., Jr., Israel, J., & Ås, D. *Arbeidernes medvirkning i industribedriften: En eksperimentell undersøkelse.* Oslo, Norway: Institute for Social Research, 1957.

11. French, J. R. P., Jr., Morrison, H. W., & Levinger, G. Coercive power and forces affecting conformity. *Journal of Abnormal and Social Psychology*, 1960, **61**, 93–101.

12. Raven, B., & French, J. R. P., Jr. Legitimate power, coercive power, and observability in social influence. *Sociometry*, 1958, **21**, 83–97.

13. Gerard, H. The anchorage of opinions in face-to-face groups. *Human Relations*, 1954, **7**, 313–325.

14. Goldhammer, H., & Shils, E. Types of power and status. *American Journal of Sociology*, 1939, **45**, 171–178.

15. Herbst, P. Analysis and measurement of a situation. *Human Relations*, 1953, **2**, 113–140.

16. Hochbaum, G. Self-confidence and reactions to group pressures. *American Sociological Review*, 1954, **19**, 678–687.

17. Hovland, G., Lumsdaine, A., & Sheffield, F. *Experiments on mass communication.* Princeton, N. J.: Princeton Univ. Press, 1949.

18. Hovland, C., & Weiss, W. The influence of source credibility on communication effectiveness. *Public Opinion Quarterly*, 1951, **15**, 635–650.

19. Jackson, J., & Saltzstein, H. The effect of person-group relationships on conformity processes. *Journal of Abnormal and Social Psychology*, 1958, **57**, 17–24.

20. Jahoda, M. Psychological issues in civil liberties. *The American Psychologist*, 1956, **11**, 234–240.

21. Katz, D., & Schank, R. *Social psychology.* New York: Wiley, 1938.

22. Kelley, H., & Volkart, E. The resistance to change of group-anchored attitudes. *American Sociological Review*, 1952, **17**, 453–465.

23. Kelman, H. Three processes of acceptance of social influence: Compliance, identification, and internalization. Paper read at the meetings of the American Psychological Association, August, 1956.

24. Kelman, H., & Hovland, C. Reinstatement of the communicator in delayed measurement of opinion change. *Journal of Abnormal and Social Psychology*, 1953, **48**, 327–335.

25. Lewin, K. *Dynamic theory of personality.* New York: McGraw-Hill, 1935. Pp. 114–170.

26. Lewin, K. *Field theory in social science.* New York: Harper, 1951.

27. Lewin, K., Lippitt, R., & White, R. K. Patterns of aggressive behavior in experimentally created social climates. *Journal of Social Psychology*, 1939, **10**, 271–301.

28. Lasswell, H., & Kaplan, A. *Power and society: A framework for political inquiry.* New Haven, Conn.: Yale Univ. Press, 1950.

29. Linton, R. *The cultural background of personality.* New York: Appleton-Century-Crofts, 1945.

30. Lippitt, R., *et al.* The dynamics of power. *Human Relations*, 1952, **5**, 37–64.

31. March, J. An introduction to the theory of measurement of influence. *American Political Science Review*, 1955, **49**, 431–451.

32. Miller, J. Toward a general theory for the behavioral sciences. *The American Psychologist*, 1955, **10**, 513–531.

33. Moore, H. The comparative influence of majority and expert opinion. *American Journal of Psychology*, 1921, **32**, 16–20.

34. Newcomb, T. *Social psychology.* New York: Dryden, 1950.

35. Raven, B. Social influence on opinions and the communication of related content. *Journal of Abnormal and Social Psychology*, 1959, **58**, 119–128.

36. Raven, B., & French, J. Group support, legitimate power, and social influence. *Journal of Personality*, 1958, **26**, 400–409.

37. Rommetveit, R. *Social norms and roles.* Minneapolis: Univ. of Minnesota Press, 1953.

38. Russell, B. *Power: A new social analysis.* New York: Norton, 1938.

39. Swanson, G., Newcomb, T., & Hartley, E. *Readings in social psychology.* New York: Holt, 1952.

40. Torrance, E., & Mason, R. Instructor effort to influence: An experimental evaluation of six approaches. Paper presented at USAF–NRC Symposium on Personnel, Training, and Human Engineering. Washington, D. C., 1956.

41. Weber, M. *The theory of social and economic organization.* Oxford: Oxford Univ. Press, 1947.

21

A Comparison of Augmentation and Reduction as Modes of Influence

KENNETH RING AND HAROLD H. KELLEY

If a teacher or trainer is to be effective in a social learning situation, he must provide a consistent schedule of reinforcements, rewarding the behavior he considers correct and/or punishing that which he considers incorrect. Being consistent is sometimes made difficult for him by the fact that the student or trainee has ways of preventing his responses from coming under the trainer's surveillance. For this reason, it is necessary for the trainer to consider the effects of his reinforcement schedule not only upon the particular response discrimination he is trying to teach but also upon the trainee's tendency to conceal or reveal his responses.

A fact that seems likely to be important in affecting concealment (and subsequent learning) is the relative magnitude of the rewards and punishments the trainer delivers when he does have information about the trainee's choices. We consider two cases: the trainer delivers large rewards for the trainee's performance of the desired behavior but only very small punishments for "errors," or he delivers only small rewards for correct responses but massive punishments for incorrect ones.

These two procedures correspond closely to two modes of influence described by McGregor (2). The first is similar to the method of *augmentation* wherein a powerful person (the trainer, to whom we will refer as A) provides rewards in order to induce the trainee, B, to perform the desired behavior, while the second is similar to the method of *reduction* under which, for the same purpose, A applies negative sanctions whenever B performs a behavior other than the desired one. McGregor was concerned with the relative effectiveness of these two influence methods, arguing that the judicious use of augmentation would be more likely to bring about the desired behavior in a

From *Journal of Abnormal and Social Psychology*, 1963, **66**, 95–102. Reprinted by permission of the authors and the American Psychological Association. This study was financed by a grant from the National Science Foundation.

subordinate than would the reliance upon reductive techniques. He did not, however, mention the implications of augmentation versus reduction for response concealment, a factor which we believe cannot be disregarded in accounting for the differences in learning and influence attributable to these two techniques.

With respect to the effect of these methods upon B's concealment of his responses, Thibaut and Kelley (3) point out that in the case of augmentation B will, if necessary, present evidence to A of his compliance with A's wishes in order to insure receiving his reward. If, however, A employs reduction as his technique, B may find it advantageous to conceal his behavior or in other ways to make it difficult for A to monitor it. The reason, of course, is that B can get the best outcomes the relationship has to offer (i.e., he can avoid punishment) through either compliance or concealment. He will be especially likely to choose the latter if he has difficulty in complying as when, for example, he simply does not know how to meet A's behavioral standards or prefers not to conform to them. In sum, augmentation should lead to showing which in turn will insure consistent feedback from A with the result that B should soon learn A's behavioral standards. In contrast, reduction should, when compliance is difficult, lead to concealment and, hence, continued ignorance of A's behavioral standards.

These two modes of influence not only have different implications for self-monitoring and the learning of A's behavioral standards, but also for B's acceptance of the standards. Where augmentation is used B should, in time, show a tendency to accept A's standards and to adopt them as his own. This would be expected on the grounds that as a consistent source of reward to B, A would take on positive value for B. Hence B will come to value what A values and to disvalue what A disvalues. Where reduction is used, however, one would expect that while public conformity might be elicited, B will not accept privately A's standards—at least not to the same extent that he would if A were employing the mode of augmentation. Thus, under reduction training, even though B might eventually learn what A's standards are (despite his concealment tendencies), he would be less likely to accept them.

Let us consider further the question of how

the differences predicted above will be affected by the difficulty B experiences in complying with the behavioral standard A regards as correct. Let us assume that, at first, B has a bias to reveal rather than conceal his responses. Such tendencies would be expected in the numerous everyday relationships which are affected by norms which encourage commitment and candidness. Person B will, then, tend to reveal his responses to A unless actively discouraged from doing so. The augmentation procedure will not increase this incidence of "showing," but the reduction technique should depress it. Furthermore, the extent to which B will be discouraged from "showing" will depend on how often he makes mistakes and is punished. If he makes them infrequently (as when A's standard or criterion—as we shall henceforth call it—is an "easy" one in the sense that B already tends to share it or for some other reason prefers to make "correct" responses), B will rarely be punished and will tend to maintain his initial bias to "show." The augmentation procedure will yield much positive feedback to B as compared to the relatively neutral reactions obtained under the reduction procedure, and while this may make for more favorable attitudes toward A, B should be able to learn A's criterion as readily in the one case as in the other.

On the other hand, if A's criterion is a difficult or implausible one for B and he makes many mistakes, he will receive a good deal of punishment under reduction in contrast to fairly neutral treatment under augmentation. The former will encourage B's tendency to conceal and thereby produce a large difference between the two procedures with respect to the degree of learning what A's criterion is. The punishment which derives from the conjunction of the reduction technique and the implausible criterion will also be expected to produce disliking of the trainer and rejection of his criterion, following the argument given earlier.

In the present study we have evaluated the effects of augmentation versus reduction as they interact with a behavioral criterion of high versus low intuitive plausibility. The plausibility of the criterion influences the probability that B will select it of his own accord without A's intervention. We have also used an interaction situation in which it would be natural for B to reveal his responses to A, at least at first. According to the reasoning outlined above, we would expect that the reduction procedure would have a particularly pronounced effect when it is combined with the low plausibility criterion.

METHOD

Subjects

Eighty males, all enrolled in introductory psychology classes at the University of Minnesota, were used in this experiment.

PROCEDURE

Each experimental session involved one subject as a trainee and a confederate serving as the trainer.[1] Each subject was greeted by the experimenter (**KR**) who informed him that he was conducting a study of conceptions of mental illness. The subject was asked to participate, he was told, in order that the experimenter would be able to teach more effectively about the subject in introductory psychology classes such as that in which the subject himself was enrolled. The experimenter said that his assistant was actually carrying out most of the work on the project and that the subject would be interviewed by him (the confederate, of course). This person was represented as being a graduate student in clinical psychology who was, naturally, interested in the problem of mental illness himself. He was also described as someone who had pretty strong opinions on the subject of mental illness and who would not be hesitant to express them. The behavior was justified on the grounds that it "tends to stimulate persons to think more critically about the subject of mental illness than perhaps they've done in the past." At this point, the subject was told that afterwards he would be rated by the interviewer on either one of two characteristics: half the subjects were told the rating would be based on "how likable you seemed to be, how cooperative and agreeable and so on" while the other half were told that they would be rated on "how frankly and honestly you express your own opinions." Everyone was encouraged to get as high a rating as possible. This manipulation was intended to affect the subject's willingness to express his opinions and his responsiveness to the confederate's praise or reproof. However, subsequent analysis showed that it did not have the desired effect; indeed, it seemed to exert no effect whatever. Consequently, we shall discuss the results of this experiment without considering it further.

The subject was then taken to another room where he was introduced to the confederate. The latter explained the experimental task to the subject. He was asked simply to go through a series of

[1] We are indebted to John Hatton for serving in this capacity.

cards on each of which were printed two statements describing symptoms of maladjustment, MMPI-style. For example, the statements on Card Number 5 read:

1. "I become pretty depressed when I fail at something important."
2. "I have nightmares every few nights."

For each pair of items on each of the cards, the subject was asked to indicate which item indicated "the greater degree of mental illness." Where he could not decide or did not know, he was encouraged to say so. (The trainer always responded to a "don't know" response with the noncommittal comment, "Go on to the next card, please.") Hence it was not necessary for the subject to commit himself on every pair of statements. There were 30 cards in all.

As the subject proceeded through the series, making choices, the trainer responded in one of two ways. If a subject had been assigned to an augmentation condition, the trainer responded very generously when the subject's choice was "correct" ("That certainly shows a lot of insight, Mr. ——; most persons don't get that one" or "For a beginning psychology student, Mr. ——, you're certainly doing very well"). Naturally, all these comments and others were made at a time when they would seem reasonable to the subject and would have a good effect. When the choice was "incorrect," the trainer would pass it off lightly ("Well, I guess I can't go along with you there" or "No, I'm inclined to choose the other one"), the comment being made in a friendly, corrective fashion without a trace of irritation. If a subject had been assigned to a reduction condition, he would get token praise for being correct such as a simple nodding of the trainer's head or a passive "um hum." If, however, the subject did not agree with the trainer, he was made to know it ("We have been conducting this survey for three months and in all that time I think you're only the second person who made that choice" or "Well, I'm sure you must have a reason for that choice, Mr. ——, but I'm darned if I can see what it could possibly be"). In such instances, the trainer would be sarcastic, critical, and—toward the end—take on an attitude of resigned exasperation.

When the subject had finished going through the stack of 30 cards, he was taken back to the experimenter's room by the confederate and the experimenter, presumably interrupting himself from his other work, asked the subject if he would be willing to do several further tasks. When he invariably consented, the experimenter had him complete the following tasks in this order:

1. Go through a series of 42 cards (30 were ones he had already seen before—although in a scrambled order—and 12 were new, but similar) and indicate which item of each pair the trainer

himself would select as representing the greater degree of mental illness.

2. Go through the original set of items—again in a new order—and indicate his own opinions (both Tasks 1 and 2 were done silently in writing).

3. Fill out a post-experimental questionnaire.

These chores completed, the subject was given a full explanation of the experiment, and before he departed was requested not to talk about it with other students.

The statements printed on the cards were constructed in such a way that for any given pair, one could be characterized as an *anxiety* statement while the other was a *depression* statement. Previous research (1) using these items has shown that the probability of a subject's selecting the depression item on any given card is substantially greater than that of his choosing the anxiety item (depression items received about 65% of the choices, anxiety items, 35%).

In this experiment, the confederate regarded as correct the anxiety statements for half the subjects; for the other half, he deemed the depression items correct. Thus, in the first case, he was choosing items in accordance with a criterion of mental illness which had been viewed by previous subjects as relatively implausible. In the second case, his criterion was a relatively plausible one.

Altogether, then, there were four conditions which may be labeled as follows, giving first the trainer's criterion and then his method of influence: plausible-augmentation (Plaus-Aug), plausible-reduction (Plaus-Red), implausible-augmentation (Implaus-Aug), implausible-reduction (Implaus-Red). The N in each condition was 20.

RESULTS

EFFECTIVENESS OF THE MANIPULATIONS

Plausibility of the Criteria. If what we have asserted about the relative plausibility of the criteria is true, we should expect to find that agreement with the depression criterion is significantly higher during the trainer-trainee interaction. The first row of Table 1 presents the relevant data giving the average number of agreements with the criterion for each condition.[2] (On trials when a subject failed to express an opinion he was given half-credit for agreement.) By analysis of variance, the criterion difference is significant at better than

[2] The difference between the Plaus-Red and Implaus-Red conditions in number of agreements is clear and unmistakable even by the end of the first 10 trials.

.001. The interaction term is not significant. (Two-tailed tests are used throughout this paper.)

Augmentation-Reduction. If our manipulation of this variable has been successful, we should expect to find that the subject perceives the augmentative trainer as more generous and the reductive trainer as more critical. On the post-experimental questionnaire, we included items to elicit the subject's perception of the trainer with respect to these characteristics. For each subject the difference between his ratings of the trainer's criticism and generosity was determined. The averages of these differences are given in the second row of Table 1, a positive score indicating that the trainer was judged relatively more critical than generous. The only significant effect is the augmentation-reduction difference which is significant at better than the .0001 level. Also relevant to this manipulation is the item on the post-experimental questionnaire which asked the subject to indicate how much he liked the trainer. The ratings made by the augmentation subjects were significantly higher ($p < .001$) on this dimension and there were no other significant effects.

EXPERIMENTAL HYPOTHESES

Concealment of Opinion. The frequency with which the subjects refused to express their opinions is indicated in the first row of Table 2 which presents the mean number of trials on which this occurred for the subjects in each condition. Since there were 30 trials altogether, it can be seen that the absolute level of failure to disclose opinions was very low— less than 10%—for both the plausible groups and the Implaus-Aug group. For the Implaus-Red group, however, the percentage is substantially higher—close to 25%. An analysis of variance shows both a significant criterion and trainer orientation effect, but, as is apparent, this is largely due to the high mean of the Implaus-Red group. The interaction sum of the squares is, in fact, greater than that of either main effect and is significant at the .01 level. As anticipated, the method of influence makes the greatest difference when the trainer uses a criterion of low plausibility.

Learning the Trainer's Criterion. The reader will remember that after the "interview" had concluded, the subject was returned to the experimenter who asked him to state which item

TABLE 1. *Tests of Effectiveness of the Manipulations*

	Experimental Condition			
Dependent Variable	Plaus-Aug	Plaus-Red	Implaus-Aug	Implaus-Red
Agreement with trainer during interaction	19.4	19.8	15.1	12.6
Ratings of trainer's criticalness	−1.8	+0.7	−1.6	+0.8

of each pair he thought the trainer would select. In some cases he was reporting on items about which the trainer might already have revealed his opinion; in other cases, he was "guessing" how the trainer would answer a "new" item. (The two sets of items give identical results and are, therefore, combined.) The index of knowledge of the trainer's criterion (average number of correct statements about how the trainer would have made his choices) is presented for each condition in the second row of Table 2. Inspection of the table reveals that all groups but the Implaus-Red have learned pretty well (a perfect score would be 42). Unfortunately, an analysis of variance showed neither main effect to be significant (the criterion effect reaches a level of significance between .05 and .10), nor was the interaction significant ($.10 < p < .20$), contrary to our predictions. Nevertheless, the trend of the data is as expected, even though the significance levels leave much to be desired.

In support of our assumption that concealment acts to retard learning, there was obtained, over all conditions, a significant negative correlation between frequency of concealment and the index of learning ($r − .33$, $p < .01$).

Acceptance of Trainer's Criterion. Another of the post-experimental chores imposed on the subject after his interview was again to indicate which item of each pair on the original 30 cards he regarded as representing "the greater degree of mental illness." When compared with the answers he gave during the interaction, these data give us some idea of the degree of adoption of the trainer's opinions. An index of this was derived by computing the difference between the number of times the subject was in agreement with the trainer on this task and the number of times he had actually voiced agreement while being interviewed, and dividing the difference by the extent of possible change in the direction of the difference. For example, if a subject agreed on 20 items afterward, but on only 10 during his interview with the trainer, his adoption score would be $\frac{20 − 10}{20} = .50$. A positive score indicates the subject is closer to the trainer in his opinions after the interview than he was during it; a negative score means the reverse.

The pattern of results yielded by the average adoption scores, shown in the third row of Table 2, is by now familiar. All groups except the Implaus-Red are influenced in a favorable

TABLE 2. *Tests of the Experimental Hypotheses*

	Experimental Condition			
Dependent Variable	Plaus-Aug	Plaus-Red	Implaus-Aug	Implaus-Red
Refusals to state opinion	2.65	2.25	2.45	6.95
Knowledge of the trainer's choices	33.0	32.6	32.8	26.7
Adoption of the trainer's opinions	+.30	+.23	+.27	−.14
Disagreement with opinions attributed to trainer	6.90	5.68	9.45	15.56

direction. An analysis of variance results in a significant criterion effect ($p < .025$), a significant effect due to method of influence ($p < .01$), and a borderline interaction ($p = .06$, approximately). In summary, the pattern of results is very much like what one would anticipate from the data presented previously.

Another analysis was performed which sought to get at the matter of acceptance from a different angle. It could be argued that the preceding analysis unfairly penalizes subjects in the Implaus-Red condition, yielding low adoption scores simply as a reflection of their lack of knowledge of the trainer's criterion and not as any indication of their tendency to reject it. To eliminate any possible effect of amount of knowledge of the trainer's criterion, actual agreement with it was disregarded and instead each person was scored in terms of his agreement with the opinions he imputed to the trainer, whether correct or not. Accordingly, the subject's own post-experimental choices on the original 30 items were compared with those attributed to the trainer and a count made of the number of instances of disagreement. The results are given in the last row of Table 2.[3] As can be seen, rejection is much greater when the criterion of low plausibility is being employed, as one would expect. However, the greatest amount of rejection occurs in the Implaus-Red group ($p < .01$ for the comparison with the Implaus-Aug group). The results of this analysis are therefore consistent with the preceding ones which show the powerful effect of the reduction procedure when coupled with an implausible criterion.

DISCUSSION

This study is the second in a series investigating the effects of certain training schedules on the performance of trainees. We wish, in this section, not only to consider the findings of the current study, but to relate them to those of the first experiment. In that experiment (1), we compared "trusting" and "suspicious" training schedules in terms of their effects on the trainee's tendency to reveal his responses and his learning to conform to the trainer's behavior standard. On each occasion during the training when the trainee made a choice between the two response categories with respect to which the trainer was trying to teach him a particular preference, he also had the option of showing or hiding his choice. The two schedules differed in the actions the trainer took when he knew that the trainee had concealed his response (but, of course, did not know what the response was). A suspicious trainer who assumed the trainee had made the incorrect choice when he hid was compared with a trusting one who under similar circumstances assumed the trainee had made the correct response. The former procedure was found to be more effective in encouraging showing and produced a higher final rate of adherence to the trainer's behavior criterion.

These results can probably be generalized to a number of real-life situations. Particularly important are their implications about the disadvantages of a trainer's providing uncontingently positive feedback (as in the trusting condition) when the trainee makes some response analogous to hiding. Some cases likely to involve such feedback would include the winsome child who says something disarming just before the parent's evaluative comment is forthcoming, the boss who in presenting his ideas to a subordinate unwittingly emphasizes his status so that the subordinate tends to become a "yes man," the disabled person who emphasizes his handicap at appropriate times in a way that makes it difficult to make any but favorable comments about his performance, and the insecure person who by his extreme self-deprecation tends to extract a perfunctory compliment no matter what his performance. Under circumstances such as these, the trainer (parent, subordinate, etc.) may be tempted to act in a manner similar to the trusting trainer, giving positive feedback regardless of the performance as long as it is

---

[3] For this analysis, the few subjects who concealed their opinions very frequently during the "interview" were eliminated because the rejection indices computed for them would have been highly unreliable, being based on few instances. One subject had to be dropped from the Plaus-Red group and four from the Implaus-Red group. It should also be noted that inasmuch as the subjects were forced to indicate what they thought the trainer's opinions were, to the extent that the Implaus-Red subjects were less *confident* of their "guesses" than the subjects in other conditions, this method of analysis does not adequately control for differences in lack of knowledge of the trainer's criterion.

accompanied by the appropriate auxiliary response (hiding in the experiment; the charming comment, allusion to status, etc., in the examples). The results of the first experiment suggest that if the trainer succumbs to this temptation, the auxiliary response may be learned and this will operate to the detriment of the trainee's learning the true evaluations others place upon his behavior.

Both the earlier study and the present one show that it is desirable for a trainer to consider whether his trainee has opportunities to make relevant choices while not under the former's surveillance. If so, he must take account of possible effects of his training schedule on encouraging the trainee to attempt such concealment. The first study deals with the case where the trainer knows about all the occasions on which the trainee has made a relevant choice. Under these conditions the suspicious schedule, which assumes the worst of the trainee, is equivalent to punishing all instances of hiding and dealing with instances of showing in terms of their merits. This method is more effective, as we have said, both in encouraging showing and learning of the trainer's criterion, than is the trusting procedure which tends to reward hiding.

The present study has application to a broader range of training situations because it involves schedules which permit the trainer to make no response or merely a noncommittal one when he fails to detect a relevant choice. Thus, he need not be aware of many of the instances on which the trainee confronts such choice situations. Our evidence suggests that as long as he uses an augmentation technique, providing large rewards for revealed compliance and being tolerant of revealed noncompliance, the trainee will tend to maintain an adequate rate of showing his responses and will, then, satisfactorily learn the trainer's criterion. On the other hand, a reduction method with its emphasis on punishment for errors will discourage showing and interfere with learning the criterion.

What are the implications of these two studies considered together? The first suggests the value of using punishment to discourage hiding and the second, the value of reward to encourage showing. Perhaps the best overall strategy which would combine the advantages of the suspicious and augmentation schedules would be one that provides punishment for detected instances of concealment, is only very mildly punishing (merely to let the trainee know he is wrong) for revealed errors, and is strongly approving for revealed correct behaviors. When it is not clear that a relevant response has been made, a neutral reaction from the trainer is probably best. To attempt any other treatment is to run the risk of providing a reinforcement schedule that affords no basis for learning either to show or to make the desired choice.

Perhaps the most important finding of the present study relates to the interaction between the trainer's influence method and the plausibility of his criterion. Specifically there was a tendency for the combination of the reduction mode of influence with the implausible criterion to depress considerably the level of revealing one's opinions, learning the trainer's criterion, and accepting the trainer's criterion. We would explain this outcome as follows. The probability that the subject would select the same items as the trainer was made deliberately small by using an implausible criterion. Finding himself often in error and being rather harshly criticized for it, the subject comes to feel rather anxious and confused about having to make any kind of choice at all—his expected outcome is not very enticing. If he refuses to make a choice he can avoid the censure of the trainer. It is true that in so doing he passes up the opportunity for a small reward (in the form of mild praise), but the probability of his receiving this small reward is substantially lower than that of his receiving condemnation from the trainer. So he begins to conceal his opinions (at least, relatively speaking, more than subjects in the other conditions do). This results, of course, in a noncommittal response from the trainer. Thus, to the extent the subject refuses to commit himself, he fails to find out anything from the trainer concerning his (the trainer's) opinions. So the trainee's learning is impaired. There are two reasons why the trainee does not adopt the trainer's opinions. One obviously derives from the fact that, because of his refusal to express his own opinions, the trainee simply does not know what the trainer's opinions are. The second factor is the negative affect that is generated by the reduction technique. The trainee just does not *care* very much what the trainer's opinions are and when he does have some ideas about them, he has no motivation whatever to accept them. It is quite possible, of course, that a lowered motivation to learn (as well as the anxiety associated with making a choice) might in part account for the low level of learning manifested by this group of subjects.

The interaction between the trainer's method and his criterion which our results so clearly indicate has one possible implication that is of considerable interest, especially as concerns practical applications of these results. Reduction is least effective, indeed most detrimental, when the trainer's standard is such that the trainee makes many errors at the outset of their interaction. Consider now a real trainer—not one who is programed to follow consistently one method or another, but one who is free to change his technique when he feels like it. Is it not likely that whatever method he starts with, a high rate of mistakes by the trainee will tend to frustrate him and cause him to turn to reduction? The point is not that this will happen every time but simply that the spontaneous adoption of reduction as an influence technique may be most likely under those very conditions where our results show it to be least effective.

A finding of some interest in this experiment is that relating to the performance of the Implaus-Aug subjects. This group learned the criterion of the trainer as well as any group and they used it (i.e., accepted it) virtually to the same extent that subjects in the plausible conditions used that criterion. This was so despite the fact that the plausibility of the anxiety criterion was decidedly lower than that of the depression criterion. Apparently, after the augmentation mode of influence these subjects received when they used this criterion, they found that it was not so implausible after all. This result seems similar to that described by Kelman (1956 unpublished [4]) as following from the process of identification. This process requires that the influencing agent be attractive to the influencee. Kelman presents evidence that the resulting influence is manifested only in situations where the influencing agent is salient in the thinking of the influencee. The present evidence is entirely consistent with this view though we have no evidence that the influence exhibited by the Implaus-Aug group would appear only under conditions of "salience." In general, the results of this experiment are consistent with the assertion by Thibaut and Kelley (3) that the distinction between augmentation and reduction parallels two of Kelman's influence processes, identification and compliance. The former is thought to yield conformity whenever the relationship with the influencer is brought to mind, as is probably the case with our augmentation data. The latter is thought to yield conformity, if at all, only under the influencer's surveillance. In the present case, the reductive influencer did not insist on compliance. He in fact permitted the influencee to avoid the consequences of his surveillance by not taking a stand. The main purpose of this study has been to demonstrate the consequences of the trainer's so doing.

References

1. Kelley, H. H., & Ring, K. Some effects of "suspicious" versus "trusting" training schedules. *Journal of Abnormal and Social Psychology*, 1961, **63**, 294–301.
2. McGregor, D. M. The staff function in human relations. *Journal of Social Issues*, 1948, 4, 5–22.
3. Thibaut, J. W., & Kelley, H. H. *The social psychology of groups.* New York: Wiley, 1959.

[4] Privately circulated monograph entitled, "Social Influence and Personal Belief: A Theoretical and Experimental Approach to the Study of Behavior Change."

22

Some Conditions Affecting the Use of Ingratiation to Influence Performance Evaluation

EDWARD E. JONES, KENNETH J. GERGEN,
PETER GUMPERT AND JOHN W. THIBAUT

The worker-supervisor relationship may be, and fruitfully has been, conceived as a power relationship in which an exchange of behavior products is involved (6). Put most simply, the worker exchanges his productive effort for such tangible rewards as wages or such intangible ones as approval and promotion prospects. The supervisor in various ways controls the giving of these rewards so as to provide optimal incentives for effective worker performance. The supervisor is said to have superior power essentially because he can help or hurt the worker more than the latter can help or hurt him. Unless his talents are in great demand elsewhere and barriers to mobility are minimal, the worker is more dependent on the supervisor than vice versa.

Because of his relative dependence, the worker is motivated to comply with the supervisor's directives and must learn and accept the latter's criteria of performance evaluation. Having done so, he is then in a position to maintain his outcomes at a high level by performing in line with these criteria. By mastering the task, then, the worker in effect exerts counterpower on the supervisor and may narrow the range of outcomes received to those at the positive end of the potential span of outcomes.

While the worker may thus effectively control the supervisor through his own operations within the task system, this means of control or counterpower is not always available. A worker who lacks appropriate talent might be unable to meet the supervisor's standards, or those standards might themselves be so ambiguous that the route to positive outcomes is obscure. In such circumstances, we might expect to find attempts to control the supervisor occurring outside the task system itself (2). Thus the ineffective or bewildered worker might attempt to present himself in a positive manner to bias

From the *Journal of Personality and Social Psychology*, 1965, **1**, 613–625. Reprinted by permission of the authors and the American Psychological Association. The research was supported by grants from the National Science Foundation and the Office of Naval Research.

the supervisor in his favor. This would effectively increase the worker's outcomes only when the supervisor was himself uncertain about good and bad performance or otherwise free to choose among competing standards in evaluating a complex task.

The present investigation was directed to some of these alternative ways of influencing a supervisor. It attempted to explore some of the conditions affecting the adoption of attraction-seeking strategies in a performance setting. For convenience these strategies are referred to under the rubric of *ingratiation*, which refers to those witting and unwitting attempts to manage an impression so as to increase one's attractiveness to a particular other (3). The basic position of the present paper is that such strategies of ingratiation may be identified in work situations where the supervisor cannot be readily controlled through the task system, and the supervisor has some freedom to develop and modify his standards of performance evaluation. The specific form that ingratiation takes is expected to be a function of the cues provided by the supervisor concerning his own values and interpersonal orientation.

The psychology of ingratiation has only recently begun to receive attention as an experimental problem. In a study closely related in method to the present ones, Jones, Gergen, and Jones (5) investigated the differential use of ingratiation tactics as a function of status in an undergraduate ROTC unit. In that study, experimentally induced pressures to make an attractive impression led all subjects to show greater opinion conformity to the target, led the high-status subjects to become more modest in describing themselves, and the low-status subjects to become more favorable in their ratings of the target. These same three tactical classes—opinion conformity, self-presentation, and other enhancement—were included as dependent variables in the present study. While these types of communication do not exhaust the tactical possibilities of ingratiation, they cover an extensive proportion of the terrain and provide convenient possibilities for quantitative measurement.

Having thus set the stage and introduced the players, we may now consider in more concrete detail the problems and opportunities created in the present experiment. Picture a worker who has just been introduced to a rather vague, complex, and ambiguous task.

The task involves a series of similar problems which he is required to solve on a trial-by-trial basis. He quickly learns that the problems are soluble, but his own prospects for solving them are clearly not good: a supervisor, whom he has only briefly met, provides a pattern of outcomes indicating poor performance over a series of practice problems. Through a plausible experimental arrangement, the worker is led into a controlled interaction with the supervisor. They exchange opinions about important and trivial issues, exchange self-ratings, and end up trading evaluative ratings of each other. This controlled interaction provides an opportunity for the worker to try to impress the supervisor if he is so inclined. What conditions are likely to entice the worker to put this opportunity to use?

As forecast by the foregoing discussion, the degree of supervisory freedom in developing and applying standards of evaluation seems critical. Thus in the experiment the worker either learns that the supervisor is free to decide after each trial whether a solution is correct, or that he is committed to a series of problem solutions which he has worked out in advance. In the former case there exists a possibility of biasing the supervisor's decisions in the worker's favor; no such possibility exists in the latter case. The general prediction would be, then, that ingratiation should occur when the supervisor is potentially open to influence but not when he is restricted to preestablished criteria in his decisions to reward or punish.

But if ingratiation does occur, what form is it likely to take and how may it be identified? Common experience suggests that ingratiation attempts occur when the prospects for success (that is, creating an attractive impression) outweigh the risks of failure. These prospects are determined both by the surrounding conditions of interaction and the apparent characteristics of the target person. Furthermore, the characteristics of the target person should actually shape the form of ingratiation once it occurs. In the present experiment, the worker received one of two patterns of preinformation about the supervisor's beliefs and values. The worker was either led to believe that the supervisor, in his leader role, especially valued togetherness, accommodation, and worker solidarity or that he was only concerned with effective performance and cared not about the frills of group cohesiveness and personal styles which contribute to it.

Knowing this much, we can predict some of the more likely variations in impression management as a function of the supervisor's openness to influence and his personal views about the leadership role. The most confident prediction is that opinion conformity or agreement between worker and supervisor should be greatest when the latter is open to influence and values accommodation, least when he is open to influence but competence and performance are admired. Under the latter circumstances, a show of independence provides some evidence of competence through the associative relationship which presumably links competence to assertiveness and self-confidence. When the supervisor is not open to influence, conformity should be moderate and more in the nature of cognitive readjustment than instrumental opinion change.

The prediction with respect to self-presentation was not so clear. The most reasonable expectation was that those subjects exercising the ingratiation option would show that they too valued whatever personal attributes were stressed by the supervisor and attempt to convince the supervisor that they possessed these attributes in fair degree. While the first part of this prediction was open to straight forward test (subjects were asked to check those attributes they considered important), the second part raises difficulties. It seems likely that blatant self-advertisement is not very winning as an ingratiation tactic, and it is difficult for a person to establish his affability or his competence through self-declaration alone. With trepidation, then, it was predicted that subjects would describe themselves more positively on attributes admired by the supervisor than on attributes belittled by him, and that this tendency would be especially strong when the supervisor was potentially open to influence.

With respect to the third dependent variable, other enhancement, it was predicted that subjects in the open-to-influence conditions would be more favorable in their supervisor ratings than those in the closed conditions. This was expected to be especially true on those personal attributes known to be prized by the supervisor.

METHOD

Subjects

A total of 50 undergraduate male volunteers participated as experimental subjects. Recruited from the introductory psychology course at the University of North Carolina, all but seven of these subjects had previously completed a Campus Opinion Survey in a group testing session. This questionnaire served as the base-line measure for inferring opinion conformity in the experiment, and thus analysis on this dependent variable was perforce restricted to those who had completed the survey. All data from four of the remaining subjects were discarded either because the subjects were clearly suspicious or because they obviously misunderstood experimental instructions. A total of 39 subjects were thus available for investigating opinion conformity, while 46 subjects provided usable data for the remaining analyses.

Procedure

Subjects appeared for the experiment in pairs and were introduced to an experimental accomplice identified as a graduate student in the School of Business Administration. The subjects were informed that they were to be players in a game designed to simulate the features of a real business concern. The graduate student was to serve as the supervisor in the game. He was to evaluate the performance of the two subjects and to give or take away points accordingly.

The experimenter then explained that the period would be divided into three parts. First there was to be a practice session in which the subjects would learn how the game was played. Then there was to be a "get-acquainted" session in which the subjects and the supervisor would get to know each other a little better as persons. Finally, the game was to be played for points. While the final game was continually referred to as the climax of the experiment, the task toward which everything else was to lead, it was not actually played.

Variation in conditions of supervisory judgment. All subject pairs were then told that the supervisor had previously looked over some relevant literature in preparation for his judging task. However, for approximately half of the pairs the experimenter emphasized both to the subjects and to the supervisor that the information was general in its implications and, he said, turning to the supervisor,

> these materials . . . won't give you the specific information you need in order to evaluate the other's decisions in the game. You'll just have to wait until you hear each worker's answer each time, and then use your best judgment in awarding points.

Because of the implied freedom of the supervisor to make on-the-spot decisions, this instructional variation will hereafter be called the open-judgment, or merely open condition.

The remaining subject pairs were told, on the

other hand, that the materials which the supervisor had been studying prior to their arrival provided much of the data on which the answers could be based. In addition, subjects in this, the closed-judgment or closed condition were told,

> He has already recorded his answers to each of the practice problems and also to each of the problems in the game to be played for real. . . . These will serve as the correct answers and each of your responses will be judged right or wrong in terms of whether they match the supervisor's sheet or not.

After the open or closed variation had been induced, the supervisor was taken to an adjoining room to finish looking over the materials.

Practice Session. The experimenter then proceeded to outline the remainder of the procedure. The subjects would be placed in individual booths and each would be provided with a manual of practice problems, a set of message forms, and a scoring sheet. The manual would contain 14 sets of four advertising slogans, each set consisting of slogans which concerned a different consumer product (for example, neckties, washing machines, skin cream). It would be the task of each subject to rank the four slogans in each set in terms of their probable effectiveness in increasing sales for the product in question. This ranking was to be recorded on a message blank to be carried by the experimenter to the supervisor. The latter would then communicate to each subject, via a microphone, the number of points won or lost on that trial. Although the subjects would not be competing in any formal way, each would be allowed to hear the number of points he won or lost as well as the outcome of the other subject.

In order to provide a meaningful incentive for doing well in the game, the subjects were further told that the research was sponsored by the American Advertising Council, and that each subject would be paid according to the number of points he received during the game. Each subject would be credited with $1 at the outset, but each could win up to $10 if the supervisor approved of his choices. It was emphasized that the supervisor had not been informed about the monetary significance of the points he would award, allegedly because this might cause him to be overgenerous in his ratings. As the game proceeded, the subjects were to use the scoring sheets to keep abreast of their gains and losses.

The subjects were then led to their respective booths and each was assigned a letter by which he was to be identified during the remainder of the procedure. Both subjects were assigned the letter A and both were led to believe that the other subject was B. The sets of slogans in the practice session were of two distinct types, and the scoring sheets were organized to emphasize the fact: one

group of slogans were for use in magazine and newspaper media, the remainder were for use with radio and television. As the subjects proceeded through the sets of slogans, each found (by prearrangement) that he was earning many points on the radio and television slogans but actually losing on the magazine and newspaper items. In addition, each was led to believe that the other subject was doing well on the magazine and newspaper slogans but doing poorly on the radio and television items. At the end of the practice session the experimenter announced that because of time limitations the actual game would concern only one of the two types of slogans. By a rigged coin toss he then indicated that in the real game only magazine and newspaper items would be used.

This elaborately controlled sequence of events was designed to serve a number of purposes. The subject had to be led to expect that he would do poorly in the real game and thus could not effectively control his outcomes by successful task performance. The fact that the other subject would probably do well in the real game presumably added some edge to the subject's motivation. And yet, each subject actually had done as well as the other on the average item of the practice game; while he was inferior on one sort of item, he was superior on the other sort. It was hoped that this arrangement would serve to minimize the personal failure implications of performance on the practice problems and inhibit such defensive reactions as autistic distortion of expected outcomes. Since his prospects were in the end determined by an arbitrary coin toss, there was presumably no ready target for blame and the subject was free to make the best of a bad situation.

Get-Acquainted Pseudointeraction. As indicated above, a get-acquainted message exchange was interposed between the practice game and the "real" game which was allegedly to climax the experiment. This exchange of personal information was introduced, according to the experimenter, in order to make the game a more valid simulation of a real business organization where

> performance . . . involves many complicated social factors. An organization can be set up to work in a certain way, but how it actually works is often affected by how the people who work together feel about each other, their mutual understanding, and so on.

The experimenter attempted to justify the artificial arrangement for the interaction by arguing that a controlled exchange of messages would make it easier to keep track of the "acquaintance process," and insure that each subject had an equal opportunity to give the supervisor information about himself.

To begin the get-acquainted session, the experimenter told the subjects that they would be able to listen over the sound system as he asked the supervisor a few questions about himself. After this, each subject would be given detailed instructions about an exchange of written messages between himself and the supervisor. The experimenter then left the room and turned on a tape recording of an interview between himself and the supervisor. Cross-cutting the variation in conditions of supervisory judgment (open versus closed), a variation in the supervisor's expressed values about leadership was introduced at this point. The general format of the interview was the same in all conditions: the supervisor was asked to discuss his thoughts on the relationship between a supervisor and his worker, to state his views on personnel selection in industry, and to comment on general criteria for determining salary differentials and promotion. The supervisor's tape-recorded response to these problems differed radically in the two halves of the subject sample.

Half of the subjects heard an interview in which the supervisor continually emphasized the "human" side of business. In his comments he stressed such factors as the spirit of cooperation, the importance of getting along with others, considerateness, and understanding. Competence and performance motivation were simply not mentioned in his discussion of relevant considerations, though they were not explicitly belittled. In view of the emphasis on accommodation and social solidarity pervading the interview, the supervisor in this condition is hereafter referred to as Sol. The remaining subjects were exposed to interview responses in which the supervisor stressed the quality and quantity of job performance above all else. The only important personal characteristics that should be considered in selecting and evaluating workers were those associated with talent and perseverance. A man's thoughts and feelings and reactions off the job were clearly his own business. In view of the emphasis on performance and productivity characterizing the interview, the supervisor in this condition is hereafter referred to as Prod. The Sol-Prod variation was chosen to reflect extreme versions of leader orientations often distinguished in the literature on role differentiation in small groups. Bales and Slater (1, 304), for example, contrast

> the person who symbolizes the demands of task accomplishment and [the] person who symbolizes the demands of social and emotional needs

and suggest that this fundamental differentiation occurs in all social systems.

The pseudointeraction which followed the interview actually involved an exchange of questionnaires between each subject and the supervisor. Since the questionnaire responses of the subject provided the main dependent variable data of the study, the nature of the questionnaires will be discussed in that context.

Measures of Opinion Conformity, Self-Presentation, and Other Enhancement

Each subject completed in the same sequence a self-rating questionnaire to be transmitted to the supervisor, a shortened version of the same opinion questionnaire he had completed earlier in the semester, and finally rated the supervisor on the same questionnaire form used for the self-ratings. He was led to believe that the supervisor was filling out the opinion questionnaire while he, the subject, was rating himself; the supervisor was filling out his self-rating form while the subject was indicating his opinions; and both were evaluating each other during the final phase of the exchange. It is important to remember that the subject was aware of the supervisor's opinions at the time he recorded his, the subject was aware of how the supervisor had rated himself before the subject rated him, and all questionnaire responses were made with the clear understanding that they would be transmitted to the supervisor.

The self-description rating form consisted of 20 pairs of attributive antonyms. Each personal attribute was separated from its opposite by three 12-point scales. On the first of these scales the subject was to rate himself, on the second he was to indicate his ideal along that dimension, and the third scale was to be left for the supervisor's use. Subjects were also asked to check those antonym pairs which they considered "especially important personal characteristics." While each item was quite clearly evaluative in connotation (that is, was composed of a favorable and an unfavorable antonym), the items fell in two predetermined content classes. Half of the items dealt with qualities connoting *affability*, warmth, or affectionateness (for example, friendly versus aloof, likable versus not likable), while the other half were more obviously centered around judgments of *respect* (for example, efficient versus inefficient, strong versus weak). Eighteen independent raters had previously classified the items as affability or respect attributes with near-unanimous agreement on the items finally chosen. The 20 items were presented in mixed order as far as content was concerned and the position of the more socially desirable attribute varied unsystematically from left to right on the page.

The opinion questionnaire consisted of 20 items taken from the 50-item Campus Opinion Survey which most of the subjects had completed earlier in the semester. From the initial battery of items, the ten items judged by the class to be most "important" as a determiner of personal attractiveness and the ten judged to be least important were combined to comprise the final shortened opinion questionnaire. Each of the 20 items was separated by two 12-point scales along which agreement or disagreement could be expressed. When he received the opinion questionnaire, each subject found that the supervisor had already used the first of the two scales to indicate his agreement or disagreement with the item statement. The subject was thus to use the second scale and return the completed questionnaire to the supervisor via the experimenter.

The opinions presented as the supervisor's had been especially prepared in advance for each subject. Working from the subject's own Campus Opinion Survey responses, the supervisors' opinion ratings were so arranged that: for half of the important and half of the unimportant items the supervisor's responses were the same as those which the subject had earlier given; on three of the important and three of the unimportant items, the supervisor disagreed with the subject's previous opinions by six scale points; on two of the important and two of the unimportant items, the supervisor disagreed with the subject's prior opinions by three scale points. The pattern of agreement and disagreement was the same for all subjects, so that the same item in the same position was always an agree, a three-disagree, or a six-disagree item. The overall effect of this procedure was to confront the subject with opinions from the supervisor which agreed with his own on many of the items (assuming little change from the previous testing) but showed some or much disagreement on other statements varying in importance.

The other description form was identical in appearance to the self-description rating form. The ideal and self-scales were already filled in, presumably by the supervisor, and the subject was left with the task of evaluating the supervisor on the same dimensions before the form was returned to him. Again by prearrangement, Sol's ideal and self-ratings were slightly closer to the positive antonym on the affability items than the respect items, and Prod's ratings were slightly closer to the positive end on respect than affability items. The mean and standard deviation of supervisor self-ratings (that is, his overall favorability in rating himself) was the same for both Sol and Prod.

A final questionnaire was also administered to inquire into the subject's "private" impressions of the supervisor, his view of the experimental setting, and his awareness of opportunities for social influence. The subjects were then told that the experiment was completed, informed of the true purpose of the experiment and of the deceptions involved, and requested not to discuss the experiment with classmates. Each received $2 for his cooperation.

RESULTS

EFFECTIVENESS OF INDUCTIONS

Open-closed Judgment Variation. Before examining the results relevant to the main experimental predictions, it is first necessary to establish the extent to which the two independent variables were successfully manipulated. The open-closed judgment variable was, of course, intended to have complex cognitive and motivational effects. To pursue all the evidence on these would carry us directly to an analysis of the pseudointeraction data. At a minimum, however, it is essential that the subjects properly understood and were able to recall the nature of the task situation for which they were preparing throughout the experiment. In the postexperimental questionnaire all subjects were asked to indicate whether the supervisor was to grade their answers (administer points) in terms of a set of previously developed solutions or whether he was free to decide on each trial whether a given answer merited credits or debits. A total of four subjects, in three conditions, were eliminated because they did not choose the alternative appropriate to their experimental condition, thus indicating gross inattention or confusion. The results for these subjects were in line with their incorrect self-assignment and not with the actual instructions to which they had been exposed. The overall effect of the differential instructions, then, was clearly as intended for more than 90% of the subjects.

Going a step beyond this minimal validation of the open-closed variation, we might ask whether the open condition in fact aroused more explicit concern with the impression created than did the closed condition. There is little indication from a set of four questionnaire items that subjects were aware of such a concern and willing to report it to the experimenter. Subjects in the two open conditions did express slightly more interest in being liked and admired by the supervisor, but not significantly more. It is not clear whether such an interest is always difficult to admit, whether judgmental openness never aroused self-conscious desires to impress the supervisor, or whether such desires were aroused initially but had declined by the time of the postexperimental questionnaire. We shall return to this question in considering, later, individual dif-

TABLE 1. *Mean Ratings of the Supervisor Following the Solidarity Versus the Productivity Interview*[a]

Trait	Condition						p_{diff}
	Solidarity			Productivity			
	Open	Closed	Total	Open	Closed	Total	
Cold (versus warm)	6.55	6.27	6.42	7.43	5.90	6.67	ns
Weak (versus strong)	5.73	6.36	6.05	3.43	4.80	4.12	.01
Incompetent (versus competent)	3.82	3.55	3.69	2.79	2.80	2.80	.05
Permissive (versus demanding)	5.54	5.54	5.50	2.79	3.80	3.30	.001
Intolerant (versus tolerant)	5.09	3.82	4.46	7.14	5.60	6.37	.01[b]
Tenderhearted (versus tough-minded)	7.09	6.91	7.00	5.14	5.00	5.07	.001
Unfair (versus fair)	3.73	3.82	3.78	4.07	3.20	3.64	ns
Not likable (versus likable)	4.27	3.91	4.09	5.57	4.20	4.89	ns

[a] Higher scores signify greater attribution of first listed trait in each pair.
[b] The difference between open and closed conditions is also significant ($p < .05$).

ferences in response to the experimental inductions.

Supervisor Values. While it might be expected that the subjects' impressions of the supervisor would be influenced by their own behavior during the experiment, gross differences in the pattern of postexperimental ratings should still have distinguished between personal attributes implied by an emphasis on solidarity versus those implied by an emphasis on productivity. Table 1 presents the mean ratings of the supervisor as a function of his expressed values, along with the probability levels of significant mean differences. From the results in this table it is clear that the two taped interviews succeeded in conveying divergent information about the supervisor and

that subjects typically used this information to construct quite different impressions of him. As expected, relative to the productivity-oriented supervisor (Prod) the solidarity-oriented supervisor (Sol) was seen as more permissive, more tolerant, and more tenderhearted. The expected difference in ratings of warmth, however, was not significant. It is perhaps not surprising that subjects saw Prod as stronger and more competent than they saw Sol. Sol, on the other hand, was better liked than Prod though not reliably so. The perceived differences between the two supervisors were, thus, largely differences on the attributes specifically emphasized in the interviews and do not seem to be strongly mediated by an evaluative halo effect.

TABLE 2. *Conformity on Discrepant Items (Total, Important Only) as a Function of Supervisor Value and Judgment Context*

	Means[a]			
	All Discrepant Items		Important Items	
	Solidarity	Productivity	Solidarity	Productivity
Open	20.78	28.40	9.67	15.20
Closed	27.60	25.60	14.70	13.10

	Analysis of Variance Summary					
Source	All Discrepant Items			Important Items		
	df	MS	F	df	MS	F
Open-closed (A)	1	4.04		1	2.15	
Solidarity-productivity (B)	1	7.80		1	3.86	
A × B	1	23.04	2.47	1	12.71	4.34[b]
Error	35	9.34		35	2.93	

[a] The lower the score, the greater the agreement with the supervisor.
[b] $p < .05$.

OPINION CONFORMITY AS AN INGRATIATION TACTIC

A major hypothesis of the present study concerned the interactive impact of both independent variables on the degree to which subjects conform to the supervisor's opinions. Specifically, it was predicted that subjects in the open-judgment conditions would conform more to Sol and less to Prod than would subjects in the closed conditions. As detailed above, conditions for estimating the degree of conformity were established by having the supervisor appear to transmit bogus opinion ratings, some of which were systematically discrepant from the earlier expressed opinions of the subject. The subject was instructed to respond to each of the supervisor's opinions with his own, degree of conformity being measured as the proximity of subject and supervisor on the discrepant items.

As Table 2 shows, the resulting means fell into the pattern predicted by the conformity hypothesis but the analysis portion of Table 2 indicates that the crucial interaction did not approach significance. It may be recalled, however, that the message exchange involved both "important" and "unimportant" issues (as determined by the normative judgments of the population from which the present subject sample was drawn). While conformity on unimportant items showed a slight (and nowhere near significant) trend in line with the hypothesis, conformity on important items resulted in a significant interaction (Table 2). Consistent with the greater statistical significance obtained, when important items only were considered, subjects in the open-solidarity condition do conform more on important versus unimportant items relative to all other subjects ($p < .10$). Thus, subjects in this crucial cell seem to attach a special meaning to the more important opinion items—whereas all subjects show a moderate and similar degree of conformity on unimportant items, open-solidarity subjects show a distinctive tendency to conform on the important items.

One difficulty with measuring conformity by summing the ultimate discrepancies between the supervisor's and the subject's opinion ratings is that much of the resulting variance may reflect opinion changes occurring prior to the experiment—that is, between taking the before measure in the classroom and being confronted with the supervisor's opinions. It was

possible for drastic changes on individual items to obscure the overall pattern of conformity or nonconformity. It was decided, therefore, to limit the contribution of individual opinion items and to assign each subject a score based on the frequency of his conformity as inferred by the direction of prepost change. Disregarding the magnitude of this change, a score of one was assigned for each rating falling between the prerating and two points beyond the supervisor's rating; all other items were simply assigned a zero. The decision to include movement slightly beyond the supervisor's rating seemed psychologically reasonable and was an a priori decision. The choice of two points beyond, rather than one or three, was arbitrary. This method reduces substantially the within-cell variance, the predicted interaction is clearly significant ($p < .05$), and interpretation does not need to be restricted to the important items (Table 3).

TABLE 3. *Opinion Conformity: Measure of Movement Toward Supervisor*

Movement Index Means[a]		
	Judgment Context	
	Open	Closed
Solidarity	8.9	6.9
Productivity	6.7	7.6

Analysis of Variance Summary			
Source	*df*	*MS*	*F*
Open-closed (A)	1	.31	
Solidarity-productivity (B)	1	.57	
A × B	1	2.09	5.08[b]
Error	35	.41	

[a]The higher the score, the greater the incidence of movement toward the supervisor. For each subject, each of the 20 discrepant items was assigned a score of + 1 for movement toward the supervisor and a 0 otherwise.
[b]$p < .05$.

POSITIVITY OF SELF-PRESENTATION

Prior to the exchange of opinion messages, subjects were instructed to describe themselves to the supervisor via a 20-item rating scale composed of evaluative personal attributes in antonym form. The content of these attributes had been preselected so that half of them connoted qualities relevant to judgments of respect or admiration for personal strength and competence (respect items) while the remaining half centered around qualities of friendliness and approachability (affability items). The apparent congruence between these two categories of item content and the qualities emphasized by the two supervisors was, of course, deliberately contrived. It was expected that the open-judgment context would give rise to ingratiating self-presentations in the particular areas stressed as important by the subject's supervisor.

It will be recalled that subjects both rated themselves and indicated their ideal position on each antonym. They were also instructed to check attribute pairs they considered especially important in determining the attractiveness of others. As mentioned in the introductory section, a clear expectation was that those subjects in the open conditions would show that they too valued whatever personal attributes were stressed by the supervisor. The most direct means to this end was, presumably, for the subject to attach more importance to these attributes.

Turning to the results, solidarity subjects did emphasize the importance of affability items whereas productivity subjects attached more importance to respect items (p = .01). While this differential emphasis was more marked in the open treatments, the interaction between judgment condition and supervisor values was not significant. This suggests that the subjects' conceptions of important attributes were shaped by the supervisor's comments during the interview, but there was no clear evidence that the subjects used agreement with the supervisor's standards to win his favor.

The remaining issue concerns evidence that the subjects in the open conditions tried to convince the supervisor that they in fact possessed the admired attributes. It was predicted that subjects would describe themselves more positively on attributes admired by the supervisor than on attributes ignored or belittled by him, and that this tendency would be especially strong when the supervisor was potentially open to influence. This prediction was proposed with some hesitance in view of the fact that a person does not necessarily convince others that he is, say, "noble" by constantly extolling his own nobility. But a study by Jones, Gergen, and Davis (4) showed that female subjects became more self-enhancing when instructed to create a good impression.

In a subsequent study by Jones *et al.* (5), low-status ROTC students became more self-enhancing when instructed to win the favor of higher status students, except on those items judged to be especially important. Because of the variation of perceived item importance as a function of experimental treatment in the present study, the effects of importance on self-ratings could not be meaningfully studied.

Table 4 presents the mean values of both ideal and self-ratings on respect and affability attributes; the lower the value, the closer the ideal or self-rating to the positive or favorable end of the scale. Several features of this rather complex table deserve comment. First of all, there is no reliable tendency for subjects to describe themselves favorably on all items or on affability items as a function of either judgmental context or supervisor values. When the analysis is restricted to respect attributes, however, there is a strong effect of the Sol-Prod variable on both ideal and self-ratings. When confronted with a supervisor who has previously emphasized performance and competence, subjects locate their ideal selves closer to the scale extremes represented by such trait names as efficient, original, well-organized, and levelheaded. In addition, they present themselves as actually having more of these characteristics when communicating to Prod.

While these systematic variations in respect to item ratings are of interest in their own right, reflecting as they do an implicit tailoring of the presented self to accommodate the characteristics of another, there is no evidence in the raw data of Table 4 that this accommodation serves as an ingratiation tactic. That is, the tendency to model themselves after the supervisor seems no greater in the open than in the closed conditions.

An unexpected finding was that those subjects confronting Sol described themselves more positively on respect items in the open than in the closed condition ($p < .06$). To the extent that this is a reliable difference, it might be argued that when there is no direct effect of the supervisor's admiration of respect attributes (such as occurred in the Prod conditions), the context of supervisory judgment does affect respect item self-ratings. In the Prod conditions, in other words, the impact of the supervisor's values may have been powerful enough to override the weaker effects of openness to influence.

TABLE 4. *Favorability of Self-Presentation (Ideal and Self-Ratings on Respect and Affability Attributes)*

	Open		Closed		Significant
Attribute	Solidarity	Productivity	Solidarity	Productivity	Comparisons
Affability					
Self	35.64	38.50	37.18	33.60	—
Ideal	21.91	25.00	25.63	25.00	—
Respect					
Self	39.91	34.86	47.00	35.40	S vs. P[a]
Ideal	22.09	15.86	25.00	16.20	S vs. P[b]
Total					
Self	75.55	73.36	84.18	69.00	—
Ideal	44.00	40.86	50.63	41.20	—
Respect-affability	4.27	−3.64	9.82	1.80	S vs. P[a]
discrepancy[c]					O vs. C[d]
Self-ideal discrepancy					
Affability	13.73	13.50	11.55	8.60	—
Respect	17.82	19.00	22.00	19.20	—
R − A[e]	4.09	5.50	10.27	10.60	O vs. C[d]

The header spans: *Experimental Condition*

[a] $p < .01$.
[b] $p < .001$.
[c] The lower the score the greater the tendency to describe self positively on respect (relative to affability) items.
[d] $p < .05$.
[e] The lower the score the greater the tendency to describe self (relative to ideal) positively on respect (relative to affability) items.

A notable (if unavoidable) weakness in the present design is its "after-only" nature. The final ratings of self and ideal are a compound of current subjective state, self-conscious strategy, scale interpretation, and other sources of idiosyncratic response bias. This is, probably, the reason why there is such excessive variability in the self-presentation scores. In an effort to get a clearer picture of the experimental effects less contaminated by these sources of response bias, the following procedure was followed as a way of using each subject as his own control. Since there were no systematic differences in either ideal or self-ratings on affability items, and since affability self-ratings were moderately correlated with respect self-ratings (r's ranging from .431 to .784), each subject was assigned a score representing favorable self-rating on respect items minus favorable self-rating on affability items. The resulting R − A difference score serves as an index of his tendency to describe himself positively on respect relative to affability items. This provides, then, a relative emphasis score and also controls for each subject's tendency to restrict himself to a particular region of the scale.

Placing these R − A scores in a factorial design yields two significant main effects: the Sol-Prod variation is highly significant and judgmental context also has a reliable effect (see Table 4). Thus not only do subjects show a general tendency to place a relative stress on their respectworthy qualities when confronted with a task-oriented, performance-centered supervisor; they also stress respect qualities when in a position to influence the supervisor to act in their behalf.

A final point needs to be considered before leaving the self-presentation results. It has been noted that both ideal and self-ratings on respect items were clearly affected by the supervisor's characteristics. This suggests that the Sol-Prod variable influenced in a general way how the scale should be used, but did not affect the relative placement of ideal and self-ratings. It is as if the supervisor, through his interview responses, defined for the subject what is "good"—it is good to be extremely competent, strong, cool-headed, etc.—but he did not affect how the subject saw himself relative to maximal goodness. The open-closed variable, on the other hand, did affect this placement of self relative to ideal so that subjects presented themselves as more competent, etc., when more strongly motivated (in the open conditions) to impress the supervisor with their worthiness.

This reasoning is supported by the last row of Table 4, where a final self-ideal discrepancy index is shown. Since the effects of shifting both ideal and self-ratings canceled each other out, only the open-closed variable remained significant.

It should be emphasized that the obtained pattern of self-presentation results was not predicted in detail. In particular, there was at the outset no theoretical reason to expect systematic variations in respect items but not affability items. It is also clear that the open-closed variables had weak effects on most indices of self-presentation, reaching substantial proportions only with a derived index of self-enhancement on respect minus affability items. Nevertheless, the significant findings reported seem provocative, and their implications will be discussed below.

OTHER ENHANCEMENT

As in the previous study by Jones *et al.* (5), the final portion of the interchange between subjects and supervisor involved ratings of the supervisor on the same sheet on which he had presumably rated himself. These ratings were presumably to be transmitted to the targets of evaluation. In the earlier study, low-status subjects showed a greater tendency than high-status subjects to evaluate their partners positively, and this was especially true when instructions emphasized the importance of compatibility. No such differential tendency was observed in the present study. That is, contrary to experimental expectations subjects in the open conditions were not more favorable in their transmitted ratings of the supervisor than those in the closed conditions. Nor were there any more subtle effects depending on the content of the items, etc. Rating variability was extremely high, and it may be that the experimental inductions had lost their potency by the time that the "other ratings" took place.

DISCUSSION

Subjects in the present study were either presented with or denied the opportunity to improve their outcomes by ingratiating themselves with the supervisor. Provision of this opportunity was implicit in the conditions which allegedly permitted the supervisor to judge each solution attempt as it was offered by the subject. Denial of this opportunity was implicit when the supervisor was allegedly committed to a set of predetermined answers in rewarding or punishing the subject's solution attempts. In the latter conditions, we would expect the subjects to be relatively unconcerned with the personal impression they may be making on the supervisor, whereas this type of concern should be heightened in the conditions of open or uncommitted supervisory judgment. The way in which this concern might manifest itself was more or less an open question, though it seemed clear that the tactics of managing a favorable impression would vary with the values and other personal attributes characterizing the supervisor. For this reason, quite different information was conveyed to subjects in the solidarity versus the production treatment, designed to emphasize radically different supervisor attitudes and orientations.

The most specific and theoretically obvious prediction involved the differential use of opinion conformity as an ingratiation tactic. It was predicted that conformity would be greatest in the open-solidarity condition and least in the open-productivity condition, the two closed conditions falling in between. The results generally support this prediction, though the degree of support depends on the particular measure employed. If one totals the item discrepancies between subject and supervisor ratings, then the interaction is significant only with the more "important" items. If one merely classifies each item as movement toward the supervisor versus residual, the interaction is significant with both unimportant and important items. Insofar as the importance distinction is worth taking seriously, it does seem reasonable to suggest that issues generally viewed as important are more useful than trivial ones for emphasizing agreeableness as well as for emphasizing independence.

The theoretical interpretation of the predicted interaction assumes that subjects in both open conditions have a special concern with being liked or admired, but that they must proceed to implement this concern in different ways. Subjects in the open-solidarity condition are invited by circumstances and the nature of the target to employ conformity for strategic purposes. Subjects in the open-productivity condition, on the other hand, are confronted with a person who seems to de-value opinion agreement as such and circumstances seem to point away from conformity as a tactic for impressing the supervisor. Some interesting, if tentative, correlational data seem to support this interpretation. Those subjects who expressed an interest in being attractive to the supervisor (as measured by a series of items on the postexperimental questionnaire) showed a special tendency to respond differently as a function of the supervisor's expressed values. In the solidarity conditions, the correlation between conformity and attraction motivation was .434; in the productivity conditions the correlation between the same two variables was − .179. In spite of the small samples involved, the difference between these correlations is almost significant ($p < .10$) suggesting that wanting to be liked leads to conformity only when the target person himself seems to value accommodation and togetherness. With a few qualifications, then, the results fit the argument developed in the introductory section: the openness of supervisory judgment provides the incentive to concentrate on creating an attractive impression; the supervisor's own emphasis on effective interpersonal relations points out the appropriate path of impression management.

The tenuous but provocative self-presentation results also merit some discussion. It is apparent that self-descriptions on traits connoting interpersonal warmth and congeniality were unaffected by the experimental variables. Ideal ratings on these traits were similarly unaffected. This is quite surprising in view of the solidarity supervisor's explicit emphasis on the value and importance of such traits in work groups. In comparison, the stated values of the supervisor had a clear effect on ratings of traits connoting competence and personal power. Both self-descriptions and ideal ratings were more favorable in the productivity conditions. The fact that both sets of ratings were more positive suggests that respect attributes are evaluated relative to a shifting standard, a standard quite sensitive to the value attached to competence and performance by a supervisor. Ideal and self-evaluations on affability attributes may be more firmly anchored in each individual's past experiences with others. Many subjects may have entered the experimental situation with the conviction that too much friendliness and warmth is a bad thing and this conviction was little influenced by the promptings of the solidarity supervisor.

Of greater theoretical interest was the tendency for subjects in the open conditions to present themselves as closer to their ideal on respect than on affection items—relative to the subjects in the closed conditions. For whatever reason, subjects in the open conditions were more anxious to impress the supervisor with their competence than their affability. Under the circumstances, if the supervisor could be led to have respect for the subject's judgment, he might begin to assign more points for the latter's solution attempts. Such an increase in respect could, of course, have no such effect in the closed conditions. Impressing the open judge with one's competence seems to be a more direct way to influence his judgment than presenting oneself as affable, and (by inference at least) dependent. It would be interesting to explore the possible conditions under which self-advertised dependence (placing oneself at another's mercy) would become a strategy to influence performance evaluation.

The expectation that subjects in the open conditions would "flatter" the supervisor—especially on those attributes he has stressed as valuable—was not confirmed by the data. It may be true that rating the supervisor in a complimentary way is viewed as a risky or inopportune strategy of influence. In our considered judgment, however, the open-closed induction had probably lost much of its strength before the final rating scales were administered. Not only had a fair amount of time elapsed since the instructions had emphasized this variable, but there were probably growing suspicions that the "real" game would never be played. Apropos of this suggestion that the induction had lost its strength by the time subjects were asked to rate their supervisors, there is evidence in the postexperimental questionnaire that at least in the crucial open-solidarity condition, those who remained interested in making themselves attractive *did* evaluate the supervisor more positively. In the open-solidarity condition only, a questionnaire measure of attractiveness motivation showed a firm positive correlation with favorability of ratings ($r = .636$); in the other conditions the correlation between the same two indexes ranged from − .131 to + .082. Perhaps if the open-to-influence induction had been stronger, the former correlation would have been lower and the tendency for subjects in the open-solidarity condition to flatter would have been more uniform.

References

1. Bales, R. F., & Slater, P. E. Role differentiation in small decision-making groups. In T. Parsons & R. F. Bales (Eds.), *Family socialization and interaction process.* Glencoe, Ill.: Free Press, 1955.
2. Blau, P. M. Patterns of interaction among a group of officials in a government agency. *Human Relations,* 1954, **7**, 337–348.
3. Jones, E. E. *Ingratiation: A social psychological analysis.* New York: Appleton-Century-Crofts, 1964.
4. Jones, E. E., Gergen, K. J., & Davis, K. E. Some determinants of reactions to being approved or disapproved as a person. *Psychological Monographs,* 1962, **76** (2, Whole No. 521).
5. Jones, E. E., Gergen, K. J., & Jones, R. G. Tactics of ingratiation among leaders and subordinates in a status hierarchy. *Psychological Monographs,* 1963, **77** (3, Whole No. 566).
6. Thibaut, J. W., & Kelley, H. H. *The social psychology of groups.* New York: Wiley, 1959.

23

Some Effects of Power on the Relations Among Group Members

JACOB I. HURWITZ, ALVIN F. ZANDER, AND BERNARD HYMOVITCH

Several experimental and field studies have been conducted in recent years to explore the effects of differential positions in power hierarchies upon various types of behavior. Back *et al.* (1), Kelley (2), and Thibaut (5) all found that individual group members occupying low status positions tend to communicate upward in a hierarchy. The explanation advanced was that individuals who want to improve their status but cannot do so will tend to communicate upward as a form of substitute locomotion. Lippitt, Polansky, and Rosen (3), in a field study of social influence among children, found that those high in attributed power make more frequent attempts to influence the behavior of others than do *lows* and are also more successful in these attempts, whereas *lows* engage in approval-seeking behavior more than do *highs*. And finally Pepitone (4), in his study of motivational effects in social perception, found that under certain conditions of power, individuals react with perceptual distortion that is facilitative with respect to their goal achievement, that is, that represents reality as a better state of affairs than actually exists for them.

These three sets of findings appear to suggest that individuals with relatively little power to influence others behave toward those with relatively more power in an essentially egodefensive manner. This defensiveness probably results from the fact that individuals high in the power hierarchy are generally regarded by other group members as being able to help them achieve some of their goals. The power to influence possessed by the *highs* makes the other group members want to be favorably regarded by them. And since these *highs* can exercise their power so as to help or hurt others they generate a feeling of uneasiness in other group members. Consequently, group

This chapter was prepared for this volume. The study was conducted under a grant-in-aid from the National Institute for Mental Health of the U.S. Public Health Service. We are indebted to Julian Morrissette, who helped analyze data.

members perceive *highs* and behave toward them in ways calculated to reduce this uneasiness.

This study was designed to check the adequacy of these conceptions among members of discussion groups in a controlled situation.

PROCEDURE

SUBJECTS AND GROUPS

The sample consisted of 42 persons working in the general field of mental hygiene in or near a medium-sized Midwestern city. Forty-eight subjects were selected and agreed to attend, but six of them were unable to attend at the last moment. The subjects were mainly social workers (including executives), teachers, counseling and guidance workers, psychiatrists, psychologists, and nurses. They were selected by two local people, qualified to judge the prestige of these persons in the eyes of fellow professionals. Half of those chosen were high in prestige and half were low. This dichotomization was made in order to maximize the likelihood of getting a reasonably good spread in the independent measure of perceived power to influence.

Perceived power of any individual to influence other members of his group was defined as the extent to which his opinions on a mental hygiene topic would, in their judgment, carry weight with them. Since it was impractical to get such ratings from the participants in advance of setting up the sample, the assumption was made that power to influence was highly correlated with prestige. As it turned out, the subsequent attributed power-to-influence scores (that is, the mean rating received by each person) conformed to this initial dichotomization for all but three individuals, thus validating the assumption.

The individuals selected (plus several alternates to allow for refusals) were invited to attend a one-day laboratory conference to discuss common and relevant mental hygiene problems and to provide data on interaction among members of different professional groups. The 48 individuals who agreed to attend were divided by a process of reshuffling into 32 six-man groups varying in their distribution by prestige. No two individuals met more than once in any group. Eight of these groups met simultaneously but separately to discuss the same topic. There were four such

discussions; hence each subject discussed four separate topics with four wholly different groups.

Since we wished to predict the effects of perceived power to influence upon degree of liking as well as upon perception of being liked, it was essential to control for liking resulting from previous acquaintance. This was done, within the limits of feasibility in such a field study, by selecting subjects from various professional groups and from different organizations, keeping apart individuals known to have definite previous acquaintance with one another.

THE CONFERENCE PROCEDURE

The flow of events during the conference was as follows. The subjects were given an orientation session which explained the general purpose of the conference and prepared them for its measurement phase. The structure of the conference, administrative details, and the nature of the measuring instruments were then described. Each subject, with the help of individual directories, rated the twenty individuals with whom he was to meet as to his perception of their power to influence him. All subjects then broke up into their assigned groups to conduct their discussions and furnish the postsession dependent measures. Group observers supervised the completion of the instruments. Lunch and a coffee period broke up the day, and in the final summary session the actual purpose and nature of the research project were candidly revealed and received with lively interest.

EXPERIMENTAL TASK

The experimental task consisted of four discussion topics selected on the basis of the following criteria. They should be (a) sufficiently general in content to avoid favoring any professional group by virtue of their particular training or experience, (b) sufficiently broad in scope and general in nature to minimize the likelihood of definite previous opinions, (c) controversial enough to insure differences in opinion, and (d) unidimensional in content to permit ratings along one continuum.

The first problem asked for recommendations concerning the type of agency or institution in the field of mental hygiene to which the subjects would prefer to make a sizable financial contribution—one emphasizing environmental change only, one emphasizing therapy only, or one emphasizing both of these. The second problem dealt with the extent to which recent changes in the role of women have had either helpful or harmful consequence to our society from the point of view of mental hygiene. The third problem had to do with the probable effect (ranging from extremely negative to extremely positive) of greater federal participation in local preventive mental health efforts. The final discussion topic concerned the effect on the mental health of the American people of an effective world-wide scrapping of atomic bombs in the coming year.

TECHNIQUES OF MEASUREMENT

The data for the independent measure of perceived power to influence were obtained by administering a preconference rating form. Each subject indicated by a rating, on a precoded seven-point scale ranging from "not at all" to "extremely much," his perception of the individuals with whom he was to meet with respect to their power to influence his opinions and judgments.

The dependent measures were obtained after each of the subgroup sessions. At the end of the half-hour discussion, each subject indicated the extent of his liking for each of the individuals with whom he had just met, his perception of how much each member liked him, and his perception of the extent of verbal participation of each of them. In all cases ratings were made on precoded seven-point scales ranging from "not at all" to "extremely much." *Liking* was operationally defined as the extent to which an individual would enjoy lunching with the other members of his group on occasions similar to the conference situation. During the discussion, an observer kept a record of the length and frequency of remarks made by each group member, as an objective measure of participation.

These measures permitted a testing of predictions about how perceived power to influence would affect (*a*) degree of liking for other group members, (*b*) degree of distortion in judgments of amount liked by others, (*c*) frequency and direction of communication, and (*d*) degree of distortion in judgments of extent of participation by other group members.

TECHNIQUES OF ANALYSIS

Since all the assumptions were of a comparative type (for example, A will be greater than B), mean values were computed for all measures of the dependent variables and the difference between appropriate pairs of means were evaluated by *t*-test or chi-square. In every case *t*-tests were done initially, but when the variances of the paired distributions were found to be significantly different by *F*-test and the *t*-test showed significant differences between means, X^2 was used since *t*-test was not permissible.

RESULTS

The theoretical conception has been advanced that group members perceive *highs* and behave toward them in an egodefensive manner, that is, in ways calculated to reduce the feeling of uneasiness they experience in their relations with *highs*. This conception was tested by examining (*a*) the extent to which group members like *highs* and *lows* in their groups, (*b*) degree of distortion in their estimations of how much *highs* and *lows* like them, and (*c*) frequency and direction of communication among group members.

DEGREE OF LIKING FOR OTHERS

It may reasonably be assumed that individuals who desire to reduce feelings of uneasiness experienced in their relations with *highs* will be ready to like these powerful persons both because of the respect and admiration usually accorded to such people and the need, realistic in these discussion groups, to feel that relations with *highs* are satisfactory and pleasant. From this assumption we may expect that

TABLE 1. *Mean Ratings of Extent of Liking for Others*[a]

Relative Power of		
Rater	Person Rated	Mean Liking
1. Low	High	5.53
2. High	High	5.42
3. Low	Low	5.31
4. High	Low	4.85

[a] Significance of differences (*p*): 1 *versus* 2 (< .60), 1 *versus* 3 (< .50), 1 *versus* 4 (< .01), 2 *versus* 3 (< .70), 2 *versus* 4 (< .02), and 3 *versus* 4 (.10).

(a) *highs* will be liked, on the average, more than *lows,* and (b) *highs* will be liked more by *lows* than will *lows* by *highs.*

In Table 1 we see that *highs* are rated somewhat higher than are *lows.* There is a marked tendency for *highs* to like *lows* less than they like other *highs. Highs* also like *lows* much less than *lows* like *lows.* As expected, *lows* like *highs* considerably more than *highs* like *lows.* In addition, there is a slight tendency for *lows* to rate *highs* higher than they rate *lows* and higher than *highs* rate *highs.* The data thus in varying degree support our theoretical expectations.

DISTORTION IN JUDGMENTS OF BEING LIKED

We have postulated a desire among group members to be favorably regarded by *highs.* Such a desire should lead to a facilitative over-rating by group members of the extent to which they are liked by *highs.*

Table 2 reveals a tendency for all subjects to underreport how much others like them. This tendency, however, is much less pronounced when the raters are judging how much *highs* like them (in comparison to *lows*). This is evident when we compare the first two rows with the last two. Comparisons between rows 1 and 3, 2 and 4, and 1 and 4 emphasize this point. It appears from these data that group members *need* to see the *highs* as liking them and report more that they do. This need

TABLE 2. *Mean Ratings of Being Liked by Others (Relative to Ratings of Liking Made by Them)*[a]

Relative Power of Rater	Person Rated	Mean Rating of Being Liked[b]
1. Low	High	−0.16
2. High	High	−0.66
3. Low	Low	−1.02
4. High	Low	−1.12

[a]Significance of differences (*p*): 1 *vs.* 2 (<.80) Chi square used, resulting in a large increase over the *p* value obtained by *t*-test, 1 *vs.* 3 (<.01), 1 *vs.* 4 (.001), 2 *vs.* 3 (<.20), 2 *vs.* 4 (<.05) and 3 *vs.* 4 (.70).

[b]*Means* are algebraic means of deviations from actual rating of liking made by person being rated. A score of 0 indicates, therefore, that the mean rating of being liked is equal to the corresponding mean rating of liking. Negative values indicate that the individual raters tend to underestimate how much they are liked.

is probably enhanced by the marked tendency shown in Table 1 for *highs* to underlike *lows.*

If we compare rows 1 and 4 in Table 1 with the same rows in Table 2, we see that there is a positive relationship between being liked and underreporting of amount liked. This suggests that the more an individual is actually liked by members of his own group, the freer he will be to underestimate the amount of this liking. Conversely, the less he is liked, the greater will be his need to see others as liking him, hence the less free will he be to underestimate this liking. The need of individuals to see *highs* as liking them thus gets added support from the data in Table 1.

Table 2 suggests that individuals distort facilitatively in an effort to reduce the uneasiness generated in them by *highs.* Whether this distortion is in *reporting* or in *perception,* however, is a question that cannot be answered by our data.

FREQUENCY AND DIRECTION OF COMMUNICATION

In group discussion, the uneasiness of *lows* in their relations with *highs* should exert a restraining force on them against communicating as frequently as do *highs.* However, the need of *lows* to be liked by *highs* should induce them, when they do talk, to communicate to *highs* more often than to other *lows.* We should thus expect *highs* both to communicate more frequently than *lows* and to receive more communications than *lows.*

By comparing, in Table 3, rows 1 and 5, 2 and 6, etc. (that is, varying the frequency of recipient's communication and holding constant power of communicator and recipient alike), we see that there is a very marked tendency for people to communicate more frequently to those who communicate to them frequently than to those who communicate to them infrequently. Given this response phenomenon, is there any evidence of the influence of power on frequency of communication?

Varying the power of the communicator and holding constant the power of the recipient and the frequency of his communication (that is, comparing rows 1 and 2, 3 and 4, etc.), we find that *highs* consistently communicate more frequently than do *lows.* And finally, varying only the power of the recipient (that is, comparing rows 1 and 3, 2 and 4, etc.), we see that *lows* tend to communicate more frequently to *highs* than to other *lows*. And since *highs* do likewise, it is of course not surprising to find that *highs* receive more communications than do *lows*.

TABLE 3. *Frequency of Communication as a Function of Frequency of Being Communicated to*[a]

Relative Power of		Frequency of Communication
Communicator	Recipient	
When Recipient Communicates Frequently to Communicator		
1. Low	High	3.61
2. High	High	4.89
3. Low	Low	2.76
4. High	Low	3.66
When Recipient Communicates Infrequently to Communicator		
5. Low	High	1.14
6. High	High	1.87
7. Low	Low	0.92
8. High	Low	1.63

[a]Significance of differences (*p*): (*a*) When only frequency of recipient's communication varies, range of *p* values is from <.01 to <.001. (*b*) When only power of communicator varies, *p*'s range from <.40 to .05 (Chi-square used in two comparisons); *p*'s based on *t*-test range from <.20 to .01. (*c*) When only power of recipient varies, *p*'s range from <.60 to <.05.

PERCEPTION OF EXTENT OF PARTICIPATION

Perception of the extent of participation by others carries with it no perceived threat to the rater. Consequently we would not expect to see in this situation the egodefensive, facilitative distortion which characterizes the judgments of extent of being liked by others. What we might reasonably anticipate, however, is distortion in judgment generated by expectation as to extent of participation of *highs* and *lows*. Let us recall for a moment that people are apparently aware of the restraints on *lows* against communicating in social situations involving individuals of unequal status and of the fact that *lows* are underliked. This awareness may lead people to expect that *lows* should participate relatively little in such situations. Consequently, when *lows* do speak up it should become relatively conspicuous, and the extent of their participation should be exaggerated.

Table 4 reveals a tendency for all subjects to overrate the amount others participate in the discussion. When we compare rows 1 and 2 with rows 3 and 4, however, we see that this tendency is much greater when the participation of *lows* is being judged than that of *highs*. This is true whether those making the judgments are *highs* or *lows*. (Compare row 1 with 3, and 2 with 4.) We also see that *lows* overrate *highs* less and other *lows* more than do *highs* with respect to other *highs*. The findings thus consistently support the expectation phenomenon described above.

TABLE 4. *Mean Ratings of Amount of Participation by Others (Relative to Actual Amount of Participation by Them)*[a]

Relative Power of		Mean Rating of Amount of Participation[b]
Rater	Person Rated	
1. Low	High	+0.23
2. High	High	+0.56
3. Low	Low	+1.38
4. High	Low	+1.42

[a]Significance of differences (*p*): 1 *versus* 2 (< .20), 1 *versus* 3 (< .001), 1 *versus* 4 (< .001) (Chi-square used), 2 *versus* 3 (< .001), 2 *versus* 4 (< .001) and 3 *versus* 4 (< .70).
[b]*Amount of participation* is defined as frequency of communication weighted by length. Means are algebraic means of deviations from observed participation (transformed linearly to a seven-point scale). A score of 0 means, therefore, that the mean rating of participation is equal to the corresponding actual amount of participation. Positive values indicate that the raters tend to overestimate how much others participate.

DISCUSSION

The explanation here advanced for upward communication does not contradict, in our judgment, the one offered by Back *et al.* (1), Kelley (2), and Thibaut (5). Their explanation, that of substitute upward locomotion, applies mainly to those situations having well-defined hierarchical structures in which individuals in low positions in the hierarchy are strongly motivated to locomote upward in it.

In such situations, of course, upward communication probably takes on an egodefensive as well as substitute goal achievement character. It is, however, in the numerous group situations in which the possibility of upward locomotion in a specific hierarchy is smaller, as for example in most informal group situations in which persons are at different status levels but not within the same hierarchy, that the egodefensive explanation we have advanced probably best applies.

Methodologically speaking, this is an experiment in a field situation, not a field study, since we were able to control experimentally the major independent variable by means of selection and assignment of subjects. As such, its chief value lies, perhaps, in that it reveals the same effects of power in a real-life situation previously found by inducing power differences in contrived laboratory situations.

SUMMARY

An experiment was conducted in a field situation to test a number of assumptions based on two theoretical conceptions concerning the effects of power possessed by individuals to influence other members of their groups. The first conception is that group members occupying low status positions will perceive and behave toward high status members in an essentially egodefensive manner, that is, in ways calculated to reduce the feeling of uneasiness experienced in their relations with *highs*. Thus, for example, due to this uneasiness *lows* will tend to like *highs*, to overrate the extent to which *highs* like them, to communicate infrequently and, when they do talk, to talk mainly to *highs*. The second conception is that awareness by people of the restraints on *lows* against communicating in social situations involving individuals of unequal status, and of their being underliked by other group members, may engender expectations that *lows* should participate relatively little in group discussions. Consequently, when *lows* speak up it becomes conspicuous, and the extent of their participation is exaggerated. No facilitative distortion operates in judgments of extent of participation of other group members (as it does in judgments of extent of being liked) since the amount of participation per se constitutes no threat.

These conceptions are stated in terms of the behavior of individuals of low status. The situation can be viewed equally well from the point of view of persons of high status. *Highs* will behave in essentially the same manner as will *lows*. They will like other *highs*, will want to be liked by them and will talk mainly to other *highs*. However, since they are more secure by virtue of their status than are *lows*, *highs* will be less threatened by participation in discussion situations. As a consequence, these tendencies will be less marked than in the case of *lows*. Moreover, because *highs* are less defensive than *lows*, they will feel more free to participate in the discussions. And finally, other members will expect that *highs* should participate actively and hence will make less exaggerated judgments as to the extent of their participation.

The reactions of *lows* and of *highs* to their respective status levels may be summarized by viewing *lows* as recipients of these behaviors. *Lows* will be liked less than *highs* by *highs* and *lows* alike; there will be less of a desire among all group members to be liked by *lows*, and fewer communications will be directed to them. And due to the lower expectations as to the amount *lows* should participate in discussions, the extent of their participation will be exaggerated by *highs* and *lows* alike.

To test these assumptions, a one-day conference was held in a Midwestern city attended by 42 persons working in the field of mental hygiene. These individuals met, each with four different groups, to discuss four topics related to mental health and to provide the necessary measures. The independent measure of perceived power to influence was obtained at the very beginning of the conference. The dependent measures, obtained at the subgroup meetings were as follows: postsession ratings of extent of liking for other group members, perceptions of extent of being liked by them, and perceptions of extent of their verbal participation. During the discussions, observers kept records of frequency and length of remarks as objective measures of participation. Since all the assumptions were of a comparative type, mean values were computed for the dependent measures and differences between appropriate pairs of means were evaluated statistically. The results support the assumptions.

References

1. Back, K., *et al.* The methodology of studying rumor transmission. *Human Relations,* 1950, **3**, 307–312.

2. Kelley, H. H. Communication in experimentally created hierarchies. *Human Relations,* 1951, **4**, 39–56.

3. Lippitt, R., Polansky, N., & Rosen, S. The dynamics of power. *Human Relations,* 1952, **5**, 37–64.

4. Pepitone, A. Motivational effects in social perception. *Human Relations,* 1950, **3**, 57–76.

5. Thibaut, J. An experimental study of the cohesiveness of underprivileged groups. *Human Relations,* 1950, **3**, 251–278.

PART FIVE

LEADERSHIP AND PERFORMANCE OF
GROUP FUNCTIONS

24

Leadership and Performance of Group Functions: Introduction

Of all the topics studied by those interested in group dynamics, the nature of leadership has been investigated most persistently over a long period of time. From the beginning it has been assumed that morale, group effectiveness, and leadership are all intimately related to one another. But as more and more research has been completed it has become increasingly clear that the relations among these different aspects of group life are exceedingly complex. As is so often true, the accumulation of facts has revealed that simple formulations are inadequate. The belief that a high level of group effectiveness can be achieved simply by the provision of "good" leaders, though still prevalent among many people concerned with the management of groups, now appears naive in the light of research findings.

In spite of the complexity of these relations, the nature of a group's leadership clearly makes a difference to many aspects of its functioning. The early work on leadership by Lewin, Lippitt, and White (reported in Chap. 25) provided striking evidence that the same group of people will behave in markedly different ways when operating under leaders who behave differently.

Subsequent research has served to support and document this general conclusion. Thus, for example, Kahn and Katz (**28**) have summarized the findings from several studies which obtained data concerning the performance of a variety of workgroups and the characteristic behaviors of each group's supervisor. They conclude: (*a*) supervisors of more effective groups were better able to play a differentiated role than the supervisors of the less effective groups, and they spent more time in planning what was to be done, in providing necessary materials, and in initiating next steps; (*b*) the better supervisors delegated authority to others more than the poorer supervisors; (*c*) the more effective supervisors checked up on the subordinates less often and were more supportive in their manner than the less effective ones; and (*d*) the supervisors of groups with better performance developed cohesiveness among their associates more than did the supervisors of poorer groups.

The intimate relation between the leadership and the qualities of a group has been emphasized by Likert (**34, 35**). On the basis of extensive research he concludes that the effective supervisor

creates a good working team which has a friendly cooperative atmosphere with high group loyalty. He seems to build this high group loyalty through using participation and other recognized methods of group leadership. Moreover, the workgroup under his leadership exercises influence upward upon organizational objectives, methods, etc., and in turn accepts as group goals those objectives which must be achieved if the group is to do its part of the total task of the organization effectively and at a high level of performance. The workgroup sets specific goals and checks its progress toward goals regularly.

Employing a rather different approach, Fiedler (Chap. 28) has shown that the leaders of more effective groups tend to be those who are concerned with successful completion of the task if the situation is either very easy or very difficult for the leader. When the situation is of intermediate difficulty, the most effective leader is one who devotes his attention primarily to friendly interpersonal relations.

From investigations like these a great many facts about the relations between leadership and characteristics of groups have been obtained. Attempts, however, to bring these all together into a coherent theoretical treatment have encountered certain basic difficulties. First, theoretical discussions of the nature of leadership have tended to confuse assumptions about what leadership "ought to be" with research oriented questions of "what produces what." It has been only in recent years that research on leadership has been concerned with cause-and-effect relations regardless of their immediately practical or ideological significance. Even today much of the research is designed to provide empirical support for some particular ideological point of view. While it is true that such research can be of great value, the social scientist whose primary motivation is to defend an ideology will almost certainly develop "blind spots" that prevent his seeing all the relevant facts.

A second problem consists of choosing an acceptable definition of the terms *leader* and *leadership*. To some, leadership is a property of a group while to others it is a characteristic of an individual. To those who emphasize the group, leadership may be synonymous with prestige, with the holding of a particular office, with the performance of activities important to the group, or with an emotional relationship between the leader and the group. To those who stress the individual, leadership may mean the possession of certain personality characteristics such as dominance, ego-control, aggressiveness, or freedom from paranoid tendencies. The variety of notions contained in these alternative conceptions makes it plain that a single meaning for the term leader that would be acceptable to all those interested in leadership cannot readily be chosen. For a discussion of the major approaches to the study of leadership reference should be made to the comprehensive reviews of the literature prepared by Bass (**2**) and by Katz and Kahn (**29**).

TRAITS OF LEADERS

The earliest approach to research on leadership was concerned with identifying the characteristics of leaders. Many studies were undertaken to determine the physical, intellectual, and personality traits of the leader (usually the person holding an office) as compared to the follower. It has been reported, for example, that leaders tend to be bigger (but not too much bigger) and brighter (but not too much brighter) than the rest of the members. Evidence has been found that well-accepted leaders tend to display better adjustment on various personality tests. Other studies have concentrated more upon the leader's skills or what he does than upon the nature of his deeper personality. Findings from such studies indicate, for example, that leaders tend to give more information, ask for more information, and make more frequent interpretations about the situation than do the rest of the members.

On the basis of ideas and findings about the traits and behaviors of leaders, various attempts have been made to develop techniques for identifying persons who have the qualities seen as important for leadership. Many different selection procedures have been invented, ranging from paper-and-pencil tests to performance tests under lifelike conditions. The usefulness of all this work depends, of course, upon establishing some agreement about the nature of "good" leadership. Values must enter at this point. Among the values more commonly invoked in determining criteria of "good" leadership are high morale, high productivity, popularity, equalitarianism, and authoritarianism. In regard to such matters as popularity, group morale, and productivity it has been possible to obtain quantitative measures and to demonstrate that certain kinds of leader behavior produce more of these valued properties than do others.

On the whole, however, the attempt to discover the traits that distinguish leaders from nonleaders has been disappointing. Bird (5) made an extensive examination of the research relevant to this problem conducted prior to 1940 and was able to compile a long list of traits which in one or more studies appeared to differentiate leaders from nonleaders. The discouraging fact, however, was that only about 5 percent of the "discovered" traits were common to four or more investigations. A more recent survey of the literature by Stogdill (53) produced only slightly more encouraging conclusions. He reports that various studies of the traits of leadership continue to result in contradictory findings. Among these studies the only conclusion that receives even fairly good support is that leaders excel nonleaders in intelligence, scholarship, dependability and responsibility, activity and social participation, and socioeconomic status. A good summary of the inadequacies of the trait approach has been provided by Gouldner (19, 23–45).

One major reason for the disappointing outcome of this approach may be that personality traits are still poorly conceived and unreliably measured. As our knowledge about the nature of personality improves and as our techniques of measurement become more dependable, it is possible that traits will be discovered that do regularly distinguish leaders from followers. It must be noted, however, that although this is a possibility that cannot be definitely rejected, the available evidence does not make it appear very probable. Another difficulty may be involved. The characteristics that get a person into a position of leadership may be rather different from those that make a person an effective leader once he has attained an office of leadership. It may well be that the study of traits of *leadership effectiveness* will reveal a greater consistency of results than has been found from comparing leaders and nonleaders.

On the whole, investigators are coming to the conclusion that certain minimal abilities required of all leaders are widely distributed among nonleaders as well. Furthermore, the traits of the leader that are necessary and effective in one group or situation may be quite different from those of another leader in a different setting. This conclusion, if adequately substantiated, would imply that the selection of leaders must consider a person's suitability for the type of functions he is to perform in a given situation, and it would raise questions about the desirability of formal arrangements that maintain the responsibilities of leadership in the same person regardless of the changing task of the group and the changing requirements of the leader.

Research on the training of leaders also suggests that a more "situational" approach to leadership is required. There is a growing recognition that little improvement in actual leadership behavior can be expected from providing people with a set of "rules of leadership." And even when efforts have been made to instill "flexibility," "sensitivity," or "good attitudes toward people," the resulting changes in behavior have been disappointing. Impressive documentation of these difficulties has been provided by Fleishmann, Harris, and Burtt (11) in their evaluation of a foreman-training program. They found marked improvement in the attitudes and skills of leaders immediately after participation in an intensive training program. Within a few months, however, the foremen had reverted to their pre-training modes of behavior. These investigators attribute this "regression" to the nature of the organization in which the foremen worked. Specifically, they show that there was often a discrepancy between the behavior taught in the program and the behavior expected by the foreman's supervisor. They conclude (11, 58) that "when what is taught in the school is at variance with what is practiced in the plant, the latter is generally the more powerful influence." Lippitt (37) was concerned with essentially the same problem when he designed an experimental training program for people working in the field of intergroup relations. He reasoned that if people were trained as members of teams they could more effectively resist "on the job" regressive pressures by giving support to one another in their post-training activities. The results of this experiment, in which some people were trained as team members while others were trained as individuals, show that those trained as teams were in fact better able to put into practice and to maintain new leadership practices than the persons who were trained as individuals.

In summary, we may conclude that the conception of leaders as people who possess certain distinctive traits has not proved to be satisfactory. A "new view" of leadership is emerging which stresses the performance of needed functions and adaptability to changing situations. According to this conception, groups are or should be flexible in assigning leadership functions to various members as conditions change. Effective leaders are sensitive to the changing conditions of their groups and flexible in adapting their behavior to new requirements. The improvement of leadership may be expected, not from improving leaders apart from the group, but by modifying the relations between leaders and the rest of the group.

LEADERSHIP AND GROUP FUNCTIONS

Dissatisfaction with the trait approach has, then, given rise to a view of leadership that stresses the characteristics of the group and the situation in which it exists. Research conducted within this orientation does not attempt to find certain invariant traits of leaders. Rather, it seeks to discover what actions are required by groups under various conditions if they are to achieve their goals or other valued states, and how different group members take part in these group actions. Leadership is viewed as the performance of those acts which help the group achieve its preferred outcomes. Such acts may be termed *group functions*. More specifically, leadership consists of such actions by group members as those which aid in setting group goals, moving the group toward its goals, improving the quality of the interactions among the members, building the cohesiveness of the group, and making resources available to the group. In principle, leadership may be performed by one or many members of the group.

This point of view has been stressed by many writers including Barnard, (3), Cattell (8), French (14), Gibb (16), Likert (34), Lippitt (36), Redl (48), and Stogdill (54).

The common denominator among these theorists includes the following points: groups differ from one another in a variety of ways, and the actions required for the achievement of valued states of one group may be quite different from those of another. The nature of leadership and the traits of leaders will accordingly be different from group to group. Situational aspects such as the nature of the group's goals, the structure of the group, the attitudes or needs of the members, and the expectations placed upon the group by its external environment help to determine which group functions will be needed at any given time and who among the members will perform them.

WHAT ARE LEADERSHIP FUNCTIONS?

Nearly every conception of leadership contains the notion that a true leader exerts more influence on the group and its activities than does the average member. There is less clear-cut agreement, however, concerning the specific kinds of influence that are uniquely those of leadership. Cattell (8) has proposed what is perhaps the most inclusive conception when he asserts that any member of a group exerts leadership to the extent that the properties of the group (syntality) are modified by his presence in the group.[1] According to this view all group functions (that is, all member actions that help the group achieve its desired states) are leadership functions. Although this conception is much broader than most popular notions of leadership, it has distinct theoretical advantages. One of the most important of these is that leadership and group performance are conceived as necessarily related to each other. In identifying acts of leadership, the research has first to determine what states are valued for the group at a given time, then to discover which functions are appropriate for the attainment of these states, and finally to determine which actions by members of the group contribute to the function. Acts of leadership thus contribute to the attainment of such things as goal achievement, viability of the group, satisfactory human relations, satisfaction of members, minimum cost to members, and the like—in short, to group perfor-

---

[1] Cattell includes both positive and negative influences under the concept of leadership. In the discussion here, however, we will consider only influences that in some sense "help" the group.

mance. Another advantage is that leadership is viewed as something that a person may display in varying degree rather than something that he has either completely or not at all. Similarly, leadership may be possessed to some degree by any member of the group regardless of his formally designated office or position. In keeping with this definition of leadership it would be rare indeed that one could properly speak of "the leader" of a group.

Some theorists prefer to stay closer to the popular notion of leadership and to restrict the term to include the performance of a more limited set of group functions such as planning, decision-making, and coordinating. This approach maintains the essentially functional conception of leadership, but it uses the word *leadership* to refer to a special class of functions. Krech and Crutchfield (31, 417–422) have listed fourteen functions a leader may perform. They propose that a leader serves to some degree as an executive, planner, policymaker, expert, external group representative, controller of internal relationships, purveyor of rewards and punishments, arbitrator, exemplar, group symbol, surrogate for individual responsibility, ideologist, father figure, or scapegoat. Redl (48), writing in the psychoanalytic tradition, has proposed a rather different list of functions that affect mainly the group's formation, maintenance, and disruption. These functions are conceived as operating through such mechanisms as identification, cathexis, guilt reduction, impulse control, and incorporation of superego.

It is not possible at the present state of research on groups to develop a fully satisfactory designation of the functions that are peculiarly functions of leadership. A more promising endeavor, at least for the present, is to identify the various group functions, without deciding finally whether or not to label each specifically as a function of leadership, and then to discover by empirical investigation such things as what determines their emergence in a group, what determines their allotment to certain offices or individuals, and what consequences stem from the execution of these functions under different conditions in the group.

The concept of group or leadership function contains two important ideas. We noted the first of these when we pointed out that, in principle, any member of a group may be a leader in the sense that he may take actions that serve group functions. The second idea is that a given function may be served by many different behaviors. According to this conception, then, one and the same leadership function may be served by a variety of actions taken by a variety of people. It is the task of research to discover the factors that determine what actions are performed by which members of the group.

If we recall the fourteen functions that Krech and Crutchfield propose a leader may perform, it becomes evident that one person could seldom be effectively responsible for them all. In most organizations, therefore, distinct functions are combined into separate offices and the occupants of these offices assume responsibility for providing their unique functions and usually no others. A person who serves in a given office, moreover, has pressures placed upon him that prescribe what he is to do and how he is to do it (see Chap. 11). These prescriptions serve to create an enduring stability in the functions available for the group and their performance by particular members. An important contribution of the Ohio State Leadership Studies (51) has been a careful examination of the duties and styles of leadership included within offices in military and industrial organizations and the documentation of how men with similar titles may vary in their behavior depending on the settings in which they work.

Under specific circumstances, of course, any given behavior may or may not serve a group function. Making "expert information available to the group," which might be expected to help the group reach a goal, can be done in such a manner that it stultifies movement toward the goal. To cite another example of usually helpful behavior, a group of children may be stimulated to self-direction at a time when they are not ready for it and when a more appropriate action would be to suggest a plan of action. Or clowning by a member of a discussion group may be exactly what is needed in a tense moment to relieve strain, but at another time such levity may seem inappropriate or may even block locomotion to the goal (18).

In a similar way we may conclude that the skills possessed by a designated leader or the holder of an office may make him well-qualified to perform important group functions under certain conditions and poorly qualified under others. The pilot of a bomber crew, for example, who is an excellent leader for the group while the plane is in the air, may be a most inadequate leader if the plane crashes and the crew is faced with the task of surviving or finding its way to safety. The specific requirements of the group's tasks demand that members possess certain skills in order to serve the appropriate functions. If the task changes, different behaviors are required, and the same person may or may not be able to perform in the new way.

In Chapter 29, Carter and his associates report experimental findings that indicate that the behavior shown by designated leaders does vary somewhat, depending upon the nature of the group task. In this experiment groups were given three different types of assignment: reasoning, mechanical assembly, and group discussion. When confronted with the reasoning task the designated leader more frequently asked for information or facts. When the group was working on mechanical assembly, he was more apt to express the desire that something be done and to work actively with the men. In a discussion group he was more likely to give information and to ask for expressions of opinion. What the leader did to help his group attain its goal, in brief, was different in each task. We recognize intuitively that reasoning, mechanical assembly, and group discussion require different behaviors from members. We cannot say precisely, however, what characteristics among these tasks, or any others, have what effects upon leadership behavior. We expect that future research will identify the properties of tasks that serve to channel leadership acts and will examine the ways they define the style of leadership. Potential candidates for study are such properties as clarity, difficulty, repetitiveness, variability, and the need for coordination among members. Thibaut and Kelley (57) provide interesting suggestions about the qualities of tasks and their consequences for group functions.

A stimulating illustration of the promise inherent in this approach is offered by Fiedler (Chap. 28). He examined the behaviors of leaders in groups engaged in many different group activities. The tasks of these groups differed primarily in their degree of structure. He assumed that a task's structure is greater the more it is possible for members to verify the correctness of the group's decisions, the more that duties of members are clearly stated, the fewer are the variety of paths to the goal, and the fewer are the number of steps necessary in

working toward the goal. Fiedler observed that an effective leader tends to be assertive and impersonal in a more structured setting whereas he gives greater freedom to members and is warmly supportive in a less structured situation.

Just as the nature of the group task influences the kinds of leadership behavior that arises in a group, so should we expect the specific needs for group maintenance to influence leadership behavior. If a group's existence is threatened by conflicting subgroups, we might expect a leading person to engage heavily in mediating behavior. If on the other hand, the group's problem is that it has such low prestige in the community that members leave, quite different leader activities would be expected. It is unfortunate that most of the carefully controlled studies of leader behavior have been conducted with temporarily organized groups where almost of necessity members are not concerned with the preservation of the group.

Although we know little of a systematic kind about the processes involved, it is apparent that the nature of the leadership behavior chosen for the performance of group functions will be influenced by situational factors both inside and outside the group.

TWO BASIC TYPES OF GROUP FUNCTIONS

It will be useful for many purposes to distinguish among various group functions according to the type of group objective to which the function contributes. It appears that most group objectives can be subsumed under one of two headings: (*a*) the achievement of some specific group goal and (*b*) the maintenance or strengthening of the group itself. Examples of member behaviors that serve functions of *goal achievement* are "initiates action," "keeps members' attention on the goal," "clarifies the issue," "develops a procedural plan," "evaluates the quality of work done," and "makes expert information available." Examples of behaviors that serve functions of *group maintenance* are "keeps interpersonal relations pleasant," "arbitrates disputes," "provides encouragement," "gives the minority a chance to be heard," "stimulates self-direction," and "increases the interdependence among members."

Any given behavior in a group may have

significance both for goal achievement and for maintenance. Both may be served simultaneously by the actions of a member, or one may be served at the expense of the other. Thus, a member who helps a group to work cooperatively on a difficult problem may inadvertently help it to develop solidarity. In another group, however, an eager member may spur the group on in such a way that frictions develop among the members, and even though the goal is achieved efficiently, the continued existence of the group is seriously endangered.

Although it is evident that goal achievement and group maintenance functions may be performed by any member, there are types of organizations in which "specialists" in these two kinds of functions emerge. Bales and Slater (1) have reported that in laboratory studies of problem-solving leaderless groups, there almost always appears a differentiation between a person who presses for task accomplishment and a person who satisfies the social and emotional needs of members. Heinicke and Bales (25) have shown that where such specialization arises the effective performance of the group depends upon the development of appropriate coordination between the specialists in their separation of labor and commonality of view.

Verba, a student of government, has proposed that such specialization is more likely to occur in informal experimental groups than in enduring organizations (60). Because the laboratory groups are leaderless, have a brief period of existence, and are composed of fairly similar college students, an effort by one person to exercise leadership is seen by others as arbitrary and a direct personal challenge. Furthermore, as noted by Carter *et al.* (Chap. 29), a person who takes control of a group in which no leader has been appointed is usually the most aggressive participant. His efforts arouse negative reactions among the members, which makes it necessary that a less assertive individual take responsibility for relieving emotional tension.

Even so, specialization has been observed in established groups. In families the father is usually the task specialist and the mother the social-emotional specialist. Grusky (21) has described the social organization of a psychological clinic in which these two types of specialist emerged. His account provides a vivid description of some of the consequences of such specialization.

Research in larger organizations has also indicated the presence of these two basic functions. Factor analytic studies reported by Halpin and Winer (22) and by Fleishmann, Harris, and Burtt (11) have shown that two factors represent 83 percent of the accountable common variance in leader behavior. These two factors have been labeled "consideration" and "initiating structure." Items with high positive loadings on "consideration" were associated with behavior indicative of friendship, mutual trust, respect, and a certain warmth between the leader and his group. Items with a high positive loading on "initiating structure" were associated with behavior on the part of the leader that tends to define the role which he expects each member to assume and that seeks to establish well-defined patterns of organization, channels of communication, and ways of getting the job done. It is interesting to note, further, that the two minor factors identified by this research, "production emphasis" and "social sensitivity," appear also to reflect the two basic functions of goal achievement and group maintenance, respectively.

Fleishmann, Harris, and Burtt (11) report results from a large industrial organization indicating that the employees liked working under foremen who were high in consideration and disliked working under those who were high in initiating structure. Proficiency ratings of the foremen revealed, however, that in production divisions the foremen with higher proficiency ratings were the ones who showed more initiation of structure but that in the nonproduction divisions those with the higher proficiency ratings manifested more consideration. In the production divisions, moreover, absenteeism was found to be positively related to initiating structure and negatively related to consideration. In summarizing the total available evidence, Shartle (51) concludes that the pattern of leader behavior that is high in both consideration and initiation of structure tends to increase group effectiveness. Confirmation of this last conclusion has been provided by Misumi and Tasaki (41) in their report of supervisory practices among Japanese coal miners. They observed that supervisors who simultaneously emphasized both goal achievement and group maintenance were more likely to generate higher production and morale than those who concentrated upon either production or maintenance alone.

Everyday experience in groups provides many examples of instances where members make group maintenance their major concern to the detriment of work to be done, or where too much interest in task achievement leads to insufficient attention to group maintenance. Managers and administrators who, for some reason, must perform both types of functions often report that a recurring problem for them is to find a proper balance between these two types of requirements.

Within a larger organization the attention that a leader will devote to goal achievement or to group maintenance may be determined by his position in the hierarchy and by the particular expectations colleagues hold for an occupant of his position; a top manager may thus reveal different leadership behavior than a lower-level supervisor. In a study of leadership in a number of hospitals, Georgopoulous and Mann (15) identified three aspects of managerial skill: administrative, technical, and human relations. They assumed that a manager would display more administrative skill than technical know-how and that a supervisor would reveal more technical than administrative skill. Competence in human relations, however, would be equally frequent at all levels in the organization. The authors asked every employee in these hospitals to rate his immediate supervisor on each of the three skills and to indicate how well he was satisfied with that person as his boss. In general, favorable ratings of the three skills were differently associated with satisfaction at separate locations in the hospital.

Satisfaction with a high status manager, for example, was greater if he was seen to be skilled in performing administrative functions but not if he was rated favorably in technical or human relations activities. Satisfaction with a supervisory nurse was primarily correlated with the skill in human relations attributed to her by her staff, and satisfaction with the head of practical nurses was almost entirely associated with her rated technical competence. The findings of Georgopoulous and Mann suggest that there are conditions where certain acts by a leader are acceptable to members and contrasting conditions where such acts are less satisfying. The task remains for research to identify what conditions, other than position in the hierarchy, generate particular expectations of a leader.

It has often been asserted that groups display a tendency to preserve themselves whenever they encounter a threat to their existence. Such a threat, so the argument goes, makes the group maintenance functions especially valuable to the group, and some person will spring to the rescue and assume the responsibilities of leadership by serving these needed functions. That this is an invariable "law of leadership" may be doubted. Nevertheless, it does appear that many groups do have tendencies toward self-preservation. When the existence of such a group is in jeopardy, member behavior is apt to arise which will strengthen the group's cohesiveness and resources. To the extent that these efforts are effective, they are by definition group functions, and most people would agree that these should also be called functions of leadership.

By similar reasoning we should expect goal achievement functions to become more valuable to the group when it accepts an important goal or when goal achievement is threatened. Under such conditions we might expect a heightened tendency for one or more members to perform acts designed to help the group achieve its goal. If one person does devote unusually great effort toward this end, or if he is especially effective in aiding the group, it would generally be agreed that he is performing functions of leadership regardless of his office in the group. Although systematic evidence is meager, Gibb's findings (16) lend support to this point of view. He reports that leadership activity occurred most frequently in the groups he studied when these groups were faced with a problem.

Countering the notion that groups invariably attempt to preserve themselves is the practical experience with groups which suggests that a group "pathology" may sometimes develop in which member behavior persistently does not contribute to the group's goal achievement or maintenance. Under some circumstances, a group may appear deliberately to escape from its problems by retreating to some relatively simple activity. In a problem-solving discussion group, for example, when the solution is difficult or when interpersonal conflict is intense, great energy may be devoted to the "safe" activity of listing on the blackboard all logical possibilities of action. Hours may be spent discussing whether a particular item falls under one heading or another, even though the decision will not bring the group any closer to its goal. It is extremely difficult, of course, to determine definitely whether or not such escape behavior makes a contribution to the maintenance of the group, since the avoidance of tension and conflict may sometimes be necessary for the preservation of the group. If, however, a group remains indefinitely "on dead center," neither improving its abilities and resources nor moving toward a goal, we may conclude that virtually no group functions and consequently no leadership functions are being performed.

LEADERSHIP AND POWER

Ever since the days of Machiavelli there have been theorists who conceive of leadership essentially in terms of the possession and exercise of power. Although few contemporary theorists would seriously maintain that leaders of most groups and organizations in modern civilized society rely on coercion or "brute force," realistic descriptions of group life must recognize that leadership inevitably involves the ability to influence other people in some way. The central concern with "authority" in theories of organization illustrates the importance of this aspect of leadership. Even in highly informal, voluntary groups, leaders are recognized by their ability to affect the course of events in the group. If, then, one accepts the view, advanced by such theorists as Russell (49), Lasswell and Kaplan (32), Simon (52), Dahl (10), and Cartwright (7), that social power consists of the ability to influence other people by whatever means, leadership clearly involves the use of power.

In the functional approach to leadership advocated here, the operation of social power should be clearly recognized. We have asserted that an act of leadership consists of contributing to some group function. Usually, if not always, such a contribution requires influencing the behavior of other people in some way: activities must be coordinated, instructions must be given and accepted, persuasion must be accomplished, motivation to strive for group goals must be generated, and harmonious interpersonal relations must be engendered. A person must have power to exert such influence if he is to contribute to group functions significantly and, thus, to perform acts of leadership.

When the performance of several important group functions is assigned to a single office, the operation of power is especially evident.

The occupant of such an office is usually provided with the resources needed for the exertion of influence: he may have the right to hire, fire, promote, and set wages; he may possess expert knowledge due to special training, experience, or access to essential information; and, in well-run organizations, his decisions are supported by other officials. The importance of the possession of power for effective leadership is well illustrated in Chapter 28, where Fiedler shows that groups are more effective when functioning under leaders who have a particular trait of personality—but only if such leaders also have adequate social power resulting from the support of other officials. A similar conclusion is suggested by Pelz (44) from research in a large manufacturing concern. He found that first-line supervisors whose orientation to subordinates was supportive of their interests received positive evaluations from these subordinates but only if the supervisor was seen as being influential in his department. Occupants of offices of leadership cannot perform the functions of leadership unless they possess sufficient power.

For some students of groups the most important attribute of the leader is his ability to provide favors for subordinates. His influence is conceived to be a consequence, then, of the appreciation subordinates develop when the leader provides a favor; followers feel obliged to reciprocate by doing what he expects of them. In a series of experiments conducted at military bases, Greer (20) noted that soldiers performed their assignments better, thereby winning approval of their leader from his superiors, the more the leader had earlier provided indulgences for the men. Greer concludes that the effectiveness of a leader is heavily determined by the tendency of subordinates to reciprocate his indulgent acts.

Even when the functions of leadership are not concentrated in formally designated offices, the possession of power is still required for their performance. The "opinion leader" of an informal group is able to influence the beliefs and attitudes of others. The "social-emotional leader" possesses the skills and resources required to make others feel comfortable and satisfied with membership in the group. And the "goal setter" is somehow capable of facilitating the conversion of personal interests into acceptable group goals.

Acts of leadership, if they are to be effective, must rely upon some basis of power. Although little research has been conducted to discover the effects upon groups of having leaders who employ predominantly one or another basis of power, the analysis of these bases presented by French and Raven (Chap. 20), suggests several interesting hypotheses about what these effects may be.

DISTRIBUTION OF FUNCTIONS AMONG MEMBERS

The conception of leadership proposed here implies that important group functions may, in principle, be performed by various members of a group. What determines whether particular people engage in behaviors relevant to group functions? What determines whether a person is allowed or urged to do so? We consider first those factors which foster the taking of initiative in leadership. Then, we shall examine some of the ways in which functions are assigned to members.

Determinants of Initiative in Leadership. In order for a member to take the initiative in attempting to serve a group function, at least two conditions appear to be necessary: (*a*) He must be aware that a given function is needed. (*b*) He must feel that he is able to perform it, that he has enough skill to do so, or that it is safe for him to attempt to do so.

Ideally one might hope that a specific behavior by a member, such as offering a summary statement, furnishing a new suggestion, or making a tension-relieving remark, will occur when it is needed. This ideal, to be sure, is seldom met, yet there is evidence that members' leadership actions are in large part determined by the group's needs. Bales and Strodtbeck in Chapter 30, for example, show that certain behaviors in a problem-solving group tend to appear at one stage in progress toward a solution while other behaviors occur in a different phase. Parker (43) reports that specialists in social-emotional leadership in a mental hospital are more likely to engage in leadership actions when a conflict develops between patients and staff which produces in the patients a need for social support. Heyns (26), Carter *et al.* (Chap. 29), and Crockett (9) observe that, when a designated leader does not perform the leadership functions he is supposed to provide, other members step in to perform them in his stead. Further evidence is provided by Kahn and Katz (28), who note that informal leaders tend to spring up in

groups where the foreman fails to furnish adequate leadership. And Haythorn (24) reports that when one member takes a large measure of initiative in a group, others are likely to show less of such behavior than they ordinarily would.

When achievement of a group goal is important to its members we should find, then, more readiness to take initiative than when the goal is unimportant to them. Results from a study by Crockett (9) are relevant. He observed that members who exerted leadership functions were those who were most interested in and concerned about the decisions to be made in the group. Hamblin (23), moreover, has noted that threats to achievement of the group goal tend to increase the frequency of leadership actions.

Other properties of the group also stimulate the spontaneous execution of group functions by members. The degree of facilitative interdependence among members, for example, increases the responsibility felt by participants for one another and, therefore, the amount of active effort they make for goal achievement, according to results reported by Thomas (59). A different group property, the channels of communication available within the group, affects the readiness of particular individuals to assume responsibility for certain functions. The studies reported by Bavelas and by Guetzkow (Chaps. 37 and 38) illustrate this point by showing that different communication networks have quite different effects on the participation of members in various group functions. In general, those members who are more central in the network tend to perform functions that others consider as constituting leadership.

To some degree people located centrally in a communication network take initiative to serve the group because they feel that their positions make others dependent upon them. An experiment by Pepitone (46) has demonstrated the effects of the awareness that one's actions are essential to the group. Certain group members were told that their job was more important to the group than were the jobs assigned to others. (In reality all members had identical work to do, though they did not know this.) The results of the experiment show that those who felt their assignments were more important developed greater feelings of responsibility to the group and were more ready to devote energy to the group task. It might be expected, in general, that whenever the members of a group experience a feeling of worth and acceptance by the group they will develop greater feelings of responsibility to the group and an increased readiness to perform group functions. This conclusion is given some support by the findings from an experiment conducted by Pepinsky *et al.* (45), in which paid participants, pretending they were regular subjects, systematically either supported or rejected the comments of other members of the group. It was found that members made considerably more leadership actions in the groups with an accepting atmosphere than in those with a climate of rejection.

A person who has had considerable experience as a leader may be expected to perform different functions in a group than one who has had little experience. McClintock (40) identified a number of college students who had previously held positions of leadership and a comparable number who had never occupied a responsible office in an organization. He then observed the behavior of these persons in small, standardized, problem-solving groups in which there were no designated leaders. The experienced leaders did not make more acts oriented to goal achievement than the nonleaders. They did, however, make significantly more friendly and agreeing acts and revealed greater concern for group achievement than the nonleaders did.

In most groups some type of discretion is used in determining who will be allowed to perform leadership acts. It is usually seen as inappropriate, for example, for a newcomer to press his views upon others. The standards of the group may designate who is to serve the group and when. Berkowitz (4) illustrates such a standard in his study of conferences in business and governmental agencies. He found a highly consistent tendency for members to prefer that the chairman exercise his designated functions concerning processes in the group without allowing others to share in them. Members were not to be excluded from expressing ideas relevant to the substantive topic at hand, but the chairman was to run the meeting. In moments of urgency, this group standard was revoked and sharing of procedural functions by members was temporarily allowed until the emergency had passed.

Certain personal characteristics are known to affect the amount of initiative individuals exercise in groups. It has been found, for example, that members participate more in the fulfillment of goal achievement efforts if they are confident of their own views (12), if they are more able than other members in performing the group's task (38), if they are high in ego strength (58), and if they have a high need for achievement (39). It has frequently been observed that a "hunger for power" brings people to assume functions of leadership. Some people, it seems, derive important satisfactions from "running things." Carter *et al.* report in Chapter 29 that persons who emerged as leaders in a leaderless group tended to be more aggressive, forceful, and dominating in their behavior than were appointed leaders under comparable conditions. It would seem probable that the emergent leaders possessed stronger need for power and found the leaderless group an ideal opportunity for gratifying this need. Guetzkow describes in Chapter 38 an experiment in which people came to assume certain roles when no explicit assignments were made. He found that those who took on the role of "keyman" scored higher on a test of "ascendance" than those who did not become this sort of leader. Additional data are provided by Veroff (61), who has attempted to measure power motivation by means of a projective test. He found that college students who obtained high scores on the test were rated by their instructors as high in argumentation and attempts to control others. Students scoring high reported more frequently than students scoring low that they would gain satisfaction from being a leader. These findings tend to support the view that initiative in leadership may derive in part from power motivation. Caution is suggested, however, by other results obtained by Veroff that lead him to conclude that the test may measure both motivation for power and motivation for recognition.

The consequences to the group of power motivation among group members may be favorable or unfavorable. It is possible for a "power grabber" to help a group achieve its goals and maintain itself. It is also possible, however, that when an individual's major motivation is the possession of power, his behavior will serve mainly his own needs without contributing to the group's locomotion or maintenance; he displays what Fouriezos, Hutt, and Guetzkow (12) call self-oriented behavior.

The needs and attitudes of those who do not assume functions of leadership constitute yet another influence upon the distribution of these functions. It is the experience of many adult leaders of youth groups that the less mature members avoid accepting responsibility by asking the adult leader to make decisions for them. If the adult leader finds personal satisfaction in having others dependent upon him, a sort of unconscious "collusion" may develop in which members and leader both gain satisfaction out of the concentration of functions in the hands of the leader. As an illustration, boys in the clubs led by an autocratic leader (Chap. 25) often developed an apathetic reaction to the person who was in charge. This accommodation of leaders and members to one another may endure in attitudes as well as behavior. In an experiment concerned with the effects of two different styles of supervision in a business office, Tannenbaum and Allport (55) obtained measures of workers' attitudes and personal characteristics at the time the supervisory styles were introduced and again a year later. As a consequence of supervision in which the foreman kept almost all leadership functions for himself it was found that the workers' attitudes and behaviors changed in ways indicating they were less willing and able to exercise leadership functions, while as a result of leadership in which the supervisor made opportunities for workers to share in group functions, the changes were in a direction indicating that members were more ready to take initiative.

Assignment of Group Functions. When offices have been designated in a group, what determines who is assigned to them? If specialized skills are required to fill a given office, the case is usually clear. A person who is sensitive to problems of human relations is often sought to perform the group maintenance functions in the personnel department of a business firm or an unexcitable person is asked to serve as mediator during a conference between disagreeing subgroups. Carter *et al.* (Chap. 29) and Kirscht *et al.* (30) report that those who are chosen as leaders more often seek to organize the group, to solicit and integrate contributions, and to propose courses of action than those who are not selected as leaders. Schrag (50) has shown the operation of a similar process with rather different consequences in a setting where the group is in conflict with its social environment. In this study the inmates of a prison were asked to nominate those whom they would want to represent them on the prisoners' council. The convicts most often named were those who were most recalcitrant, most violent, and with a record of such infractions of prison regulations as escape, attempted escape, fighting, and assault. Since the relations between prisoners and the management of the traditional sort of prison are characterized by conflict and hostility, the prisoners were choosing as leaders those men who might be expected best to carry on the fight.

It appears that the person who is most able to meet the needs of a group is more likely to be granted leadership. A revealing test of this assumption was conducted in Holland by Mulder and Sterding (42). In a number of medium-sized cities the authors created local groups of grocers who were to consider what they might do about a rumored development of a well-financed chain of supermarkets throughout the country. The grocers were independent merchants who theretofore had not formed city-based units of their national association. Half of the groups were told that it was very certain that a supermarket would be placed in their town (a high threat condition) and the other half were told that it was unlikely that a supermarket would appear locally (a low threat condition). During the group's discussions two experimental assistants, each of whom was said to own a local shop, showed contrasting behavior. One, the strong member, advocated certain aggressive actions and took a large part in the discussion; the other, the weak member, proposed a softer line in a rational and restrained manner. The two assistants, with the collusion of the experimenter, were subsequently nominated as potential officers of the newly created chapter. In the ensuing election, the grocers in the high threat condition more often voted for the strong member while those in the low threat condition chose the weaker member. The effects of threat in determining members' preferences for authoritarian or for democratic forms of leadership are described by Korten in Chapter 27.

It sometimes happens, of course, that a person is chosen for a position of leadership even though he clearly lacks ability for the job. An example would be the youth group that elects a popular but incapable athlete as chairman. Although defects in the machinery for selecting leaders may account for some inappropriate assignments (and little is known about these), there is evidence that certain conditions in the group affect members' willingness to accept a valuable contributor as leader. Theodorson (56) has described, for example, how group cohesiveness may affect the evaluation of participants in adult discussion groups. He reports that members of highly cohesive groups felt that their personal needs and those of the group were one and the same, with the result that effective participants in the group were seen as helpful to all members in gratifying their own needs. Members in less cohesive groups had disparate needs, and a good contributor was less likely to satisfy these many different needs. A somewhat similar conclusion has been reached by Israel (27) in investigations of cooperative and competitive groups. In the cooperative group a valuable member is accepted and wanted, but in a competitive group he is not appreciated and is seen, instead, as a rival. These effects may be more fully understood in the context of our discussion of group goals and personal evaluation in Chapter 31.

If a person is granted the right to exercise important leadership functions for a group, he must meet to some degree the group's expectations or he will lose his following. Hamblin (23) reports that influential persons who were not effective in helping the group during a time of crisis were soon replaced.

Effects of Different Distributions of Functions. In some groups all members are expected to take over as much responsibility for any functions as conditions will allow. At the other extreme, some groups may concentrate all functions in one person and punish any member who attempts to usurp any of them. What are the consequences of restricting the functions to a few offices in a group? What are the results of distributing them more widely? These are questions that have stimulated much debate, but few answers can be supported by indisputable facts. There are those who believe that greater efficiency results when all leadership functions are concentrated in a few roles—the officers. They maintain that "too many cooks spoil the broth." And there is much reasonableness in the argument that if everyone has a final say in running the group, chaos will result unless all want to say the same thing. On the other hand, it is argued that the concentration of authority in the hands of a few undermines the motivation of the rest, thus destroying enthusiasm, morale, and creativity and engendering conflicts and hostility between leaders and followers (34).

There is undoubtedly some justification for each position. Bavelas (Chap. 37) reports that when experimental groups are working on certain tasks, the concentration of leadership results in both more efficient group performance and lower morale. It should be noted, however, that in these experiments the groups did not exist long enough for any demoralizing effects to show up in reduced efficiency. Gilchrist *et al.* (17) have observed that a central person can even be a detriment to a group's accomplishments if he has too much work (information) to handle so that he cannot effectively help others. Research reported by Kahn and Katz (28) also indicates that the concentration of functions may have mixed results. They found, for example, that high producing groups in business and industry tend to have supervisors who take responsibility for planning the work, providing materials, and coordinating, but the supervisors of these productive groups also are more inclined to delegate responsibilities to others in the group and to encourage members to make decisions and to take initiative in many activities.

The same issue is often raised on more ideological or ethical grounds. Many writers have insisted that group procedures are more democratic if the functions of leadership are widely shared. Others have replied, however, that the essence of democracy is not the wide distribution of leadership functions, but rather the fact that groups are allowed to assign and reassign leadership functions without arbitrary dictation. We shall not engage here in this debate over the meaning of democracy. Important empirical findings are available, however, in the studies reported by White and Lippitt (Chap. 25), Preston and Heintz (47), Bovard (6), Coch and French (Chap. 26), and Levine and Butler (33). All of the leaders in these experiments were externally imposed upon the group, but even so those leaders who tended to distribute the functions of leadership more widely obtained group performances generally regarded as "better" in our society. When production was measured, it was higher. When interpersonal affect was measured, it was more friendly. And when cohesiveness was measured, it was stronger.

In order to clarify this issue further, it will be necessary to rephrase the question. Rather than ask, "How much concentration should there be?" we should ask, "What things result when functions are combined in certain ways under specified circumstances?" Then we shall almost certainly conclude that different degrees of concentration are required for the accomplishment of different purposes under different circumstances.

OVERVIEW OF RESEARCH REPORTED IN PART FIVE

It should be apparent from the preceding discussion that the problem of leadership cannot be sharply separated from many other problems of group functioning. All of the other sections in this volume contain materials relevant to the topic of leadership. In this section we present six papers that focus upon the twin tasks of describing leadership behavior and discovering the consequences of leadership.

The experimental study reported in Chapter 25 by White and Lippitt has now become a classic. It has added great impetus to the functional approach to leadership and has served to stimulate much of the research in this field. The leaders in this investigation were not peers of the group members but were adult leaders of youth groups. They were trained to be capable autocratic, democratic, or laissez faire leaders. The behavior of the leaders and of all the members was carefully observed and recorded in quantitative terms. The results show clearly that the different patterns of leadership style resulted in distinctive kinds of behavior among group members. Both group solidarity and group productivity differed markedly, and a characteristic emotional atmosphere developed in each group.

The field studies described by Coch and French in Chapter 26 were conducted in an industrial firm with the purpose of comparing the reactions of workers who had differing opportunities to participate in discussions about their work procedures. The authors observe that changes are better accepted and put into practice the more that members have a voice in determining changes to be introduced in their work. This research demonstrates that it is possible to introduce different styles of leadership in ongoing institutions and to determine the consequences of each style. Although the settings studied are quite different

from those of the laboratory experiments reported elsewhere in this section, the two sorts of settings yield consistent findings.

The situational factors that determine the form of leadership which will arise and be accepted in a group is considered in Chapter 27. Korten traces the forces leading a group or society from democratic to authoritarian forms of leadership and compares these with forces that lead the group in the opposite direction from an authoritarian to a democratic form. He proposes that an authoritarian form of leadership will be sought where group goals assume greater importance than do individual goals and where there are ambiguities obscuring the path to attaining these goals. A more democratic leadership will be sought where there are no ambiguities standing in the way of goal attainment and the attainment of group goals is not seen as a necessary prior event to the attainment of individual goals. His model provides a framework for further experimentation and theoretical development that has previously been lacking.

Fiedler presents in Chapter 28 the major results from an extensive series of carefully planned and integrated field and laboratory studies that cast light on the relations between the personality of leaders, their social position in the group, and group effectiveness. In all of these studies he administers a test to leaders designed to reflect how much they esteem their coworkers. This measure is interpreted by Fiedler to indicate the degree that the leader is considerate of others and desires approval from others or the degree that the leader gains satisfaction from successful performance of the task. Fiedler then demonstrates that the effectiveness of groups is contingent upon the appropriateness of the leader's style to the specific situation in which he operates and upon the degree to which that situation enables the leader to exert influence.

The last two chapters in this section are concerned with observations of interpersonal behavior among leaders and members. In Chapter 29, Carter, Haythorn, Shriver, and Lanzetta report an attempt to record the actual behavior of group members "in such a fashion as to allow definitive statements regarding the activities of one member relative to those of other members." Using a standardized scheme of observation, they noted the behavior of members in groups both with a designated leader and without. They found that certain kinds of behavior were more typical of leaders while other kinds were displayed more often by ordinary members, and the actions of designated leaders were not exactly the same as those of leaders who emerged from the group to take over leadership.

Finally, Bales and Strodtbeck present in Chapter 30 data relevant to the task of isolating and describing group functions in discussion groups. They have recorded in great detail the kinds of interactions that take place among the members of such groups using a standardized observation scheme that has been widely employed in investigations of interpersonal behavior. As a result of this work they are able to show that certain types of groups go through definite phases in the course of solving problems when there is no designated leader. These phases are defined in terms of certain group functions that are required for the group to reach a solution to its problem.

The reaction one derives from all this work is one of optimism and encouragement. Although leadership is a confusing and complicated concept, a beginning has clearly been made in isolating some of its major components. As our understanding of the nature of these phenomena is advanced, the practical problems of improving group life will be more readily solved. An excellent beginning has now been made toward settling ideological arguments about how leaders should behave. When the consequences of different leadership procedures can be regularly predicted, then those procedures may be chosen which best lead to preferred criteria of group performance. Finally, it is becoming evident that problems of leadership and group performance cannot be safely separated from problems of followership and effective membership. As our understanding of groups broadens, the mystery of leadership diminishes.

References

1. Bales, R., & Slater, P. Role differentiation in small decision-making groups. In T. Parsons, et al. *Family, socialization, and interaction process.* Glencoe, Ill.: Free Press, 1955.
2. Bass, B. *Leadership, psychology, and organizational behavior.* New York: Harper, 1960.
3. Barnard, C. I. *Functions of the executive.* Cambridge, Mass.: Harvard Univ. Press, 1938.
4. Berkowitz, L. Sharing leadership in small decision-making groups. *Journal of Abnormal and Social Psychology,* 1953, **48**, 231–238.
5. Bird, C. *Social psychology.* New York: Appleton-Century, 1940.
6. Bovard, E. Group structure and perception. *Journal of Abnormal and Social Psychology,* 1951, **46**, 398–405.
7. Cartwright, D. A field theoretical conception of power. In D. Cartwright (Ed.), *Studies in social power.* Ann Arbor, Mich.: Institute for Social Research, 1959.
8. Cattell, R. New concepts for measuring leadership in terms of group syntality. *Human Relations,* 1951, **4**, 161–184.
9. Crockett, W. Emergent leaders in small decision-making groups. *Journal of Abnormal and Social Psychology,* 1955, **51**, 378–383.
10. Dahl, R. The concept of power. *Behavioral Science,* 1957, **2**, 201–215.
11. Fleishmann, E., Harris, E., & Burtt, H. *Leadership and supervision in industry: An evaluation of a supervisory training program.* Columbus: Ohio State Bureau of Educational Research, 1955.
12. Fouriezos, N., Hutt, M., & Guetzkow, H. Measurement of self-oriented needs in discussion groups. *Journal of Abnormal and Social Psychology,* 1950, **45**, 682–689.
13. French, J. R. P. Jr., & Snyder, R. Leadership and interpersonal power. In D. Cartwright (Ed.), *Studies in social power.* Ann Arbor, Mich.: Institute for Social Research, 1959.
14. French, R. L. Morale and leadership. *Human factors in undersea warfare.* Washington, D. C.: National Research Council, 1949.
15. Georgopoulos, B., & Mann, F. *The community general hospital.* New York: Macmillan, 1962.
16. Gibb, C. The principles and traits of leadership. *Journal of Abnormal and Social Psychology,* 1947, **42**, 267–284.
17. Gilchrist, J., Shaw, M., & Walker, L. Some effects of unequal distribution of information in a wheel group structure. *Journal of Abnormal and Social Psychology,* 1954, **49**, 554–556.
18. Goodchilds, J., & Smith, E. The wit and his group. *Human Relations,* 1964, **17**, 23–32.

19. Gouldner, A. (Ed.), *Studies in leadership.* New York: Harper, 1950.
20. Greer, F. L. Leader indulgence and group performance. *Psychological Monographs,* 1961, **75** (12).
21. Grusky, O. A case for the theory of familial role differentiation in small groups. *Social Forces,* 1957, **35**, 209–217.
22. Halpin, A., & Winer, B. *The leadership behavior of the airplane commander.* Columbus: Ohio State Univ. Research Foundation, 1952.
23. Hamblin, R. Leadership and crises. *Sociometry,* 1958, **21**, 322–325.
24. Haythorn, W. The influence of individual group members on the behavior of co-workers and on the characteristics of groups. Unpublished doctoral dissertation, Univ. of Rochester, 1952.
25. Heinicke, C., & Bales, R. Developmental trends in the structure of small groups. *Sociometry,* 1953, **16**, 7–38.
26. Heyns, R. Effects of variation in leadership on participant behavior in discussion groups. Unpublished doctoral dissertation, Univ. of Michigan, 1958.
27. Israel, J. *Self-evaluation and rejection in groups.* Stockholm: Almquist, Wiksell, 1956.
28. Kahn, R., & Katz, D. Leadership practices in relation to productivity and morale. In D. Cartwright & A. Zander (Eds.), *Group dynamics research theory.* New York: Harper & Row, 1960.
29. Katz, D., & Kahn, R. *The social psychology of organizations.* New York: Wiley, 1966.
30. Kirscht, J., Lodahl, T., & Haire, M. Some factors in the selection of leaders by members of small groups. *Journal of Abnormal and Social Psychology,* 1959, **58**, 406–408.
31. Krech, D., & Crutchfield, R. *Theory and problems of social psychology.* New York: McGraw-Hill, 1948.
32. Lasswell, H., & Kaplan, A. *Power and society.* New Haven, Conn.: Yale Univ. Press, 1950.
33. Levine, J., & Butler, J. Lecture vs. group decision in changing behavior. *Journal of Applied Psychology,* 1952, **36**, 29–33.
34. Likert, R. *New patterns of management.* New York: McGraw-Hill, 1959.
35. Likert, R. An emerging theory of organization, leadership, and management. In L. Petrullo & B. Bass (Eds.), *Leadership and interpersonal behavior.* New York: Holt, Rinehart and Winston, 1961.
36. Lippitt, R. An experimental study of authoritarian and democratic group atmosphere. *Univ. of Iowa Studies in Child Welfare,* 1940, **16** (3), 43–195.
37. Lippitt, R. *Training in community relations.* New York: Harper, 1949.
38. Marak, G. E. The evaluation of leadership structures. *Sociometry,* 1964, **27**, 174–182.
39. McClelland, D. *The achieving society.* Princeton, N. J.: Van Nostrand, 1961.
40. McClintock, C. Group support and the behavior of leaders and nonleaders. *Journal of Abnormal and Social Psychology,* 1963, **67**, 105–113.
41. Misumi, J., & Tasaki, T. A study on the effectiveness of supervisory patterns in a Japanese hierarchical organization. *Japanese Psychological Research,* 1965, **7**, 151–162.
42. Mulder, M., & Sterding, A. Threat, attraction to group, and need for strong leadership. *Human Relations,* 1963, **16**, 317–334.
43. Parker, S. Leadership patterns in a psychiatric ward. *Human Relations,* 1958, **11**, 287–301.
44. Pelz, D. Influence: A key to effective leadership in the first line supervisor. *Personnel,* 1952, **3**, 3–11.
45. Pepinsky, P., Hemphill, H., & Shevitz, R. Attempts to lead, group productivity, and morale under conditions of acceptance and rejection. *Journal of Abnormal and Social Psychology,* 1958, **57**, 47–54.
46. Pepitone, E. A. Responsibility to the group and its effects on the performance of members. Unpublished doctoral dissertation, Univ. of Michigan, 1952.
47. Preston, M., & Heintz, R. Effects of participatory vs. supervisory leadership on group judgment. *Journal of Abnormal and Social Psychology,* 1949, **44**, 345–355.
48. Redl, F. Group emotion and leadership. *Psychiatry,* 1942, **5**, 573–596.
49. Russell, B. *Power.* London: Allen & Unwin, 1938.
50. Schrag, C. Leadership among prison inmates. *American Sociological Review,* 1954, **19**, 37–42.
51. Shartle, C. *Executive performance and leadership.* Englewood Cliffs, N. J.: Prentice-Hall, 1956.

52. Simon, H. A. *Models of man.* New York: Wiley, 1957.
53. Stogdill, R. Personal factors associated with leadership: A survey of the literature. *Journal of Psychology,* 1948, **25,** 35–71.
54. Stogdill, R. Leadership, membership, and organization. *Psychological Bulletin,* 1950, **47,** 1–14.
55. Tannenbaum, A., & Allport, F. H. Personality structure and group structure. *Journal of Abnormal and Social Psychology,* 1956, **53,** 272–280.
56. Theodorson, G. The relationship between leadership and popularity roles in small groups. *American Sociological Review,* 1957, **22,** 58–67.
57. Thibaut, J., & Kelley, H. *The social psychology of groups.* New York: Wiley, 1959.
58. Thomas, E. J. Effects of role interdependence and ego-strength on group functioning. Unpublished doctoral dissertation, Univ. of Michigan, 1956.
59. Thomas, E. J. Effects of facilitative role interdependence on group functioning. *Human Relations,* 1957, **10,** 347–366.
60. Verba, S. *Small groups and political behavior, a study of leadership.* Princeton, N. J.: Princeton Univ. Press, 1961.
61. Veroff, J. Development and validation of a projective measure of power motivation. *Journal of Abnormal and Social Psychology,* 1957, **54,** 1–8.

25

Leader Behavior and Member Reaction in Three "Social Climates"

RALPH WHITE AND RONALD LIPPITT

This investigation was carried out in two different parts: an exploratory experiment and a second, more extensive research. The primary aim of the first study was to develop techniques for creating and describing the "social atmosphere" of children's clubs and for quantitatively recording the effects of varied social atmospheres upon group life and individual behavior. Two degrees of control of group life, labeled "democratic" and "authoritarian," were used as the experimental variables. The second study had a number of purposes. The one most relevant to this report is to examine the effects upon individual and group behavior of three variations in social atmosphere, labeled "democratic," "authoritarian," and "laissez-faire." The actual meaning of the adjectives used to label these social climates is necessarily somewhat different from the meanings attributed to them in political and economic discussions. The accompanying tabulation describes briefly the chief characteristics of these three treatment variations.

In the first study (Experiment I), the same leader met with two clubs. One group was led in a democratic manner, the other in an autocratic style. Both groups had five members, ten years of age. The behavior of the leader and the members was recorded by observers. A fuller description of the experimental plan for this investigation may be found in Lippitt (1).

In the second study (Experiment II), four groups of ten-year-old boys were used. These were also five-member clubs which met after school to engage in hobby activities. The groups were roughly equated on patterns of interpersonal relationships, intellectual, physical, and socio-economic status, and personality characteristics. Four

Condensed from a fuller discussion contained in Chapters 3 and 5 of a book by the same authors, *Autocracy and Democracy*. New York: Harper, 1960. Reprinted by permission of the authors and the publishers.

Authoritarian	Democratic	Laissez-faire
1. All determination of policy by the leader	*1.* All policies a matter of group discussion and decision, encouraged and assisted by the leader	*1.* Complete freedom for group or individual decision, with a minimum of leader participation
2. Techniques and activity steps dictated by the authority, one at a time, so that future steps were always uncertain to a large degree	*2.* Activity perspective gained during discussion period. General steps to group goal sketched, and when technical advice was needed, the leader suggested two or more alternative procedures from which choice could be made	*2.* Various materials supplied by the leader, who made it clear that he would supply information when asked. He took no other part in work discussion
3. The leader usually dictated the particular work task and work companion of each member	*3.* The members were free to work with whomever they chose, and the division of tasks was left up to the group	*3.* Complete nonparticipation of the leader
4. The dominator tended to be "personal" in his praise and criticism of the work of each member; remained aloof from active group participation except when demonstrating	*4.* The leader was "objective" or "fact-minded" in his praise and criticism, and tried to be a regular group member in spirit without doing too much of the work	*4.* Infrequent spontaneous comments on member activities unless questioned, and no attempt to appraise or regulate the course of events

adult leaders were trained to proficiency in the three leadership treatments. The leaders were shifted from club to club every six weeks, each one changing his leadership style at the time of this transition. Thus, each club experienced each of the leadership styles under different leaders. All clubs met in the same place and did the same activities with similar materials. The behavior of the leaders and the reactions of the boys were observed during every meeting. The members and their parents were also interviewed concerning their feelings about the club in the case of the boys and the nature of parent-child relations in the case of the home visits. A more complete description of the experimental plan for the second study may be found in Lippitt and White (2).

In the following pages we shall first describe in some detail the nature of the leadership behavior typically used in each of the three leader treatments. The second part of this report describes the behavior of the members when under the direction of a leader using each of the variations.

LEADER'S BEHAVIOR

To some extent, the observation of what the leaders actually did was a process of discovery, both for the observer and for the leaders themselves. As we shall see, some of the statistically significant differences in leaders' behavior could not have been directly deduced from our central definitions, although they tend to be consistent with these role definitions. The adult who was faced with the constantly changing problems of leading a group of children found himself doing things which he could never have anticipated he would do. And the unanticipated things which the leader with the predetermined autocratic philosophy did were quite different from the things which he did in the same situations when he changed to the democratic role. The data described the different types of leader-behavior which resulted from the attempts at consistent application of the varying philosophies of leadership represented by the definitions of autocracy, democracy, and laissez-faire.

Figure 1 presents a summary graph of the

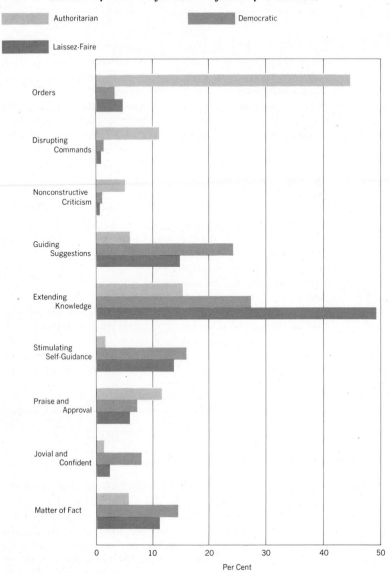

FIGURE 1. Comparison of behavior of average authoritarian, democratic, and laissez-faire leader.

leader behavior in terms of the percentage of total behavior in each category. These percentages are based upon the grand total of behavior in a given style of leadership over six meetings. All differences concerning leadership behavior which are discussed are statistically significant at the 5% level of confidence or better.

GIVING ORDERS

Statistically, the chief single characteristic of our autocratic leader role, as distinguished from both democracy and laissez-faire, is the giving of orders. Forty-five per cent of the verbal behavior of the autocrats, in contrast to 3% in democracy and 4% in laissez-faire, consisted of this simplest form of the imposition of one human will upon another. Many of these were direct orders or statements in the imperative form:

"Get your work aprons on." [1]
"All right, put your brush away."

[1] The illustrations used throughout this chapter are sample episodes or units of descriptions taken from the continuous research records of the group process.

"Each of you turn yours over and try on the back."

And many were indirect orders, not in the imperative form, but recognizable as autocratic if given in certain contexts and in certain tones of voice:

"Now we need some plaster."

"That should be about two-thirds full."

"Today we've got to paint and letter the sign."

"Before we start there's something we have to do. That's to make work aprons."

Such orders clearly correspond to the part of our strict experimental definition of autocratic leadership which calls for "high goal and means control."

DISRUPTING COMMANDS

A more ambiguous criterion of means and end control is the giving of "disrupting commands"—commands which cut across an expressed wish or ongoing activity of a member of the group, and substitute for it some wish of the leader. Such commands represented 11% of the verbal behavior of our autocratic leaders, as contrasted to 1% or less for our democratic and laissez-faire leaders. For example:

"I want to saw."

"No, Bill, you and Hamil make another leg." Mr. Bohlen says he wants "two fellows." Fred volunteers, "Let Reilly and me do it." But Mr. Bohlen appoints two others: "I'm going to let Sam and Leonard do this." Mr. Bohlen consistently refuses to let Fred do what he wants to do—painting on the sign.

The data show that the laissez-faire leaders were consistent in restraining themselves from initiating goals and means.

NON-OBJECTIVE CRITICISM AND PRAISE

A third type of behavior which was more characteristic of our autocratic leaders was "non-objective criticism"—criticism which was adverse and personal in character and which did not point objectively toward improvement by suggesting a reason for failure or a way of doing the thing better. Such criticism constituted 5% of the leaders' behavior in our auto-

cratic atmospheres and 1% in the democratic and laissez-faire atmospheres. For example:

"You're not making a sack, you're making an apron."

"No, you can't make it like that. That isn't a good job at all."

"Who was it left the tool box on the floor again?"

Praise was also found more often in the autocrats' behavior (11%) than in that of the democratic (7%) or laissez-faire (5%) leaders. For example:

Fred is doing a nice job of lettering, and Mr. Bohlen compliments him on it—the second compliment he has given him today. "That's the best side view there. But I think I want a front view."

(In democracy) Bill to Mr. Rankin: "Eddie really did a swell job on that, didn't he? I couldn't do as good a job as that."

Mr. Rankin: "Yeah, it's swell."

Different kinds of praise in different contexts can obviously (like different kinds of criticism) have widely different psychological meanings. Yet it is probably significant, from more than one standpoint, that *both* praise and criticism were especially characteristic of our autocratic leaders. From our present standpoint, however, the most interesting implication of the large amount of both praise and criticism is that both suggest an emphasis on *personal evaluation from the leader's standpoint.* Both suggest an emphasis on a status-hierarchy, and both suggest that the leader is setting himself up as chief judge of the status and achievement of the members of the group.

GUIDING SUGGESTIONS

We come now to the forms of leader-behavior that were more characteristic of democratic or of laissez-faire leadership than of autocratic. For example, as a direct counterpart of the order-giving which was characteristic of the autocratic style, we find "guiding suggestions" to be one of the two most frequent forms of verbal behavior on the part of democratic leaders. It represents 24% of the democratic leaders' behavior, as compared with 6% of the autocrats' behavior. The line between "guiding suggestions" and the indirect type of order-giving is, of course, somewhat difficult to draw. However, the reliability of making this distinction in the coding of the conversation was satisfactory. The way in which we defined "guiding suggestions" can be seen from the following examples, which were classified in this way:

> "Did you ever try going the other way—with the grain?"
>
> "That's a knife-sharpener so you can have sharp knives to carve wood with."
>
> Bill holds up his model for Mr. Rankin to see. "That's pretty weak there." Mr. Rankin: "If you don't get it any thinner I think it will be all right."
>
> Mr. Rankin sits down beside Van as he works. "That's good, Van, because if you leave as big a piece as that you can try again."

The distinguishing characteristic in each of these examples is that a given course of action is implicitly or explicitly related to one of the boy's *own* purposes. Very similar in psychological meaning is the *clarifying of alternatives*, between which the boys themselves are free to choose (which was included in this same category):

> "Motion carried. Now the question is, who wants to be the G-man?" (All speak.) "Should we choose from everybody that wants to be, or just those that haven't had a chance yet?"

And similar, too, is the giving of suggestions by example rather than by precept:

> Reilly discovers that Mr. Rankin is making papier-mâché, and stops throwing to join him. He tears up paper too, and so does Fred. Leonard stops throwing. The group is gathered around Mr. Rankin and is listening to him and paying attention.
>
> Bill: "Let's get ready to go home."
>
> Mr. Rankin (picking up a broom): "We don't have much cleaning up to do today."

It should be especially noticed that a very active readiness to give guiding suggestions at precisely those moments when they are appropriate and appreciated, and to point out the operating procedure which lies behind the efficient action, was in practice the chief single difference between the democratic and laissez-faire leaders. In laissez-faire such suggestions made up only 14% of the leader's verbal behavior, as compared with 24% in democracy and 6% in autocracy.

In other words, democracy (as distinguished from laissez-faire) did not imply freedom alone, i.e., a relatively passive "regard" for the child's welfare, in the sense that the child's desires were not needlessly thwarted. If either individual welfare or group achievement is to be fully attained, the democratic leader took the viewpoint that it is necessary to have also a very *active* respect for those individual desires in the sense of a constant active thinking about how they can best be realized. Only by such full participation in the life of the group can the leader really lead. For instance, the following are examples in which a boy wanted guidance and did not get it. In some situations exactly the same behavior by the leader—throwing back the question the boy asked—would be a constructive device for stimulating self-guidance. In these situations, however, it seemed to be merely a result of insensitivity to the boy's legitimate needs for goal or means suggestions:

> Reilly: "Where can we put this up?"
>
> Mr. Rankin: "Where would you like to put it up?"
>
> Leonard: "How do you cut it?"
>
> Mr. Rankin: "What do you think? Cut it in the right shape. . . ."

But, at the other extreme, the democratic leader had to avoid overcomplicated suggestions, such as the following, both of which are double-barreled and at least slightly confusing:

> "Who wants to help who to get things finished up?"
>
> "Have you been thinking about a G-man Club? Do you want a meeting now, fellows?"

The effective use of guiding suggestions seems to depend on timing. The democratic leader had to have a keen sense of awareness of the shifting momentary needs and interests of the boys so that he could make his suggestions at just the moments when they fitted into those interests.

GIVING INFORMATION

Another major activity of the democratic leader was simply giving information, or extending the knowledge of the members of his group. This constituted 27% of the democratic leaders' behavior, and 15% of the autocratic leaders'. (In laissez-faire it was 49%, which is natural in view of the fact that the laissez-faire leaders' role was explicitly confined very largely to the giving of technical information when asked for it.) Actually the amount of technical information given by the three leader types was not significantly different, even though the proportion was so much greater in laissez-faire. Here are some typical examples of information-giving:

Finn (holding up orangewood stick): "What's this for?"

Mr. Rankin: "That's an orangewood stick, and the flat end is for smoothing down this way." (Demonstrates.) "This is more curved here, and you can get a smoother tip of soap because it's narrower than this."

There is a dispute between the two groups about the ages of the knives. . . . Reilly, Sam and Fred listen to Mr. Rowe talk about the ages of the knives. They are all very much interested.

(In laissez-faire) Finn (very plaintively): "Why can't we have a crime?"

Mr. Davis: "I could have a crime for you next week if you wanted me to."

One meaning of information-giving, as compared with either orders or guiding suggestions, is that there is almost no chance of its being a form of social influence or pressure. The information is simply there. The boy can take it or leave it, use it or not use it, depending on his needs at the moment.

STIMULATING SELF-DIRECTION

Less frequent numerically is a group of leader-behaviors which we have called "stimulating self-direction." This type of behavior was fairly frequent in democracy and almost nonexistent in autocracy; the percentages were, respectively, 16 and 1.2. Although this made up 13% of the behavior of the laissez-faire leaders, this only represented an average of 30 such acts per meeting, as compared with 59 by democratic leaders. The meaning also tended to be quite different. In laissez-faire this type of leadership act tended to be a throwing back of responsibility on the individual member. In the democratic style it was more frequently a teaching of the total group to learn to depend on itself as a group.

One way of stimulating democratic self-direction in setting new goals and choosing means is to inculcate the democratic procedure directly: group decision, majority vote, free discussion with an opportunity for every interested person to have his say, secret ballot when appropriate, delegation of special tasks to committees, minority acceptance of majority decisions, etc. For example:

Finn: "Guess I'll change the name of our club."

Bill: "No, it's still the Law and Order Patrol."

Mr. Rankin: "If the group wants to change the name, they can—if a majority wants."

Bill: "Eddie should be captain and Van should be a lieutenant-assistant."

Van: "Hey, that's lower than I am now, and I got a high score!"

Mr. Rankin: "In an army, the general decides the promotions; but here, even if it is organized like an army, it seems to me the group ought to decide who should get the promotion."

Bill: "Now you stay out of it and we three will vote." Mr. Rankin steps in to confer with Bill about taking a vote. He gives him a formal wording. "All in favor say aye, opposed, no," etc. (Bill is especially keen on formality and "having things regular.")

Finn votes for adjournment, and the motion passes. Bill starts to ignore the vote and keep on with the discussion. Mr. Rankin: "All right we don't have any meeting now if the majority votes to adjourn."

It will be noticed that in some of the above examples the role of the democratic adult leader is chiefly one of supporting or bringing to clear expression the feeling of the majority. He is a catalyst, releasing energies that already exist in the group. This was done formally by insisting on a majority when dispute had arisen and backing up the majority with his own prestige. It was also done informally by simply listening to and drawing out the less articulate or less vociferous members of the group. It is also sometimes necessary to support a minority, especially if it is opposed by an even smaller minority. This occurred, for instance, when Finn and Hamil were refusing to accept the arbitrary leadership of Bill. The other two members did not take part in this contest so that it was actually a conflict of two against one.

Bill: "It's time for our meeting. The second half of our meeting will come to order. Come on boys."

Hamil: "That's what you think." He and Finn go just outside the burlap curtain surrounding the enclosure, but lift the curtain; it is cooler outside because the moving-picture lights make the enclosure itself very warm.

Finn: "We'll just listen from out here." Bill doesn't get the response he wants and pouts while he takes up his whittling again.

Mr. Rankin: "I shouldn't think a good chairman would whittle while the meeting was going on."

Bill: "Well, I can't get any of the guys to come." Mr. Rankin goes over to the other two and holds up the curtain. Eddie and Van go too so that four of the five boys are gathered at the edge of the enclosure.

Mr. Rankin: "The meeting is going on over here." (A satisfactory meeting is held, with Bill fully participating, as well as Hamil and Finn.)

The commonest form of stimulating self-direction, however, was simply to follow up a particular boy's ideas, encouraging him to elaborate them and think them through:

Mr. Rowe: "Let's all sit down and talk it over. Sam suggested glass painting. How does it go, Sam?"

Sam: "Get a picture under a piece of glass."

Mr. Rowe: "How would it be if I got a big piece of glass and a big painting? Does the paint come in tubes?"

Sam: "The stuff in bottles is better."

Mr. Rowe: "Would everybody like to do it?"

Reilly: "I'd like to do it."

Lyman: "I think I'd like to do it."

Van (in a doubtful tone): "I was thinking of a canoe [for soap carving]."

Mr. Rankin: "I think a canoe is probably the best idea. Can you see there [picture of canoe model] how almost straight it is for a distance in the middle?"

"JOVIAL" AND "CONFIDING" BEHAVIOR

The last type of conversation that was measured and that significantly distinguished the democratic club atmosphere from the other two is one which, for the want of a better term, has been characterized by the two terms "jovial" and "confiding." It represents the purely social aspect of the leader's behavior and was far more characteristic of our democratic situation than of either autocracy or laissez-faire (8% as compared with less than 1% in autocracy and in laissez-faire). For example:

Fred talks and laughs with Mr. Rowe—far different from his behavior with Mr. Bohlen.

There is a very nice relationship between Mr. Rowe and the group. . . . He seems to be having the most fun of all. . . .

(The acute conflict between Fred and Mr. Bohlen is still fresh in everybody's mind, and on this day Fred is absent. The following topic of conversation is therefore a natural one.) Mr. Rowe: "Does Fred get into much trouble with the teacher?"

Sam says, "I'll say!" and Lyman adds, "He got sent out of the room two times. He always does something."

This is the clearest instance of a type of behavior which was not consciously planned, but which developed as sort of a by-product of the democratic leader's total relationship to his group, usually by the initiative of group members. It has nothing directly to do with freedom or lack of freedom, but it obviously does have something to do with openness of communication which develops as a result of the relationship created by the other types of leadership behavior described above.

This completes our list of the types of conversation which were statistically analyzed and which clearly differentiated one or more of the three atmospheres. A number of incidental observations can be added, however, which were not statistically analyzed, but which help to round out the picture.

DEMOCRATIC CRITICISM AND PRAISE

Although it did not occur frequently enough for statistical comparison, the observer noted that the democratic leaders tended to use praise and criticism in a different way from the autocratic leaders. The democratic leaders recognized that "training in procedures" seemed to mean (a) helping individuals to learn the criteria and methods for evaluating their own work without dependence on the adult as well as (b) helping the group to learn the methods of mutual support and cooperative operation as a group. This first type of training we find exemplified in such illustrations as:

Mr. Rankin: "That's good,——, because if you leave as big a piece [of soap during soap-carving period] as that you can try again [if the first try fails]."

Leader: "I think that's going to be pretty wobbly [piece of box furniture]. Can you guess why I think so?"

Boy: "Maybe because there are so many bent nails and none that go through."

By this type of praise and criticism, the democratic leaders attempted to extend their assigned function of teaching a group procedure for setting goals and means to teaching of criteria and methods for *evaluating* goals and means. This seemed to be a natural part of the same leadership role.

EQUALITARIAN BEHAVIOR

It may be worth while also to cull a number of illustrations not falling under any one topic that has already been discussed, but illustrating again, in a variety of ways, some additional implications of respect for own member's goals and means which seem to flow from the leadership patterns that were defined for the leaders. There are, for instance, some egotistical uses of the pronoun "I" by autocratic leaders which are clearly lacking in that sort of respect:

"I'm going to pick out the best one when you get done."

"Guess you'll have to put some more powder in that. I don't like it yet."

By contrast, the democratic leaders often showed equalitarian or even self-effacing behavior, and an absence of concern about their status and dignity. They took off their coats; they sat or squatted instead of standing; they worked just as the boys did and showed that they were enjoying the work just as the boys did. Other illustrations:

Mr. Rowe subordinates himself to the newly elected boy-leader. "What should I do for cleanup, Sam?"

Mr. Rankin, on the first day of democracy in the Law and Order Patrol (after a period of laissez-faire), finds Bill in a position of temporarily revived leadership. He does not challenge this leadership, but helps Bill when he can do so without antagonizing the others.

Bill is administering a test which he has carefully made up on crime-detection agencies in the community, safety rules, etc. Mr. Rankin asks: "Are you testing me too?"

Bill: "No."

Mr. Rankin (with a smile): "I'd probably get the worst grade."

Observer writes: "Another characteristic of the democratic behavior of Rankin is his emotional expressions with the boys—'Oh,' 'Aha'—and his going thoughtfully into everything the children think they want to do."

On the other hand, the democratic leaders sometimes did not hesitate to accept delegated authority when it was unequivocally handed to them. Mr. Rankin suggests a committee to make up the crime, but the group wants to leave it to him this next time. He agrees.

In other words, the democratic leader's lack of concern about his own dignity was not a blind or compulsive self-effacement; it was a sensitive awareness of and respect for the status needs (own social goals) of the boys in the group as well as of the various other social needs that they might have in this situation.

ROLE-CHANGES BY THE SAME PERSON

Did the four leaders in this experiment actually change their behavior to be consistent with the leadership policy they were supposed to be representing, or did they primarily "keep on being like themselves" in each of the three clubs they led? The data clearly reveal that each leader was more like the others in the same role than he was like himself from one role to another. The interviews with each boy, in which the boy compared his leaders, also indicate that the boys were actually reacting to these behavioral differences rather than to other, unchanging aspects of the leaders' personalities. Certainly there must have been a core of enduring characteristics which each individual leader took with him from one club to the other. These characteristics probably exerted some influence on the perceptions and reactions of the club members, but these were evidently minor or irrelevant as far as the leader effect on the club life was concerned in the dimensions we have studied.

SUMMARY OF LEADER BEHAVIOR

We have reviewed the statistical analysis of leader behavior, with illustrations of leader behavior taken from the club records. It is clear that the leaders did behave differently in carrying out their three types of role-assignment. These differences seem to represent consistent behavioral definitions of the three types of leadership policy which we want to compare.

MAJOR DIFFERENCES IN BOYS' BEHAVIOR

The glimpses given above may have conveyed some of the "feel" of the atmosphere resulting from the three types of leadership. We will now present the results of the experiments more fully and systematically, in terms of the chief statistical differences between the boys' behavior under autocratic, democratic, and laissez-faire types of leadership. Summary graphs will be found at the end of the chapter. The findings can be grouped under six major generalizations, which are discussed in the remainder of this chapter.

LAISSEZ-FAIRE WAS NOT THE SAME AS DEMOCRACY

Laissez-faire was less organized, less efficient, and definitely less satisfying than democracy to the boys themselves. Since there is a general tendency to attribute to democracy certain results which are actually results of laissez-faire, it is necessary to make this distinction very clearly before going on to any further thinking about differences between democracy and autocracy. The boys' behavior in laissez-faire differed from their behavior in democracy in the following ways:

1. *Less work was done, and poorer work.* In democracy, the time periods during which there was general absorption in constructive activity or psychological involvement in the work situation, represented 50% of the total time; in laissez-faire, 33%. In democracy, the time periods of general out-and-out loafing constituted 0.2% of the total time; in laissez-faire, 5%. And in *quality* of work accomplished, the difference was considerably greater than these figures indicate. The lack of active guiding suggestions in laissez-faire often resulted in disorganization and in failure and setbacks in work, which were discouraging and exasperating. Some outright aggression can be directly attributed to such work failures, as well as much loss of interest in the job that was being done. For instance:

> Eddie and Bill have mixed the plaster-of-Paris before getting the sand and making a

print. Mr. Davis doesn't step in to tell them it will soon get hard. Van tries the plaster-of-Paris and finds it quite stiff. Eddie, Bill, and Van finish a handprint and go to pour the plaster-of-Paris, but find it has hardened in the can. Bill pounds at it. Eddie stamps in the sand with his shoe, spoiling the print they had prepared. Finn and Hamil finish some new guns. Everybody is now milling around idly except Bill, who keeps on trying to get the hard plaster-of-Paris out of the can. Horseplay is about to begin.

> Fred breaks his cast, is discouraged, goes on and tears up the whole thing. (Later in the same hour, he was the leader in destroying the work of the "Monday gang.")

> Fred watches, sitting on a stool he made. A leg falls off. He breaks up the rest of it.

2. *They played more.* Play-minded conversation with other boys was more than 2.5 times as frequent in laissez-faire (33 as compared with 13 in democracy; significant at the 1% level). Pure silliness was included in this category. For instance:

> Leonard (hearing the term "orange sticks"): "Orange sticks—pick up sticks."
> Ray: "Hooray, hooray—I-O-W-A!"

DEMOCRACY CAN BE EFFICIENT

Since arguments for autocracy often take the form of claiming that democracy is not efficient enough to accomplish a certain end (such as winning a war, reducing production costs, or educating a child in necessary basic skills), it is of interest to consider the degree of efficiency of the democratic groups in our experiments. Did these groups achieve the ends the boys themselves wanted to achieve?

On the whole, they did. The question is not a simple one, since the boys did not want work achievement to the exclusion of other goals. (And in this respect, of course, the situation was also not comparable with the many situations in which society demands that a certain end be accomplished by methods that are inherently distasteful.) Our clubs were recreational clubs. They were "to have fun," and the boys came to them expecting to have fun through sociability, and probably through occasional good-natured horseplay, as well as through carpentry, painting, and organized crime-games. A respect for the boys' own legitimate goals would perhaps necessitate evaluating "efficiency" as much in terms of the achievement of these social goals as in terms of the achievement of work goals. And certainly from this combined standpoint democracy was decidedly more "efficient" than either autocracy or laissez-faire, since it achieved simultaneously both goals, while autocracy, in the main, achieved only work goals, and laissez-faire achieved (if anything) only social goals. But even from the narrow standpoint of work goals alone, the evidence suggests that in our situation the democratic groups were about *as* efficient as the autocratic ones.

This conclusion is based upon an over-all impression of the observers and experimenters. It is also based on a balancing of certain factors of efficiency which appeared to be more prominent in autocracy and others which appeared to be more prominent in democracy. On the one hand, there was a large quantity of work done in autocracy—or at least, in those autocratic groups in which the reaction to autocracy was a submissive one. In such groups the time periods of general absorption in work constituted 74% of the total time, as compared with 50% in democracy, and 52% in the one instance (in the second experiment) of an aggressive group reaction to autocracy. On the other hand, the amount of genuine interest in work was unquestionably higher in democracy. This was shown by a somewhat larger amount of "work-minded" conversation in democracy (63 such remarks per child as compared with 53 in the aggressive reaction to autocracy and 52 in the submissive reaction). This difference is not significant at the 1% level, but it does strongly suggest that work-mindedness was at least *as* great in democracy as in autocracy. Some illustrations of "work-minded" remarks:

"Let's see, who's got the saw?"

"I'm going to get a chisel to chisel that out with."

"How come some of these pieces are bigger than others?"

"Because they belong to the end of the wing out here."

"I guess all these pieces go together."

"Well this is supposed to stand up straight."

More significantly, the difference in amount of genuine, spontaneous work interest was shown by the difference in the boys' behavior *when the adult leader left the room.* Typically, the boys in democracy kept right on working while their leader was present or not, while in autocracy when the leader left, the boys stopped working as if glad to be relieved of a task which they "had" to do. In democracy there was a very slight drop in proportion of general work involvement during the leader-out periods—from 50% to 46%. On the other hand, in the one group which reacted aggressively to autocratic leadership, the drop in work involvement was from 52% to 16%, and in the three groups reacting submissively it was from 74% to 29%.

There was, finally, an impression on the part of the experimenters that both work and play showed a higher level of *originality* or creative thinking in the democracies than under either of the other types of leadership. There was a larger amount of creative thinking about the work in progress than in autocracy, and it was more sustained and practical than in laissez-faire.

AUTOCRACY CAN CREATE MUCH HOSTILITY AND AGGRESSION, INCLUDING AGGRESSION AGAINST SCAPEGOATS

The word "can" is important here, because this reaction did not always occur. It occurred to a very marked degree in Experiment I, and to some degree in one of the four groups that took part in Experiment II; but the other three groups in Experiment II showed, instead, a "submissive" reaction in which there was significantly *less* overt aggression than in democracy.

The clearest evidence comes from Experiment I. For example:

1. "Dominating ascendance" occurred 392 times in the autocratic group and only 81 times in the democratic group. The category "ascendance" showed no significant difference between the groups (63% of all child-to-child behavior in autocracy, and almost as much—57%—in democracy). But the reason for this apparent similarity was that the term "ascendance" was so broad as to be somewhat meaningless psychologically. When three kinds of ascendance were distinguished, "dominating," "objective," and "friendly" ascendance, it was found that dominating ascendance was highly characteristic of the autocratic group, while objective and friendly ascendance were characteristic of the democratic group. Some illustrations of dominating ascendance follow.

"Shut up."

Two children look in, and Sarah and Jack repulse them with comments of "not wanted."

"You put them away; you dumped them."

"Give me some of that paint." (Remarks of this sort are classified as dominating or objective, depending upon context and upon tone of voice. In this case it was classed as dominating.)

"Get a pan of water, Jack."

"Why don't you get it yourself?"

Friendly ascendance, on the other hand, occurred 24 times in the autocratic group and 230 times in the democratic group:

> "Let's do coloring."
> "Carry the bottles over there."
> "You've got to get all the cracks filled in."
> "Better fill in your side there."

2. Definite hostility occurred 186 times in the autocratic group and only 6 times in the democratic group. It represented 18% of all the recorded social interactions in the autocratic group, and less than 1% of all the interactions in the democratic group. (This category is included in the larger category of "dominating ascendance.") Some illustrations:

> "You guys haven't got nothing done yet."
> "Hey, you, don't throw water on my hair."
> "Look out, Tom, quit throwing things."
> "Don't start crabbing. I wouldn't talk too much yourself."
> "Oh God, Tom, don't you know anything?"

3. Aggressive demands for attention occurred 39 times in the autocratic group and 3 times in the democratic group. For example:

> Joe (in a loud voice): "I guess this is a mighty fine job I'm doing!"
> Tom: "I'm a lot smarter than you are. Boy-oh-boy, can I ever brag."
> Harry: "I'll say you can."
> Joe: "Sure, I've got three radios; I ought to know."
> All the others: "You have not!"
> Joe: "Oh yes I have."

4. Destruction of own property was conspicuous at the end of the meeting of the autocratic group, and did not occur at all in the democratic group:

> Peculiar actions begin after the leader (in the autocratic group) announces that there will be

no more meetings. The leader asks Harry and Jack to put more paper on the floor to work on. They put it down and then run and jump on it time and again in a wild manner. The masks are divided out as had been decided by the voting, and Jack immediately begins to throw his around violently, pretending to jump on it. He throws it down again and again, laughing. Ray wants to know if it won't break, then starts to throw his down too. Later Jack and Harry chase each other around the room wildly with streamers of toweling.

5. Scapegoat behavior was conspicuous in the autocratic group, and scarcely occurred at all in the democratic group. "Scapegoat behavior" is here defined as the concentration or polarization of group aggression against a single "innocent" object, i.e., a person or group which does not actually threaten or frustrate the group to an extent comparable with the aggression that occurs. Presumably in this case the autocratic leader was the source of most of the frustration in the autocratic group, yet only a small part of the resulting aggression was directed against him; most of it was directed by the club members against each other. It could therefore be called "displaced aggression." When this displaced aggression is concentrated against a single person, as occurred twice during the course of the meetings of the autocratic group in Experiment I, it can be called "scapegoat behavior."

AUTOCRACY CAN CREATE DISCONTENT THAT DOES NOT APPEAR ON THE SURFACE

Less dramatic but more fundamental than the question of aggression is the question of total need satisfaction. Under which major type of leadership is there likely to be more satisfaction of the boys' own needs, and why?

The answer is far from simple. There is no reason to think that democracy is necessarily superior from the standpoint of immediate personal satisfaction. It is a well-established fact that autocracy is often satisfying to some of the needs—the regressive needs, perhaps—of the ruled as well as the rulers. There can be satisfactions in passivity, satisfactions in not having to think, satisfactions in identifying (on an irreal level) with a strong, dominating leader image. On the other hand, it is also obvious, and needs no proof, that autocracy is always frustrating insofar as it imposes barriers to the satisfaction of individual needs. The real problem, then, is to pin down and describe scientifically the specific factors that determine whether, in a given case, the regressive need satisfactions or the frustrations will predominate. Some of the evidence bearing on this point has already been presented. The aggression shown in some of the autocratic groups points to probable frustration—if the frustration-aggression hypothesis has any weight. Also, the lack of spontaneous work interest in autocracy is a relevant fact. If the boys stopped work when the autocrat left the room, it was an indication that they had not been particularly enjoying it when he was in the room. It meant that the work has become merely a task, rather than something to be done with spontaneous zest and enjoyment. In this section, we shall present additional evidence, and in doing so we shall focus on an aspect of the matter which has not hitherto been emphasized: the fact that much of the discontent which existed was not immediately obvious.

The deceptiveness of autocracy in this respect is a fact that needs more emphasis than it has usually received. For example, out of our six autocratic setups (one in Experiment I, and five in Experiment II), five were in some degree deceptive, insofar as the discontent which existed did not show itself to any appreciable extent in protests to the autocrat himself. The evidence that latent discontent did exist in at least some of the other five autocratic situations can be summarized as follows:

1. Four boys actually dropped out, and all of them did so during those autocratic club periods in which overt rebellion did not occur.

2. Of 20 boys who made direct comparisons between their autocratic and democratic leaders, 19 preferred the democratic leader. These comparisons were, of course, made in private interviews with a third person who was not identified in any way with the leader who was being explicitly or implicitly criticized. It was also noticeable that most of the criticisms that did occur were mild and qualified. Nevertheless, when forced to make a choice, their vote was almost unanimous.

3. Discontent in autocracy was occasionally expressed even during the meetings themselves. In Experiment II, the average number of discontented remarks to other boys was 4.4 per meeting in autocracy (aggressive reaction), 2.1 in autocracy (submissive reaction), 3.1 in laissez-faire, and only 0.8 in democracy.

The difference between democracy and the submissive reaction to autocracy is significant at the 1% level. Similar, but not as significant statistically, is the difference in number of expressions of discontent directly to the adult leader. In autocracy (aggressive reaction) these averaged 11.1 per meeting; in autocracy (submissive reaction) the average was 2.0; it was 1.5 in laissez-faire and again only 0.8 in democracy. In this case, the difference between democracy and the submissive reaction to autocracy is significant at only the 10% level.

4. "Release" behavior on the day of transition to a freer atmosphere suggested the presence of previous frustration. There were three occasions when a group which had shown the submissive reaction to autocracy came out of this somewhat repressive atmosphere into the freer atmosphere of democracy or laissez-faire. In two of these cases, the first day of freedom was marked by an especially large amount of aggressive behavior (much of it, of course, playful in character). The first explanation that suggests itself is that on these days the boys were "blowing off steam"; discontent in autocracy had led to bottled-up tension, and when the lid was off, the tension discharged itself in a more or less explosive way. Actually, the explanation is probably somewhat more complex than this. On the first day of permissive leadership, the boys apparently still had the status needs and self-assertive impulses which were frustrated by autocracy, but they no longer felt any great need to inhibit these impulses. They were in the same general situation so that they were reminded of their former frustration, and yet their new freedom contrasted with the old restraint in such a way as to make itself prominent in the psychological field, as if each boy had said to himself, "Aha! *Now* I can do what I've been wanting to do in this club!" On later days the thrill of new-found freedom apparently wore off, and, in addition, the spontaneous interest in work which tended to develop in democracy was stronger on later days than it was at first.

THERE WAS MORE DEPENDENCE AND LESS INDIVIDUALITY IN AUTOCRACY

1. In autocracy, more of the boys' behavior was classified as "submissive" or "dependent." In Experiment I, the number of "submissive" actions toward the adult leader was 256 in autocracy and 134 in democracy. In Experi-

ment II, the number of "dependent" remarks to the leader by each boy averaged 14 in the aggressive reaction to autocracy, 16 in the submissive reaction, 4 in laissez-faire, and 6 in democracy. The difference between democracy and either type of autocracy is significant at the 1% level. Some illustrations:

"Is this O.K.?"

Bill starts to hold up his hand for advice. "Mr. Rowe, shall I paint the bottom of this or not?"

2. Conversation in autocracy was less varied—more confined to the immediate club situation. In Experiment II, the amount of "out-of-field" conversation was significantly less in the submissive reaction to autocracy than in any of the other three group atmospheres. The figures: democracy 14, laissez-faire 13, aggressive reaction to autocracy 12, and submissive reaction 5. The difference between the last figure and any of the other three is significant at the 1% level. Some illustrations of what was called "out-of-field" conversation:

Bill: "Some day I'm going to get me a job at the glass works."

Van: "I wish I could get a job."

Bill: "You should get out and get a job in the newspaper and then work yourself up. That's what I did." (He sells papers on the corner.) "And maybe someday you'll be able to get a good job."

Big conversation about pussy willows; then about places where the boys had traveled.

Leonard: "I saw your girl's picture in the paper, in the Press Citizen. She's fat, boy."

Reilly: "She's not fat, boy. You probably didn't see her."

Leonard: "She is fat. She's not slender."

No figures are available for Experiment I, but the impression of the experimenter is that the same difference held good there also.

3. In the submissive reaction to autocracy there was an absolute (though not a relative) reduction in individual differences in the various behavior categories. The essential fact here is that the total volume of conversation was significantly lowered in the submissive reaction to autocracy, even though the adult did not tell the boys to "keep still" or directly discourage sociability in any way. The mean total amount of recorded child-to-child conversation was 298 in laissez-faire, 220 in democracy, 200 in the aggressive reaction to autocracy,

and, in the submissive reaction to autocracy, only 126. The difference between this and the figure for democracy is significant at the 1% level. In other words, there was a sort of general subduedness in the atmosphere, the animal spirits of the boys were damped down, and they kept rather soberly at work. With this reduction in total amount, the range of individual differences in amount of "aggressiveness," or "demands for attention," was correspondingly reduced. Whether this absolute reduction in individual differences has any psychological significance, apart from the general reduction of volume with which it coincided, is a question which we prefer to leave open.

THERE WAS MORE GROUP-MINDEDNESS AND MORE FRIENDLINESS IN DEMOCRACY

1. The pronoun "I" was used less frequently. One highly objective approach to the problem of group-mindedness is simply to count the number of times that the members of the group use the pronoun *I* (or *me,* or *mine*) in comparison with the number of times that they use the pronoun *we* (or *us,* or *ours*). Which is more frequent, I-centered remarks such as "I want this," or we-centered remarks such as "We need that"? In Experiment I, this appeared to be a very promising index. In the autocratic group the proportion of singular pronouns in the total of all first person pronouns was 82%, and in the democratic group only 64%. In Experiment II, however, although there was some difference in the same direction, it was not statistically significant.

2. Spontaneous subgroups were larger. In Experiment I, a count was made of the frequency of subgroups representing the highest amount of unity possible in a five-person group (5 and 4–1) and the lowest possible amount of unity (2–1–1–1 and 1–1–1–1–1). The high-unity structures occurred 14 times in the autocratic group and 41 times in the democratic group, while the low-unity structures occurred 41 times in the autocratic group and 19 times in the democratic group. This difference is in spite of, rather than because of, the direct influence of the leader; he exerted his influence in the autocratic group much more often in the direction of higher group unity than in the opposite direction. But in autocracy his direct influence was more than balanced by a strong spontaneous tendency to group fragmentation

or disintegration. (In Experiment II, this type of data was not obtained.)

3. "Group-minded" remarks were much more frequent. The "We/I ratio" is atomistic insofar as it deals with words out of context. The word *I*, for instance, may be used in the sentence, "I think we'd better pour in the water now." Here it does not indicate egotism or individualistic competition; in its context it is clearly subordinate to a wholly group-minded idea. More significant than the We/I ratio, therefore, is the number of remarks which were classified as "group-minded." This was done only in Experiment II. The results showed that the highest percentage of group-minded remarks was in laissez-faire—which is paradoxical, in view of the low amount of effective group cooperation in laissez-faire. But an analysis of the actual remarks showed that many of them expressed not the existence of group unity but a *desire* for it:

> "Hey, how about us having a meeting?"
> "Well, we have to do something."
> "Now if we just had a club. . . ."

On the other hand, the contrast between democracy and both forms of autocracy seems to show a genuine difference in effective group-mindedness. The figures are: democracy 18, aggressive reaction to autocracy 7, submissive reaction to autocracy 4. The difference between democracy and each of the others is significant at the 1% level. Some illustrations:

> Finn: "I wish that guy [the "hostile stranger"] would stop telling us stuff and tearing down our work. We won't be able to finish it."
> Eddie: "We're going to vote about it."
> Finn: "We can't leave it here. It's our last day. We're all in charge of this airplane from now on."
> Leonard: "I'll take it home and hang it up."
> Reilly: "You won't if the club doesn't say so."

4. "Friendly" remarks were slightly more frequent. In Experiment I, as we have already noted, "friendly ascendance" occurred 24 times in the autocratic group and 34 times in the democratic group. Similarly, "submissive" behavior of one child to another (which might better have been called "agreeable" or "cooperative" behavior in many cases) occurred 120 times in autocracy and 188 times in de-

mocracy. The category of "friendly" behavior was not used in the analysis.

In Experiment II, the category of "friendly" was used, and a slight difference was found in favor of democracy as compared with either form of autocracy, but it was not statistically significant. The figures were: democracy 26, submissive reaction to autocracy 17. The difference between democracy and the submissive reaction was significant at only the 5% level, and the difference between democracy and the other two atmospheres does not even reach the 5% level of significance. It should also be noted that the proportion of friendliness in the total of all conversation was actually larger in the submissive reaction to autocracy than it was in democracy.

How can we account for this surprisingly large amount of mutual friendliness in the submissive reaction to autocracy? It seems likely that the unfriendliness which would naturally result from frustration is here counterbalanced by one or both of two factors: the general atmosphere of moral goodness which the presence of the leader seems to have inculcated (the boys were "on their good behavior"), and perhaps also a sort of drawing-together of the group because of the feeling that "we're all in the same boat." The common experience of being subjected to the same frustrating experience may have created a sort of feeling of comradeship similar to that which has often been described as existing in army groups subjected to a common danger and a common discipline. In our experiments this did not result in any responsible type of group cooperativeness ("group-minded" remarks) but it does seem to have resulted in a certain amount of individual friendliness ("friendly" remarks). Many joking and half-joking remarks are included. For instance:

> Finn: "Well, so long, I'm going to get my hair cut."
> Van: "Look at Finn, he's going to get his head cut off."
> "Now, my fine feathered friend, does this suit you O.K.?" (Friendliness to individual in outgroup.) Finn is over near the box, and Rudy (in the other group) holds up the work he is doing in a friendly manner for Finn to see.
> Finn: "What is it?"
> Rudy: "It's a tin can thing."

5. Mutual praise was more frequent. In Experiment I there were three instances of child-

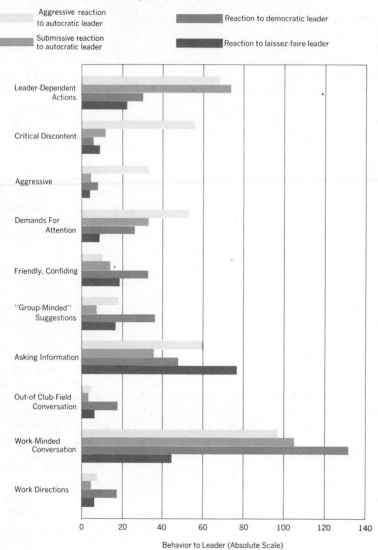

FIGURE 2. Four patterns of child-to-leader relationship.

to-child praise in the autocratic group and 16 in the democratic group. In Experiment II praise was not counted as a separate category, but was included in the category of "friendliness." Some instances of its occurrence under democratic leadership:

> Finn: "Well, nice going, Bill—such an idea. You could take a bit more out of that one." (Bill is Finn's archenemy, but Finn is also changeable, and he is now in the best of spirits.)
> Bill (reciprocating, a minute or two later): "Oh, that's good Finn. That's a good idea. Mine's too weak."
>
> Bill: "Oh, Van, that's coming good."
> Bill (to Mr. Rankin): "Eddie really did a swell

job on that, didn't he? I couldn't do as good as that."

6. Friendly playfulness was more frequent. In number of "play-minded" remarks the figures for Experiment II were: laissez-faire 33, democracy 13, submissive reaction to autocracy 8, and aggressive reaction to autocracy 3. The difference between democracy and the submissive reaction is significant at only the 5% level. Here again autocracy may have brought out a paradoxical type of irresponsible we-mindedness. (Illustrations of "play-mindedness" have already been given in differentiating laissez-faire from democracy.)

7. There was more readiness to share group

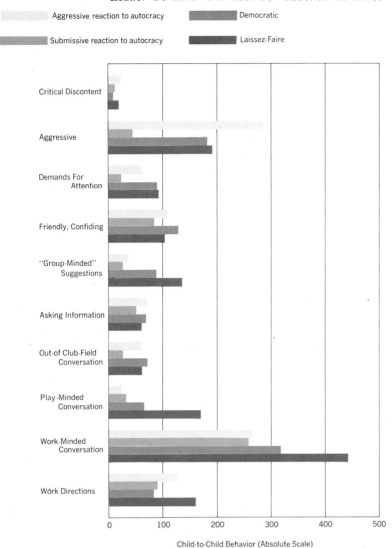

FIGURE 3. Four patterns of child-to-child relationship.

property. This was shown most conspicuously in Experiment I. At the end of the meeting series, each of the two groups was asked to vote, with individual secret ballot, on the question, "What would you like to have done with the masks?" In the autocratic group (in which each child had already identified with one mask), three out of four gave wholly "individualistic" answers: "Give us our masks," and "Let me have mine." In the democratic group, not one of the five regular members gave a completely individualistic answer.

SUMMARY

A bird's-eye view of the more important results of Experiment II is given in Figures 2 and 3, which represent, respectively, the boys' behavior toward their leader and toward each other. The chief differences to be noted here are: (a) the large number of leader-dependent actions in both reactions to autocracy; (b) the large amounts of critical discontent and of aggressive behavior in the aggressive reaction to autocracy; (c) the frequency of "friendly, confiding" conversation and of group-minded suggestions in democracy; and (*d*) the contrast between democracy and laissez-faire in work-minded conversation.

Here the following differences should be noticed: (*a*) the large difference between the two reactions to autocracy in amount of aggressive behavior, and the intermediate position of democracy and laissez-faire in this respect; (*b*) the generally subdued atmosphere in the submissive reaction to autocracy, as shown by the small absolute totals of aggressive behavior, attention demands, group-minded suggestions, out-of-club-field conversation, and play-minded remarks; (*c*) the small proportion of group-minded suggestions in both reactions to autocracy; and (*d*) the small amount of play-minded conversation in both reactions to autocracy, and the very large amount in laissez-faire.

Summarizing, then, we can say that the above diagram and several other types of evidence tend to support the following descriptive generalizations.

1. *Laissez-faire was not the same as democracy.*
    (*a*) There was less work done in it, and poorer work.
    (*b*) It was more characterized by play.
    (*c*) In interviews, the boys expressed preference for their democratic leader.
2. *Democracy can be efficient.*
    (*a*) The quantity of work done in autocracy was somewhat greater.
    (*b*) Work motivation was stronger in democracy as shown, for instance, when the leader left the room.
    (*c*) Originality was greater in democracy.
3. *Autocracy can create much hostility and aggression, including aggression against scapegoats.*
    (*a*) In Experiment I, the autocratic group showed more dominating ascendance, much more hostility (in a ratio of 30 to 1), more demands for attention, more destruction of own property, and more scapegoat behavior.
    (*b*) In Experiment II, one of the four clubs showed a similar reaction.
4. *Autocracy can create discontent that does not appear on the surface.*
    (*a*) Four boys dropped out, and all of them did so during autocratic club periods in which overt rebellion did not occur.
    (*b*) Nineteen out of 20 boys preferred their democratic leader.
    (*c*) There was more discontent expressed in autocracy—even when the general reaction was submissive—than in democracy.
    (*d*) "Release" behavior on the day of transition to a freer atmosphere suggested the presence of previous frustration.
5. *There was more dependence and less individuality in autocracy.*
    (*a*) There was more "submissive" or "dependent" behavior.
    (*b*) Conversation was less varied—more confined to the immediate situation.
    (*c*) In the submissive reaction to autocracy, there was an absolute (though not relative) reduction in statistical measures of individual differences.
    (*d*) The observers' impression was that in autocracy there is some loss of individuality.
6. *There was more group-mindedness and more friendliness in democracy.*
    (*a*) In Experiment I, the pronoun "I" was used relatively less frequently in the democratic group.
    (*b*) Spontaneous subgroups were larger.
    (*c*) In Experiment II, group-minded remarks were much more frequent in democracy.
    (*d*) Friendly remarks were slightly more frequent.
    (*e*) In Experiment I, mutual praise was more frequent in the democratic group.
    (*f*) In Experiment II, friendly playfulness was more frequent in democracy.
    (*g*) In Experiment I, the democratic group showed more readiness to share group property.

References

1. Lippitt, R. An experimental study of the effect of democratic and authoritarian group atmospheres. *Univ. of Iowa Studies in Child Welfare,* 1940, **16,** 43–195.
2. Lippitt, R., & White, R. The "social climate" of children's groups. In R. G. Barker, J. Kounin, & H. Wright (Eds.), *Child behavior and development.* New York: McGraw-Hill, 1943. Pp. 485–508.

26

Overcoming Resistance to Change

LESTER COCH AND JOHN R. P. FRENCH, JR.

It has always been characteristic of American industry to change products and methods of doing jobs as often as competitive conditions or engineering progress dictate. This makes frequent changes in an individual's work necessary. In addition, the markedly greater turnover and absenteeism of recent years result in unbalanced production lines, which again makes for frequent shifting of individuals from one job to another. One of the most serious production problems faced at the Harwood Manufacturing Corporation has been the resistance of production workers to the necessary changes in methods and jobs. This resistance expressed itself in several ways, such as grievances about the piece rates that went with the new methods, high turnover, very low efficiency, restriction of output, and marked aggression against management. Despite these undesirable effects, it was necessary that changes in methods and jobs continue.

Efforts were made to solve this serious problem by the use of a special monetary allowance for transfers, by trying to enlist the cooperation and aid of the union, by making necessary layoffs on the basis of efficiency, etc. In all cases, these actions did little or nothing to overcome the resistance to change. On the basis of these data, it was felt that the pressing problem of resistance to change demanded further research for its solution. From the point of view of factory management, there were two purposes to the research: (a) Why do people resist change so strongly? and (b) What can be done to overcome this resistance?

Starting with a series of observations about the behavior of changed groups, the first step in the program was to devise a preliminary theory to account for the resistance to change. Then, on the basis of the theory, a real-life action experiment was devised and conducted within the context of the factory situation. Finally, the results of the experi-

From *Human Relations*, 1948, **11**, 512–532. Reprinted by permission of the authors and *Human Relations*.

ment were interpreted in the light of the preliminary theory and the new data.

BACKGROUND

The main plant of the Harwood Manufacturing Corporation, where the present research was done, is located in the small town of Marion, Virginia. The plant produces pajamas and, like most sewing plants, employs mostly women. The plant's population is about 500 women and 100 men. The workers are recruited from the rural, mountainous areas surrounding the town, and are usually employed without previous industrial experience. The average age of the workers is 23. The average education is eight years of grammar school.

The policies of the company in regard to labor relations are liberal and progressive. A high value has been placed on fair and open dealing with the employees and they are encouraged to take up any problems or grievances with the management at any time. Every effort is made to help foremen find effective solutions to their problems in human relations, using conferences and role-playing methods. Carefully planned orientation, designed to help overcome the discouragement and frustrations attending entrance upon the new and unfamiliar situation, is used. Plant-wide votes are conducted where possible to resolve problems affecting the whole working population. The company has invested both time and money in employee services such as industrial music, health services, lunchroom, and recreation programs. In the same spirit, the management has been conscious of the importance of public relations in the local community; they have supported, both financially and otherwise, any activity which would build up good will for the company. As a result of these policies, the company has enjoyed good labor relations since the day it commenced operations.

Harwood employees work on an individual incentive system. Piece rates are set by time study and are expressed in terms of units. One unit is equal to one minute of standard work: 60 units per hour equal the standard efficiency rating. Thus, if on a particular operation the piece rate for one dozen is 10 units, the operator would have to produce six dozen per hour to achieve the standard efficiency rating of 60 units per hour. The skill required to reach 60 units per hour is great. On some jobs, an average trainee may take 34 weeks to reach the skill level necessary to perform at 60 units per hour. Her first few weeks of work may be on an efficiency level of 5 to 20 units per hour.

The amount of pay received is directly proportional to the weekly average efficiency rating achieved. Thus, an operator with an average efficiency rating of 75 units per hour (25% more than standard) would receive 25% more than base pay. However, there are two minimum wages below which no operator may fall. The first is the plant-wide minimum, the hiring-in wage; the second is a minimum wage based on six months' employment and is 22% higher than the plant-wide minimum wage. Both minima are smaller than the base pay for 60 units per hour efficiency rating.

The rating of every piece worker is computed every day, and the results are published in a daily record of production which is shown to every operator. This daily record of production for each production line carries the names of all the operators on that line arranged in rank order of efficiency rating, with the highest rating girl at the top of the list. The supervisors speak to each operator each day about her unit ratings. Because of the above procedures, many operators do not claim credit for all the work done in a given day. Instead, they save a few of the piece rate tickets as a "cushion" against a rainy day when they may not feel well or may have a great amount of machine trouble.

When it is necessary to change an operator from one type of work to another, a transfer bonus is given. This bonus is so designed that the changed operator who relearns at an average rate will suffer no loss in earnings after change. Despite this allowance, the general attitudes toward job changes in the factory are markedly negative. Such expressions as, "When you make your units [standard production], they change your job," are all too frequent. Many operators refuse to change, preferring to quit.

THE TRANSFER LEARNING CURVE

An analysis of the after-change relearning curves of several hundred experienced operators rating standard or better prior to change showed that 38% of the changed operators recovered to the standard unit rating of 60 units per hour. The other 62% either became chronically substandard operators or quit during the relearning period.

The average relearning curve for those who recover to standard production on the simplest type of job in the plant is eight weeks long, and, when smoothed, provides the basis for the transfer bonus. The bonus is the percentage difference between this expected efficiency rating and the standard of 60 units per hour.

The relearning period for an experienced operator is longer than the learning period for a new operator. This is true despite the fact that the majority of transfers—the failures who never recover to standard—are omitted from the curve. However, changed operators rarely complain of "wanting to do it the old way" after the first week or two of change, and time and motion studies show few false moves after the first week of change. From this evidence it is deduced that proactive inhibition, or the interference of previous habits in learning the new skill, is either nonexistent or very slight after the first two weeks of change.

An analysis of the relearning curves for 41 experienced operators who were changed to very difficult jobs gives a comparison between the recovery rates for operators making standard or better prior to change, and those below standard prior to change. Both classes of operators dropped to a little below 30 units per hour and recovered at a very slow but similar rate. These curves show a general (though by no means universal) phenomenon: the efficiency rating prior to change does not indicate a faster or slower recovery rate after change.

A PRELIMINARY THEORY OF RESISTANCE TO CHANGE

The fact that relearning after transfer to a new job is so often slower than initial learning on first entering the factory would indicate, on the face of it, that the resistance to change and the slow relearning is primarily a motivational problem. The similar recovery rates of skilled and unskilled operators tend to confirm the hypothesis that skill is a minor factor and motivation is the major determinant of the rate of recovery. Earlier experiments at Harwood by Alex Bavelas (3) demonstrated this point

conclusively. He found that the use of group decision techniques on operators who had just been transferred resulted in very marked increases in the rate of relearning, even though no skill training was given and there were no other changes in working conditions.

Interviews with operators who have been transferred to a new job reveal a common pattern of feelings and attitudes which are distinctly different from those of successful nontransfers. In addition to resentment against the management for transferring them, the employees typically show feelings of frustration, loss of hope of ever regaining their former level of production and status in the factory, feelings of failure, and a very low level of aspiration. In this respect, these transferred operators are similar to the chronically slow workers studied previously.

Earlier unpublished research at Harwood has shown that the nontransferred employees generally have an explicit goal of reaching and maintaining an efficiency rating of 60 units per hour. A questionnaire administered to several groups of operators indicated that a large majority of them accept as their goal the management's quota of 60 units per hour. This standard of production is the level of aspiration according to which the operators measure their own success or failure, and those who fall below standard lose status in the eyes of their fellow employees. Relatively few operators set a goal appreciably above 60 units per hour.

The actual production records confirm the effectiveness of this goal of standard production. The distribution of the total population of operators in accordance with their production levels is by no means a normal curve. Instead there is a very large number of operators who rate 60 to 63 units per hour, and relatively few operators who rate just above or just below this range. Thus we may conclude that:

PROPOSITION 1

There is a force acting on the operator in the direction of achieving a production level of 60 units per hour or more. It is assumed that the strength of this driving force (acting on an operator below standard) increases as she gets nearer the goal—a typical goal gradient.

On the other hand, restraining forces operate to hinder or prevent her reaching this goal. These restraining forces consist, among other things, of the difficulty of the job in relation to the operator's level of skill. Other things being equal, the faster an operator is sewing the more difficult it is to increase her speed by a given amount. Thus we may conclude that:

PROPOSITION 2

The strength of the restraining force hindering higher production increases with increasing level of production.

In line with previous studies, it is assumed that the conflict of these two opposing forces— the driving force corresponding to the goal of reaching 60 and the restraining force of the difficulty of the job—produces frustration. In such a conflict situation, the strength of frustration will depend on the strength of these forces. If the restraining force against increasing production is weak, then the frustration will be weak. But if the driving force toward higher production, i.e., the motivation is weak, then the frustration will also be weak. Probably both of the conflicting forces must be above a certain minimum strength before any frustration is produced, for all goal-directed activity involves some degree of conflict of this type; yet a person is not usually frustrated so long as he is making satisfactory progress toward his goal. Consequently we assume that:

PROPOSITION 3

The strength of frustration is a function of the weaker of these two opposing forces, provided that the weaker force is stronger than a certain minimum necessary to produce frustration (3).

From Propositions 1, 2, and 3, we may derive that the strength of frustration (a) should be greater for operators who are below standard in production than for operators who have already achieved the goal of standard production; (b) should be greater for operators on difficult jobs than for operators on easy jobs; and (c) should increase with increasing efficiency rating below standard production. Previous research would suggest:

PROPOSITION 4

One consequence of frustration is escape from the field (2). An analysis of the effects of such frustration in the factory showed that it resulted, among other things, in high turnover and absenteeism. The rate of turnover for successful operators with efficiency ratings above standard was much lower than for unsuccessful operators. Likewise, operators on the more difficult jobs quit more frequently than those on the easier jobs. Presumably the effect of being transferred is a severe frustration which should result in similar attempts to escape from the field.

In line with this theory of frustration and the finding that job turnover is one resultant of frustration, an analysis was made of the turnover rate of transferred operators as compared with the rate among operators who had not been transferred recently. For the year September, 1946, to September, 1947, there were 198 operators who had not been transferred recently; i.e., within the 34-week period allowed for relearning after transfer. There was a second group of 85 operators who had been transferred recently; i.e., within the time allowed for relearning the new job. Each of these two groups was divided into seven classifications according to their unit rating at the time of quitting. For each classification the percentage turnover per month, based on the total number of employees in that classification, was computed.

The results are given in Figure 1. Both the levels of turnover and the form of the curves are strikingly different for the two groups. Among operators who have not been transferred recently the average turnover per month is about 4½%; among recent transfers the monthly turnover is nearly 12%. Consistent with the previous studies, both groups show a very marked drop in the turnover curve after an operator becomes a success by reaching 60 units per hour, or standard production. However, the form of the curves at lower unit ratings is markedly different for the two groups. The nontransferred operators show a gradually increasing rate of turnover up to a rating of 55 to 59 units per hour. The transferred operators, on the other hand, show a high peak at the lowest unit rating of 30 to 34 units per hour, decreasing sharply to a low point at 45 to 49 units per hour. Since most changed operators drop to a unit rating of around 30 units per hour when changed and then drop no further, it is obvious that the rate of turnover was highest for these operators just after they were changed and again much later just before they reached standard. Why?

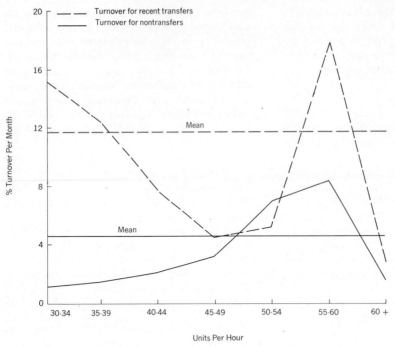

FIGURE 1. The rate of turnover at various levels of production for transfers as compared with nontransfers.

It is assumed that the strength of frustration for an operator who has not been transferred gradually increases because both the driving force toward the goal of reaching 60 and the restraining force of the difficulty of the job increase with increasing unit rating. This is in line with Propositions 1, 2, and 3, above. For the transferred operator, on the other hand, the frustration is greatest immediately after transfer when the contrast of her present status with her former status is most evident. At this point, the strength of the restraining forces is at a maximum because the difficulty is unusually great due to proactive inhibition. Then, as she overcomes the interference effects between the two jobs and learns the new job, the difficulty and the frustration gradually decrease and the rate of turnover declines until the operator reaches 45–49 units per hour. Then at higher levels of production the difficulty starts to increase again and the transferred operator shows the same peak in frustration and turnover at 55–59 units per hour.

Though our theory of frustration explains the forms of the two turnover curves in Figure 1, it seems hardly adequate to account for the markedly higher level of turnover for transfers as compared to nontransfers. On the basis of the difficulty of the job, it is especially difficult

to explain the higher rate of turnover at 55–59 units per hour for transfers. Evidently, additional forces are operating.

Another factor which seems to affect recovery rates of changed operators is the amount of cohesiveness. Observations seem to indicate that a strong psychological subgroup with negative attitudes toward management will display the strongest resistance to change. On the other hand, changed groups with high cohesiveness and positive cooperative attitudes are the best relearners. Collections of individuals with little or no cohesiveness display some resistance to change, but not so strongly as the groups with high cohesiveness and negative attitudes toward management.

An analysis of turnover records for changed operators with high cohesiveness showed a 4% turnover rate per month at 30 to 34 units per hour, not significantly higher than in unchanged operators, but significantly lower than in changed operators with little or no cohesiveness. However, the acts of aggression are far more numerous among operators with high cohesiveness than among operators with little cohesiveness. Since both types of operators experience the same frustration as individuals but react to it so differently, it is assumed that the effect of the ingroup feeling is to set up a restraining force against leaving the group and perhaps even to set up driving forces toward staying in the group. In these circumstances, one would expect some alternative reaction to frustration rather than escape from the field. This alternative is aggression. Strong cohesiveness provides strength so that members dare to express aggression which would otherwise be suppressed.

One common result in a cohesive subgroup is the setting of a group standard concerning production. Where the attitudes toward management are antagonistic, this group standard may take the form of a definite restriction of production to a given level. This phenomenon of restriction is particularly likely to happen in a group that has been transferred to a job where a new piece rate has been set, for they have some hope that, if production never approaches the standard, the management may change the piece rate in their favor.

A group standard can exert extremely strong forces on an individual member of a small subgroup. That these forces can have a powerful effect on production is indicated in the production record of one presser during a period of 40 days:

In the Group

Days	Efficiency Rating
1–3	46
4–6	52
7–9	53
10–12	56

Scapegoating Begins

13–16	55
17–20	48

Becomes a Single Worker

21–24	83
25–28	92
29–32	92
33–36	91
37–40	92

For the first 20 days she was working in a group of other pressers who were producing at the rate of about 50 units per hour. Starting on the 13th day, when she reached standard production and exceeded the production of the other members, she became a scapegoat of the group. During this time her production decreased toward the level of the remaining members of the group. After 20 days the group had to be broken up and all the other members were transferred to other jobs, leaving only the scapegoat operator. With the removal of the group, the group standard was no longer operative, and the production of the one remaining operator shot up from the level of about 45 to 96 units per hour in a period of four days. Her production stabilized at a level of about 92 and stayed there for the remainder of the 20 days. Thus it is clear that the motivational forces induced in the individual by a strong subgroup may be more powerful than those induced by management.

THE EXPERIMENTS

On the basis of the preliminary theory that resistance to change is a combination of an individual reaction to frustration with strong group-induced forces, it seemed that the most appropriate methods for overcoming the resistance to change would be group methods. Consequently, an experiment was designed (Experiment I) employing three degrees of participation in handling groups to be transferred. The first variation, the control group, involved *no participation* by employees in planning the changes, though an explanation was given to them. The second variation involved *participation through representation* of the workers in designing the changes to be made in the jobs. The third variation consisted of *total participation* by all members of the group in designing the changes. Two experimental groups received the total participation treatment. The four experimental groups were roughly matched with respect to (*a*) the efficiency ratings of the groups before transfer, (*b*) the degree of change involved in the transfer, and (*c*) the amount of cohesiveness observed in the groups.

In no case was more than a minor change in the work routines and time allowances made. The no-participation group, 18 hand pressers, had formerly stacked their work in half-dozen lots on a flat piece of cardboard the size of the finished product. The new job called for stacking their work in half-dozen lots in a box the size of the finished product. The box was located in the same place the cardboard had been. An additional two minutes per dozen was allowed (by the time study) for this new part of the job. This represented a total change of 8.8%.

The group treated with participation

through representation, 13 pajama folders, had formerly folded coats with prefolded pants. The new job called for the folding of coats with unfolded pants. An additional 1.8 minutes per dozen was allowed (by time study) for this new part of the job. This represented a total change of 9.4%.

The two total participation groups, consisting of eight and seven pajama examiners, respectively, had formerly clipped threads from the entire garment and examined every seam. The new job called for pulling only certain threads off and examining every seam. An average of 1.2 minutes per dozen was subtracted (by time study) from the total time on these two jobs. This represented a total job change of 8%.

The no-participation group of hand pressers went through the usual factory routine when they were changed. The production department modified the job, and the new piece rate was set. A group meeting was then held in which the group was told that the change was necessary because of competitive conditions, and that a new piece rate had been set. The new piece rate was thoroughly explained by the time-study man, questions were answered, and the meeting dismissed.

The group which participated through representatives was changed in a different manner. Before any changes took place, a group meeting was held with all the operators to be changed. The need for the change was presented as dramatically as possible, showing two identical garments produced in the factory; one was produced in 1946 and had sold for 100% more than its fellow in 1947. The group was asked to identify the cheaper one and could not do it. This demonstration effectively shared with the group the entire problem of the necessity of cost reduction. A general agreement was reached that a savings could be effected by removing the "frills" and "fancy" work from the garment without affecting the folders' opportunity to achieve a high efficiency rating. Management then presented a plan to set the new job and piece rate:

1. Make a check study of the job as it was being done.
2. Eliminate all unnecessary work.
3. Train several operators in the correct methods.
4. Set the piece rate by time studies on these specially trained operators.

5. Explain the new job and rate to all the operators.
6. Train all operators in the new method so they can reach a high rate of production within a short time.

The group approved this plan (though no formal group decision was reached) and chose the operators to be specially trained. A sub-meeting with the "special" operators was held immediately following the meeting with the entire group. They displayed a cooperative and interested attitude and immediately presented many good suggestions. This attitude carried over into the working out of the details of the new job, and when the new job and piece rates were set the "special" operators referred to the resultants as "our job," "our rate," etc. The new job and piece rates were presented at a second group meeting to all the operators involved. The "special" operators served to train the other operators on the new job.

The total participation groups went through much the same kind of meetings. The groups were smaller, and a more intimate atmosphere was established. The need for a change was once again made dramatically clear. The same general plan was presented by management. However, since the groups were small, all operators were chosen as "special" operators; that is, all operators were to participate directly in the designing of the new jobs, and all operators would be studied by the time-study man. It is interesting to observe that in the meetings with these two groups suggestions were immediately made in such quantity that the stenographer had great difficulty in recording them. The group approved of the plans, but again no formal group decision was reached.

RESULTS

The results of the experiment are summarized in graphic form in Figure 2. The gaps in the production curves occur because these groups were paid on a time-work basis for a day or two. The no-participation group improved little beyond their early efficiency ratings. Resistance developed almost immediately after the change occurred. Marked expressions of aggression against management occurred, such as conflict with the methods engineer, expression of hostility against the supervisor, deliber-

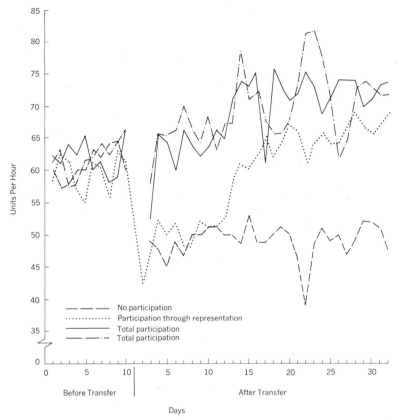

FIGURE 2. The effects of participation through representation and of total participation on recovery after an easy transfer.

ate restriction of production, and lack of co-operation with the supervisor. There were 17% quits in the first 40 days. Grievances were filed about the piece rate, but when the rate was checked, it was found to be a little "loose."

The representation group showed an unusually good relearning curve. At the end of 14 days, the group averaged 61 units per hour. During the 14 days, the attitude was cooperative and permissive. They worked well with the methods engineer, the training staff, and the supervisor. (The supervisor was the same person in the cases of the first two groups.) There were no quits in this group in the first 40 days. This group might have presented a better learning record if work had not been scarce during the first seven days. There was one act of aggression against the supervisor recorded in the first 40 days. We should note that the three special representative operators recovered at about the same rate as the rest of their group.

The total participation groups recovered faster than the others. After a slight drop on

the first day of change, the efficiency ratings returned to a prechange level and showed sustained progress thereafter to a level about 14% higher than the prechange level. No additional training was provided them after the second day. They worked well with their supervisors and no indications of aggression were observed from these groups. There were no quits in either of these groups in the first 40 days.

(A fifth experimental group, composed of only two sewing operators, was transferred by the total participation technique. Their new job was one of the most difficult jobs in the factory, in contrast to the easy jobs for the other four experimental groups. As expected, the total participation technique again resulted in unusually fast recovery rate and a final level of production well above the level before transfer.)

In the first experiment, the no-participation group made no progress after transfer for a period of 32 days. At the end of this period the group was broken up, and the individuals were reassigned to new jobs scattered

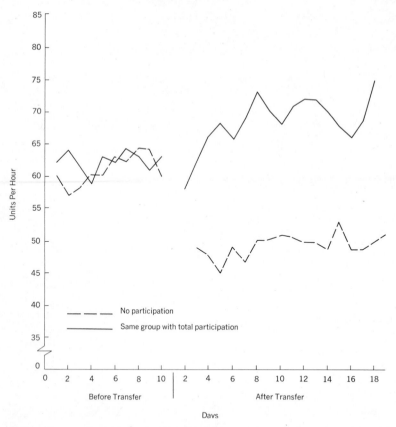

FIGURE 3. A comparison of the effect of no participation with the total participation procedure on the same group.

throughout the factory. Two and a half months after their dispersal, the 13 remaining members of the original no-participation group were again brought together as a group for a second experiment (Experiment II).

This second experiment consisted of transferring the group to a new job, using the total participation technique. The new job was a pressing job of comparable difficulty to the new job in the first experiment. On the average, it involved about the same degree of change. In the meetings, no reference was made to the previous behavior of the group on being transferred.

The results of the second experiment were in sharp contrast to the first (see Figure 3). With the total participation technique, the same group now recovered rapidly to their previous efficiency rating and, like the other groups under this treatment, continued on beyond it to a new high level of production. There was no aggression or turnover in the group for 19 days after change, a marked modification of their previous behavior after

transfer. Some anxiety concerning their seniority status was expressed, but this was resolved in a meeting of their elected delegate, the union business agent, and a management representative.

INTERPRETATION

The purpose of this section is to explain the drop in production resulting from transfer, the differential recovery rates of the three experimental treatments, the increases beyond their former levels of production by the participating groups, and the differential rates of turnover and aggression.

The first experiment showed that the rate of recovery is directly proportional to the amount of participation, and that the rates of turnover and aggression are inversely proportional to the amount of participation. The second experiment demonstrated more conclusively that the results obtained depended on the experimental treatment rather than on personality factors like skill or aggressiveness, for identical individuals yielded markedly different results in the no-participation treatment as contrasted with the total-participation treatment.

Apparently total participation has the same type of effect as participation through representation, but the former has a stronger influence. In regard to recovery rates, this difference is not unequivocal because the experiment was unfortunately confounded. Right after transfer, the latter group had insufficient material to work on for a period of seven days. Hence, their slower recovery during this period is at least in part due to insufficient work. In succeeding days, however, there was an adequate supply of work and the differential recovery rate still persisted. Therefore, we are inclined to believe that participation through representation results in slower recovery than does total participation.

Before discussing the details of why participation produces high morale, we shall consider the nature of production levels. In examining the production records of hundreds of individuals and groups in this factory, one is struck by the constancy of the level of production. Though differences among individuals in efficiency rating are very large, nearly every experienced operator maintains a fairly steady level of production, given constant physical conditions. Frequently the given level will be maintained despite rather large changes in technical working conditions.

As Lewin has pointed out, this type of production can be viewed as a quasi-stationary process—in the on-going work the operator is forever sewing new garments, yet the level of the process remains relatively stationary (3). Thus there are constant characteristics of the production process permitting the establishment of general laws.

In studying production as a quasi-stationary equilibrium, we are concerned with two types of forces: (*a*) forces on production in a downward direction, and (*b*) forces on production in an upward direction. In this situation we are dealing with a variety of both upward forces tending to increase the level of production and downward forces tending to decrease the level of production. However, in the present experiment we have no method of measuring independently all of the component forces either downward or upward. These various component forces upward are combined into one resultant force upward, and the several downward component forces combine into one resultant force downward. We can infer a good deal about the relative strengths of these resultant forces.

Where we are dealing with a quasi-stationary equilibrium, the resultant forces upward and the forces downward are opposite in direction and equal in strength at the equilibrium level. Of course either resultant forces may fluctuate over a short period of time, so that the forces may not be equally balanced at a given moment. However, over a longer period of time, and on the average, the forces balance out. Fluctuations from the average occur, but there is a tendency to return to the average level.

Just before being transferred, all of the groups in both experiments had reached a stable equilibrium level at just above the standard production of 60 units per hour. This level was equal to the average efficiency rating for the entire factory during the period of the experiments. Since this production level remained constant, neither increasing nor decreasing, we may be sure that the strength of the resultant force upward was equal to the strength of the resultant force downward. This equilibrium of forces was maintained over the period of time when production was stationary at this level. But the forces changed markedly after transfer, and these new constellations of forces were distinctly different for the various experimental groups.

For the no-participation group the period after transfer is a quasi-stationary equilibrium at a lower level, and the forces do not change during the period of 30 days. The resultant force upward remains equal to the resultant force downward, and the level of production remains constant. The force field for this group is represented schematically in Figure 4. Only the resultant forces are shown. The length of the vector represents the strength of the force, and the point of the arrow represents the point of application of the force, that is, the production level and the time at which the force applies. Thus the forces are equal and opposite only at the level of 50 units per hour. At higher levels of production the forces downward are greater than the forces upward, and at lower levels of production the forces upward are stronger than the forces downward. Thus there is a tendency for the equilibrium to be maintained at an efficiency rating of 50.

The situation for the other experimental

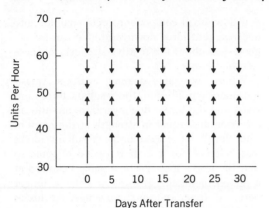

FIGURE 4. A schematic diagram of the quasi-stationary equilibrium for the no-participation group after transfer.

groups after transfer can be viewed as a quasi-stationary equilibrium of a different type. Figure 5 gives a schematic diagram of the resultant forces for all the participation groups. At any given level of production, such as 50 units per hour or 60 units per hour, both the resultant forces upward and the resultant forces downward change over the period of 30 days. During this time the point of equilibrium, which starts at 50 units per hour, gradually rises until it reaches a level of over 70 units per hour after 30 days. Yet here again the equilibrium level has the character of a "central force field" where, at any point in the total field, the resultant of the upward and the

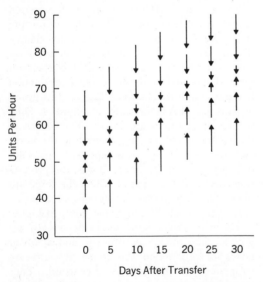

FIGURE 5. A schematic diagram of the quasi-stationary equilibrium for the experimental groups after transfer.

downward forces is in the direction of the equilibrium level.

To understand how the differences among the experimental and the control treatments produced the differences in force fields represented in Figures 4 and 5, it is not sufficient to consider only the resultant forces. We must also look at the component forces for each resultant force.

There are three main component forces for each resultant force.

There are three main component forces influencing production in a downward direction: (*a*) the difficulty of the job, (*b*) a force corresponding to avoidance of strain, and (*c*) a force corresponding to a group standard to restrict production to a given level. The resultant force upward in the direction of greater production is composed of three additional component forces: (*a*) the force corresponding to the goal of standard production, (*b*) a force corresponding to pressures induced by the management through supervision, and (*c*) a force corresponding to a group standard of competition. Let us examine each of these six component forces.

JOB DIFFICULTY

For all operators, the difficulty of the job is one of the forces downward on production. The difficulty of the job, of course, is relative to the skill of the operator. The given job may be very difficult for an unskilled operator but relatively easy for a highly skilled one. In the case of a transfer a new element of difficulty enters. For some time the new job is much more difficult, for the operator is unskilled at that particular job. In addition to the difficulty experienced by any learner, the transfer often encounters the added difficulty of proactive inhibition. Where the new job is similar to the old job, there will be a period of interference between the two similar but different skills required. For this reason a very efficient operator whose skills have become almost unconscious may suffer just as great a drop as a much less efficient operator. Except for the experiment on only two operators, the difficulty of these easy jobs does not explain the differential recovery rates, because both the initial difficulty and the amount of change were equated for these groups. The two operators probably dropped further and recovered more slowly than any of the other three groups under total participation because of the greater difficulty of the job.

STRAIN AVOIDANCE

The force toward lower production corresponding to the difficulty of the job (or the lack of skill of the person) has the character of a restraining force; i.e., it acts to prevent locomotion rather than as a driving force causing locomotion. However, in all production there is a closely related driving force towards lower production, namely, "strain avoidance." We assume that working too hard and working too fast is an unpleasant strain; and corresponding to this negative valence there is a driving force in the opposite direction, namely, towards taking it easy or working slower. The higher the level of production the greater will be the strain and, other things being equal, the stronger will be the downward force of strain avoidance. Likewise, the greater the difficulty of the job, the stronger will be the force corresponding to strain avoidance. But the greater the operator's skill, the smaller will be the strain and the strength of the force of strain avoidance. Therefore:

PROPOSITION 5

The

$$\text{strength of the force of strain avoidance} = \frac{\text{job difficulty} \times \text{production level}}{\text{skill of operator}}$$

The differential recovery rates of the three experimental groups in Experiment I cannot be explained by strain avoidance because job difficulty, production level, and operator skill were matched at the time immediately following transfer. Later, however, when the experimental treatments had produced a much higher level of production, these groups were subjected to an increased downward force of strain avoidance which was stronger than in the no-participation group in Experiment I. Evidently other forces were strong enough to overcome this force of strain avoidance.

THE GOAL OF STANDARD PRODUCTION

In considering the negative attitudes toward transfer and the resistance to being transferred, there are several important aspects of the complex goal of reaching and maintaining a level of 60 units per hour. For an operator producing below standard, this goal is attractive because it means success, high status in the eyes of her fellow employees, better pay, and job security. On the other hand, there is a strong force against remaining below standard because this lower level means failure, low status, low pay, and the danger of being fired. Thus it is clear that the upward force corresponding to the goal of standard production will indeed be strong for the transfer who has dropped below standard.

It is equally clear why any operator who accepts the stereotype about transfer shows such strong resistance to being changed. She sees herself as becoming a failure and losing status, pay, and perhaps the job itself. The result is a lowered level of aspiration and a weakened force toward the goal of standard production.

Just such a weakening of the force toward 60 units per hour seems to have occurred in the no-participation group in Experiment I. The participation treatments, on the other hand, seem to have involved the operators in designing the new job and setting the new piece rates in such a way that they did not lose hope of regaining the goal of standard production. Thus participation resulted in a stronger force toward higher production. However, this force alone can hardly account for the large differences in recovery rate between the no-participation group and the experimental groups; certainly it does not explain why the latter increased to a level so high above standard.

MANAGEMENT PRESSURE

On all operators below standard the management exerts a pressure for higher production. This pressure is no harsh and autocratic treatment involving threats; rather, it takes the form of persuasion and encouragement by the supervisors. They attempt to induce the low rating operator to improve her performance and to attain standard production.

Such an attempt to induce a psychological force on another person may have several results. In the first place the person may ignore the attempt of the inducing agent, in which case there is no induced force acting on the person. On the other hand, the attempt may succeed so that an induced force on the person exists. Other things being equal, whenever there is an induced force acting on a person, the person will locomote in the direction of the force. An induced force which depends on the power field of an inducing agent—some other individual or group—will cease to exist when the inducing power field is withdrawn. In this respect it is different from an "own" force which stems from a person's own needs and goals.

The reaction of a person to an effective induced force will vary depending, among other things, on the person's relation to the inducing agent. A force induced by a friend may be accepted in such a way that it acts more like an own force. An effective force induced by an enemy may be resisted and rejected so that the person complies unwillingly and shows signs of conflict and tension. Thus in addition to what might be called a "neutral" induced force, we also distinguish an *accepted* induced force and a *rejected* induced force. Naturally, the acceptance and the rejection of an induced force can vary in degree from zero (i.e., a neutral induced force) to very strong acceptance or rejection. To account for the difference in character between the acceptance and the rejection of an induced force, we make the following propositions.

PROPOSITION 6

The acceptance of an induced force sets up additional "own" forces in the same direction.

PROPOSITION 7

The rejection of an induced force sets up additional "own" forces in the opposite direction.

The grievances, aggression, and tension in the no-participation group in the first experiment indicate that they rejected the force toward higher production induced by the management. The group accepted the stereotype that transfer is a calamity, but the no-participation procedure did not convince them that the change was necessary, and they viewed the new job and the new piece rates set by management as arbitrary and unreasonable.

The other experimental groups, on the contrary, participated in designing the changes and setting the piece rates so that they spoke of the new job as "our job" and the new piece rates as "our rates." Thus they accepted the

new situation and accepted the management-induced force toward higher production.

From the acceptance by the experimental groups and the rejection by the no-participation group of the management-induced forces, we may derive (by Propositions 6 and 7 above) that the former had additional "own" forces toward higher production, whereas the latter had additional "own" forces toward lower production. This difference helps to explain the better recovery rate of the participation groups.

GROUP STANDARDS

Probably the most important force affecting the recovery under the no-participation procedure was a group standard, set by the group, restricting the level of production to 50 units per hour. Evidently this explicit agreement to restrict production is related to the group's rejection of the change and of the new job as arbitrary and unreasonable. Perhaps they had faint hopes of demonstrating that standard production could not be attained and thereby obtain a more favorable piece rate. In any case there was a definite group phenomenon which affected all the members of the group. We have already noted the striking example of the presser whose production was restricted in the group situation to about half the level she attained as an individual. In the no-participation group, we would also expect the group to induce strong forces on the members. The more a member deviates above the standard, the stronger would be the group-induced force to conform to the standard, for such deviations both negate any possibility of management's increasing the piece rate and at the same time expose the other members to increased pressure from management. Thus individual differences in levels of production should be sharply curtailed in this group after transfer.

An analysis was made, for all groups, of the individual differences within each group in levels of production. In Experiment I, the 40 days before change were compared with the 30 days after change; in Experiment II, the 10 days before change were compared to the 17 days after change. As a measure of variability, the standard deviation was calculated each day for each group. The average daily standard deviations before and after change were as follows.

Experiment I	*Before Change*	*After Change*
No participation	9.8	1.9
Participation through representation	9.7	3.8
Total participation	10.3	2.7
Total participation	9.9	2.4
Experiment II		
Total participation	12.7	2.9

There is, indeed, a marked decrease in individual differences within the no-participation group after their first transfer. In fact, the restriction of production resulted in a lower variability than in any other group. Thus, we may conclude that the group standard at 50 units per hour set up strong group-induced forces which were important components in the central force field shown in Figure 4. It is now evident that for the no-participation group the quasi-stationary equilibrium after transfer has a steep gradient around the equilibrium level of 50 units per hour—the strength of forces increases rapidly above and below this level. It is also clear that the group standard to restrict production is a major reason for the lack of recovery in the no-participation group.

The table of variability also shows that the experimental treatments markedly reduced variability in the other four groups after transfer. In the group having participation by representation, this smallest reduction of variability was produced by a group standard of individual competition. Competition among members of the group was reported by the supervisor soon after transfer. This competition was a force toward higher production which resulted in good recovery to standard and continued progress beyond standard.

The total-participation groups showed a greater reduction in variability following transfer. These two groups were transferred on the same day. Group competition developed between the two groups, and this competition, which evidently resulted in stronger forces on the members than did the individual competition, was an effective group standard. The standard gradually moved to higher and higher levels of production, with the result that the groups not only reached but far exceeded their previous levels of production.

Probably a major determinant of the strength of these group standards is the cohesiveness of the group (1). Whether this power of the group over the members was used to increase or to decrease productivity seemed to depend upon the use of participation (4).

TURNOVER AND AGGRESSION

Returning now to our preliminary theory of frustration, we can see several revisions. The difficulty of the job and its relation to skill and strain avoidance has been clarified in Proposition 5. It is now clear that the driving force toward 60 is a complex affair: it is partly a negative driving force corresponding to the negative valence of low pay, low status, failure, and job insecurity. Turnover results not only from the frustration produced by the conflict of these two forces, but also from a direct attempt to escape from the region of these negative valences. For the members of the no-participation group, the group standard to restrict production prevented escape by increasing production, so that quitting their jobs was the only remaining escape. In the participation groups, on the contrary, both the group standards and the additional own forces resulting from the acceptance of management-induced forces combined to make increasing production the distinguished path of escape from this region of negative valence.

In considering turnover as a form of escape from the field, it is not enough to look only at the psychological present; one must also consider the psychological future. The employee's decision to quit the job is rarely made exclusively on the basis of a momentary frustration or an undesirable present situation. She usually quits when she also sees the future as equally hopeless. The operator transferred by the usual factory procedure (including the no-participation group) has, in fact, a realistic view of the probability of continued failure because, as we have already noted, 62% of transfers do fail to recover to standard production. Thus, the higher rate of quitting for transfers as compared to nontransfers results from a more pessimistic view of the future.

The no-participation procedure had the effect for the members of setting up management as a hostile power field. They rejected the forces induced by this hostile power field, and group standards to restrict production developed within the group in opposition to management. In this conflict between the power field of management and the power field of the group, the group attempted to reduce the strength of the hostile power field relative to the strength of their own power field. This change was accomplished in three ways: (a) The group increased its own power by developing a more cohesive and well-disciplined group. (b) They secured "allies" by getting the backing of the union in filing a formal grievance about the new piece rate. (c) They attacked the hostile power field directly in the form of aggression against the supervisor, the time-study engineer, and the higher management. Thus the aggression was derived not only from individual frustration, but also from the conflict between two groups. Furthermore, this situation of group conflict both helped to define management as the frustrating agent and gave the members strength to express any aggressive impulses produced by frustration.

CONCLUSIONS

It is possible for management to modify greatly or to remove completely group resistance to changes in methods of work and the ensuing piece rates. This change can be accomplished by the use of group meetings in which management effectively communicates the need for change and stimulates group participation in planning the changes.

For Harwood's management, and presumably for managements of other industries using an incentive system, this experiment has important implications in the field of labor relations. A majority of all grievances presented at Harwood have always stemmed from a change situation. By preventing or greatly modifying group resistance to change, this concomitant to change may well be greatly reduced. The reduction of such costly phenomena as turnover and slow relearning rates presents another distinct advantage.

Harwood's management has long felt that action research, such as the present experiment, is the only key to better labor-management relations. It is only by discovering the basic principles and applying them to the true causes of conflict that an intelligent, effective effort can be made to correct the undesirable effects of the conflict.

References

1. Festinger, L., *et al. Theory and experiment in social communication.* Ann Arbor, Mich.: Institute for Social Research, 1950.
2. French, John R. P., Jr. The behavior of organized and unorganized groups under conditions of frustration and fear. *Univ. of Iowa Studies in Child Welfare*, 1944, **20**, 229–308.
3. Lewin, Kurt. Frontiers in group dynamics. *Human Relations*, 1947, **1**, 5–41.
4. Schachter, S., *et al.* An experimental study of cohesiveness and productivity. *Human Relations*, 1951, **4**, 229–238.

27

Situational Determinants of Leadership Structure

DAVID C. KORTEN

Leadership has long been a topic of considerable interest in the social sciences. Nearly every aspect of leadership has been the subject of some degree of study. The present paper is concerned with some of the situational factors which determine the form of leadership which will arise and be accepted in a group. Two basic questions will be considered:

1. Under what conditions will there be pressure toward centralized authoritarian leadership?
2. Under what conditions is a more participative democratic form of leadership likely to arise?

While this is certainly not a new topic, this paper attempts to develop a somewhat more systematic approach than has ordinarily been undertaken toward this subject. I feel that the "model" developed in this paper provides a framework or structure for further experimentation and theoretical development that has perhaps previously been lacking.

My initial interest in making such a study was stimulated by observations made last summer in Indonesia and Burma of a strong desire, particularly among certain high government officials, for centralized control. I observed this same trend beginning to develop in Malaya. Recent releases from Ghana suggest that this situation is not confined to Asia.

Particularly in Indonesia, which is the situation most familiar to me, there was an original attempt at developing a free society and a free enterprise economy. In each of the countries mentioned there was no revolution in depth establishing the centralized control over more democratic institutions, nor has there been any other single totally

From *The Journal of Conflict Resolution*, 1962, **6**, 222–235. Reprinted by permission of the author and *The Journal of Conflict Resolution*.

disrupting occurrence which might account for the shift toward centralization. Though stress is certainly present, the overt crisis situation which is usually used to account for the rise of dictatorship is not entirely relevant. A more refined approach is needed.

Although each of these countries is unique in its own way, they all seem to have certain common elements in their situations which may be very important in exerting pressure for these centralizing trends. Mention of these seems helpful as a starting point for discussion.

1. Each of them is in a sense in a high drive state. There is a great desire, at least among major elements of the population, for improvement and development.
2. In addition to the drive for development, there is a related but separate drive for national status to compensate for feelings of inferior status developed through years of colonial suppression.
3. A sense of crisis exists which is closely related to the high drive state and results in part from the self-imposed adverse results of many of the programs which have been attempted.
4. A reasonably definite goal structure is established which may be spelled out in great and specific detail as evidenced in the five-year plans, eight-year plans, etc., which establish production goals and welfare measures to be attained at specific points in time.
5. All possess a low level of technical skill and an ill-developed understanding of the economic forces with which they must deal. The path to their goal is unclear and they are attempting to force clarity through control, although they lack the real understanding in many cases which is needed to accomplish effective control.

DEVELOPMENT OF A CONCEPTUAL MODEL

The first problem is one of developing a framework within which the important variables causing pressure for structural shifts can be studied and interrelated. From this framework, or model, it may then be possible to trace the forces leading a group or society from democratic to authoritarian forms of leadership and to compare these with the forces which lead the group in the opposite direction from an authoritarian to a democratic form.

This paper offers a very simplified proposal in order to facilitate initial study, even though simplification to the extent currently proposed may not be entirely realistic and certainly does not cover all possible cases. For example, no attempt has been made at this point to deal with laissez-faire forms of leadership.

We will, for the present, think in terms of a two-dimensional space represented by a four-cell matrix. The purpose is to represent discrete dimensions of authoritarian and democratic leadership against discrete dimensions of high goal structure and low goal structure. This is illustrated in Figure 1. The reasons for including the high and low goal structure dimensions should become clear later in the discussion.

	High Goal Structure	Low Goal Structure
Democratic		
Authoritarian		

FIGURE 1. Two dimensions of leadership.

In the following discussion the attempt is made to characterize each of these dimensions. While it is realized that these dimensions in fact exist as continua, they are treated here as discrete for purposes of simplicity.

GOAL STRUCTURE

Although I am not really satisfied with the terms *high* and *low goal structure* as being clearly descriptive of the concepts which I have in mind, I have not yet found a term which is substantially better in this respect. For this reason I suggest that preconceptions as to what the terms represent be avoided and their meaning instead be developed from the following discussion.

The consideration of goals came into the study at the very beginning in a comparative discussion of Russian communism with its presently authoritarian leadership and American democracy. In the United States approach we stress more *how* we want progress, rather than *where,* thus placing somewhat more emphasis on the method than on the outcome. Our goal is actually a continuing one and although we look for continual material and spiritual progress, we set no specific terminal goals and establish no time schedule. Our goals are to a large extent *non-operational*.[1]

On the other hand, the Russians seek to build a way of life not yet attained. Their stated orientation is toward future attainment and involves emphasis on change rather than on preservation. Their goals are fairly concrete or *operational* in such things as surpassing free world industrial output and communizing the world. Such terminal goals as these assume great importance and lead to the establishing of a definite time-table of accomplishment.

I feel these goal differences may have a great importance in helping to explain the differences in the forms of government adopted. It was consideration of these factors which led to adopting the terms high and low goal structure which referred to the clarity of expression or structuring of future goals which the group was seeking to attain. As the model developed further, this description broke down to some extent as it was found that the cognitive clarity was not so essential as the terminal quality. Still no alternative has been suggested which seems to be a real improvement. The original concept still fits very nicely into the final model, but the present model is not so limiting as the original concept.

HIGH GOAL STRUCTURE

In this situation we are concerned with groups which have rather specific goals which are of importance in the consensus of group opinion. The group is looked upon as a means of carrying out tasks or operations which will lead to these goals. It is not generally characterized by the desire to maintain the status quo, but rather by the desire to work toward a new situation or to attain something which the group has not presently attained. Group goals assume considerably more importance than individual goals. Individuals see the attainment of the group goal as prerequisite to the attainment of their own goals.

In some situations there may be a specific

[1] March and Simon (**10**, 155) developed the concept of *operational* and *non-operational* goals. "When a means of testing actions is perceived to relate a particular goal or criterion with possible courses of action, the criterion will be called operational. Otherwise the criterion will be non-operational."

threat to the status quo which is introduced from a source external to the group. In this case the "new situation" would be the status quo with the threat removed. If a crisis has already occurred, the goal might be *reattainment* of the *old* status quo, but it would *not* be *maintenance* of the *present* status quo.

LOW GOAL STRUCTURE

The group in the low goal structure situation will have fewer or much less important shared *achievement* goals. Such goals as exist will more likely relate to maintaining routine functions necessary to maintaining the status quo or making slight readjustments in it. There will be less commonality of individual goals, and attraction to the group might be considered more social in nature. Emphasis will tend to be on individual rather than on group goals. To the extent that the person does identify with the group, the identification is likely to be based on personal attractiveness or on the means which the group offers for the facilitation of personal efforts to attain individual goals.

DESCRIPTIVE EXAMPLES

A study carried out by Back (**1**) is very useful in describing or characterizing the interactions expected in the high and low goal structure situations. This study provides a discussion of differences in social interactions under different orientations toward group membership.

Two of the situations studied were cohesiveness based on the performance of a task and cohesiveness based on personal attraction.

It may be expected that interaction in the high goal structure group will be most closely characterized by that found in Back's task-oriented group where "group members wanted to complete the activity quickly and efficiently; they spent just the time necessary for the performance of the task, and they tried to use this time for the performance of the task only." There was an absolute minimum of social as opposed to task-oriented interaction.

The low goal structure situation would probably be more closely characterized by the group where cohesiveness was based on personal attraction and there was little emphasis on the group task. This group was essentially interested in enjoying the status quo. The activity of these groups tended toward "longish, pleasant conversation."

Sussman's study (12) of the "Calorie Collectors," an organization of women supposedly drawn together to participate in weight losing activities, also provides a similar characterization of the two goal structure situations.

The members of this club could be divided into one of two classes. The first were those who were primarily interested in looking for social support and sympathy for their problem. These would be in the low goal structure situation. The other group was described as the serious dieters who were really interested in undertaking activities leading to the loss of weight. These would be in the high goal structure situation.[2]

A reasonably clear example could be described at the level of the local community. In the usual case, the function and orientation of this unit of organization will be toward providing the services upon which individuals are dependent for maintenance of their personal pursuits. Emphasis would be on such relatively routine functions as maintenance of the streets, law enforcement, fire protection, garbage collection, provision of utilities, and other common services. This would be an example of a low goal structure situation.

This same community might be considered in the high structure situation if the citizens were strongly intent upon making certain changes in their community. These might take the form of a massive community beautification campaign or an all-out effort to attract new industries, etc. Individual goals of having personal prosperity would be aroused and their attainment would be seen as dependent upon accomplishment of these group goals.

[2] It might be pointed out that a group can be in both of the goal structure situations at the same time as suggested by the Sussman observations. This is probably always true to some extent, but it also seems from the study that there were essentially two distinct groups within the "Calorie Collectors." When such a situation exists, the two subgroups may tend to work at cross purposes and the total effect may be very disruptive of group performance as was the case in this situation. This may account for the ineffective performance of many small informal organizations. While this would make a very interesting area for further study, it does not appear directly relevant to the present discussion.

LEADERSHIP

In the discussion of democratic and authoritarian leadership, I have relied on the operational definitions developed by White and Lippitt (16, 26). Further elaboration will be made at a later stage concerning additional characteristics. For the present these operational definitions seem appropriate for either large or small groups. Since these are both well-known concepts, little further elaboration at this point seems necessary.

AUTHORITARIAN LEADERSHIP

1. All determination of policy by the leader.
2. Techniques and activity steps dictated by the authority, one at a time, so that future steps are always uncertain to a large degree.
3. The leader usually dictates the particular work task and work companion of each member.
4. The leader tends to be 'personal' in his praise and criticism of the work of each member, but remains aloof from active group participation except when demonstrating.

DEMOCRATIC LEADERSHIP

1. All policies a matter of group discussion and decision, encouraged and assisted by the leader.
2. Activity perspective gained during discussion period. General steps to group goal sketched, and where technical advice is needed the leader suggests two or more alternative procedures from which the choice can be made.
3. The members are free to work with whomever they choose, and the division of tasks is left up to the group.
4. The leader is "objective" or "fact-minded" in his praise and criticism, and tries to be a regular group member in its spirit without doing too much of the work.

THE DYNAMIC CHARACTERISTICS OF THE MODEL

So far we have been concerned only with the development of static definitional concepts. The real interest, however, is in the dynamic characteristics of the model—the forces causing shifts from one to another of the cells of the matrix.

THE INFLUENCE OF STRESS

The term stress is used here to include actual stress, motivation, desire, etc., regardless of the source from which it might arise. The stress may have one of two origins. First would be from natural disaster or from some other form of externally imposed threat. The second would be motivation arising from increased level of expectation, changes in values, etc. In other words stress arising in the first case is essentially a threat to the status quo as in the cases of the crisis studies where a present equilibrium is threatened. In the second case stress results rather from an increase in the level of equilibrium along some dimension of desire.

The outcome seems much the same regardless of the source of the stress, but the two situations may appear somewhat different when they are experienced and may have later implications for refinements in the model. Probably the first will tend to be more severe in its effects.

Our attention will be directed first to movements along the goal structure continuum, or rather shifts between high and low goal structure cells while the leadership pattern remains constant. At this point the assertion will be tested that an increase in situational stress will cause an increase in goal structuring, while reduction in stress will lead to a reduction in goal structuring. This is diagramed in Figure 2.

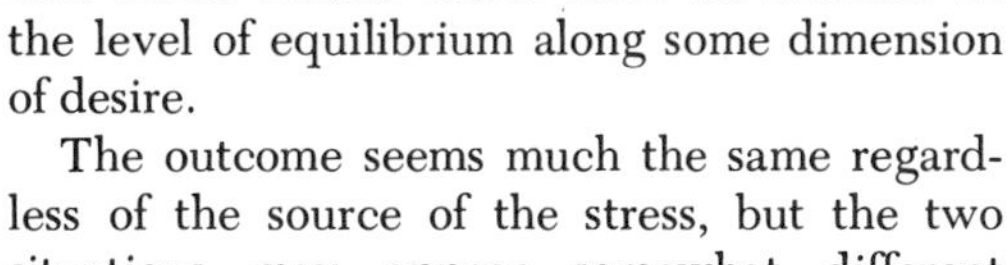

	High Goal Structure	Low Goal Structure
Democratic	← Stress ———	——— Non-Stress →
Authoritarian	← Stress ———	——— Non-Stress →

FIGURE 2. Effects of situational stress on goal structuring.

STRESS AND TOLERANCE FOR AMBIGUITY

There have been a number of studies attempting to relate stress and tolerance of ambiguity. Wispe and Lloyd (17) did a study of 43 life insurance representatives in which they related sales productivity, preference for permissive or structured group organization, and amount of threat perceived in the organizational environment. They find a significant tendency for persons who perceived little threat in their environment to prefer permissiveness in the group organization. Those with a higher threat orientation preferred the more highly structured group situation.

Smock (11) found that groups placed under stress showed a greater tendency to make an early attempt to recognize structure in an ambiguous situation. Furthermore, they tended to adhere more strongly to their pre-recognition hypothesis in spite of increasing incongruity between their hypothesis and the stimuli.

Cohen (3) reports, from a study using an interview situation, that a highly significant relationship exists between lack of situational structure and the perception of threat in the power exercised by others. This experiment seems to suggest that a perception of threat and the anxiety or stress caused by such a perception can be reduced by seeking to increase situational structure.

STRESS AND GOAL CLARITY

Though specific empirical evidence has not been found, it might be suggested that in the absence of stress a group will tend to maintain less-structured goals or objectives. This is only to say that we tend to seek to maintain the status quo when our drives are satisfied and we feel secure. The development of specific goals which might be difficult to attain develops the possibility of failure and creates anxiety or the pressure for attaining these goals. A less-structured goal situation is safer and less threatening.

When stress is introduced, the status quo is no longer satisfactory and change is sought to reduce the anxiety. The highly non-operational goal of anxiety reduction is introduced. If the cause of the stress is ambiguous this in itself will further serve to increase the anxiety. It can be expected that the first efforts will be made to reduce the ambiguity by attempting to identify or give structure to the source of the anxiety.

Another source of ambiguity will be present when, even though the source of the stress is clear, it is not exactly clear what actions can be taken to remove the source of the stress.

Anxiety seems to serve as a motivation for three actions, which must logically be made in sequence. The completion of any one of these will serve to reduce a part of the anxiety.

1. Identify the source of the anxiety.
2. Identify the steps which must be taken to remove the anxiety.
3. Carry out the steps identified in 2.

The first two parts of the sequence are concerned primarily with reduction of ambiguity but are nearly essential to successful purposeful (as opposed to random) actions to reduce the anxiety. The ambiguity is a frustrating experience because it stands as a barrier to successful action. As Lewin (8, 255) points out, "An unstructured region has the same effect as an impassable obstacle. Being in unstructured surroundings leads to uncertainty of behavior because it is not clear whether a certain action will lead to or away from a goal."

Torrance (13), who studied a group of 200 Air Force personnel downed over enemy territory during World War II or Korea, relates the results of situations where the ambiguity is not reduced. He found that in this very stressful survival situation two types of structural unclarity were likely to be evident: (a) unclear structure of paths to survival and (b) unstabilized relations among persons. He found that these were likely to lead to either random, trial-and-error behavior, or to development of a feeling of hopelessness which usually led to surrender to the enemy.

Studies have found that in stressful situations where goal and path clarity is not established, there will be a tendency to avoid the situation or to leave the group.

Gerard (4, 397) reported that low-status subjects whose group goals were unclear tended to withdraw from their group, become dissatisfied with their roles, and devaluate their own effectiveness.

Weitz (15) conducted a study of 474 life insurance salesmen who tend, as the nature of their occupation, to be under considerable competitive stress. A detailed book describing the work to be done was given to 226 of them. The other 248 were not given the book. There was a considerably higher rate of termination among those for whom the situation was not clearly defined.

It should be quite clear that once a goal is attained, it is no longer a goal. If the goal has been attained and the anxiety reduced, the group has almost automatically relocated itself in the low goal structure situation. Of course this is looking to a sort of "pure" case. Particularly in a larger organization it would be highly unlikely that all goals would be attained and all anxieties removed at any particular point in time. It seems at least conceptually possible, however, to think in terms of an over-all index of anxiety and degree of goal structuring in order to place the group along the goal structure continuum.

CHANGES IN LEADERSHIP

The shifts from one goal structure cell to another are merely incidental to a unified hypothesis regarding the development of pressures for shifts between democratic and authoritarian leadership.

THE "NATURAL" SHIFTS IN LEADERSHIP PATTERNS

While it is possible for these shifts between democratic and authoritarian leadership to take place at either the high or low goal structure levels, the hypothesis to be tested suggests that *unless outside pressure or force is exerted,* the direction of the shifts in the high goal structure situation will be only from democratic to authoritarian and in the low goal structure situation it will be only from authoritarian to democratic. This is represented very simply in Figure 3.

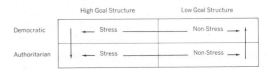

FIGURE 3. Direction of shifts in leadership patterns.

HIGH STRESS SHIFT FROM DEMOCRATIC TO AUTHORITARIAN LEADERSHIP

We have already established that under stressful conditions there will be strong pressures exerted for the development of clear goals and clearly defined methods of attaining them. In going one step further, we may also expect that the more compelling and/or the more clearly structured the goal, the greater will be the desire to take a direct approach to the attainment of the goal. Pleasant socializing is replaced with more intense emphasis on achievement. This would suggest attempting to attain complete control over any ambiguities in the environment, especially those ambiguities which take the form of deviant individuals or subgroups. The greater the immediacy or urgency, the greater the demand that all available resources be channeled directly toward the attainment of this goal. This is sometimes difficult to do while still attempting to maintain truly democratic institutions.

Deviants loom as frustration-creating barriers to the goal attainment. The most direct way to remove the barrier is to control it and move it at will. There are two basic forms which this control may take. Of course, here again we must realize that we are in reality dealing with a continuum. The first is the control common to democratic institutions where certain limits are set on action, and control is carried out by the policing of exceptions. Actual attainment of goals is more likely to depend on conformity attained through perceived commonality of interest or through group social pressures. The second form of control is the authoritarian form which seeks to maintain absolute control over every action taking place within the organization. The greater the pressures for collective action and the greater the tendency for deviation within the group, the more likely it is that this form of control will have the greater appeal.

The assertion is explicit in the model that a democratic organization can maintain itself with a well-defined goal structure. It now remains to establish the conditions under which this is likely to be the case, as well as stating those conditions under which the appeal of authoritarianism will be more overpowering.

When is democracy retained?

We can see from the nature of the control methods available under democracy that the success of democracy in the face of crisis depends to large degree on the cohesiveness of the group and its ability to apply sanctions through social pressure. This is most assured if the goal is clear, the path to the goal is clear, and individuals identify their own objectives with group objectives and agree on the methods of attaining these. This means essentially a minimum of unresolved ambiguity. The statement is to some extent redundant in that when the goal and path are clear it is almost a definitional matter that all who agree on the goal or identify with the group will also agree on the path. To the extent that there is disagreement, we might consider the goal or the path to contain elements of ambiguity.[3]

When is there a shift to authoritarianism?

Stress reduction in itself does not provide a unifying group goal due to its rather extreme non-operational, ambiguous character. Cohesiveness under stress is dependent on some agreement as to the source of the stress, or on the goal, the attainment of which will reduce the stress. Further cohesiveness can be developed through agreement on the path to the attainment of the goal. Since the cohesiveness of the group becomes more and more task-oriented as the stress increases, the group will be evaluated in terms of its potential for providing a means of completing the task-stress reduction. Thus the less the agreement within the group with regard to how the objective may be attained, the less the individual who disagrees with the group view will be attracted to the group and the more he will attempt to take independent action, form opposition groups, etc.

This situation may be expected to lead to more overt action on the part of leaders to control these deviants in order to reduce the ambiguity which they face in their decision-making. Control over the deviants gives them greater control over their environment and removes impediments to what they consider to be effective action. The greater the stress, and the less the clarity and general agreement on goals and path, the greater the compulsion among the group members to give power to a central person who in essence promises to remove the ambiguity and reduce the stress. Hook (**7**, 13) points out that, ". . . insofar as alternatives of action are open, or even conceived to be open—a need will be felt for a hero to initiate, organize, and lead."

That there is a tendency toward reliance on a power figure in ambiguous situations may be demonstrated at even very low levels on the continuum, as is demonstrated in a study by Waring, Dwyer, and Junkin (**14**). They found that during meals on the first day of nursery school, children were more ready to acquiesce to the advice of the adult than later on when they felt themselves to be on better-

---

[3] Although this seems the situation most conducive to maintaining democratic leadership in time of stress or even crisis, it may be seen that there is also a danger in complete agreement, because in this case there may be too little concern with maintaining restrictions on the power of leaders. If those in power are opportunists, this provides their opportunity to establish authoritarian control. Thus even when the real crisis is passed, the peo-

ple may find that now they are unable to regain the power which they originally passed to the central authority. "Where a democracy is wise, it will wholeheartedly cooperate with its leaders and at the same time be suspicious of the powers delegated to them—a difficult task but one which must be solved if democracy is not to become, as often in the past, a school for tyrants" (**7**, 14).

known ground for resisting. In other words, during the period of initial ambiguity, they tended to submit to an authoritarian leader on whom they relied to help structure the situation.

Hamblin (5) found in laboratory groups subjected to apparent crisis in a problem-solving experience a tendency to replace the old leader with a new leader if the old leader did not have an obvious solution to the crisis problem. Hertzler (6) did an analysis of 35 historical dictatorships. Although his method was not as systematic and objective as might be desired, his conclusion is consistent with the one reached here (6, 160).

A befuddled and fearsome mass in time of crisis is nearly always ready, nay anxious, to give over control to anyone who gives evidence of ability to wield it efficiently. This situation, in turn, both demands and provides the opportunity for a leader or a cohesive minority group which offers a ready made formula of social procedure and which promises a dynamic attack upon the problems.

Other experiments have demonstrated increased suggestibility in situations of ambiguity which point up the increased possibility for an authoritarian leader to introduce distorting suggestions when ambiguity is present. Luchins and Luchins (9) presented subjects with a picture identification task. Subjects were influenced by an overheard judgment and by the experimenter's evaluation of the communication as right or wrong. Although there was more agreement with the true than with the false communications, the conformity with false communications, and failures to respond were higher for the ambiguous than for the clear-cut pictures.

Coffin (2) conducted a series of studies which are relevant to the present problem. In one case he used the Rorschach ink-blot tests as the ambiguous stimulus. Subjects were given a fictitious journal article stating that business and professional men would see the blots in one way while laborers would see them in another way. Using college students as subjects, the conclusion was reached that "subjects may be influenced by suggestion not only to accept or assent to a suggested statement, but actively to construct the imaginative situation in accordance with the suggestion given." From this not-very-surprising conclu-

sion we see a laboratory demonstration of an often-used political technique to force judgments in unfavorable situations. "A good American will recognize that . . . etc."

Another experiment by Coffin (2) revealed low but consistent correlation between suggestibility and difficulty of a set of math problems. The degree of suggestibility declined with years of mathematical training. This may have particular relevance in the underdeveloped countries where the tasks are indeed difficult yet the level of training is very low. It is in these countries where there seems to be the greatest susceptibility to authoritarian leadership.[4]

Still another experiment conducted by Coffin (2) used sound stimuli and again found that suggestibility increased as the ambiguity of the assigned task increased.

SHIFTS FROM AUTHORITARIAN TO DEMOCRATIC LEADERSHIP UNDER LOW STRESS

In the low stress situation, it would seem difficult for authoritarian leadership to maintain itself. We can expect that the power held by the authoritarian figure will be reduced as was found in a study by Hamblin (5). He found that the person with highest influence in a group had the greatest influence (relative to other members of the group) during periods of crisis. This influence decreased as the goal was attained and the crisis was thereby reduced or removed.

Once major group goals have been attained, the cohesiveness of the group will once again come to depend more upon the socializing process. Greater importance will be placed on the attempt to satisfy individual needs which may have been either sacrificed or frustrated by the authoritarian leadership.

As in the case of the White and Lippitt study there will be decreased satisfaction with the authoritarian structure and the opportunity for greater individual participation and self-

[4] When Hook (7, 238) points out that "A successful democracy . . . may honor its statesmen: but it must honor its teachers more . . ." he is in a way suggesting that a democracy must be able to decrease situational ambiguity through increased knowledge of the situations likely to be encountered rather than relying upon a hero leader to provide this structure.

determination will be desired. In many cases the surface expressions of this discontent exhibited in the presence of the authoritarian leader are such as to probably go unnoticed, but at least in the White and Lippitt study these showed up clearly in careful analysis.

The following expressions of the discontent were noted (**16**, 74–76).

1. Four boys dropped out of the clubs during the experimental situation and all did so during periods of autocratic leadership.
2. Nineteen of twenty boys who made direct comparisons between the autocratic and democratic leaders stated preferences for the democratic leader.
3. The boys made significantly more discontented remarks to each other under autocratic than under democratic rule.
4. There were more expressions of discontent directed at the leader.
5. There was more ignoring of the leader's approaches.

Over a longer period of time as these resentments built up under the confining authority, we might expect that more overt signs of discontent would develop.

"UNNATURAL!" SHIFTS IN LEADERSHIP PATTERNS

One can hardly imagine shifts between democratic and authoritarian leadership taking place in directions opposite to those just discussed *if* indeed the important variables are as they have been described. Cases can easily be found, however, of shifts counter to the direction indicated. It might be established that *these* shifts do not usually take place as a matter of group acceptance or from other internal pressures, but rather are forced upon the group through superior strength. A military dictator may arise in a time of indifference and establish military control; a department or office of a larger firm may be suddenly assigned a new administrator who introduces a more centralized control, etc. These shifts do take place, but they are of a somewhat artificial nature compared with the processes which we have been discussing.

A shift from authoritarian to democratic leadership in a situation of high stress would also seem to be very unlikely unless an outside force dedicated to democratic leadership overthrew or replaced the former leaders and then significantly reduced the source of the stress that had kept the authoritarian leader in power. Other special cases might be presented where an authoritarian leader apparently gave up his power voluntarily in time of high stress, but such occurrence is rare and such cases would have to be examined individually to determine their relationship to the present model.

THE EQUILIBRIUM CELLS

It should be clear that there are resistances to shifts in leadership patterns taking place. These are created by tradition and vested interest. There are thus important restraining factors involved to prevent the shifts previously indicated. The hypothesis we have developed establishes only the direction of the pressures which exist for change, but does not promise that the change will actually take place.

The direction of the pressures suggests that in the highly structured goal situation the equilibrium cell is one in which authoritarian leadership is exercised, while in the low goal structure situation, it is democratic leadership which exists in the equilibrium situation. In the low goal structure group, the emphasis will be on individual subgoals rather than super organization goals. In a sense this might be considered the characteristic nature of the democracy with its emphasis on the individual rather than the group. In this situation the group leadership will be sought which will serve the advancement of the individual. The autocrat will be hard put to maintain his position.

When a more all-consuming group goal is developed, the individual's role becomes subservient to the group and his only importance comes in his contribution to the group. This is the situation in the high goal structure condition and it is here that the autocracy will be in equilibrium. The democratic government will be in constant danger of running into new ambiguities and losing its consensus support.

MAINTAINING AUTHORITARIAN EQUILIBRIUM

It seems that authoritarian leaders have a particular appreciation of the equilibrium acting to maintain their power in the high stress, highly structured goal situation. Thus it can be seen that one of the most important activities of a dictatorship is that of stressing the threats created by both external and internal enemies in order to maintain the stress and produce the super goals which can be used to unite the populace. These must be constantly internalized by the people.

In Indonesia this is represented by the "struggle for West Irian" which is reiterated in nearly every public utterance by every public official. For the Communist countries, the "foe" is the menace of capitalism, represented by the United States in particular. The most extreme emphasis is placed on this in Communist China, where the internal problems are much more severe than in Russia, for example. Considerable dependence is placed on these central goals in directing the people's attention away from the frustrations experienced in satisfying their true personal goals.[5]

In Sussman's study (12, 354) we find a case where a group leader was attempting to maintain an essentially authoritarian leadership position; however, this leader made little pretense of establishing or working toward group goals. "Leadership as it existed in Calorie Collectors was one of attainment of personal influence and power by Mrs. Lott rather than achievement of group goals. The result was ultimate factionalism and disorganization." The group disintegrated and later reformed around another woman who was oriented more toward group objectives of planning programs to encourage weight reduction. This gives one example of loss of control by an authoritarian leader in a situation where the leader did not identify with group goals.

It is interesting to note a further technique used by the authoritarian to maintain his leadership. This is mentioned in the operational definition by White and Lippitt (16, 26). "Techniques and activity steps dictated by the

---

[5] It will be noted that China is an especially complex case, as the "manufactured" crisis is used to structure the stress created by a real internal crisis. The attempt is to develop a structure more consistent with retaining the present government in power than would be the case if the structure were allowed to develop around the true source of the stress.

authority, one at a time, so that future steps are always uncertain to a large degree."

This serves several functions. It provides reduction of immediate anxiety, but retains dependence on the authoritarian leader for further reduction of the ambiguity when the present step is completed. It also makes it difficult for failure to be evaluated, as it is not possible to determine the actual importance of any particular step that is taken. It is further not possible to certainly establish whether or not the current step is truly leading toward the *stated* goal. Considerable faith must be placed on the authoritarian. If his work is not accepted, the situation again becomes intolerably ambiguous.

IMPLICATIONS

It is difficult at this point to discuss specific applications of detailed knowledge of the influence of these situational pressures on leadership. However, it is possible to suggest where applications might be sought.

This study was undertaken from the point of view of an advocate of democratic or participative leadership. In order to insure the preservation of the democratic structure, it seems essential to understand the forces which cause pressure for a shift from democratic structure to more highly authoritarian structure.

Through greater understanding, possibly either the situations leading to the pressures may be avoided or effective countermeasures can be established to resist the pressures expected under certain circumstances. Not only does this have implication at the national and international political level and in particular in dealings with newly independent nations, but it might also prove of value in the implementation of the relatively new group-centered theories of management and organization. Systematic study and organization of the forces which resist the successful introduction and application of participative management are the first steps in finding suitable implementation techniques and in establishing the situation or environment in which such types of organization can persist in equilibrium.

More could be done at this point to discuss the problems of leadership in underdeveloped countries which served as the introduction of the paper. Most of the implications should, however, be reasonably clear and will for the present be left as they were presented—the initiating stimulus for undertaking the study. The important problem was to provide the model or "structure" which could then be adapted for application to these specific situational problems. The same statement could be made with regard to the applications to participative management.

SUMMARY

A model was developed showing how certain situational forces develop to produce shifts between democratic and authoritarian forms of leadership. It was established that where group goals assume greater importance than do individual goals and there are ambiguities obscuring the path to attaining these goals, an authoritarian leadership will be sought to reduce these ambiguities. Where ambiguities are not of a stress-creating nature, that is, not standing in the way of goal attainment, and the attainment of group goals is not seen as a necessary *prior* event to the attainment of individual goals, a more democratic leadership will be sought.

References

1. Back, K. W. The exertion of influence through social communication. *Journal of Abnormal and Social Psychology*, 1951, **46**, 9–24.
2. Coffin, T. E. Some conditions of suggestion and suggestibility: A study of some attitudinal and situational factors influencing the process of suggestion. *Psychological Monographs*, 1941, No. 241.
3. Cohen, A. R. Situation structure, self-esteem, and threat-oriented reactions to power. In D. Cartwright (Ed.), *Studies in social power*. Ann Arbor, Mich.: Institute for Social Research, 1959.
4. Gerard, H. Unpublished study reported in D. Cartwright and A. Zander (Eds.), *Group dynamics research and theory*. Evanston, Ill.: Row, Peterson, 1960.
5. Hamblin, R. L. Leadership and crises. *Sociometry*, 1958, **21**, 322–335.
6. Hertzler, J. O. Crises and dictatorship. *American Sociological Review*, 1940, **5**, 157–169.
7. Hook, S. *The hero in history*. New York: John Day Co., 1943.
8. Lewin, K. *Field theory in social science*. New York: Harper, 1959.
9. Luchins, A. S., & Luchins, E. H. Previous experience with ambiguous stimulus under various social influences. *Journal of Social Psychology*, 1955, **42**, 249–270.
10. March, J. G., & Simon, H. A. *Organizations*. New York: Wiley, 1958.
11. Smock, C. D. The influence of stress on the intolerance of ambiguity. *Journal of Abnormal and Social Psychology*, 1955, **50**, 177–182.
12. Sussman, M. B. The calorie collectors: A study of spontaneous group formation, collapse, and reconstruction. *Social Forces*, 1956, **34**, 351–356.
13. Torrance, E. P. The behavior of small groups under stress conditions of survival. *American Sociological Review*, 1954, **19**, 751–755.
14. Waring, E. S., Dwyer, F. M., & Junkin, E. Guidance: The case of Ronald. *Cornell Bulletin for Homemakers*, 1939, **418**, 1–112.
15. Weitz, J. Job expectancy and survival. *Journal of Applied Psychology*, 1956, **40**, 245–247.
16. White, R. K., & Lippitt, R. *Autocracy and democracy: An experimental inquiry*. New York: Harper, 1960.
17. Wispe, L. G., & Lloyd, K. E. Some situational and psychological determinants of the desire for structured interpersonal relations. *Journal of Abnormal and Social Psychology*, 1955, **51**, 57–60.

28

Personality and Situational Determinants of Leadership Effectiveness

FRED E. FIEDLER

What are the leader's personality traits, behaviors, or attitudes that determine whether his group will be successful?

This is a central question in contemporary leadership theory and research. The answer determines how millions of dollars and thousands of man hours each year are spent on management development and on leadership recruitment, selection and training.

This chapter summarizes a fifteen-year research program that has covered more than thirty-five studies and sixteen hundred groups. It will attempt to make three major points.

1. The effectiveness of a group is contingent upon the appropriateness of the leader's style to the specific situation in which he operates. Most people are effective leaders in some situations and ineffective in certain others.
2. The type of leadership style that will be most effective depends upon the degree to which the group situation enables the leader to exert influence.
3. If leadership effectiveness depends not only upon leadership style but also the group situation, we can either make the leader fit a specific group situation by selection or training or we can engineer the group situation to fit the leader. Since it is extremely difficult to change a man's personality and leadership style, but relatively easy to change his work situation, we will examine "an organizational engineering" approach to leadership and management development.

MEASUREMENT OF LEADERSHIP STYLE

Leadership is a process of influencing others for the purpose of performing a shared task. This process requires to a greater or lesser extent that one person direct, coordinate, or motivate others in the group in order to get the assigned task accomplished. In grossly oversimplified terms, the leader may use the power of his posi-

This chapter was prepared especially for this volume. The research was supported by grants from the Office of Naval Research and the National Institute for Mental Health, U. S. Public Health Service.

tion to enforce compliance or he may persuade and cajole his members to do his bidding.

Ever since Lewin and Lippitt's classical leadership studies (20), investigators in this area have concentrated on these two important aspects or clusters of leadership behaviors and attitudes. The poles of this general dimension have been given such various labels as autocratic versus democratic, authoritarian versus equalitarian, production versus human relations oriented, and task versus group oriented. (See McGrath and Altman, 21.)

The measures we utilized to tap these two styles of exerting influence were interpersonal perception scales called the "Assumed Similarity between Opposites" (ASo) and the esteem for the least-preferred co-worker (LPC) scores. The ASo and LPC scores are highly correlated (.80 to .93) and will therefore be interpreted interchangeably.

The ASo score, which we used in earlier studies, is obtained by asking the individual to think of everyone with whom he has ever worked. He then describes (a) the person whom he considers his most-preferred co-worker (MPC) and (b) the person whom he considers his least-preferred co-worker (LPC). This does not need to be someone with whom he works at the time. This score can be obtained, therefore, to select leaders in advance, when this is desired.

The descriptions are made on eight-point, bipolar adjective check-lists similar in form to Osgood's Semantic Differential (23), but using items descriptive of personality attributes, for example:

Pleasant:—:—:—:—:—:—:—:—:Unpleasant
    8 7 6 5 4 3 2 1

Friendly:—:—:—:—:—:—:—:—:Unfriendly [1]
    8 7 6 5 4 3 2 1

ASo scores are derived by scoring each of the items from most to least favorable and computing a measure of profile similarity between the two descriptions. A person who perceives his most- and least-preferred co-workers as very similar will, therefore, have a high as-

[1] Other scale items typically used are: rejecting-accepting, helpful-frustrating, unenthusiastic-enthusiastic, tense-relaxed, distant-close, cold-warm, cooperative-uncooperative, supportive-hostile, boring-interesting, quarrelsome-harmonious, self-assured-hesitant, efficient-inefficient, gloomy-cheerful, open-guarded.

sumed similarity score (or, in operational terms, a small discrepancy score), while a person who strongly differentiates between these two "opposites" on his co-worker continuum will have a low ASo (and thus a large discrepancy) score. The LPC score is one component of ASo. It is obtained by simply summing the item scores on the scale sheet describing the least-preferred co-worker.

A person with a high LPC score tends to see even a poor co-worker in a relatively favorable manner ("Even if I cannot work with him, he may still be a very nice and valuable person"). A low LPC leader perceives his least-preferred co-worker in a highly unfavorable, rejecting manner ("If I cannot work with him, he is probably just no good"). LPC and ASo scores have a high internal consistency with split-half coefficients of over .90. The scores are reasonably stable over time, although changes occur depending upon intervening experiences.

LPC and ASo have been very difficult to interpret since they do not correlate with commonly used personality and attitude scores. We originally thought that we were dealing with a measure of psychological distance. It has become clear recently that we are dealing with a motivational measure that manifests itself in different behaviors as the situation changes. In brief, the individual who rates his least-preferred co-worker in relatively favorable terms tends to be considerate of the feelings and opinions of his co-workers. However, his primary motivational pattern is to obtain recognition and rewards from others. He tends to gain self-esteem by being esteemed by others and having good relations with them. The low LPC leader, who describes his least-preferred co-worker in very negative, rejecting terms, gains self-esteem and need satisfaction from performing the task. He tends to be task-oriented and structuring in his behavior and concerned with productivity rather than with interpersonal relations. We will return to this interpretation later in this chapter.

THE RESEARCH PROGRAM

INFORMAL GROUPS

Basketball Teams. Our first study (4) was conducted on fourteen high school basketball teams. These seemed especially well suited for our purposes since an excellent criterion of team effectiveness is readily available. Teams that win most of their games are obviously better than teams that lose most games. Moreover, teams that play in the same league are fairly well matched on the basis of size of school and resources in coaching staff and the pool of potential players.

A sample of fourteen squads was tested at the beginning of the season. In this first study each player was asked to name and describe the member of the team with whom he could work best and the member with whom he could work least well. These descriptions, as already mentioned, yielded ASo scores. Since these scores were interpreted at that time as measures of psychological closeness and warmth, we had expected to find that close-knit teams in which members perceived each other as very similar would also have the best performance record. As it turned out, only the ASo scores of the sociometrically most-preferred team member, its informal leader, correlated very highly with group performance, but in the negative direction (− .69, *p* < .01). Thus, the leader who was presumed to be psychologically distant tended to have the best team.

These results were checked toward the end of the season in a second study of basketball teams, which compared seven teams that had won most of their league games with five teams that had lost most of their games. The informal leaders were again identified by means of sociometric preference questions. Their ASo scores correlated negatively with team performance (− .58, *p* < .05) thus confirming the results of the first study.

Surveying Teams. To test the generality of our findings, we studied twenty-two student surveying parties during a field course (4). Each team consisted of three to four civil engineering students. The main criterion of effectiveness was the instructor's evaluation of the accuracy with which the team had measured and mapped the assigned plots of land.

Sociometric preference ratings again identified the informal leader of each group. As in the basketball studies, the ASo score of the informal leader correlated negatively with the criterion of team effectiveness (4).

FORMALLY ORGANIZED GROUPS

The data we had obtained on informal groups showed a correlation between the ASo score of the sociometrically chosen leader and the team's performance. But were groups effective because their leaders happened to have the attributes measured by low ASo scores? Or did groups that were effective prefer the task-motivated low ASo person over the more relationship-oriented high ASo person? We hoped to answer this question by investigating groups in which the leader was appointed by the organization rather than identified *post hoc* by sociometric questionnaires.

Bomber Crews. The first study in this second series (5) utilized 53 B-29 bomber crews, each consisting of eleven men. The aircraft commander, as the formally appointed leader, commanded four specialist officers (the co-pilot, navigator, radar observer, and bombardier) as well as five enlisted men. The primary mission of these crews was to deliver bombs on targets, guided either by radar equipment or by visual bomb sights. The main criterion was an average circular error score for radar bombing which indicated the distance by which a bomb would have missed a target in hypothetical radar bomb runs. These scores, based on complex radio gear and corrected for weather and equipment variation, had a reliability of .45 (19).

We expected to find a negative correlation between the ASo score of the aircraft commander and group performance. However, the relationship, while negative, was at best marginal (*r* = − .23). Extensive further analyses of the data suggested that the hypothesized results could be obtained only in crews in which the aircraft commander had a very good relationship with his crew. These were crews in which the aircraft commander and his keymen sociometrically endorsed each other, or in which (*a*) the crew members sociometrically chose their aircraft commander as the most-preferred member of the crew and (*b*) the aircraft commander sociometrically endorsed his keymen. The keymen who most directly influenced the success of the mission in this situation were the radar observer and the navigator who manned the radar equipment. Quite unexpectedly, we obtained a positive correlation between the aircraft commander's ASo and radar-bombing scores in crews in which the aircraft commander was accepted by his crew but did not endorse his keymen. The correlations were negative in crews that did not accept their crew commander and in which the crew commander did

TABLE 1. *Correlation of the Aircraft Commanders' ASo with Radar-Bombing Criterion Under Selected Sociometric Relations Between the Aircraft Commander and the Keyman*

Sociometric Condition [a]	Rho	N	p
AC = MPC ⟶ VO/N	−.81	.10	(.01)[b]
⎯⎯ VO/N	−.14	6	
⟶̸⟶	.43	6	
AC = MPC ⟶ VO/N	−.03	18	
⎯⎯ VO/N	−.80	5	
⟶̸⟶ VO/N	−.67	7	

[a] AC = aircraft commander; MPC = most-preferred co-worker; VO = radar observer; N = navigator. ⟶ = high sociometric choice. ⎯⎯ = neutral sociometric choice. ⟶̸⟶ = low sociometric choice.

The high sociometric choice symbol indicates that either the VO and N or both were given ranks 1 to 2 by the AC. The low sociometric choice indicates that both the VO and N were given ranks 3.5 to 10. All other cases are in the neutral category. These cutoff points are in part based on the desire to divide the groups into three equal subsamples; however, the second rank is considered indicative of high preference, even though this makes the highly liked group somewhat larger than the other two subgroups.

[b] As this study explored many hypotheses, tests of significance are not interpretable.

not endorse his keymen (Table 1). The significance of these findings became obvious to us approximately ten years later.

In the meantime we were able to perform several replication studies. One of these used results from the same sample of crews but with an uncorrelated criterion of performance—namely, the percent of satisfactory visual bomb runs. Since over 50 percent of the crews obtained perfect scores, the test was at best suggestive. However, we again found that the ASo scores of sociometrically accepted leaders who endorsed the bombardier correlated negatively with crew performance; groups in which the accepted commander did not endorse his keyman yielded positive correlations.

Tank Crews. A completely independent cross-validation study of the bomber crew findings was possible in connection with an Army experiment conducted by the Ballistics Research Laboratory (5). A group of twenty-five tank crews were assembled for the purpose of comparing the performance of five different models of tanks on twenty-five different target runs. Crews and equipment were matched, and extraneous factors were experimentally controlled by means of a partial Greco-Latin square design. The crew members were assembled and tested shortly before the experiment was begun. These pretests included interpersonal perception measures from which we derived ASo scores.

The criteria of crew effectiveness were (*a*) the average time required to hit each of twenty-five targets and (*b*) the average time needed to travel from one target to the next. These two criteria correlated −.08, indicating that we were dealing with independent performance measures. The keymen for these two tasks were, of course, also different. The gunner was primarily involved with the "time-per-hit" criterion, while the driver was the keyman for the "travel-time" score.

Sociometric preference scores were obtained from all crew members three times during the experiment. These indicated that 17 of the 25 tank crew commanders were also the most-chosen crew members. A cross-validation

TABLE 2. *Correlations Between Tank Commanders' ASo Score and Crew Performance in Crews that Accept Their Leaders*

		Leader's Preference for Keyman					
		High		Neutral		Negative	
Criterion	Keyman	Rho	N	Rho	N	Rho	N
Average time to hit target	Gunner	−.60	6	.11	6	.60	5
Average time to travel to target	Driver	−.33	5	.39	6	.43	6

was therefore possible for crews that accepted their leader.

We hypothesized that the low ASo commanders would have the most effective crews if they were sociometrically accepted and if they sociometrically endorsed their keymen. Sociometrically accepted commanders with high ASo scores would be more effective if they did not sociometrically endorse the keyman. As can be seen from Table 2, these results yielded data closely corresponding to those obtained in analogous bomber crew samples. It was, therefore, obvious that the relationship between leader and group members played an important part in determining whether the crew would perform more effectively under high or under low ASo leaders.

A number of subsequent studies (2, 15, 18) showed that the prediction of group performance required not only the leaders' ASo scores but also sociometric measures to indicate the leader's relations with his group members.

Anti-Aircraft Crews. Similar results were obtained in a study of anti-aircraft artillery crews conducted by Hutchins and Fiedler (17). The criterion of group performance was the "acquisition and lock-on" of unidentified targets flying over the defense area. These data were recently subjected to a re-analysis. We selected ten crews with the most highly chosen crew commanders, ten with the least-chosen or rejected commanders, and ten intermediate in this respect.

Correlations were then obtained between the commander's LPC score and the crew's performance rating. Low LPC leaders performed best in crews in which they were highly chosen and in which they were rejected. High LPC leaders performed best in crews in which they had only moderately good relations. These results were, thus, similar to those obtained in the bomber crew study when we take into account the entire range of leader-member relations (Table 3).

Complex Organizations. It now became important to ask whether (a) the results would generalize to complex organizations that consist of a policy- and decision-making group as well as a subordinate task group and (b) the direction of the relationship would be affected by the nature of the tasks that these two types of groups were required to perform.

An investigation (12) was conducted in 32 small consumer cooperative organizations that sell supplies and petroleum products to farmers within their sales area. Each of the companies has its own board of directors and two or more assistant managers in charge of operating various departments of the company. All companies in this group belonged to the same federation. The headquarters of the federation maintained accurate records of sales and operating costs that served as criteria of company performance. The most important measure was the company's net income (adjusted for gross sales) averaged over a three-year period to minimize the effects of seasonal and yearly fluctuations over which management had no control.

All available general managers and assistant managers and all but three available members of the 32 boards of directors completed the interpersonal perception and sociometric preference questionnaires. The companies were grouped on the basis of the sociometric preference patterns that would indicate the relationship between the general manager and the key personnel of the company. The manager's relations were considered to be excellent if he was sociometrically endorsed by both the board's leader and his assistant managers, considered to be intermediate if he was endorsed by the board but not by his staff or vice versa, and considered to be poor if he was endorsed by neither his board leader nor by his staff of assistant managers. Within each group the general manager's LPC score was then correlated with his company's net income (Table 4).

As can be seen, the low LPC managers performed best in companies in which their relations with other key members were very good and in which their relations were very poor.

TABLE 3. *Correlations Between Leaders' LPC Scores and Anti-Aircraft Artillery Crew Performance*

	Rho	N
Most highly chosen crew commanders	$-.34$	10
Middle range in sociometric choices	.49	10
Lowest chosen crew commanders	$-.42$	10

TABLE 4. *Correlations Between General Managers' LPC Score and Company Net Income*

	Rho	N
General manager is most chosen by board and staff	−.67	10
General manager is chosen by board but rejected by staff	.20	6
General manager is rejected by board but chosen by staff	.26	6
General manager is rejected by board and staff	−.75	7

High LPC managers performed best in the companies in which their relations were only moderately good. These findings are thus similar to those obtained in the bomber-crew and anti-aircraft artillery studies.

This study also provided data about the difference between effective leadership styles in policy-making and in executive groups. The policy- and decision-making group appeared to require considerate, permissive, relationship-oriented leadership under conditions of good group climate. The executive functions of running the company demanded a more task-motivated leadership in groups in which leader member relations were good or very poor, but relationship-oriented, considerate leadership in groups with only moderately good group climate. Obviously, the task as well as the nature of the leader-member relationship seemed to determine the type of leadership style that led to effective group performance. It became important, therefore, to study more intensively groups that had to perform highly unstructured, vaguely defined, or creative tasks.

GROUP CREATIVITY

The Dutch Creativity Study. An opportunity to conduct studies of group creativity presented itself in Holland (9). The country has approximately eleven million inhabitants of whom slightly more than half are protestants, mostly Calvinists, living in the northern part of the country, and about 40 percent are Roman Catholics who live primarily in the south. A considerable amount of political tension exists between these two population sectors, and it carries over into social relations. As a result, Calvinists and Catholics tend to keep apart in most areas of life; however, almost all governmental and public committees are constituted in large part on the basis of religious affilia-

tion. It was of considerable interest, therefore, to determine the effects of religious and cultural heterogeneity on group creativity.

The study utilized a total of 32 four-man groups. Half of these contained two men from each of the two religious and regional backgrounds; the other half contained either four Calvinists or four Catholics. The groups were further subdivided so that half the groups had appointed leaders while the other half were given no instructions about determining leadership. The emergent (or informal) leader of the group was identified after the session by means of sociometric questionnaires. The leaders in these latter groups obviously had a very weak position compared with leaders who were formally appointed by the experimenters.

The groups were given creative tasks—that is, Guilford's Alternative Uses and Plot Titles tests (13)—and the groups were also required to compose three different stories on the basis of one Thematic Apperception Test picture which they were shown. These stories were rated on the basis of a manual on originality and creativity by two independent judges. The reliability of judgments was .88.

The results of correlating the leader's LPC score with group creativity are shown on Table 5. As can be seen, the correlation between leader LPC and group performance was high and positive only in the homogeneous formal groups but high and negative in groups that were heterogeneous or had informal leadership. A content analysis as well as the results from post-session questionnaires showed that the homogeneous formal groups tended to be quite relaxed and tension free. The other groups tended to be relatively more stressful and tense, presumably because of the social strain caused by the heterogeneous composition of the group or because of the

TABLE 5. *Correlations Between Leaders' LPC and Productivity Scores in the Dutch Creativity Study*

Group Structure	Group Composition	
	Homogeneous	Heterogeneous
Formal	No competition for leadership status	No competition for leadership status
	Little social strain; few problems in communication	Much social strain; impeded communication
	$\overline{X}^a$ 105.28	$\overline{X}^a$ 116.62
	SD^a 37.23	SD^a 34.37
	N 7	N 8
	$rho_{\text{LPC Creativity}}$ $+.75^b$	$rho_{\text{LPC Creativity}}$ $-.72^c$
Informal	Competition for leadership status	Competition for leadership status
	Little social strain; few problems in communication	Much social strain; impeded communication
	$\overline{X}^a$ 87.50	$\overline{X}^a$ 105.75
	SD^a 16.64	SD^a 10.30
	N 6	N 8
	$rho_{\text{LPC Creativity}}$ $-.67$	$rho_{\text{LPC Creativity}}$ $-.21$

[a] Means and standard deviations refer to creativity scores.
[b] $p < .10$.
[c] $p < .05$.

rivalry for leadership status that arose in informal groups.

This study turned out to be one of the critical turning points in our program. It suggested the importance of group climate, as well as the leader's position power, in determining the relationship of leadership style and group performance in situations involving an unstructured task.

Two additional experiments (6) confirmed the finding that the relationship-oriented, considerate leaders performed better in situations they considered relaxed and free of tension, while task-oriented, directive leaders were more effective in situations they considered tense and less pleasant. These studies also showed that it is the leader's, not the member's, reaction to the group atmosphere that determined the direction of the relationship. This suggested that it was primarily the leader's reaction to the group, rather than the objective reality of the situation, that determined the appropriateness of the leadership style.

It was painfully apparent at this point that we were dealing with a very complexly inter-

acting set of determinants, all of which played their part in making the group effective or ineffective. A sound theory of leadership effectiveness or group performance was obviously required. This demanded (*a*) the development of a meaningful system for categorizing group-task situations, (*b*) an underlying model that would integrate the various results obtained in our studies, and (*c*) adequate tests to determine the validity of the model.

DEVELOPMENT OF THE CONTINGENCY MODEL

DEFINITIONS

We shall limit our discussion to interacting rather than co-acting or counteracting task groups. By an *interacting* task group we mean a face-to-face team situation, as a basketball team or a tank crew in which the members work interdependently toward a common goal. In groups of this type, the individual's contribution determines the performance of the other group members, and it cannot be separated from total group performance. In a *coacting* group, such as a bowling team or a rifle team, the group performance is generally determined by summing the members' individual performances. In *counteracting* groups, subgroups negotiate or reconcile competing or partially incompatible goals (7).

The leader is the group member officially appointed or elected to direct and coordinate group action. In groups in which no one has been so designated, we have identified the informal leader by means of sociometric questions that ask group members to name the person who was most influential or whom they would most like to have as a leader in a similar task.

The leader's effectiveness is defined in terms of the group's performance of the primary task. Thus, a company manager may have a job description that includes the maintenance of good public relations or low personnel turnover. But the criterion on which he is likely to be evaluated in the final analysis is the long-range profitability of the company. Good relations with employees and customers, high morale, and low turnover may all contribute to performance, but they would not be the primary criterion that defines company success.

CATEGORIZATION OF GROUP-TASK SITUATIONS

We have defined leadership as essentially a problem of wielding influence and power. When we say that different types of groups require different types of leadership, we imply that the leader has to use different means to influence his group members. It is obviously easier to wield influence and power in some situations than in others. Other things being equal, a military group will be more easily influenced by a general than by an army private; a group will be influenced more easily by a person who is liked and trusted than by someone who is hated and rejected.

An attempt to categorize group-task situations might reasonably begin, therefore, by specifying the aspects of the group situation that determine the influence the leader is likely to have. On the basis of our previous work, we postulated three important aspects of the situation that influence the leader's role.

Leader-Member Relations. The leader who is personally attractive to his group members and respected by his group enjoys considerable power (11). In fact, if he has the confidence and loyalty of his men he has less need of official rank. This dimension can generally be measured by means of sociometric indices or by group atmosphere scales (6) that indicate the degree to which the leader experiences the group as pleasant and well-disposed toward him.

Task Structure. The task generally implies an "order from above" that incorporates the authority of the superior organization. The group member who refuses to comply must be prepared to face disciplinary action by the higher authority. For example, a squad member who fails to perform a lawful command of his sergeant may have to answer to his regimental commander. However, compliance with a task order can be enforced only if the task is relatively well structured—that is, if it is capable of being programmed. One cannot effectively force a group to perform well on an unstructured task such as developing a new product or writing a good play.

Thus, the leader who has a structured task can depend on the backing of his superior organization, but if he has an unstructured task the leader must rely on his own resources to inspire and motivate his men. The unstructured task thus provides the leader with much less effective power than does the highly structured task.

We made this dimension operational by utilizing four of the aspects that Shaw (25) recently proposed for the classification of group tasks: (*a*) *decision verifiability,* the degree to which the correctness of the solution can be demonstrated objectively; (*b*) *goal clarity,* the degree to which the task requirements are clearly stated or known to the group; (*c*) *goal path multiplicity,* the degree to which there are many or few procedures available for performing the task (reverse scoring); and (*d*) *solution specificity,* the degree to which there is one rather than an infinite number of correct solutions (for example, solving an equation versus writing a story). Ratings based on these four dimensions have yielded interrater reliabilities of .80 to .90.

Position Power. The third dimension is defined by the power inherent in the position of leadership irrespective of the occupant's personal relations with his members. This includes the rewards and punishments that are officially or traditionally at the leader's disposal, his authority as defined by the group's rules and by-laws, and the organizational support given to him in dealing with his men. This dimension can be operationally defined by means of a check list (7) containing items such as "Leader can effect promotion or demotion" and "Leader enjoys special rank and status in real life which sets him apart from, and above, his group members." The median interrater agreement of four independent judges rating thirty-five group situations was .95.

A THREE-DIMENSIONAL GROUP CLASSIFICATION

Each group-task situation can now be rated on each of the three dimensions of leader-member relations, task structure, and position power. This locates each group in a three-dimensional space. By dividing each dimension into a high and a low half we obtain an eight-celled cube (Figure 1). We can now determine whether the correlations between leader attitudes and group performance within each of these eight cells, or octants, are relatively similar in magnitude and direction. If they are, we can infer that the group classification has been successful since it shows that groups falling within the same cell require a similar leadership style.

An analysis of all interacting groups on which we had data from previous studies led to 59 group-task situations that were assigned to the various octants. As Table 6 shows, sets of

groups falling within the same octant have similar correlations between the leader's LPC or ASo score and group performance scores showing that this classification is meaningful.

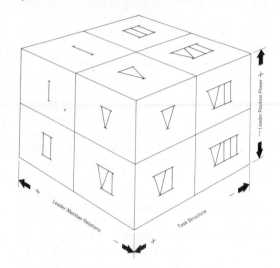

FIGURE 1. A model for the classification of group-task situations.

We can further order the group-task situations on the basis of how favorable they are for the leader's exercise of power and influence. A liked and trusted leader with high rank and a structured task is in a more favorable position to influence his group than a disliked and powerless leader who is faced by a nebulous, unstructured task. The intermediate steps pose certain theoretical and methodological problems. Ordering a three-dimensional system into

TABLE 6. *Median Correlations Between Leader LPC and Group Performance in Various Octants*

Octant	Leader-Member Relations	Task Structure	Position Power	Median Correlation	Number of Relations Included in Median
I	Good	Structured	Strong	−.52	8
II	Good	Structured	Weak	−.58	3
III	Good	Unstructured	Strong	−.41	10
IV	Good	Unstructured	Weak	.47	10
V	Moderately poor	Structured	Strong	.42	6
VI	Moderately poor	Structured	Weak		0
VII	Moderately poor	Unstructured	Strong	.05	10
VIII	Moderately poor	Unstructured	Weak	−.43	12
V–A	Very poor	Structured	Strong	−.67	1

a unidimensional one implies a partial order or a lexicographic system (3) for which there is no unique solution.

We have made the assumption that the leader-member relationship is the most important dimension in the classification system. This seems appropriate since the liked and respected leader has little need of position power or the power that the higher authority (usually the organization) incorporates in the structured task. Empirical support for this assumption has recently been obtained in a study by Fishbein *et al.* (**10**). The second most important dimension is assumed to be the task structure, since a leader with a highly structured task does not require a powerful leader position. (For example, lower ranking officers and noncommissioned officers are at times called upon to lead and instruct higher ranking officers in certain highly structured tasks, such as demonstrating a new weapon or teaching medical officers close order drill, but not in unstructured tasks such as planning new policies.) The resulting ordering of group-task situations constitutes a reasonable continuum, although we recognize that specific conditions and future studies may well call for extensive modifications as new data become available. For example, in a situation in which leader position power is very strong it may well be more important than task struc-

ture or affective leader-member relations: a high-ranking officer working with recruits.

As shown in Table 6, the type of leadership style most conducive to group effectiveness is contingent upon the nature of the group task situation. The eight octants have been ordered on the basis of favorableness for the leader, and the correlations between leader LPC or ASo and group performance have been plotted for each of the octants. Each point on the plot is a correlation coefficient predicting leadership performance or group effectiveness. The plot, therefore, represents 59 *sets of groups*, totaling over 800 separate groups.

As Figure 2 shows, the task oriented (low LPC) leaders perform most effectively under the very favorable situations of Octants I, II, and III or under the relatively unfavorable situations (Octant VIII). Hence, we obtain negative correlations between LPC or ASo and group performance scores. Considerate, relationship-oriented (high LPC) leaders obtain optimal group performance under situations intermediate in favorableness (Octants IV and V). These are situations in which (*a*) the task is structured but the leader is disliked and must, presumably, be diplomatic and concerned with the feelings of his men and (*b*) the liked leader has an unstructured task and must, therefore, depend upon the

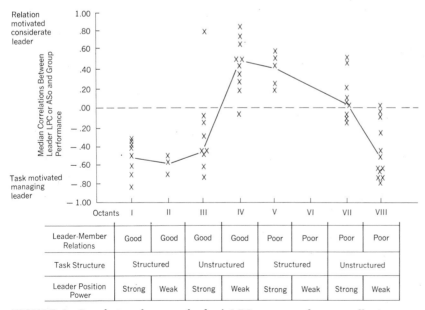

FIGURE 2. Correlations between leaders' LPC scores and group effectiveness plotted for each cell.

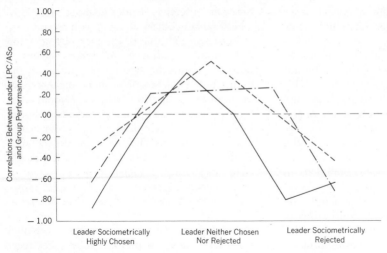

FIGURE 3. Correlations between leader LPC or ASo scores and group performance under three conditions of leader acceptance by the group in studies of bomber crews, anti-aircraft artillery crews, and consumer cooperatives.

creativity and willing cooperation of his members. Where the leader is well liked, considerate, nondirective, relationship-oriented leadership behavior is unnecessary and probably inappropriate.

REANALYSIS OF EARLIER DATA

The model leads to the major hypothesis that leadership effectiveness is contingent upon the leader's style of interacting with his group members and the favorableness of the group-task situation. Specifically, low LPC leaders who are task-motivated and task-controlling perform best under conditions that are very favorable or are relatively unfavorable for them. Considerate, relationship-motivated leaders perform best under conditions that are intermediate in favorableness.

We can now more readily interpret the results obtained in the bomber-crew, anti-aircraft, and farm supply company studies. It should be noted that the leader-member relations are especially important in real-life groups where individuals must spend a major portion of each working day in close association. In contrast to laboratory groups, in which we rarely if ever find really poor interpersonal relations, or even expressions of overt annoyance or hostility directed against another group member, these do occur in real-life groups. Occasionally, these very poor relations deteriorate to the point where they may result in subtle or even overt sabotage of the task.

The groups in these studies are characterized by having highly structured tasks and high leader position power. These situations will, therefore, be quite favorable for the accepted leader; they will be moderately unfavorable for the leader who is tolerated but not rejected. However, these real-life group situations will be quite unfavorable for the strongly rejected leader. We would expect, therefore, that low LPC leaders will perform best in groups in which they are highly accepted or in which they are rejected, while high LPC leaders will perform better in groups intermediate in this respect. We have again plotted the correlations. The resulting family of curves (Figure 3) shows that this set of data conforms to the hypothesis. These data do not constitute a test of the hypothesis in the strict sense of the word since the bomber crew data had been analyzed before and the other sets of data had been obtained earlier. These data do, however, constitute corroborative evidence.

FIT WITH EVERYDAY EXPERIENCE

These findings fit rather well with our everyday experience. When the group backs the leader and the task is straightforward, the leader is expected to give clear directions and orders. The leader who under these conditions acts in a passive, nondirective manner will tend to lose the esteem of his group. We do not want the pilot of an airliner to strive for consensus on landing procedures while he is making his final approach. Similarly, when the task is confused, when the leader has little power, and when he is disliked, he would be better off paying attention to the task than waiting until he can get better interpersonal relations with his group. In fact, unless the leader takes charge of the task under these unfavorable conditions, his group is likely to fall apart. This is reflected in the old army advice that the leader in an emergency is better off giving wrong orders than no orders.

The considerate, human relations oriented approach seems most appropriate when the liked leader deals with a group engaged in a highly unstructured task such as a committee engaged in creative work or in decision-making and problem-solving tasks. Here the liked leader must be considerate of the feelings and opinions of his members; he must be permissive and nonthreatening. The task-oriented, low LPC leader is likely to be too impatient to get on with the work and perhaps too intolerant of side comments and off-beat suggestions. Another type of situation that requires a human-relations oriented, considerate leadership is one in which the leader has a structured job but his relations with his group or key members are not too good. Even though the leader's position may be powerful, he may have to be diplomatic and defer to his group to avoid being completely rejected by his members.

The interaction between appropriate leadership and the group-task situation also is apparent whenever a major change in an organization disrupts the structure of the task. This happens, for example, in business organizations during a crisis. By definition, a crisis implies a situation that does not provide ordinary guidelines for behavior. The typical response, under these circumstances, is for the manager to call his assistants together for consultation. After the crisis has passed, the organization generally returns to routine and fairly well structured tasks that again require task-oriented leadership.

The opposite situation exists in such organizations as research and development groups. Here the task begins in a very unstructured manner. The research director and his assistants typically plan, discuss, consult, and weigh various approaches. This situation requires a high degree of permissiveness. However, during the data collection phase—a highly structured activity in which no deviation or "creativity" is permitted—the research director is likely to become very authoritarian and directive. After the data have been analyzed there is again room for discussion about the interpretation of data, and the leader's behavior again tends to be more permissive, considerate of others' opinions, and human-relations oriented (24).

VALIDATION OF THE CONTINGENCY MODEL

BELGIAN NAVY TEAMS

The original model classified group-task situations on the basis of three major dimensions: the leader-member relations, the leader's position power, and the task structure. The more general hypothesis that this model suggests is, however, that the type of leadership attitude and behavior that will be most effective is contingent upon the favorableness of the group and the task situation.

It is obvious that the three dimensions in the original model are not the only factors determining the degree to which the leader will be able to influence his group members. Other aspects of the situation undoubtedly also play an important part. One of these is the degree to which the group members share similar or dissimilar technical training, as is the case in interdisciplinary research teams. Also important is the degree to which group members have the same cultural background, as we already saw in the Dutch study. In groups in which members have different language backgrounds this problem is especially acute since it is very easy to "misunderstand" instructions or to let antagonistic attitudes toward fellow group members interfere with the task. As a consequence, the leader's job becomes more difficult since he has to watch not only over the task but also over the potentially explosive social situation.

We recently tested the contingency model in multilingual military groups of the Belgian Navy (8). The study involved Flemish and French-speaking petty officers and men who were assigned to three-man teams of which half had petty officers and half had recruits as leaders, thus varying the leader's power of position. Each team performed two types of tasks. One was a relatively unstructured task that required the composition of a recruiting letter urging 16 to 17 year old boys to join the Belgian Navy. Two short structured tasks were given which required the group to compute the shortest route for ships, one through ten ports, the other through twelve ports, given certain conditions as a result of fuel capacity and obligatory sections of route.

Group climate measures, to determine the leader-member relations, were obtained from the leader after each task. Up to this point, the study tested the model presented in Figure 1. In addition, however, the study also involved groups with homogeneous membership—three Flemish-speaking men or three French-speaking men—and groups with heterogeneous membership—a Flemish-speaking leader and two French-speaking members, or a French-speaking leader and two Flemish-speaking members.

A further factor affecting the difficulty of the group-task situation arose because the leader of the newly assembled group had a more difficult job than the leader of a group that had had some practice in working together. Thus, the first task would present a more difficult problem than the same task after the group had had some practice in working together. Secondly, the study involved two structured tasks. Here again, the leader would find it easier to handle his group on the second structured task than on the first. These three tasks—the two ship-routing problems and the recruiting letter—were statistically independent and were thus treated as separate criteria.

The study used a total of 96 three-man groups, all of which were tested on the same day to prevent the groups from communicating with each other about the tasks or procedures. There were 48 homogeneous and 48 heterogeneous groups, half with petty officers as leaders and half with recruit leaders, half beginning the study with the structured tasks and half with the unstructured task. The groups were matched on the basis of preliminary tests on LPC, intelligence, and attitude toward the other language group. We again correlated each leader's LPC score with the group's performance with each of the 48 group-task conditions in the study (see Figure 4).

Figure 4 includes all group-task situations by giving to three of the factors—homogeneity, high leader position power, and high group atmosphere—a weight of three, to structured tasks a weight of one, to the second task and the second structured task an additional weight of one point. Each group participated in three tasks and was therefore classified in three group-task situations. For all groups within the same group-task situation we correlated the leader's LPC score and the group performance. These were then plotted against the score of favorableness of the situation for the leader. As can be seen, the results of this study give a very close fit to the hypothesized curve, thus supporting the contingency model.

Other tests based on data from this study likewise have supported this hypothesis. Only

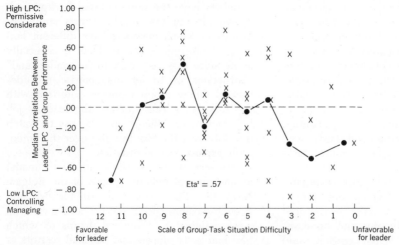

FIGURE 4. Performance curve indicating the relationship of leader LPC and performance with task-group situation difficulty for all tasks, split on leader group climate factor.

one will be mentioned, which involved the ordering of group-task situations on the basis of only three factors: homogeneity, group climate, and position power. Separate curves are shown for the unstructured task and the second and more reliable structured task (Figure 5).

INDUSTRIAL WORK GROUPS

Recent research by Hunt (16) provides further evidence supporting the contingency model in ongoing industrial organizations. Hunt obtained LPC scores as well as ratings of position power, task structure, and leader-member relations in four different industrial organizations: shops in a large farm implement company, production groups of a paint manufacturing concern, research and development teams at a national physical sciences laboratory, and meat departments in a chain of supermarkets.

Ratings of these departments classified them into four of the eight octants of the contingency model. Correlations were then obtained between the foreman's or the supervisor's LPC scores and the performance of his department or work group. These correlations are plotted and super-imposed on the performance curve originally obtained on the total sample of American groups. As can be seen in Figure 6, the fit of the data is quite close, suggesting the generalizability of the model to interacting groups in real-life industrial and business organizations.

GROUP PROCESS

What is the underlying group process? How can we explain why low LPC or ASo leaders perform more effectively in very favorable or very unfavorable situations, while the high LPC leaders are more effective in situations intermediate in favorableness?

The key to the problem is, of course, in the interpretation of the LPC score, the esteem of the leader for his least-preferred co-worker, and the dimension we have labelled "favorableness for the leader."

The LPC score measures the individual's motivation to satisfy his need for recognition and self-esteem as a consequence of having good interpersonal relations. As Bishop (1) has shown, the high LPC person becomes more adjusted when he feels that he has been successful in interpersonal relations. The low LPC person is motivated by the task itself. His self-esteem and adjustment depend upon the mastery or the successful completion of a task. As one would expect, therefore, the high LPC person is more considerate, more concerned with the feelings of his fellow group members. The low LPC person tends to be more task-oriented, more concerned with task-relevant interpersonal relations.

Our society values leadership highly, and this value is clearly present in most people who are in supervisory or leadership positions. Almost everyone becomes quite ego-involved and concerned about his leadership performance even in role-playing situations lasting only a few minutes or a few hours. A difficult leadership situation will, therefore, be experienced as anxiety-arousing and threatening. Thus, when the situation is highly favorable for the leader—when he can readily influence the members of his group by virtue of his good relationship with them, the power of his position, or the nature of the task—the leader will be quite relaxed. The high LPC leader will be at ease because he has the position that provides him with the ego-satisfactions he seeks. The low LPC leader will also be at ease in such a situation because he has the influence that allows him to get his group members to work. He will, therefore attend to the task, and his chances of outperforming the high LPC leader in this very favorable situation are good.

As the situation becomes less favorable the leader will become aware of the threat which this poses to his potential need satisfaction. Under these conditions, the high LPC leader engages more intensively in interpersonal relations, he concentrates on maintaining good relations with others and on maintaining good relations among them. The low LPC leader becomes more and more concerned with the task performance. In situations of intermediate difficulty, typified by the committee or the creative group, the high LPC leader tends to establish a considerate, friendly, permissive atmosphere which is required for good performance of these tasks. The low LPC leader will seem to be too impatient, too task-oriented to take care of the relationship and self-oriented needs of his group members, and hence less effective.

Under conditions still more unfavorable and

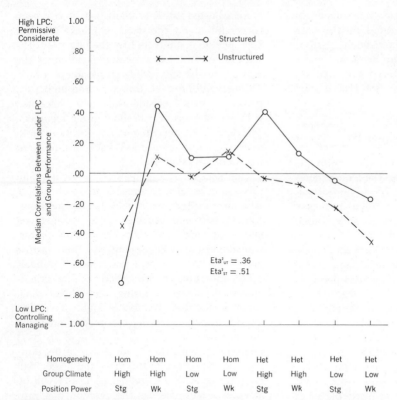

FIGURE 5. Correlations between leader LPC and group performance in unstructured and second structured tasks, classified by homogeneity, group climate, and position power of teams.

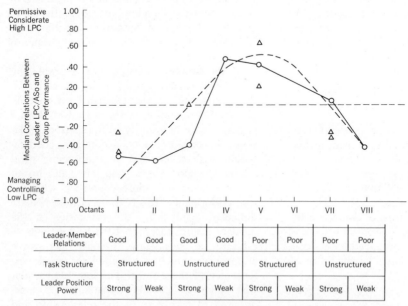

FIGURE 6. Preliminary validation results obtained in a chemical research laboratory, meat departments of a grocery chain, and departments of a farm implement manufacturing company. Validation results, indicated by triangles, are superimposed on original contingency model curve.

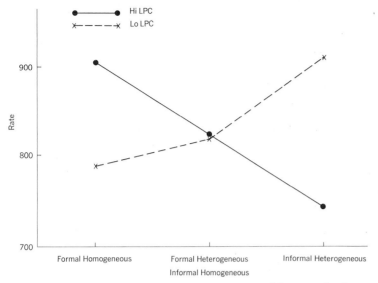

FIGURE 7. Task relevant comments by high LPC and low LPC leaders under conditions of different stress in the Dutch study.

threatening, still more difficult to control (where the leader has low power and an unstructured task or where he feels disliked and not accepted by his group), the high LPC leader may become too anxious, too concerned with his position in the group. We see an increase in the intensity of his interpersonal relations and a correspondingly lower rate of task-relevant behavior. The leader with low LPC, on the other hand, becomes more task-oriented, less concerned with the relationship, and hence more effective in such unfavorable situations. The interaction between the behaviors of high and low LPC leaders under conditions of varying favorableness can be readily seen by one example provided by the Dutch study. Leader behaviors were classified as being task- or relationship-oriented. The rates of task-relevant and relationship-oriented comments in each of these three conditions of favorableness were then plotted for homogeneous-formal groups, heterogeneous-formal and homogeneous-informal groups, and heterogeneous-informal groups. As can be

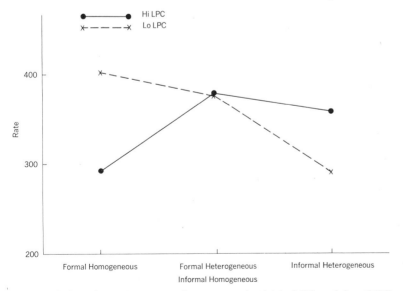

FIGURE 8. Relationship-oriented comments by high LPC and low LPC leaders under conditions of different stress in the Dutch study.

seen in Figures 7 and 8, the two sets of curves cross, indicating that the high LPC leaders are more relationship-oriented in unfavorable situations and that low LPC leaders are more concerned with the task under these conditions. Similar results have been obtained with data from other studies.

ORGANIZATIONAL ENGINEERING

Our program of leadership research has presented evidence that the effectiveness of the group is contingent upon the appropriateness of the leader's style to the group-task situation. Thus, effective group performance depends upon the interaction of leadership style and situation. What do these results and the theory mean for executive selection and training? What implications do they have for the leadership and management of large organizations?

Leadership has always been a scarce manpower resource. Leadership and management training has, therefore, been a focus of attention in industry and government as well as in the military services. Yet we know that it is very difficult to change a man's leadership style or interpersonal behavior. Studies by Harris and Fleishmann (14), as well as a review of the literature by Mann (22), have not been able to produce any evidence that leadership training promotes the productivity and effectiveness of groups or industrial departments. This was also shown in the Belgian Navy study (8) to which we have referred. We compared the 48 groups of trained and experienced petty officers with the performance of the 48 groups led by inexperienced and untrained recruit leaders. On none of the tasks did the groups led by petty officers perform significantly better than groups led by recruits. This finding is all the more striking since the petty officers had an average of ten years of leadership experience. It is equally interesting that the amount of experience (that is, the number of years of Navy service of petty officers) did not correlate with group performance on any of the tasks. How can we explain these results?

One explanation is suggested by the contingency model. Leadership training is likely to indoctrinate supervisors to adopt one particular type of leadership style. Even if we make the questionable assumption that the

typical leadership training succeeds in every case in modifying leadership style in the desired direction (either more human-relations oriented or more task-oriented), the contingency model would point out that the man's leadership style will be effective only under some situations but not others. Moreover, as the situation changes, or as the individual changes from one type of managerial job to another, his leadership style might become more or less appropriate to the situation. This would explain why some managers are eminently successful in one position but fail in another.

The model also throws new light on the many findings that group performance criteria are so often uncorrelated (22, 5, 19). Why, for example, should groups differ so markedly in their performance of nearly parallel tasks? The model suggests that the situation becomes more favorable for the leader as the group moves from the novel and unusual situation to the situation that is already known. The leader already knows his men on later tasks, and he has more control over planning and division of work. This is also reflected in the fairly common observation that some managers are excellent in routine management but do not bear up too well under crisis, while others are excellent trouble-shooters and organizers of new companies or branch offices but go stale under routine operating conditions.

What then are the implications of this theory for selection and training of leaders? Business and industry, as well as government and military services, are now trying to attract an increasingly large share of highly intelligent and technically well trained men. Many of these are specialists whose talents are in critically short supply. Can we really afford to select only those men who have a certain style of leadership in addition to their technical training? Can we afford to fire highly creative specialists because they do not have the style of leadership they "ought to have"? The answer is obvious.

Can we then train the men who have the necessary technical qualifications to adopt one style rather than another? This is, of course, the orthodox solution, even though our past experience with leadership training does not give much cause for optimism. We could, however, train managers to diagnose the group-task situation in which they find themselves and to adopt a strategy that will enable them to perform best given their type of leadership style. It is always possible for the manager to place his prime emphasis on developing better interpersonal relations with members of his group. He can decide to increase his own authority by becoming an expert in his task, or he can decide that he would be better off by treating his subordinates as equals and concentrating on a permissive, nonthreatening group climate.

A more explicit recognition of this alternative is the "organizational engineering" approach that the results of our research suggest. This approach involves the explicit recognition that it is considerably more difficult to change a man's personality or leadership style than it is to change the situation within which he operates. Rather than fitting the manager to the job, we should, therefore, aim to fit the job to the manager.

We have already shown that the type of leadership called for depends on the favorableness of the situation for the leader—the degree of influence he potentially has in the group. This favorableness, in turn, depends on a number of factors. These include the leader's relations with his men, the power of his position, the homogeneity of the group, the degree to which the job is structured, and the routineness of the problems. It is quite clear that management or the larger organization can change the favorableness of the leadership situation in most, if not all, cases to a greater or lesser extent. Higher management may be able to do this in many cases more easily than it could transfer the leader from one job to another or train him in a different style of interacting with his members.

Although we must stress that this type of organizational engineering is still in an exploratory stage, we know that organizations have been well aware of this possibility in an informal way. This is implied when we say that Mr. X needs more authority, that Mr. Y can't handle interdisciplinary teams, that Mr. Z would be better off working on a job that gives him more scope (that is, that is less structured). The answer has generally been to move the man from one job to another. Let us suggest some ways of changing the group situation.

1. *We can change the leader's position power.* We can give him more authority or less authority; we can let him make the final decision or have him consult with his subordinates. We can allow him to hire and fire, or we can limit his authority over personnel matters. We can give him subordinates who are two or three steps below him in rank (the apprenticeship situation) or subordinates who are equal or nearly equal to him in rank and power (the committee situation).

2. *We can change the task structure.* One leader may be given detailed operating instructions while another may be given problems that require new procedures; one man's group may be given planning and development functions while another man's may be assigned to the production functions in the organization. One man may need to be told what to do and how to do it while another may have to be given the new and unfamiliar problems for which he will need to work out his own procedures.

3. *We can change the leader-member relations.* We can assign "trouble-makers" to one man and keep them out of groups headed by another. We can assign one manager to tasks likely to create dissension and we can assign another the types of tasks likely to increase harmony and cohesiveness in the group (18). We can, as we have seen in the Belgian Navy study, increase the difficulty of the situation by assigning linguistically and culturally heterogeneous groups or groups whose members differ in technical background, relevant opinions, and attitudes, or we can increase the homogeneity of the leader's work group by assigning him men who are similar to him in background, training, and attitudes.

These are, of course, only examples of what could be done. All of these must be tried out in real-life situations before they can be applied in practice. We have presented a model and a set of principles that may permit predictions of leadership effectiveness in interacting groups and that may allow us to take a look at the factors affecting team performance. This approach, as applied to organizational management, goes beyond the traditional notions of selection and training. It focuses on the more fruitful possibility of organizational engineering for the more effective utilization of available leadership and managerial manpower.

References

1. Bishop, D. W., Alsobrook, J. M., & Fiedler, F. E. The effects of intergroup competition in quasi-therapeutic leaders on the adjustment of small military groups. University of Illinois, Group Effectiveness Research Laboratory, Urbana: 1966, Technical Report No. 20, Contract DA-49-193-MD-2060.
2. Cleven, W. A., & Fiedler, F. E. Interpersonal perceptions of open-hearth foremen and steel production. *Journal of Applied Psychology,* 1956, **40,** 312–314.
3. Coombs, C. H. *A theory of data.* New York: Wiley, 1964.
4. Fiedler, F. E. Assumed similarity measures as predictors of team effectiveness. *Journal of Abnormal and Social Psychology,* 1954, 381–388.
5. Fiedler, F. E. The influence of leader-keymen relations on combat crew effectiveness. *Journal of Abnormal and Social Psychology,* 1955, **51,** 227–235.
6. Fiedler, F. E. Leader attitudes, group climate, and group creativity. *Journal of Abnormal and Social Psychology,* 1962, **65,** 308–318.
7. Fiedler, F. E. A contingency model of leadership effectiveness. In L. Berkowitz (Ed.), *Advances in experimental social psychology.* Vol. 1. New York: Academic Press, 1964, 149–190.
8. Fiedler, F. E. The effect of leadership and cultural heterogeneity on group performance: A test of the contingency model. *Journal of Experimental and Social Psychology,* 1966, **2,** 237–264.
9. Fiedler, F. E., Meuwese, W., & Oonk, S. Performance of laboratory tasks requiring group creativity. *Acta Psychologica,* 1961, **18,** 100–119.
10. Fishbein, M. A preliminary test of the contingency model. Unpublished research.
11. French, J. R. P., Jr. A formal theory of social power. *Psychological Review,* 1956, **63,** 181–194.
12. Godfrey, E. P., Fiedler, F. E., & Hall, D. M. *Boards, management, and company success.* Danville, Ill.: Interstate Printers and Publishers, 1959.
13. Guilford, J. P., Berger, R. M., & Christiansen, P. R. A factor analysis study of planning. I. Hypotheses and description of tests. Los Angeles: Univ. of Southern California, Psychol. Laboratory, 1954.
14. Harris, E. F., & Fleishmann, E. A. Human relations training and the stability of leadership patterns. *Journal of Applied Psychology,* 1955, **39,** 20–25.
15. Havron, M. D., *et al.* The assessment and prediction of rifle squad effectiveness. Washington, D. C.: The Adjutant General's Office, Personnel Research Branch, November 1954, Technical Research Note 31.
16. Hunt, J. A test of Fiedler's leadership contingency model in four organizational settings. Unpublished doctoral dissertation, Univ. of Illinois, 1966.
17. Hutchins, E. B., & Fiedler, F. E. Task-oriented and quasi-therapeutic role functions of the leader in small military groups. *Sociometry,* 1960, **23,** 293–406.
18. Julian, J. W., Bishop, D. W., & Fiedler, F. E. Quasi-therapeutic effects of intergroup competition. *Journal of Personality and Social Psychology,* 1966, **3,** 321–327.
19. Knoell, D., & Forgays, D. G. *Interrelationships of combat crew performance in the B-29.* U.S.A.F. Human Resources Research Center, *Research Note,* 1952, CCT 52-1.
20. Lewin, K., & Lippitt, R. An experimental approach to the study of autocracy and democracy: A preliminary note. *Sociometry,* 1938, **1,** 292–300.
21. McGrath, J. E., & Altman, I. *Small group research.* New York: Holt, Rinehart and Winston, 1966.
22. Mann, F. C. Studying and creating change: A means to understanding social organization. In C. M. Arensburg *et al.* (Eds.), *Research in industrial human relations: A critical appraisal.* New York: Harper, 1957, 146–167.
23. Osgood, C. E., Suci, G. A., & Tannenbaum, P. H. *The measurement of meaning.* Urbana: Univ. of Illinois Press, 1957.
24. Sample, J. A., & Wilson, T. R. Leader behavior, group productivity, and rating of least preferred co-worker. *Journal of Personality and Social Psychology,* 1965, **1,** 266–270.
25. Shaw, M. E. *Annual Technical Report, 1962.* Gainesville, Fla.: Univ. of Florida, 1962.

29

The Behavior of Leaders and Other Group Members

LAUNOR CARTER, WILLIAM HAYTHORN, BEATRICE SHRIVER, AND
JOHN LANZETTA

The psychological literature is replete with lists of behaviors or traits which purport to characterize leaders. *Psychology for the Armed Services* (4) has a section on "The Attributes of Leadership," which suggests that a leader exercises authority, is competent, industrious, confident, responsible, etc. Bird (3) reviewed "approximately twenty inquiries bearing some resemblance to controlled investigations" and compiled a list of 79 traits which were said to characterize the behavior of leaders. As he points out, "surprisingly little overlapping is found from study to study."

More recently there have been careful investigations attempting to characterize the followers' opinions regarding typical leadership behavior. Notable among these studies are those of Hemphill (9), Roff (13), and Sanford (14). In each of these studies respondents were asked to describe things leaders did or, as in part of Sanford's study, the things that leaders should do. While such reports are very useful in giving the non-leaders' perceptions of what they think leaders do or should do, they may not adequately represent the actual behavior of the leaders on which the respondents are reporting. This problem seems particularly acute in those studies in which information was collected some months after the respondents had left the groups on which they were reporting. It would at least seem reasonable that these results include a mixture of actual behavior, the respondents' rationalizations regarding the behavior, and cultural stereotypes of good and poor leadership.

There have been surprisingly few attempts to describe the behavior exhibited by persons in a group setting by direct observation with immediate recording. Parten

From *Journal of Abnormal and Social Psychology*, 1950, **46**, 589–595. Reprinted by permission of the authors and the American Psychological Association. The work reported here was done under a contract between the Office of Naval Research and the University of Rochester.

(12) and Murphy (11) have made such observations on young children, and more recently Bales (1) has given a more detailed characterization of the activities of the members of one group of five persons. Lippitt (10) has presented some data showing the relative contributions of leader and delegate in a discussion group but uses only very molar descriptive categories. As far as is known, there is no detailed description of the actual behavior of group members obtained in such a fashion as to allow definitive statements regarding the activities of one member relative to those of other members. This study reports such results. Lest there be misunderstanding, it should be emphasized that the particular results obtained are certainly not characteristics of leaders in all situations or for groups of any size. They are thought to be characteristic of individuals working in small homogeneous groups on tasks similar to those described.

PROCEDURE

The subjects were 40 NROTC junior students. By means of sociometric measures of friendship and leadership, the subjects were formed into five groups of eight with as equal leadership potential and as low mutual friendship ratings as possible. Each of these groups of eight was then run in a leaderless group session on three tasks: reasoning, mechanical assembly, and discussion. The tasks are described in some detail in a previous publication (5). On the basis of leadership ratings based on this performance, each group was broken into two smaller groups of four, selected so that each group would have an approximately equal distribution of leadership ability. These groups of four were then run on three similar tasks. In the results this group will be referred to as working in "the emergent situation." [1] At the second meeting of the group one member had been withdrawn and replaced by an individual having a similar leadership rating but from another group. This new individual was appointed as the leader in

___

[1] "Emergent situation" refers to what has been frequently called the "leaderless situation." It is felt that "emergent" is more appropriate, since "leaderless" connotes a lack of leadership, whereas in our groups a leader usually emerged.

the presence of the other three group members.

While the subjects were working on the tasks, they were observed through one-way mirrors by two independent observers who classified their behavior in terms of a coding system involving 53 categories. This system and the categories are described in detail elsewhere (6). At the completion of each task, the observers rated each of the subjects on a seven-point rating scale on a number of characteristics, including leadership. The reliability of the ratings and categorizations is generally adequate and is fully presented in (7).

RESULTS AND DISCUSSION

Since one of the major comparisons to be made is between leaders and other group members, it is important to define carefully how the subjects designated as the leaders were selected. In the case of groups working in the appointed situation, the subject appointed as the leader is considered the leader. In certain of these groups, the individual who was appointed was not the real or functional leader in the sense that some other person in the group was rated as the more effective group leader. However, an analysis of the ratings made by the observers shows that the average leadership ratings of the appointed leaders were significantly higher than the average rating of the remaining group members. (The difference was significant at past the .01 level for reasoning, at .02 for mechanical assembly, and at .02 for discussion.) The average ratings of the appointed leader and those of the best other leader in the group are essentially the same with all the *t*s being less than 1.

In the case of groups working in the emergent situation, the leaders were determined by selecting the individual in each group who received the highest leadership rating from the group observers. There is some problem of circularity in the treatment of our results for these leaders, although we believe it to be largely mitigated. The observers categorized the subjects' behaviors into a continuous ongoing record; for a typical group this might involve some 200–300 categorizations per task. Before these categorizations were even transcribed, the ratings were made by the observers. Thus the ratings are based on over-all, global impressions of performance, not on a consideration of the detailed categorizations.

The subjects we have called the "leaders" are simply the individuals so designated in the appointed situation or the individuals receiving the highest ratings in the emergent situation. The problem is: What do such leaders do which differentiates them from the other group members?

The results for the appointed situation are based on an analysis of the complete records for 10 groups. Thus, throughout the analyses the comparison is between 10 leaders and 30 other group members. For the emergent situation, the comparisons are for 8 leaders and 24 others on the reasoning task, for 7 leaders and 21 others on the mechanical assembly task, and 9 leaders and 36 others on the discussion task. While more groups were run in the emergent situation, defective tape recordings reduced the number of cases on which complete data were available. (Incidentally, the use of modified Stenographs (6) has almost completely eliminated defective records and is less expensive.) Levels of significance throughout this paper are based on *t*s calculated from the distribution of frequencies for a particular category attributable to each individual with *N*s as indicated above. Thus where significant differences are indicated they were conservatively determined, and the number of degrees of freedom is not inflated by considering each act as the base unit for analysis.

Since there were 53 categories, 3 work tasks, 2 types of situations and the totals analyzed, there were 324 possible comparisons. Of these possible comparisons, 159, or about half, were automatically eliminated because of the very small number of behaviors falling in these categories. It was arbitrarily decided that no category would be considered unless there was an average of at least one such behavior per task-session. As Bales (1) points out, an act such as a bald command or a crucial insight may happen only once and yet be most important in determining a long sequence of action. Even so, we as yet have no adequate way of handling behavior which occurs with such small frequency.

Of the 165 actual comparisons made, the leader's behavior differed from that of the other group members with a frequency which was significant at the 1% level or beyond in 34 comparisons, at the 2–5% level in eight cases, and at the 6–10% level in 12 comparisons. Table

1 shows the average number of behaviors falling in any category (col. 1 for each task), the percentage of such behavior attributable to the leader (col. 2), and the percentage attributable to the average of the other three group members (col. 3). This table includes only the categories for which at least one of the six possible comparisons was significant at the 10% level or better. In other words, there were only 20 categories in which any significant differences occurred when as liberal a criterion as the 10% level of significance is used. There were 10 categories which had less than an average of one behavior per task for any task and 23 other categories in which there was considerable behavior recorded, but where there were no appreciable differences between the leaders and others. In other words, there is a considerable number of categories, probably well over one-half, in which the leader's behavior does not differ significantly from that of the other members of the group. The exact nature of this similar behavior will be considered later.

First let us consider the kinds of behavior which seem to differentiate leaders from the other group members over all the tasks and group situations. Category 23, "diagnoses situation—makes interpretation," and category 50, "gives information on carrying out action," are the only two categories in which the leader consistently shows a statistically significant different level of activity from the other group members. Thus, the type of behavior which characterizes the leader, whether he is appointed or emerges, without regard to the task involved, is the making of interpretations about the situation and giving information on how to carry out the activity. There are other items which also seem to be similarly related although they do not always reach acceptable levels of statistical significance, usually due to their relatively infrequent occurrence. Such categories are number 26, "proposes course of action for others," number 29, "initiates action toward problem-solving which is continued or followed," number 33, "gets insight," and number 55, "integrates group behavior." These categories, along with the two previously mentioned, definitely imply that leaders are characteristically concerned with (*a*) getting insight or analyzing the situation and (*b*) with initiating the action required.

It seems that in some cases the leader's behavior is determined by the task on which the

TABLE 1. *Behavior of Group Members Which Differentiates Leader from Others*

Category	Leadership Situation	No. Behaviors in Av. Session	Reasoning Per Cent Attributable to Leader	Av. Per Cent Attributable to Non-Leaders
21. Calls for attention	Appt.	2.3	27	24
	Emerg.	5.0	49	17 [a]
22. Asks for information	Appt.	39.6	43	19 [c]
	Emerg.	43.8	30	23 [c]
23. Diagnoses situation	Appt.	38.4	35	22 [b]
	Emerg.	39.2	36	21 [c]
24. Asks for expression of opinion	Appt.	4.2	53	16 [c]
	Emerg.	1.3	38	21
26. Proposes course of action for others	Appt.	8.4	45	18 [c]
	Emerg.	8.8	45	18 [c]
27. Supports his proposal	Appt.	2.3	30	23
	Emerg.	2.3	31	23
28. Defends his proposal from attack	Appt.	1.5	37	21
	Emerg.	1.8	39	20
29. Initiates action	Appt.	4.5	66	11 [c]
	Emerg.	2.5	33	22
31. Agrees or approves	Appt.	11.2	32	23
	Emerg.	8.1	32	23
32. Gives information	Appt.	30.2	27	24
	Emerg.	10.5	28	24
33. Gets insight	Appt.	14.1	34	22 [c]
	Emerg.	8.9	35	22 [a]
35. Expression of opinion	Appt.	7.9	32	23
	Emerg.	4.4	39	20 [a]
40. Disagrees or skeptical	Appt.	7,1	17	28
	Emerg.	6.9	23	26
41. Argues with others	Appt.			
	Emerg.	2.5	20	27
50. Gives information on carrying out action	Appt.	2.7	65	12 [c]
	Emerg.	3.3	52	16 [b]
52. Desires something to be done	Appt.			
	Emerg.			
55. Integrates group behavior	Appt.	1.7	45	18 [a]
	Emerg.	1.8	56	15 [c]
61. Offers to help	Appt.			
	Emerg.			
66. Performs simple work unit	Appt.	56.6	24	25
	Emerg.	69.9	24	25
90. Stands around doing nothing	Appt.			
	Emerg.			
Total	Appt.	269.0	32	23 [b]
	Emerg.	248.0	31	23 [c]

[a] Significant at .06–.10 level
[b] Significant at .02–.05 level
[c] Significant at .01 level or better

| Mechanical Assembly | | | Discussion | | |
No. Behaviors in Av. Session	Per Cent Attributable to Leader	Av. Per Cent Attributable to Non-Leaders	No. Behaviors in Av. Session	Per Cent Attributable to Leader	Av. Per Cent Attributable to Non-Leaders
1.1	23	26			
2.9	25	25			
11.2	26	25	7.8	33	22
6.3	34	22	6.4	28	24
32.8	37	21[c]	10.2	47	18[c]
27.9	35	22[c]	9.8	43	19[c]
1.0	26	25	6.7	46	18[c]
			11.8	41	20[c]
10.6	36	21[a]	6.0	37	21
10.1	43	19[c]	6.2	59	14[c]
2.2	47	18[c]	30.1	18	27
			30.8	46	18[c]
1.0	47	18[a]	6.0	14	29[a]
			8.5	36	21
3.0	45	18[c]	1.2	64	12[c]
4.7	39	20[b]	2.3	36	21
3.7	40	20[c]	11.2	34	22
2.6	17	28	13.2	34	22[a]
16.4	30	23	14.0	35	22[b]
11.7	25	25	6.8	41	20[c]
5.7	32	23			
9.6	38	21[b]			
6.0	31	23	37.3	23	26
2.6	30	23	35.2	38	21[c]
4.8	35	22	10.3	18	27[b]
4.0	27	24	9.6	19	27
			2.3	12	29
			3.3	39	20[a]
11.3	45	18[c]	2.1	76	8[c]
11.4	52	16[c]	3.0	62	13[c]
1.2	50	17[c]			
1.0	46	18			
			2.0	73	9[c]
			1.1	40	20
8.4	22	26			
15.3	17	28[a]			
68.5	27	24	5.7	55	15[c]
70.0	27	24	6.3	15	28
13.8	11	30			
10.3	12	29[a]			
294.9	29	24[a]	197.0	29	24
289.6	28	24[b]	192.7	38	21[c]

group is working, whatever the situation. Uniquely associated with the reasoning task is category 22, "asks for information or facts," which is to be expected, since in this task information from each of the subjects must be coordinated to obtain a solution to the syllogistic reasoning problems. Specifically related to the mechanical assembly task are category 52, "expresses a desire that something be done," and probably category 90, "stands around doing nothing." Again these behaviors are the kind that would be expected from the nature of the task. The mechanical assembly task involves a large number of work units. Once the general plan of construction is perceived, there are sufficient work units for all to participate. Thus, we find the leader on this task "expressing the desire that something be done" and not "standing around doing nothing," since the task demands that the leader be active in getting others to enter into the work. Associated with leader activity on the discussion task are category 24, "asks for expression of feeling or opinion," category 31, "agrees or approves," and category 32, "gives general information," and perhaps a low score on category 40, "disagrees or skeptical." Here the discussion leader seems typically to give information, and to ask for expressions of opinion, but he does not disagree; rather he approves or agrees. These are the types of behavior in discussion that the leader has freedom to engage in because of the kind of task involved.

Finally, there seem to be interesting differences in behavior depending on whether the group was working under emergent or appointed leader conditions. It appears that in the appointed situation the leader may perceive his role as that of a coordinator of activity or as an agent through which the group can accomplish its goal. In the emergent group, on the other hand, the person who becomes the leader may take over the leadership by energetic action and by trying to get the other members to accept his leadership. The leaders of the emergent group discussion tasks show much greater over-all activity than the leaders in any other situations or tasks, as may be seen from the "total" row in Table 1. Category 21, "calls for attention," is significant only for the reasoning task in the emergent situation. Category 27 is "supports or gives information regarding his proposal." For the discussion task in the appointed situation, a considerable amount of behavior is classified as 27, but the

individuals showing most of this behavior are the non-leaders. In contrast, in the emergent situation the leader has many more 27s attributable to him than do the non-leaders. Similarly for category 28, "defends self (or his proposal) from attack," for category 35, "expression of opinion," and for category 41, "argues with others." Exactly the reverse is found for category 66, "performs a simple work unit," where the appointed leader shows a great deal of such behavior and the emergent leader very little. In the discussion task, this category was used to indicate the routine recording of opinions and writing of conclusions. In the emergent situation, the leader had someone else do this routine work, whereas in the appointed situations the leader tended not to impose the writing chore on someone else.

All these results were contrary to expectations. It was assumed that the appointed situation would be structured more in an "authoritarian" direction than the emergent situation would be. The reverse seems to have occurred. The results for the appointed situation may be explained by speculating that the appointed leader conceives his role as one of coordinator rather than as a director or controller of the group's activities. This would apparently be the role expected of him by the majority of group members. Some incidental evidence bearing on this point was obtained in interviews with subjects dealing with their behavior when they are appointed leaders. In general, they felt that as leaders they should not interfere with the group's activity, that the other members of the group were as capable of doing the tasks as they were, and that their main job was merely "to keep things moving." It can probably be said, then, that the appointed leaders conceive their chief function to be that of moving their groups toward agreeing on a solution to the problem presented and initiating action toward this solution. The appointed leaders attempted to do this by eliciting the opinions of the group members, minimizing conflicts, and integrating in written form those opinions on which there was general agreement. The leaders of the emergent groups, on the other hand, had to establish their positions of leadership by being forceful and strongly supporting their own proposals in competition with other potential leaders. It may be that individuals rated as leaders in the emergent situations were competing for high status positions, whereas the individuals appointed as leaders had their status positions secured, and the nature of their positions required, that they become more involved in the goals of the group as a whole.

In some respects the categories on which the leader does not differ from the other members of the group are of equal interest with those areas where there is a difference. Categories 1 through 12 included "personal feelings of," i.e., such things as confusion, aggressiveness, and friendliness. Unfortunately, not a large number of behaviors were recorded in this area, but of those recorded, there seemed to be no outstanding differences between leaders and others. Item 30, "supports proposal of another," while used fairly frequently is shown about equally by the leader and by the other members. However, just as some leaders' differential behaviors were specific to particular tasks, so some similarities seem to be related to specific tasks. In the reasoning task, the leader did not give information (category 32) significantly more frequently than others, nor did he perform simple work units

(category 66) more frequently. For the mechanical assembly task, it is particularly noticeable that of 17 comparisons made on categories 60 through 68, only one comparison was significant at even the 10% level of confidence. In other words, the leader did not differ from others in the amount of helping with work, performing simple work units, etc. There seem to be no outstanding similarities for the discussion task, which reinforces the belief that in this task being appointed or not is a very important determinant of the behavior elicited.

An incidental but very important conclusion indicated by the above findings is that the generality of the results of small group research will often be limited by the kind of task used. Much of the work in this field, such as that of Bales (1), Bass (2), and French and Bell (8), has been done on discussion groups. It seems apparent that the requirements of the task and the formal characteristics of the group structure will importantly determine the results observed.

SUMMARY

Using a system of categorization, individuals were observed working in small groups on reasoning, mechanical assembly, and discussion tasks. Some groups worked with an appointed leader and others in an emergent situation. The behavior of the leaders is compared with that of other group members. The unique behavior of leaders over all situations and tasks was concerned with (*a*) analyzing the situation and (*b*) initiating action required. Other leader behaviors seemed to be associated with specific tasks or situations. In the discussion task, and to some extent on other tasks, the leaders who emerged in the emergent situation were more "authoritarian" than were the leaders who were appointed. Except in the discussion task, leaders and other group members do not tend to differ greatly in the amount of work performed. It is emphasized that the behavior of group members is considerably determined by situational and task-dictated requirements.

References

1. Bales, R. F. *Interaction process analysis.* Cambridge: Addison-Wesley Press, 1950.
2. Bass, B. M. The leaderless group discussion technique. *Personnel Psychology*, 1950, **3**, 17–32.
3. Bird, C. *Social psychology.* New York: Appleton-Century, 1950.
4. Boring, E. G. (Ed.), *Psychology for the armed services.* Washington, D. C.: Infantry Journal, 1945.
5. Carter, L., Haythorn, W., & Howell, M. A further investigation of the criteria of leadership. *Journal of Abnormal and Social Psychology*, 1950, **45**, 350–358.
6. Carter, L., *et al.* A note on a new technique of interaction recording. *Journal of Abnormal and Social Psychology*, 1951, **46**, 258–260.
7. Carter, L., *et al.* The relation of categorizations and ratings in the observation of group behavior. *Human Relations*, 1951, **3**, 239–254.

8. French, R. L., & Bell, B. Consistency of individual leadership position in small groups of varying membership. *Journal of Abnormal and Social Psychology,* 1950, **45,** 764–767.

9. Hemphill, J. K. Relations between the size of the group and the behavior of "superior" leaders. *Journal of Social Psychology,* 1950, **32,** 11–22.

10. Lippitt, R. *Training in community relations.* New York: Harper, 1949.

11. Murphy, L. *Social behavior and child personality.* New York: Columbia Univ. Press, 1937.

12. Parten, M. Leadership among preschool children. *Journal of Abnormal and Social Psychology,* 1933, **27,** 430–440.

13. Roff, M. A study of combat leadership in the Air Force by means of a rating scale: Group differences. *Journal of Psychology,* 1950, **30,** 229–239.

14. Sanford, F. H. *Authoritarianism and leadership.* Philadelphia: Institute for Research in Human Relations, 1950.

30

Phases in Group Problem-Solving

ROBERT F. BALES AND FRED L. STRODTBECK

The idea that groups go through certain stages or phases in the process of solving problems, or that problem-solving would somehow be more effective if some prescribed order were followed, has been current in the literature for some time (4, 5, 8). However, the distinction between predicting an empirical order of phases under given conditions and prescribing an ideal order in terms of value judgments has not in all cases been clearly drawn. Furthermore, it has not always been recognized that different types of conditions or problems may result empirically in different sorts of phase movement. The persistence of these confusions has probably been related to the fact that until recently empirical methods which would give operational substance to the ideas have been lacking.

This paper presents a method of testing for the empirical existence of differentiated phases in group process and some evidence that under certain particular conditions a certain type of phase movement does tend to appear. The type of phase movement described is *not* held to be universal in an empirical sense. Whether it appears empirically depends upon a large number of conditions. Whether this type of phase movement is "optimum" under certain conditions in terms of value standards is a different problem and is not discussed in this paper.

By *phases* in the hypothesis presented below, we mean qualitatively different subperiods within a total continuous period of interaction in which a group proceeds from initiation to completion of a problem involving group decision.

From *The Journal of Abnormal and Social Psychology*, 1951, **46**, 485–495. The research was facilitated by the Laboratory of Social Relations, Harvard University. The article, in somewhat condensed form, is reprinted by permission of the authors and the American Psychological Association.

A PHASE HYPOTHESIS FOR FULL-FLEDGED PROBLEMS

The present phase hypothesis is restricted to instances in which groups work toward the goal of a group decision on a full-fledged problem. Briefly stated, the phase hypothesis is the proposition that under these conditions groups tend to move in their interaction from a relative emphasis upon problems of *orientation*, to problems of *evaluation*, and subsequently to problems of *control*, and that concurrent with these transitions, the relative frequencies of both *negative reactions* and *positive reactions* tend to increase. The terms used in the statement of the hypothesis have as their operational referents the acts which are briefly defined in Figure 1. There are 12 categories on the observation list. The present hypothesis is stated in terms of five groups of these categories, identified by the brackets on the left and right of the list. Categories 6 and 7 are grouped as dealing with problems of orientation; 5 and 8 deal with problems of evaluation; 4 and 9 with problems of control; 10, 11,

and *12* with negative reactions; and *1, 2,* and *3* with positive reactions. This is a relatively crude grouping, and it seems likely that further experience will enable us to state the hypothesis in a way which treats each category separately.

This particular phase hypothesis is expected to hold only under *certain conditions,* which we try to identify and state below. In general, we believe that the rates of activity we observe in each of the categories, and the way these rates move, over time, vary with changes in the conditions under which the interaction takes place. A major distinction can be drawn between those conditions which may be regarded as constituted prior to the period of observation and those which arise and change during the actual period of observation.

Under prior conditions we tend to think of three broad classes of variables: (*a*) the personalities of the individual members in their idiosyncratic aspects; (*b*) those characteristics the members have in common, as part of their parent culture, as well as of the subculture of the particular group under observation; and (*c*) the organization of the group, that is, the

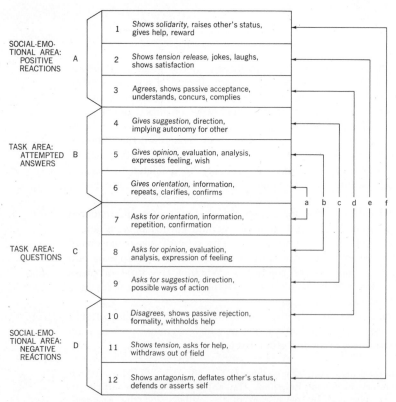

FIGURE 1. Interaction process categories defined and grouped by types.

expectations the members have established concerning their social relationships with each other and their different positions in this total constellation of expectations.

In addition to these prior conditions, we recognize (*d*) a series of conditions arising from the nature of the problems faced during the specific period of observation, which change as the group interaction moves through time.

Obviously, we are not able to specify the content of these four classes of conditions with the degree of refinement we should like, but as a first approximation we sketch the following requirements as the conditions under which the present phase hypothesis is expected to hold. Whenever the group or the problem does not meet the requirements, the particular phase movement described above is not expected to appear.

We have no experimental evidence as to the effects of variations in personality composition of the group on phase movement. Our data are all obtained from groups of persons assumed to be "normal." There are more or less obvious reasons for supposing that the hypothesis should not be expected to apply to groups involving persons of subnormal intelligence or seriously disturbed personalities.

We assume the participants will be adult, or near-adult, members of our own culture. This gives us some expectation that they will speak English, have some formal education, etc. As to the particular subculture of the groups, if the group has met before, it seems possible that such features as special procedural customs and training in group discussion methods might directly affect the phase movement. Hence, it may be that certain groups could deliberately evolve procedures to circumvent the expected movement, or to follow it in spite of conditions which would otherwise prevent it. Obviously, it is necessary to exclude cases of this type.

We require a group in which there is some minimum pressure to maintain its solidarity so that joint decision will have some binding power over the members after the sequence observed and so that the presence of disagreement, tension, and antagonism will be negatively valued. The status differences among members of the group should not be so great as to deny each member the right to participate and influence the choice of the ultimate decision. It appears likely that serious status

struggles within the group may modify the phase movement, although this has not yet been explored. The group size may vary from two to twenty, or may be even larger, perhaps, if there is the possibility of face-to-face interaction among the participants over a common problem.

As to the duration of the period of observation itself, we require the selection for analysis of a single complete "topical cycle of operations," from the recognition of a topical problem to its disposition by the group. We do not mean this requirement to exclude periods in which a group considers several topics involved in a single major decision, but we do require that, when topical problems are considered serially as items on an agenda, the period of discussion on each topic be analyzed separately. Thus, an entire meeting in some cases may be an appropriate period for analysis; in other cases, discussion of a single agenda item may be appropriate. (In addition, we exclude groups not concerned with a fairly specific problem of group planning and decision. For example, we exclude groups in which the aim or main emphasis is on expressive personal interaction, such as therapeutic interviews, play groups, meetings of friends at a cocktail party, and the like.)

Finally, we require a task in which it may be assumed that the functional problems of *orientation, evaluation,* and *control* are each to a major degree unsolved at the beginning of observation and are solved in some degree during the period of observation. More specifically:

With regard to *orientation,* members of the group must have some degree of ignorance and uncertainty about the relevant facts but individually possess facts relevant to decision. A clear example of a group which meets this requirement is a diagnostic council, where the members have seen the patient separately and have made different tests relevant to a decision as to what to do with the patient.

With regard to problems of *evaluation,* we require that the problem not be what is sometimes called an "open and shut" case. We need to be able to assume that the members possess somewhat different values or interests and that the problem is such that it involves several different values and interests as criteria by which the facts of the situation and the proposed course of action are to be judged.

With regard to problems of *control* (of the

members over one another and over the common environment), we require that there be both pressure for a group decision and the expectation of further joint action. It is also assumed that there are a number of possible alternatives with different, and perhaps uncertain, degrees of potential frustration or satisfaction associated with various choices.

When problems lack or greatly minimize any of these three characteristics, we speak of them as being *truncated*. When the three characteristics are present, we speak of the problem as being *full-fledged*. We do not expect the particular phase hypothesis stated above to hold for truncated problems. Presumably, it may be possible to formulate other phase hypotheses which will describe the phase movement for particular kinds of truncated problems.

The above conditions may seem formidable at first glance, but it is our opinion that they are met in group conferences, committees, and the like with sufficient frequency to insure the practical importance of investigating situations of this type.

In order to test the hypothesis empirically, it is necessary to specify the length of a phase. In the absence of any compelling rationale, we have adopted a simple convention: After the observations have been recorded on a moving tape (3), we divide into thirds the cycle of operations which constitutes the total period to be analyzed, producing the *first, middle,* and *final* phases. The total period is divided so that each phase includes one-third of the acts of the total set. (This is approximately equivalent to a time division into thirds, though not quite, since we have observed that there is some tendency for the interaction to speed up toward the latter part of topical cycles.) Since we have no basis for predicting the absolute number of acts by type for each phase, we implement the hypothesis by designating the phase in which we expect the number of acts of a particular type to be high, intermediate, or low when rank-ordered.

We have drawn Figure 2 on the basis of the summary data for all group sessions examined in the present study in order to illustrate something of the magnitude of the variation which may be expected. It should be emphasized that, when we say there is a shift in relative emphasis from problems of orientation in the first phase, to problems of evaluation in the second phase, to problems of con-

trol in the third phase, we do not mean that the absolute magnitude for the selected activity is greater than all others in that phase—we mean, rather, that the rate of the selected activity is at its own high point in the designated phase. (It should be noted that the cases upon which Figure 2 is based include a number in which the conditions for the hypothesis are not fully met, and yet the phase movement of the aggregate is of the type we specify will hold for individual cases only under full-fledged conditions. This apparent paradox will be discussed later.)

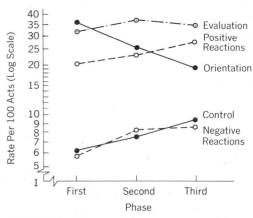

FIGURE 2. Relative frequency of acts by type and phase, based upon twenty-two sessions.

RATIONALE FOR THE HYPOTHESIS

For an interacting group, the solution of problems of orientation is assumed to bear an enabling relation to the solution of problems of evaluation and control and, in this sense, to be functionally prerequisite to their solution. That is, an individual may be cognitively oriented to a situation and speak of it to others in cognitive terms without committing himself overtly either to evaluation of it or to an attempt to control it; but speaking to the other in evaluative terms implies previous orientation, and the attempt to control the situation by joint action implies both previous orientation and evaluation. Something like this sequence of process may be characteristic of individual human problem-solving on the nonovert level. Historically speaking, most of the theories about steps or stages in group problem-solving seem to be more or less direct extrapolations of steps or stages assumed to exist in individual mental processes. The present rationale is based directly on conditions present in the overt process of social interaction between individuals through an appreciable lapse of time, and it may be compatible with any number of theories regarding the mental processes of individual problem-solving.

In the most general rationale of the whole set of categories (see Fig. 1), *3* and *10* are thought of as dealing with problems of *decision; 2* and *11*, with problems of *tension management;* and *1* and *12*, with problems of *integration* or *reintegration* of the group. For the present phase hypothesis, these categories have been grouped not according to the type of functional problem with which they deal, but according to their implication, positive or negative, for the solution of these types of problems. These problems we call social-emotional problems, to distinguish them from those which are more directly task-connected (see Fig. 1, brackets on left).

It is our assumption that efforts to solve problems of orientation, evaluation, and control (that is, attempts to accomplish the task) tend to lead to differentiation of the roles of the participants, both as to the functions they perform and their gross amounts of participation. Both types of differentiation tend to carry status implications which may threaten or disturb the existing order or balance of status relations among members and thus impair the basic solidarity of the group.

This impairment, we assume, tends to grow more marked as the group passes from emphasis on problems of orientation to problems of evaluation and still more acute as it passes on to its heaviest emphasis on problems of control. This assumption seems to be a more generalized way of stating the findings of certain other studies. For example, Lippitt (9) found negative reactions to autocratic control or leadership in boys clubs under certain conditions, and Rogers and his associates (**10**) tend to find a minimization of negative reactions on the part of clients when the counselor confines himself to nondirective (or, in our categories, orienting) types of activity. Thus, the present assumption may be regarded as a generalization of this connection between degree of control and negative reactions and as applying to different points in the process of the same group, not simply to differences between groups.

Thus, as we conceive the process, a series of changes in the social-emotional relationships of the members tend to be set in motion by pressures arising initially from the demands of the external problem or outer situation. As they grow more acute, these social-emotional problems, as well as the task problems, tend to be expressed or dealt with in overt interaction. These, in brief, are the theoretical reasons for expecting that with our crude division of the cycle of operations into three phases, rates in Categories 10, 11, and 12 will be lowest in the initial period and highest in the final period, moving concomitantly with the emphasis on problems of control.

However, at the extreme end of the final period, assuming that the members' attempts at control over the outer situation and over each other are successful and a final decision is reached, we expect the rates in Categories *1, 2,* and *3* also to rise to their peak. In other words, the group tends to confirm its agreement and to release in diffuse ways the tensions built up in its prior task-efforts, repairing the damage done to its state of consensus and social integration. We note joking and laughter so frequently at the ends of meetings that they might almost be taken as a signal that the group has completed what it considers to be a task effort and is ready for disbandment or a new problem. This last-minute activity completes the hypothetical cycle of operations both for the task problems and social-emotional problems. The apparent incongruity of predicting a peak for both negative and positive reactions in the third phase is thus explained. Negative and positive reactions tend to be successive emphases within the crudely defined third phase.

TESTING THE PHASE HYPOTHESIS

To test the phase hypothesis, we have considered *all* the protocols available in our files which had been scored in a form appropriate for this investigation. The number is small, only 22 cases. Some of these cases represent several hours of sustained interaction by one group, while others represent the discussion of single topics taken from longer sessions. The groups involved were originally observed for a number of different purposes. Some were experimentally formed groups with assigned

TABLE 1. *Transpositions Required to Establish the Order Predicted by the Phase Hypothesis for 22 Sets of Observations*

Case No.	Fulfills Conditions	Description of Group and Task	No. of Transpositions Required
1	Yes	Five-man chess novice group planning first move of seven-move problem	0[a]
2	Yes	Three-man group on first group projective story	1[a]
3	Yes	Eight-man academic group planning thesis	2[a]
4	Yes	Four-man chess club evaluating past performance and planning future performance	2[a]
5	Yes	Seven-man college group in discussion skills planning own operations	2[a]
6	Yes	Four-man steering committee planning arrangements for Christmas party	3[a]
7	Yes	Four-man chess club evaluating past performance and planning future operation	4
8	No	Four-man chess club solving two-move problem	4
9	No	Three-man group on third group projective story	4
10	No	Four-man chess club solving two-move problem	5
11	No	Four-man chess club solving two-move problem	5
12	No	Three-man group on fourth group projective story	5
13	Yes	Seven-man college group on discussion skills	5
14	No	Three-man chess club constructing chess problem	6
15	No	Four-man chess club solving two-move problem	6
16	No	Three-man group on fifth group projective story	6
17	No	Three-man group on second group projective story	6
18	No	Three-man role-playing group deciding between two fictional alternative purchases	6
19	No	Eight-man academic discussion group on theory	7
20	No	Three-man chess club constructing a chess problem	8
21	No	Three-man chess club constructing a chess problem	10
22	No	Five-man chess novice group planning second move of seven-move problem	11

[a]Significant at or beyond the .05 level.

tasks. Some were operating groups that allowed us to sit in and observe. We have given a brief description of the task considered by each of these groups in Table 1.

The writers have judged each of the 22 cases separately and have agreed that 8 of the 22 satisfactorily fulfill the conditions outlined in earlier paragraphs. The distinction between cases which meet and cases which fail to meet the conditions can be illustrated by discussion of a few concrete ones.

Cases 8, 10, 11, and 15 were chess problem solving groups in which the participants were well oriented to the factual aspects of the problem before beginning interaction. Chess problems are almost uniquely "full information" problems, and the participants were skilled chess players. The profile of scores generated in these sessions was uniformly below the expected limit on giving information

and orientation, according to empirical norms we have published elsewhere (2). On this basis, the writers classified this problem as being *truncated;* it was assumed not to have the necessary requirement for orientation.

An interesting and partially parallel instance is Case 1. Here, again, a chess problem which the group solves cooperatively is involved, but the participants are novices who have just been instructed for one hour in the rules of the game. They have their instruction manuals with them, and they are still uncertain about the identity of the pieces and the best mode of attack. The phase sequence of their interaction up to their decision as to their first move is in complete accord with the hypothesis. In the planning of their second move, however, they were able to draw upon their earlier discussion in which they had discussed future moves as well, and the problem was truncated for them in terms of the reduced emphasis on orientation, just as it had been for the previous chess group described above.

A similar sequence of topical cycles which seemed to involve successively less orientation is seen in Cases 2, 9, 12, 16, and 17. In these cases the same group made up stories to the five cards of the Guetzkow and Henry Group Projection Sketches (6). The interaction only up to the point of completion of the first card (Case 2) was markedly in the expected phase order.

In Cases 14, 20, and 21, members of a chess club were confronted with the task of *constructing* an original chess problem, starting from an empty board. They were fully oriented to the task at the beginning of the sequence, since they were quite familiar with chess problems. They began with suggestions in order to determine initial placements of pieces on the board, and they became more concerned with problems of orientation as more pieces were added to the board and the complications thus increased. Two of these three sequences were the direct reverse of the phase order expected under full-fledged conditions on problems of orientation and control. It may be that certain types of creative problems typically produce this type of approach and that a different sort of phase hypothesis could be evolved for such tasks. An increasing complexity of orientation needed as the task evolves might be a basic factor in limiting the number of persons who may work together successfully on creative problems.

To test the conformity between the observed orderings and the orderings predicted by our original theoretical analysis, we have employed a model based upon the occurrence of the maxima and minima in the predicted phase rather than a model in which absolute magnitudes were considered. Table 2 presents the hypothesis in a form appropriate for this type of test. Table 2 may be compared with Figure 2 to clarify its meaning.

The following hypothetical example, which involves only one type of act, illustrates this method of analysis.

Phases in Which Acts of Orientation Are:

	High	*Intermediate*	*Low*
Predicted:	First	Middle	Final
Observed:			
Example I	First	Middle	Final
Example II	Middle	First	Final
Example III	Final	Middle	First

In Example I, the observed values match exactly with the prediction; that is, the high, intermediate, and low values occur in the periods in which they were predicted to occur. In Examples II and III there are departures from the prediction. The main point of this discussion of the model is the justification of the method adopted to evaluate the degree of departure. We believe that it is inappropriate to consider the goodness of fit in terms of the number of instances in which the predicted values match the observed values. In terms of matches alone, there is no distinction between II and III; in each example one element corresponds with the predicted placement. This is not a satisfactory description, however, since one feels that there is a more serious departure from expectation if the predicted high is interchanged with the predicted low, as in III, than if the predicted high is interchanged with the predicted median, as in II. Fortunately, if we count not the number of matches but the number of *transpositions* of adjacent values required to establish the predicted order, we may take account of the distinction between II and III.

TABLE 2. *Expected Phase in Which Frequencies of Acts by Type Will Be High, Intermediate, and Low Under Conditions of the Full-fledged Problem*

Type of Act	High	Intermediate	Low
Orientation	First	Middle	Final
Evaluation	Middle	Final	First
Control	Final	Middle	First
Negative	Final	Middle	First
Positive	Final	Middle	First

To illustrate the counting of transpositions, Example II can be modified to fit the predicted order by exchanging the middle and first element, whereas for Example III there are three transpositions required: first with middle, first with final, and middle with final. A statistical evaluation of the difference between the predicted and observed orders can be made on the basis of the number of transpositions required. It can be demonstrated [1] that if there are three or fewer transpositions,

[1] The statistic employed is essentially a repeated application of Kendall's rank correlation coefficient *tau* (7). Persons wishing to perform computations for orderings of other sizes can obtain the appropriate coefficients of the powers of *x* to be inserted in the formula from Kendall (7, 388–437).

the null hypothesis may be rejected at the .05 level.

By reference to Table 1, it may be noted that six of the eight sessions which were judged to have fulfilled the stated necessary conditions were also significant in the sense that they would require only the three transpositions or less required to reject the null hypothesis of random distribution at the .05 level. Two sessions which we judged to meet the conditions were not significantly different from random expectations.

It is thus apparent that cases which meet the conditions do deviate significantly from random expectations and that cases which do not meet the conditions do not deviate significantly. In short, one or more alternative phase hypotheses, accompanied by corresponding specification of conditions, are required before we can duplicate the relatively accurate predictions of the occurrence of maxima and minima which we have made for the eight individual cases in question.

DISCUSSION OF RESULTS

The 14 cases which failed to meet the conditions also failed to conform to the phase movement predicted for full-fledged conditions. Nevertheless, when all of the acts of the 22 cases are summed together by type of act and phase, the values for each type of act have maxima and minima which correspond exactly with the particular phase movement under discussion. These data are presented in Table 3 and earlier, graphically, in Figure 2. How is this paradoxical finding to be interpreted?

It may be that we simply have a sample of cases in which compensating differences happen to exist and that new aggregates of cases would fail to show the pattern. On the other hand, it may be that certain conditions are operating which tend to be similar from case to case, in spite of particular differences. There are certain conditions which seem to be more or less inherent in the nature of the process of interaction or communication itself. If this were not so, it would be difficult to produce a set of categories of the sort used in the present observations, which we believe to be very general and applicable in formal terms at least, to any interaction.

We suggest that parts of the interaction process itself tend to affect other parts in such a way that, at the time of any given act, the acts which have gone before, or which have not yet occurred but are expected to come, constitute a set of "internal" conditions which operate in addition to whatever "external" conditions there may be of the sorts specified in the statement of the hypothesis. We know that in the more microscopic act-to-act sequences this is the case. Questions tend to be followed by attempted answers, and these in turn tend to be followed by positive or negative reactions or more questions (1, 129–131). These are "internal tendencies" of the process itself on a microscopic time span. It may be that similar internal tendencies operate on the more molar level of longer chains of sequences leading to group decision.

It can now be pointed out that the rationale of the phase hypothesis presented earlier is essentially an argument based on an assumption that there are internal tendencies of interaction considered as a system distributed between persons and through time. If one started with the assumption that interaction does constitute a social system and that it will tend to exhibit certain systematic properties on that account, how would he go about demonstrating this empirically? The critical logical difficulty would seem to be that the system he is trying to investigate never operates apart from external conditions which are expected to influence the behavior which actually occurs. The effects of the external conditions are always compounded with, or confounded with, the effects of the internal conditions.

One approach, perhaps, is to attempt to observe the system operating in a set of conditions complete enough and balanced in such a way as to call out the full range of internal tendencies or possibilities of the interaction

TABLE 3.   *Acts by Type and Phase, Total for 22 Cases*

	Phase			
Type of Act	First	Middle	Final	*Total*
Orientation	1,668	1,170	916	3,574
Evaluation	1,550	1,792	1,656	4,998
Control	285	364	429	1,078
Negative	275	374	408	1,057
Positive	984	1,058	1,361	3,403
Total[a]	4,762	4,758	4,770	14,290

[a] The totals in phases are not quite equal, due to the fact that no systematic technique was employed to distribute the extra acts when the total acts of a session were not divisible by three.

process, so that the empirical observations might display in most articulate form the effects of the internal conditions. Here it may be pointed out that the description of the set of conditions we have called the *full-fledged* problem is essentially an attempt to specify a set of external conditions which might meet this methodological requirement so far as the problem the group is working on is concerned.

The other approach which suggests itself is an attempt to randomize in some fashion the kinds of external conditions involved and to deal with large aggregates of cases. If there are internal tendencies characteristic of interaction as a systematic process or social system, the similarity of these tendencies from case to case, in spite of the differences due to external conditions, would be expected to exert a constant "biasing" effect away from randomness. In aggregates of cases, then, where the external conditions of individual cases are varied enough to average out, one would expect the effects of the internal-system tendencies to become apparent.

In short, the present reasoning suggests that there are two ways of detecting the presence and nature of rather general internal tendencies, if, indeed, they exist: first, by letting them operate under *full-fledged* rather than *truncated* external conditions, and second, by averaging out various kinds of truncation and accentuation by adding many widely varied cases together.

If later research indicates the general methodological position taken here to be tenable, the problems of experimentally investigating how particular types of external conditions influence the course of interaction are greatly simplified. It may be that empirically average phase tendencies like those presented in Table 3 can be taken as sufficiently representative of the effects of parts of the process on other parts, that is, the social system effects. In experimental designs, then, where a full-fledged problem is used as the basic testing situation, deviations from the empirical norm might be used as evidences of the effects of known or experimentally introduced conditions. For example, the experimental introduction of persistent difficulties of communication or orientation might upset the phase sequence expected on the basis of the internal tendencies of the interaction system alone.

Conversely, in using the method for clinical analysis or training of particular groups, groups might be set up under full-fledged conditions, and the deviations from the empirical norm used as diagnostic indicators of otherwise unknown characteristics of the group or the members. For example, the appearance of a high rate of negative reactions in the first phase of a standard full-fledged problem might indicate the presence of hostilities not arising out of the present interaction itself, but existing as a prior condition.

SUMMARY

A set of categories for the firsthand observation of group process has been presented. A set of conditions has been described which we believe to be characteristic of many staff conferences, committees, and similar groups dealing with problems of analysis and planning with the goal of group decision. We have presented a hypothesis which states that under these specified conditions the process tends to move through time from a relative emphasis upon problems of *orientation*, to problems of *evaluation*, and subsequently to problems of *control;* and that concurrent with these transitions, the relative frequencies of both *negative reactions* and *positive reactions* tend to increase.

It has been shown that all 22 sessions available to the experimenters from prior observations, when considered as an aggregate, show a significant departure from a random distribution of acts between phases. It has been shown further that the observed significance is attributable to the inclusion of cases which meet the specified conditions. Individual cases which do not meet the conditions do not show a significant departure from a random distribution of phase movements.

However, when all of the acts of the 22 cases are summed together by type of act and phase, the values for each type of act have maxima and minima which correspond exactly with the particular phase movement postulated for individual cases under the specified full-fledged conditions. This finding may be accidental. The suggestion is offered, however, that in addition to the external conditions specified, the interaction process should be considered as a system, with internal tendencies which make each part of the process a condition to other parts. These "internal" conditions are assumed to be similar to some degree from case to case and to exert a constant "biasing" effect. This biasing effect becomes apparent either in individual cases under full-fledged external conditions or in aggregates of cases in which differences in external conditions average out.

It is suggested that if the phase movement described here does represent the effect of conditions internal to the process itself, it may be used with some advantage as a baseline for the detection of discrepancies or accentuations due to known or experimentally introduced external conditions or, conversely, as diagnostic indicators of the presence of otherwise unknown conditions.

Finally, the general method of testing for the existence of any given phase pattern seems to open the way for an experimental attack on problems of determining the effects of various patterns of process under various conditions—effects on the motivation and satisfaction of participants and on their performance of the group task.

References

1. Bales, R. F. *Interaction process analysis: A method for the study of small groups.* Cambridge, Mass.: Addison-Wesley Press, 1950.
2. Bales, R. F. A set of categories for the analysis of small group interaction. *American Sociological Review*, 1950, **15**, 257–263.
3. Bales, R. F., & Gerbrands, H. The interaction recorder: An apparatus and check list for sequential content analysis of social interaction. *Human Relations*, 1948, **1**, 456–463.
4. Dewey, J. *How we think.* Boston: Heath, 1910.
5. Elliott, H. S. *The process of group thinking.* New York: Association Press, 1928.
6. Guetzkow, H., & Henry, W. *Group projective sketches.* Ann Arbor, Mich.: Univ. of Michigan Press, 1949.
7. Kendall, M. G. *The advanced theory of statistics.* London: Lippincott, 1943.
8. Lasker, B. *Democracy through discussion.* New York: H. W. Wilson Co., 1949.
9. Lippitt, R. An experimental study of authoritarian and democratic group atmospheres. *Univ. of Iowa Studies in Child Welfare*, 1940, **16** (3), 43–195.
10. Rogers, C. R. *Counseling and psychotherapy: New concepts in practice.* Boston: Houghton Mifflin, 1942.

PART SIX

MOTIVATIONAL PROCESSES IN GROUPS

31

Motivational Processes in Groups: Introduction

Everyone has belonged, at one time or another, to a group that seemed to have no clearly identifiable goals or objectives. Because it has no criterion by which to evaluate alternative courses of action, such a group finds it difficult to organize a coherent program of activities. Members come to feel that the group "never gets anywhere" and that they have no way of deriving satisfaction from group accomplishment. As a result, their behavior in the group is guided mainly by personal needs and interests.

Quite a different situation arises when a group has a clearly specified goal. Now members have a basis for evaluating alternative courses of group action and for considering how their own behavior may contribute to group accomplishment. A member who accepts the group goal is motivated to collaborate with other members in order to facilitate its attainment. He experiences satisfaction from evidences of group success and frustration from group failure. Concern for the welfare of the group is likely to be high.

What do we mean when we assert that a group does or does not "have a goal" or "accomplish something"? The terms used in everyday language to describe the goal-directed behavior of groups suggest that a group can be said to have a location of some sort, that it may change its location from time to time, and that certain locations are preferred by all or some segment of the membership to others. As a first step, then, toward conceptualizing the phenomena related to group goals, we assume that a group may be conceived as an undifferentiated entity which at any given time has a particular location in its environment. Whenever it is possible to assert that some location is relatively preferred for a group and that a sequence of efforts to change the group's location will terminate when it is reached, we will designate that location as the group's goal. If a group changes its location, we will speak of group locomotion. For group locomotion to occur it is usually necessary for the group to perform a sequence of group actions; a sequence that leads to a preferred location may be thought of as a path through the group's environment to its goal. Group actions, although carried out by means of the behavior of individuals, are appropriately described at the group level. Thus, for example, if a fraternity sets the goal of "having a dance," it must take such actions as "appropriating funds," "renting a ballroom," "hiring a band," and "getting a chaperone."

In order to give these rather abstract terms more concrete meaning, let us consider how they may be applied to a fund-raising committee that has explicitly decided to attempt to collect a certain sum of money. The committee may be conceived as having a location on a scale indicating the amount of money received at any given time, and the committee's goal is the location on this scale corresponding to the amount specified by the decision. Upon receiving a contribution, the committee as a whole undergoes a locomotion toward its goal. Since its location is specified in terms of the amount of money collected, there is usually little difficulty in identifying the group's location or its rate of locomotion.

A laboratory experiment conducted by Horwitz (Chap. 34) indicates another way in which our conceptualization may be employed. Horwitz assigned groups the task of putting together a jig-saw puzzle by taking a group vote concerning where each piece should be placed. Here, the group may be conceived as existing in a "task environment." Each time it correctly places a piece of the puzzle, the group may be said to move a step toward its preferred location—its goal—of "completing the task." Horwitz was able to demonstrate that the motivational tensions of individual members depend in a systematic way upon the position of the group relative to its preferred location.

An investigation carried out by Leavitt (Chap. 37) provides a further illustration. Groups formed in the laboratory were given the task of assembling information so as to arrive at the answer to an intellectual problem. Although it was rather difficult to identify each step in the progress toward the goal, the transition from "no solution" to "having the answer" was clear, and Leavitt could construct a group-learning curve indicating how the group shortened the time required to reach its goal with repetition of the group task.[1]

In these examples, it is not especially difficult to identify the group's goal, the group's location in relation to its goal, and the group actions required for goal attainment. It is evident, however, that the situation is not always so clear-cut. Indeed, one of the most common practical problems of group management arises from the difficulty often encountered in knowing precisely where a group is located in relation to a goal and what steps need be taken by the group to reach it. We will return to this problem when we discuss the "operationality" of group goals. It often happens, too, that a group appears to have a particular goal in the sense that group actions are directed by it even though the members are not consciously aware of the goal. Situations of this sort have been of special interest to investigators who approach the study of groups from a psychoanalytic background. Bion (6) and Ezriel (11), for example, have asserted that "unconscious group goals" are important in the functioning of groups organized for purposes of individual therapy. A further difficulty in ascertaining the goals of a group arises from the fact that these are sometimes effectively established by some subpart of the group rather than by consensus. Thus, for example, a church may "decide" to build a new edifice and thus commit the congregation, as a whole, to a particular sequence of group actions even though only the members of the executive committee actually participate in the decision.

The fact that group goals may be vaguely formulated, known only to some of the members, or not consciously recognized by any presents problems to the investigator. Since these problems are especially difficult in research on groups in naturalistic settings, much of our knowledge about motivational processes in groups has come from laboratory investigations, but important contributions have also been made by such students of organizations as Cyert and March (10), March and Simon (24), and Shartle (31).

In the remainder of this chapter, we will

[1] Hays and Bush (15) have explored the possibility of predicting the learning curves of groups by means of a "group-actor" mathematical model in which the same properties are attributed to a group, as an entity, as have been found to characterize an individual. The results of an experiment conducted on three-man groups conform rather well to those predicted by the model, but they also indicate that the specific nature of the relationships among group members undoubtedly have an effect upon group learning.

examine in more detail the nature of group goals, their effects upon the functioning of groups, and some of their consequences as reflected in the behavior of members. More specifically, we will consider three basic aspects of group motivation: (*a*) *Goal formation.* How are group goals established? What are the processes of group decision-making? What conditions facilitate or inhibit the formation of group goals of various kinds? How do goals of individuals become "converted" into group goals? (*b*) *Group goals and group action.* How does a group goal affect the choice of actions to be taken by the group? What conditions help or hinder a group's locomotion toward its goals? What characterizes the acts of individuals that result in group locomotion? (*c*) *The effects of goal-directed group action.* What motivational consequences for members stem from the nature of a group's goals and its success or failure in attaining them? How are the gains or losses resulting from a group's goal-directed actions distributed among its members? How do different "rules" for their distribution affect the functioning of the group?

FORMATION OF GROUP GOALS

We turn our attention first to the question of how group goals are formed. What are the factors that influence the selection of goals by a group? Although this question has stimulated speculation and, especially, proposals as to how groups *should* go about selecting a goal, remarkably little evidence is available to provide an answer. In an effort to simplify thinking about the complexities that are obviously involved, we will distinguish two aspects of the process of group goal-formation. The first concerns the way in which individuals develop goals for a group. The second focuses attention on the conversion of goals for a group into a group goal. Although these two aspects of the process can be considered separately, it should be clear that in any concrete situation they may occur simultaneously and in interaction.

INDIVIDUAL GOALS FOR A GROUP

It is reasonable to assume that one necessary condition for a group goal to come into existence is that at least some members have a goal for the group—that is, a conception of an outcome they prefer for the group. Thus, for example, a Rotary club may establish the goal of raising funds for crippled children because of the special interests of certain influential members. Or a civil rights group may decide to embark upon a drive for new members because its policy committee believes that the group's political power depends upon the size of its membership. In general terms, three classes of influence appear to determine a member's goal for a group: the nature of his motives, his conception of the group's preestablished (or superordinate) goals, and his view of relations between the group and its social surroundings.

Motives of Members. In its broadest meaning a motive is a disposition to be satisfied by a specific class of outcomes. A person with a particular motive will engage in a certain activity if he believes it will bring about satisfying consequences. It is convenient to distinguish between two types of such motives, which we will call "person-oriented" and "group-oriented." By a *person-oriented motive* we mean a more-or-less enduring interest that exists whether or not the person is a member of the group under consideration. This motive is activated in a group if the person believes that satisfying consequences for himself will be provided by the group's actions. Many groups exist mainly for the purposes of satisfying person-oriented motives; groups in recreational, educational, and therapeutic agencies usually serve such ends. By a *group-oriented motive* we refer to a disposition to be satisfied by group outcomes favorable to the group as a unit. The operation of group-oriented motives is illustrated by instances of loyalty to one's political party, team, or firm, where a particular group goal is accepted even though its accomplishment promises no personal benefit to the member.

The nature of these two types of motives may be exemplified by considering how they motivate achievement behavior. An individual who is satisfied by personal success has a person-oriented motive for personal achievement (**2**), whereas an individual who is gratified by his group's success has a group-oriented motive for group achievement (Chap. 32). The person-oriented achievement motive is likely to be aroused by any task in which the person's performance will be compared to some standard of excellence. The group-oriented motive for achievement, on the other hand, tends to be activated by an awareness that the group's performance will be evaluated. In a situation capable of activating both types of motives, an individual with a strong person-oriented achievement motive may be expected to be especially concerned with the quality of his own performance whereas one with a strong group-oriented achievement motive will be particularly interested in the quality of the group's performance. There is evidence indicating that members who have more responsible roles in the group or who are otherwise more committed to the group are likely to develop a stronger group-oriented motive.

The role of person-oriented motives in the formation of group goals may be better understood if we consider more closely the process of group decision-making. For this purpose, let us examine a hypothetical example of three boys who select the group goal of building a lemonade stand. We assume that each boy has a single individual goal based on a person-oriented motive: one boy wants to make enough money to buy a baseball glove, the second wants to use his new carpentry tools, and the third simply wants to play with the other two. It should be evident that nothing about these separate motives requires that the group goal be "to build a lemonade stand." And yet it appears that this goal is a rather natural outcome, considering the nature of the several motives. How is this "fitting" of person-oriented motives and group goal accomplished? Obviously many different sequences of events might take place, but the following appears not unlikely.

When the three boys first get together they soon ask the inevitable question, "What shall we do?" In other words, they seek to establish a group goal and its associated group activities. Various suggestions might be proposed: "Let's play ball," "Let's collect bottles and sell them," "Let's build a club house," "Let's build a lemonade stand," and so on. Each suggestion constitutes simultaneously a possible individual goal and a possible alternative for the group as an entity. After several alternative goals for the group have been proposed, the boys face the task of evaluating the relative merits of each: "I don't want to play ball because I don't have a glove," "If we sell bottles, we could earn enough money for me to buy a glove," "Let's build something so that I can use my tools," and so forth. In other words, each boy attempts to evaluate each alternative

at least partially in terms of its potential satisfaction for his own person-oriented motives. The result of this process is a more-or-less explicit preference ranking by each boy of the alternative group goals. Finally, by a process that we will consider later, the boys somehow combine their personal preferences to form a group goal that will then steer their collective activities.

A member's group-oriented motives enter into his formation of a goal for the group in much the same way as do his person-oriented motives. A person with a strong group-oriented motive may be expected to favor a particular goal for the group whenever he believes its attainment will benefit the group, and he may do so even though he realizes that the consequences will not be beneficial to him personally. Thus, for example, the chairman of the finance committee of a church who is convinced that the congregation needs a new edifice may advocate embarking upon a building campaign even when he knows that this decision would require him to neglect his own business interests. When a group-oriented motive is dominant, the critical considerations are whether the attainment of a particular goal will benefit the group and how likely it is that the group can in fact attain the goal.

The distinction suggested between person-oriented and group-oriented motivation is, of course, an ancient one. People have long been characterized as "selfish" or "altruistic." But research has only begun to provide systematic knowledge about the determinants of these orientations and their consequences. An excellent beginning was made by Lewis and Franklin (20, 21) in their experimental studies of the different motivational consequences of a "task orientation" and an "ego orientation." Fouriezos, Hutt, and Guetzkow (12) extended the analysis and applied it more explicitly to groups in their study of "self-oriented needs" in committee meetings. From observations of 72 decision-making conferences in business and government they concluded that "groups which exhibited more self-oriented need behavior were least satisfied with the meeting in general, with the decisions reached, with the way in which the group reached its decision, and with the chairmanship of the meeting." It was found that groups with high scores on self-oriented need behavior completed fewer items on the agenda but held longer meetings.

The willingness of a person to work for the

benefit of another even when there is not the slightest possibility of personal gain has been studied by Berkowitz and Daniels (4). They led individuals to believe that they were receiving written instructions from a person in another room, a complete stranger, whose skill as a supervisor was being appraised. There was in fact nobody in the other room, and all the messages, provided by the experimenter, were exactly alike. Some of the participants were told that the evaluation of the supervisor would depend upon how much work the participant completed; others were not given this understanding. The workers who knew that their output would determine the fate of the supervisor worked harder than those who were not so informed. In interpreting this result, the authors proposed that the subjects behaved in accord with a cultural norm which prescribes that a person should help anyone who is directly dependent upon him. They tested this view in a further study (5) and report that the tendency to work in behalf of a dependent individual is stronger if the potential helper is reminded of this norm ahead of time (by receiving help himself) or if he is a "socially responsible" individual in his way of life. It seems reasonable that members who agree upon a goal for their group become aware that the benefits for all depend upon the efforts of each, and thus a norm to help one another is aroused.

On the basis of available evidence, then, we may make the following summary statement. The attractiveness for any given member of a particular goal for the group is influenced by the nature of the member's person-oriented and group-oriented motives, by his judgment of the rewards and costs involved for him and the group in activities relevant to the goal, and his subjective probability that the group will attain this goal. It should be recognized, however, that both the motives and the judgments of the group members are themselves usually influenced by membership in the group.

Superordinate Group Goals. If we restrict our attention to established and formalized groups, it becomes clear that another set of influences is also operative in the formation of group goals. One important feature of established groups is that their members when engaged in group decision-making refer their evaluations of alternative goals for the group not only to their own desires but also to exist-

ing longer-range goals, objectives, or purposes of the group. For example, the members of a service club, in considering the program for the coming year, will tend to evaluate proposed alternatives in terms of their appropriateness to the objectives of the club and their compatibility with prior commitments of the club. In most established groups, decision-making has more the character of selecting subgoals that are subordinate to an existing goal than that of constructing group goals *de novo*. Unfortunately, almost no systematic research has been conducted on the ways in which superordinate goals influence the selection of subgoals in groups, and little is known about the ways in which these influences work.

The Group and Its Social Surroundings. Another important feature of enduring groups is that they have certain relationships with other groups and institutions that appear to exert pronounced influence upon the setting of goals for the group. This aspect of goal-setting is considered in some detail by Thompson and McEwen (37), who emphasize the fact that when a group or organization embarks upon the setting of goals it is attempting, in part, to establish a desired relationship between the group and its social environment. They point out that a change in either the properties of the group or its social environment requires review and perhaps alteration of goals. The necessary interaction between a group and its social environment introduces an element of environmental control over the group. To the degree that a group must please or satisfy those in its social environment, its goals must be acceptable: schools must teach what is congenial to the community; companies must manufacture what will sell; and TV studios must provide what people will watch. It follows that the selection and appraisal of goals is more difficult as the "product" of the group becomes less tangible and harder to measure and as society finds it more difficult to decide upon and express its acceptability of the product.

Members may be influenced, then, in selecting their goals for the group at least partially by anticipated reactions from the social environment of the group. The attitudes and behaviors of people in the group's environment may well be a function, in turn, of the degree to which the group is seen as relevant to furthering or obstructing the objectives of these people. It is not uncommon for groups to spend considerable energy and talent in convincing the significant elements of their social environment that their goals should be accepted by society, nor for society to invent ways to curb or destroy groups whose goals are viewed as threatening.

CONVERTING GOALS FOR THE GROUP INTO A GROUP GOAL

The formation of a group goal requires that the various goals for the group held by the different members be somehow converted into a single goal capable of steering group activities. A review of the literature on this problem reveals that no comprehensive understanding of it has yet emerged, although certain aspects have been studied in rather great detail.

Normative Approaches. There has been a long-standing interest, especially among political theorists, economists, and mathematicians, in formulating criteria for the way in which the preferences of individuals should be combined into a group decision. One of the most influential approaches within this tradition seeks, by means of mathematical reasoning and formal models, to construct rules of decision-making that will conform to the democratic doctrine that group decisions should optimally represent the individual interests of all participants. Probably the earliest mathematical treatment of this sort was that of the French scholar Borda, who published his results just shortly before the French Revolution. His work was extended in various ways during the period 1873–85 by C. L. Dodgson (Lewis Carroll), who sought to improve the quality of group decisions made by faculty committees at Oxford.[2] With the recent rise of the theory of games and decisions a high level of mathematical sophistication has been achieved, as may be seen in the publications of Arrow (1) and Luce and Raiffa (23). The purpose of this work has been formulated in the following way (23, 368):

Given the preference rankings (ties allowed) of m alternatives by the members of a society of n individuals, define "fair" methods for aggregating this set of individual rankings into a single rank-

[2] An interesting description of these early treatments may be found in a book by Black (7).

ing for the society. Such a rule for transforming an n-tuple of rankings—one for each individual—into a ranking for the society is called a social welfare function.

A rather different criterion than "fairness to individuals" is to be found, implicitly at least, in other discussions of how group decisions should be made. This criterion might be labeled "group effectiveness." Here the point of view is taken that group goals should be formed by whatever method will best assure that the group will effectively realize its most basic objectives. Thus, if one of the members of the group is an "expert," it might be argued that his goal for the group should be given complete weight in selecting the group goal. It is not surprising, perhaps, that this view is found most commonly among executives and management theorists.

It is possible, of course, that the two criteria of "fairness" and "group effectiveness" will turn out to be compatible. Many advocates of democracy claim that in the long run a group decision that best reflects the preferences of the members will also result in optimal group effectiveness.

Participation and Power. Instead of asking how individual goals for the group should be converted into a group goal, one may ask how the conversion actually takes place. Research conducted to date combines with everyday experience to focus attention on one aspect of group goal-setting: most groups fail, in some degree, to meet the "fairness" criterion in forming their goals. Two interrelated factors—differences among members in participation and differences among participants in the amount of influence exerted—appear most commonly to produce deviation from the state where the preferences of all members have equal weight in the formation of group goals.

With respect to the first factor, it is clear that the determinants of participation in group goal-setting are many and varied. Research like that of Stephan and Mishler (33) demonstrates that even when conditions are optimal—the group is small and group standards call for full participation—members do not usually participate equally. Many groups, especially larger and more formalized ones, have specialized the function of decision-making. Goals in such groups are set by committees, boards, and executives. The participation of others in setting the goals of the group is not expected and may even be prohibited.

Even if we confine our attention to the people who participate directly in the setting of a group goal, we find that differences may exist among them in the influence exerted by each. A person who, for any reason, gets others to accept his point of view is able to increase the likelihood that his personal preferences for the group will be reflected in the group goal selected.

The many determinants, both formal and informal, of participation and power combine in some fashion to create among the members of a group a particular distribution of influence over each group decision. Tannenbaum and Kahn (35) have developed a method for studying the perceptions people have of the customary locus and distribution of control in a group over decision-making. On the basis of interviews with group members, these investigators are able to construct a "control graph" of the group. Along its horizontal axis are indicated subparts of the group; for example, in a labor union these might be "local membership," "plant bargaining committee," "executive board," and "president." On the vertical axis is shown the amount of control over group decisions (how much "say") each subgroup is reported to have. Groups may differ greatly in the shape and general level of the control curves. Employing this method in the investigation of union locals, Tannenbaum and Kahn have found that the membership may gain a sense of control over group decisions in at least four ways: attending meetings of the local, participating in various informal and representational activities, having the right to ratify decisions made by others, and being able to recall from office those in decision-making positions. A belief by the membership that they have a reasonable control over group decisions seems to generate an interest on their part in the goals of the union, but this does not appear to be a necessary condition for the development of loyalty to the union.

Cognition and Motivation. A close look at what goes on among a group of people when they are attempting to form a group goal reveals both cognitive and motivational aspects. Cognitive processes are evident in the search for agreement about the facts relevant to the decision. "If we were to engage in this project, would we actually achieve our goal?" "How

would others react?" "Would the group's resources be sufficient to assure success?" The search for answers to questions such as these involves an exchange of information and opinions, and the sources of pressures to uniformity discussed in Chapter 11 may be expected to be operative. But agreement is ordinarily not enough; the members want to achieve a "correct" consensus. The quality of any group decision will depend in part upon the degree to which it rests upon an accurate assessment of facts and reflects intelligent problem-solving. Kelley and Thibaut (19) provide an excellent treatment of the many factors that affect the quality of group problem-solving.

It is possible, of course, for a group of people to agree on the pertinent facts, solve their cognitive problems effectively, and still disagree as to what the group goal should be. If members have conflicting interests, the selection of a group goal will be difficult. The members are likely to bargain, maneuver for power, and form coalitions in which some part of the larger group acts in concert to determine the outcome. The mathematical theory of games has been used extensively in treatments of motivational conflicts in group decision-making. The strengths and weaknesses of this general approach have been evaluated by Rapoport (28), who has also advanced an insightful distinction among types of conflicts, which he labels "fights," "games," and "debates." Research and theory concerned with the formation of coalitions has been reviewed by Gamson (13).

The relative emphasis on cognitive and on motivational processes in decision-making may vary from one group to another and within the same group at different times. One might expect, for example, that greater emphasis would be placed on cognitive aspects the more members are "task-oriented" or "group-oriented" rather than "self-oriented" and the more they see their basic relationships as promotively interdependent.

LEVEL OF ASPIRATION AND RISK-TAKING

It frequently happens that a group in setting a goal confronts a set of alternatives that can be arrayed along a scale of difficulty: the chosen goal is referred to as *the group's level of aspiration*. Subsequent group performance at or above this level is taken by the members to indicate "group success"; performance below it has the meaning of "group failure." When the members of an athletic team agree at the beginning of a tournament to try to win a certain number of their games, they are establishing a level of aspiration against which they then evaluate their performance in the tournament. Similar processes are involved when a fund-raising committee chooses the goal of collecting a specific sum of money, when a work group agrees to try to reach a particular level of production, or when a club sets as its target the recruitment of a certain number of new members. It is evident that the motivation, morale, and self-evaluation of members will depend greatly upon the relation between the group's level of aspiration and its subsequent performance.

Research has revealed that the level of aspiration of a group functions in a way quite similar to that of an individual. Thus, for example, both individuals and groups tend to raise their levels following "successful" performance and to lower them after "failure." Both individuals and groups may be motivated primarily either by a hope for success or by a fear of failure. When hope for success is dominant, the level of aspiration of an individual or a group tends to fall at an intermediate level of difficulty, but when fear of failure is dominant it tends to lie either at a very high or a very low level of difficulty. A theoretical analysis of these effects has been presented by Atkinson and Feather (**2**, 13–24).

The level of aspiration members set for their group is especially susceptible to influences from persons outside the group. Strong forces are aroused within a group to raise or lower its goals when members become aware that other groups similar to their own are performing better or worse than themselves. In many instances, it appears, participants will pay more attention to the performance of other groups than to the performance of their own when deciding what their group ought to be able to accomplish. In general, external agents who have power over the group exercise strong influence over the level of aspiration of the group. The choice made by the group influenced by external agents may be unrealistically high or low and thus may lead to unintended consequences (**44, 45**). A more detailed discussion of the determinants and consequences of a group's level of aspiration is given in Chapter 32.

The alternatives considered by a group when it is choosing a goal often entail different amounts of risk. In making such choices, do groups differ from individuals in the amount of risk they favor? It has been found in a number of experiments that the alternatives selected following a group discussion typically involve more risk than ones chosen by an individual making the choice by himself (**3, 8, 38, 39**, Chap. 33). It appears from this research that the greater riskiness of group decisions arises from the process of group discussion, although the exact way in which this happens has not been conclusively established. One plausible hypothesis holds that individuals become more willing to support risky alternatives when they participate in a group discussion because of a "diffusion of responsibility" arising from knowledge that others are participating in the decision. Whatever the ultimate explanation of the greater riskiness of groups, it has been shown that the effect cannot be fully accounted for by a tendency for leaders to be riskier than nonleaders or by an expectation on the part of members that they will be approved by others for favoring risky decisions. On the other hand, it has been found that those members who are initially more conservative change more as a result of group discussion and that those who are initially more confident of their recommendations favor riskier decisions, dominate the discussion more, and consequently exert more influence on the group's choice.

The repeated finding that group decisions are riskier than individual decisions does not, of course, demonstrate that they are invariably so. In fact, there is reason to believe that groups are sometimes more conservative than individuals. Further research is required to discover the conditions determining the relationship between the amount of risk preferred by individual members and the amount involved in decisions reached by the group.

STEERING GROUP ACTION

An essential feature of a group goal is that it steers group activities toward a preferred location. An adequate understanding of how this process works requires that we examine the relationships between group goals and group activities.

GROUP GOAL AND GROUP ACTION

Suppose that the local congregation of a church has selected the goal "to build a new edifice." The congregation will have to engage in a number of group actions such as "raising funds," "obtaining a mortgage," "acquiring a site," "employing an architect," and "hiring a contractor." Each of these actions requires that individual people engage in particular behaviors that are so constituted that they in fact bring about the group action. Thus, for example, the group action of "acquiring a site" may require a great variety of individual behaviors such as talking with real estate agents, inspecting available sites, bargaining with owners concerning price, and signing a contract. We see, then, that in order for group locomotion toward a goal to take place, appropriate group actions must occur. Each such group action, moreover, requires that particular individuals engage in suitable individual behaviors. Efficient group locomotion ordinarily demands that group actions and their associated individual behaviors be carried out in a particular sequence. Their coordination and synchronization often present basic problems for a group.

It is important to recognize that many group goals are of such nature that it is difficult to specify group activities that will contribute to their attainment. A governmental agency may have as its basic purpose "advancing the general welfare," a business may seek "to maximize profits in the long run," a professional society may exist "to advance the field in which members work," and a women's club may have as its objective "to raise the cultural level of the community." It would be difficult to evaluate alternative group activities in terms of their relative contribution to the attainment of these goals.

In view of these considerations, March and Simon (**24**, 155) have proposed that a distinction should be made between *operational* and *nonoperational* goals according to whether there exists some basis for relating the goal to possible courses of group action. If there is some way of determining whether and to what extent a goal will be realized by a particular sequence of group actions, then the goal is operational; otherwise it is not. March and Simon offer the hypothesis that when a group goal is nonoperational there is a tendency to steer group activities by means of operational subgoals that have some plausible linkage to the general goal. They suggest that (**24**, 156)

a business firm may understand to some degree how its specific actions affect its share of the market, but may understand less surely how its actions affect long-range profits. Then the subgoal of maintaining a particular share of the market may become the effective criterion of action—the operational goal.

Another example of this tendency might be the professional society whose goal is "to advance the field in which members work." Since this goal has a low degree of operationality, more operational subgoals might be set up, such as "large attendance at annual meetings" or "a full program of papers." The success of the society would then be evaluated in terms of these more tangible criteria.

It has also been proposed by March and Simon that when a group has an operational superordinate goal, differences of opinion concerning the choice of subgoals will be resolved by predominantly analytic processes—that is, by the analysis of expected consequences of courses of action directed toward each subgoal. On the other hand, when superordinate goals are nonoperational, the decision will be reached primarily by bargaining processes. However, empirical documentation of this interesting hypothesis is yet to be established.

On the basis of practical experience one may doubt that all groups display a tendency to select highly operational goals. It appears likely that whenever there is difficulty in mobilizing group activities (because of intragroup conflict, member apathy, inadequate resources, etc.) there will be a tendency to avoid the establishment of operational group goals; nonoperational goals are "safe" in the sense that group activities cannot unequivocally be termed a failure under these conditions. It seems, too, that if the principal basis for attraction to the group is simply to be with other people, there will be a tendency to avoid operational goals that might mobilize efforts toward different purposes. Other possible advantages in keeping long-range objectives vague have been proposed by Gross (**14**), who believes that overprecise goals often stifle initiative, restrict flexibility in responding to changing conditions, or rule out the possibility of reaching compromises among conflicting views.

The content of a group's goals, whether operational or not, may have broad ramifications for the characteristics of the group. In a study of institutions devoted to the care of juvenile delinquents, Zald (41) found that the roles and social relations among staff members depended largely upon whether the institution sought to provide "treatment" or "custody" for the inmates. The institution emphasizing treatment employed numerous professional workers who were given considerable autonomy to provide therapy as they saw fit and to work as a team in rehabilitating the young offenders. In the institution oriented toward custody, most of the power remained with the superintendent who kept close control over the actions of the staff and who depended mainly upon nonprofessional people to enforce his rules. The relations between staff members and inmates were also strikingly different in the two types of institution.

GROUP GOAL AS AN INDUCING AGENT

In order to account for the fact that a group goal can steer the behavior of group members to perform certain activities rather than others, it is necessary to recognize that the group goal itself can be a source of influence upon the group members. Once a particular group goal has been established, "good" group members are expected to work toward its attainment even when their preferred goal has not been chosen. In actual fact, of course, various group members are influenced to various degrees by various group goals. For this reason, a satisfactory conception must recognize that a group goal can arouse motivational forces within members and the magnitude of such influence can vary quantitatively among goals and among members.

In Chapter 34 Horwitz reports the results of an experiment in which groups selected a goal and attempted to attain it. He found great individual differences in the degree to which members accepted the group's decision concerning its goal. He found also that those who most fully accepted the group goal displayed most strongly need tensions to have the group achieve its goal, those who merely acquiesced mobilized less need tension, and those who rejected the group decision tended to persist in their personally determined motivation. These findings make it clear that when a group goal is fully accepted by the members it will influence their behavior. If the group goal is not accepted by a significant portion of the group, we should expect to find relatively poor coordination of efforts and a relatively high incidence of self-oriented rather than group-task oriented behavior.

Many factors undoubtedly influence how readily a member accepts a group goal. One of the more important of these would seem to be the member's assessment of the consequences to him of accepting it. If he believes that the group goal represents satisfactorily his own motives, he should readily accept it, since attainment of the goal by the group promises him satisfaction. To the extent that a member's satisfaction does depend upon the group's successful achievement of its goal, his assessment of the probability of group success will also influence his acceptance of the group goal. Raven and Rietsema (30) report findings from an experiment that varied the clarity of the subjects' understanding of the group goal and path to the goal. They found that those with a clear picture had a closer involvement with the group goal, more empathy with group emotions, and a greater readiness to accept influence from the group than those who were unclear about the goals and paths of their group.

Findings like those reported in Chapters 13 and 14, which show that group cohesiveness heightens the power of the group over its members, suggest that acceptance of group goals will also depend upon the degree to which members are attracted to membership in the group. Although it is not definitely known whether all bases of attraction to a group have precisely the same effects upon the power of the group, there is good reason to believe that groups whose members like one another as people, groups that mediate personal need-satisfaction, and groups having high prestige can all exert strong pressures upon members to accept group goals. If members have a correct understanding of the group actions required for goal attainment and of how their own behaviors contribute to group actions, they should perform with relatively good effectiveness.

It has often been observed that the motivation of members to work for the attainment of group goals is heightened by participation in goal-setting. The reasons are undoubtedly complex, but it appears that the increase in motivation derives in part from the fact that participation produces (*a*) a better fitting of the motives of members and the chosen group goal, and hence a greater acceptance of this goal, (*b*) a better understanding of group actions required for goal attainment, and (*c*) a better appreciation of how the behavior of individuals contributes to the required group actions. Because of considerations of this sort, a number of management theorists have advocated a group-centered approach to supervision whereby the leader encourages his subordinates to form cohesive groups through frequent meetings in which explicit group goals are formulated, appropriate group actions are identified, and individual responsibilities are assigned (16, 22, 25, 45).

In considering the ways in which group goals come to steer the behavior of members, we must recognize that the management of groups is frequently such that members remain unaware of group goals, uninterested in them, or both. Such a state of affairs is more likely in larger groups or when membership is involuntary or is maintained merely as a means of earning a living. It is not uncommon for employees of a business firm to view their relationship to the organization as a purely contractual one in which their time and talents are purchased by the firm; they expect to do whatever their supervisors tell them to do without being concerned about the contribution of their behavior to group locomotion. The quality of their contribution will depend primarily on their relations with supervisors and on the skill of supervisors in designing behaviors that will successfully meet the task requirements. The burden of supervision may be expected to be especially great under these conditions.

CONSEQUENCES OF GROUP ACTION

When a group adopts a goal and embarks upon a program of actions intended to bring about goal attainment, it may encounter success or failure. If the group's efforts are successful, members who have accepted the group goal have reason to experience gratification. They may be expected to increase their

evaluation of the group, to become more attracted to it, and to set higher aspirations for its future performance. A group that is unsuccessful in attaining its goal encounters quite a different situation. Members are likely to experience frustration, to decrease their evaluation of the group, to become less attracted to it, and to set lower goals for its future performance. Group failure also stimulates members to engage in a variety of coping behaviors designed to minimize the negative consequences of failure. Such behaviors include efforts to shift responsibility for the group outcome from oneself to others, depreciation of the value of the unattained goal, and derogation of the criteria employed in evaluating the performance of the group and its members. These and other reactions to group success and failure are discussed more fully in Chapter 32.

If a group has a clear operational goal, members will tend to evaluate one another in accordance with their apparent contributions to goal attainment. The specific nature of the goal and its associated group actions may be expected, then, to influence the social ranking of members of the group. Research (34, 42) has shown, further, that when a group undertakes a program of goal-directed actions it tends to establish a standard for the performance of its members. An individual member's level of aspiration for his own performance is more likely to conform to this standard the more his performance is seen as contributing to group performance and the more influence he has in setting the group's goal. Since a member's experience of personal success or failure depends upon the relation between his performance and his own level of aspiration, the nature of a group's goal and its related standards of performance for individual members can have a marked effect upon the self-evaluation of members.

DISTRIBUTION OF REWARDS WITHIN A GROUP

It is evident that the members of a group ordinarily experience certain gains or losses when the group engages in goal-directed activities. These "payoffs," as they are called in the language of game theory, may take various forms ranging from such intangibles as prestige, recognition, and affection to something as concrete as money. The conditions or "rules" that govern the awarding of payoffs will have important motivational consequences for the members and for the functioning of the group as a whole. If, for example, a group is operating under a rule whereby the magnitude of each member's payoff depends directly upon the quality of the group's performance, we should expect the members to want to engage in whatever behaviors they believe will contribute to this end (such as working hard, helping others, making suggestions about ways to improve the group's efficiency, or even "playing second fiddle"). We should expect, however, a fundamentally different motivational situation to be created by a rule that makes each member's payoff contingent upon the quality of his own individual performance. Here, it is to each person's advantage to be concerned with his own performance alone; no incentive is provided for helping others, seeking ways to improve the group's efficiency, or doing anything that might lower his level of performance.

To illustrate the variety of rules that may govern the distribution of payoffs within a group and some of their consequences, let us consider how a researcher might compensate subjects for participating in a laboratory experiment designed to study group productivity. We assume that each experimental group consists of five individuals who are told that their task is to work as a group to manufacture a particular product. The experimenter informs the members of each group that he will keep a record of the number of units produced by the group during each work period (group output) and that he will observe the behavior of members so that he can assign each a number of points according to the quality of his performance (individual score). Given this setting, the experimenter might employ a compensation system based on any of the rules below.

Rule 1. Each member's pay is independent of group output and his score. The experimenter decides to allocate $10.00 to each group for a work period, and he informs the subjects that each will be paid $2.00 for his time. This system of compensation is analogous to one commonly found in organizations where each employee is paid a certain wage or salary regardless of the group's output or his own performance. It should be noted, however, that this rule does not require that all members receive the same amount; individual payments might be made to depend upon

such "irrelevant" criteria as age, marital status, or tenure. But whether the members receive the same or different amounts, neither an individual's score nor the group's output has any effect upon his compensation. We should not expect the experimenter's payments, then, to provide a member with any incentive to raise his own score or to have the group increase its output.

Rule 2. Each member's pay is independent of group output but contingent on his score. This rule may be applied in two different ways.

a. Total payoff to group is fixed. The experimenter tells the members of each group that he has a total of $10.00 that he can pay them and that each will receive a share equal to his proportion of the total number of points earned by the members of the group. If, for example, the total number of points earned is 100, an individual earning 25 will receive $2.50. This system of compensation provides each person with a financial incentive to increase his own score, and we should expect members to try to engage in behaviors they believe will lead the experimenter to award them more points regardless of their effect on group output. It is obvious, of course, that since the total amount of money available to the group is fixed, one member's gain is another's loss. Because of this competitive interdependence, each member should be motivated not simply to increase his score but to earn a higher score than others. A member could, in fact, increase his pay merely by causing other members to obtain lower scores. We shall return later to a discussion of the consequences produced by this kind of competitive situation.

b. Total payoff to group is not fixed. Here, the experimenter informs the subjects that each will be paid ten cents for each point he earns. No restriction is placed on the total amount of money that will be paid. This system is analogous to piece rates sometimes employed in industrial organizations (provided that rates are not adjusted to keep the total payoff to a work group constant). Under this plan, each member's pay is determined entirely by his own score; the scores of others have no effect on the amount he receives. We should expect, then, that each member will be motivated to impress the experimenter with the high quality of his own behavior and to be relatively uninterested in the behavior of others (unless it has some influence on his own) or in the output of the group.

Rule 3. Each member's pay is contingent upon group output but independent of his score. The subjects are told that the experimenter will allocate $1.00 to the group for each unit it produces and that each member will be paid one-fifth of what the group earns. Thus, if the group produces 10 units, each member will receive $2.00, and if the group produces 20 units, each will receive $4.00. As under Rule 1, the members could be given different shares in accordance with some "irrelevant" criterion, but whether the shares are equal or different this rule creates a situation in which each member benefits whenever any member makes a contribution to the group's output. And since a member's individual score has no bearing upon his earnings, he should be willing to sacrifice his score in the interest of group performance. We shall discuss more fully the consequences brought about by this rule when we consider the nature of cooperative interdependence.

Rule 4. Each member's pay is contingent upon both group output and his scores. Again, the experimenter informs the subjects that he will allocate to the group $1.00 for each unit produced, but now each member's share will equal his proportion of the total number of points earned by all members. If, for example, a group produces 10 units and the sum of individual scores is 100, a member whose score is 25 will receive $2.50 whereas a member whose score is 10 will receive $1.00; but if the group produces 20 units while the distribution of scores is the same, these two members will receive $5.00 and $2.00, respectively. This rather complex plan of compensation combines the cooperative features of Rule 3 with the competitive ones of Rule 2a. It provides an incentive to each member both to contribute to the group's output and to engage in behavior that he believes will increase his own score relative to others. But it also poses a motivational dilemma: a member should want others to perform acts that will contribute maximally to the group's output, but he should not want these acts to raise the others' scores relative to his own.

In Chapter 35, Deutsch presents a conceptual scheme for predicting various consequences stemming from cooperative interdependence, such as that created by Rule 3, and from competitive interdependence, as produced by Rule 2a. We now consider briefly his analysis of each.

The critical feature of the situation confronting the members of a group who are cooperatively interdependent is that whenever one member performs an act beneficial to himself he simultaneously benefits all other members. Since each person gains from the occurrence of appropriate acts regardless of who performs them, members should be willing to let one individual's actions substitute for those of another, and it should be easy for a specialization of functions to develop. And since each member contributes to the payoff received by others when he behaves so as to increase his own, the other members should come to evaluate his behavior positively and to like him as an individual. These positive feelings, together with the fact that each member can trust the others to be helpful, should lead, in turn, to a readiness on the part of the members to be influenced by one another. Finally, each member should be motivated to help others, since he sees that he will benefit from improving the effectiveness of the others' behavior.

A group whose members are competitively interdependent should be expected to display characteristics of an opposite kind. Here, whenever a member acts so as to benefit himself, he reduces the payoff that the others will receive. Since each member will want to be sure that he gets credit for what he does, members should be reluctant to let one individual's actions substitute for those of another, and there should be resistance to specialization of functions. The fact that a member reduces the others' rewards when he behaves so as to increase his own should lead others to react negatively to such behavior and to him as an individual. They should be expected, moreover, to resist his influence attempts or to act in a way opposite to what he wants. Finally, it is in each member's interest not to help anyone else or even to hinder the behavior of others.

On the basis of this analysis, Deutsch proposes a number of more specific hypotheses concerning differences that should be observed between groups whose members are cooperatively interdependent and groups whose members are competitively interdependent. Thus, for example, he predicts that a cooperative situation, in comparison with a competitive one, should show more coordination of efforts, less homogeneity with respect to amount of participation, more specialization, more rapid decisions, more achievement pressure, more effective communication, better productivity, and more positive interpersonal relations.

To test these hypotheses, Deutsch conducted an experiment in which he employed two different methods for awarding grades to students taking a course in introductory psychology. Cooperative interdependence was established by telling the students that the performance of their group would be compared with that of four other similar groups and that every member of the group would be given the rank that his group received. To create competitive interdependence, the students were told that each member of the group would be evaluated individually and given a grade corresponding to his rank within the group. We see, then, that the "cooperative" groups operated in accord with Rule 3, whereas the "competitive" ones functioned under Rule 2a. Two additional features of this experiment should be noted, however: (a) in the cooperative situation all members of a particular group received the same payoffs whereas in the competitive situation they received different ones and (b) the "cooperative" groups were also engaged in intergroup competition but the "competitive" groups were not.

The results obtained from this experiment generally support Deutsch's theoretical analysis. Subsequent research, conducted in a variety of settings by Thomas (36), Raven and Eachus (29), Myers (27), Julian, Bishop, and Fiedler (17), and Crombag (9), lends additional support. It has become clear, however, that the effects brought about by a particular rule for the distribution of payoffs are dependent to some extent upon other conditions under which a group functions. Thus, there is reason to believe, as suggested by Miller and Hamblin (26) and others, that the effects of competitive versus cooperative interdependence upon group productivity depend upon the specific nature of the group's task. If this task is carried out in such a way that the members' activities are independent of one another (for example, each works alone in a separate room), they have no opportunity to help or hinder one another. A member can increase his payoff in either the cooperative or the competitive situation only by improving his own productivity. We should expect, then, that under conditions of low task interdependence group productivity will not depend upon the group's rule for the distribution of payoffs. If, on the other hand, the group's task is organized so as to make the member's activities interdependent, then the effects predicted by Deutsch may be expected to bring about greater group productivity under cooperative than under competitive conditions.

The difficulty in maintaining a coordination of the activities of individuals when they are competitively interdependent is dramatized by instances of panic behavior when a collection of people are simultaneously threatened by danger. Under such conditions each person is strongly motivated to seek his own safety and is likely to be less interested in the welfare of the total collection of people. Even when it is actually in the interest of each individual for there to be a coordination of their behaviors (such as forming queues or taking turns), effective coordination often fails to occur. In a laboratory experiment designed to create conditions of this sort, Kelley *et al.* (18) found that coordination (taking turns) decreases and behavior analogous to panic increases as the threat of danger increases, as the size of the group increases, as optimism about the chances of successfully escaping the danger decreases, and as lack of confidence in escaping is communicated among members.

Many groups are large enough to contain subunits, which may be cooperatively or competitively interdependent. Walton, Dutton, and Fitch (40) have examined the consequences of collaboration and rivalry among departments of a business firm and report intergroup relations not unlike those already noted among individuals. As part of a field experiment in a summer camp, Sherif *et al.* (32) observed the development of intergroup hostility during competition between two cabin groups. When they brought these antagonistic groups together under pleasant circumstances, they found that intergroup activities did not reduce the hostility. They discovered, however, that positive intergroup relations did develop when the separate groups came to adopt a single common goal which required collaborative effort by the two groups for its attainment. The existence of this "superordinate goal," it appears, made the members of the two groups cooperatively interdependent and brought about consequences of the sort postulated by Deutsch.

OVERVIEW OF RESEARCH REPORTED IN PART SIX

The four chapters that follow take up several problems related to group goals and the motivation of group members. The first two are concerned with processes of group goal-setting and decision-making; the third considers some of the motivational consequences for members stemming from the existence of a group goal; and the final chapter deals with the effects on group functioning of two different rules for the distribution of rewards among members.

In Chapter 32, Zander reports a summary of findings from a series of studies on the origins and effects of group aspirations. The results reveal that under appropriate conditions a member develops a concern about the success of his group that affects the goals he prefers for the group, his willingness to work in the group's behalf, and his evaluation of the group's performance and of his own. In general, the determinants of the goal a member chooses for his group are similar to those that guide an individual's personal aspirations.

The process of goal setting often involves a choice among alternatives that entail different degrees of risk. In Chapter 33, Wallach, Kogan, and Bem report an experiment comparing the riskiness of alternatives chosen by individuals and by groups. They find that choices resulting from group consensus are riskier on the average than are those reached by the same individuals when making decisions by themselves. The authors suggest several possible interpretations of these interesting results.

In Chapter 34 Horwitz asks the fundamental question: Can the motivational concepts that have been developed for individuals who are acting for their own goals be applied to individuals who are acting so that a group will achieve group goals? He reports the results of an experiment which support an affirmative answer to this question. Employing the Zeigarnik technique for detecting the presence of need tension in an individual, he examines the influence of overt goal-setting by a group upon the need systems of individual members. Of special interest are those situations in which personal goals for the group come into conflict with the goal overtly chosen by the group.

Chapter 35 contains Deutsch's conceptual analysis of two basic types of motivational interdependence that may exist among a collection of people. He develops several hypotheses contrasting the effects of cooperative versus competitive interdependence upon the motivations of individuals, interpersonal evaluations, processes of communication, and group productivity. He also reports the results of an experiment designed to test these hypotheses.

References

1. Arrow, K. J. *Social choice and individual values.* New York: Wiley, 1951.
2. Atkinson, J. W., & Feather, N. *A theory of achievement motivation.* New York: Wiley, 1966.
3. Bem, D., Wallach, M., & Kogan, N. Group decision-making under risk of aversive consequences. *Journal of Personality and Social Psychology,* 1965, **1,** 453–460.
4. Berkowitz, L., & Daniels, L. Responsibility and dependency. *Journal of Abnormal and Social Psychology,* 1963, **66,** 429–436.
5. Berkowitz, L., & Daniels, L. Affecting the salience of the social responsibility norm: Effects of past help on the response to the dependency relationship. *Journal of Abnormal and Social Psychology,* 1964, **68,** 275–281.
6. Bion, W. R. *Experiences in groups.* New York: Basic Books, 1959.
7. Black, D. *The theory of committees and elections.* Cambridge, Eng.: Cambridge Univ. Press, 1958.
8. Clausen, G. T. Risk-taking in small groups. Unpublished doctoral dissertation. Univ. of Michigan, 1965.
9. Crombag, H. F. Cooperation and competition in means-interdependent triads: A replication. *Journal of Personality and Social Psychology,* 1966, **4,** 692–695.

10. Cyert, R., & March, J. *A behavioral theory of the firm.* Englewood Cliffs, N. J.: Prentice-Hall, 1963.

11. Ezriel, H. A psychoanalytic approach to group treatment. *British Journal of Medical Psychology,* 1950, **23**, 59–74.

12. Fouriezos, N. T., Hutt, M. L., & Guetzkow, H. Measurement of self-oriented needs in discussion groups. *Journal of Abnormal and Social Psychology,* 1950, **45**, 682–690.

13. Gamson, W. Experimental studies of coalition formation. In L. Berkowitz (Ed.), *Advances in experimental social psychology.* Vol. 1. New York: Academic Press, 1964. Pp. 82–110.

14. Gross, B. M. What are your organization's objectives? *Human Relations,* 1965, **18**, 195–216.

15. Hays, D. G., & Bush, R. R. A study of group action. *American Sociological Review,* 1954, **19**, 693–704.

16. Hughes, C. L. *Goal setting.* New York: American Management Association, 1965.

17. Julian, J. W., Bishop, D. W., & Fiedler, F. E. Quasi-therapeutic effects of intergroup competition. *Journal of Personality and Social Psychology,* 1966, **3**, 321–327.

18. Kelley, H. H., *et al.* Collective behavior in a simulated panic situation. *Journal of Experimental Social Psychology,* 1965, **1**, 20–54.

19. Kelley, H. H., & Thibaut, J. W. Experimental studies of group problem-solving and process. In G. Lindzey (Ed.), *Handbook of social psychology.* Cambridge, Mass.: Addison-Wesley, 1954. Pp. 735–785.

20. Lewis, H. B. An experimental study of the role of the ego in work. I. The role of the ego in cooperative work. *Journal of Experimental Psychology,* 1944, **34**, 113–126.

21. Lewis, H. B., & Franklin, M. An experimental study of the role of ego in work. II. The significance of task orientation in work. *Journal of Experimental Psychology,* 1944, **34**, 195–215.

22. Likert, R. *New patterns of management.* New York: McGraw-Hill, 1959.

23. Luce, R. D., & Raiffa, H. *Games and decisions.* New York: Wiley, 1957.

24. March, J., & Simon, H. A. *Organizations.* New York: Wiley, 1958.

25. Marrow, A. *Making management human.* New York: McGraw-Hill, 1957.

26. Miller, L. K., & Hamblin, R. L. Interdependence, differential rewarding, and productivity. *American Sociological Review,* 1963, **28**, 768–778.

27. Myers, A. E. Team competition, success, and adjustment of group members. *Journal of Abnormal and Social Psychology,* 1962, **65**, 325–332.

28. Rapoport, A. *Fights, games, and debates.* Ann Arbor, Mich.: Univ. of Michigan Press, 1960.

29. Raven, B. H., & Eachus, H. T. Cooperation and competition in means-interdependence triads. *Journal of Abnormal and Social Psychology,* 1963, **67**, 307–316.

30. Raven, B. H., & Rietsema, J. The effects of varied clarity of group goals and group path upon the individual and his relation to his group. *Human Relations,* 1957, **10**, 29–44.

31. Shartle, C. L. Leadership and executive performance. *Personnel,* 1949, **25**, 370–380.

32. Sherif, M., *et al. Intergroup conflict and cooperation.* Norman, Okla.: Univ. of Oklahoma Book Exchange, 1961.

33. Stephan, F. F., & Mishler, E. The distribution of participation in small groups: An exponential approximation. *American Sociological Review,* 1952, **17**, 598–608.

34. Stotland, E., *et al.* The effects of group expectations and self-esteem upon self-evaluation. *Journal of Abnormal and Social Psychology,* 1957, **54**, 55–63.

35. Tannenbaum, A. S., & Kahn, R. L. *Participation in union locals.* Evanston, Ill.: Row, Peterson, 1958.

36. Thomas, E. J. Effects of facilitative role interdependence on group functioning. *Human Relations,* 1957, **10**, 347–366.

37. Thompson, J., & McEwen, W. J. Organizational goals and environment: Goal setting as an interaction process. *American Sociological Review,* 1958, **23**, 23–31.

38. Wallach, M., & Kogan, N. The roles of information, discussion, and consensus in group risk taking. *Journal of Experimental Social Psychology,* 1965, **1**, 1–19.

39. Wallach, M., Kogan, N., & Bem, D. Diffusion of responsibility and level of risk taking in groups. *Journal of Abnormal and Social Psychology,* 1964, **68**, 263–274.

40. Walton, R., Dutton, J., & Fitch, H. A study of conflict in the process, structure, and attitudes of lateral relationships. In A. Rubenstein & C. Haberstroh (Eds.), *Some theories of organization.* Homewood, Ill.: Irwin, 1966.

41. Zald, M. Organizational control structures in five correctional institutions. *American Journal of Sociology,* 1962, **38,** 305–345.

42. Zander, A., & Curtis, T. Effects of social power on aspiration setting and striving. *Journal of Abnormal and Social Psychology,* 1962, **64,** 63–74.

43. Zander, A., & Medow, H. Individual and group levels of aspiration. *Human Relations,* 1963, **16,** 89–105.

44. Zander, A., Medow, H., & Efron, R. Observers' expectations as determinants of group aspirations. *Human Relations,* 1965, **18,** 273–287.

45. Zander, A., & Wolfe, D. Administrative rewards and coordination among committee members. *Administrative Science Quarterly,* 1964, **9,** 50–69.

32

Group Aspirations

ALVIN ZANDER

In many groups members must periodically select a goal for their joint action. When the chosen goal is one among a set of alternative possibilities, some of which are more difficult than others, it is called a group level of aspiration. Examples of such aspirations are: the number of units a production committee decides to have manufactured in the next month, the quota of contracts a sales force schedules for the coming quarter, and the amount of money the officers of a community fund plan to raise during the year ahead.

This report contains a summary of findings from a series of studies in the origins and effects of group aspirations. The program has sought to determine in a preliminary way whether certain assumptions and concepts are useful in explaining these matters. The basic ideas under study have been limited, however, to ones having a reasonably clear conceptual link with the motives of individual members. Readers familiar with the theories concerning personal aspirations advanced by Lewin *et al.* (5), McClelland (6), and Atkinson and Feather (1) will recognize that many ideas have been borrowed from those sources for the present purposes.

The daily work of individuals is largely affected by their striving to achieve individual aims. Much of what people do accomplish, however, is through the coordination of their efforts with others in group settings and through the achievement of their group as a unit. It seems reasonable, then, to suppose that members will be interested in helping to decide the aspirations of their group. When they discuss aspirations, however, it is not immediately clear who is deciding what about whom. Where do the decisions lie? They certainly must be in the expectations of separate members, yet how are these

This statement was prepared as part of a project sponsored in the Research Center for Group Dynamics by the Air Force Office of Scientific Research. It reports research financed by that agency and by the United States Office of Education.

expectations joined to form a group's aspiration? Let us assume that each member has a notion about the aspiration he prefers his group to choose and call this the *member's aspiration for his group*. When the members of a group discuss and agree upon a joint level of aspiration, they create an aspiration of the group for the group, or more simply, the *group's level of aspiration*. Thus, a group level of aspiration is the level of performance members agree they expect their group to attain at some time in the future.

DETERMINANTS OF A GROUP'S LEVEL OF ASPIRATION

What do the members of a group consider when selecting a level of aspiration for their unit? How do different considerations determine which level they choose? We can conveniently seek answers to these questions by creating a situation in the laboratory that contains features typically met when groups set goals. We will give a group an activity to perform for a series of trials, urge them to see how well they can do, tell them their team's score after each attempt, and ask the members to decide after each trial what score they believe their group will be able to attain next time. In order to rule out extraneous matters, a simple activity will be used in which all members do exactly the same thing simultaneously and in which each person obtains no clear evidence about how much he or others individually contribute to the group's score.

A group ball-propelling task is suitable for this purpose. It requires all members to stand in a single file, to grasp a long pole, and to swing it in unison so that the end of the shaft strikes a wooden ball and rolls it down an extended channel. The ball stops next to one of several numbers painted on the side of the channel, providing a score for that shot. Five shots make a trial, and the group may earn up to fifty points on each trial.

When a group performs this task for a series of trials, we observe that each level of aspiration agreed upon by the members tends to be close to the immediately preceding score. If the performance improves, the aspiration goes up. If the performance worsens, the aspiration goes down (3, 14). One can make a pretty good guess then about the level of aspiration a group will choose from knowing the group's most recent score. But there is a modifier. As-

piration levels are raised more often when the performance increases than they are lowered when the performance decreases. Thus, new goals, on the average, tend to be higher than past levels of performance. Why?

When an individual is faced with the choice of engaging or not engaging in a solo activity, he makes his decision on the basis of the satisfaction he may obtain. The more certain he is that participation will provide him satisfaction, the greater is the likelihood that he will engage in the activity. In deciding upon a personal level of aspiration, his preference is likewise determined by the perceived satisfaction and the probability that satisfaction will occur from engaging in the task. When choosing a level of aspiration for his group, we assume, a member considers in an analogous fashion both the satisfaction to be derived and the probability that this satisfaction will follow from the group's participation in that task.

When a group is faced with a challenging activity in which the performance of the unit will be compared with some standard of excellence, we may assume, members will view a successful group performance as satisfying. In deciding upon a group level of aspiration, then, they will weigh the chances of attaining such satisfaction and will prefer a goal they believe the group can successfully achieve. A sensible estimate by the members is that their group can do as well in the future as it has done in the past. But the amount of satisfaction members expect to derive from a group success is not the same for all potential levels of aspiration. Participants characteristically expect more satisfaction from success on a more difficult task than from success on an easier one. Thus, their group aspiration is chosen to maximize expected satisfaction and is a balance between what would be a most satisfying outcome (success at a very difficult goal) and what would be an achievable outcome (success at a recently achieved level).

Returning to the ball-propelling test, we see why members raise their group's aspiration more often than they lower it (they wish to maximize satisfaction from success) and why they keep the future goal close to the group's past level of performance (they wish to ensure that success will indeed occur). Several hypotheses follow from the above assumptions.

1. Because more difficult tasks are more attractive than easier tasks, members

select increasingly more difficult group aspirations over a series of trials if reliable evidence about the group's performance, and thus about the probability of group success, is not available to them. This hypothesis was tested by asking groups to perform a card-making test in which each member circled a set of numbers on each of a supply of cards and the cards were passed from member to member (**15**). A successful performance required that they complete marking the cards within a standard but not stated period of time that was the same for every trial. Before a trial they decided how many sets of numbers their group proposed to mark on the cards. This was the group's level of aspiration; the more sets they selected, the more difficult the level. The members were given no information about their group's time on any trial or about their successes or failures. It was found, in accord with the hypothesis, that on each new trial members chose a more difficult task, repeatedly placing the group's level of aspiration higher than it had been on the previous trial.

2. Members in groups with a difficult task will be more attracted to their group's activity than members in groups with an easy task. To test this prediction, the experimenter assigned groups either difficult tasks or easy ones. The activity required members to work together and to create, in the center of a table, a series of designs composed of dominoes; the more difficult designs were slightly more complicated than the easier ones. The results revealed that those who worked on the more difficult tasks were as expected more favorable toward the activity than those who worked on the easier ones, regardless of the group's success or failure (**13**). It is relevant that in another experiment members felt more favorably toward observers of their group who suggested it should set higher aspiration levels than toward observers who suggested it should set lower levels (**17**).

3. Because they prefer more difficult aspirations that are yet attainable, members will raise their group's aspiration after it has achieved a prior goal and will lower the aspiration after it has failed. Strong support for the rule "succeed, raise; fail, lower" has been found in the majority of experiments discussed in later pages. As would be expected, the "succeed, raise" part of the rule has typically received better support than the "fail, lower" part.

4. The amount the level is raised after a successful trial will be larger than the amount the level is lowered after a failing trial. This prediction has been supported in a number of investigations (**13, 15, 17, 19**). An interesting illustration was observed in a study of official goals and changes in them for United Fund financial campaigns in 149 cities over four years (**18**). A failing campaign in one year was seldom followed by a lowered goal in the next year, whereas a successful campaign was almost always followed by a higher goal.

It is noteworthy, in passing, that results reported thus far occur whether the members are setting a goal for their own group to achieve or are setting one for persons outside the group to attain (**17**).

MEMBER MOTIVES AND GROUP ASPIRATIONS

In selecting a level of aspiration for his group, a member considers both the probability of satisfaction and the amount of satisfaction he will derive from his group's attainment of that aspiration. His choice indicates which level he prefers out of a set of alternatives but says nothing about the degree of his preference or about his inclination to move toward that goal. The strength of a member's preference for a given group aspiration depends upon the strength of the motive he brings to the unit or develops through his membership in it.

A motive, broadly speaking, is a disposition to be satisfied by a specific set of outcomes. A person who experiences the arousal of a particular motive enters into an activity if it appears likely to provide the outcomes he desires. In the present instance, the member learns only the score of his group as an entity and is asked to agree upon and work toward a goal for the group as a unit. His satisfaction, therefore, is determined by outcomes in the group and whether these are the kind he wishes them to be. Two group-oriented motives are of primary interest.

1. The member is mainly attentive to favorable consequences following group success. Examples of such consequences are pride in the group, positive evaluation of the group, and rewards to the group because of its accomplishment. This motive is designated as a *desire for group achievement of success.*

2. The member is primarily alert to the unfavorable consequences from group failure. Examples of such consequences are humiliation, derogation of the group, and costs to the group because of failure to reach its goal. This motive is called a *desire to avoid group failure.*

These motives are aroused by certain conditions in a group, concern events in that group alone, and are not relevant to membership in any other. What effects do they have in determining the level of a group's aspiration? Although both motives may simultaneously be aroused in members, their effects will be clearer if we examine them separately.

These motives are aroused by certain conditions in a group, concern events in that group alone, and are not relevant to membership in any other. What effects do they have in determining the level of a group's aspiration? Although both motives may simultaneously be aroused in members, their effects will be clearer if we examine them separately.

DESIRE FOR GROUP ACHIEVEMENT OF SUCCESS

Let us suppose that the more members desire achievement of group success the more they are attentive to both the probability of success and the consequences of succeeding. Thus, members who have a strong desire for group success will not be attracted to an extremely difficult aspiration level because their group is not likely to succeed and success is important. They will not be attracted to a very easy level, even though success for the group would then be assured, because such a success would not be wholly satisfying and satisfaction is important. As a result, members with a greater desire for group achievement will be more attracted to group goals in the intermediate range of difficulty than to very difficult or very easy goals. The preference for intermediate group goals was examined in several experiments in which contrasting conditions were created to arouse separate degrees (high or low) of the desire for group achievement of success.

A set of persons who are strongly bound together is more likely to be interested in the score of the group on a challenging task than is a set of persons who are weakly connected. It follows that a greater desire for group success should be aroused in strong groups than in weak ones when members are urged to do as well as they can and that members of strong groups should prefer intermediate aspirations more than members of weak groups.

To create strong groups, high school boys were brought to the laboratory three at a time and seated at a table facing one another (**15**). They were told by the experimenter that they were a group; references were often made to "this group"; they were asked to discuss and decide on a name for their unit, which was then printed in large letters on a card and hung on the wall; and they were informed that school records available about them indicate that they will work together smoothly. In order to create weak groups, participants were seated at a table hidden from one another by wooden screens, they were not called a group but instead were addressed as "you," they were given a unit number instead of an opportunity to decide on a group name, and they were told that school records suggest they will not work together smoothly.

Following these instructions members in both the strong and the weak groups worked on the card-marking task in which they had to pass cards from one to another around the table. All participants were separated by screens and were allowed no verbal interaction. The groups performed a series of trials and were asked before each trial to agree, balloting repeatedly until unanimity was reached, on the level of difficulty they preferred to attempt out of twenty possibilities.

Members in the strong condition preferred neither the very easy nor the very difficult tasks; instead they favored ones at about the middle in the range of difficulty. Those in the weak condition preferred easier or more difficult tasks and avoided those at the medium level. Thus, the greater was the strength of the group, the more there was a tendency to select group aspirations of intermediate difficulty.

It has been reported by Pepitone (**8**) and

Thomas (10) that a person who is more responsible for the score of his group is more eager to have his group perform well and works harder on a challenging group activity than a member who contributes less to the group's outcome. Thus, a member who is in a more responsible position in a group should more often choose intermediate aspirations than a member in a less responsible position.

Participants in small laboratory groups were informed that their group was being tested. They were told that the test required each member to produce on the table before him a domino design that was to be an exact replica of any one of fourteen patterns available for him to copy. These patterns ranged from very simple ones using a few dominoes to very complex patterns requiring a large number of pieces. Although the members worked separately, each on his own design behind wooden screens, they all had to work on the same pattern chosen within the group. The group's quality of performance was measured by the time needed for all participants to finish (7).

One participant, the central member, was asked to announce his progress as he moved through the steps in his design. The other persons, the peripheral members, could not put a piece in their designs until the central person had placed that piece and stated that fact. The actions of the central member thus preceded the group on the path to completion of the task and were more responsible for the group's score than were the actions of the peripheral members.

All groups were required to begin on a task of intermediate difficulty (number seven) and thereafter were allowed to choose their own levels of aspiration. Our interest is in the aspirations for the group that members privately reported to the experimenter before each trial. The private aspirations of the central person showed less movement away from level seven, thus remaining more in the middle range of difficulty, than did the aspirations of the peripheral members.

The responsibility of the central person was further increased by an additional feature. In half of the groups the central person selected the group's task without knowing the wishes of his colleagues, and in the other half all members participated in this selection. The additional decision-making responsibility of the central person increased his tendency to prefer intermediate levels of difficulty for the group.

Effects of Personal Need for Achievement. Some members may have a stronger need for individual achievement than others. Persons who have a greater need for achievement, it is known, more often choose intermediate levels of aspiration on solo tasks than do those with less need for achievement (1). Will they also differ in this way when they choose aspirations for a group? Will those with low need for achievement become interested in group achievement if they have a more responsible position in the group?

To answer these questions, the main features of the centrality-peripherality experiment were repeated. This time, however, each three-person group had one member who was high in need for achievement, one who was low, and one who was in between these two, as measured prior to the experiment. Each of the high- and low-need achievement members had a turn in both the central and peripheral positions for a series of trials. It was found that members with higher need for achievement more often preferred intermediate goals for the group when they were in either the peripheral position or the central one. Among those with low need for achievement, the members had a greater preference for intermediate group aspirations while occupying the central position and a preference for aspirations away from the medium level while occupying the peripheral position. A person with a greater need for achievement, then, chooses group aspirations as he would for himself alone. A central position causes persons with a low need for achievement to choose group goals similar to those chosen by persons with a high need for achievement.

Maintaining Group Motivation. If it is true that groups with a greater desire to achieve success are more ready to engage in tasks of an intermediate probability, it follows that members will seek to maintain and encourage one another's interest in such a level of aspiration. Consider a group activity in which a single trial takes a long time to finish. The attainment or nonattainment of the goal will occur only after extended effort. In order to prevent a flagging of interest in completion of the task, members should foster the perception that the outcome is uncertain (that is, the perceived probability of success is .50). They can do this by, for example, replying to optimistic remarks about the future with pessimistic answers, thereby pressing one another to view potential events as maximally unpredictable. A study by Emerson, a member of the American team engaged in climbing Mount Everest, provided support for this hypothesis (4). In that drawn-out and stressful group effort in which there was a strong desire for group success, the climbers maintained their motivation by repeatedly commenting to one another that the outcome was uncertain and by fostering this view in their conversations. The members' responses to standardized pessimistic or optimistic remarks made to individuals by Emerson further indicated their desire to keep an open mind about the outcome.

Motive Arousal. At least two conditions seem necessary for a member to develop a desire for group achievement of success: he must perceive that he is a member of a group and he must perceive that the group faces a challenge in which its score will be compared to some standard of excellence. Thus, setting a group aspiration in itself arouses some of this desire. Other conditions help to heighten it. Among them are an awareness that group-mates are concerned about the group's success, that the group has frequently experienced success, that the group is attractive to the members, that the member has a central role, that the member has personal need to achieve success, and that external agents will provide rewards for success. In brief, it appears that the more members are committed to the group or are responsible for its fate, the more they will develop a desire for group achievement of success.

One further condition noteworthy as a potential source of this desire is the member's perception of his competence in the group task. In two experiments members were privately told after each trial how well they individually had performed their part of the group's activity. Those who learned they were more competent became more concerned about the group's welfare than those who discovered they were less competent (19, 20).

DESIRE TO AVOID GROUP FAILURE

Members who desire to avoid group failure are attentive to both the probability of failure and the negative consequences of failing.

Doubtless they wish to avoid the dissatisfaction that group failure creates. Dissatisfaction ordinarily is greater after failure on an easy task than after failure on a difficult task. It follows that members who have a strong desire to avoid failure will prefer either an easy task, because the group is not likely to fail at such a level, or a very difficult task, because failure at a difficult level is less dissatisfying. Thus, members with a greater desire to avoid failure will be less attracted to tasks of intermediate difficulty than to tasks at either extreme.

Do members who wish to avoid the consequences of group failure select different goals than those who wish to attain success? The answer to this question was sought in an experimental investigation (15). To generate an awareness of the consequences of failure each participant was given a similar supply of poker chips and told that each chip was worth one point toward the total score of the group. The group worked on the previously described card-making task and members were allowed to choose any level of difficulty they wanted their group to attempt. They were warned, however, that each time the group failed to attain its goal all members and thus the group as a unit would lose a number of chips; the number the group might lose depended upon the difficulty of the aspiration level—the easier the task, the more it would lose. Nothing was said to them about consequences from successfully performing the task. These instructions made the possibility of failure salient and stressed that failure at an easy task would cause more negative consequences than failure at a difficult one.

In order to generate an interest in group success, the members were not given chips at the outset. All other matters were the same except that the group could win chips every time it succeeded. The number of chips it might win depended upon the difficulty of the task on which it succeeded—the greater the difficulty of the task, the greater the number of chips. In this case, members were induced to be aware of the value of succeeding at more difficult levels; nothing was said to them about failure or the effects of failure.

There were distinct differences in the levels of aspiration chosen by members in these groups. Those who presumably were concerned about the negative effects of failure did not prefer tasks in the intermediate range of difficulty. Those who apparently were aware of the advantages from success preferred tasks in the intermediate range of difficulty.

The motive to avoid group failure was invoked in quite a different way in another experiment (20) in which it was assumed that persons individually may be disposed either to engage in a challenging task because they view it as an opportunity for success (low test-anxiety) or to avoid such a task because they view it as a likely source of failure (high test-anxiety). It was expected that groups composed of persons who meet challenges in these contrasting ways would select different group aspirations. More specifically, members who have high test-anxiety will have little interest in group aspirations in the middle range of difficulty, whereas members with low test-anxiety will prefer tasks in that range.

The amount of anxiety in taking tests was measured by a standardized instrument developed for that purpose by Judith Cowen (2) and the two kinds of groups were created. The members participated in the ball-propelling activity and before each trial discussed and voted upon a group level of aspiration. The groups whose members had low test-anxiety preferred tasks of medium difficulty and those with high anxiety preferred tasks away from the middle.

The trend of the results seems clear. The members of a group who have a stronger concern about failure will tend to select either very easy tasks or very hard ones. Which of these two will they prefer?

Let us consider the future level chosen by a group immediately after it has failed, since any latent uneasiness about failure is likely to be aroused among members after such an experience. In the condition where groups were promised a loss after failure, members tended reliably to "jump" their group aspirations after their group had failed toward the difficult end of the scale. In contrast, among groups promised a reward for success there was almost no change in goals after a failure, and in both the reward and the cost conditions there were only small shifts in goals after the groups had succeeded. The groups composed of persons with high test-anxiety also made larger upward jumps after failure than did groups composed of persons with low test-anxiety, but after a successful trial there was little shift in goals away from prior levels of performance.

In sum, the desire to avoid failure invokes a tendency to choose more difficult tasks after the group has failed. The location of these goals, in addition, is higher than that the group has achieved in the past. Thus, members who are concerned about failure select conditions conducive to another failure immediately after they have failed. What they wish to avoid, it seems, is not the failure itself as much as embarrassment after failure. Such humiliation is more likely to be avoided if the failure is on a difficult task than on an easy one.

As in the case of desire for group success, certain conditions may strengthen the desire to avoid group failure. Among these are awareness that the group has often failed in the past, that groupmates wish to avoid the consequences of failure, that the group is unattractive for members, that the member has a peripheral role in the group, that the members personally are anxious about failure, and that external agents will provide punishments for failure.

The effect of achievement-oriented motives on readiness to approach a given group aspiration can now be briefly stated. The tendency of group members to select a given level of aspiration for their unit is a multiplicative function of the strength of the members' desire to attain group success or to avoid group failure, the perceived probability that engaging in the task will provide desired outcomes, and the value placed upon these outcomes. The resultant tendency to engage in any given task is determined by the strength of the members' tendency to approach that task minus their tendency to avoid it.

INFLUENCE OF EXTERNAL AGENTS ON GROUP ASPIRATIONS

Many goal-setting groups experience pressures originating outside their membership. These pressures may, for various reasons, support unreasonably difficult or much-too-easy aspirations compared to the group's past levels of performance. When these pressures occur, and when they influence the goals chosen by the group, it is evident that the members are no longer choosing group aspirations solely on the basis of what is most probable or attractive for them; they are reacting, instead, to the pressures. The members, moreover, cannot readily lower the goal if it is too difficult or raise it if the goal is too low.

Several experiments have examined conditions that might facilitate the tendency of members to place their group's aspiration distant from past levels of performance as a response to pressures from outside the group. In these studies, as we shall see, the induced level was apparently accepted by members since it was used by them as the criterion for evaluating the success of their group's effort and of their own personal performance as well.

In the first study, members were given an opportunity to compare their group's performance with that of similar groups (14). At the conclusion of each trial on the ball-propelling test, when recording the group's score on the blackboard the experimenter also recorded what was alleged to be the average performance on that trial for all groups in the school attended by the subjects. These average scores were fictitious and preplanned. In one-third of the groups the averages were so high that they could seldom be attained, in another one-third the averages were so low that they could easily be exceeded, and in the remaining one-third no averages were reported (control condition). The reported averages were remarkably powerful in determining the group's level of aspiration. When the average of the other groups was said to be high the subject-groups chose higher goals and when it was low they chose lower goals than control groups. Their higher goals, moreover, were placed far above their past levels of group performance and their lower goals were put well below their past levels of group performance.

In another study (16) the hypothesis was tested that external social pressures will more often determine group goals when these pressures are accompanied by sanctions than when they are not. Teams worked on the ball-propelling test and received, along with the report of their score for each trial, a message said to come from an attractive and respected committee of students who had previously established standards of performance for all participating teams with the legitimate right to do so. Each message described a particular level of aspiration that the committee asked the workers to achieve on each trial. The requests were always higher than the group was likely to earn. One-third of the groups was promised

a reward if they performed as requested, one-third was promised a punishment if they failed to do as asked, and the remaining third was given requests without any sanction being offered. A fourth set of groups, a control condition, received no requests at all. The findings were clear: the levels of aspiration more closely adhered to the requested scores if sanctions were promised than if they were not. In setting their group's aspirations the members apparently ignored the fact that their group could not attain the goals suggested for them.

In an additional experiment the suggestions given to the group came from observers who were sitting in the room and who obviously were aware of the group's performance on every trial. Prior to each trial on the ball-propelling test the observers privately discussed and decided what level of performance they expected the workers to achieve in the future. The hypothesis was that group aspirations would more often be influenced by the observers when the latter were to share in a reward potentially available to the goal-setters than when the observers were not eligible for a share in the reward (17). The groups working on the task received what they thought were the observers' estimates before they set each level of aspiration. The messages did not in fact contain what the observers had decided but rather were standardized statements substituted by the experimenter so that some groups received high observer-expectations and other groups low ones. It was found that performers set their group aspirations to match the expectations of observers, high or low. It made no difference, however, whether the observers were dependent on the performing groups for a share in a reward. If the group's performance failed to attain the observers' expectations, furthermore, the members tended not to lower their group aspirations for the next trial, and if the group's score exceeded the observers' expectations they tended not to raise their future aspirations.

In these last experiments, it should be added, the external agent was more influential in determining the performers' aspirations when the group failed to attain its goal than when it succeeded. Apparently it is easier to induce unsuccessful groups to set unreasonable goals than to get successful groups to do so.

There is ample evidence, then, that external

sources can have a strong effect upon the collective goals of members and can lead groups to establish and accept unrealistic aspirations. The consequences of these events may not always be beneficial to the group.

CONSEQUENCES OF GROUP ASPIRATIONS

EVALUATION OF GROUP PERFORMANCE

When a member derogates his group after it fails to attain its goal or praises it after it attains its goal, we may assume that he has taken the group's aspiration seriously as an appropriate objective. In the present studies the members consistently used their group's aspiration as a criterion for judging their group's performance. These differential ratings occurred after success and failure even when there was no difference in the actual level of performance (7, 14, 16, 17, 20). Of greater interest is the finding that members evaluated their group's score in the light of their group's aspiration level whether the members had agreed on the group's aspiration without external influence, had aspiration levels pressed upon them from the outside, or had imitated the goals of others.

We see then that under the conditions studied, group aspirations are taken as criteria for judging the quality of a unit's performance regardless of how the aspirations are reached or influenced. Induced aspirations have as much meaning for members as ones they have freely selected in the absence of social pressures originating outside the group.

SELF-EVALUATION BY MEMBERS

It is a common belief that the quality of a group's performance affects the members' personal self-regard: members of highly successful groups evaluate their individual contributions favorably and those in unsuccessful groups rate them poorly. When members have no reliable evidence about the amount they individually provided toward the group's score, this belief is not always upheld. Experimental studies have found that under this condition a member's evaluation of his own performance is more strongly determined by the group's score when the group succeeds than when it fails

(3, 7, 14). In other words, a member is less likely to evaluate his personal performance unfavorably when the group fails. A member of a failing group, it appears, can protect his self-esteem by denying that he performed as ineptly as the group's score suggests.

A participant who has a more responsible position or one who is otherwise committed to his group may, however, be less able to deny that he performed poorly since his efforts and desires are more closely identified with those of the group. A more-involved member, therefore, may have lower self-regard when his group fails to attain its level of aspiration. The results of several experiments have supported this hypothesis. It was discovered that the members of a group evaluated their personal performance more negatively after the group had failed if they had a central position in the work of the group, had tried hard in the group's behalf (a self-judgment), had worked for a potential group reward, or had been in a group with high unity. In contrast, a member rated his performance positively, regardless of whether the group had succeeded or failed, when he had a peripheral role in the work of the group, admitted taking it easy on the group's activity, and when the group was low in unity (7, 13, 20).

These last results suggest several useful derivations. The conditions that cause a member to evaluate his personal competence in accord with the quality of the group's performance resemble the sources of a desire for group achievement of success. It follows that a member who strongly desires his group to be successful is more likely to perceive that the success or failure of his group is his own success or failure. A member who has less desire for group success, in contrast, is more inclined to rate his personal performance well in spite of his group's performance. Since an agent outside the group is more able to determine its level of aspiration as his social power over the group is greater, it seems likely that members of a failing group will have a larger loss of self-regard as the power of the external agent becomes stronger. This hypothesis has not as yet been tested.

MEMBER ATTITUDES FOLLOWING GROUP SUCCESS OR FAILURE

The members of a successful group obtain desirable consequences from their group's success—a sense of satisfaction, favorable self-appraisal, and perhaps more tangible rewards. The members of a failing group receive opposite and less-desirable consequences. One may expect, therefore, that participants in successful groups will wish to ensure that the group continue, maintain, or pursue the activity on which it has done so well. The members of failing groups, however, may be expected to avoid, discontinue, or devalue the group's activity. These dispositions to approach or avoid are called *coping tendencies*. They are frequently evident in the attitudes members display during or following their group's performance.

When a group succeeds, for example, members more strongly believe that the group's score is a reliable indicator of the group's ability, that it is important to get a good score, and that they are willing to engage in further work on the group's task. When a group fails, on the other hand, members are inclined to derogate the reliability of their score or the importance of doing well and dislike the idea of repeating that activity (7, 13, 14, 15).

No doubt the discussion among members in a work group frequently concerns views relevant to coping tendencies. As is often true, the result of this discussion may be an intensification of the member's attitudes. One may expect, then, a strengthening of these attitudes after a conversation about such matters. An illustration of this intensification was evident in an experiment in which members openly discussed attitudes indicative of coping tendencies. Stronger attitudes were developed in these discussions—approaching after a group success and avoiding after a group failure—than the same members had expressed in private prior to the group discussion (13).

It seems likely that these coping tendencies serve to assure members that potentially favorable outcomes will occur after a success and unfavorable outcomes will be avoided after a failure.

GROUP ASPIRATIONS AND GROUP PERFORMANCE

The ultimate importance of a group's level of aspiration lies in its capacity for stimulating group effort. The members of an organization may be expected to work harder toward their group's level of aspiration than toward any alternative level. We earlier noted that group goals are most often placed slightly above past levels of performance. When the group's goal is moved upward, does the group's score improve on the next trial? Results from a study of changes in United Fund goals suggest that this is so (18). The amount that the goal for a given year exceeded the performance of the prior year was followed by a comparable amount of improvement in performance. But the goal must not be placed too far from the past level of performance, for then it appears to depress performance rather than improve it.

We have seen that members who have a stronger desire for their group to be successful prefer group aspirations in the intermediate range of difficulty. Such a group should perform better on a task of medium difficulty than on an easier or more difficult one. A study by Stedry and Kay (9) in an industrial setting supports this hypothesis. The foremen of a number of work crews were given particular goals their groups were to attain within six months. One-third of the crews was given "very easy" assignments, one-third was given "impossible" assignments, and the remaining third was given goals of moderate difficulty. At the end of six months the crews with the moderately difficult tasks had improved more than those with the easier and those with the more-difficult goals.

It is important, however, that the participants understand that the task is in fact, easy, medium, or hard for their group. To do this they must have reliable information about their group's typical level of performance and how that performance compares to the goal they are trying to reach. In a laboratory experiment (12) that repeated the major features of the study by Stedry and Kay, the subjects did not develop a clear understanding of their group's typical level of performance. In this instance the performance at the middle level was somewhat better than that at the easier or harder levels, but not significantly so.

We have noted that members with a greater desire for achievement of group success appear to be more eager to approach the group's task than those who have less of this desire. Groups of the former type should therefore perform better than the latter ones. In an experiment to test this hypothesis, each member simultaneously squeezed a hand-held dynamometer, creating an electronically "accumulated" group score (12). The hand dynamometer is a measure of grip-strength but was used in this instance as a simple indicator of effort exerted. Half of the groups were led to believe that the members had a very strong desire for the group to perform well on the test, the other half that members had little desire for success. In accord with the above hypothesis, the groups in the former condition exerted considerably greater effort and persistence on the task.

It is noteworthy that the members with the stronger desire for group success did not perform better when working on a complicated task in which they were required to coordinate their efforts, make decisions, take turns, and keep out of one another's way. There was instead a nearly significant tendency in the opposite direction—groups with the stronger desire did less well, even though they talked more and in many ways expressed greater enthusiasm for the group's activity. These results suggest, as Zajonc has elsewhere proposed (11), that a stronger desire may lead to more frequent errors on activities that are not well learned and require thought and coordination of effort among members.

SUMMARY

Findings have been presented from a series of studies in the origins and consequences of group aspirations. The following conclusions emerge from these investigations.

1. The tendency of group members to select a given level of aspiration is a function of the perceived probability of succeeding on it and the attractiveness of doing so.
2. The more members are committed to their group or are responsible for its fate, the more they develop a desire for group achievement of success. The greater this desire, the more they prefer the group to attempt tasks in the intermediate range of difficulty rather than easier or more demanding ones.
3. The members of a group who have a strong concern about the consequences of failure tend to select either easier tasks or harder ones. After any specific failure they are likely to choose unreasonably difficult goals in order, apparently, to avoid the embarrassment following from failure.
4. Social pressures arising outside the group can cause members to choose unreasonably high or unrealistically low group aspirations.
5. Group aspirations are used as criteria for judging the quality of a unit's output regardless of how the aspirations are reached or influenced.
6. A member who has a more responsible position or is more committed to his group is more likely to perceive his group's performance to be a reliable indicator of his own personal quality of performance.
7. Coping tendencies indicating the members' attitudes toward approaching or avoiding the task are apparently used by members to assure themselves that potentially favorable outcomes will occur after a success and unfavorable outcomes will be avoided after a failure.
8. Moderate increases in aspiration level generate comparable increases in performance.
9. Groups with tasks of intermediate difficulty produce more than those with easier or more difficult goals.
10. Groups whose members have a stronger desire for achievement of group success perform better on simple tasks than groups whose members have less of this desire.

References

1. Atkinson, J. W., & Feather, N. *A theory of achievement motivation.* New York: Wiley, 1966.
2. Cowen, J. Test anxiety in high school students and its relationship to performance on group tests. Unpublished doctoral dissertation, Harvard Univ., 1957.

3. Dustin, D. Member reactions to team performance. *The Journal of Social Psychology,* 1966, **69,** 237–243.

4. Emerson, R. Mount Everest: A case study of communication feedback and sustained group goal striving. *Sociometry,* 1966, **29,** 213–227.

5. Lewin, K., *et al.* Level of aspiration. In J. McV. Hunt (Ed.), *Personality and behavior disorders.* New York: Ronald Press, 1944.

6. McClelland, D. *The achieving society.* Princeton, N. J.: Van Nostrand, 1961.

7. Medow, H., & Zander, A. Aspirations for the group chosen by central and peripheral members. *Journal of Personality and Social Psychology,* 1965, **1,** 224–228.

8. Pepitone, E. A. Responsibility to the group and its effects on the performance of members. Unpublished doctoral dissertation, Univ. of Michigan, 1952.

9. Stedry, A. C., & Kay, M. *The effects of goal difficulty on performance.* Crotonville, N. Y.: General Electric Co., Management Development and Employee Relations Services, 1964.

10. Thomas, E. J. Effects of facilitative role interdependence on group functioning. *Human Relations,* 1957, **10,** 347–366.

11. Zajonc, R. Social facilitation, *Science,* 1965, **149,** 269–274.

12. Zander, A., & Forward, J. Desire for group achievement and group performance. Unpublished report.

13. Zander, A., & Ledvinka, J. Difficulty of group's task and collective coping behavior. In A. Zander & H. Medow (Eds.), *Group aspirations and group coping behavior.* Ann Arbor, Mich.: Institute for Social Research, 1964.

14. Zander, A., & Medow, H. Individual and group levels of aspiration. *Human Relations,* 1963, **16,** 89–105.

15. Zander, A., & Medow, H. Strength of group and desire for attainable group aspirations. *Journal of Personality,* 1965, **33,** 122–139.

16. Zander, A., Medow, H., & Dustin, D. Social influences on group aspirations. In A. Zander & H. Medow (Eds.), *Group aspirations and group coping behavior.* Ann Arbor, Mich.: Institute for Social Research, 1964.

17. Zander, A., Medow, H., & Efron, R. Observers' expectations as determinants of group aspirations. *Human Relations,* 1965, **18,** 273–287.

18. Zander, A., & Newcomb, T., Jr. Group levels of aspiration in United Fund campaigns. *Journal of Personality and Social Psychology,* 1967, **6,** 157–162.

19. Zander, A., Stotland, E., & Wolfe, D. Unity of group, identification with group, and self-esteem of members. *Journal of Personality,* 1960, **28,** 463–478.

20. Zander, A., & Wulff, D. Members' test anxiety and competence: Determinants of a group's aspirations. *Journal of Personality,* 1966, **34,** 55–70.

33

Group Influence on Individual Risk-Taking

MICHAEL A. WALLACH, NATHAN KOGAN, AND DARYL J. BEM

What are the effects of group interaction on risk and conservatism in decision making? By risk and conservatism we mean the extent to which the decision maker is willing to expose himself to possible failure in the pursuit of a desirable goal. Consider the situation in which several individuals working separately arrive at a series of decisions and then are brought together to arrive at a group consensus regarding those decisions. What relationship should one expect to find between the individual decisions and the group consensus?

On the basis of prior experimental studies of individual and group judgment (4, 17), we should predict an averaging effect, i.e., group decisions randomly distributed around the average of the prediscussion individual decisions. Such an effect would seem to imply a process of minimizing individual losses or minimizing the maximum individual concession. The cited studies report that inducements toward compromise and concession seem to be exerted most strongly toward group members whose initial individual views are most deviant from the central tendency.

An equally, if not more, compelling alternative hypothesis is that the group discussion will lead to increased conservatism, relative to the average of the prior individual decisions. One may cite the observations of Whyte (27), among others, concerning the outcomes of conferences and meetings in bureaucratic organizations. Whyte argues that the use of committees and teams in the management of business and other kinds of enterprises leads inexorably to an inhibition of boldness and risk-taking, a concentration on the conservative course when a choice must be made between more and less risky courses of action. How are such effects to be explained? First, it may be that the very

From *Journal of Abnormal and Social Psychology*, 1962, **65**, 75–86. The research was supported by a grant from the National Science Foundation. Reprinted by permission of the authors and the American Psychological Association.

nature of the group process or atmosphere encourages such a trend: there may be a fear, for example, of appearing foolhardy to others. Alternatively, or in addition, it is possible that the mechanism underlying an increase in conservatism is one of greater influence being exerted within the group by members whose individual conservatism tendencies are stronger. These two interpretations are not incompatible, of course, since the group process, if encouraging of conservatism, will enhance the influence of the initially more conservative members.

Finally, consideration should be given to the remaining and least likely possibility—that group interaction will eventuate in increased risk-taking relative to the average of the prior decisions of the group members working separately. In this regard, Osborn (15) has reported that group interaction may lead to quite radical, bold, problem solutions. While Osborn claims that special conditions must exist if such effects are to be observed, attempts to produce such conditions experimentally by Taylor, Berry, & Block (21) have yielded no evidence whatever for the so-called "brainstorming" phenomenon. Thibaut and Kelley (22) discuss the conflicting evidence on this issue. We might, in passing, also mention mass or crowd phenomena, in which extreme actions taken by groups are well beyond the capacities of the members of such groups considered individually (3, 23). The relevance of such mass phenomena to group decision making in a laboratory context, however, is probably quite remote. In sum, increased risk-taking as a consequence of group interaction appeared to us to be the least feasible of the three possibilities discussed above.

An examination of the literature reveals little experimental research which addresses itself explicitly to the problem of the present investigation. Lonergan and McClintock (12) report that membership in an interdependent group led to no significant move toward greater conservatism or risk-taking in a betting situation involving monetary gain or loss. Since the group situation was so structured that a consensus was not required, however, this experiment is not directly relevant to the aims of the present study. Hunt and Rowe (7) report no difference between three-person groups and individuals in riskiness of investment decisions. However, the brevity of the group interaction (15 minutes) and the

disruptive influence of having the various groups meet within sight of each other in a large room render their results inconclusive. Atthowe (1), comparing individual and dyadic decisions in the choice of the better of two alternative wagers, found greater conservatism in the dyadic decisions. But the relevance of this result to the problem at hand is called into question when we learn that the alternative wagers were presented to the subjects as "problems taken from the mathematical reasoning section of an advanced intelligence test and arranged as wagers" (p. 115). This could well contribute to a conservative strategy.

We turn, finally, to a study by Stoner (19), which provides the starting point for the research to be reported. Using male graduate students of industrial management as subjects, Stoner observed that a group consensus regarding degree of risk to be taken in resolving a "life dilemma" situation deviated from the average of prediscussion decisions in the direction of greater risk-taking. These results took us by surprise. We wondered whether the finding could be generalized to other subject populations, whether it was an enduring effect, and whether it might have anything to do with relationships between risk-taking and perceived group influence.

One issue that arises in interpreting Stoner's study concerns the effect that expectations about one's role might have on the results. Thus, a group of male graduate students of industrial management might make more risky decisions qua group than would each such student individually—the result obtained by Stoner—because the presence of their peers reminds each that one of the positively sanctioned attributes of the business manager role which they occupy or aspire to occupy is a willingness to take risks in their decision making. Stoner's use of a male business school sample, therefore, leaves open the possibility that his results may be a function of this particular group's self-assigned professional role alone. It also is possible that a group of males, regardless of their professional role, might make more risky decisions when gathered together because the presence of other males serves as a reminder that one of the expected indications of manliness in our society is a willingness to be bold and daring in decision making. Conversely, a group of females might make more conservative decisions when gathered together or at least might fail to shift in a risky direction, since risk-taking tendencies are not likely to be mutually reinforced in groups for whom risk is not a positive social value (10, 14, 24).

In the present experiment, we shall employ samples of male and female undergraduates enrolled in a liberal arts curriculum at a large state university. If the effects observed by Stoner are found to hold for both of the above samples, this would constitute strong evidence for the generality of the phenomenon and its independence of occupational and sex role considerations. Furthermore, the use of previously unacquainted subjects whose ascribed status is initially equal will insure that whatever effects are obtained cannot be attributed to an association between initially high or low status, on the one hand, and risk or conservatism, on the other. If initial status levels were unequal, low status individuals might simply adopt the standards of those whose status is high—an outcome which would tell us nothing about the effect of group interactional processes as such on individual risk-taking.

One should distinguish initially ascribed status from status indices (e.g., perceived influence and popularity) derived from the group experience. Since such indices may bear some relation to initial risk-taking level, the necessary sociometric-type judgments will be obtained.

Finally, evidence will be presented with regard to the following two questions: Is the group-induced effect on risk-taking limited only to the group member's overt compliance in the group setting or does it also extend to his covert acceptance when he makes post-group decisions as an individual (5, 8)? To what extent are group effects on individual decision making relatively enduring or short-lived?

METHOD

Assessment of Level of Conservatism or Risk-Taking

The instrument used for assessing level of conservatism or risk-taking, as developed in some of our prior research (9, 25, 26), is called an "opinion questionnaire" and contains descriptions of 12 hypothetical situations. The central person in each situation must choose between two courses of action, one of which is more risky than the other but also more rewarding if successful. For each situation the subject must indicate the lowest probability of success he would accept before rec-

ommending that the potentially more rewarding alternative be chosen. The probabilities listed are 1, 3, 5, 7, and 9 chances of success in 10, plus a final category (scored as 10) in which the subject can refuse to recommend the risky alternative no matter how high its likelihood of success.

The situations were so designed as to cover a wide range of content and may be summarized as follows:

1. An electrical engineer may stick with his present job at a modest but adequate salary or may take a new job offering considerably more money but no long-term security.
2. A man with a severe heart ailment must seriously curtail his customary way of life if he does not undergo a delicate medical operation which might cure him completely or might prove fatal.
3. A man of moderate means may invest some money he recently inherited in secure "blue chip" low return securities or in more risky securities that offer the possibility of large gains.
4. A captain of a college football team, in the final seconds of a game with the college's traditional rival, may choose a play that is almost certain to produce a tie score or a more risky play that would lead to sure victory if successful, sure defeat if not.
5. The president of an American corporation which is about to expand may build a new plant in the United States where returns on the investment would be moderate or may decide to build in a foreign country with an unstable political history where, however, returns on the investment would be very high.
6. A college senior planning graduate work in chemistry may enter university X where, because of rigorous standards, only a fraction of the graduate students manage to receive the PhD, or may enter university Y which has a poorer reputation but where almost every graduate student receives the PhD.
7. A low ranked participant in a national chess tournament, playing an early match with the top-favored man, has the choice of attempting or not trying a deceptive but risky maneuver which might lead to quick victory if successful or almost certain defeat if it fails.
8. A college senior with considerable musical talent must choose between the secure course of going on to medical school and becoming a physician or the risky course of embarking on the career of a concert pianist.
9. An American prisoner-of-war in World War II must choose between possible escape with the risk of execution if caught or remaining in the camp where privations are severe.
10. A successful businessman with strong feelings

of civic responsibility must decide whether or not to run for Congress on the ticket of a minority party whose campaign funds are limited.

11. A research physicist, just beginning a 5-year appointment at a university, may spend the time working on a series of short-term problems which he would be sure to solve but which would be of lesser importance, or on a very important but very difficult problem with the risk of nothing to show for his 5 years of effort.

12. An engaged couple must decide, in the face of recent arguments suggesting some sharp differences of opinions, whether or not to get married. Discussions with a marriage counselor indicate that a happy marriage, while possible, would not be assured.

The response categories are arrayed from chances of 1 in 10 upward for the odd items and in the reverse order for the even items, thus, counter-balancing for any possible order-preference effect in choice of probability levels. An overall conservatism–risk-taking score is derived by adding the scores for the separate items. The larger his score, the greater the subject's conservatism.

Our prior research, cited above, yielded split-half Spearman-Brown reliability coefficients ranging from .53 to .80 for various age and sex samples, suggesting that the instrument possesses satisfactory internal consistency. The results of the present experiment will provide evidence, furthermore, of high test-retest reliability.

Regarding the instrument's construct validity as a risk-taking measure, our earlier studies, cited above, have yielded findings consistent with a risk-taking interpretation. For example, degree of conservatism as measured with the present instrument increases with age from young adulthood to old age for both males and females and increases with degree of subjective probability of personal failure in a motor skill game with actual motor skill controlled.

Experimental Condition

Subjects. The subjects were invited to participate in an experiment which would take no longer than 2 hours and for which remuneration would be provided. Six subjects were scheduled for any one time, with every effort being made to insure that previously acquainted persons were not signed up for the same session. A total of 167 subjects participated in the experimental condition—14 all-male groups and 14 all-female groups.[1] The subjects were liberal arts students

[1] Of the 14 male groups, 13 contained six subjects each, and one contained five subjects. A subject in one of the six-person male groups misun-

enrolled in summer session courses at the University of Colorado in Boulder.

Prediscussion Individual Decisions. The experiment was run in a seminar room around a very long table. For the initial administration of the questionnaire, subjects took alternate seats with the experimenter at one end. The six subjects were requested to read the instructions to the questionnaire and to look over the first item. The experimenter then emphasized two points in further standard instructions: that the more risky alternative is always assumed to be more desirable than the safer course, if the former should prove successful; that the odds which the subject marks indicate the lowest odds the subject would be willing to take and still advise the central figure to give the risky alternative a try. The subjects were told there was no time limit, that they should consider each of the 12 situations carefully, and that they could return to an earlier question if they wished to. The conservatism-risk instrument then was filled out individually by each of the six subjects in a group administration session that took about 20 minutes. To avoid giving any of the subjects the feeling that they were being rushed, the questionnaires were not collected until all had finished.

Group Discussion and Consensual Group Decisions. Without having had any prior expectation that they would be requested to discuss their decisions, the six subjects were then asked to move together into a discussion group at one end of the table. They now each were given another copy of the questionnaire, and a stand-up cardboard placard with the identification letter K, L, M, N, O, or P on it was placed before each subject. The experimenter then told them that the questionnaire now before them was the same one they just finished taking. They had taken it, he continued, to familiarize them with all the situations and to give them some idea where they might stand on each. Now he wanted the group to discuss each question in turn and arrive at a unanimous decision on each. This time they could not return to a question, but rather had to discuss each one until the group decision was reached before going on to the next. When the group reached its decision on a question, all subjects were to mark it on their questionnaires in order to have a record. The group would be completely on its own, the experimenter not participating in the discussion at all.

The experimenter then retired to the other end

derstood instructions for the prediscussion individual decisions, so that his decision scores were removed prior to analysis. All 14 of the female groups contained six subjects each. A subject in each of 2 female groups misunderstood instructions for the prediscussion individual decisions, so that the decision scores of these two females were removed prior to analysis.

of the table in order to be as far from the group as possible. A question that often arose before discussion had started was what to do if a dead-lock occurs. The experimenter's standard reply was:

Most groups are able to come to some decision if those who disagree will restate their reasons and if the problem is reread carefully.

Most groups succeeded in reaching a unanimous decision on most items, although an occasional deadlock did occur on one or another item. The group discussions were of such a nature as to indicate that the participants were highly involved in the decision tasks.

Postdiscussion Individual Decisions. After the discussion was over, the experimenter proceeded to ask the group members to spread apart for some further individual work and to take their questionnaires and identification placards with them. In standard instructions, he requested them to go back over the situations and indicate their own present personal decisions with a "P." He noted that while in some cases the subjects may have agreed with the group decision, in other cases they may have disagreed with it. In the former cases the P would be placed on the same line as the check mark; in the latter cases, on a different line.

While the consensual decisions by the group would indicate the public effect of the discussion process, the private postdiscussion decisions made once again on an individual basis would indicate whether the discussion process had influenced covert acceptance as well as public compliance.

Rankings for Influence and Popularity. After the postdiscussion individual decisions had been made, a ranking sheet was passed out to each subject requesting that he rank everyone in the group (identified by their letter placards), including himself, in terms of how much each influenced the final group decision. Then each subject was requested to rank everyone in the group (except, of course, himself) in terms of how much he would like to become better acquainted with each.

The rankings for influence provided the information needed for examining possible relationships between strength of individual risk-taking or conservatism tendencies, on the one hand, and degree of influence in the group, on the other. If such relationships existed, it seemed to be of interest to determine whether they were specific to perceived influence or would prove to be dependent upon the subject's popularity; hence the second set of rankings.

Secrecy Instructions. After the ranking sheets were collected, the experimenter told the group that the research would be carried out in coming weeks, and that they could now appreciate why it would be important for the content of the experiment to be kept secret, since a person who even knew that the group would be discussing the same questions which he had filled out individually would have a tendency to mark logically defensible answers instead of his true opinion, etc. The subjects therefore all were sworn to secrecy. Various indications suggest that this pledge was faithfully kept.

Post-Postdiscussion Individual Decisions. A further session of individual decision making took place approximately 2–6 weeks later for some subjects. These subjects individually were given the conservatism-risk questionnaire a third time and were asked to reconsider the situations. The standard instructions emphasized that the experimenter was not interested in testing the subject's memory, but rather wanted the subject truly to *reconsider* each situation. The instructions thus oriented the subjects away from simply trying to recall their prior decisions. Each subject was paid for this further work.

Control Condition

Subjects. Control subjects were obtained in the same way as the experimental subjects and likewise received remuneration for their work. The controls were signed up to participate in two sessions: the first to last about 20 minutes; the second, exactly 1 week later, to last about 15 minutes. A total of 51 subjects participated in the control condition—24 males and 27 females. Like the experimental subjects, the controls were liberal arts students enrolled in summer session courses at the University of Colorado in Boulder.

First Individual Decision Session. The first session was identical to the prediscussion individual decision part of the experimental condition. From six to eight subjects of the same sex, scheduled for the same time, filled out the conservatism-risk instrument while sitting together in physical conditions identical to those of the experimental subjects and at approximately the same time of day as the experimental subjects had worked. Exactly the same instructions were provided as had been given the experimental subjects.

After the first session, the control subjects were sworn to secrecy. They also were told that they would be taking a similar questionnaire the next week and that it was extremely important that they not discuss it with one another nor with anyone else, since such discussion might affect the way they filled out next week's questionnaire.

Second Individual Decision Session. The same control subjects who had participated in a particular first individual decision session came back exactly 1 week later. After checking that no discussion had taken place in the intervening week among the controls, the experimenter handed out new copies of the questionnaire and explained that this questionnaire was identical to the one taken last week. Each subject was requested to go back over the situations and reconsider them, the experimenter emphasizing that he was not interested in testing the subject's memory but rather wanted the subject truly to *reconsider* each situation. The instructions were so designed, therefore, as to dissuade the subject from assuming that the most socially acceptable thing to do would be to try to make the same decisions that he had made a week ago. Change was encouraged rather than discouraged. Control subjects were sworn to secrecy again at the end of the second session.

RESULTS

CONSENSUAL GROUP DECISIONS COMPARED WITH PREDISCUSSION INDIVIDUAL DECISIONS

Tables 1 and 2 examine, for male and female groups, respectively, the significance of the conservatism difference between the mean of the prediscussion individual decisions made by the members of each group and that group's consensual decisions. The basic test is carried out using the total conservatism score, which consists of all 12 item scores combined. Tests also are carried out for each item separately.

In the case of the total score, a group's difference score is the sum of the 12 unanimous group decision scores minus the average of the prediscussion total individual decision scores for the six members.[2] Since larger scores indi-

cate greater conservatism, a negative difference (or score decrease) indicates a shift in the risky direction. A *t* test is used to determine whether the 14 difference scores for the groups of each sex are significantly different from zero (13).[3] These total score data indicate a move in the risky direction significant beyond the .001 level for the 14 male groups, and a move in the risky direction significant beyond the .005 level for the 14 female groups. Furthermore, the degree of shift is not significantly different for the two sexes.

In the case of the scores for a single item, a group's difference score consists of the unanimous group decision on that item minus the average of the prediscussion individual decision scores on that item for the six members. Once again a negative difference or score decrease indicates a shift in the risky direction, and a *t* test is applied to determine whether the difference scores for all groups that reached a unanimous decision on the item in question are significantly different from zero. For both the male and female groups, we find that 10 of the 12 items show shifts in the risky direction, 7 of them significant in each case. Five of those 7 are the same for both sexes. Only 2 items show any indication for either

TABLE 1. *Significance of Conservatism Difference Between Mean of Prediscussion Individual Decisions for a Group's Members and Group's Consensual Decision: Males*

Item	Mean Difference[a]	Number of Groups[b]	t
All combined	−9.4	14	6.46[f]
1	−1.0	14	4.34[f]
2	−0.2	14	<1.00
3	−1.1	13	2.19[c]
4	−1.8	13	6.18[f]
5	+0.1	13	<1.00
6	−1.2	13	3.35[d]
7	−2.0	14	9.64[f]
8	−1.1	14	1.97
9	−1.0	10	3.67[d]
10	−0.4	13	<1.00
11	−1.1	12	4.37[e]
12	+0.8	11	2.34[c]

[a] In Tables 1, 2, 3, 4, 6, and 7, a negative difference signifies a risky shift, a positive difference signifies a conservative shift.
[b] In Tables 1 and 2, number of groups for an item is less than 14 when one or more groups deadlocked on that item. Any deadlocked item is, of course, not included when calculating scores for all items combined.
[c] *p* < .05.
[d] *p* < .01.
[e] *p* < .005.
[f] *p* < .001.

[2] Any deadlocked item is, of course, not included in either term for the group in question.

[3] All significance levels cited in this study are based on two-tailed tests.

TABLE 2. *Significance of Conservatism Difference Between Mean of Prediscussion Individual Decisions for a Group's Members and Group's Consensual Decision: Females*

Item	Mean Difference	Number of Groups	t
All combined	−9.4	14	3.91 [c]
1	−1.0	13	4.17 [c]
2	−0.6	14	1.65
3	−0.4	14	1.12
4	−1.4	14	2.60 [d]
5	+0.7	14	1.90
6	−0.8	13	2.63 [d]
7	−2.0	12	3.21 [b]
8	−1.7	14	5.26 [e]
9	−0.8	12	1.19
10	−1.5	13	3.18 [b]
11	−0.9	13	2.28 [a]
12	+0.6	6	2.00

[a] $p < .05$.
[b] $p < .01$.
[c] $p < .005$.
[d] $p < .025$.
[e] $p < .001$.

sex of not sharing in the general shift toward greater risk taking: Items 5 and 12. It should be noted that these two items exhibited, in our previous research, the lowest correlations with the overall risk-conservatism score, suggesting that they are relatively impure measures of the psychological dimension being tapped by the other 10 items.

In sum, the evidence from Tables 1 and 2 indicates a strong move toward greater risk-taking when groups arrive at unanimous decisions, compared with the risk levels ventured by the same persons in prediscussion individual decisions. Furthermore, this move toward greater risk-taking obtains for females as well as for males.

A further question concerns the extent to which the risky shift is consistent from one group to another. Consider one example of several consistency tests that have been conducted, all of which yield highly similar results. Suppose we define a group as showing a risky shift from prediscussion individual decisions to consensual group decisions if the difference score for its total score, as defined above, is a negative one. Fourteen out of 14 male groups and 12 out of 14 female groups are found to move in the risky direction, both results being very significant by a sign test. Such a finding demonstrates, therefore, that the risky shift phenomenon is quite consistent across groups.

POSTDISCUSSION INDIVIDUAL DECISIONS COMPARED WITH PREDISCUSSION INDIVIDUAL DECISIONS

In Tables 3 and 4 we present, once again for male and female groups, respectively, the significance of the difference between the mean of the prediscussion individual decisions and the mean of the postdiscussion individual decisions made by the members of each group. The basic test once again is provided by the total conservatism score, but tests also are presented for each item separately.

For the total score, a group's difference score consists of the average of the postdiscussion total individual decision scores for the members minus the average of the prediscussion total individual decision scores for the same members. Negative difference scores again indicate risky shifts, and a t test is applied to determine whether the 14 difference scores for the groups of each sex are significantly different from zero. We find, once again, a shift in the risky direction significant beyond the .001 level for the 14 male groups and a risky shift significant beyond the .005 level for the 14 female groups. As before, the degree of shift is not significantly different for the two sexes.

Turning to the scores for each separate item, a group's difference score consists of the

TABLE 3. *Significance of Conservatism Difference Between Mean of Prediscussion Individual Decisions for a Group's Members and Mean of Postdiscussion Individual Decisions for a Group's Members: Males*

Item	Mean Difference	Number of Groups	t
All combined	− 10.4	14	9.12[d]
1	− 1.0	14	4.32[d]
2	− 0.6	14	2.87[a]
3	− 1.1	14	3.04[b]
4	− 1.7	14	8.14[d]
5	+ 0.1	14	<1.00
6	− 1.1	14	3.79[c]
7	− 1.8	14	7.80[d]
8	− 1.1	14	3.54[c]
9	− 1.1	14	3.99[c]
10	− 0.3	14	<1.00
11	− 0.8	14	4.36[d]
12	+ 0.1	14	<1.00

[a] $p < .02$.
[b] $p < .01$.
[c] $p < .005$.
[d] $p < .001$.

average of the postdiscussion individual decision scores on that item minus the average of the prediscussion individual decision scores on that item. With a negative difference score indicating a risky shift and a t test applied to indicate whether the 14 difference scores for each sex on an item are significantly different from zero, we find that 9 of the 12 items show separate significant shifts in the risky direction for the male groups (with one additional item shifting nonsignificantly in the same direction), and that 8 of the 12 items show separate significant shifts toward greater risk-taking for the female groups (with two additional items shifting nonsignificantly in that direction). The 8 items showing significant risky shifts for the females are among the 9 showing significant risky shifts for the males. Items 5 and 12 once again are the only ones for either sex showing any indication of not sharing in the general

TABLE 4. *Significance of Conservatism Difference Between Mean of Prediscussion Individual Decisions for a Group's Members and Mean of Postdiscussion Individual Decisions for a Group's Members: Females*

Item	Mean Difference	Number of Groups	t
All combined	−8.2	14	3.67[b]
1	−0.9	14	5.09[d]
2	−0.7	14	2.67[a]
3	−0.6	14	2.58[c]
4	−1.4	14	3.40[b]
5	+0.6	14	1.85
6	−0.8	14	2.90[a]
7	−1.7	14	3.56[b]
8	−1.2	14	4.44[d]
9	−0.5	14	<1.00
10	−0.7	14	1.95
11	−0.9	14	2.89[a]
12	+0.7	14	3.66[b]

[a] $p < .02$.
[b] $p < .025$.
[c] $p < .005$.
[d] $p < .001$.

TABLE 5. *Comparability of Experimental and Control Subjects in Initial Conservatism and Age*

Subject	Males		Females	
	M	N	M	N
Mean initial overall conservatism				
Experimental	66.9	82[a]	65.6	82[a]
Control	68.3	24	64.6	27
t	0.41		0.34	
Mean age				
Experimental	20.7	82[b]	20.3	84
Control	21.0	24	20.7	27
t	0.41		0.67	

[a] Initial overall conservatism scores were available for 164 of the experimental subjects. See Footnote 2 in text.
[b] One subject forgot to list his age, and one group contained five rather than six subjects.

shift toward greater risk-taking found in both sexes.

There is clear evidence, therefore, that postdiscussion individual decisions exhibit a strong move toward greater risk-taking when compared with prediscussion individual decisions arrived at by the same persons, and do so for both sexes. The group discussion process, in other words, seems to have an effect on private attitudes (postdiscussion individual decisions) that is just as significant as its effect on publicly expressed views (unanimous group decisions).

Once again we may inquire about the extent to which the risky shift is consistent from group to group. Several consistency tests have been carried out, all yielding highly similar results. As an example, suppose we define a group as exhibiting a shift in the risky direction from prediscussion to postdiscussion individual decisions if the difference score for its total score, as defined in this section, is a negative one. Fourteen out of 14 male groups and 12 out of 14 female groups are found to shift in the risky direction, both results being quite significant by a sign test. Such a finding demonstrates, therefore, that the risky shift phenomenon is quite consistent across groups in regard to covert acceptance as well as overt compliance.

CONTROL SUBJECTS

To insure that the move toward greater risk-taking just described actually is a result of the

group discussion process, we must turn to the findings for the control subjects. The comparability of control and experimental subjects is indicated in Table 5. We note that, in the case both of males and females, the experimental and control subjects have approximately the same initial total conservatism scores and also are approximately the same in age.[4] Item-by-item comparisons of experimental and control subjects of each sex on initial conservatism scores also were carried out and show that controls and experimentals within sex obtain highly similar scores.

In Tables 6 and 7 we present, for male and female control subjects, respectively, the significance of the difference between decisions made during the first and the second sessions. It will be recalled that one week intervened between these two sessions, and that instructions for the second session requested the subjects not to try simply to remember what they had marked before, but to reconsider their decisions. It is evident that the total conservatism score shows no shift from first to second session for either sex. Turning to the separate tests carried out on each item, we find that none of the 12 items shows a significant shift for the males, and only 1 of the 12 items shows a significant shift for the females. When no group discussion and achievement of group

[4] It might also be mentioned that, in confirmation of earlier findings, there is no sex difference in initial total conservatism scores for either the experimental or the control subjects.

TABLE 6. *Significance of Conservatism Difference Between First and Second Decisions by Male Control Subjects*

Item	Mean Difference	Number of Subjects	t^a
All combined	+1.5	24	<1.00
1	+0.4	24	<1.00
2	−0.3	24	<1.00
3	+0.3	24	<1.00
4	+0.8	24	2.00
5	−0.4	24	1.06
6	0.0	24	<1.00
7	+0.4	24	1.03
8	+0.5	24	1.63
9	−0.1	24	<1.00
10	+0.1	24	<1.00
11	+0.1	24	<1.00
12	−0.4	24	1.42

[a] All *t* values *ns.*

consensus intervenes, then, there is no systematic shift toward greater risk-taking or greater conservatism, and this despite instructions that encourage shifts by emphasizing that we are not interested in the subjects' memories.

The data for the control subjects also provide us with an opportunity for determining the test-retest reliability of the conservatism-risk instrument, with one week intervening and under instructions that encourage change rather than constancy. For the 24 male subjects, the product-moment correlation coefficient between total conservatism scores in the first and second sessions is .78. For the 27 female subjects, the same correlation coefficient is .82. Test-retest reliability of the instrument, therefore, is quite high.

PREDISCUSSION RISK-TAKING AND INFLUENCE IN THE GROUP

Our data concerning perceived influence within the group consisted in each individual's ranking of all group members, including himself, in terms of how much each influenced the group's decisions. A first question to ask of these influence rankings is: How consistent are they from member to member within a group? To determine the degree of agreement among a group's members in their rankings of one another for influence, Kendall's coefficient of concordance (18) was applied to each group's influence rankings. If the members of a group agree regarding who among themselves are more influential and who less so, then W will be significantly large. Table 8 presents

TABLE 7. *Significance of Conservatism Difference Between First and Second Decisions by Female Control Subjects*

Item	Mean Difference	Number of Subjects	t
All combined	−2.2	27	1.26
1	−0.4	27	<1.00
2	−0.2	27	<1.00
3	−1.0	27	2.61[a]
4	−0.4	27	1.12
5	−0.3	27	<1.00
6	−0.2	27	<1.00
7	0.0	27	<1.00
8	0.0	27	<1.00
9	+0.2	27	<1.00
10	+0.3	27	1.03
11	−0.3	27	<1.00
12	+0.1	27	<1.00

[a] $p < .02.$

TABLE 8. *Degree of Agreement Among Group Members in Rankings of One Another for Influence*[a]

Group	*Males* N	W	Group	*Females* N	W
1	6	.64[c]	1	6	.85[c]
2	6	.55[c]	2	6	.61[c]
3	6	.74[c]	3	6	.31
4	6	.72[c]	4	6	.79[c]
5	6	.70[c]	5	6	.47[c]
6	6	.50[c]	6	6	.67[c]
7	5	.56[b]	7	6	.13
8	6	.50[c]	8	6	.59[c]
9	6	.62[c]	9	6	.59[c]
10	6	.66[c]	10	6	.69[c]
11	6	.66[c]	11	6	.83[c]
12	6	.55[c]	12	6	.80[c]
13	6	.54[c]	13	6	.70[c]
14	6	.73[c]	14	6	.30

[a] Kendall's coefficient of concordance.
[b] $p < .05$.
[c] $p < .01$.

the results of these tests for all 28 groups. It is evident that agreement in influence rankings is quite high: the degree of agreement is significant for all 14 of the male groups and for 11 of the 14 female groups.

Given this high agreement among group members in their rankings of one another for influence, an approximate overall estimate of degree of influence for a given group member was obtained by averaging the influence ranks that had been assigned to that person by all members of the group (including that person). The lower the average, the greater that subject's perceived influence (i.e., the higher the assigned influence ranks for that person). These average influence scores for the subjects of each sex were correlated with the initial total conservatism scores obtained by the same subjects. The resulting product-moment correlation coefficients are shown in Table 9. They are significant beyond the .005 and .05 levels for the 82 males and the 82 females,

TABLE 9. *Product-Moment Correlations Among Initial Conservatism, Influence, and Popularity*[a]

	Males $(N = 82)$[b]	*Females* $(N = 82)$[b]
Initial overall risk-taking and influence	.32[g]	.22[d]
Initial overall risk-taking and popularity	.15	− .04
Influence and popularity	.72[h]	.54[h]
Initial overall risk-taking and influence, popularity held constant[c]	.30[f]	.28[e]

[a] Small score values signify greater risk-taking, greater influence, and greater popularity.
[b] While all influence and popularity scores are based on the 167 subjects in the experimental condition, the correlations are based on the 164 of those subjects for whom initial overall risk-taking scores were available.
[c] Partial correlation coefficients.
[d] $p < .05$.
[e] $p < .02$.
[f] $p < .01$.
[g] $p < .005$.
[h] $p < .001$.

respectively: persons higher in initial risk-taking are rated as having more influence on the group decisions.

Average popularity scores for each group member were constructed by averaging the popularity rankings assigned by all the other members of the group. We note in Table 9 that there emerges a very strong relationship between this average popularity score and the average influence score for both the male and the female group members: persons rated high in influence also tend to be rated high in popularity. This general relationship has, of course, been known for some time (2, 6, 20), so that our obtaining it here increases our confidence in the respective measures being used to assess influence and popularity. It is further evident in Table 9, however, that degree of initial risk-taking is *not* related to degree of popularity within the group for either sex.

Finally, we also find from Table 9 that risk-taking and influence are significantly related for each sex when popularity ratings are held constant. The partial correlation coefficients are significant beyond the .01 and .02 levels for the males and females, respectively. It is evident, therefore, that the relationships obtained for both sexes between degree of initial risk-taking and degree of influence on group decisions are not dependent upon members' popularity.

MAINTENANCE OF THE RISKY SHIFT OVER A SUBSEQUENT PERIOD OF TIME

An interesting further question concerns the extent to which the shift toward greater risk-taking, which we have found to result from group discussion, is maintained over a subsequent period of time. We were able to gather evidence on this point for males but not for females. In the case of the former, but not in the case of the latter, a random sample of subjects from the original groups could be obtained for further study. The 22 males who were available for further work were approximately evenly distributed among the 14 original male groups. After a time interval of roughly 2–6 weeks had elapsed since the group session, these subjects individually were given the conservatism-risk questionnaire a third time, as described in the section on procedure.

The comparability of the random male sub-sample of 22 to the original male experimental condition sample of 82 is evident from the following data on total conservatism scores. The mean prediscussion total conservatism score was 66.9 for the sample of 82 and also was 66.9 for the subsample of 22. The mean postdiscussion total conservatism score, in turn, was 56.6 for the whole sample and 56.2 for the subsample. The t test of the difference scores had yielded a t significant beyond the .001 level ($t = 9.12$) for the whole sample, and it also yielded a t significant beyond the .001 level ($t = 4.70$) for the subsample.

Turning now to the total conservatism scores obtained by this subsample when they took the questionnaire again 2–6 weeks after the group discussion (call these scores the "post-postdiscussion" individual decisions), the mean score is 54.6. The mean of the difference scores obtained by subtracting each subject's prediscussion total conservatism score from his post-postdiscussion total conservatism score is -12.3, with a t test of these difference scores yielding a t value of 4.92 ($p < .001$), hence indicating a risky shift from the prediscussion individual decisions to the post-postdiscussion individual decisions. The mean of the difference scores obtained, in turn, by subtracting each subject's postdiscussion total conservatism score from his post-postdiscussion total conservatism score is only -1.6, and a t test of these difference scores is not significant, hence indicating no further change from the postdiscussion individual decisions to the post-postdiscussion individual decisions. Item-by-item analyses tell the same story: the only significant item shifts are risky ones, and they are as strong from prediscussion to post-postdiscussion sessions as they are from prediscussion to postdiscussion sessions.

In sum, the data available on the point indicate that the shift in the risky direction found to occur as a result of the group discussion process is maintained over a subsequent period of time.

DISCUSSION AND CONCLUSIONS

The following conclusions may be drawn from the preceding evidence:

1. Unanimous group decisions concerning matters of risk show a shift toward greater risk-taking when compared with prediscussion individual decisions made by the same persons

and concerning the same matters. This holds for both sexes.

2. Postdiscussion individual decisions that follow unanimous group decisions exhibit the same kind of shift toward greater risk-taking as appears in the group decisions. This is the case for both sexes. Covert acceptance as well as overt compliance, thus, are affected in the same manner by the discussion process.

3. This shift toward greater risk-taking as a result of the discussion process is still maintained when 2–6 weeks have elapsed since the discussion occurred. Evidence on this point was available only for males.

4. No shift in risk-taking level of individual decisions occurs over time in the absence of the discussion process. This holds for both sexes.

5. There is a positive relationship between degree of risk-taking in prediscussion individual decisions and the extent to which group members are perceived by one another as influencing group decisions. This relationship is specific to judgments of influence, in that it obtains when judgments of popularity are held constant, and also no relationship is found between prediscussion individual risk-taking and the extent to which group members are judged to be popular. These statements all hold for both sexes.

The present study indicates, then, that group interaction and achievement of consensus concerning decisions on matters of risk eventuate in a willingness to make decisions that are more risky than those that would be made in the absence of such interaction. Furthermore, although initial ascribed status levels of the group members are equal, it is found that persons with stronger individual risk-taking proclivities tend to become more influential in the group than persons who are more conservative. Two alternative interpretations of these findings can be suggested; one more group centered, the other more person centered. It is possible that there is at work in these groups a process of diffusion or spreading of responsibility as a result of knowing that one's decisions are being made jointly with others rather than alone. Increased willingness to take risk would eventuate from this decreased feeling of personal responsibility. That initial risk-taking and judged influence within the group are positively related could well occur as a consequence of this process, since

one of its effects would be for the views of high risk-takers to be given more weight by the rest of the group. Alternatively, the fact that high risk-takers exert more influence may be a cause of the group's movement toward greater risk-taking. It is possible that high risk-takers are also more likely to take the initiative in social situations. Of course, these two interpretations are not necessarily mutually exclusive. Both of them may contribute to the group effect.

That females as well as males show the same change toward greater risk-taking as a result of the group interaction condition, and that the samples of both sexes were liberal arts university students, renders it unlikely that the results can be explained on the basis of reinforcement by others of one's expectation as to whether one's appropriate role is to be more or less of a risk-taker. We noted earlier that Stoner (19) found a move toward greater risk-taking in group as compared to individual decision-making by male graduate students of industrial management, and we pointed out that this result might be accounted for in terms of the professional role that they had assigned themselves by becoming graduate students in a business school. Presence of peers might be expected to increase the salience of their business manager role, and a greater willingness to take risks in decision-making might well be perceived as one of the attributes of that role. Such a role-expectation interpretation is ruled out for the present study, however, through our use of liberal arts students as subjects. In addition, the possibility of explaining the results in terms of males' perceiving their appropriate role as one of willingness to be bold and daring, and being reinforced in this view by interaction with other like-minded males, is ruled out by the present study's obtaining the same results for females as for males. This outcome would not be expected if the findings depended on sex-linked role-expectations as to whether one should be more risky or more conservative. This outcome also, of course, rules out interpretation in terms of any possible sex-linked differences in major fields of study.

That the group induced move toward greater risk-taking in individual decisions is still maintained 2–6 weeks after the discussion, provides evidence, incidentally, which supports Lewin's view (11) that "group carried" attitudinal changes maintain themselves (see also Pelz, 16).

References

1. Atthowe, J. M., Jr. Interpersonal decision making: The resolution of a dyadic conflict. *Journal of Abnormal and Social Psychology*, 1961, **62**, 114–119.
2. Back, K. W. Influence through social communication. *Journal of Abnormal and Social Psychology*, 1951, **46**, 9–23.
3. Brown, R. W. Mass phenomena. In G. Lindzey (Ed.), *Handbook of social psychology.* Vol. 2. Cambridge, Mass.: Addison-Wesley, 1954. Pp. 833–876.
4. Cartwright, D., & Zander, A. (Eds.), *Group dynamics.* Evanston, Ill.: Row, Peterson, 1960. Pp. 165–319.
5. Festinger, L. An analysis of compliant behavior. In M. Sherif & M. O. Wilson (Eds.), *Group relations at the crossroads.* New York: Harper, 1953.
6. Horowitz, M. W., Lyons, J., & Perlmutter, H. V. Induction of forces in discussion groups. *Human Relations*, 1951, **4**, 57–76.
7. Hunt, E. B., & Rowe, R. R. Group and individual economic decision making in risk conditions. In D. W. Taylor (Ed.), *Experiments on decision-making and other studies.* Arlington, Va.: Armed Services Technical Information Agency, 1960. (Technical Report No. 6, AD 253952)
8. Kelley, H. H., & Thibaut, J. W. Experimental studies of group problem-solving and process. In G. Lindzey (Ed.), *Handbook of social psychology.* Vol. 2. Cambridge, Mass.: Addison-Wesley, 1954.
9. Kogan, N., & Wallach, M. A. The effect of anxiety on relations between subjective age and caution in an older sample. In P. Hoch & J. Zubin (Eds.), *Psychopathology of aging.* New York: Grune & Stratton, 1961.
10. Komarovsky, M. Functional analysis of sex roles. *American Sociological Review*, 1950, **15**, 508–516.
11. Lewin, K. Frontiers in group dynamics. *Human Relations*, 1947, **1**, 2–38.
12. Lonergan, B. G., & McClintock, C. G. Effects of group membership on risk-taking behavior. *Psychological Reports*, 1961, **8**, 447–455.
13. McNemar, Q. *Psychological statistics.* New York: Wiley, 1955.
14. Milner, E. Effects of sex role and social status on the early adolescent personality. *Genetic Psychology Monographs*, 1949, **40**, 231–325.
15. Osborn, A. F. *Applied imagination.* New York: Scribner's, 1957.
16. Pelz, E. B. Some factors in "group decision." In E. E. Maccoby, T. M. Newcomb, & E. L. Hartley (Eds.), *Readings in social psychology.* New York: Holt, 1958.
17. Schachter, S. Deviation, rejection, and communication. *Journal of Abnormal and Social Psychology*, 1951, **46**, 190–207.
18. Siegel, S. *Nonparametric statistics for the behavioral sciences.* New York: McGraw-Hill, 1956.
19. Stoner, J. A. F. A comparison of individual and group decisions involving risk. Unpublished master's thesis, Massachusetts Institute of Technology, School of Industrial Management, 1961.
20. Tagiuri, R., & Kogan, N. Personal preference and the attribution of influence in small groups. *Journal of Personality*, 1960, **28**, 257–265.
21. Taylor, D. W., Berry, P. C., & Block, C. H. Does group participation when using brainstorming facilitate or inhibit creative thinking? *Administrative Science Quarterly*, 1958, **3**, 23–47.
22. Thibaut, J. W., & Kelley, H. H. *The social psychology of groups.* New York: Wiley, 1959.
23. Turner, R. H., & Killian, L. M. (Eds.), *Collective behavior.* Englewood Cliffs, N.J.: Prentice-Hall, 1957.
24. Wallach, M. A., & Caron, A. J. Attribute criteriality and sex-linked conservatism as determinants of psychological similarity. *Journal of Abnormal and Social Psychology*, 1959, **59**, 43–50.
25. Wallach, M. A., & Kogan, N. Sex differences and judgment processes. *Journal of Personality*, 1959, **27**, 555–564.
26. Wallach, M. A., & Kogan, N. Aspects of judgment and decision-making: Interrelationships and changes with age. *Behavioral Science*, 1961, **6**, 23–36.
27. Whyte, W. H., Jr. *The organization man.* New York: Simon & Schuster, 1956.

34

The Recall of Interrupted Group Tasks: An Experimental Study of Individual Motivation in Relation to Group Goals

MURRAY HORWITZ

The general problem considered in this research is the following: Can the motivational concepts which have been developed for individuals who are acting for their *own goals* be applied to individuals who are acting so that a group will achieve *group goals?*

The concept of group goals appears in one form or another in most theories of group functioning. Barnard's (2) concept of group effectiveness and Homans' (7) of group activities both involve the notion of particular outcomes which the group can achieve in its external environment. French (5), in his studies of group productivity, makes explicit use of the concept of group goals but distinguishes conceptually the two types of goals by locating each in a different type of environment. He follows Lewin (11) in describing the individual's behavioral environment in terms of the possible activities existing for the person, and locomotion through this environment as a change in the person's position in the sense of moving from one activity to another. The individual's goal is treated as a consummatory activity which terminates a sequence of other activities which lead up to it. Analogously, the group's behavioral environment is regarded as consisting of possible activities in which the group can engage. Group activities, however, are carried on, not by the separate activities of individual members, but by the organization of these individual actions within the group. Locomotion toward a group goal involves a change of position by the group, and for this reason, although a member may contribute in some degree to the group's moving toward its goal, neither the locomotion nor the goal can be said to be achievable by any individual in the group. As in the case of an individual goal, the group goal is consummatory in that it terminates a sequence of group activities.

This chapter is condensed from a fuller article appearing under the same title in *Human Relations*, 1954, **7**, 3–38. It is reprinted here by permission of the author and *Human Relations*.

A number of studies have examined the motivation of group members as related to group goals. Lippitt (16) found that in certain types of children's groups members persisted in working on a group task although the leader had left the room, while in others work ceased when pressure from the leader was removed. The studies by Katz (9) and the numerous investigations of "group identification" reported by Sherif and Cantril (21) indicate that under some conditions members can become motivated in terms of group goals, while under other conditions they act without such motivation. From the standpoint of motivational theory in individual psychology, these studies raise the problem of how goals which represent changes in the state of a group can be conceptually linked with goals which are consummatory activities of the person himself.

In individual psychology, the existence of some internal system in tension, e.g., a need, is usually taken as a necessary condition for the person's having a goal. According to this view tension systems result in the individual's "cathecting" some goal in the environment, and tendencies are then aroused for the person to locomote toward this desirable outcome. Lewin (13) has given a rather elaborate systematic treatment of the properties of tension systems, based primarily on experiments which have treated the individual in isolation from the social field. In measuring tension systems, the Lewinian experiments on individuals involve the general procedure of providing the subject with a series of tasks which he desires to complete, having the subject engage in activities directed to this end, and interrupting some of the tasks but allowing others to be completed. There are several features of this experimental procedure which prevent our generalizing the results obtained to the behavior of individuals in a goal-setting group:

1. The "interrupted task" experiments indicate that individuals develop tension systems coordinated to reaching their own goals. Group goals, as we have seen, cannot be attained by an individual. The question is raised whether individuals can develop tension systems coordinated to the group's attaining its goal; and, if so, does the group's reaching its goal reduce tension in the same way as "consumption" by the individual?

2. In experiments with individuals the subject engages in a sequence of activities which will enable him to complete the task. The individual's environment is regarded as a stable and relatively invariant frame of reference, locomotion being treated as the person's changing his position within this environment. A characteristic of behavior in a social field, however, is that desirable or undesirable states of affairs may come about by changes in the social environment, independently of the individual's action. A change in the person's position, i.e., locomotion, can occur not only by his entering into a new activity, but by the "ground moving under his feet." Even though the person is himself inactive, he may find himself psychologically "carried" toward or away from a goal or toward or away from an avoidance by the action of the group. The results of experiments with individuals do not permit us to answer the question: Will tension systems be reduced where the person has not actively completed the task but has to some degree been "carried" by the group into a condition in which the task has been completed?

3. In the individual experiments the tension systems which are measured are coordinated to completing a task. In a group situation a person may wish to avoid completing a task which he may nevertheless be obliged to complete by virtue of his membership in the group. If tension systems exist coordinated to avoiding a task, one would expect these avoidance tensions to have somewhat different properties from goal tensions; for where nonentry into the region of negative valence should reduce an avoidance tension, non-entry into the region of positive valence should leave the goal tensions unreduced. On the other hand, entering a region of negative valence should leave an avoidance tension unreduced, although entering a region of positive valence should reduce the goal tension. The experimental procedure used with individuals has made it difficult to investigate avoidance tensions. Do tension systems, in fact, exist for avoidances as well as goals? If so, what are the properties of avoidance tensions?

4. In the individual experiments, the subject is either allowed to choose his own tasks or is provided tasks in which he will be interested. However, a group may set a goal in the absence of an individual member's tension system, or even in opposition to it. Thus, differences may occur between the particular goals set by the group and the goals which the individual desires the group to set. What, if any,

are the effects on tension systems of members' attitudes toward undesired group goals?

PREVIOUS RESEARCH

Zeigarnik (22), in the earliest experimental work using the tension system construct, coordinated an inner-personal system in a state of tension to the person's striving toward a goal. If the person reaches the goal, the tension is assumed to be reduced; if he is interrupted short of the goal, the system remains in a state of tension. Zeigarnik demonstrated that interrupted tasks are more frequently recalled than completed tasks.

The question of the effects of events in the social field on the arousal of tension systems in the person was first explicitly raised by Adler and Kounin (1). These investigators found that another person's unfinished task failed to arouse tension systems in an observer. Lewis (14) was justly critical of the conclusions drawn from the negative results of this experiment, in which there was little interdependence between the two individuals involved. Lewis set up an experimental situation in which a subject worked on a set of tasks, half of which he finished, the other half being interrupted by a cooperating partner who proceeded himself to finish the tasks. No significant difference was found between recall by a subject of tasks which he completed personally and those which were interrupted and completed by his partner. The result is interpreted to mean that one's tension-system can be reduced by another's reaching his own goal. This still leaves open the question whether tension systems can be aroused for nonpersonal goals. In a second experiment, Lewis and Franklin (15) had the subject and one of the experimenters work together on the tasks. The second experimenter interrupted half the tasks, setting them aside. The number of subjects who recalled more interrupted than finished tasks proved to be significantly above chance. This experiment touches directly on the question: Given a group goal does an individual develop tension systems coordinated to the group's reaching its goal?

Unfortunately, although this second experiment points to a method for investigating the question, it does not provide the answer. In analyzing the task structures of the 18 problems, Lewis indicates that some of the problems were seen by the subjects as allowing the two partners differential responsibility for the results. Tasks which required an exchange of ideas between the partners might not, for example, incorporate some of the subject's ideas in the solution. They might, therefore, be regarded by him as unfinished, leaving him with an undischarged tension. Other tasks might be seen as consisting of separate halves, one belonging to one partner and the other to the other. In the words of one subject, "Some we divided up. You finished your part and I finished mine." One cannot, therefore, determine whether the tension systems aroused in Lewis' experiment were related to a desire to complete a group task or to complete some part of a group task which was regarded by the individual as his personal goal.

EXPERIMENTAL PROCEDURE

SUBJECTS

The subjects were female students recruited in groups of five from sororities at the University of Michigan. There were 18 such groups, two of which lacked one member. The experiment was explained as a test of group cooperativeness which would be judged by the quality of the group's performance in working together on a number of jigsaw puzzles. The situation was presented as a contest in which each team represented its sorority. In the main the teams consisted of volunteers, although in some instances they contained persons specifically designated by sorority officers.

DEVELOPING MOTIVATION FOR THE GROUP TASK

Upon entering the experimental room the subjects were engaged in a group discussion for about 15 minutes, designed to heighten their awareness as group members. After the five subjects appeared to be thoroughly involved in the discussion about their group, they were asked to take seats in one of five booths set side by side. Partitions between them prevented subjects seeing one another, but all could see the experimenter who took his place at a table in front of the booths. At each workplace within a booth was a one-page questionnaire, entitled "Test on Group Loyalty," which was aimed at increasing the subjects' involvement in working toward a group goal. The questionnaire contained five scales on which the subjects were asked to rate "the loyalty and team spirit of your group," "your respect for the will of the group," "your readiness to go along with a group decision with which you disagree," and finally, "how much you desire the group to do well on this test."

EXPLAINING THE PROCEDURE ON THE TASK

A cardboard poster (size 14″ × 14″) was attached by means of a spring clip to a display board on the experimenter's table. Drawn on the poster was the outline of a figure, sectioned into five parts to represent a jigsaw puzzle. There were 17 such figures, two of which were used for demonstration purposes. The group's task was to attempt to direct the experimenter in filling in each of these "target" figures one piece at a time. Each subject communicated with the experimenter by a system of signals without knowledge of what others in the group were signaling.

In an envelope at her workplace each subject had four differently shaped pieces of cardboard, each of which was cut out to correspond with a section of the jigsaw "target" figure. By holding up one of these pieces, the subject could signal to the experimenter which section of the figure should be filled in. According to the instructions, if a given number of people and *no more* than that held up the same piece then the corresponding section of the jigsaw figure would be filled in by the experimenter. The effect of this rule was that those subjects who had not held up the piece could claim credit for keeping the number below the maximum, so that it was impossible to say that any member contributed more than another to the successful placing of a piece. The subjects would hold up their choices on successive trials, and the experimenter would announce whether or not the correct number of subjects were holding up the same piece. The trials were continued until the experimenter announced that the correct number of subjects were holding up a given piece, whereupon the experimenter would fill in the corresponding section of the jigsaw figure. The group then engaged in a second series of trials until they succeeded in filling in another section of the figure. This process continued until the entire figure was completed.

EXPLAINING THE METHOD OF VOTING AND SCORING

After the procedure had been explained to the group, the method of scoring was described. The method entailed taking a vote at the midpoint of each of the 15 puzzles, and was designed to allow members to express their personal decisions either for or against completing the puzzle.

Each puzzle was said to have a *basic score* of fifty points which a group could obtain on the basis of only *part* of its performance. Thus, a group could stop without completing a puzzle and still earn the basic score. If the group wished to complete the puzzle, however, it could do so. This was entirely up to the group to decide.

There was also a system of bonus points. If the group decided to complete the puzzle, and if it did well, they were told, it would obtain a bonus of ten points. If it did not do well, it would be penalized five points.

Two demonstrations were given to enable the subjects to learn the procedure in solving the task and to set up the routine on voting. Votes were always taken after two of the five pieces had been placed on the figure, the experimenter announcing, "I have the basic score. Does the group want to stop here or complete the puzzle?" The subjects voted, without knowledge of how their fellow members were voting, by raising their right hands if they wished to continue work or their left hands if they wished to stop. The experimenter then announced the outcome of the vote. If the announced majority decision was to "complete the puzzle," work was continued in trying to place the third piece; if the announced decision was to stop, the puzzle was set aside, and work was begun on the next puzzle.

ADMINISTERING THE EXPERIMENT

In signaling their individual choices, both in filling in the figure and in voting, the subjects could not see one another and had to depend entirely on the experimenter for announcement of the results. The experimenter was therefore able to make his announcements according to a prearranged experimental plan. Standard sequences for filling in the various sections of the figure were planned in advance for all groups. After from four to six trials, irrespective of the actual pieces being held up by the subjects, the experimenter would announce that the correct number of subjects were holding up the piece which had been selected in advance, and the experimenter would then set this piece on the figure. Although nothing the group did made any difference in how the pieces were being placed on the figure, the experimenter's control of the "feedback" served to maintain the illusion that the group was solving the task in its own way. In a similar fashion, it was possible to follow a prearranged experimental plan in announcing the results of the voting. On five puzzles selected in advance, no matter how the group actually voted, the group was told that a majority had voted "no," or *not* to go on with the work. On 10 selected puzzles, the group was told that a majority had voted "yes," in favor of continuing work. Of these 10 tasks, the group completed half, and half were interrupted by the experimenter. The interruption, which came in the middle of work on the third piece, was described as temporary and the subjects were told they would return to their work later.

There were thus three treatments for the 15 tasks: an announced "yes" vote, followed by completion of the task (designated hereafter as Y-C); an announced "yes" vote, followed by partial completion and interruption (designated as Y-I); and an announced "no" vote, with work stopping (designated as N). At the end of the series of tasks, the subjects were requested individually to recall the names of the jigsaw figures. The instructions were designed to minimize the recall as a "memory test" which, as Zeigarnik (22) has shown, tends to equalize recall of finished and unfinished tasks.

The lists of recalled tasks constitute the basic data of the experiment. Each task on a subject's list could be identified as receiving a specific one of the three experimental treatments. Each type of task could be further broken down into two groups, according to whether the subject's personal vote had been "yes" or "no."

EXPERIMENTAL DESIGN

The strength of recall of tasks *for a given treatment* is measured by the ratio:

$$\frac{\text{number of recalled tasks}}{\text{total number of tasks in treatment}}$$

Since recall will be affected by the serial order of the tasks and by the "intrinsic" recall value of each figure, it was necessary to equalize these two factors among the three treatments. This could be achieved by presenting the 15 figures in the same order for all 18 groups but alternating the treatment in successive groups. Thus a given task would be treated in one group as a Y-C task, in the next group as a Y-I task, and in the next as an N task.

Certain departures from this scheme were required by the following additional experimental requirements:

1. The first puzzle in the series should be a Y-C task, since an initial "no" vote might suggest to the subjects that their fellow members were rejecting the experiment, and an initial Y-I treatment, in which the experimenter interrupted the task, might cast doubt on his intention to respect the group's decision.
2. No two Y-I tasks should succeed each other without the interposition of a Y-C task in order to avoid any suggestion that the experimenter intended consistently to deny the subjects' decision to complete a task.
3. No contiguous tasks in the series should receive the same treatment.

In summary, each subject was exposed to 15 tasks, five tasks in each of the three treatments Y-I, Y-C, and N. The ratio of tasks recalled within a given treatment to total tasks within that treatment was computed for each subject. The means of these recall ratios were computed for the 15 subjects belonging to the three groups within a complete rotation. This yielded three scores representing strength of recall of Y-I, Y-C, and N tasks, respectively. Since 18 groups were employed, we have a total of six rotations or, in effect, six replications of the experiment.

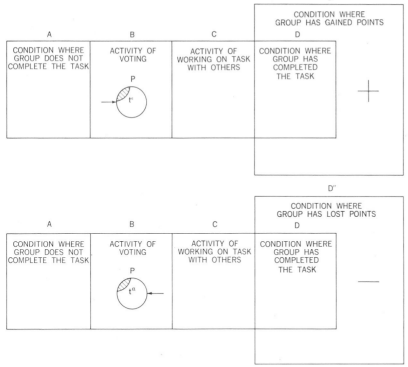

FIGURE 1*a*. The psychological situation of the member in case of a "yes" vote.
b. The psychological situation of the member in case of a "no" vote.

THEORY AND RESULTS

THE PSYCHOLOGICAL SITUATION OF THE GROUP MEMBER

The group goal for these competing teams can be characterized as "getting as many points as possible." This goal can be represented in a social space as a consummatory activity toward which the group is locomoting. If the group votes "yes," the path along which the group is acting may be represented as one in which the activity, "completing the task," is connected with the goal. If the group votes "no," the activity of "completing the task" is connected with a region of negative valence, namely, "losing points."

One can deal with these group activities entirely within a social space without reference to the life space of any individual member. Nevertheless, to the extent that the instructions and recruiting procedures of the present experiment were effective, we can say that each subject had a personal goal of seeing the group obtain the best possible score. Within

the individual's life space this goal can be represented as a state region [1] which can be designated, "condition where the group has gained points." Whether or not the person finds himself "carried" into this region of his life space depends in the present situation on events in the group or social space.

At the time of voting whether or not to complete the puzzle, the psychological situation of members who vote "yes" can be represented as in Figure 1*a*. This representation indicates that any one person so voting believes that he can locomote through activity region C, "working on the task with others," into the state region D, "condition where the group has completed the task." In view of the member's belief about the consequences of completing the task, region D is included in the region of positive valence, D, "condition where the group has gained points." The shaded region inside the person, *t* (ten-

---

[1] We follow Lewin here as opposed to Leeper (**10**) in coordinating states as well as activities to regions in the life space.

sion for completion), indicates the existence of a tension system corresponding to the person's desire to see the task completed. If the person enters the region of task-completion, D, the tension system, t^c, should be reduced.

Figure 1b represents the situation of members who vote "no." Here the person believes that entering region D will entail a loss of points. Therefore region D is included in a region of negative valence. The tension system, t^a (tension for avoidance), corresponds to the individual's desire to avoid completing the task. We hypothesize that tensions for avoidance are reduced where the person locomotes into a position which removes the possibility of his entering the region of negative valence. In the situation of the present experiment the direction of locomotion is irreversible after the first step along the path, and t^a should be reduced upon P's entering region A, "condition where the group does not complete the task."

The concept of a state region has been used in these representations to deal with the fact that if a group attains its goal, or in any other way changes its position within its social space, this event will produce a change in the member's position within his own space. Even though the member has been passive, and has taken no active part in the group's reaching its goal, he will have been "carried" by the group action into a new condition or state. State regions are distinguished from activity regions in that locomotion into or through the former depends, at least in part, on the person's being transported by some outside agent. In all other respects we assume that they have the same properties as activity regions.

TENSION SYSTEMS FOR GROUP GOALS AND AVOIDANCES

An individual may disagree with the group's decision to complete or to avoid a given task. For simplicity, however, we make the working assumption—which will be evaluated below —that following the announcement of the group decision members will tend to agree with the group about the desirability or undesirability of completing the task.

On this assumption, if the group sets a goal of task-completion, the corresponding state region of the member will tend to have a positive valence. The member will thus have a

tension system for completion which (a) will be reduced if the member is transported into the state region "condition where the group has completed the task" (experimental treatment Y-C) or (b) will remain in a state of tension if the member is not transported into this desired state region (treatment Y-I).

If the announced group decision is "no," we assume that in the subject's life space the region "condition where the group has completed the task" tends to have a negative valence, and that the member has an avoidance tension system which (a) will be reduced if the member is transported into the state region, "condition where the group has not completed the task," and there is no longer any possibility of the individual's being transported into the region of negative valence (treatment N), or (b) will remain in a state of tension if the member remains in a position from which it is possible that he will be transported into the region of negative valence (which might result if the group were told that they would return to tasks on which they had voted "no").[2]

These hypotheses assert that tensions are reduced for tasks in the Y-C and N treatments and that tensions are not reduced in the Y-I treatment. Assuming that the level of recall of tasks within a treatment is directly related to tension level, there follows:

Hypothesis 1.   % recall Y-I > % recall Y-C = % recall N.

Table 1 gives the data on recall of tasks for the three treatments, Y-I, Y-C, and N. The mean percentages of tasks recalled by the subjects in each of the six rotations are .559 for treatment Y-I, .444 for treatment Y-C, and .460 for treatment N. By analysis of variance into three components, the influence of treatments on strength of recall is found to be highly significant ($P < .01$). By t-tests we find that the mean recall score for Y-I tasks is significantly greater than either the mean recall

---

[2] No direct test was attempted for the hypothesis that avoidance tensions would remain unreduced if the group were told they would return to N tasks. It was feared that if the group were made to act against its expressed decision to halt work, the members would become skeptical of the genuineness of their power to make decisions. However, we show below that avoidance tensions remain unreduced where individuals desire to avoid a task but are moved toward task-completion by the action of the group.

TABLE 1. *Percentage of Tasks Recalled Under Three Different Experimental Treatments*

| | Treatment | | | | | | | | |
| | Y-C | | | Y-I | | | N | | |
Rotations	Total Tasks	Re-called	X (%)	Total Tasks	Re-called	X (%)	Total Tasks	Re-called	X (%)
1	75	35	.467	75	40	.533	75	31	.413
2	70	31	.443	70	35	.500	70	36	.514
3	75	33	.440	75	42	.560	75	35	.467
4	70	35	.500	70	41	.586	70	29	.414
5	75	32	.427	75	42	.560	75	38	.507
6	75	29	.387	65	40	.615	70	31	.443
Mean			.444			.559			.460

scores for Y-C tasks ($P < .01$) or for N tasks ($P < .01$). On the other hand, there is no statistically significant difference between the mean recall scores for Y-C and N tasks ($P = .59$). These results confirm the hypothesized relationships expressed in Hypothesis 1, above.

EFFECTS OF THE INTERACTION OF INDIVIDUAL AND GROUP DECISIONS ON TENSION SYSTEMS FOR GROUP GOALS

We made the working assumption above that members will tend to agree with the announced group decision. It is to be expected in some instances at least that members whose votes were opposed to announced results of the group voting would adhere to their original points of view.

Where a member's original vote is "yes," we designate this vote in combination with each of the three experimental treatments as y Y-C, y Y-I, and y N, respectively. Individual and group decisions are in agreement for the situations y Y-C and y Y-I, and we should expect as above that completion of the task will reduce tension systems for y Y-C tasks and that interruption of the task will leave the tension unreduced for y Y-I tasks. In situation y N, individual and group votes are in disagreement. If the person persists in holding to his own "yes" vote, his tension system for completion will remain unreduced where the group votes "no" and halts work. If, however, the individual "changes his mind," and accepts the judgment expressed by the group, then the avoidance tension which is aroused should be reduced by the group's halting work. On the

assumption that sometimes individuals will change their minds and sometimes not, tensions will sometimes be reduced in the y N situation and will sometimes remain unreduced. The level of recall of y N tasks should, therefore, be somewhere between recall of y Y-I tasks (where tension is not reduced) and recall of y Y-C tasks (where tension is reduced). This may be formulated as:

Hypothesis 2. % recall y Y-I > % recall y N > % recall y Y-C.

The percentages of tasks recalled are .560 for y Y-I tasks, .477 for y N tasks, and .412 for y Y-C tasks (Table 2), analysis of variance indicating that the influence of these situations upon recall is highly significant ($P < .001$). Testing pairs of means by the t-test, it is found that recall of y Y-I tasks exceeds the recall of both y N tasks ($P < .01$) and y Y-C tasks ($P < .001$). Recall of y N tasks, moreover, is greater than recall of y Y-C tasks ($P < .02$). The results confirm the relationships expressed in Hypothesis 2.

Turning now to the situation where the person's original vote is "no," the three possible situations are designated n Y-C, n Y-I, and n N. In situation n N, individual and group decisions are in agreement, and the avoidance tension coordinated to a "no" vote should be reduced by the group's stopping work. In situation n Y-C, if the individual persists in his personal vote of "no," the avoidance tension will not be reduced; for the task is completed by the group, and the individual is transported into the region he desires to avoid. If, on the other hand, this member accepts the group vote of "yes," the resulting tension system for completion will be reduced upon the group's

TABLE 2.   *Percentages of Tasks Recalled Under Situations y Y-I, y N, and y Y-C, Based on Pooled Data for All Individuals Within Each of Six Rotations*

	y Y-I			y-N			y Y-C		
Rotations	Total Tasks	Re-called	X (%)	Total Tasks	Re-called	X (%)	Total Tasks	Re-called	X (%)
1	53	27	.509	43	22	.512	48	18	.375
2	53	28	.528	44	21	.477	56	25	.446
3	55	32	.582	55	29	.527	54	22	.407
4	48	27	.562	48	19	.396	55	25	.454
5	63	36	.571	52	26	.500	54	23	.426
6	51	31	.608	56	25	.446	58	21	.362
Mean			.560			.476			.412

completing the task. Since, however, tension should not be reduced where the person rejects the group decision, the recall of tasks in situation *n Y-C* should be greater than recall of tasks in situation *n N*. In situation *n Y-I*, it is to be expected that tension systems will remain unreduced whether the person accepts or rejects the group vote. If the person adheres to his "no" vote, his avoidance tension will not be reduced, because treatment *Y-I* implies that it is still possible that the group will complete the task, transporting him into the region of negative valence. If the person accepts the group vote of "yes," interruption on the task prevents reduction of the tension for completion. With tensions remaining unreduced in both cases, recall of *n Y-I* tasks should exceed recall in either of the other two situations. This may be expressed as:

Hypothesis 3.   % recall *n Y-I* > % recall *n Y-C* > % recall *n N*.

Percentages of recall are .547 for *n Y-I* tasks, .525 for *n Y-C* tasks, and .427 for *n N* tasks

(Table 3). The results are in the predicted rank order, although analysis of variance applied to these data does not permit us to reject the null hypothesis ($P = .20$). The data give partial confirmation of the relationships involved in Hypothesis 3, but the recall of *n Y-C* tasks is unexpectedly high, approaching within two percentage points the level of recall for *n Y-I* tasks.

We shall present here an interpretation of the relatively high level of recall of *n Y-C* tasks, which it will be possible to test by additional data in the experiment. Both *n Y-C* and *y N* tasks, as we have noted, are characterized by disagreement between personal and group decisions. In both, our theory requires that tensions should be reduced if the person accepts the group vote which disagrees with his own; and, in both, tensions should not be reduced if the person rejects the group vote.

An analysis of situation *y N* is presented in Figure 2*a*. At Time 1, when the person casts his original vote, a tension system for task-completion exists, and a force is acting on the

TABLE 3.   *Percentages of Tasks Recalled Under Situations n Y-I, n Y-C, and n N, Based on Pooled Data for All Individuals Within Each of Six Rotations*

	n Y-I			n Y-C			n N		
Rotations	Total Tasks	Re-called	X (%)	Total Tasks	Re-called	X (%)	Total Tasks	Re-called	X (%)
1	22	13	.591	27	17	.630	32	9	.281
2	17	7	.412	14	6	.428	26	15	.577
3	20	10	.500	21	11	.524	20	6	.300
4	22	14	.636	15	10	.667	22	10	.454
5	12	6	.500	21	9	.428	23	12	.522
6	14	9	.643	17	8	.470	14	6	.428
Mean			.547			.524			.427

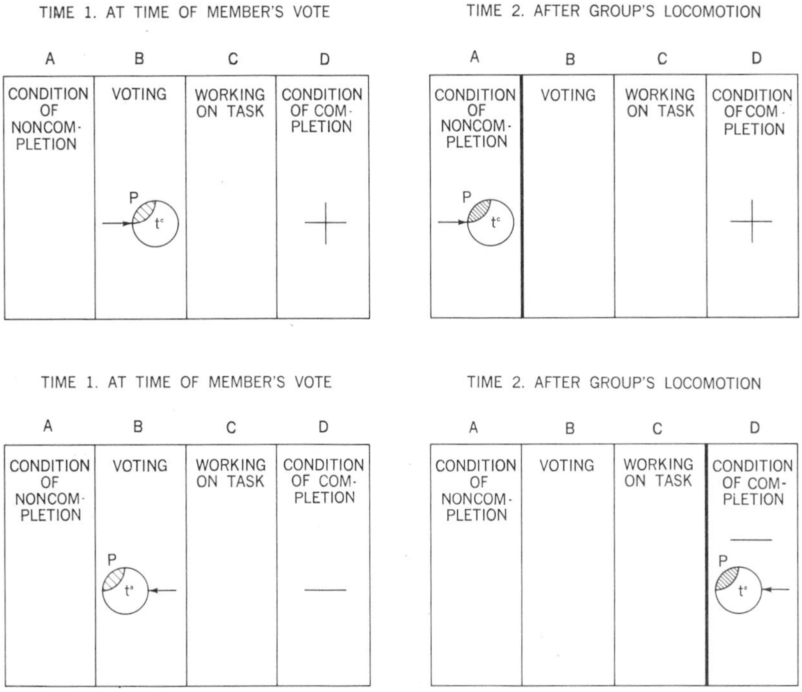

TIME 1. AT TIME OF MEMBER'S VOTE   TIME 2. AFTER GROUP'S LOCOMOTION

TIME 1. AT TIME OF MEMBER'S VOTE   TIME 2. AFTER GROUP'S LOCOMOTION

FIGURE 2a. The psychological situation of the member who votes "yes" and rejects the group vote of "no" (situation $y\ N$). Representation is based on Figure 1a. Region D' is omitted for economy of presentation. b. The psychological situation of the member who votes "no" and rejects the group vote of "yes" (situation $n\ Y\text{-}C$). Representation is based on Figure 1b. Region D'' is omitted for economy of presentation.

person in the direction of the positively valent region, "condition where the group has completed the task." At Time 2, the group has voted "no" and has halted work. This is conceptually equivalent to introducing an impassable barrier in the individual's life space, which blocks locomotion toward this goal. The significant feature of this situation for our purposes is that the person has not been moved closer to the goal as a result of the group action. There should, therefore, be no increase of the force acting on him by virtue of the goal-gradient effect (17). Indeed, we may regard the person as having been moved by the group to a greater psychological distance from the goal, in which case the force toward the goal will be decreased.

In situation $n\ Y\text{-}C$ there is a marked difference. Here the person wishes to avoid completing the task, but he is not merely blocked by the group action; he is coerced into working on the task "against his will." The conceptual analysis is presented in Figure 2b. At Time 1, when the member casts his original

"no" vote, there is a tension-system for task-avoidance. A force is acting on the person in the direction away from the region "condition where the group has completed the task," which is now represented as having a negative valence. The effect of the group's completing the task at Time 2 is to transport the person into this region of avoidance, after which he is blocked from leaving it by an impassable barrier (since in the present experiment the completed task cannot be undone). The feature of the situation we wish to stress here is that the person has been moved closer to—in fact, inside—the region of avoidance. By the goal-gradient hypothesis, the magnitude of an avoidant force increases steeply as the person approaches a region of avoidance. In consequence, the force *away* from region D should be greater in situation $n\ Y\text{-}C$ (Fig. 2b) than the force toward region D in situation $y\ N$ (Fig. 2a).

Lewin (12) presents evidence that where the person is in an "equilibrium" situation, i.e., an impassable barrier, there will be a rise in tension level. The amount of this rise is hypothesized to be directly related to the magnitude of the force acting on the person to locomote against the barrier. It follows that, if an individual rejects a group decision which conflicts with his own decision, there will be a greater rise in tension where the individual has voted "no" (situation *n Y-C*) than where the individual has voted "yes" (situation *y N*). Such a rise in tension would account for the relatively high level of recall in situation *n Y-C*.

ATTITUDES TOWARD DISAGREEMENT BETWEEN INDIVIDUAL AND GROUP DECISIONS

After the recall phase of the experiment, open-ended questionnaires were administered to determine whether different subjects had perceived the experimental situation in similar ways. Considerable uniformity appeared among responses to questions dealing with such matters as feelings of success or failure, views about the reasons for interruption of tasks, and desire to do well on the test. A variety of responses were given, however, to the questions, "In general, how did you feel when you voted 'no' and the group voted 'yes'?" and "In general, how did you feel when you voted 'yes' and the group voted 'no'?"

Some indicated that they consistently accepted or rejected group decisions different from their own. Others responded differentially according to whether the contrary group decision was "no" or "yes." Thus some individuals, who tended to stress the value of being cautious, indicated that they resolved disagreements between their own and the group's votes by adopting a "no" position. Individuals who stressed the value of being venturesome resolved disagreements by adopting a "yes" position. The result was that some individuals whose votes differed from the group's accepted group votes of "no" and rejected group votes of "yes," while some accepted group votes of "yes" and rejected group votes of "no."

The attitudes expressed toward group decisions which differed from their own were coded under four categories:

1. *Accept group decision.* Subject explicitly adopts the contrary group decision, disavowing his own, e.g., "The group knew best; I reconsidered and thought I was wrong; I guess I really wanted to do it anyway."

2. *Acquiesce in group decision.* Subject does not explicitly adopt the group decision but explicitly states his willingness to comply with the group action, e.g., "I tried my best even though my vote was different; it was O.K. with me if that's the way they wanted it."

3. *Reject group decision.* Subject does not state his willingness to comply with the group decision and discusses (*a*) his having disagreed with the group or (*b*) his continuing to disagree with the group.

4. *Fear group decision.* Subject indicates "anxiety" about complying with the group decision, e.g., "I felt I was a liability to the group; I didn't know how to contribute to the puzzle, and felt I had to try especially hard."

We assume that persons who *accept* a group decision which differs from their own change the valence, whether positive or negative, which they have originally attributed to completing the task. Persons who *acquiesce, reject,* or *fear* the contrary group decision are assumed to maintain the original valence of the task. Let us examine in more detail how each of these attitudes may be expected to influence tension systems in each type of experimental situation.

Situation y N. The member votes "yes," the group votes "no," and the work is halted. Thus, it follows:

1. If the person *accepts* the group decision, he develops a tension system for avoidance. The outcome—quitting work on the puzzle—reduces this tension system.

2. If the person *acquiesces* in the group decision, he maintains his original tension system for completion. Quitting work constitutes an impassable barrier to this goal, and this equilibrium condition should produce some rise in tension level.

3. If the person *rejects* the group decision his original tension system is maintained. This system is initially stronger than in the case of acquiescence. Like acquiescent persons, the rejective individual is in a condition of equilibrium, but since task-completion has a greater positive valence for the rejective person, the positive driving force acting upon him against the impassable barrier is greater. Rejection should, therefore, produce a greater rise in

tension than acquiescence. Both because of the greater original tension level and the greater expected rise in tension, persons who reject the group decision should have stronger tension systems than those who acquiesce.[3]

Transforming level of tension into percentage of tasks recalled, we obtain:

Hypothesis 4. % recall *y* N accept < % recall *y* N acquiesce < % recall *y* N reject.

The data of Table 4 confirm the predicted rank order. The mean percentages of tasks recalled are .292 for acceptant individuals, .424 for acquiescent individuals, and .574 for rejective individuals. Independently of the predicted rank order, the null hypothesis applied to these means, tested by an analysis of variance weighted for unequal size of groups, can be rejected at the .05 level of confidence.

Situation n Y-C. The person votes "no," the group votes "yes," and the task is completed. Thus, it follows:

1. If the person *accepts* the group decision, he develops a tension system coordinated to the group's completing the task. The outcome, completing the task, reduces this tension system.

2. If the person *acquiesces* in the group decision, he maintains his original tension system for avoidance. Completion by the group introduces an impassable barrier which blocks avoidant locomotion. A rise in level of tension should follow.

3. If the person *rejects* the group decision, the initial avoidance tension is assumed to be greater than in acquiescence. Again action by the group introduces an impassable barrier. The rise in tension should be greater here than in acquiescence, since the negative driving force away from completion is assumed to be greater.

4. If the person *fears* the group decision, the avoidance tension is assumed to be greatest. The negative driving force against the impassable barrier is likewise assumed to be greatest. Accordingly, the level of tension should be at a maximum.

Measuring tension level by recall, we have:

Hypothesis 5. % recall *n* Y-C accept < % recall *n* Y-C acquiesce < % recall *n* Y-C reject < % recall *n* Y-C fear.

The predicted rank order is confirmed in Table 4, the mean percentages of recall cor-

TABLE 4. *Mean Per Cent Recall of Tasks in Three Different Situations of Disagreement for Four Attitudes Toward Disagreement*

Situation		Attitude Toward Group Vote[a]			
		Accept	Acquiesce	Reject	Fearful
*y*N	Mean % recall for individuals	.292	.424	.574	
	Number of individuals	6	36	25	
n Y-C	Mean % recall	.167	.597	.660	.900
	Number of individuals[b]	10	32	12	5
n Y-I	Mean % recall	.467	.577	.667	.500
	Number of individuals	10	25	11	8

[a] Note that an individual's attitude toward a group vote of N may be independent of his attitude toward a group vote of Y, and conversely. A person, for example, may accept group N votes and reject group Y votes (see text).

[b] The corresponding scores for *n* Y-C and *n* Y-I are each based on the same class of subjects, namely, those with the specified attitudes toward group Y votes. Frequently, however, individuals were exposed to one or more *n* Y-C tasks and not to *n* Y-I tasks, and vice versa—hence the different frequencies of individuals in the same attitude column.

---

[3] The attitude of *fear* cannot occur in situation *y* N, since where the group halts work the person is not required to do anything with respect to which he feels inadequate.

responding to the terms of Hypothesis 5 being .167, .597, .661, .900, respectively. The differences among these means are significant at a high level of confidence ($P < .01$).

Situation n Y-I. The person votes "no," the group votes "yes," and the task is interrupted. Thus, it follows:

1. If the person *accepts* the group decision, he develops a tension system coordinated to the group's completing the task. Since the task is interrupted, this tension system remains unreduced. However, the tension level for these acceptant individuals is assumed to be relatively low.

2. If the person *acquiesces* in the group decision, he maintains his original tension system for avoiding work, which is at a higher level than the tension associated with acceptance. Moreover, the group action prior to the interruption transports the person closer to the region of negative valence, and the person is blocked from quitting the task, since he has been told that work will be resumed. Again, this condition of equilibrium should produce a rise in level of tension.

3. If the person *rejects* the group decision, the level of tension should be greater than in acquiescence (for the same reasons given in the discussion of *n Y-C* reject).

4. If the person *fears* the group decision, the level of tension should be greatest (for the same reasons given for *n Y-C* fear).

From these considerations we may propose:

Hypothesis 6. % recall *n Y-I* accept < % recall *n Y-I* acquiesce < % recall *n Y-I* reject < % recall *n Y-I* fear.

The rank order of the first three terms in Hypothesis 6 is predicted correctly (Table 4). However, the level of recall for *n Y-I* fear is lower than predicted. A possible explanation for this discrepancy may be suggested in terms of the partial reduction of avoidance tensions corresponding to feelings of relief in fearful persons that appear to occur when completion of the task is postponed.

FREQUENCY OF INDIVIDUAL AND GROUP DISAGREEMENT

Up to this point, we have examined a number of the ways by which motivational processes in the individual can be affected by group goal-setting and locomotion. The focus of treatment throughout has been in terms of goals or avoidances which members hold in relation to the group's completing or not completing a task.

In addition, it seems likely that group members would have another goal in this situation, namely, voting in such a way that they would be generally in agreement with their fellow members. The studies by Festinger *et al.* (4) indicate that groups induce pressures on members to conform to standards and ways of behaving which are relevant to group functioning and that deviants from these standards tend to be rejected by the group. Sherif's (20) work suggests that, particularly where the grounds for individual judgment are vague or ambiguous, individuals will want their judgments to be reinforced by "social reality."

The judgments which members were obliged to make in this situation were both relevant to the group's functioning and based on relatively vague criteria. We would therefore expect that concurrently with goals related to the task, members would want their own decisions to be in more or less general agreement with the group decisions. Members could tell on the basis of the announced group vote whether or not they were agreeing with the group. If the member found himself agreeing often enough, i.e., if the goal of being in agreement were reached, tension systems coordinated to this goal should be reduced. With "agreement" tensions reduced, one would expect no effects of these tension systems on "task" tensions. If the member finds himself in frequent disagreement with the group, however, the tension system corresponding to a desire for agreement should not be reduced. How does this affect tension systems for the group task?

Each subject voted 15 separate times, and found in the course of the experiment that group votes differed from his own votes with greater or lesser frequency. Subjects were exposed to the announcement of five group "no" votes and ten group "yes" votes. One would expect that persons who more frequently voted "no" would more frequently find themselves in opposition to the group. Paradoxically, however, a large number of disagreements with the group vote could arise because of the person's desire to agree with the group. If, for example, the announced group vote was "no" on a given puzzle, and the subject then voted "no" on the next puzzle, anticipating that the group would repeat its vote, the subject's own vote would necessarily be in disagreement, since the sub-

TABLE 5. *Comparison of Percentages of Recall of Agreements Versus Disagreements in Treatments Y-C, Y-I, and N, Based on Pooled Data for Groups of Individuals with Different Numbers of Total Disagreements*

Comparison	Total Number of Disagreements			
	5	6	7	8
(%n Y-C) − (%y Y-C)	(44.7 − 38.0)	(57.2 − 37.5)	(67.0 − 48.9)	(44.4 − 55.9)
Difference (%)	+ 6.7	+ 19.7	+ 18.1	− 11.5
(%n Y-I) − (%y Y-I)	(57.9 − 56.2)	(60.0 − 55.8)	(59.3 − 52.0)	(41.6 − 57.2)
Difference (%)	+ 1.7	+ 4.2	+ 7.3	− 15.6
(%y N) − (%n N)	(44.6 − 46.8)	(49.0 − 46.6)	(44.5 − 36.4)	(55.0 − 66.7)
Difference (%)	− 2.2	+ 2.4	+ 8.1	− 13.7
(% Total Disagr.) − (% Total Agr.)	(49.1 − 47.0)	(55.4 − 46.6)	(56.9 − 45.8)	(46.3 − 59.9)
Total Difference (%)	+ 2.1	+ 8.8	+ 11.1	− 13.6

sequent announcement was always "yes." We were, in fact, able to find no clear-cut relationship between a person's tendency to vote "yes" or "no" and the frequency with which group votes differed from his own votes. We can conclude that in general subjects had little control over the frequency of their disagreements.

As the number of their disagreements with the group became greater, however, several subjects could be observed to be losing their interest in the group tasks. They appeared, instead, to become concerned with whether the group votes were turning out the same as their own. After casting their votes, they would appear to await the announcement of the group vote with great expectancy. If the group vote agreed with their own, they would give evidences of feelings of satisfaction; if it turned out differently, they would show disappointment. In the postexperimental questionnaire, subjects who felt the group vote had differed from their own too frequently expressed a variety of doubts and misgivings about themselves, asking such questions as—"What's wrong with me? Am I a bad group member? Am I too different from the others?"

Most subjects found the announced group vote differed from their own votes from five to eight times over the 15 tasks. In examining the recall of tasks in relation to the number of such disagreements, it was noticed that with very frequent disagreements (a) recall appeared to diminish in certain cases where theoretically we would expect the presence of unreduced tension systems; (b) recall appeared to increase for tasks on which his own and group vote were in agreement. Such results seemed to have a prima-facie reasonableness

in terms of the qualitative observations reported above. For, if frequent disagreements with the group vote created a situation where members lost their task-orientation, then there should be no arousal of tension systems for the tasks. If the member in this situation now desired to be in agreement with the group, agreements would be experienced as rewards, and it might be expected that rewarded tasks will tend to be better remembered (3).

In order to determine whether effects of this sort were present in the data, tasks were grouped in Table 5 according to whether they had been worked on by individuals whose own votes had differed from the group vote five, six, seven, or eight times. For each of the three group treatments comparisons were then made of the percentages of tasks recalled where the individual's vote on the task had been the same as the group's and where the individual's vote had been different. The scores presented in Table 5 are the differences between these percentages. Friedman's (6) test is applied to these data because of heterogeneity of variance and indicates that frequency of disagreements significantly affects type of recall ($P < .02$). Where subjects differ from the group five, six, or seven times, disagreements are either about equally recalled or somewhat more frequently recalled than agreements. But where subjects differ on eight occasions, i.e., on over half the total votes cast, a sharp reversal occurs and the recall of agreements exceeds that of disagreements.

It seems plausible to interpret this phenomenon as reflecting a loss of task-orientation by subjects and the replacement of this with a new goal, namely, the goal of finding themselves in the condition of being in agreement with the group. However, to say that this goal of being in agreement with the group will lead subjects to recall agreements raises a difficult problem in terms of tension system theory. Agreement for these subjects represents the attainment of their goal; disagreement represents non-attainment. We would then have to say that subjects with the goal of being in agreement recall more finished tasks (i.e., agreements) than unfinished ones (i.e., disagreements).

A brief statement may be in order about a possible way of resolving this paradox. Within Lewinian theory tension systems may result in a person's attempting to locomote toward a goal, or, if the medium is fluid or more "irreal," some form of restructuring of the situation may occur. On the level of action, interruption of the task leaves the person with tendencies to resume locomotion (18). The Zeigarnik effect, according to Lewin (13), is based on the fact that where thinking is related to action the person tends to continue to think about the task which is to be resumed and that this will be reflected in increased recall. However, thinking about unfinished tasks is not functionally related to tension-reduction if the person feels unable to act, but feels obliged to *wish* for a satisfactory outcome. For it is likely that persons operating on a wish-level will obtain a greater measure of tension-reduction by thinking about successes (finished tasks) rather than failures (unfinished

tasks). This should manifest itself in tendencies to recall finished tasks by persons who feel unable actively to locomote to their goals —which is a possible interpretation of findings such as those of Rosenzweig's (19) with handicapped children.

In the present experiment, among those subjects who experienced frequent disagreements with the group, one would expect to find some, at least, who would be doubtful that action on their part could bring them into agreement. If, with frequent disagreements, they become discouraged about their ability to predict the group vote, they can only cast their votes and wait passively, *wishing* that the group vote will turn out the same as their own. The hypothesis that persons who are behaving on a wish-level will tend to recall finished tasks, will then account for the finding that these subjects recall more agreements than disagreements.

To test this interpretation of the results, one could design an experiment in which the only goal of the member is to vote in such a way that he will be in agreement with group vote. Recall of agreements and disagreements could then be compared in situations where the individual believes he can actively locomote toward this goal and where he believes he is unable actively to locomote. Theoretically, recall of agreements should exceed recall of disagreements in the latter case; disagreements should exceed agreements in the former case.[4]

SUMMARY

A method for conceptually treating the relations between individual and group goal-striving has been presented, and a technique for measuring individual motivation in relation to group goals has been described.

The conceptual treatment—within the framework of Lewin's topological and vector constructs—is designed to handle the fact that individuals may find themselves psychologically "carried" toward or away from goals, or toward or away from avoidances by the action of a group. The effects of the group action are represented in the individual's life space as locomotions by the person into or through state regions. Goals or avoidances which the individual holds for the *group* are represented as state regions with positive or negative valences, respectively.

The measurement technique employed is an adaptation of Zeigarnik's method of recall of interrupted tasks to the group situation. An experiment was designed in which a number of individuals worked together on a series of group tasks. Votes were taken on whether or not the individual desired the group to complete each task, and after these votes work on the tasks was either halted, partly completed, or fully completed. The major findings may be indicated as follows.

---

[4] This experiment has since been performed with positive results (8).

1. Tension systems can be aroused for goals which the individual holds for the group. If the individual accepts the group goal, tension is reduced where the group completes the task; tension is not reduced where the group activity is interrupted. Just as with tension systems for goals which the person holds for himself, these can be measured by the relative recall of finished versus unfinished group tasks.

2. Tension systems can be aroused for avoidances which the individual holds for the group. Avoidance tensions will be reduced if the possibility of the individual's being "carried" into the region of avoidance is removed; they will be unreduced if this possibility persists. It was shown that recall of tasks can be used to measure avoidance tensions as well as goal tensions.

3. A member's attitude toward disagreement between his own and group decisions will have systematic effects on the arousal and reduction of tension systems. The same person's attitudes toward group decisions which differ from his own may vary according to whether the group decision is to complete a task or to abandon it. Four attitudes affecting tension systems were distinguished, "acceptance," "acquiescence," "rejection," and "fearfulness," the latter arising only in cases where the group decision is to complete a task.

Where an individual votes "yes" (to complete a task), the consequence of a contrary group vote is that a barrier is interposed along the individual's path to the goal (frustration). Where the individual votes "no" (to avoid a task), the consequence of disagreeing with the group is that the person will be "carried" by the group toward the avoidance (coercion). The theoretical derivations that individuals will develop higher levels of tension in situations of coercion than in situations of frustration were confirmed.

4. Evidence was found for the interpretation that tension systems to be in agreement with other members exist concurrently with tension systems for the group task, and that frequent deviations from the group vote will leave tension for agreement unreduced. This *agreement* tension system tends to supplant *task* tension systems in deviant members.

References

1. Adler, D. L., & Kounin, J. S. Some factors operating at the moment of resumption of interrupted tasks. *Journal of Psychology,* 1939, **7**, 255–267.

2. Barnard, C. I. *The functions of the executive.* Cambridge, Mass.: Harvard Univ. Press, 1938.

3. Beebe-Center, J. G. *The psychology of pleasantness and unpleasantness.* New York: Van Nostrand, 1932.

4. Festinger, L. Informal social communication. *Psychological Review,* 1950, **57**, 271–282.

5. French, J. R. P., Jr. Group productivity. In H. Guetzkow (Ed.), *Groups, leadership, and men.* Pittsburgh: Carnegie Press, 1951.

6. Friedman, M. Use of ranks to avoid the assumption of normality implicit in the analysis of variance. *Journal of the American Statistical Association,* 1937, **32**, 675–701.

7. Homans, G. C. *The human group.* New York: Harcourt, Brace, 1950.

8. Horwitz, M., & Lee, F. J. Effects of decision-making by group members on recall of finished and unfinished tasks. *Journal of Abnormal and Social Psychology,* 1954, **49**, 201–210.

9. Katz, D. Morale and motivation in industry. In W. Dennis (Ed.), *Current trends in industrial psychology.* Pittsburgh: Univ. of Pittsburgh, 1949.

10. Leeper, R. *Lewin's topological and vector psychology.* Eugene: Univ. of Oregon, 1943.

11. Lewin, K. *Principles of topological psychology.* New York: McGraw-Hill, 1936.

12. Lewin, K. The conceptual representation and the measurement of psychological forces. *Contributions to psychological theory,* 1938, **1** (4).

13. Lewin, K. *Field theory in social science.* New York: Harper, 1951.

14. Lewis, H. B. An experimental study of the role of the ego in work. I. The role of the ego in cooperative work. *Journal of Experimental Psychology,* 1944, **34,** 113–127.

15. Lewis, H. B., & Franklin, M. An experimental study of the role of the ego in work. II. The significance of task orientation in work. *Journal of Experimental Psychology,* 1944, **34,** 194–215.

16. Lippitt, R. An experimental study of authoritarian and democratic group atmospheres. *Univ. of Iowa Studies in Child Welfare,* 1940, **16** (3), 43–195.

17. Miller, N. E. Experimental studies of conflict. In J. McV. Hunt (Ed.), *Personality and the behavior disorders.* New York: Ronald Press, 1944.

18. Ovsiankina, M. Die Wiederaufnahme unterbrochener Handlungen. *Psychologische Forschung,* 1928, **11,** 302–379.

19. Rosenzweig, S. The recall of finished and unfinished tasks as affected by the purpose with which they were performed. *Psychological Bulletin,* 1933, **30,** 698.

20. Sherif, M. *The psychology of social norms.* New York: Harper, 1936.

21. Sherif, M., & Cantril, H. *The psychology of ego-involvements.* New York: Wiley, 1947.

22. Zeigarnik, Bluma. Das Behalten erledigter Handlungen. *Psychologische Forschung,* 1927, **9,** 1–85.

35

The Effects of Cooperation and Competition upon Group Process

MORTON DEUTSCH

The concept of *cooperation* and the interrelated concept of *competition* are rarely missing in discussions of interpersonal and intergroup relations. Implicitly, they play a key role in the writings of many social theorists. Yet, despite the obvious significance of these concepts for the understanding and control of social process, there has been little in the way of explicit theorizing and virtually no experimental work with respect to the effects of cooperation and competition upon social process. The work in this area has largely been concerned with the effects of the individual's motivation to achieve under the two different conditions. None of the experimental studies has investigated the interactions between individuals, the group process that emerges as a consequence of the cooperative or competitive social situation.

The purpose of this article is to sketch out a theory of the effects of cooperation and competition upon small (face-to-face) group functioning and to present the results of an experimental study of such effects.

PART I. A CONCEPTUALIZATION OF THE COOPERATIVE AND COMPETITIVE SITUATIONS WITH A DEVELOPMENT OF SOME OF ITS LOGICAL AND PSYCHOLOGICAL IMPLICATIONS

In a *cooperative social situation* the goals for the individuals or subunits in the situation under consideration have the following characteristics: the goal regions for each of the individuals or subunits in the situation are defined so that a goal region can be entered (to some degree) by any given individual or subunit only if all the individuals or

This chapter is a condensation of two separate articles. The reader is referred to the original articles for more complete treatment: *Human Relations*, 1949, **2**, 129–152 and 199–231. This material is reprinted by permission of the author and of *Human Relations*.

subunits under consideration can also enter their respective goal regions (to some degree). For convenience's sake, the phrase *promotively interdependent goals* will be used to identify any situation in which the individuals or subunits composing it have their goals interrelated by the characteristic defined above.

In a *competitive social situation* the goals for the individuals or subunits in the situation under consideration have the following characteristic: the goal regions for each of the individuals or subunits in the situation are defined so that, if a goal region is entered by any individual or subunit (or by any given portion of the individuals or subunits under consideration), the other individuals or subunits will to some degree, be unable to reach their respective goals in the social situation under consideration. For convenience's sake, the phrase *contriently interdependent goals* will be used to identify any situation in which the individuals or subunits composing it have their goals interrelated by the characteristic defined immediately above.

It should, perhaps, be noted that there are probably very few, if any, real-life situations which, according to the definitions offered above, are "purely" cooperative or competitive. Most situations of everyday life involve a complex set of goals and subgoals. Consequently, it is possible for individuals to be promotively interdependent with respect to one goal and contriently interdependent with respect to another goal. Thus, for example, the members of a basketball team may be cooperatively interrelated with respect to winning the game but competitively interrelated with respect to being the "star" of the team.

It is also rather common for people to be promotively interdependent with respect to subgoals and contriently interdependent with respect to goals, or vice versa. For instance, advertising concerns representing different cigarette companies may be cooperatively interrelated with respect to the subgoal of increasing the general consumption of cigarettes but competitively interrelated with respect to the goal of increasing both the relative and absolute sales of a specific brand of cigarette.

No attempt will be made here to describe and analyze further the wide variety of "impure" cooperative and competitive situations which are found in everyday life. The theoretical development to be presented will be primarily concerned with "pure" cooperative and competitive situations. However, it is believed that in many circumstances not much theoretical extrapolation is necessary to handle the more complex situations.

From the definitions of promotively and contriently interdependent goals, it appears to follow that (a) any person, X, who has promotively interdependent goals with persons A, B, C, etc., will come to have promotively interdependent locomotions in the direction of his goal with persons A, B, C, etc.; (b) any person, Y, who has contriently interdependent goals with persons A, B, C, etc., will come to have contriently interdependent locomotions in the direction of his goal with persons A, B, C, etc.

The above statements are based on the following considerations. Locomotion in the direction of the goal, from any point not in the goal region, may be thought of as a condition for entry into the goal region. Entry into the goal region may be thought of as a part of locomotion in the direction of the goal, entry being the final step in locomotion. It follows that a locomotion by X or Y in the direction of his goal can be considered to be promotively or contriently interdependent with the locomotions of A, B, C, etc., in the direction of their goals, the nature of the interdependence with respect to locomotions depending upon the nature of the interdependence with respect to goal regions.

Several major differences reveal themselves as inherent in the distinctions between the cooperative and competitive social situations. The analysis of the cooperative situation reveals that all the individuals in such a setting occupy the same relative positions with respect to their goals. If any one individual locomotes, the others must also locomote in the same direction. In the competitive situations, the various individuals may occupy the same or different positions with respect to their goals. Locomotion by any individual has no necessary effect on the locomotions of others, though it may affect the relative positions of the various individuals.

Up to this point we have stated some of the consequences logically inherent in the conceptualizations of simple cooperative and competitive situations. No statements have been made which have a direct psychological reference, i.e., a reference in terms of individual life spaces. The statements have had reference only to an objectively defined social space.

The next step called for is to derive psychological implications from these statements by introducing additional psychological assumptions which will somehow relate these statements about events in objective social space to events in individual life spaces. It should be apparent that very complex assumptions are required to make any rigorously derived predictions about behavior from an analysis of the characteristics of an objective social situation. However, as this problem relates to the specific conditions of the experiment to be reported here, we shall make the relatively simple assumption that the perceptions and expectations of an individual are likely to be veridical to his environment if he has had enough experience with the situation, if he has intelligence, and if the situation is simple enough.

We may now proceed to state certain specific hypotheses.

BASIC HYPOTHESES

Hypothesis 1. Individuals who are exposed to the cooperative social situation (*Indiv coop*) will perceive themselves to be more promotively interdependent (in relation to the other individuals composing their group) with respect to goal, locomotions, facilitations, and similar matters, than will individuals who are exposed to the competitive social situation (*Indiv comp*).

Hypothesis 1a. *Indiv comp* will perceive themselves to be more contriently interdependent (in relation to the other individuals composing their group) with respect to such matters as goal, locomotions, and facilitations than will *Indiv coop*.

For convenience's sake, let us direct our attention to the psychological implications of locomotion in the cooperative and the competitive situations. Let us analyze a hypothetical instance with respect to locomotion in the direction of the goal, in which A locomotes in the direction of his goal and the other individuals in the social situation perceive that A is locomoting.

The Cooperative Situation. Under these conditions X would be likely to perceive that he has locomoted toward his goal as a consequence of A's actions. Several implications seem directly to follow, if we accept certain additional psychological assumptions:

Substitutability. Since X has locomoted toward his goal as a consequence of A's actions, there is no longer any necessity for X to perform any action which is similar to A's.

Positive cathexis. If we make a rather widely accepted assumption that an entity will acquire positive valence or cathexis if that entity is seen to be promotively related to need satisfaction, it is possible to derive that A's action (which results in locomotion in the direction of the goal) will be positively cathected by X. That is, X is likely to accept, like, or reward A's action.

Positive inducibility. Let us assume that inducibility derives from the fact that the inducible person perceives the inducing entity to be such that it can cause the intensification, continued persistence, or lowering of need tension within himself. Positive inducibility [1] occurs when the inducing entity is seen to be promotive rather than contrient with respect to tension reduction (or when the inducing entity is seen as capable of producing even more tension than before).

Making the above assumption, one can derive that X will stand in the relationship of positive inducibility to A insofar as A's action contributes towards X's locomotion in the direction of his goal.

Facilitations and hinderings. If X facilitates the locomotion of A in the direction of his goal, he also facilitates his own locomotion. Thus, X's facilitations of others are likely to result in his own locomotion and therefore are also likely to result in tension reduction with respect to that locomotion. His own actions of facilitation (helpfulness) will become positively cathected and will be likely to be manifested in appropriate situations. By similar reasoning, we conclude that acts hindering locomotion in the direction of the goal (obstructiveness) will be negatively cathected and will be avoided.

The Competitive Situation. Under conditions of competition essentially opposite conclusions to those above are to be drawn:

Substitutability. It is evident that there will be no substitutability.

Negative cathexis. The assumption here is parallel to that made in deriving positive ca-

---

[1] Positive inducibility is meant to include two related phenomena, (*a*) the production of additional *own* forces in the direction induced, and (*b*) the channeling of existing *own* forces in the direction induced.

thexis. An entity will acquire negative cathexis if that entity is seen to be contriently related to need satisfaction (and therefore is seen to decrease the probability of need satisfaction). A's locomotions in the direction of his goal will, therefore, be negatively cathected by Y.

Negative inducibility. Assuming that negative inducibility [2] occurs when the inducing entity is seen as contrient with respect to tension reduction, one can derive that Y will stand in the relationship of negative inducibility to A insofar as A's actions lead to locomotions by A which decrease Y's probability of reaching his goal. However, another factor, cognitive in nature, may come into play, making Y's relation to B one of ambivalence or noninducibility—the cognition that going in a direction opposite to or away from A's would be going in a direction opposite to or away from his own goal.

Facilitations and hinderings. When others locomote in the direction of the goal, helpfulness will become negatively cathected, obstructiveness positively cathected. The converse should be true for locomotion in a direction opposite to that of the goal.

We can, with the same kinds of assumptions, analyze a hypothetical instance in which B locomotes in a direction away from his goal. Without detailing the analysis, it is evident that in the cooperative situation, substitutability is not expected, but one would expect negative cathexis and negative inducibility. The competitive situation is not so unequivocal. Here one would expect positive cathexis and ambivalent inducibility or noninducibility.

Our statements about substitutability, cathexis, inducibility, and helpfulness are somewhat different in the two social situations, depending upon whether locomotions are made in the direction of the goal or away from it. To test the theory experimentally, it is necessary, therefore, to make some assumption about the incidence of these two directions of locomotion. We assume that, under the experimental conditions set up to test the theory, in both social situations there will be more locomotions in the direction of the goal than in a direction away from the goal. From this assumption and the foregoing analysis it is

possible to assert the following hypotheses:

Hypothesis 2. There will be greater substitutability for similarly intended actions among *Indiv coop* as contrasted with *Indiv comp*.

Hypothesis 3. There will be a larger percentage of actions by fellow members positively cathected by *Indiv coop* than by *Indiv comp*.

Hypothesis 3a. There will be a larger percentage of actions by fellow members negatively cathected by *Indiv comp* than by *Indiv coop*.

Hypothesis 4. There will be greater positive inducibility with respect to fellow members among *Indiv coop* than among *Indiv comp*.

Hypothesis 4a. There will be greater internal (self) conflict among *Indiv comp* than among *Indiv coop*.

Hypothesis 5. There will be more helpfulness towards one another among *Indiv coop* than among *Indiv comp*.

Hypothesis 5a. There will be more obstructiveness towards one another among *Indiv comp* than among *Indiv coop*.

IMPLICATIONS FOR GROUP FUNCTIONING

Let us turn now to the next step, that of applying some of the psychological implications of the hypotheses derived in the preceding section to the functioning of small face-to-face groups.

Organization. From Hypothesis 4 (positive inducibility), it seems evident that one would expect greater coordination of effort, as well as more frequent interrelationship of activity, among *Indiv coop* than among *Indiv comp*.

Hypothesis 6. At any given time there will be more coordination of efforts (working together, interrelation of activities) among *Indiv coop* than among *Indiv comp*.

Hypothesis 6a. Over a period of time, there will be more frequent coordination of efforts among *Indiv coop* than among *Indiv comp*.

If we assume that the individuals composing the various groups in both the cooperative and competitive situations differ from one another with respect to ability or personal inclinations to contribute, it is possible from the substitutability hypothesis (Hyp. 2) to derive the following.

[2] Negative inducibility is meant to include two related phenomena: (*a*) the production of additional *own* forces and (*b*) channeling existing *own* forces in the direction opposite to that desired by the inducer.

Hypothesis 7. There will be more homogeneity with respect to amount of contributions or participations among *Indiv comp* than among *Indiv coop.*

The above hypothesis follows from the consideration that the contribution of an *Indiv coop* can substitute for similarly intended contributions by another *Indiv coop.* This does not hold for *Indiv comp.* In the cooperative situation, if any individual has ability and contributes, there is less need for another individual to contribute, producing greater heterogeneity in amount of contributions.

Making the same kinds of assumptions as above, plus the additional ones that the individuals comprising the various groups differ in respect to either ability, interest, or both, in performing the various functions necessary for successful task completion, it is possible from the substitutability hypothesis to derive:

Hypothesis 8. There will be greater specialization of function (i.e., different individuals fulfilling different functions) among *Indiv coop* than among *Indiv comp.*

If we assume some time or achievement pressure, from the substitutability hypothesis it is also possible to derive:

Hypothesis 9. There will be greater specialization with respect to content or activity (i.e., different individuals taking different aspects of the task and working on them simultaneously) among *Indiv coop* than among *Indiv comp.*

The structure of certain kinds of tasks makes it extremely difficult for this type of specialization to take place. Thus, one would expect fewer differences between *Indiv coop* and *Indiv comp* on some tasks than on others.

If specialization of function occurs, and we assume that expectations are established as a result of this specialization and that these expectations act as a determinant of behavior, we would expect:

Hypothesis 10. There will be greater structural stability (from like situation to like situation) with respect to functions assumed among *Indiv coop* than among *Indiv comp.* This difference will increase with time.

From the lack of substitutability among *Indiv comp* one can derive a rigidity, each individual always trying to fulfill all the functions. Stability of structure among *Indiv coop* may result in some perseverance but there does not seem to be any reason to equate rigidity and stability.

Hypothesis 11. In the face of changing circumstances, more organizational flexibility (change of roles to adapt to circumstances) will be manifested among *Indiv coop* than among *Indiv comp.*

Motivation. From the hypothesis about positive inducibility one can expect:

Hypothesis 12. The direction of the forces operating on *Indiv coop* will be more similar than the direction of the forces operating on *Indiv comp.*

From this hypothesis one would expect more rapid locomotions, i.e., more rapid decisions and reaching of agreements by cooperative groups. Another point to be considered here is that of the frame of reference with respect to locomotion in the cooperative and competitive situations. In the latter situation, the individual is oriented to locomotions relative to those of other individuals with whom he is competing; in the cooperative situation, meaningful locomotion units are defined in relation to task completion. One can therefore expect:

Hypothesis 13. The directions of the forces on *Indiv coop* will be more toward task closure than will the forces on *Indiv comp*, i.e., there is more achievement pressure on *Indiv coop.*

From the hypothesis of positive inducibility we can assert that a force of any *Indiv coop* is likely to be paralleled by a force on other *Indiv coop.* Thus, if we define *group* motivation as some complex function of the strength of forces that operate simultaneously on all individuals in the group, there follows:

Hypothesis 14. The group force in the direction of the goal in a cooperative group will be stronger than such a group force in a competitive group.

From positive inducibility we would expect more additional own forces to be induced on *Indiv coop* once he is exposed to induction by other members. In the competitive situation, due to combined negative and positive induction, one would also expect the production of additional own forces. If to the concept of the sum of the strength of forces operating on an individual we coordinate interest, or involvement, there does not seem to be any clear-cut rationale for predicting differences between the situations.

Hypothesis 15. There will not be a significant difference in the total strength of the forces (interest, involvement) operating on *Indiv coop* and *Indiv comp.*

Communication. From the substitutability hypothesis and the additional assumptions that (*a*) it is perceived that locomotion takes place either through the utterance of many good ideas, i.e., the production of many signs that will be evaluated highly, or through the frequent persuasion or informing of others via communication; (*b*) quantitative efforts do not seriously interfere with quality or that, if they do, quantity is seen to be as important as or more important than quality; and (*c*) the time available allows for more production of signs than are necessary for optimal solution of any problem, it is possible to derive:

Hypothesis 16. When the task structure is such that production in quantity of observable signs is perceived to be a means for locomotion, there will be a greater total of signs produced per unit of time by *Indiv comp* than by *Indiv coop.*

From the hypothesis about the coordination of effort in tasks (Hyps. 6 and 6a), one would expect:

Hypothesis 17. When the task structure is such that locomotion is possible without the production of observable signs, there will be a greater total production of such signs per unit time by *Indiv coop* than by *Indiv comp.*

If from the communicator's point of view communication can be considered a locomotion or a means of locomotion, the state of receptivity, i.e., the readiness to be aroused, in the communicatee can potentially facilitate or hinder the locomotions of the communicator. From the hypotheses concerning helpfulness and obstructiveness (Hyps. 5 and 5a) one can derive:

Hypothesis 18. There will be less attentiveness to one another's productions of signs among *Indiv comp* than among *Indiv coop.*

If attentiveness is a condition for the arousing of common significata, there follows:

Hypothesis 19. The production of signs will less frequently result in common significata among *Indiv comp* than among *Indiv coop.*

Even when attentiveness is present, there probably will be a greater likelihood of distortion by communicatees in the competitive situation, since in this situation locomotion is likely to be perceived in terms of its effect on relative position, while in the cooperative situation the locomotion of any individual is likely to be perceived as resulting in the locomotion of the others. The consequence of this difference is that the expressive characteristics of the production of signs are likely to be more significant to *Indiv comp.* A sign if expressive if the fact of its production is itself a sign to its interpreter of something about the producer of the sign.

Hypothesis 20. Common signification, even when attentiveness is optimal, will be less prevalent among *Indiv comp* than *Indiv coop.*

From the hypothesis of positive inducibility, there follows directly:

Hypothesis 21. There will be more common appraisals (mutual agreements and acceptances) of communications by communicators and communicatees among *Indiv coop* than among *Indiv comp.*

Orientation. From the hypothesis about communication, one can assert:

Hypothesis 22. Indiv coop will have more knowledge about other active members than will *Indiv comp.*

Group orientation, as we define it, exists to the extent that there is commonality of perception among the members. It can be assessed in relation to goals, position at a given time, direction to the goal, or steps in the path to the goal. From the hypotheses concerning communication and positive inducibility, one can derive:

Hypothesis 23. There will be more group orientation among *Indiv coop* than among *Indiv comp.*

Group Productivity. From the hypothesis with respect to strength of group motivation (Hyp. 14), assuming that locomotion will proceed more rapidly the stronger the motivation, one can derive:

Hypothesis 24. Indiv coop as a group will produce more per unit of time than will *Indiv comp* as a group.

Hypothesis 24a. It will take less time for *Indiv coop* as a group to produce what *Indiv comp* as a group produce.

Let us assume that any or all of the following are negatively related to group productivity in respect to quality of product: lack of group orientation. We can then derive:

Hypothesis 25. The qualitative productivity of *Indiv coop* as a group will be higher than that of *Indiv comp* as a group.

From the hypotheses about communication and about positive inducibility, with the additional assumption that the individuals in the various groups have information and experience that can benefit the others, it is possible to derive:

Hypothesis 26. Indiv coop will learn more from one another than will *Indiv comp.* (The more knowledgeable and experienced of *Indiv coop* will, of course, learn less than the not so well informed *Indiv coop.*)

Interpersonal Relations. From the hypotheses about cathexis (Hyps. 3 and 3a), we expect the actions of fellow members to be more positively cathected among *Indiv coop* than among *Indiv comp.* We also expect the perceived source of these actions to acquire, to some extent, a cathexis similar to that held with respect to the actions. Thus, there follows:

Hypothesis 27. There will be more friendliness among *Indiv coop* than among *Indiv comp.*

By similar reasoning, it follows that the cathexis will be generalized to the products of the joint actions of fellow members and oneself, i.e., the group products. Thus, we propose:

Hypothesis 28. The group products will be evaluated more highly by *Indiv coop* than by *Indiv comp.*

If we define *group functions* as any actions which are intended to increase the solidarity of the group, or to maintain and regulate the group so that it functions smoothly, and assert that group functions are seen to be helpful, from the hypothesis about helpfulness (Hyp. 5a) there follows:

Hypothesis 29. There will be a greater percentage of group functions among *Indiv coop* than among *Indiv comp.*

If we define *individual functions* as any actions of the individual which are not immediately directed toward task solution and which are not group functions (actions which are obstructive, blocking, aggressive, or self-defensive are individual functions), from the hypothesis about obstructiveness (Hyp. 5a) there follows:

Hypothesis 30. There will be a greater percentage of individual functions among *Indiv comp* than among *Indiv coop.*

From the hypothesis concerning communication, it was developed (Hyp. 22) that over a period of time *Indiv coop* should know more than *Indiv comp* about the attitudes of (active) fellow members. Using the same reasoning, and making the assumption that the communication difficulty with respect to this content is also greater for *Indiv comp,* there follows:

Hypothesis 31. The perception of the attitudes of the others towards aspects of one's own functioning in the group by *Indiv coop* should be more realistic than such perceptions by *Indiv comp.*

From the hypothesis about inducibility, there also follows:

Hypothesis 32. The attitudes of any individual with respect to his own functioning should be more similar to the attitudes of the others with respect to his functioning among *Indiv coop* than among *Indiv comp.*

From Hypothesis 31 and the hypothesis about cathexis, we can derive with respect to *Indiv coop* that he has a favorable effect on the others in the group. If we make the assumption of *autistic hostility,* that is, that hostile impulses under conditions of reduced communication tend to create the expectation of counter-hostility, we can demonstrate:

Hypothesis 33. Indiv coop will perceive himself as having more favorable effects on fellow members than will *Indiv comp.*

The term *attitude of the generalized other* refers to an internalized structure which is developed as a result of introjecting the mutually interacting attitudes of those with whom one is commonly engaged in a social process. From our preceding discussion, it is clear that the development of the attitude of the generalized other requires communication and positive inducibility. There follows, then:

Hypothesis 34. Incorporation of the attitude of the generalized other will occur to a greater extent in *Indiv coop* than in *Indiv comp.*

For present purposes, the *feeling of obligation* to other members will be taken as an operational definition of the degree of internalized attitude of the generalized other.

The Concept of Group. In concluding this theoretical analysis, let us suggest a linkage between the conceptualization of the cooperative situation and the concept of *group.* We propose a linkage similar to certain proposals of Koffka (3) and Barnard (1).

We present the following definitions:

1. A sociological group exists (has unity) to the extent that the individuals composing it are pursuing promotively interdependent goals.

2. A psychological group exists (has unity) to the extent that the individuals composing it perceive themselves as pursuing promotively interdependent goals.

3. A psychological group has cohesiveness as a direct function of the strength of goals perceived to be promotively interdependent and of the degree of perceived interdependence.

The following definitions are reformulations of the above definitions from the point of view of membership:

1a. Individuals or subunits belong in a sociological group to the extent that they are pursuing promotively interdependent goals.

2a. Individuals or subunits possess membership in a psychological group to the extent that they perceive themselves as pursuing promotively interdependent goals.

3a. Individuals or subunits possess membership motive in a psychological group as a direct function of the strength of goals perceived to be promotively interdependent and of the degree of perceived interdependence.

The conceptualization of the cooperative situation is, of course, identical with the definition of social group. It follows that if *Indiv coop* and *Indiv comp* are equated in other respects, *Indiv coop* will possess more unity as a sociological group than will *Indiv comp.* From the logical and psychological considerations advanced above it also follows that *Indiv coop* will possess more unity as a psychological group than will *Indiv comp.* Since all our hypotheses are relative statements based on the assumption that *Indiv coop* and *Indiv comp* are equated in other respects, it is possible to substitute for *Indiv coop* the phrase *a psychological group with greater unity* and to substitute for *Indiv comp* the phrase *a psychological group with lesser unity.*

PART II. AN EXPERIMENTAL STUDY OF THE EFFECTS OF COOPERATION AND COMPETITION UPON GROUP PROCESS

THE EXPERIMENTAL DESIGN

In setting up the experiment to test the hypotheses it was necessary to have the following: (*a*) intelligent and reasonably well adjusted subjects who would regularly attend experimental sessions over a period of time; (*b*) some degree of control over the goals the subjects strove for (to be able, through manipulations of these goals, to place the subjects in cooperative or competitive situations); and (*c*) a readily observable situation.

The somewhat unorthodox Introductory Psychology course offered by the Industrial Relations Section at the Massachusetts Institute of Technology appeared to provide the needed conditions. Through the excellent cooperation of the Industrial Relations Section, it became possible to make the experimental sessions an integral part of the course. Regular attendance was thus assured. The experimenter-instructor's control over grades and assignments also provided the needed degree of control over the goals of the subjects.

At the first meeting of the various sections, it was announced that the department was interested in doing research on the course and wanted to form some small sections to be composed of five students and one instructor. These sections would meet once weekly as a substitute for the regularly scheduled three one-hour meetings. Nothing was stated about the research except that it had the purpose of improving the course. Volunteers were requested and over 50 were obtained, which was more than enough. The volunteers were then formed into 10 tentative groups on the basis of their available meeting times. Though this very much limited the possibility of matching personalities as well as groups, some flexibility still remained because of the large overlappings of time schedules.

All the volunteers were administered the following tests: The A-S Reaction Study, Wide Range Vocabulary Test, and the University of California ideology questionnaires. On the basis of these tests and other face-sheet data about the individuals, the most deviant students were eliminated as subjects. The time schedules of the remaining subjects did not allow for further shifting of subjects from group to group.

The next step was to match pairs of groups. Each group, at its first meeting together, was told, "You are to be constituted as a board of human relations experts. As experts, each week you will be presented a human relations problem. Your job is to analyze and discuss the problem and to formulate, in letter form, some written recommendations." They were then given a human relations problem having to do with a question of discipline in a children's camp. A total of 50 minutes for the discussion and writing of recommendations was allowed. Each of the groups was rated by the experimenter on a nine-point scale in terms of the productivity of their discussion of the problem. Groups were then paired off in terms of these ratings, and by a random procedure one of each pair was assigned to the cooperative treatment and the other to the competitive treatment.

EXPERIMENTAL PROCEDURES

Instructions designed to produce the cooperative or the competitive situation were given at the beginning of the second meeting to the appropriate groups. The two sets of instructions are presented below.[3]

Instructions to Cooperative Groups

Puzzle Problems. Every week you will be given a puzzle to solve as a group. These puzzles are, in effect, tests of your ability to do clear, logical thinking as a group. Your effectiveness in handling the problem will be evaluated by ranking you as a group in comparison with four other groups who will also tackle the same problems. Each of the five groups will be ranked. The group that works together most effectively will receive a rank of 1, the next most effective group will receive a rank of 2, the least effective group will receive a rank of 5. The ranks that each group receives on the weekly problems will be averaged. At the end of it all, we should be able to have a pretty good picture of each group's ability to do clear, logical thinking.

To motivate you to contribute your best efforts, we will have a reward. The group that comes out with the best average will be excused from one term paper and will receive an automatic *H* for that paper. That is, if your group receives the highest rank, all of you will receive an automatic *H*.[4]

You are to come out with one solution as a group. When you have decided as a group that you have reached a solution, let me know by handing me your answer written on this answer sheet.

Human Relations Problems. There are two principal factors determining your grade for this

course: (*a*) the discussions in class of the human relations problems and (*b*) the papers you hand in periodically.

Your grade for the discussions in class will be determined in the following manner:

Each week the plans or recommendations that the group comes out with as a result of discussion will be judged and evaluated by ranking them in comparison with the efforts of four other similar groups. The group whose discussions and recommendations are judged to be best (in terms of both quality and quantity of ideas) will receive a rank of 1, the next best group a rank of 2, and so on; the worst group will receive a rank of 5.

Every member of the group will be given the rank that his group receives. That is, all members of a group will receive the same rank, the rank being determined by how good their group discussions and recommendations are.

The ranks that are received weekly will be averaged and used in making up that part of the grade which is based on class discussion.

Thus, in effect, you are to consider the discussions of these human relations problems presented to you weekly as a test in which your group rank or grade is determined by your ability to effectively apply insight to these problems. Remember, the group whose discussions and recommendations are best in quality and quantity will get the highest grade; the group whose discussions and recommendations are worst will get the lowest grade.

In this meeting, as in all the other meetings, you will consider yourself to be a board of human relations experts. As such, you have been presented with the following problem which I will read to you. You may glance at your copies of the problem as I read, if you wish to do so. (*The problem was then read by the experimenter.*)

You will be allowed a total of 50 minutes for both the discussion and the writing of recommendations. You are to write your recommendations in letter style, on this form which I have provided.

You will be notified when you have only 20 minutes, 10 minutes, and 5 minutes left.

Instructions to Competitive Groups

Puzzle Problems. Every week you will be given a puzzle to solve as a group. These puzzles are, in effect, tests of your individual abilities to do clear, logical thinking. The contributions that each of you make to solving the weekly puzzle will be ranked, so that the person who contributes most to the solution will receive a rank of 1, the one who contributes next most will receive a rank of 2, etc. The one who contributes least will receive a rank of 5. The ranks that each of you receive on the

---

[3] "Pure" cooperative and competitive situations were not created by the instructions. Other goals, related to such needs as recognition and affiliation, made it possible for these instructions to produce only relative differences of cooperation and competition.

[4] An *H* at M.I.T. is the highest grade obtainable.

weekly problems will be averaged. At the end of it all, we should have a pretty good picture of each individual's ability to do clear, logical thinking.

To motivate you to contribute your best individual efforts, we will have a reward for the individual who comes out with the best average. He will be excused from one term paper and will receive an automatic *H* for that paper.

You are to come out with one solution as a group. When you have decided as a group that you have reached a solution, let me know by handing me your answer written on this answer sheet.

Human Relations Problem. There are two principal factors determining your grade for this course: (*a*) the discussions in class of the human relations problems and (*b*) the papers you hand in periodically.

Your grades for the discussion in class will be determined in the following manner:

Each week the contributions that each of you makes to the plan of recommendations that the group comes out with as a result of discussion will be ranked so that the individual contributing the most (in terms of both quality and quantity of ideas) to the group plan will receive a rank of 1, the individual contributing next most will get a 2, and so on; the individual who contributes least will get a 5.

The ranks that each individual receives from week to week will be averaged and will be used in making up that part of his grade which is based on class discussion.

Thus, in effect, you are to consider the discussions of these human relations problems presented to you weekly as a test, in which each of you is being ranked and graded on your individual ability to effectively apply insight to these problems. Remember, the individual who contributes most in quality and quantity to the discussions and recommendations will get the highest grades; the individual who contributes least will get the lowest grades.

In this meeting, as in all the other meetings, you will consider yourself to be a board of human relations experts. As such, you have been presented with the following problem which I will read to you. You may glance at your copies of the problem as I read, if you wish to do so. (*The problem was then read by the experimenter.*)

You will be allowed a total of 50 minutes for both the discussion and the writing of recommendations. You are to write your recommendations in letter style, on this form which I have provided.

You will be notified when you have only 20 minutes, 10 minutes, and 5 minutes left.

The cooperation of the subjects in not discussing problems and procedures outside of the group meetings was solicited. The same instructions were repeated at each group meeting. Subjects in both the cooperative and competitive groups were not informed about their weekly grades until the end of the experiment.

During the five weeks of experimentation, each of the groups met once weekly for a period of approximately three hours. The schedule of a meeting was as follows: (*a*) The experimenter read the appropriate instructions for the puzzles. (*b*) The group undertook the solution of the puzzle. (*c*) The students filled out a brief questionnaire while the observers made various ratings. (*d*) The experimenter read the appropriate instructions for the human relations problem. (*e*) The group was allowed a total of 50 minutes for the discussion and writing of recommendations. (*f*) The students then filled out a lengthy questionnaire. (*g*) There was a 10–15 minute break. (*h*) The rest of the three hours the experimenter lectured, encouraging active discussion, on psychological principles such as are involved in "need theory," "level of aspiration," and "conflict." Each of the 10 groups received the same informal lectures in any given week.

It should be clear that the discussion and solution of both the puzzles and the human relations problems were undertaken by the various groups without the participation of the experimenter-instructor. During these discussions he sat at a table with the other observers and functioned as an observer.

It should be emphasized that the only differences introduced into the three-hour meetings by the experimenter-instructor were the differences in instructions read to the cooperative and competitive groups. The experimenter-instructor tried to create a friendly, informal, but impersonal relationship with all groups.

The Problems. The background considerations previously outlined dictated that human relations problems be used as group tasks. In addition, for comparative purposes, it was thought that it would be interesting to have the groups confronted with problems of a rather different type. The human relations problems are tasks in which there are no clearly discernible objective criteria of locomotion; they are tasks in which the group itself, through consensus, provides the criteria for judging locomotion. In addition, the content of these problems is likely to evoke strongly held personal value systems. The puzzle problems were, for convenience, chosen for contrast. Due to their objective (i.e., logically demonstrable) solutions, locomotion could take place without group consensus. This, of course, provided the possibility for relatively more individual work in the puzzles than in the human relations problems. The relative lack of ideological relevance of the content of the puzzle problems also made conflict more likely in the human relations problems.

It is possible that the sequence in which the problems were presented might influence the results obtained. Care was taken, therefore, to control this influence. With the limited number of subjects and groups available it was decided that a Latin-square design would be most appropriate. This design makes it possible to vary systematically from group to group the sequence in which the different problems were presented. It permits the effective elimination and estimation (by statistical methods) of the effect of differences among groups, due to the effect of sequence in which the problems are presented, and the effect of different kinds of problems.

MEASURING INSTRUMENTS

Instruments Used by the Observers. For most of the experiment there were four observers. Two major tasks, among others, were assigned to the different observers.

The Functions Observations Sheet. The job of the observer was to categorize each participation of the members in terms of the following: (a) who spoke (or gestured), (b) to whom the remark was addressed, (c) the intent of the participant, and (d) the length of the participation. Arbitrarily it was decided to use the *utterance* to define a unit of participation, with the exception that if more than one function distinctly occurred in any utterance two or more categorizations would be made. To provide the possibility of cross-analysis with other instruments, a new *functions sheet* was used for each five-minute period. To facilitate tabulation no attempt was made to retain sequence of utterances or the linkage "who-to-whom."

The categories used in the Functions Obser-

vations Sheet were divided into three broad groupings:[5]

Task functions include participations which are directed toward the task with which the group is confronted. These functions have as their immediate purpose the facilitation of problem solution. Included in this grouping are such functions as "initiator-contributor," "information-giver," "position-stater," "elaborator," "coordinator," "orientor," "evaluator-critic," "energizer," and "information-seeker."

Group functions include participations which are directed toward the functioning of the group. They have for their immediate purpose the maintenance, strengthening, regulation, or perpetuation of the group. Included here are such functions as "encourager-rewarder," "harmonizer-mediator," "good group member," "gate-keeper," "standard-setter," "follower," and "group observer."

Individual functions include participations which are directed toward the satisfaction of the participant's individual needs. They have for their immediate purpose the reaching of an individual goal which is neither task nor group relevant. The goal is individual in the sense that the satisfaction aimed at by the participant cannot be participated in by the others, either at all or in the same way. Such functions are grouped here as "play-boy," "sympathy-seeker," "aggressor," "dominator," "blocker," "recognition-seeker," "self-defender," and "self-observer."

The observer, using this instrument, was trained for approximately 30 hours before observing the experimental group meetings.

The Over-all Rating Scales. These are a series of nine-point rating scales which were rated by each observer at the end of each problem. They covered such things as group-discussion productivity, group orientation, self-centeredness, involvement, communication difficulties, attentiveness, and acceptance-rejection. All the rating scales apply to the entire discussion of any given problem.

In considering the various ratings, we

---

[5] This classification was developed by the present author in conjunction with this research project. It was also used by the National Training Laboratory in Group Development and was the basis for an article appearing under the authorship of Benne and Sheats (2). For fuller description of this system of classification, see the article by Benne and Sheats.

should keep in mind that it was impossible to maintain any absolute standards. The ratings more or less presumed a standard of judgment based on experience with groups of introductory psychology students. Thus, the emphasis throughout will be primarily on the direction of the obtained differences rather than on size of differences between the two types of groups.

The results themselves give prima-facie evidence that the observing instruments have sufficient reliability for many of the present purposes. The validity of the observations and ratings, however, cannot be directly determined from the results. One of the primary questions that may arise with respect to the validity of the observations may be concerned with a possible bias among the observers. Thus, if the observers were disposed to see the cooperative groups as being better than the competitive groups, any significant results might be a reflection of this predisposition rather than of real differences.

There is no simple way to insure that the observers had no such predispositions. However, two kinds of evidence support the belief that the observers did not bias their observations in terms of any preconceptions about cooperation and competition: [6] (a) The observers made impromptu statements to the effect that, if they were allowed to keep the instructions in mind, they would have a better interpretive frame of reference for their observations. (b) The second kind of evidence is indirect but, nevertheless, quite convincing. Data collected from the subjects strongly agree with the results from data collected by observers. Since there is no reason to suspect the subjects of bias (they did not know what the experiment was about), this is good indication of lack of bias in the observers.

Instruments Used by the Subjects. 1. The Weekly Questionnaire. At each meeting after the discussion of the human relations problems, the subjects filled out a questionnaire. The items on the questionnaire consisted for the most part of rating scales which roughly paralleled those in the observers' Over-all Rating Scales. In addition to such scales as attentiveness, communication difficulties, and acceptance-rejection, the subjects rated inter-

est, group-feeling, amount of group cooperation, group productivity, individual productivity, and anticipated reactions of the others to their own contributions.

2. The Postexperimental Questionnaire.[7] One week after the last experimental group meeting, the subjects filled out a lengthy questionnaire covering a range of topics. The questionnaire attempted to get at such things as (a) when first and last names were learned; (b) amount and kinds of social activities mutually engaged in by group members outside of class hours; (c) reactions to the small group meetings, the instructor, and the course; (d) the importance of different factors in motivating the subjects to achieve during the solution of the problems; (e) reaction to the grading system; and (f) reaction to being observed.

EXPERIMENTAL RESULTS

Effectiveness of Instructions. It is perhaps important to start out by inquiring about the reactions of the subjects to the two different sets of instructions. Clearly, if the instructions never· "got over," one could reasonably question their efficacy in producing differences.

All subjects, when requested (D)[8] to "describe the method by which you were being graded on the human relations problems," responded with an appropriate description. That is, each subject understood and could recall the essentials of the instructions.

In answer to the question (D), "If you had had completely free choice as to the method of grading discussion in class, which would you have preferred?" the following results were obtained:

Grading Method Preferred	Cooperative	Competitive	No Preference
By *Indiv coop*	11	6	2
By *Indiv comp*	6	11	3

[7] Due to unavoidable circumstances, this questionnaire was given to only four cooperative groups, totaling 19 subjects, and four competitive groups, totaling 20 subjects.

[8] From this point on, (A) will refer to the *Over-all Rating Scales*, (B) to the *Functions Observations Sheet*, (C) to the *Weekly Questionnaire* filled out by subjects, and (D) to the *Postexperimental Questionnaire*.

[6] The observers were never informed by the experimenter of the hypotheses being investigated.

TABLE 1. *Differences Between Cooperative and Competitive Groups on Data Relevant to Hypotheses of Perceived Promotive and Contrient Interdependence*[a]

Variable	Problem Type	Total	
		M diff	*p*
Group-centeredness (A)	H. R.	+2.98	.001
Group-centeredness (A)	P	+2.54	.001
Group-feeling (C)	H. R.	+1.20	.01
Competitiveness (C)	H. R.	−0.37	b
Desire to excel others (D)	H. R.	−2.30	.03
Desire to excel others (D)	P	−2.20	.01

[a] The following symbols are being used in the various tables: P = Puzzles; H. R. = Human Relations problems; (A), (B), (C), or (D) = the measuring instrument (see footnote 8); Total *M diff* = average of the differences (cooperative minus competitive) between each of the five paired groups for each of the five experimental weeks. A plus sign indicates that the cooperative groups had more of the variable than did the competitive groups. Total *p* = the *p* value obtained by combining the *p* values for each of the five pairs. A combined value is given only when the direction of the differences for all five pairs is the same as that of the total mean difference.

[b] The differences for three of the pairs are in the same direction as the total mean difference; these differences have *p* values of .01, .01, and .13 respectively. The differences for the other two pairs are in an opposite direction; these differences have *p* values of .14 and .23.

Assuming these differences did not exist at the beginning of the experiment, one can conclude that roughly the same percentage of individuals were satisfied with the method of grading to which they were exposed.

Clearly, then, the instructions "got over" to the subjects in both kinds of groups and in such a way as to seem satisfactory to approximately the same percentage in both groups.

Perceived Interdependence. Hypothesis 1 asserts that *Indiv coop* will perceive themselves to be more promotively interdependent than will *Indiv comp*. Table 1 presents some relevant data.

Group-centeredness (we-feeling) was rated by the observers to be considerably higher in the cooperative groups for both the puzzles and the human relations problems. The ratings of the subjects, in the questionnaire pertaining to the human relations problems, give the same results. *Indiv coop* give themselves credit for more "group feeling" than do *Indiv comp*. These differences with respect to group-centeredness and group-feeling are significant at the 1% level for both the puzzles and human relations problems. Thus, the evidence gives support to the first part of the hypothesis (perceived promotive interdependence).

The second part of the hypothesis (*Indiv comp* will perceive themselves to be more contriently interdependent than will *Indiv coop*) is partly supported by the same evidence.

Thus, the competitive group members were rated to be more self-centered by the observers. Likewise, *Indiv comp* rated themselves as being more self-oriented than did *Indiv coop*. "Perceived contrient interdependence," however, seems to include, in addition to "self-centeredness," the notion of "I" versus "the others." To measure this component, the subjects were asked (C), in reference to the human relations problem, "How competitive with the other members in your group did you feel you were, during the discussion?"

The results obtained here are not so conclusive, though they tend to support the hypothesis (see Table 1, competitiveness). It seems probable that the lack of clean-cut results is a reflection of the differing interpretations placed on the word *competitiveness* by *Indiv coop*. This interpretation is supported by the fact that when the question was phrased, "How much did you desire to excel others?" on the Postexperimental Questionnaire, significant differences were obtained in the predicted direction.

To sum up, the data support the predictions that perceived promotive interdependence would be greater among *Indiv coop* and that perceived contrient interdependence would be greater among *Indiv comp*.[9]

[9] We proposed in our theoretical discussion that *Indiv coop* has greater unity as a *sociological*

TABLE 2. *Differences Between Cooperative and Competitive Groups on Data Relevant to the Hypothesis Concerning Coordination of Effort*

Variable	Problem Type	Total	
		M diff	p
Working-together (A)	H. R.	+2.42	.001
Working-together (A)	P	+2.68	.001
Degree of coordination (A)	H. R.	+2.62	.001
Degree of coordination (A)	P	+2.57	.001
Group cooperation (C)	H. R.	+1.18	.001

Organization.   Coordination of efforts. Hypothesis 6 asserted that there would be greater degree of coordination of efforts and that coordination would occur more frequently among *Indiv coop* than among *Indiv comp.* Table 2 presents the relevant evidence.

The observers rated that the cooperative groups worked together more frequently (A) and were more highly coordinated (A) than were the competitive groups. In answer to the question (C), "How cooperatively did the group work together on this problem?" the ratings of *Indiv coop* indicated more working together than did the ratings of *Indiv comp.*

Thus the data give rather definite support to the coordination hypothesis.

Homogeneity of participation. Hypothesis 7 states that there will be less homogeneity with respect to amount of contribution among *Indiv coop* than among *Indiv comp.* The data presented in Table 3 provide the evidence relevant to this hypothesis. The variance in amount of contributions among members has been used as the measure of homogeneity. The differences between variances of paired groups were then entered as scores in the Latin square

and the customary statistical treatment was made.

The data give support for the hypothesis, although the results are not conclusive. In both the puzzles and human relations problems, there is greater homogeneity of participation within competitive groups. Four out of the five pairs in the human relations problem and all of the five pairs in the puzzles go in the direction predicted by the hypothesis.

Further support is given the hypothesis by some additional data which are directly relevant to the basic substitutability hypothesis. On the Weekly Questionnaire the subjects were asked to indicate the reasons they had for not offering suggestions or thoughts to the group discussion. Of the reasons checked by *Indiv coop,* 47% were in the category "Somebody else said pretty much the same thing," compared to 33% for *Indiv comp.*

Thus, though the results are not conclusive, support is given to the hypothesis that there will be more homogeneity in amount of participation among *Indiv comp* than among *Indiv coop.*

Specialization. A cursory inspection of the

TABLE 3. *Differences in Homogeneity of Amount of Participation Between Cooperative and Competitive Groups*

Variable	Problem Type	Total	
		M diff	p
Homogeneity of participation (B)	H. R.	−2593	a
Homogeneity of participation (B)	P	−518	.16

[a] The differences for four of the pairs are in the same direction as the total mean difference; these differences have p values of .005, .07, .13, and .67 respectively. The pair going in the opposite direction has a p value of .16.

group than does *Indiv comp.* Also, *psychological unity as a group, cohesiveness of a group,* and *strength of membership motives* were defined to be direct functions of the degree of perceived promotive interdependence. Thus, it is possible to state the results here more generally. The data

support the hypothesis that a sociological group with greater unity will possess more psychological unity than a sociological group with lesser unity. In further comparisons of *Indiv coop* and *Indiv comp,* one should keep in mind the possibility of making similar more general statements.

TABLE 4. *Average Number of Persons Simultaneously Engaged in Writing Recommendations for the Different Human Relations Problems in Cooperative and Competitive Groups*

	Barber Shop	Cheating	W.W. II Vet.	Negro Workers	Supervisors[a]
Coop[b]	1.8	2.4	2.0	2.8	2.8
Comp	1.2	1.0	1.2	1.8	1.2

[a] For all problems, but the Supervisors, only three persons could write simultaneously; it was possible for four persons to write simultaneously on this one.

[b] In none of the 25 paired experimental sessions were there more members simultaneously engaged in writing in a competitive group than in its paired cooperative group. In sixteen of the sessions there were more members in cooperative groups engaged in simultaneous writing; in the remaining nine sessions there were no differences between the paired groups.

data collected on the Functions Observations Sheets revealed a low reliability of the data needed to test Hypothesis 8 (specialization with respect to function). In the statistical tests that were made the data revealed no clear-cut significance (though with respect to all functions there is, on the average, greater specialization of functioning within cooperative groups than within competitive groups).

The evidence relevant to specialization with respect to content or activity (Hyp. 9) is much more clear-cut. Table 4 presents the data. The results definitely indicate that with respect to the job of writing the letter of recommendations, asked for in the human relations problems, there were significantly more instances of division of labor in the cooperative groups. Faced with the problem of achievement in a limited amount of time, cooperative members were able to organize themselves so as not to duplicate one another's efforts. Substitutability of one for the other permitted the members to divide up the job into its different aspects and allowed the various members to

work on these components simultaneously. In the competitive situation, writing procedure generally followed either of two extremes: (a) One man was assigned the job, usually on the basis of a rotation scheme, and the other members took an active part in supervising the writing. The getting of ideas into written form was seen as a path; thus everyone was actively concerned with what was being written. Since the number of pages, always less than five, prevented the possibility of any compromise— "we each do one"—it was necessary for all to focus on the same activity. As a consequence, it was rare that two members were writing simultaneously. When two or more recorders are shown in the competitive groups, their time of writing did not overlap much. (b) A conscientious member took the form and wrote up recommendations while the others discussed. The discussants showed no interest in the write-up, never examining it, their whole attention being directed to the discussion. The written product was, more or less, considered to be an irrelevant side issue for some consci-

TABLE 5. *Differences Between Cooperative and Competitive Groups on Data Relevant to the Motivation Hypotheses*

Variable	Problem Type	Total	
		M diff	p
Effect of other's ideas (C)	H. R.	+.78	.001
Achievement pressure (A)	H. R.	+1.00	.01
Achievement pressure (A)	P	+.49	a
Strength of motivation to achieve (D)	H. R.	+.83	.01
Strength of motivation to achieve (D)	P	+.20	not sig.
Involvement (A)	H. R.	+.15	not sig.
Involvement (A)	P	+.23	not sig.
Interest (C)	H. R.	−.10	not sig.

[a] The differences for four of the five pairs are in the same direction as the mean differences; these differences have p values of .04, .13, .24, and .68. The p value for the pair going in the opposite direction is .66.

entious soul to handle. It was not seen as a necessary path; thus it was perfectly permissible for anyone who wished to do so to take over the function of writing.

Motivation. Hypothesis 12 asserts that the directions of the forces operating on *Indiv coop* should be more similar than the directions of the forces on *Indiv comp.* If this hypothesis is correct, one should expect greater speed in group locomotion for the cooperative groups. The data with respect to locomotion are presented under the heading of *Productivity* below. The data give strong support to the hypothesis.

The validity of the hypothesis presupposes the validity of the basic hypothesis with respect to positive inducibility. The following questions (C), "How did you react to the ideas or suggestions of others?" and "How frequently was your own thinking or reaction affected by what the others were saying?" are relevant. Table 5 indicates that *Indiv coop* were affected by the ideas of others significantly more often than were *Indiv comp.* Table 7 indicates, further, that *Indiv coop* were markedly more agreeable and acceptant towards the ideas initiated by others. These two sets of facts provide direct support for the basic hypothesis with respect to positive inducibility and indirect evidence for Hypothesis 12.

From Hypothesis 13 one would predict that there would be more pressure for achievement in the cooperative groups than in the competitive ones. The ratings of the observers and of the subjects both produce significant differences in the predicted direction for the human relations problem. The direction of the differences obtained for the puzzles is in line with the hypothesis, but the size of the differences is not significant.

Hypothesis 15 states that there is nothing inherent in the cooperative or competitive situations which should produce differences in the strength of force operating on individuals in the two situations. *Interest* or *involvement* is considered to be an operational measure of total situationally relevant forces. The data of Table 5 clearly provide no basis for rejecting the hypothesis. The differences between cooperative and competitive groups with respect to involvement or interest in the problems at hand were negligible.

Communication. Hypotheses 16 and 17 assert that the volume of participation of the cooperative as contrasted with the competitive groups will be (Hyp. 16) smaller for the human relations problems and (Hyp. 17) greater for the puzzles. The relevant data are presented in Table 6.

The observers rated that there were significantly fewer communication difficulties among *Indiv coop* than among *Indiv comp* for both the human relations problems and puzzles. Further support for Hypothesis 19 is obtained

TABLE 6. *Differences in Participation Volume, Attentiveness, and Communication Difficulties Between Cooperative and Competitive Groups*

Variable	Problem Type	Total	
		M diff	p
Participation volume [a](B)	H. R.	−22.8	[b]
Participation volume (B)	P	+118	.001
Attentiveness (A)	H. R.	+1.04	.01
Attentiveness (A)	P	+1.50	.001
Attentiveness (C)	H. R.	+.42	[c]
Communication difficulties (A)	H. R.	−1.94	.001
Communication difficulties (A)	P	−1.39	.01
Difficulty in communicating to others (C)	H. R.	−.81	.001
Difficulty in understanding others (C)	H. R.	−.67	.001

[a] *Participation volume* has the meaning of Total Number of Participations per 45 Minutes. Thus, all participation volumes are equaled in terms of a constant time unit.

[b] The differences for three pairs are in the same direction as the total mean difference; these differences have p values of .007, .06, and .20. The other two pairs go in the opposite direction; these differences have p values of .12 and .73.

[c] The differences for three pairs are in the same direction as the total mean difference; these differences have p values of .03, .04, and .72. The other two pairs, in the opposite direction, both have p values of .83.

TABLE 7. *Differences Between Cooperative and Competitive Groups on Data Relevant to the Hypothesis About Common Appraisals of Communications*

Variable	Problem Type	Total	
		M diff	p
Acceptance of each other's ideas (A)	H. R.	+1.80	.001
Acceptance of each other's ideas (A)	P	+.95	.01
Agreement with others (C)	H. R.	+.81	.001
Agreement by others (C)	H. R.	+.61	a
Follower (B)	H. R.	+4.34	.01
Follower (B)	P	+2.05	.25
Evaluator-critic (B)	H. R.	−3.36	.04
Evaluator-critic (B)	P	−.95	not sig.

[a] The differences for four of the five pairs are in the same direction as the total mean difference; these differences have *p* values of .01, .02, .04, and .38. The other pair, in the opposite direction, has a *p* value of .92.

from the subjects. In answer to the question (C), "Did you find that you had difficulty in getting your ideas across to others?" the ratings of *Indiv coop* expressed significantly less difficulty than did the ratings of *Indiv comp.* The same results were obtained in answers to the following question (C), "Did you find that you had difficulty in trying to follow or get the point of what the others were saying?" Thus, the competitive subjects experienced more difficulty with respect to the spread of common signification, both in the roles of communicators and communicatees.

Hypothesis 21 asserts that there will be more common appraisals of communications in the cooperative groups than in the competitive groups. Table 7 presents the evidence for the hypothesis.

The observers rate greater acceptance of one another's ideas in the cooperative groups than in the competitive groups in both kinds of tasks. The subjects' ratings also strongly support the hypothesis. In answer to the questions (C), "How did you react to the suggestions of others?" and "How did the others tend to react to your ideas or suggestions?" the ratings made by *Indiv coop*, as contrasted with those of *Indiv comp*, indicate both significantly more

agreement with the ideas and suggestions of others and perception of more agreement from other group members.

Two categories on the Functions Observation Sheets, "evaluator-critic" and "follower," also provide some relevant data, although it should be kept in mind that both categories may contain a few items which are not specifically related to the notion of *common appraisal*. Thus, "evaluator-critic" probably contains some items which are positive evaluations and "follower" includes some items which connote understanding but not necessarily agreement. Nevertheless, for both categories there are significant differences between the cooperative and competitive groups on the human relations problems in the direction of the hypothesis. The differences with respect to the puzzles are in the predicted direction but are not significant.

Orientation. Hypothesis 23 asserts that there will be more commonality of perception with respect to position and direction to the goal among *Indiv coop* than among *Indiv comp.* The relevant data are presented in Table 8.

According to the observers' ratings the co-

TABLE 8. *Differences in Degree of Orientation and Orderliness Between Cooperative and Competitive Groups*

Variable	Problem Type	Total	
		M diff	p
Orientation (A)	H. R.	+1.70	.001
Orientation (A)	P	+1.92	.01
Orderliness (A)	H. R.	+1.99	.001
Orderliness (A)	P	+1.96	.001

operative groups were significantly more oriented ("aware of where they are and where they are going") than the competitive groups for both kinds of tasks. The hypothesis is also given indirect support by the observers' ratings which indicate that the cooperative groups were also significantly more orderly and systematic in their approach to the various problems.

Productivity. Hypothesis 24 asserts that, since speed of locomotion will be greater in cooperative groups, quantitative productivity per unit of time will be less in the competitive groups. The evidence in Table 9 provides striking support. Cooperative groups solve the puzzle problems more rapidly than do the competitive groups and they also produce more on the human relations problems (number of words written in the recommendations are taken as a crude measure of quantity of productivity).

Hypothesis 25 states that qualitative productivity will be higher for the cooperative groups. Clear support is given to this hypothesis by the observers' ratings of discussion productivity (Table 9) and by the judges' ratings of written recommendations for the human relations problems (Table 10). According to observer ratings, the discussions of the cooperative groups not only came out with more fruitful ideas for handling the problem presented to them, but also their group discussions showed more insight and understanding of the nature of the problem being posed to them. These

differences with respect to group productivity and group insight are significant for both kinds of tasks.

Average individual productivity must not be confused with group productivity. Group productivity ratings referred to the ideas that were agreed upon and accepted as a basis for action by the group. The ratings of average individual productivity show no significant difference for the cooperative and competitive groups on the human relations problems. For the puzzles, there is a difference approaching significance favoring *Indiv coop.* The latter result is probably explained by the fact that the greater communication within cooperative groups meant that individuals were less likely to stay in blind alleys for long periods of time.

Table 10 presents the ratings of each group for each of the five different problems, as made by three different judges. Although it is evident that there is a considerable unreliability in the ratings, it is also clear that despite this there are significant differences between the paired cooperative and competitive groups.

Hypothesis 26 states that *Indiv coop* will learn more from one another than will *Indiv comp.* Table 9 indicates that the cooperative group members in three of the five pairs rated themselves as learning more from the discussion of the human relations problem than did the competitive members rate themselves.

The same kind of results are obtained when one examines the grades obtained by the individuals exposed to each of the experimental conditions. The grades being considered were

TABLE 9. *Differences Between Cooperative and Competitive Groups on Various Measures of Productivity*

Variable	Problem Type	Total	
		M diff	*p*
Discussion productivity (A)	H. R.	+1.86	.001
Discussion productivity (A)	P	+1.90	.01
Discussion insight (A)	H. R.	+1.25	.001
Discussion insight (A)	P	+1.72	.02
Time per solution	P	−7.35 minutes	.01
Number of words in written product	H. R.	+299 words	.001
Average individual productivity (A)	H. R.	+.15	not sig.
Average individual productivity (A)	P	+.58	.07
Learning from discussion (C)	H. R.	+.25	a
Grades on term paper		+2.85	.18

[a] Differences for three pairs are in the same direction as the total mean difference; these differences have *p* values of .07, .07, and .39. The two pairs, in the opposite direction, have *p* values of .30 and .45.

TABLE 10. *Data Relevant to Hypothesis that Qualitative Productivity Will Be Higher in Cooperative Groups*

Correlations Among Ratings of Group Products by Three Judges			
Judges 1 & 2	Judges 1 & 3	Judges 2 & 3	Average of Correlations
.42	.46	.61	.50

Differences Between Cooperative and Competitive Groups on Mean of Judges' Ratings						
	Total	Pair 1	Pair 2	Pair 3	Pair 4	Pair 5
M diff	+2.04					
p	.001	.02	.001	.54	.01	.05

those obtained on the first term paper handed in by all the subjects. The paper was due on the final week of the experiment. Statistical analysis reveals that the differences are in the predicted direction but not statistically significant.

Thus, the hypotheses predicting greater group productivity for the cooperative groups have received strong support from the data, but the evidence with respect to the hypothesis predicting greater learning for *Indiv coop* is far from conclusive. It should be noted that the discussions took place at the very beginning of an introductory psychology course. Perhaps at such an early stage the subjects were not particularly ready to have cognitive changes induced by fellow members under either of the two conditions.

Interpersonal Relations. From the basic hypothesis with respect to cathexis, it was derived that *Indiv coop* would be more friendly towards one another in the group meetings

than would *Indiv comp* (Hyp. 27). Table 11 presents the relevant data.

Observers' ratings reveal that *Indiv coop* were significantly more friendly than *Indiv comp* during discussions of both types of problems. The hypothesis receives additional support from the observation of functions during discussion of the human relations problems. A greater percentage of encouraging or rewarding remarks was made in cooperative groups, and a significantly larger proportion of aggressive remarks was made in the competitive groups. The puzzle problems yielded such a low frequency of all emotionally laden functions that no significant differences could be established between groups.

The cooperative subjects in answer to the question (C), "How good were the contributions of others?" rated one another's contributions to be better than did the competitive subjects. This result can also be taken to indicate greater positive cathection among *Indiv coop*.

TABLE 11. *Differences Between Cooperative and Competitive Groups in Friendliness, and Other Related Data*

Variable	Problem Type	Total	
		M diff	p
Friendliness (A)	H. R.	+1.26	.001
Friendliness (A)	P	+.89	.01
How good were contributions of others (C)	H. R.	+.70	a
Encourager (B)	H. R.	+.96	b
Encourager (B)	P	+.20	not sig.
Aggressor (B)	H. R.	−1.16	.01
Aggressor (B)	P	−.64	not sig.
Time taken to learn last names (D)		−.20	.06
Correctness of spelling of last names (D)		+5.3	.11

[a] Differences for four pairs are in the same direction as the total mean difference; these differences have p values of .005, .01, .01, and .07. The other pair, in the opposite direction, has a p value of .87.

[b] Differences for four pairs are in the same direction as the total mean difference; these differences have p values of .001, .18, .57, and .62. The other pair has a p value of .57.

The next question of interest has to do with the extent of the generalization of the friendliness shown during the experimental meetings. The question (D), "How much did the weekly small group meetings stand out for you in contrast with the other classes you attend during the week?" is the only relevant measure. The average responses for the cooperative and the competitive groups were not significantly different. On the average, the subjects rated the weekly meetings as, "Thought about some—more prominent in my thinking than some of my other courses, but not more prominent than most of my other courses." Since the experimental sessions were not especially prominent in the lives of the subjects, there is little reason to expect much generalization of cathexis to other areas.

Various measures were taken to test the extent of generalization: ratings of fellow members with respect to desirability as a friend, rating of amount of friendly feeling toward others, time taken to learn first and last names, correctness of spelling of last names, amount of time spent together in outside activities and kinds of activities jointly engaged in outside of class. Table 11 presents most of the evidence.

Indiv coop learned one another's last names sooner than did *Indiv comp* (as reported on the final questionnaire). They also spelled one another's names more nearly correctly, but the size of this difference is significant at only the 11% level of confidence. No differences were obtained with regard to learning first names nor in the frequency or kinds of outside activities undertaken together. At the end of the experiment, *Indiv coop* rated themselves as being more friendly toward one another than did *Indiv comp*. These differences, however, are clearly not statistically significant. The data thus indicate that little generalization of cathexis occurred. The relative lack of generalization was probably due to (a) the relative lack of importance of the goals involved in the experiment and (b) strong restraining forces against any inclinations toward increased sociability which might have resulted from the experimental situation.

Hypothesis 28 states that the group and its products will be evaluated more highly by *Indiv coop* than by *Indiv comp*. Table 12 presents the relevant data. In answer to the question (C), "Did the group help your thinking?" the ratings revealed significantly more help among the cooperative than among the competitive members. Similar results were obtained from the question (C), "How good do you think the group's product was?"

According to Hypotheses 29 and 30 there should be a greater percentage of group functions among *Indiv coop* and a greater percentage of individual functions among *Indiv comp*. The data in Table 12 support these hypotheses with respect to the human relations problems but not the puzzles. The lack of difference for the puzzles suggests that (a) the objectively demonstrable solution of the puzzles makes it more difficult for individuals to produce the rationalizations necessary for "civilized" blocking or aggressive behavior and (b) a demonstrable solution compels a certain degree of agreement and acceptance, making group functions more likely. Thus, the competitive groups have a significantly greater percentage

TABLE 12. *Differences Between Cooperative and Competitive Groups on Kinds of Functions Performed and Evaluations of the Group*

Variable	Problem Type	Total	
		M diff	p
Group help to thinking (C)	H. R.	+ 1.03	.001
How good was group product (C)	H. R.	+ 1.22	.01
Total group functions (B)	H. R.	+ 4.64	a
Total group functions (B)	P	+ .08	not sig.
Total individual functions (B)	H. R.	− 3.87	.05
Total individual functions (B)	P	− 2.10	not sig.
Blocker (B)	H. R.	− 1.40	.01
Blocker (B)	P	− .25	not sig.
Self-defender (B)	H. R.	− 1.03	.05
Self-defender (B)	P	− .10	not sig.

[a]Differences for four pairs are in the same direction as the total mean difference; these differences have p values of .001, .001, .01, and .01. The other pair, in the opposite direction, has a p value of .05.

TABLE 13. *Differences Between Cooperative and Competitive Groups in Perception of Effects on Others and in Feeling of Obligation to Other Members*

Variable	Problem Type	Total	
		M diff	p
How did others react to your ideas? (C)	H. R.	+.61	a
How frequently did others react? (C)	H. R.	+.49	b
How will others rate your contributions? (C)	H. R.	+.49	c
Strength of feeling of obligation to others (D)	H. R.	+2.80	.01
Strength of feeling of obligation to others (D)	P	+1.55	.10
Strength of desire to win respect of others (D)	H. R.	+1.53	.09
Strength of desire to win respect of others (D)	P	+2.38	.001

[a] Four pairs are in the same direction as the total mean difference; the differences for these pairs have p values of .01, .04, .12, and .38. The other pair has a p value of .92.

[b] Four pairs are in the same direction as the total mean difference, with p values of .01, .03, .04, and .18. The other pair has a p value of .02.

[c] Four pairs are in the same direction as the total mean difference, with p values of .01, .02, .06, and .28. The other pair has a p value of .33.

of group functions in the puzzles than in the human relations problems and a slightly smaller percentage of individual functions in the puzzles. Similar, but less-marked, differences are found for the cooperative groups on the two kinds of problems.

Hypothesis 33 states that *Indiv coop* will perceive themselves as having more favorable effects on fellow members than will *Indiv comp*. Table 13 indicates that the cooperative subjects saw their fellow members as reacting more positively to their ideas, the competitive members perceived that their ideas were being ignored more frequently, and the cooperative members felt that their contributions would be evaluated more highly.

Hypothesis 34 asserts that there will be greater internalization of the attitude of the generalized other by *Indiv coop* than by *Indiv comp*. Most of the experimental data already discussed are relevant to this hypothesis, but, in the more restricted sense of identification with the attitudes of others, two complementary measures, the feeling of obligation to others and the desire to win the respect of others, are especially pertinent. Table 13 presents data which indicate that *Indiv coop* felt more obligated as members of a group to participate in joint effort than did *Indiv comp*. The desire to win the respect of the other members also played more of a role in the motivation of *Indiv coop* than *Indiv comp*.

SUMMARY AND CONCLUSIONS

Basic Hypotheses. The evidence for the basic hypotheses is, for the most part, indirect.

Data collected to test the more specific hypotheses about group functioning also, in effect, test the basic hypotheses.

The experimental findings give support to the following hypotheses:

1. *Indiv coop* will perceive themselves to be more promotively interdependent, and *Indiv comp* will perceive themselves to be more contriently interdependent (Hyp. 1).

2. There will be greater substitutability for similarly intended actions among *Indiv coop* than *Indiv comp*. This hypothesis is supported by data obtained in connection with Hypotheses 7 and 9, but the data are ambiguous with respect to Hypotheses 8 and 16.

3. A larger percentage of actions of others will be positively cathected among *Indiv coop*; a larger percentage of actions of others will be negatively cathected among *Indiv comp* (Hyp. 3).

4. There will be a greater positive inducibility among *Indiv coop* than among *Indiv comp* (Hyp. 4).

5. *Indiv coop* will exhibit more helpfulness and *Indiv comp* will exhibit more obstructiveness (Hyp. 5).

Thus, all in all, the theory of cooperation and competition has been given considerable backing by the present experimental investigation.

Group Functioning. The results with respect to aspects of group functioning, indicate that *Indiv coop* showed more of the following characteristics than did *Indiv comp*: (*a*) coordination of efforts; (*b*) diversity in amount of contributions per member; (*c*) subdivision of activity; (*d*) achievement pressure; (*e*) production of signs in the puzzle problem; (*f*) attentiveness to fellow members; (*g*) mutual comprehension of communication; (*h*) common appraisals of communication; (*i*) orientation and orderliness; (*j*) productivity per unit time; (*k*) quality of product and discussions; (*l*) friendliness during discussions; (*m*) favorable evaluation of the group and its products; (*n*) group functions; (*o*) perception of favorable effects upon fellow members; and (*p*) incorporation of the attitude of the generalized other.

Indiv comp showed more (*a*) production of signs in the human relations problem and (*b*) individual functions.

No significant differences were found in the (*a*) amount of interest or involvement, (*b*) amount of specialization of function, and (*c*) amount of learning (though the trend is in favor of *Indiv coop*). Nor did the data reveal any striking developmental differences with time.

Practical Implications.   To the extent that the results have any generality, greater group or organizational productivity may be expected when the members or subunits are cooperative rather than competitive in their interrelationships. The communication of ideas, coordination of efforts, friendliness, and pride in one's group which are basic to group harmony and effectiveness appear to be disrupted when members see themselves to be competing for mutually exclusive goals. Further, there is some indication that competitiveness produces greater personal insecurity through expectations of hostility from others than does cooperation. The implications for committees, conferences, and small groups in general appear fairly obvious.

Also, in light of the results of this study, it seems that educators might well reexamine the assumptions underlying their common usage of a competitive grading system. One may well question whether a competitive grading system produces the kinds of interrelationships among students, the task-directedness, and personal security that are in keeping with sound educational objectives.

References

1. Barnard, C. I. *The functions of the executive*. Cambridge, Mass.: Harvard Univ. Press, 1938.
2. Benne, K. D., & Sheats, P. Functional roles and group members. *Journal of Social Issues*, 1948, **4** (2), 41–49.
3. Koffka, K. *Principles of gestalt psychology*. New York: Harcourt, Brace, 1935.
4. Newcomb, T. M. Autistic hostility and social reality. *Human Relations*, 1947, **1**, 69–86.

PART SEVEN

STRUCTURAL PROPERTIES OF GROUPS

36

The Structural Properties of Groups: Introduction

Suppose that you, as a person interested in group life, have the chance to visit a staff meeting of a department within a large business concern. All of the members of the conference are strangers to you, but you happen to know that one is a vice-president of the company and another is a junior executive just a few years out of college. You decide to see if you can determine, on the basis of the interactions in the conference, which person is the vice-president and which the junior executive. These two, of all the participants, will be the farthest separated on the company's table of organization. Soon you begin to note that two of the participants act in quite different ways. The man whom you believe to be the junior executive addresses the majority of his remarks to the man you believe to be the vice-president. Moreover, he chooses his words with care in order that he not seem to imply any criticism of the other man or appear inadequate. He listens carefully to what the vice-president has to say and is usually ready to see the reasonableness of the arguments made by him. He is friendly toward the boss, ready to tell a joke or talk about his family, and to copy some of the older man's mannerisms.

In contrast, the vice-president talks pretty much to the entire group. He freely offers information, advice, and even criticism to others. He seldom makes critical remarks about himself. Nor is he nearly so ready as the younger man to listen to statements made by the rest of the group. He is more likely to defend his own position than to see the value in the points made by the staff. And on the whole he is less inclined to idle talk than is the junior executive.

You may come away from the meeting feeling that the two men acted the way they did because they had quite different personalities, and you would undoubtedly be partly correct. If, however, you were to see the junior executive in a meeting with his staff in which he is now the boss, you would probably be surprised to see how differently he behaves. Now it is likely that you would find the young man acting toward others in a way very similar to that shown by the vice-president in the earlier meeting. What are the features of the two situations that produce such marked differences of behavior? To answer this question we must carefully examine what is commonly called the *structure* of the group and the *position* each person occupies in the structure.

It appears to be almost impossible to describe what happens in groups without using terms that indicate the "place" of members with respect to one another. Various words have been employed, but the most common are position, status, rank, office, role, part, clique, and subgroup. Although these do not all convey intuitively quite the same meaning, all do refer to the fact that individual members of a group can be located in relation to other members according to some criterion of placement. The prevalence of such terms in the literature on groups, moreover, suggests that such placement of individuals is important for understanding what happens in and to groups.

Consider the following statements that might be used to communicate something about a person's place in a group: he is central in this group but marginal in that one; he is part of the ruling clique; from where he stands he can learn about anything going on in the organization; you can't reach the president except through one of the vice-presidents; since he moved from line to staff no one even notices him at the departmental meetings; everything he does is with an eye toward promotion; his chances of getting an ulcer have increased 50 percent since becoming an executive. The various terms employed in such descriptive sentences refer to phenomena that cannot be conceived satisfactorily as "properties of an individual" nor as "properties of an undifferentiated group." They refer to distinguishable parts of a group whose nature and arrangement constitute "internal properties" of the group.[1] These properties, along with other determinants, influence the behavior of individuals and the performance of groups; people behave as they do partly because of their particular locations within a differentiated group, and groups perform as they do partly because of the particular type of internal structure they possess.

These rather abstract considerations may be made more concrete by considering the communication structure of a group. When organizations are large, their formal structure usually does not provide for direct communication from each office to every other. In a military organization, for example, one cannot communicate with the commanding officer without first talking to one's immediate superior. In governmental agencies it is quite common for direct communication with a person in another bureau to be forbidden. One must "go through channels," which means that a communication must go "upstairs" in the agency, across to the top level in the other, and then down to the person addressed. The totality of such channels constitutes one aspect of the group's communication structure.

Once we have determined the communication structure of a group, we may locate every member in it. The locations may then be characterized in various ways. One person, for example, may be in a central position, connected to everyone else through a relatively small number of communication links, and will be quite likely to hear about nearly everything. Another may be in a peripheral position, removed by many links from several other members, and will tend to be out of touch with things. A third may be located in the only position connecting two parts of the group and is a potential "bottleneck" in the flow of information between the two subgroups. It should be evident that a person's location in a communication structure will affect him in important ways.

When a group acquires some stability in the arrangement of relationships among members, it may be said to be structured.

Research and everyday experience in organizations have made it quite clear that the stable structures of groups may differ greatly in how formally they are specified. In highly formalized groups there may be detailed written statements concerning the structure. The by-laws of an organization may specify all the positions within it together with the duties of each as well as the types of relationships expected among them. Some organizations have written regulations governing who can communicate with whom. A few organizations even go so far as to ban social interactions among certain positions. To the extent that these formal, written statements of structure are taken seriously, they are known by members and enforced by organizational sanction.

---

[1] This designation of three kinds of "properties" is similar to the three "panels of group description" proposed by Cattell (7).

In contrast to these groups with highly formalized structures, there are others that display stable structures without there ever having been any explicit description of them or any formal agreement concerning them. In Chapter 18, for example, Lippitt, Polansky, Redl, and Rosen show how boys in summer camp are in common agreement concerning which boy has the greatest power in the group, although they probably have never discussed this fact among themselves. Similarly, Mills (33) describes how, in three-person discussion groups, different stable patterns of interaction develop without any explicit agreement. And Hare (25) has shown how the size of the discussion group influences such things as tendencies to split into factions and the amount of power exerted by the leader, even though the group's adjustment to its size is seldom explicitly discussed. From all available evidence, there is yet no reason to conclude that informal structures are any less demanding upon group members than formal ones.

In many cases a formal organization may have within it, or parallel to it, an informal organization that is quite different. Thus, the members of a group may be expected to do certain things, or relate to others in certain ways, according to the formal organization, but may also feel quite different influences stemming from the informal organization. Roethlisberger and Dickson (41) provide dramatic illustrations of the conflicts created for a worker when he must decide between conforming to the pressures coming from the formal organization and those deriving from the informal one. To the degree that the worker's behavior is mainly influenced by the informal social structure, it may appear quite unexplainable to the management, who expect strict conformity to the formal structure.

ORIGINS OF STRUCTURE

Much has been written about the reasons that groups become structured but there have been few empirical investigations in the origins of structure as such. It will be useful to note briefly that three rather different kinds of factors tend to produce stable differentiations within groups. The first set stems from requirements for efficient group performance, the second arises from the different motivations and abilities of different individuals, and the third derives from physical and social characteristics of the group's environment.

EFFICIENT GROUP PERFORMANCE

As a group organizes to do work, it often finds that it is more effective if it "specializes" the tasks of its members. Thus, one subgroup of a fraternity becomes responsible for maintenance of the house, another arranges social activities, another maintains liaison with the interfraternity council, another supervises the pledges, and so on. In large, formal organizations this specialization is quite self-consciously supervised by a specialist in specialization. It is the objective of this person to construct a structure that will result in optimal organizational performance. Usually he is primarily concerned to see that each position (*a*) consists of a set of functions that can readily be performed by one individual (or sometimes a group), (*b*) has unambiguous responsibility to some other position, (*c*) has clear authority over other positions, and (*d*) is directly connected in a communication network with some positions but not with others. Whether or not a group recognizes explicitly any relation between the way it is structured and its effectiveness, most groups find it advantageous to develop some specialization, some regularity of assignments and responsibilities, and some dependability in its internal communication and coordination.

ABILITIES AND MOTIVATIONS OF INDIVIDUALS

Many writers have looked for the origin of group structure in the characteristics of the individuals composing the group. Barnard (2), for example, stresses heavily the way in which individual differences in ability and temperament lead people to prefer to do certain group tasks themselves and to give other tasks to other people. Similarly, some people like to assume responsibility while others prefer to be told what to do. Some gain satisfaction from fame and exhibitionism while others are shy and retiring. It has been observed frequently in informal discussion groups that one person "naturally" tends regularly to be perhaps the compromiser, the scapegoat, or the joker. From observations of this sort and everyday experience in groups, it is clear that individual abilities and predispositions do result in regularities of interaction and differentiation among the parts of a group.

Another facet of individual motivation has also been proposed as a source of group structure. It has been suggested by Bales (1) and others that an individual's security derives largely from his being able to count upon a stable social environment. All members of a group, whether their purposes are exploitative or cooperative, share a common need for being able to predict how other members will behave toward them. Out of this need for predictability come strong pressures on each member to assume certain stable relations with all other members. In a similar vein, Wispé and Lloyd (49) have proposed that subordinates may desire formally structured relations between themselves and superiors to protect themselves from any impulsive or "personal" application of negative sanctions for failure to perform well. To account for findings resulting from their analysis of interviews with the sales personnel of a life insurance company, they advance the hypothesis that (49, 60)

behind the desire for structure lies a permeating anxiety which results from the intense competition through which the agents must live and their inability to meet it efficaciously. The desire for structured personal interaction is thus a defense mechanism which attempts to control the behavior of those individuals in the system who have the authority to initiate negative sanctions.

The distribution among group members of needed resources or of the control over resources may be expected to influence the pattern of relations that develops among them. If, for example, one person has sole possession of expert knowledge needed by the others, a centralized structure may tend to arise in which each member depends on the central person, communicates primarily with him, and identifies with him. Experiments by Bavelas and Hastorf (Chap. 37) and by Burnstein and Zajonc (5) demonstrate that members will alter the structure of their group as the abilities of their colleagues change. In the former investigation, while experimental groups engaged in discussion, the experimenters sent approving messages to some members and disapproving messages to others, thus raising or lowering

the recipients' confidence in their skill as participants. The more confident members thereafter talked more often in the meetings of their group and subsequently were placed in more central positions in the group structure by their peers. In the latter investigation, the experimenters arranged matters so that some participants apparently improved and others decreased in ability while working on a motor task for the group. As a result, the members changed the group's structure to take advantage of these shifts in ability. Quite a different structure may be expected if valuable information is shared by two people or if two types of resources (for example, expertness and emotional warmth) are possessed by different people. This latter situation is essentially the one cited in our discussion (Chap. 24) of "task leader" and "social-emotional leader." We are suggesting here that the structure of the whole group (that is, the pattern of relations among group members) may be affected by the degree of concentration and the nature of distribution of resources in the group.

ENVIRONMENT OF THE GROUP

It is a common observation of the leaders of children's groups that physical environment, including such things as the amount of space available for play or the type of recreational equipment, greatly influences the structure of the group. Several studies have indicated, too, that the opportunity for social contact provided by the geographical arrangement of houses affects the way friendships develop and consequently the sociometric structure of a neighborhood (15). The sociometric structure, in turn, has been shown to influence the kind of communication network that arises —people are less restrained in talking to close friends than to mere acquaintances (14). In discussion groups the physical limitations imposed by the fact that only a few people can be heard at once makes the absolute size of the group an important determinant of group structure. Finally, making available to a group certain technological facilities, such as telephones for communication or equipment for simultaneous interpretation at international conferences, may modify its structure in a fundamental way.

The social environment of a group also exerts an influence on the structure of a group. Thus, for example, the stratification of society into social-economic classes or racial groups may be reflected in the sociometric structure of a neighborhood (**17**). Similar influences, of course, may be seen in groups at school, in church, and throughout the community.

PROBLEM OF CHARACTERIZING STRUCTURES

If we are to compare the structure of one group with that of another, or if we are to study how the structure of the same group changes over time, we must develop some way of describing the characteristics of any given structure, whether it be formal or informal. Although much has been written about the structure of groups and a good deal of research has been completed, a fully satisfactory theoretical conception of group structure has not yet gained general acceptance. Four rather different, though not entirely incompatible, approaches to conceptualizing group structure may be distinguished.

OFFICE, POSITION, STATUS, AND SUBGROUP

Much of the thinking found in the literature on group structure accepts the general approach outlined by Linton (**32**). One of his central points is that both structural (spatial) and dynamic properties are interwoven in the phenomena of group differentiation. Linton proposes to keep these aspects separate by treating them under two terms: status and role. Thus, he writes (**32**, 113–114):

A status, as distinct from the individual who may occupy it, is simply a collection of rights and duties. . . . . A role represents the dynamic aspects of a status. The individual is socially assigned to a status and occupies it with relation to other statuses. When he puts the rights and duties which constitute the status into effect, he is performing a role.

Various revisions and refinements of this approach can be found in current theoretical writings. Perhaps the most important of these is that of Newcomb (**36**), who has developed Linton's general point of view and incorporated it into a broad theory of social psychology. He employs the concept of position rather

than status and views position as the "smallest element—the construction block" of societies and organized groups. He views role as the behavior of people "as occupants of the position." Newcomb notes further that (**36**, 277) "every position which is recognized by the members of a group contributes in some way to the purposes of the group; this contribution represents its *function*." The similarities should be apparent between this approach and our treatment of "offices" in Chapter 24.

There is general agreement among those who adopt this approach that, whenever a group continues to exist for some time with group activities to perform, there arises a tendency for divisions of responsibility to come about. Different parts of the group are made regularly responsible for different group activities and functions. These parts may be given various labels such as status, position, and office. Whatever the label, however, they are conceived as having two properties: (*a*) each member of the group may be located as "inside" or "outside" each part and (*b*) expected, permitted, and prohibited behaviors are associated with the occupancy of each part.

The structure of a group consists, however, not only of differentiated parts but also of relations, sometimes called "links" or "bonds," between parts. Four *types of relations* among the parts of a group have received most attention, especially from theorists concerned with workgroups and organizations: (*a*) the flow of information, (*b*) the flow of work, (*c*) authority, and (*d*) the mobility of people. It may be found with respect to each of these for any specific pair of parts that the relation between them is symmetrical, asymmetrical, or absent. Thus, for example, information may flow freely in both directions between two offices, in one direction only, or not at all. Or the personnel practices of the group may permit people to move from either position to the other, only from one to the other, or not directly from either to the other. It should be clear that these different types of relations may, in principle, be quite independent of one another. To illustrate, the positions of president and secretary may be related symmetrically with respect to the flow of information; information reaching either the president or his secretary is likely to be passed on to the other. The same two positions may be asymmetrically related with respect to the flow of work and authority; both work and commands can go only from the president to the secretary. And the positions may be unrelated with respect to mobility; it is not possible for a person to move from being secretary to being president and vice versa. In actual practice, of course, we should expect to find a tendency for relations of certain types to be associated; the flow of work and the distribution of authority, for example, might be expected to "require" certain communication channels. The discovery of what types of relations tend to go together under various conditions of group life is an interesting topic for research.

In order to describe the structure of a group, it is necessary to determine the nature of each of these types of relation (and perhaps others) between all pairs of parts of the group. Each type of relation may be thought of as generating a corresponding *type of structure*. From an examination of the *pattern* of authority relations, for instance, one might characterize the authority structure of the group as hierarchical, equalitarian, or anarchical. Or one might describe the communication structure in terms of its completeness, degree of connectedness, or its provision for "feedback loops." Unfortunately, no comprehensive system for characterizing the many patterns of relations that may constitute group structure has yet gained general acceptance, although, as we shall see later, certain mathematical treatments of structure appear to hold great promise.

INTERPERSONAL RELATIONS

A somewhat different approach to the study of group structure concentrates, not upon the relations between positions or offices, but directly upon the relations between individuals. The procedure followed is, however, essentially the same as the previous one if we consider individual members as the "parts" of the group: the relations between each pair of members are specified, and the interpersonal *structure of the group* is defined as the pattern of these interpersonal relations. Needless to say, this second approach is better suited than the first to the study of groups that do not have clearly identifiable offices, but it may also be used even when they do. When a group does have specified offices and definite relations among them, this structure may be thought of as one of the determinants of the interpersonal structure of the group, since re-

lations between offices may be expected to influence relations between individuals who occupy these offices. It should be noted, though, that at least under certain conditions the structure of offices may be properly conceived as a resultant of stabilized interpersonal relations. And the possibility should not be overlooked that the two kinds of structure are always interdependent to some degree.

To date, the research conducted on interpersonal structures of groups has investigated primarily four types of relations. (*a*) The relation A *chooses* B (sociometric choice) was one of the earliest to be used in describing the interpersonal structure of groups. Moreno (34) employed a criterion of choice intended to reveal the desire of the chooser to associate with the person chosen in some particular activity. In subsequent research many different criteria of choice have been employed, such as selection of a colleague for work on a given task, a leisure-time companion in various settings, a roommate, a superior, and so on. It is now clear that many different aspects of interpersonal relationships may be revealed by the technique of having people "choose" one another and that a person may select one individual in one situation and another individual in a different setting. The most preferred person, Rosenfeld has shown (42), may be quite different from the one chosen as an actual associate because actual choices, in contrast to wishful preferences, are more regularly based upon the chooser's belief that the chosen person will reciprocate the choice. Moreover, Newcomb reports in Chapter 41 that the judged as well as the actual relationships are largely determined by efforts to maintain a balance among separate elements such as personal values, estimates of one another's attitudes, and interpersonal attraction. The general relation A chooses B must therefore be viewed as including several specific relationships whose particular nature depends upon the criterion of choice employed. (*b*) The relation *can communicate to* has been studied intensively, especially in experiments where individuals are assigned to groups having some degree of restriction on who can communicate to whom. The nature of the interpersonal communication network of a group has been found to have marked effects on many other aspects of the group. (*c*) The interpersonal relation *has power over* has also been investigated in a variety of settings. The interpersonal power structure of a group is undoubtedly one of its most important features. We have seen, however, that a person may be said to have, or not to have, power over another depending upon what criterion of influence is employed—he may be able to influence a particular person with respect to some things but not others. It follows, then, that the exact nature of the interpersonal power structure of a group will depend upon the "topic" of influence being considered. (*d*) Finally, a few experiments have varied the flow of work among group members and thus the pattern of *task interdependence* among individuals in the group.

One of the difficulties in characterizing group structure in terms of interpersonal relations lies in the fact that there are so many possible types of relations between people. The four listed here constitute but a small proportion of the total that might be studied. DeSoto and Kuethe (9) have developed an ingenious method for systematizing "the myriad interpersonal relationships that are named in English." They present data on some of the properties people attribute to ten interpersonal relationships: likes, trusts, feels superior to, is happier than, confides in, dominates, lies to, dislikes, is afraid of, and hates. Specifically, they asked respondents to estimate the likelihood that these relationships exist among three hypothetical persons, and, given an instance in which a certain relationship does exist among two members of the trio, to state the likelihood that this same relationship exists among the others. The results revealed that people more often predict positive relationships to exist than negative ones and that certain relations are more often seen as symmetric or transitive than others. It appears, then, that people think about interpersonal relationships in terms of preconceived schemas. Subsequent work by DeSoto (10) and Zajonc and Burnstein (50, 51) indicate that individuals employ such schemas in their perceptions of more complicated group structures and tend to make correct or incorrect deductions about aspects of the structures that are not objectively evident but are in accord with their preconceptions. Research like this is beginning to lay the groundwork for solving the problem of how to establish a satisfactory basis for determining which of the many possible relationships can meaningfully be employed to specify group structures. No satisfactory solution, however, has yet been achieved.

RANKING

A rather different way of describing the structure of groups is commonly employed. This method consists in essence of designating some dimension, or attribute, in terms of which people can be ranked and defining a person's "status" or "standing" in the group as his rank on one or more of these dimensions. The nature of this conception and its relation to the previous two may be seen in the following statement by Homans concerning the concept *status* (**26,** 179):

When a sociologist says that a man has high status in an organization, he may mean any or all of the following: (*a*) the man is close to the center of the web of communication in the organization; (*b*) he is carrying on a particular kind of activity or maintaining a certain level of activity; and (*c*) by reason of his position in the web of communication and the kind of job he does, he is highly ranked or valued. Thus in a certain manufacturing firm, the General Manager reports to the President, is in charge of manufacturing, and has high prestige. We do not want to lump all three aspects of his position together under the name of *status*, but to separate them and see the relations among them. And of the three aspects, we give the name of *rank* to the evaluation or prestige aspect. . . .

The essential feature of this third approach to defining structure, in contrast to the other two, is that it is based on the ranking of group members with respect to some characteristic they possess. In its most general form it would permit the assignment of a rank to members with respect to any characteristic that has the logical properties required for constructing an ordering of people. Thus, a member might be said to have a certain rank with respect to age, intelligence, height, wealth, duration of membership, popularity, frequency of attendance at meetings, and so on endlessly.

In actual practice very few orderings have been considered by theorists to constitute group structure. But, just as we found in considering interpersonal relations as a basis for defining structure, no satisfactory general principle has yet been formulated for selecting among the many possibilities. Bales (**1**) has proposed that four kinds of differentiation are most common in small groups: (*a*) the degree to which members have access to resources, (*b*) the degree to which they have control over other persons, (*c*) the degree to which they have importance or prestige, and (*d*) the degree of solidarity or identification each has with the group. The third of these, the one labeled *rank* by Homans, has been employed most widely in research on groups. From this research it has been consistently reported that a person's rank in an ordering of people according to prestige makes a great deal of difference to his behavior, his interactions with others, his level of aspiration, and his self evaluation. Caution is required, however, in interpreting results like these because it is almost certain that various orderings of people are positively associated. We should expect, for instance, that a person who is high on one of the four kinds of differentiation identified by Bales will tend to be high on the others. Unfortunately, most of the research on the effects of prestige has not eliminated the possibility that other bases of differentiation also contribute to observed effects.

MATHEMATICAL TREATMENTS OF GROUP STRUCTURE

In recent years a great deal of attention has been devoted to the possibility of using mathematics in the treatment of group structure. We will undertake here only a brief description of some of the general approaches that have been made and provide references to the more technical literature. The most promising developments, to date, have employed the second conception mentioned above, which defines group structure in terms of interpersonal relations. The major part of this work has been motivated by an interest in sociometric choices (interpersonal liking), communication networks, and power structures. In all these, group structure is conceived as a pattern of dyadic relations. The mathematical formulations are, of course, entirely abstract and could be applied to any kind of interpersonal relation.

Much of the early work on group structure made use of the sociometric test, in which each member of the group indicates his preferences for associating with other members of the group. Originally these choices were converted into a picture, or sociogram, in which circles represented people and arrows represented choices. The sociometric structure of a given group could be examined by inspecting this picture. The first major step in the mathematical treatment of sociometric material, as pointed out by Glanzer and Glaser (19) in their review of mathematical representations of group structure, was the observation by Forsyth and Katz (18) that sociometric choices could be cast in the form of matrixes and thereby subjected to the operations of matrix algebra.

In its simplest form a matrix is constructed so that each member of the group is represented as both a row and a column of the matrix. If person A chooses person B, the number 1 is entered in the cell where row A and column B intersect. If person A does not choose person B, the number 0 is entered in this cell. Once the choices of a group have been converted to a matrix, the operations of matrix algebra can be performed, and various properties of the sociometric structure of the group can be specified rigorously. For example, Festinger (12) and Harary and Ross (24) have developed methods for detecting "cliques" by matrix operations, and Ross and Harary (43) have demonstrated how to identify the "liaison persons" in a group by means of matrixes. Glanzer and Glaser (19) have summarized the many indexes that can be constructed, which provide a basis for comparing groups with one another and individuals within groups.

It is apparent from this and similar work that matrix algebra can be a useful tool in research on group structure. Since matrixes can be dealt with by high-speed computers, it is possible to handle large quantities of complex material rather easily, not only sociometric data but data on any type of interpersonal relation.

Another mathematical treatment of structure was introduced by Bavelas (3), who wanted to be able to characterize rigorously such structural properties of a group as its segmentation into central and peripheral layers and the distance from its innermost part to the outside. He constructed a formal system by which he could do so and initiated a program of work on the effects produced by placing people in communication networks with different structural properties. Examples of this research may be found in Chapters 37 and 38.

It has subsequently been shown that Bavelas' formal system can be incorporated into the more general mathematical theory of linear graphs (known more briefly as "graph theory"). The basic terms of this mathematical system are *point* and *line,* and the system is concerned with the patterns that can be constructed from these two abstract elements. The usefulness of graph theory for treating structural properties of groups lies in the possibility of coordinating each member of a group to a point of a graph and a relation between a pair of people to a line connecting the corresponding points. A drawing of a graph looks like a sociogram, since the points of a graph may stand for people and the lines for sociometric relations. The same sort of drawing would result from coordinating points to people and lines to permissible communication links between people.

The essential contribution of graph theory, however, stems from the fact that it is a mathematical system consisting of undefined terms ("point" and "line") and axioms and theorems derived from them. Specifically, three major results from the mathematical work on graphs are of value in the treatment of group structure. First, graph theory contains certain "higher order" concepts that are rigorously defined in terms of the mathematical system. Since these terms refer to more complex properties of graphs, the coordination of graphs to groups of people yields a set of precisely defined concepts for describing group structures and thereby for comparing different structures. Thus, for example, one can speak with exact meaning about the diameter of a group, the number of levels it has, its degree of connectedness, its vulnerability to splitting, and its degree of balance. The availability of rigorously defined concepts makes it unnecessary to rely upon such ambiguous labels as "hierarchical," "decentralized," or "loosely connected" in characterizing group structures. Second, graph theory supplies techniques of computation and formulas for calculating certain quantitative features of group structure. Third, graph theory contains theorems that specify features of graphs, and thus of group structures, that follow necessarily from the undefined terms and the axioms of graph theory. In this connection, however, it should be noted that graph theory per se has nothing to say about empirical tendencies. In order to derive theorems about the "behavior" of group

structures, it is necessary to add to graph theory additional axioms or postulates about the psychological or sociological determinants operating in any given situation. More complete accounts of graph theory and its possible uses in group dynamics are presented by Harary and Norman (**22**), Cartwright (**6**), and Harary, Norman, and Cartwright (**23**).

It should be apparent from this discussion that a given set of empirical data (for example, sociometric choices and communication links among the members of a group) can be represented as both a matrix and a graph. To illustrate, if person A chooses person B, this fact may be represented both in a matrix by the number 1 in the cell where row A and column B intersect and in a graph by a directed line from point A to point B. For this reason, the two mathematical treatments of group structure are not incompatible alternatives for the group dynamics theorist. Instead, they provide different, but supplementary, methods for dealing rigorously with various aspects of structure. Which method is preferable in dealing with a particular problem depends upon the specific nature of the problem.

We noted earlier that matrixes and graphs have been employed primarily in connection with the view of group structure that deals with interpersonal relations. It should now be apparent that they are equally applicable when group structure is viewed as a pattern of relations among offices; we merely represent an office as a row and a column of a matrix or as a point on a graph. In fact, the organization chart may be conceived as a pictorial representation of a graph of the relations among offices. The conception of group structure in terms of the ranking of people also relates to the other two broad conceptions. Both matrix algebra and graph theory permit the construction of indexes that assign numerical values to each member of a group and, of course, it is then possible to rank people according to these values, which are derived strictly from the structural properties of the relations between people. Harary (**21**), for example, has defined the status of a person in terms of an index calculated from the graph representing the interpersonal relations in a group. There is, thus, reason to believe that by the aid of mathematics the three approaches to group structure may eventually be consolidated into one. Much more theoretical and empirical work will be required, however, before a fully satisfactory conception of group structure can be achieved.

SOME EFFECTS OF STRUCTURE

Empirical research on the structure of groups has tended to concentrate on a few aspects of the total topic. We will consider here four general questions that have motivated much of the research conducted to date: (*a*) How are different types of structure interrelated in a particular group? (*b*) What consequences for the individual group member stem from his location in the group structure? (*c*) What effects on the performance of a group are produced by its structure? (*d*) What characteristics of a group tend to change as it changes in size?

RELATIONS BETWEEN TYPES OF STRUCTURE

In the discussion thus far, different "types" of structure have been identified. Any given group may be structured according to the flow of communication, flow of work, mobility of people, authority and power relations, sociometric relations, and ranking on such dimensions as importance, prestige, popularity, identification with the group, and ownership of resources. Although empirical research has only begun to examine the nature and consequences of these many different kinds of structure, there is evidence that most of those listed here do in fact exert an influence on the behavior of group members and the performance of groups. In studying group structure we seem almost embarrassed by an abundance of riches; the number of "types" of structure is too great. Is it possible ever to speak of "the structure" of a group or even of a few dominant structures? An affirmative answer would require interrelations among the many types such as to make them regularly associated with one another in some definite way.

Discussions of status have suggested that there may be a tendency in groups to "equilibrate" the rankings of members of different dimensions. Benoit-Smullyan (**4**, 160) has proposed, for instance, that there is a tendency "for a man's position in the economic hierarchy to match his position in the hierarchy of prestige." Lasswell and Kaplan (**30**, 56) have advanced essentially the same hypothesis in their proposition that "the positions of a person or group in different value patterns tend to approximate one another" so that "the rich tend also to be the healthy, respected, informed, and so on, and the poor to be the sickly, despised, ignorant." Case studies of groups have provided a wealth of anecdotal evidence supportive of this general point of view.

A more controlled study of the nature of status equilibration has been undertaken by Exline and Ziller (**11**), who experimentally created different combinations of status in groups by means of instructions designed to show that a subject was either congruent or incongruent in status on ability to carry out the task successfully and on voting power. Their results show in several different ways that interpersonal conflict was significantly greater in the groups having status incongruence. It appears, moreover, that the status structure of these groups was unstable and that, if allowed to change, they might modify their structures so as to bring about congruence. Finally, there is evidence that status-congruent groups had a better quality of group performance.

It seems not unreasonable to assume from the available evidence that future research will be able to show that groups do in fact develop a "core" system for ranking individual members and that discrepancies from this system generate tendencies to bring about a more congruent status system.

Conceptions of group structure that are based on interpersonal relations rather than ranking also tend to assume interdependence among the different "types" of relations. French and Raven (Chap. 20) assume, for example, a definite relation between the sociometric structure and the power structure of a group. As the popularity of a member increases, his ability to exercise influence within the group increases, and as his influence increases (for whatever reason) he becomes more attractive. We shall see in our discussion of communication networks that there appear to be communication structures that are optimal for effective influence and coordination of effort among members.

In an enduring group, it seems, a compatibility exists among its separate forms of structure, and some formal or informal means obtains among the members for making the necessary adjustments whenever incompatibility appears in its different structures.

CONSEQUENCES OF LOCATION

From the point of view of the individual member, one location in a group may be associated with rather different opportunities, demands, and experiences than another. Because of these differing attributes, a member's position in a group's structure is of great importance. For one thing, he will probably not find all locations equally attractive or satisfying. He may want to have many people "beneath" him in the power structure, or he may desire to have a central location in the communication structure. If his location is not the one he prefers, there will be forces on the member to change either his location or the structure itself. But if he is satisfied with his location, he may make great efforts to maintain it and resist anything that might bring about a change in the structure of the group. An interesting example of this kind of situation has been provided by Festinger *et al.* (14) in their description of a small community in which a hostile rumor, started by people who were opposed to an impending change of group structure, served to retard developments leading to such a change. In general, the degree of satisfaction that a person derives from his location in a structure, and the degree of frustration of his desire to change location, may be expected to influence his beliefs, morale, and productivity.

We have seen that persons who have positions of higher status tend to be more satisfied with their jobs than those of lower status (Chap. 7). There is additional evidence indicating that as people move up in a hierarchy, their jobs become increasingly important to them. Festinger (13) measured the attitudes among managers in a large manufacturing firm on two occasions separated by a period of three and one-half years. The managers who were promoted during that interval shifted their attitudes so that they subsequently placed greater importance on their careers, perceived their families to be less sympathetic to their careers, and believed the wishes of their families to be less compelling. The greater the size of promotion, moreover, the larger were these shifts. Managers who were not promoted changed their attitudes in the opposite direction; on the second measure-

ment they believed that their careers were less important, that their families concurred in this view, and that the wishes of their families were more important.

The pressures acting upon a person in a given location have consequences for his opinions, attitudes, and behavior aside from those aroused by satisfaction with his role. These effects have been examined most intensively in studies comparing the behavior of persons at different status levels in the hierarchy of an organization.

A person's position within an organization exposes him to a particular group and to that group's pressures toward uniformity. An interesting illustration of the effects of membership in groups at different status levels was noted earlier in an account of a study by Lieberman (Chap. 2). It will be recalled that he observed the changes in attitudes among workers, some of whom were promoted to the position of foreman while others were elected stewards in their union. The neophyte foremen developed attitudes more sympathetic to management and the newly elected stewards developed views more pro-union. Because of financial problems in the company, some of the foremen were demoted a year or so later, and at about the same time the shop stewards finished their terms of office. In each case, after returning to the status of worker, the respondent's attitudes became similar to the ones they had initially held as workers.

There are indications that members' views about methods of managing are modified as they move into higher positions. In business firms at least, persons at higher levels believe it is more important to make up one's own mind than to conform to the wishes of others (38), to initiate structure than to display consideration (16), and to achieve success in work than to strive for approval or rewards (37).

Persons of superior status appear to have more access to channels of interpersonal communication. It has been observed that individuals in higher positions talk more often in face-to-face meetings, are more often the target of communication in such meetings, send more messages to those who are not near at hand, and receive more messages from people at lower levels.

A higher-ranking official must solve problems quite different from those met by a lower-ranking member. Managers, compared to foremen, for example, look farther into the future in their daily work and develop an understanding of a wider array of functions performed by a larger number of people within the organization. Thus, the state of a superior's knowledge should be different from that possessed by a subordinate. Zajonc and Wolfe (**52**) asked members at several levels of management in a small company about the aspects of their organization that were most prominent for them. It was found that persons located at higher levels had more differentiated cognitions and that these fitted together into a more coherent whole than did those at the lower levels. Among those at the higher levels, comments about the company were also more objective and less laden with affective and evaluative views than among those at lower ranks. In a similar vein are the observations of several different investigators that the officers of a group make more accurate estimates than does the average member about what the membership desires or believes (**8, 46**).

A striking consequence of location in a group's structure has been reported by Kasl and French (**29**), who found that employees with higher status in a large company had fewer medical complaints and made fewer visits to the company clinic than did those with lower status. In a national survey, Kahn et al. (**28**) discovered that respondents who occupied higher positions in their places of employment more often perceived themselves to be in excellent health. To explain these results the authors propose that individuals of higher rank develop more favorable self-esteem, which has beneficial consequences in turn for their physical and mental health.

Persons at different status positions in a group, it is clear, display interesting differences in behavior. It is not at all clear, however, why this is so. Two separate locations in a group's table of organization may be widely separated on power or prestige but close together in communication or flow of work. Which locations in which type of structure generate the differences in behavior? We expect that a person's behavior will change when he moves from line to staff, from a position which requires few contacts outside his group to one in which he must often deal with outsiders, from being popular to being less well liked, or from being a newcomer to being a veteran. Future studies in ongoing organizations will need to observe the consequences of

one's location on several different simultaneous relationships.

Carefully controlled research on the effects of location in a structure has been conducted in several laboratory experiments. We have already noted differences in behavior among members of laboratory groups who had different amounts of social power (Chaps. 21, 23). Closely allied to the studies of social power are experimental investigations on *communication networks*. The common procedure, illustrated in Chapters 37 and 38, has been to create in the laboratory groups consisting usually of four or five people, to assign them a group task, and to establish certain patterns of permissible communication among them while they are working on the task. The group task is typically an intellectual problem which requires that information, initially distributed among the members, be collected into one place and processed so as to provide an "answer" to the problem. As a rule, the experiment is conducted so that when an answer is achieved a new problem is given, and the group repeats the process several times.

The independent variable in these experiments is the *pattern of permissible communication links* between the members of the group. Of major interest has been the *degree of centrality or peripherality* of each person in the network. Although several slightly different formal definitions of "centrality" have been employed, the intuitive notion involved is not difficult to grasp. If for example, five people, A, B, C, D, and E, are placed in a communication network so that the only communication links are A-B, B-C, C-D, and D-E, the network then resembles a chain with C in the central location and with A and E in the most peripheral ones. If to this network we add the communication link A-E, then the network resembles a circle (known in graph theory as a cycle) and all locations become central. It is possible to determine the centrality of each person in any specified network. Some of the networks employed are illustrated in Chapter 37.

These studies show quite consistently that the degree of centrality of a person's location in communication networks is related to the satisfaction he experiences from participating in the group. In general, the greater the centrality (or the degree of centrality relative to that of others), the greater the satisfaction. And, as might be expected, the average satisfaction among the members of a group is related to the average degree of centrality of the positions of the group's network.

Why should personal satisfaction be positively associated with centrality of location? Several hypotheses have been advanced. The first was proposed by Leavitt (31), who reasoned that a person in a central location will be seen by himself and by others as having the greatest potential for getting the information required for arriving at the answer to the group's problem. Perception of each member's "answer-getting potential" will, in turn, affect the roles of members and accordingly the degree of each person's dependence on others or independence from them. Leavitt then concludes (31, 48): "In our culture, in which needs for autonomy, recognition, and achievement are strong, it is to be expected that positions which limit independence of action (peripheral positions) would be unsatisfying." A rather similar hypothesis has been advanced by Trow (47). He proposes that the relationship between satisfaction and centrality may be accounted for largely by two variables: (*a*) the autonomy of positions in the group and (*b*) the members' need for autonomy. Autonomy here means "independence from others with respect to direction of one's own activities." Trow has demonstrated experimentally that people in positions of higher autonomy are more satisfied and that the relationship between autonomy and satisfaction is stronger among people with a higher need for autonomy.

Mulder (35) has presented a critique of these and other hypotheses designed to account for the relation between centrality and satisfaction. He concludes that the research evidence tends, on the whole, to be consistent with hypotheses broadly similar to those of Leavitt and Trow. However, he argues that independence and autonomy are essentially negative conceptions. What is it, he asks, that people want to be free to do? He suggests three possibilities that might be applicable to the experimental situations employed in this type of research: "freedom to unfold activity," "freedom to exert power," and "freedom to have responsibility for completion of one's own task." On the basis of the results of an experiment he conducted and of others reported in the literature, Mulder concludes that it is the freedom to exert power (that is, to influence the behavior of others) that produces the relationship between centrality in the communication network and satisfaction. Although Mulder's findings and arguments are impressive, it is hardly likely that the general problem has yet been finally solved. Further research is needed before a fully satisfactory understanding of these phenomena will be achieved.

Another finding from this general line of research is that when one location is distinctly more central than the rest there is a strong tendency for the person in this location to become the leader of the group. This finding is, of course, relevant to the question of satisfaction, for a central person by being a leader may gain satisfaction of such motives as those for power, independence, autonomy, recognition, and perhaps others. The research reported by Guetzkow in Chapter 38 makes it clear, however, that a more complex differentiation of roles is involved than simply a dichotomy of "leader" and "follower." Guetzkow shows that the nature of the network, the nature of the group task, and certain characteristics of the people in the group all affect the development of the role structure. It is important to recognize, nevertheless, that some communication networks seem to be so restrictive that an individual member's role is almost completely determined by his location in the network.

Although laboratory experiments have thus far been confined to quite small groups working on one particular sort of group task, their findings point to a significant feature of group life. They suggest that the morale and behavior of members of "natural" groups may be better understood through a knowledge of their communication structures. Satisfactory methods for determining the communication structures of natural groups, however, have yet to be developed.

A member's rank in a group can affect how well he performs the task assigned to him. Burnstein and Zajonc (5) required members of four-person groups to engage in a simple task in which each person pressed a button, after a given signal, as quickly as he could. This activity was repeated during a long series of trials. A very brief time was allowed for each person's reaction and a red light was turned on, visible to all in the group, if he failed to respond fast enough. Differences in status were generated by varying the amount of weight each member's score contributed to the total score of the group; the greater the weight, the higher the status. Members were allowed to determine, by secret ballots, which one should have each of the four status positions and typically assigned these positions in accord with the quality of performance among the members. Throughout the study changes were made in the status ordering as the members wished. Because the time intervals were exceedingly small, it was possible for the experimenter secretly to make it appear that members were either failing or succeeding on the task regardless of how well they actually were performing. In one experiment the persons who were originally chosen as the highest ranking members were demoted by their groups because the quality of their work appeared to decrease and the persons who were the lowest ranking members were promoted because their performances appeared to improve. In a second experiment members who were originally of intermediate rank were either promoted or demoted. Careful records were kept of the actual performances by the participants throughout all trials. As a member's status level was increased his actual performance improved, and as his status level was decreased his performance suffered.

GROUP PERFORMANCE

The experimental studies on communication networks have consistently shown that group performance—whether measured in terms of time required to reach a solution, number of messages sent, number of errors made, or rate of group learning—is affected by the communication structure imposed on the group. The formulation of general principles to account for these effects, however, has proved to be quite difficult. The findings of Guetzkow and Simon (20) suggest one important lead for further research. These investigators employed a technique similar to that used by Bavelas, but in addition they directed their attention to the ways in which the groups organized themselves to perform the task. They found that the different networks did not create differences in time needed to solve the problems when comparisons were made only among groups that achieved an optimal work organization. The communication structure appears, therefore, to affect performance by the relative difficulty it creates for the group in establishing an effective work organization.

From a review of dozens of experiments on

communication networks, Shaw (44) concludes that groups without a central person (as in a circle) tend to solve problems faster than groups containing a central person (as in a chain). Although the magnitude of these effects is modified by other conditions such as the amount of "noise" in the system, the location of the relevant information among members, and the kind of prior experience the members have had in other networks, it is clear that the most pronounced effect is created by the kind of task the group must perform. Centralized groups appear to do better on a task requiring little use of logic or deduction, such as in the accumulation of information at one point in the group, whereas decentralized groups are more efficient when the task requires logical operations to be performed upon the information after it is accumulated in one place. Further research is now needed to examine in greater detail how groups adjust their working arrangements to meet the requirements of group tasks in different communication networks. The analysis presented by Guetzkow in Chapter 38 indicates some of the ways in which this research might proceed.

GROUP SIZE

The most visible aspect of a group's structure is the number of persons in the organization. When a group expands or shrinks in size, various properties of the group change. Thus, it is common for members to be concerned about how rapidly their group should grow, whether it should break into smaller units, and what effects changes in size will have upon the individual members and the group's productivity.

Virtually all of the quantitative research on the effects of a group's size have been descriptive investigations in which the properties of larger and smaller groups are compared. Excellent reviews of these investigations, each with a somewhat different approach, are available. Willems (48) has summarized studies that reveal the effects of size on the behavior of members. Porter and Lawler (39) have considered changes in the characteristics of subunits within larger organizations and the effects of size on the larger bodies as well. Indik (27) has discussed size in larger industrial organizations, and Thomas and Fink (45) have summarized the findings from laboratory investigations in which size was one of the variables. Certain general findings are pertinent to our interests.

As groups increase in size, a smaller and smaller proportion of persons become central to the organization, make decisions for it, and communicate to the total membership. A familiar example is a discussion group. As the group becomes larger, a smaller percentage of those present can have the floor, the chairman tends to exercise stronger control, and remarks from the chair are more often made to the group as a whole than to separate members. As a consequence of such tendencies toward centralization, more members become peripheral and engage in activities that are less crucial for a group's outcome as the size of a group increases.

A smaller proportion of members keep in touch with one another as an organization grows; there are too many persons for complete communication to occur among them, and many members do not know one another. Complaints about poor communication are thus more often heard in larger organizations than in smaller ones, consensus is harder to develop, splits within the group are more likely to occur, and there tends to be less satisfaction with administrative decisions.

It has been shown that larger agencies depend more often upon impersonal means for communicating rules and policies, such as published statements or posters, than do smaller organizations. This impersonal promulgation of group standards probably is made necessary by the increased centralization of authority and the complexities in communication. . There are those who believe that the pressures toward uniformity tend to have less weight for members as the institution increases in size. If this is so, it may be due to the weak impact of a printed rule compared to one proposed and supported by present peers. A relevant example is found in a study of safety and accidents in coal mines of England and America (40). In England larger mines presumably had weaker standards of safety since they had considerably more accidents than smaller mines. In America the opposite was true; larger mines were safer than smaller ones. The investigator explains these contrasting results by demonstrating that in America the larger mines more often had a staff who were responsible for developing, promoting, and enforcing standards of safety but that this was not the case in England. The

safety specialists presumably overcame the impersonal nature of the rules in the larger mines.

We noted in Chapter 7 that a larger group tends to be less cohesive, a condition that also weakens the pressures toward uniformity in larger groups. The evidence is consistently strong that larger groups have more absenteeism as well and more turnover of membership. There is no clear indication, however, that groups of different sizes tend to be reliably different in their productivity.

We conclude that members find participation more satisfying and that group processes are more effective in smaller groups than in larger ones. But the results of available research on these matters probably does not tell the whole story. The increasing number of larger organizations in all parts of our society suggest that there are advantages in larger size that may well outweigh the disadvantages and that may not have been measured in the research conducted thus far. Two issues remain for further study. One is to determine what contrasting outcomes for an organization are enhanced and what ones are attenuated by larger and smaller size. The other issue is to explain why it is that a given size has particular effects. The volume of descriptive research on the consequences of group size suggests that solutions for these two issues may soon be attained.

OVERVIEW OF RESEARCH REPORTED IN PART SEVEN

The following six chapters examine, in a variety of settings and with several different techniques of research, some of the major phenomena related to group structure.

The first two chapters report research concerned with the communication structure in groups. In Chapter 37 Bavelas describes the original experiments on communication networks whose methods and findings have stimulated so much subsequent research. In these experiments groups were required to perform while operating with certain communication structures. It was found that speed and accuracy in problem-solving, morale, and the emergence of a leader were all affected by the nature of the communication network. For information about the findings from subsequent research, reference may be made to the excellent review by Shaw (44).

An interesting extension of this type of investigation is reported in Chapter 38 by Guetzkow. Attention is directed to the question of how the different communication networks influence the differentiation of roles within the group and the interlocking of roles into a work structure. Guetzkow shows how the communication network combines with other variables to influence the way the work is carried out by the group.

The problem of altering the structure of a group is considered by Bavelas, Hastorf, Gross, and Kite in Chapter 39. These authors demonstrate that the verbal output of selected members during a group discussion can be changed in a desired direction by either positively or negatively reinforcing the members' actions. As a result of changes in this verbal output, a member's position in the group's sociometric structure also changes. A series of experiments are reported in which the conditions necessary for such shifts and the persistence of them in subsequent meetings of the group are examined.

When a person attains higher status within a group, the members are likely to perceive that compared to a regular member he is in a better position to affect the group's outcomes. Members expect him to use this ability toward attaining the group's outcomes. In Chapter 40, Wiggins, Dill, and Schwartz observe the reactions of members to persons whose behavior is detrimental to the group rather than helpful.

They report that the reactions are more negative toward higher status persons who behave in detrimental manner than toward lower status persons who do the same things.

Although we are accustomed to think of a group's structure as a rather stable aspect of a group, we see that changes do occur in a group's structure under appropriate conditions. In Chapter 41 Newcomb reports on the shifts in interpersonal attraction among students who lived together in the same rooming house for many months. He notes that changes in interpersonal attraction develop as the members get to know one another's values and attitudes better or as these personal attributes change. The members seem to prefer a psychologically balanced relationship among the three elements—personal values, estimates of one another's attitudes, and interpersonal attraction—and shifts in interpersonal attraction apparently are made in order to maintain this balance.

In Chapter 42 French presents a formal theory, employing the mathematical theory of linear graphs, concerning the ways in which the power structure of a group determines the influence processes within the group and the outcome of these processes. This theory is especially interesting in the way it extends the analysis presented by Festinger in Chapter 14 to suggest ways in which certain aspects of group structure may affect the content and strength of group standards.

References

1. Bales, R. F. *Interaction process analysis, a method for study of small groups.* Cambridge, Mass.: Addison-Wesley, 1950.
2. Barnard, C. I. Functions and pathology of status systems in formal organizations. In W. F. Whyte (Ed.), *Industry and society.* New York: McGraw-Hill, 1946.
3. Bavelas, A. A mathematical model for group structures. *Applied Anthropology,* 1948, **7** (3), 16–30.
4. Benoit-Smullyan, E. Status, status types, and status interrelations. *American Sociological Review,* 1944, **9,** 151–161.
5. Burnstein, E., & Zajonc, R. Individual task performance in a changing social structure. *Sociometry,* 1965, **28,** 16–29.
6. Cartwright, D. The potential contribution of graph theory to organization theory. In M. Haire (Ed.), *Modern organization theory.* New York: Wiley, 1959.
7. Cattell, R. B. New concepts for measuring leadership, in terms of group syntality. *Human Relations,* 1951, **11,** 41–53.
8. Chowdry, K., & Newcomb, T. M. The relative ability of leaders and nonleaders to estimate opinions of their own groups. *Journal of Abnormal and Social Psychology,* 1952, **47,** 51–57.
9. DeSoto, C., & Kuethe, J. L. Subjective probabilities and interpersonal relationships. *Journal of Abnormal and Social Psychology,* 1959, **59,** 290–294.

10. DeSoto, C. Learning a social structure. *Journal of Abnormal and Social Psychology,* 1960, **60,** 417–421.

11. Exline, R., & Ziller, R. C. Status congruency and interpersonal conflict in decision-making groups. *Human Relations,* 1959, **12,** 147–161.

12. Festinger, L. The analysis of sociograms using matrix algebra. *Human Relations,* 1949, **2,** 153–158.

13. Festinger, L. Some changes in attitudes and values following promotion in General Electric. A preliminary report. Crotonville, N. Y.: General Electric Co., Management Development and Employee Relations Services, 1965.

14. Festinger, L., *et al.* A study of rumor: Its origin and spread. *Human Relations,* 1947, **1,** 464–486.

15. Festinger, L., Schachter, S., & Back, K. *Social pressures in informal groups.* New York: Harper, 1950.

16. Fleishmann, E. A. The measurement of leadership attitudes in industry. *Journal of Applied Psychology,* 1953, **37,** 153–158.

17. Form, W. H. Stratification in low- and middle-income housing areas. *Journal of Social Issues,* 1951, **7,** 109–131.

18. Forsyth, E., & Katz, L. A matrix approach to the analysis of sociometric data: Preliminary report. *Sociometry,* 1946, **9,** 340–347.

19. Glanzer, M., & Glaser, R. Techniques for the study of group structure and behavior. I. Analysis of structure. *Psychological Bulletin,* 1959, **56,** 317–332.

20. Guetzkow, H., & Simon, H. The impact of certain communication nets upon organization and performance in task-oriented groups. *Management Science,* 1955, **1,** 233–250.

21. Harary, F. Status and contrastatus. *Sociometry,* 1959, **22,** 23–43.

22. Harary, F., & Norman, R. Z. *Graph theory as a mathematical model in social science.* Ann Arbor, Mich.: Institute for Social Research, 1953.

23. Harary, F., Norman, R. Z., & Cartwright, D. *Structural models, an introduction to the theory of directed graphs.* New York: Wiley, 1965.

24. Harary, F., & Ross, I. C. A procedure for clique-detection using the group matrix. *Sociometry,* 1957, **20,** 205–215.

25. Hare, A. P. Interaction and consensus in different-sized groups. *American Sociological Review,* 1952, **17,** 261–267.

26. Homans, G. C. *The human group.* New York: Harcourt, Brace, 1950.

27. Indik, B. Some effects of organization size on member attitudes and behavior. *Human Relations,* 1963, **16,** 369–384.

28. Kahn, R., *et al. Organizational stress.* New York: Wiley, 1964.

29. Kasl, S. V., & French, J. R. P., Jr. The effects of occupational status on physical and mental health. *Journal of Social Issues,* 1962, **18,** 67–89.

30. Lasswell, H. D., & Kaplan, A. *Power and society.* New Haven, Conn.: Yale Univ. Press, 1950.

31. Leavitt, H. J. Some effects of certain communication patterns on group performance. *Journal of Abnormal and Social Psychology,* 1951, **46,** 38–50.

32. Linton, R. *The study of man.* New York: Appleton-Century, 1936.

33. Mills, T. M. Power relations in three-person groups. *American Sociological Review,* 1953, **18,** 351–357.

34. Moreno, J. L. *Who shall survive?* Washington, D. C.: Nervous and Mental Disease Publishing Co., 1934.

35. Mulder, M. Power and satisfaction in task-oriented groups. *Acta Psychologica,* 1959, **16,** 178–225.

36. Newcomb, T. M. *Social psychology.* New York: Dryden, 1950.

37. Pellegrin, R., & Coates, C. Executives and supervisors: Contrasting definitions of career success. *Administrative Science Quarterly,* 1957, **1,** 506–517.

38. Porter, L., & Henry, M. Job attitudes in management. V. Perceptions of the importance of certain personality traits as a function of job level. *Journal of Applied Psychology,* 1964, **48,** 31–36.

39. Porter, L., & Lawler, E. E. Properties of organization structure in relation to job attitudes and job behavior. *Psychological Bulletin,* 1965, **64,** 23–51.

40. Revans, R. W. Human relations, management, and size. In E. M. Hugh-Jones (Ed.), *Human relations in modern management.* Amsterdam: North Holland Publishing Co., 1958.

41. Roethlisberger, F. J., & Dickson, W. J. *Management and the worker.* Cambridge, Mass.: Harvard Univ. Press, 1939.

42. Rosenfeld, H. Social choice conceived as a level of aspiration. *Journal of Abnormal and Social Psychology,* 1964, **68,** 491–499.

43. Ross, I. C., & Harary, F. Identification of the liaison persons of an organization using the structure matrix. *Management Science,* 1955, **1,** 251–258.

44. Shaw, M. Communication networks. In L. Berkowitz (Ed.), *Advances in experimental social psychology.* Vol. I. New York: Academic Press, 1964.

45. Thomas, E. J., & Fink, C. Effects of group size. *Psychological Bulletin,* 1963, **60,** 371–384.

46. Talland, G. H. The assessment of group opinion by leaders and their influence on its formation. *Journal of Abnormal and Social Psychology,* 1954, **49,** 431–434.

47. Trow, D. B. Autonomy and job satisfaction in task-oriented groups. *Journal of Abnormal and Social Psychology,* 1957, **54,** 204–210.

48. Willems, E. P. Review of research. In R. Barker & P. V. Gump (Eds.), *Big school, small school.* Stanford, Calif.: Stanford Univ. Press, 1964.

49. Wispé, L. G., & Lloyd, K. E. Some situational and psychological determinants of the desire for structured interpersonal relations. *Journal of Abnormal and Social Psychology,* 1955, **51,** 57–60.

50. Zajonc, R., & Burnstein, E. The learning of balanced and unbalanced social structures. *Journal of Personality,* 1965, **33,** 153–163.

51. Zajonc, R., & Burnstein, E. Structural balance, reciprocity, and positivity as sources of cognitive bias. *Journal of Personality,* 1965, **33,** 570–583.

52. Zajonc, R., & Wolfe, D. Cognitive consequences of a person's position in a formal organization. *Human Relations,* 1966, **19,** 139–150.

37

Communication Patterns in Task-oriented Groups

ALEX BAVELAS

When the nature of a task is such that it must be performed by a group rather than by a single individual, the problem of working relationships arises. One of the more important of these relationships is that of communication. Quite aside from a consideration of the effects of communication on what is generally called "morale," it is easily demonstrated that for entire classes of tasks any hope of success depends upon an effective flow of information. But on what principles may a pattern of communication be determined which will in fact be a fit one for effective human effort? Administrative thinking on this point commonly rests on the assumption that optimum patterns of communications for a task-group may be derived from the specifications of the task to be performed. Students of organization, however, have pointed out repeatedly that working groups— even if one considers only communications relevant to the work being done—invariably tend to depart from formal statements of the patterns to be employed. One may take the view that this departure is due to the tendency of groups to adjust toward that class of communication patterns which will permit the earliest and most satisfying flow of ideas, information, and decisions. In groups which are free of outside control, it is clear that the interaction patterns which emerge and stabilize are products of the social process within the group. A group which exists as a part of a larger organization, however, seldom has the freedom to make such an adjustment. In most organizations the maintenance of the stated—and presumably optimum—patterns of communication is regarded as a first principle of effective performance. It is easy to understand this tendency of administration to inhibit changes in formal communication patterns. One

From *Journal of the Acoustical Society of America*, 1950, **22**, 725–730. Also, from a chapter with the same title in *The policy sciences*, Daniel Lerner & Harold D. Lasswell (Eds.), Stanford, Cal.: Stanford University Press, 1951. Reprinted by permission of the author, the Acoustical Society of America, and Stanford Univ. Press.

need only remember how intimate the relation is between communication, control, and authority.

In these organizational situations, the imposed patterns of communication may determine certain aspects of the group process. This raises the question of how a fixed communication pattern may affect the work and life of a group. Do certain patterns have structural properties which may limit group performance? May it be that among several communication patterns—*all logically adequate for the successful completion of a specified task*—one will result in significantly better performance than another? What effects might pattern, as such, have upon the emergence of leadership, the development of organization, and the degree of resistance to group disruption?

These questions have prompted a series of exploratory studies which have grown into a program of research. The findings are incomplete at present, but are of interest in their possible implications. In this chapter, the attempt will be made to describe the areas of present experimental activity and the general direction which the work is taking.

SOME GEOMETRIC PROPERTIES OF COMMUNICATION PATTERNS

If we consider who may communicate with whom in a task-group, without regard for the nature or medium of communication, we can ask a number of simple but important questions. Let us vary the ways in which five individuals are linked [1] to one another (it being understood that every individual in the group will be linked to at least one other individual in the same group). What different kinds of communication patterns may we produce, and

how may we describe quantitatively the difference between them? Obviously, this would more properly be an exercise for a topologist. For the social scientist it is more to the point to ask, "What differences among these patterns appear (quite intuitively) to be of a kind that would affect human beings in some way?" If we look at the patterns shown in Figure 1, we find that intuitive notions come easily— perhaps, too easily. Students commonly remark, upon seeing patterns C and D for the first time, that pattern C is "autocratic," while pattern D is a typical "business setup." Actually, of course, insofar as linkage goes they are identical, the only difference being the arrangement of the dots on this paper. Among patterns A, B, and C, however, we may point to some real differences. For instance, in pattern A each individual can communicate with two others in the group directly—that is, without relaying a message through some other person. In patterns C and D there is only one individual in the group who can communicate directly with all the others.

To make another comparison, any individual in pattern A can communicate with any one of the others with no more than a single "relay." In pattern B two individuals must relay messages through three others in order to communicate with each other.

In a sense, the comparisons just made involve the notion of "distance" between individuals in a pattern. If we adopt some method of counting the "distances" between individuals, we can make some statements regarding differences between and within patterns. In Figure 2 a method of counting is illustrated as applied to pattern B in Figure 1. The summation of all internal distances for pattern B is 40 ($\Sigma d_{x,y} = 40$). In a similar way, we find that the same summation for pattern A is 30 and for pattern C, 32. (Figure 3 shows the tabulations of distances in pattern C.)

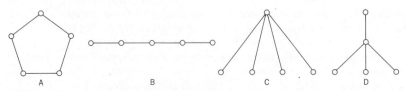

FIGURE 1. Some different communication patterns. Each line represents a communication linkage.

[1] For purposes of this discussion, if individual p is linked to individual q it will mean that p may communicate to q and that q may communicate to p—that is, the link is symmetrical.

p — 4.0   q — 5.7   r — 6.7   s — 5.7   t — 4.0

p to q =1	q to p =1	r to p =2	s to p =3	t to p =4
p to r =2	q to r =1	r to q =1	s to q =2	t to q =3
p to s =3	q to s =2	r to s =1	s to r =1	t to r =2
p to t =4	q to t =3	r to t =2	s to t =1	t to s =1
p to all = 10	q to all =7	r to all =6	s to all =7	t to all = 10

FIGURE 2. A method of counting "distances" as applied to pattern B of Figure 1.

Turning to the question of differences among positions in the same pattern, we see clearly that position q in the pattern shown in Figure 2 is different from position p in the same pattern. One aspect of this difference is shown by the tabulation in Figure 2: $d_{p,x} = 10$, $d_{q,x} = 7$. Position q in Figure 2 has a total distance of 7, just as position q in Figure 3. In this case the distance from q to all others does not differentiate between the two positions. Yet we cannot but feel from an inspection of the patterns that there is a difference between the two q positions. We could, of course, point to the fact that in one case q has two "neighbors" and in the other case has only one. But let us consider further the question of distance as such. Since the two patterns in question have different $\Sigma d_{x,y}$ values, it may help if we express the distance "q to all others" in a relative manner. One way of doing this is to calculate for each position the value of the expression $\dfrac{\Sigma d_{x,y}}{\Sigma d_{q,x}}$. For position q in Figure 2, this quantity would be equal to 5.7; for position q in Figure 3, the quantity would be equal to 4.6. In Figure 4 are shown such similar values for each of the positions in pattern A of Figure 1.

If we were to summarize the preceding discussion, we could say that comparisons between two patterns might be made on the basis of "dispersion" (sum of internal distances) defined as $\Sigma d_{x,y}$, and that comparison between positions within the same pattern might be made on the basis of "relative centrality" defined as $\dfrac{\Sigma d_{x,y}}{d_{x,y}}$ (the sum of all internal distances of the pattern divided by the total sum of distances for any one position in the pattern).

OPERATIONAL POSSIBILITIES OF PATTERNS

Let us turn now to the question of how these patterns of communication might be used by a group. Any sensible discussion of "operation" must, of course, be in terms of some specified task. A simple but interesting one would be the following: each of five subjects is dealt five playing cards from a normal poker deck and has the task of selecting from his hand the one card which, together with the four cards similarly selected by the other four subjects, will make the highest-ranking poker hand possible

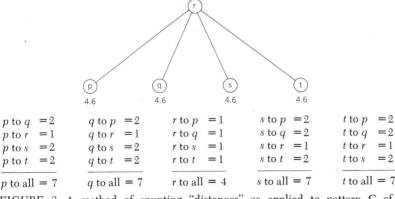

r

p — 4.6   q — 4.6   s — 4.6   t — 4.6

p to q =2	q to p =2	r to p =1	s to p =2	t to p =2
p to r =1	q to r =1	r to q =1	s to q =2	t to q =2
p to s =2	q to s =2	r to s =1	s to r =1	t to r =1
p to t =2	q to t =2	r to t =1	s to t =2	t to s =2
p to all = 7	q to all = 7	r to all = 4	s to all = 7	t to all = 7

FIGURE 3. A method of counting "distances" as applied to pattern C of Figure 1.

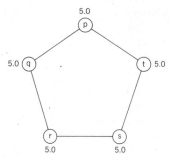

FIGURE 4. Index of "relative centrality" for each position in pattern A of Figure 1.

under these conditions.[2] The cards may not be passed around, but the subjects may communicate over the indicated channels, in the particular pattern being tested, by writing messages.

It is clear that pattern *B* in Figure 1 may be operated in a number of ways, or "operational patterns." Two of the possible operational patterns for communicating necessary information are shown in Figure 5. Obviously, it is possible for pattern *B* to be so operated that the subject in any one of the five positions will be the one to have all the necessary information first (and presumably decide which card each subject should select). There are no linkage structures which would force a given method of operation into use. We might ask, however, whether there are differences in efficiency between different operational patterns. Two measures of efficiency come naturally to mind: the number of messages required for task completion and the time required for task completion.

With respect to the number of messages required, it is possible to make a general statement. In terms of the task given above, one may say that each of the subjects has in his possession one-fifth of the information neces-

sary for a solution. Also, all of the information must at some time be present at one position in the pattern. It can be shown that four messages are necessary and sufficient to accomplish this. Since each subject must know the correct card for him to select, an additional four messages will be required. One may say, therefore, that for any patterns with *symmetrical linkage* the number of messages required will be equal to $2(n-1)$, where n stands for the total number of positions, and that this requirement is completely independent of the linkage pattern as such.

With respect to the time it would take to reach a solution in different patterns, we have a somewhat different situation. We must, of course, for any general discussion of speed of solution assume some standard unit of time to be associated with a message.[3] Let t equal the time it takes for information to go from one person to another when they are linked, i.e., when they occupy neighboring positions in the pattern.

(Before going on to a consideration of the patterns under discussion, a relationship between t and the number of individuals in a group should be pointed out. If any linkage pattern is allowed, then it may be stated that the minimum time for solution will have the following relation to the number of individuals in the pattern:

$$t^{\min} = x + 1 \text{ when } 2^x < n \leq 2^{x+1}$$

This relationship leads to some rather interesting conclusions. Let us consider two groups with unrestricted linkage—one group of nine members and one group of 16 members. With a task such as that of selecting the best poker hand, the minimum time necessary for completion would be the same for both groups, although in the first case we would have nine individuals each possessing one-ninth of the information, and in the second case we would

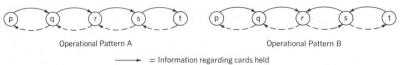

Operational Pattern A   Operational Pattern B

——————▶ = Information regarding cards held
— — —▶ = Information regarding the card selection to be made

FIGURE 5. Two possible "operational patterns" with the same communication pattern.

[2] We assume subjects with perfect knowledge of poker-hand ratings.
[3] This is not intended to exclude the possibility

that in certain patterns "morale" effects will materially affect the speed with which an individual might perform.

have 16 individuals each with one-sixteenth of the information.)

With t defined in this way, it is easy to see that operational pattern A in Figure 5 will require eight time units, while operational pattern B in the same figure will require five time units. Obviously, when more than one message is sent in the same time unit, time is saved. However, if individual p sends a message simultaneously with individual r (as in Figure 6),

FIGURE 6. Relation between timing of message and transmission of information. If r and p send messages simultaneously, p's message cannot contain r's information.

his message to q cannot possibly contain the information contained in the message from r. We can expect, therefore, that in certain patterns time will be saved at the expense of messages; and doing the task in minimum messages will involve the use of more time units. This is nicely illustrated by pattern A in Figure 1. In this pattern the problem may be done in as few as three time units, but to do this requires 14 messages; if the problem is done in eight messages (the fewest possible), the number of time units required increases to five.

SOME EXPERIMENTS WITH SELECTED PATTERNS

An analysis such as this must sooner or later lead to the question: "Granted that kind of difference has been demonstrated between one pattern and another, is it a difference which will make a difference?" Such a question can be answered only by experiment. Without attempting a detailed account, a brief mention of two experimental studies would be helpful here.

Sidney Smith conducted an experiment [4] at the Massachusetts Institute of Technology with eight groups of college students, using patterns A and B shown in Figure 1. He gave his groups a task which in its essentials was similar to the poker-hand problem described earlier. Instead of playing cards, each subject

[4] Unpublished manuscript.

was given a card upon which had been printed five symbols taken from among these six:

○   △   ✳   □   ✛   ◇

While each symbol appeared on four of the five cards, only one symbol appeared on all five cards. Each group's task was to find the common symbol in the shortest time possible. In each subject's cubicle was a box of six switches, each switch labeled with one of the six symbols. The task was considered finished when each member of the group indicated that he knew the common symbol by throwing the appropriate switch. The switches operated a board of lights visible to a laboratory assistant who recorded individual and group times and errors (an error being the throwing of an incorrect switch). The subjects communicated by writing messages which could be passed through slots in the cubicle walls. The slots were so arranged that any desired linkage pattern could be imposed by the experimenter. No restriction whatever was placed upon the content of the messages. A subject who had the "answer" was at liberty to send it along. The cards upon which the messages were written were coded so that a reconstruction of the communicatory activity could be made.

Each experimental group worked on 15 successive problems. The same six symbols were used throughout, but the common symbol varied from trial to trial. Four groups worked in pattern A, and four other groups worked in pattern B. No group worked in more than one pattern.

Of the detailed analysis which Smith made of the experimental data, only two findings will be presented here: errors, and the emergence of recognized leaders (see Table 1 and Figure 7).

TABLE 1. *Number of Errors in Two Communication Patterns* [a]

Error Category	Pattern A	Pattern B
Average total errors	14.0	7.0
Average group errors	5.0	1.5

[a] Total errors = number of incorrect switches thrown. Group errors = number of problems which on completion contained at least one error. (All figures are averages from the performance of four groups in each pattern. Each group did 15 problems.)

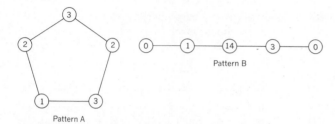

FIGURE 7. Emergence of recognized leaders in different communication patterns. The number at each position shows the total number of group members who recognized the individual in that position as the leader (Smith's data).

With respect to the emergence of recognized leadership, Smith had each of his subjects answer a questionnaire immediately after the end of the fifteenth trial. One of the questions read: "Did your group have a leader? If so, who?" The answers are shown in Figure 7.

While no good theory could be formulated for the differences in numbers of errors, the findings suggested that the individual occupying the most central position in a pattern was most likely to be recognized as the leader. Also, from observation of the subjects while they worked, it appeared that the morale of the individuals in the most peripheral (least central) positions of pattern *B* was the poorest.

In order to explore these possibilities further, Harold Leavitt did a more detailed study [5] of the same two patterns plus two others. The four patterns he used are shown in Figure 8. Leavitt used the same problems and the same experimental setting used by Smith. His findings on errors and leadership recognition are presented in the same form as Smith's data (Table 2 and Figure 8).

TABLE 2. *Number of Errors in Four Communication Patterns*

Error Category	Patterns			
	A	B	E	F
Average total errors	17	10	3	10[a]
Average group errors	3	2	1	1

[a]Leavitt attributes almost all of this error figure to one of the five pattern *F* groups which became confused over the meaning of one member's method of reporting his information.

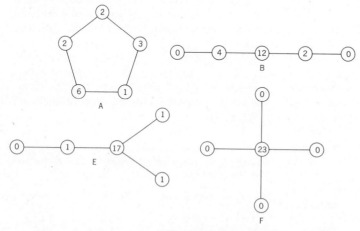

FIGURE 8. Emergence of recognized leaders in different communication patterns. The number at each position shows the total number of group members who recognized the individual in that position as the leader (Leavitt's data).

[5] For a detailed account of this experiment, see Leavitt (1).

TABLE 3. *Differences of Morale Among Four Communication Patterns*

Questions	Average Rating by Pattern			
	A	B	E	F
How much did you like your job?	6.6	6.2	5.8	4.7
How satisfied are you with the job done?	8.0	5.8	6.0	5.4

Leavitt's findings considerably strengthen the hypothesis that a recognized leader (under the conditions of the experiment) will most probably emerge at the position of highest centrality. His findings also lend some support to the hypothesis that errors may be related to pattern properties.

In addition to errors and leadership, Leavitt was interested in the question of morale differences between and within patterns. His subjects were asked two questions to which they responded by ratings from 0 (very unfavorable) to 10 (very favorable). The data are given in averages of all ratings for subjects in the same pattern (Table 3).

In order to check the hypothesis that morale differences exist within patterns and are related to relative centrality, the following analysis of the responses to the same two questions was made (Table 4). The ratings of men who occupied the most peripheral positions in patterns B, E, and F were averaged together; the ratings made by men in the most central positions of the same three patterns were also averaged together. All ratings made by subjects in pattern A were omitted from these calcula-

tions for the obvious reason that no one is most central or most peripheral in that pattern.

On the basis of a detailed study of all the data yielded by his experiments, Leavitt makes the following comments.

Pattern F [6] operated as expected in all five cases. The peripheral men sent their information to the center where the answer was arrived at and sent out. This organization usually evolved by the fourth or fifth trial and was maintained unchanged throughout the remaining trials.

Pattern E operated so that the most central man got all the information and sent out the answer. Organization evolved more slowly than in pattern F, but, once achieved, was just as stable.

Pattern B was not as stable as patterns E and F. Although most of the times the answer was sent out by the individual in the most central position, this function was occasionally performed by one of the men on either side of him. Organization was slower to evolve than in patterns E and F.

Pattern A showed no consistent pattern of

TABLE 4. *Differences of Morale Related to Relative Centrality of Position*

Questions	Average Rating by Position in Pattern	
	For 35 Individuals in the Most Peripheral Positions[a]	For 15 Individuals in the Most Central Positions[b]
How much did you like your job?	3.2	8.8
How satisfied are you with the job done?	4.6	7.8

[a] As represented here (black dots):

[b] As represented here (black dots):

[6] In this question, pattern letters used in Figure 8 have been substituted for the letters used in Leavitt's report.

FIGURE 9. Experimental puzzle. The 15 pieces may be arranged as shown to form five squares.

organization. Subjects, for the most part, merely sent messages until they received or could work out the answer themselves.

A PROPOSED EXPERIMENT USING THE SAME PATTERNS BUT A DIFFERENT TASK

In the Leavitt experiment, the normal behavior of a subject in working toward a solution was to send to the others a list of the five symbols appearing on his card. Occasionally, however, something quite different would occur. The subject would send, instead, the one symbol (out of the total six symbols) [7] which was *not* on his card. The advantages of this method in saving time and avoiding possible error are obvious. In a sense, this procedure is a "detour" solution of the problem confronting the subject. The whole task situation was such as to suggest strongly the straightforward action of sending along the symbols one had, rather than the symbol one had not. Although the frequency of occurrence of this insight was fairly even in the groups, its adoption by the group as a method of work was not. It was used by two of the five groups in pattern A, by one of the five groups in pattern B, and by none of the groups in patterns E and F. While these differences could not be demonstrated to be significant, they excited considerable speculation. In individual psychology, it has been shown repeatedly that an individual's frame of reference may be such as to inhibit effectively the solving of a problem requiring a detour. With the groups in question, the insight invariably occurred to some member or members. Why, then, did it not spread throughout

the group in every case? Might it be that in certain communication patterns the probability of effective utilization of the insights that occur is greater than in others? It was felt that if a more suitable task could be devised, some relationship between the occurrence and utilization of insights and communication pattern might be uncovered.

A task has been constructed which seems to be a step in the right direction. Preliminary trials with it are encouraging. The task consists essentially of forming squares from various geometric shapes. In Figure 9 are shown the 15 pieces which make up the puzzle and how they go together to form five squares.

Out of these shapes, squares may be made in many ways. Some of the possible combinations are: *ccaa, eaaaa, eaag, ffaaaa, ffca, ffgaa, ica,* etc. However, if, using all 15 pieces, five squares must be constructed, there is only one arrangement that can succeed—that shown in Figure 9. In the experimental situation the pieces are distributed among the five subjects. They are told that the task will be successfully completed when each subject has a square before him and no unused pieces. Messages and pieces may be passed along open channels.

The initial distribution of the pieces may be made so that the probability of "bad" squares being formed is increased ("bad" squares being any which, perfect in themselves, make a total of five squares impossible). A possible distribution is given in Figure 10.

As can be seen, the pieces with which an individual starts may suggest a particular composition. Or, the pieces an individual starts with may suggest nothing at all and therefore be speedily traded. Let us look at the situation at position A in Figure 10. The pieces *i,h,e* do not readily suggest a combination of them-

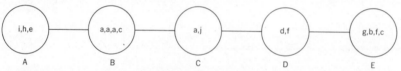

FIGURE 10. A possible distribution of the pieces of the puzzle (Figure 9) among the positions of a communication pattern.

[7] He could see all six symbols on his box of six switches.

selves. We may assume that the subject will pass one of the three to position *B*. At position *B*, however, the situation is quite different. The combinations *ace*, or *aaah*, or *aci* all form squares which if completed will lead to group failure, so that any piece received from position *A* merely suggests possible "wrong" squares. In preliminary trials the "bad" squares appear with great regularity. The point of the experiment is what happens once these deceptive "successes" occur. For an individual who has completed a square, it is understandably difficult to tear it apart. The ease with which he can take a course of action "away from the goal" should depend to some extent upon his perception of the total situation. In this regard, the pattern of communication should have well-defined effects.

A formal experiment using this task has not yet been done. Preliminary runs (making use of various communication patterns and concerned primarily with experimental method) have revealed, however, that the binding forces against restructuring are very great and that, with any considerable amount of communication restriction, a solution is improbable.

CONCLUDING REMARKS

The studies, so briefly discussed in this chapter, if they do nothing more, suggest that an experimental approach to certain aspects of social communication is possible and that, in all probability, it would be practically rewarding. Although the problem of effective communication is an old one, recent trends are bringing to it a new sense of urgency. More and more it is becoming clear that any fundamental advance in social self-understanding must rest upon more adequate intercommunication. In areas where effective and highly integrated social effort is required, the problem is particularly critical. This is nowhere better illustrated than in scientific work. In many fields, it has become impossible to think in terms other than research teams. These groups, aside from the ordinary problems of communication which attend organization,

face a whole new set of problems arising from the current emphasis upon "security." In practice, security is invariably translated into "communication restriction." In a sense, the experiments discussed above explore precisely this question: What happens to the performance and morale of working groups when communication is restricted in one way rather than another?

The experimental evidence is provocative. Generalization at such an early stage of work is dangerous, but one is tempted to make a tentative step. It would seem that under the conditions imposed in the experiments, differences between certain patterns very probably exist. The differences most clearly revealed by the experiments are with respect to (*a*) the location, in the pattern, of recognized leadership; (*b*) the probability of errors in performance; and (*c*) the general satisfaction of group members.

Further, we note that in patterns with a high, localized centrality, organization evolves more quickly and is more stable, and errors in performance are less. At the same time, however, morale drops. It is conceivable that poor morale would, in the long run, affect stability and accuracy negatively. The experimental runs of 15 trials conducted by Smith, if extended to a larger number of trials, might well begin to show this effect.

More speculative, at present, is the question of the occurrence and utilization of insight. The preliminary trials with the "five squares" puzzle, while few, are dramatic. Every group succeeded in forming two or three or four squares. But the ability to restructure the problem, to give up the partial successes, varied widely from pattern to pattern. If the indications of the few experimental runs that have been made to date are any guide, both occurrence and utilization of insight will be found to drop rapidly as centrality is more and more highly localized. In one group, the individual to whom the necessary insight occurred was "ordered" by the emergent leader to "forget it." Losses of productive potential, in this way, are probably very common in most working groups, and must be enormous in society at large.

Reference

1. Leavitt, H. J. Some effects of certain communication patterns on group performance. *Journal of Abnormal and Social Psychology*, 1951, **46**, 38–50.

38

Differentiation of Roles in Task-oriented Groups

HAROLD GUETZKOW

An important feature in the development of groups is the differentiation of roles into an organizational structure.[1] In newly forming groups such differentiation often accompanies the occupancy of the developing positions by particular persons. In this work on the development of experimental organizations in a laboratory, factors related to these two processes have been isolated.

The first part of this inquiry demonstrates the distinction between role differentiation and development of organizational structure. The second part analyzes group processes and personal characteristics associated with role differentiation.

DESCRIPTION OF EXPERIMENT

The experiments reported in this paper used the communication situation initially suggested by Bavelas (2). The two laboratory "runs" analyzed in this report involved 76 groups of five men each operating in the experimental problem-solving situation designed by Leavitt (8), but modified to permit study of the group's handling of its operating task separately from its organization problem.

This chapter was prepared especially for this volume.

[1] See Guetzkow and Simon (6), and Guetzkow and Dill (5); full details of the experimental procedures are described in a microfilm (1). The research was supported by a grant from the research funds of the Graduate School of Industrial Administration, Carnegie Institute of Technology. Hearty thanks are due to Messrs. K. Hellfach, A. D. Martin, and F. Metzger and to Mrs. Martha Pryor, Miss Anne E. Bowes, Mrs. Marion Bement, and to Mrs. Janet Stein for aid in conducting the investigation and help in analyzing its results. The manuscript was prepared during 1956–57, at the Center for Advanced Study in the Behavioral Sciences. My collaborators, Professors W. R. Dill and H. A. Simon, helped in the development of ideas included in this paper in their usual stimulating way.

 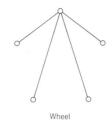 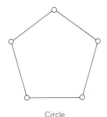

All-Channel   Wheel   Circle

FIGURE 1. Open channels used in the three nets.

The task was identical to that used by Leavitt: the five subjects each had five pieces of a standard set of six pieces of information; their task on a given trial was to determine which piece was common and then to identify this common piece for the experimenter.

None of the participants had been exposed to this laboratory situation before. Each group worked for about two hours during which time the operating task was repeated twenty times. The time needed for each completion of the repeated task varied from over two minutes to less than one minute. The five subjects were seated around a circular table, screened from each others' view by five radial partitions. Intertrial periods of not more than two minutes each provided opportunity for work on the group's organizational problems. After the preliminary instruction period, there was no oral communication among the participants. During the task trials, the subjects passed messages through slots in their partitions to each other on precoded cards. During the intertrials, messages were written by the subjects on blank cards and then exchanged among themselves. Each subject was given a letter, which was used by him in identifying his message and the slots which opened into each cubicle. When the missing information had been obtained by each, the experimenter was so informed and the task trial was ended by the automatic sounding of a bell. By a signaling arrangement, the subjects were allowed to terminate the intertrial period at any time they wished before the end of the two minutes allowed them.

Three hundred and eighty male freshmen engineering students at Carnegie Institute of Technology served as subjects for the experiments. The groups were equated with respect to the average and the spread of intellectual ability among their five members through the use of ACE Psychological Examination scores.

Each group was composed of one man from each of the Carnegie quintiles.

The task problem had been reduced to a routine through the preexperimental instructions and practice period. The urgent problem before each group was how to organize itself, given its communication net. Three types of nets were used in a quartet of variations (see Figure 1). Twenty of the groups operated without restriction, *all-channels* being open for communication ("All-Channel" groups). Twenty-one groups were placed in a *circle* net in which the members could communicate only with those immediately to their left and right ("Circle" groups). Twenty groups were placed in the circle net during the task trials, but these communication restrictions were removed during the intertrial period ("Circle-all-channel" or "Circle-AC" groups). Fifteen of the groups operated with severe restrictions in a *wheel* arrangement in which the four spokes could communicate only with the hub ("Wheel" groups). The apparatus could be easily rearranged for the different groups by mechanically closing and opening the communication slots. The subjects were not told by the experimenter of the pattern used in arranging their net either before or during their work period in the laboratory.

ORGANIZATION AS TASK SPECIALIZATION

There were large differences among the 76 groups in the four nets as to whether and how they organized themselves for the performance of their operating tasks (**5**, 178–179). In the groups which differentiated, it was possible for the experimenter to distinguish three roles on the basis of the interactions portrayed in their task messages.

1. Some participants performed the specialized functions of receiving information, forming the

TABLE 1.   *Distribution of Roles (Number of Persons in Role)*

Role	All-Channel		Circle and Circle-AC, Organized[a]		Circle and Circle-AC, Unorganized[a]		Wheel	
Keymen	23[b]	23%	15[b]	21%	30[b]	23%	15	20%
Relayers	17	17%	28	40%	39	30%	0	0
Endmen	46	46%	27	38%	35	27%	60	80%
Persons without roles	14	14%	0	0%	26	20%	0	0%
Totals	100		70		130		75	

[a] One Circle-AC group was omitted from this and subsequent tabulations because of its marginality to both the organized and the unorganized categories. The Circle group which developed a "chain" in sending information while using a three-level hierarchy arrangement for returning the answers (**6**, 246) was classified as "organized" in the study, although it was omitted in an earlier analysis (**5**, Tables 3 and 4).

[b] The classification of more than one person per group as a keyman results when two persons within a single group played that role at different times.

solution, and then sending answers; these organized activities may be thought of as constituting a "keyman" role.

2. Other participants would merely send their own missing information to others and then later receive the answer to the problem; this package of actions is designated as the "endman" role.

3. Some individuals usually passed on the missing information of others as well as their own, and then, if they received the answer, relayed the answer to one or more neighbors; this grouping of activities is designated as the "relayer" role.

When two or three roles are performed simultaneously in an interlocked fashion within a group, one obtains hierarchical structures (**5**). In the Wheel and All-Channel groups, one typically obtained a two-level hierarchical organization, with four endmen sending their information to the keymen, who in turn formed the solution and communicated the answer to the endmen. In the third of the Circle and Circle-AC groups which organized, the hierarchical structure had three levels, with two relayers serving as intermediaries between two endmen and the keyman.

In the so-called unorganized Circle and Circle-AC groups, the subjects eventually all received information about the four missing symbols and then each formed his own solution to the problem. In such situations there was no need to exchange answers. Sometimes the information exchanges became stable, developing quite systematic "each-to-all" patterns. But because each participant performed identical functions (often in an identical way), there sometimes was no role specialization in these "unorganized" groups.

As has been argued elsewhere (**4**, 380–381), it seems fruitful to distinguish "organizations" from face-to-face, "small" groups, by virtue not of their size but of the relatively large amount of indirect, mediated interaction which occurs among the members of the former. When these mediated interactions are more or less stably structured in somewhat elaborate arrangements in "organized" groups, it is convenient to distinguish them from the "unorganized" groups in which the interactions, although mediated, are unstable and less involved. As is usually the case in working with a set of multi-dimensional characteristics, these bipolar typologies are not discrete.

A quantitative description of the extent and type of role specialization which occurred in the various groups is presented in Table 1. The coder assigned individuals to roles by following the definitions given above. To be classified as occupying a role, it was necessary for an individual to have performed the specified behaviors for four or more consecutive trials. Sometimes an individual occupied two or three roles during the course of the twenty trials. To avoid multiple classifications, a keyman who sometimes also behaved as endman or relayer, was classified only as "keyman," as long as the keyman role had been occupied for a minimum of four consecutive trials. If an individual qualified both as relayer and endman, he was "classified according to the role he held for the longer period of time" (quotation from coding instructions).

A second person, using the code written by the first coder, agreed in assigning the same role (including "no role") to 85 percent of the subjects represented in Table 1. There was variation in the accuracy with which different types of groups could be categorized. The agreement among the coders was 100 percent for the Wheel groups, 95 percent for the organized Circle and Circle-AC groups, and 85 percent for persons in the All-Channel groups. Persons in the unorganized Circle and Circle-AC groups were more difficult to classify, as is indicated in an agreement of 71 percent by the two coders. The accuracy of classification of persons in the three different roles varied too: 85 percent for keymen, 63 percent for relayers, and 78 percent for endmen.

Examine the results presented in Table 1. In the All-Channel groups, the inability of three of the twenty groups to organize is reflected in 14 percent of the subjects having differentiated no roles for any four consecutive trials. In these All-Channel groups, six of the seventeen organized groups used a three-level hierarchy in returning answers from keymen to endmen, as evidenced in the relayers reported in Table 1. The organization of two-level hierarchies in all of the Wheel groups after the fourth or fifth trial is reflected in the assumption of keymen roles by 20 percent of the members and occupancy of endmen roles by the remaining 80 percent.

Compare the role specialization in the 14 organized groups with that which occurred in the 26 unorganized groups in the Circle and the Circle-AC nets. Although only 20 percent of the members of the latter groups failed to develop operationally identifiable roles, all of these groups were unorganized. Had the 26 persons without roles been members of common groups, one still could account for only five or six of the 26 groups which failed to organize. Nor can one account for the failure to organize because of an insufficiency of keymen—there being slightly more in the unorganized than in the organized Circle and Circle-AC groups (23 percent to 21 percent). There is a deficit of relayers and endmen. But if the persons who did differentiate relayer and endman roles were collected into common groups (along with sufficient keymen), 18 to 19 of the 26 "unorganized" groups might have been organized. Examination of the actual distribution of the roles in the 26 unorganized groups in the Circle and Circle-AC nets reveals there is a full complement of one keyman, two relayers, and two endmen in 14 of the groups. The difficulty, then, is not in the

failure of the members to develop individually appropriate role behaviors.

The failure lay in the groups' inabilities to interlock their roles appropriately at the proper times. Further analysis (5, 202) revealed that this inability was largely caused by the failure of the groups to communicate during the intertrial periods about their organizational problem. Thus, the development of unorganized groups is due fundamentally to the failure to interlock roles into an organization, not to a dearth of differentiated roles.

FACTORS ASSOCIATED WITH ROLE DIFFERENTIATION

The finding that roles emerge before groups become organized indicates that conditions associated with the differentiation of roles may be different from those associated with the macro-organization of the group. Let us first explore factors that are associated with role differentiation. In the discussion we will compare them with our hypotheses about macro-organizational development, as analyzed elsewhere (5). In displaying the co-relations that exist among the variables in this chapter, we will conform to the common practice of stating many of our hypotheses in the form of causal interrelationships. It is understood that the data supporting the hypotheses do not demonstrate the existence of causality.

Factors associated with role differentiation may be viewed as of two kinds—those *external* environmental factors that induce role formation because of the task components and those *internal* processes involved in the establishment of particular persons in particular roles.

ROLE FORMATION AS INDUCED BY REQUIREMENTS OF EXTERNAL ENVIRONMENT

Task Characteristics. Role formation would seem to be intimately associated with the functions demanded by the tasks. Our operational description of the three roles in terms of the components of the task is information exchange, solution formation, and answer exchange. But the task characteristics did not determine just how the components should be assembled into differentiated roles—nor whether these roles need be continuously played by one set of individuals or interchanged among

TABLE 2. *Functional Roles as A Priori Combination of Task Components*

Task Components	Role Descriptions
Information Sending (IS) alone	Endmen
Solution Forming (SF) alone	No role exists
Answer Sending (AS) alone	Relayers in structures in which 2-level hierarchies are used for information exchange and 3-level ones for answer exchange
IS and SF combinations	All persons in "round-robins" used for information exchange and in many "each-to-all" groups
IS and AS combinations	Relayers in groups using 3-level hierarchies for both information and answer exchanges
IS and SF and AS combinations	Persons in "each-to-all" and "round-robin" groups, in which exchanges include both information and answers

them. In Table 2 we have hypothesized the various combinations in which the task components might have been assembled in functional roles. All but one were found to have occurred. By its very nature, the task did not allow persons to specialize only in solution formation, for to form solutions on receipt of information from one's colleagues was imperative. The selection of particular combinations, with the one exception, therefore was not due to the task characteristics themselves.

Communication Restrictions.   The communication restriction was an important factor in inducing particular forms of role differentiation. The use of a circle net by the Circle and Circle-AC groups necessitated the use of three- rather than two-level hierarchies. But these restrictions did not necessitate the use of hierarchy roles, as was demonstrated in the evolution of a set of interlocked but identical roles in a "round-robin." In this form of organization, each participant received missing information, added his own symbol to the compilation, and then routed it around the "robin" so that each could form his own solution. The all-channel net was not nearly so restrictive—and other ways of interlocking roles were developed (5, 178). Even the most restrictive variation used—the wheel net—did not prescribe completely the nature of the role differentiation as one of the subjects in the "spokes" of the wheel (who in our experiments actually all played endman roles) could have been "keyman" with the evolution of a "lieutenant keyman" at the hub.

The time of role differentiation also seems to have been prescribed in part by the communication restrictions. In the All-Channel groups, the average of the numbers of the trials on which the keymen first differentiated their roles was 5.2 ($\sigma = 4.2$). The endmen differentiated their roles soon thereafter, averaging 5.7 trials ($\sigma = 3.4$). The relayers lagged, averaging 8.1 ($\sigma = 3.9$) as the trial of their differentiations. The differences between relayers and both keymen and endmen are significant (relayers versus keymen, $t = 2.13$, $p < .05$; relayers versus endmen, $t = 2.33$, $p < .05$). Contrariwise, there were no such contrasts in the times at which the three roles were differentiated in the communication-restricted Circle and Circle-AC groups. The average of the first trials at which differentiation occurs for the keymen, relayers, and endmen in these two types of organized groups were 6.9 ($\sigma = 2.7$), 6.2 ($\sigma = 3.2$), and 6.5 ($\sigma = 4.2$), respectively, with none of the differences significant.

Thus, two pieces of evidence indicate that the development of roles is prescribed to an extent by differences in communication restriction. The type of role which may be developed is prescribed in part by the communication restrictions; the time at which the roles emerge also is determined in part by the same communication restriction.

Group Goal.   The differentiation of roles in these experimental groups would seem to have its central origin in the efficiency goals posited by the experimenter in the instruction, "Your team is competing with the other five-man groups to see which group is fastest at getting the answer. The shorter the time, the better your team score." Two preconceptions may have been evoked in our subjects: a crude notion of the inverse relation of the volume of messages to efficiency of performance and a cultural bias favoring hierarchical arrangements. Groups adopting an each-to-all solution averaged .84 minutes per task trial during their three fastest trials; groups adopting a hierarchical organization averaged .47 minutes. The division of labor increased for efficient group performance. This division of labor was expressed in the differentiation of relatively stable roles. Role stability may have been enhanced by the goal, for with but twenty trials in all there may have been reluctance to experiment with change.

That such role specialization need not be attached stably to particular persons is evidenced in one pilot variation (3) in which the goal instruction was changed to induce interindividual instead of intergroup competition. In four pilot groups run within an all-channel net, the members were informed their success would be evaluated individually in terms of the rapidity with which each reported the solution to the experimenter rather than in terms of their group's overall performance. Three of the groups bogged down, developing no organization. The members of the fourth group developed a quasi-stable coalition among themselves, the terms of which were to organize a two-level hierarchy in which the keyman role was passed trial-by-trial from person to person—so that each member could report the solution first on one out of every five trials.

Summary. Three facets of the task environment, as imposed by the experimenter, seem to be orderable in terms of their impact on the role formation in the experimental situations as follows: task characteristics (weakest) communication restrictions, and group goal (strongest).

INTERNAL PROCESSES INVOLVED IN THE DIFFERENTIATION OF ROLES

Had the experimenter so chosen, it probably would have been comparatively easy—given the authority relationships obtaining between experimenters and subjects (6, 235)—to have designated that three functional roles should be employed and then to have assigned particular subjects to these roles. Had that been done, both role formation and occupant assignment would have been an initial condition in the experiment constituting part of the external environment. Although research work is needed on the impact of different modes for the designation of positions and their occupancy, these experiments focused on organizational development without formal designation devices.

The mechanisms involved in the establishment of certain persons in particular positions may be divided into those rooted in the action characteristics of the group and those rooted in the personal characteristics of the members. These experiments yield more information about the former than the latter, as no detailed personality assessments were made of the participants.

MECHANISMS RELATED TO GROUP INTERACTION

In the wheel net, selection of particular people for keyman and endman roles was a function of communication restrictions. In the other three nets, however, the five persons were placed in functionally equivalent communication points at the beginning of the first trial. What happens as the group develops to establish particular persons in particular roles?

Establishment by Chance. During the first few trials there was much random activity; the subjects seemingly sent information to each other without rhyme or reason. These initial chance-like events, then, might be thought of as selecting a person who, once having served as solution-former, continues thereafter in the key position. On the basis of this "chance" hypothesis, the persons forming the solution on the first trial eventually would occupy keyman roles as the organization differentiated.

In those 18 All-Channel, 18 Circle, and 18 Circle-AC groups in which one or more keymen become differentiated, it is possible to check the extent to which the solution-formers on the first trial become keymen in the semistabilized or fully stabilized organizational structures. The hypothesis is tested in Table 3. There is no significant difference between the proportion of persons who become keymen from among those who formed solutions on the

TABLE 3.   *Selection of Keymen by Chance on First Trial*

	All-Channel	Circle	Circle-AC
Total number of persons who formed solutions	42	46	45
Number who became keymen	10	15	11
Percent keymen	24	33	24
Total number who failed to form solutions:	43	44	45
Number who became keymen	12	10	10
Percent keymen	38	23	22
Total number of group members	85	90	90
Number who became keymen	22	25	21
Percent keymen	26	28	23

first trial and the proportion who become keymen from among those who fail to form solutions. "Being lucky" in becoming a solution-former "by chance" on the initial trial does not help one become keyman in subsequent trials. These results contradict the hypothesis and indicate that some other mechanisms must be involved in selecting out the keymen.

Establishment by Withholding Information. The "common symbol" problem made it possible for an individual to ensure himself of the key role by withholding his information from the others, provided the latter did not try to use the same device. This procedure was used by only one subject. In fact, there was only a gradual decline in the number of information messages the keymen sent, even after they had become the solution-formers and answer-senders. This means we must look elsewhere for an explanation of how certain persons became the keymen.

Role Differentiation on the Basis of Situational Perceptions.   Was role development associated with differences in the adequacy of the sub-jects' perception of the organizational situation? Our procedures yielded two sets of data from which estimates of such perceptions were obtained. During the intertrial periods participants exchanged messages in efforts to perceive the structure of the communication net and their emerging organization. At the end of the experiment, the participants were asked to explain how their groups were organized and to diagram the communication net.

The All-Channel, Circle, and Circle-AC groups devoted an average of 16, 29, and 21 percent of their intertrial messages, respectively, to understanding the nature of their communication net and to inquiries about and evaluations of proposed organizational plans. The average numbers of such units in their messages over the 19 intertrials for persons within the three roles are presented in Table 4. These findings indicate that keymen and relayers, in general, tend to send more messages concerning their perception of the structure than do endmen, although the differences are significant only in the All-Channel groups.

The coding used on the intertrial messages

TABLE 4.   *Intertrial Messages About Situation by Roles (Numbers of Units in Nineteen Intertrials)*[a]

Role	All-Channel		Circle and Circle-AC, Organized		Circle and Circle-AC, Unorganized	
	Mean	SD	Mean	SD	Mean	SD
Keyman	5.1	4.6	8.1	6.3	5.0	4.3
Relayer	6.8	6.4	6.4	5.5	6.5	5.4
Endman	3.3	3.5	5.8	4.7	5.2	5.1

[a]Significance tests: In the All-Channel groups a t-test of relayers *versus* endmen was significant ($t = 2.7$, $p < .01$), as was the t-test of (keymen + relayers) *vs.* endmen ($t = 2.6$, $p < .02$). Number of persons occupying each role is given in Table 1.

TABLE 5. *Accuracy of Organizational Perception by Roles (Correct Minus Incorrect Role Identifications over Total Roles Present)*[a]

Role	All-Channel		Circle and Circle-AC, Organized		Circle and Circle-AC, Unorganized	
	Mean	SD	Mean	SD	Mean	SD
Keyman	.52	.35	.68	.46	.16	.42
Relayer	.50	.37	.58	.45	.18	.35
Endman	.50	.39	.37	.47	.02	.29

[a]Significance tests: *t*-tests of (keymen + relayers) *versus* Endmen were significant both in the Circle and Circle-AC, organized groups ($t = 2.1$, $p < .05$), and in the Circle and Circle-AC, unorganized groups ($t = 2.0$, $p < .05$). Number of persons occupying each role is given in Table 1.

indicates the amount of effort the subjects devoted to perceiving their situation. This measure has ambiguity in its meaning—more effort may be stimulated by the inadequacy of perceptions, and, contrariwise, more effort may yield superior levels of perception. At the end of the experiment, open-ended questionnaires were given the participants about the functioning of the group, about each participant's own role within the group, and about the group's communication net. On the basis of this information, it was possible to decide whether each participant described his own role and that of his colleagues correctly or incorrectly or omitted mention of some persons. The accuracy of organizational perceptions of the subjects was conceived as a ratio of the number of correct observations minus the incorrect observations to the total number of roles operationally identified by the experimenters (Table 2). The average of these ratios for persons occupying various roles is presented in Table 5. In interpreting these figures, it must be remembered that an omitted response on the part of the subject does not necessarily imply lack of knowledge—it may indicate communication failure in the open-ended questionnaire, as no individual probing was undertaken by the experimenters. The results are somewhat disparate with those obtained from the intertrial message measure (Table 4). This is not unexpected, since the correlation between the two estimates is but .13 (significant at the 5 percent level), based on 258 of the subjects.

The superiority found in Table 4 of the keymen and relayers compared with the endmen holds for the organized Circle and Circle-AC groups in Table 5 but fails to be the case in the All-Channel groups. This discrepancy between Tables 4 and 5 may reflect the differ-

ence in time at which the two measures sampled perceptual adequacy. Did the complete absence of communication restrictions allow endmen in the All-Channel groups finally to gain knowledge of the organization situation equal to that of their keyman and relaying colleagues, even though they did not *send* messages about these matters during the course of their organizational development?

A second discrepancy between Tables 4 and 5 is that in the unorganized Circle-AC groups there was no significant difference between the keymen-relayers and the endmen in intertrial messages (Table 4), while there was in the accuracy measure obtained at the end of the experiment (Table 5). This finding confirms the time-honored proposition that effort does not always bring achievement. The new findings, thus, do not entirely contradict our earlier hypothesis that relative adequacy of perceiving the organizational situation is associated with occupancy of keyman and relayer roles.

Role Differentiation on the Basis of Organizational Planning. Although there was no designation of roles by the experimenter, did the participants overtly plan roles for themselves and for others in the course of their intertrial communications? Members of the All-Channel, Circle, and Circle-AC groups respectively devoted 30 percent, 12 percent and 14 percent of their intertrial messages to organizational planning activities. These planning message units were of three kinds—specific messages, either (*a*) proposals of oneself or another individual as keyman or (*b*) promulgations of specific suggestions and (*c*) more general, somewhat abstract proposals, such as "Why don't we all send our messages clockwise?" The

TABLE 6. *Intertrial Messages Concerned with Specific Organizational Proposals by Roles* (*Number of Units Sent in Nineteen Intertrials*)[a]

Role	All-Channel		Circle and Circle-AC, Organized		Circle and Circle-AC, Unorganized	
	Mean	SD	Mean	SD	Mean	SD
Keyman	7.1	2.1	4.0	3.2	0.6	1.4
Relayer	2.9	3.4	1.7	2.4	0.5	0.9
Endman	2.8	4.2	1.2	1.8	0.4	0.7

[a] Significance tests: keymen versus relayers, All-Channel, $t = 4.7$, $p < .001$; Circle and Circle-AC, organized, $t = 2.6$, $p < .02$. Keymen versus (relayers + endmen), All-Channel, $t = 3.2$, $p < .01$; Circle-AC, organized, $t = 3.6$, $p < .001$. Number of persons occupying each role is given in Table 1.

average numbers of these three types of planning messages sent during the course of the 19 intertrials by persons within each role are presented respectively in Tables 6, 7, and 8.

In the specific messages incorporating organizational proposals (Table 6), the differences between the keymen and the other roles are dramatic. About half of these messages are particular plans, proposing oneself as keyman, and most of these proposals were disseminated by the endmen and the relayers (Table 7).

The more general planning messages (Table 8) indicate an ordering of the roles somewhat similar to those found in the intertrial messages concerned with perceiving the organizational situation (Table 4). As in the perceptual messages, the keymen were more given to generalized planning than the endmen.

So far, no use has been made of comparisons between the All-Channel and organized Circle and Circle-AC groups versus the unorganized Circle and Circle-AC groups, exhibited in Tables 4 through 8. These data, along with the role differences already discussed, enable us to

distinguish between factors that induce role formation versus those that relate to both role formation and the interlocking of roles into a social structure. The volume of intertrial messages displayed in Table 4 is approximately the same for both organized and unorganized groups. However, in Tables 5 through 8, there are impressive differences between the two types of groups, ranging from a ratio of 1 to 2 to a ratio of 1 to 6. Thus, the accuracy and planning measures are related not only to role formation, but as importantly to the interlocking of roles into group structures.

Summary. The role of keyman clearly is not determined by chance factors operating in the initial trial. Nor did the persons who became keymen bludgeon their way into occupancy of the role by withholding their own piece of information from the other members of their group. It seems that keymen and relayers establish themselves by having more-adequate perceptions of their organizational situations than do endmen—and that keymen, in turn, gain their special position of leadership in these experimental situations by self-

TABLE 7. *Intertrial Messages Concerned with Promulgation of Specific Proposals by Roles* (*Number of Units Sent in 19 Intertrials*)[a]

Role	All-Channel		Circle and Circle-AC, Organized		Circle and Circle-AC, Unorganized	
	Mean	SD	Mean	SD	Mean	SD
Keyman	1.2	1.6	1.1	2.0	0.4	0.7
Relayer	1.8	2.3	1.2	1.8	0.3	0.6
Endman	2.7	3.0	1.4	2.1	0.5	1.3

[a] Significance tests: In the All-Channel groups a t-test of keymen versus endmen was significant ($t = 2.2$, $p < .05$). Number of persons occupying each role is given in Table 1.

TABLE 8. *Intertrial Messages Concerned with General Organizational Matters by Roles* (*Number of Units Sent in 19 Intertrials*)

Role	All-Channel		Circle and Circle-AC, Organized		Circle and Circle-AC, Unorganized	
	Mean	SD	Mean	SD	Mean	SD
Keyman	2.8	3.8	1.7	2.2	1.0	2.2
Relayer	2.1	2.2	1.3	1.4	0.5	1.2
Endman	0.7	2.1	1.1	2.2	1.1	2.2

[a] Significance tests: In the All-Channel group *t*-tests of the endmen versus keymen ($t = 3.0$, $p < .01$) and versus the relayers ($t = 2.2$, $p < .05$) are both significant. Number of persons occupying each role is given in Table 1.

designation of the key role to themselves, the designation being relayed by the other members of the group to each other.

MECHANISMS RELATED TO PERSONAL CHARACTERISTICS

ROLE DIFFERENTIATION BY MEANS OF INTELLECTUAL ABILITY

Intellectual ability is often related to role occupancy, as documented in Stogdills' survey of the leadership literature (11). An American Council on Education Psychological Examination score was obtained on each subject.[2] The ACE is a general aptitude test of intellectual ability, both quantitative and verbal. These data allow us to check whether role occupancy is associated with intelligence in these experimental situations, as well as to determine indirectly whether intelligence

played a part, *per se,* in the interlocking of the roles into organizational structures. In composing the groups, the experimenters matched subjects so that each group had one person coming from each of five ACE levels. Thus, no group could fail to organize because of low intellectual ability.

Did the varying intellectual ability of the subjects induce differences in role occupancy among the five persons all of whom initially had equipotential locations within the social situation? The average raw ACE scores for persons in the three roles are presented in Table 9. In the All-Channel groups, there is a significant difference ($t = 2.0$, $p < .05$) between the ACE scores of the keymen and both the relayers and the endmen. These differences are not calculational artifacts; the raw scores place the "average" keyman (average = 138.5) at the 89th percentile, with the relayers and endmen (average = 124.4) at the 74th percentile on national, four-year college

TABLE 9. *Intellectual Ability by Roles (Raw Scores for Total ACE Test)*[a]

Role	All-Channel		Circle and Circle-AC, Organized		Circle and Circle-AC, Unorganized	
	Mean	SD	Mean	SD	Mean	SD
Keyman	138.5	18.8	129.9	22.9	131.9	21.2
Relayer	122.1	16.9	132.5	20.3	125.1	18.8
Endman	125.3	20.3	123.2	18.8	125.1	23.3

[a] Significance tests: *t*-tests of keymen versus (relayers + endmen) are significant both in the All-Channel groups ($t = 3.0$, $p < .01$) and in the Circle and Circle-AC, unorganized groups ($t = 5.3$, $p < .001$). Number of persons occupying each role is given in Table 1.

[2] Through the courtesy of Drs. Roland Moore and Robert Morgan of Carnegie Institute of Technology's Bureau of Measurement and Guidance, scores were provided for approximately 90 per-

cent of our subjects; the remaining 10 percent were tested by the experimenters in a special session before they were assembled with the others into the groups.

norms.[3] In the Circle and Circle-AC groups
that organized, the keymen and relayers are
associated in intellectual level, being superior
to the endmen at the 10 percent level
($t = 1.7$), not as sharply as the keymen are
superior to the relayers and endmen in the All-
Channel groups. Thus, role differentiation is
associated with intellectual ability.

Can these contrasting results, in which relayers and endmen are similar in the All-
Channel groups while keymen and relayers are
associated in the organized Circle and Circle-
AC groups, be related to our earlier findings
with regard to accuracy of organizational perceptions and amount of planning activity?
Both keymen and relayers in the Circle and
Circle-AC groups who finally were successful
in organizing themselves were shown to have
been more adequate in their perceptions of the
organization, as they differentiated their roles.
Gaining such superior perception of the organizational structure was not difficult in the All-
Channel groups, as there were no communication restrictions. Superior intelligence was
not necessary in the All-Channel groups for
perceptual accuracy.

Further, consider the strong association between ACE scores and success in designating
oneself as keyman in the All-Channel groups.
This state of affairs is reflected also, in a di-
luted way, in the superior ability of the keymen in the unorganized Circle and Circle-AC
groups. Thus, it would seem that superior intellectual ability is a prerequisite to the establishment of oneself in both keyman and relayer
roles in the more restricted Circle and Circle-
AC groups.

These interpretations would be less tenuous
had the data revealed a clear relationship between intelligence and accuracy in perception
of organizational structure and planning the
specific role establishment. Then one might
argue that intelligence expresses itself in superior organizing activity. But the product-
moment correlations between ACE scores and
the accuracy measure ($r = .03$) and the volume of specific planning ($r = .06$) are nearly
zero. This would seem, then, to mean that although intelligence may be a necessary pre-

requisite for role differentiation its presence
does not ensure the effective occupancy of
roles and their intermeshing into a social system. This latter interpretation is further supported by the fact that, although all groups
were equated in intelligence, 66 percent of the
Circle and Circle-AC groups failed to organize
by interlocking their roles.

ROLE DIFFERENTIATION BECAUSE
OF PERSONAL ASCENDANCE

If intellectual ability is a limiting rather
than an enhancing factor, what personal characteristics might be responsible for inducing
the heightened activity in organizational development? The important part self-desig-
nation played in role establishment for the
keymen suggests that social ascendance might
be a fruitful variable to explore. The Guilford-
Zimmerman "A" scale was administered to
participants in the second "run" before they
developed their groups. When a table analogous to the one made for ACE scores is constructed for these self-rated questionnaires
(Table 10), the keymen are seen to be clearly
more ascendant than the relayers and endman.

Note the relation between ACE scores for
the organized Circle and Circle-AC groups
and the importance of ascendance. It would
seem that, although superior intelligence is
needed for both keymen and relayers, higher
amounts of personal ascendance distinguish
the keymen from the relayers. Personal ascendance predicts the occurrence of self-
nomination as keyman.

The fact that identical findings were obtained for both organized and unorganized
Circle and Circle-AC groups indicates that ascendance was *not* associated with the interlocking of roles into organizational structures.
This contrasts with the parts played by perceptual accuracy, planning, and intellectual
ability—all three of which were integrally involved in the development of structure as well
as in the distribution of occupants in differentiated roles.

Summary. Only two variables were available for the analysis of the relation of personal
characteristics to the development of roles. Intellectual ability seems to be a necessary, but
not sufficient, factor. Ascendance, on the other
hand, seems necessary for the distribution of
persons among the differentiated roles but

---

[3] Percentiles based on Table 5, data for men in
94 four-year colleges, *Norms bulletin American
council in education psychological examination for
college freshmen.* Princeton, N. J.: Educational
Testing Service, 1949.

TABLE 10. *Personal Ascendance of Subjects by Roles (Raw Sums on G–Z A Scale)*[a]

Role	Circle and Circle-AC, Organized		Circle and Circle-AC, Unorganized	
	Mean	SD	Mean	SD
Keyman	5.9	2.1	6.0	2.0
	(n = 11)		(n = 13)	
Relayer	4.2	2.0	4.8	1.5
	(n = 20)		(n = 24)	
Endman	4.6	1.2	4.9	1.4
	(n = 19)		(n = 23)	

[a] Significance tests: *t*-tests of keymen versus (relayers + endmen) are significant both in the organized ($t = 2.4$, $p < .05$) and in the unorganized ($t = 2.2$, $p < .05$) Circle and Circle-AC groups. Number of persons occupying each role is given in parentheses under each mean. Ascendance scores are not available for either the All-Channel or Wheel groups, as the bulk of the All-Channel groups and all the Wheel groups were completed during the first experimental run (see (5, footnote 3) for further details).

does not determine whether groups with differentiated roles will develop interlocked structures of their roles.

DISCUSSION

PLANNING OF THE ORGANIZATION VERSUS INTERLOCKING ROLES

In the previous macro-analysis of these data it was concluded (5, 186–187): "although some explicit understanding of the net and of the evolution of the organization is necessary, understanding *per se* is not sufficient to induce the development of continuing, differentiated organizations." An analogous state of affairs seems to prevail with respect to the existence of roles: although differentiation of roles is imperative for articulation, such differentiation is not sufficient in itself to induce an interlocking of the roles. Murray puts it vividly (9, 451): "It is not so much that a man is obliged (expected) to do certain things, but that he is obliged (in order to integrate his actions with others) to do them at a fixed time."

In the earlier report, considerable support was adduced for the conclusion that communication restriction operates by reducing the planning (5, 194–195). The results of the present role-analysis indicate that in this experimental situation planning is deficient, not in securing behavioral differentiation of the functional roles, but in its failure to plan the interlocking of the performed roles.

In the previous paper it was hypothesized (5, Table 4) that the sending of specific proposals for organizing the groups was a necessary condition for induction of organization. This analysis indicates that those specific proposals were related integrally to achievement of an interlocking of already differentiated roles. Thus, it is now less difficult to understand why only the specific planning messages rather than the more general ones were found in the macro-analysis to be crucial (5, Table 4). Participants cannot articulate roles by exchanging notes about general organizational plans. To interlock particular roles, it seems, one must get specific.

The discrepancy noted in Tables 4 and 5 dramatically supports an interpretation that the participants must have highly specific knowledge of each other's roles in planning. The unorganized Circle and Circle-AC groups at the end of the experiment (Table 5) only minimally understood the roles that were being played—even though they devoted almost as many of their intertrial messages to such activity (Table 4). Those individuals who had a more accurate (averaging approximately 53 percent) knowledge of the roles were able to interlock their roles much more adequately than those without such detailed knowledge (averaging approximately 12 percent).

Examination of the accuracy averages presented in Table 5 suggests that the knowledge needed for interlocking the roles is relatively widespread throughout the group, as would necessarily be the case if the hypothesis that roles are systems of reciprocated interactions is valid. The equal need for knowledge about the other individuals' roles is vividly exhibited in the startling equality of role perceptions among all participants, regardless of their performed role, in the All-Channel groups. The

TABLE 11. *Accuracy with Which Particular Roles Are Perceived (Correct Minus Incorrect Role Identifications over Total Roles Present)*

Role	All-Channel		Circle and Circle-AC, Organized		Circle and Circle-AC, Unorganized	
	Mean	SD	Mean	SD	Mean	SD
Keyman	.71	.31	.68	.28	.04	.29
Relayer	.48	.50	.43	.30	.07	.30
Endman	.35	.44	.45	.31	.03	.39

[a]Significance tests: keymen versus relayers, All-Channel, $t = 2.7$, $p < .05$; Circle and Circle-AC, organized, $t = 3.0$, $p < .02$. Keymen versus (relayers + endmen), All-Channel, $t = 6.2$, $p < .001$; Circle and Circle-AC, organized, $t = 2.8$, $p < .02$. The number of perceptions made of each role is the number of persons in each role, as given in Table 1, multiplied by five (as each person in the group had opportunity to observe each role, including the instance when the role was his own).

modification that certain minimal amounts of such knowledge can make is indicated in the gradient of knowledge exhibited among persons in different functional roles. In Table 5, for the Circle and Circle-AC groups that organized, the endmen seem to be able to articulate themselves into the organization, even though they possess but half (37 percent) of the knowledge possessed by the keyman (68 percent). Note, however, that the 37 percent is twice that possessed by the persons (that is, relayers) with the greatest amount of knowledge (18 percent) in the unorganized Circle and Circle-AC groups.

The ease with which various roles are perceived may be calculated from the accuracy scores used originally for Table 5 by re-averaging the accuracies with which particular roles are perceived by all the members of the group. These new calculations are presented in Table 11. The keymen are more easily visible in the All-Channel and in the organized Circle and Circle-AC groups than are the relayers or endmen.

The figures used to generate Table 11 also yield the accuracy with which one perceives one's own role as contrasted with the accuracy with which one perceives the roles being played by the others. The average overall accuracy with which each participant described his own role was 45 percent. This compares with an accuracy of 29 percent for these same participants in perceiving the roles of others, a statistically significant difference ($t = 3.9$, $p < .001$). Thus, not only do roles have varying visibility, but in this experimental situation persons see their own roles with more accuracy than they perceive the roles of others.

Newcomb has shown that self-perceptions are the result of interactions (10, 316–318). By noting the different accuracies of participants in the three communication situations, we have empirical evidence to support this long-held proposition. In the All-Channel groups, the participants had no communication restrictions imposed by the net within which they operated; in this situation the group members perceived their own roles with an accuracy of 59 percent. In the organized Circle and Circle-AC groups, despite the net imposed restriction, the members had worked out relatively stable communication patterns at the end of the experiment; their accuracy of self-perception was 51 percent. In the unorganized Circle and Circle-AC groups, however, where adequate communications were never developed, the accuracy of self-perceptions was but 29 percent. The difference between the organized and unorganized Circle and Circle-AC groups is statistically significant ($t = 2.0$, $p < .05$). These findings about role self-perception are analogous to those obtained for group opinion by Travers (12), who presents evidence that group members estimate group opinion more accurately with more interaction.

POSITION CONSENSUS VERSUS ORGANIZATION INTEGRATION

This experiment generated evidence on the relation of perception to behavior in a way impossible when one is restricted to an interview or questionnaire. For example, members of the Survey Research Center at The University of Michigan (7, 20) have studied whether "the degree of integration existing within an organization at any time stems in part from the degree of consensus or sharing of expectations about the behavior of people who occupy various positions." But, using a verbal survey methodology, they necessarily limited their definition of "integration" to personal judgments by role-occupiers of such variables as felt conflict, feelings of "easy relations," and satisfaction with participation. In this study it was possible to relate consensus to two objective measures of "integration"—namely, organizational complexity and organizational efficiency.

The test of the relation of consensus to organizational complexity is contained in Table 5. We may use our accuracy measure as an index of the extent to which role expectations were shared, for at least to the extent the participants agreed with the experimenter, to that extent they share their expectations about the roles. If we measure organizational complexity by the extent to which the Circle and Circle-AC groups were organized, we find that the "integrated" groups (that is, the "organized" groups) have some four times as much consensus ("accuracy") as did the less "integrated" groups (that is, the "unorganized" groups).

By correlating the efficiency with which each of 68 groups performed its task (average time on three fastest trials) with the overall accuracy of the members of the groups in perceiving their roles, it is established $(r = -.73)$ that consensus relates to integration, when one measures integration through an objective performance index, too.

It is reassuring to find that both methodologies lead to the same conclusion—namely, that greater consensus about position is associated with greater degrees of organization integration, defined subjectively or objectively.

As this discussion intimates, the term "integration" is ambiguous. The three subjective meanings ("felt conflict," "easy relations," and "participation satisfaction") and the two objective meanings ("organizational complexity" and "performance efficiency") suggest that much further work will be needed to delineate

useful definitions of integration so that the scope of the proposition relating consensus to integration may be specified more adequately.

CONCLUSIONS

This experimental study of the differentiation of roles in task-oriented groups allowed the separation of processes involved in role formation from those involved in interlocking roles into organizational structures. In both phases, the establishment of role systems was related to external and internal factors operating on the group. Within the internal processes, it was possible to distinguish further those factors that operated to allow role formation as well as those which induced interlocking roles into organizational structures.

The study tapped only a few of the totality of the mechanisms involved. The findings may, however, be summarized as hypotheses about the processes which were uncovered.

1. In task-oriented groups which begin their existence with no *a priori* roles, the development of performed roles does not necessarily provide the group with the ability to interlock these roles into organizational structures.

2. The possibility of an interlocked role system is increased: (*a*) when the activities comprising the tasks can be assembled into functional positions, (*b*) when the perception of the role differentiation processes by the members is more explicit, (*c*) when there is planning of a more specific nature, (*d*) and when greater intellectual ability is available in the group.

3. The establishment of individuals in leadership-followership roles is related to the same intragroup factors as those related to the establishment of the organizational structure (2*b*, 2*c*, and 2*d*), with the addition that persons characterized by personal ascendance tend to occupy leadership roles.

References

1. ADI Auxiliary Publication Project, Photo-duplication Service, Library of Congress, Washington 25, D. C., Document No. 4590.
2. Bavelas, A. Communication patterns in task-oriented groups. *Journal of Acoustical Society of America*, 1950, **22**, 725–730.

3. Dill, W. R., & McKee, R. L. An experiment to compare the effects of competitive and of cooperative motivations on group behavior. May 1953, unpublished manuscript.

4. Guetzkow, H., & Bowes, A. E. The development of organizations in a laboratory. *Management Science,* 1957, **3**, 380–402.

5. Guetzkow, H., & Dill, W. R. Factors in the organizational development of task-oriented groups. *Sociometry,* 1957, **20,** 175–204.

6. Guetzkow, H., & Simon, H. A. The impact of certain communication nets upon organization and performance in task-oriented groups. *Management Science,* 1955, **1,** 233–250.

7. Jacobson, E., Charters, W. W., Jr., & Lieberman, S. The use of the role concept in the study of complex organizations. *Journal of Social Issyes,* 1951, **7,** 18–27.

8. Leavitt, H. J. Some effects of certain communication patterns on group performance. *Journal of Abnormal and Social Psychology,* 1951, **46,** 38–50.

9. Murray, H. Toward a classification of interactions. In T. Parson & E. A. Shils (Eds.), *Toward a general theory of action.* Cambridge, Mass.: Harvard Univ. Press, 1951. Pp. 434–464.

10. Newcomb, T. M. *Social psychology.* New York: Dryden, 1950.

11. Stogdill, R. M. Personal factors associated with leadership: Survey of the literature. *Journal of Psychology,* 1948, **25,** 35–71.

12. Travers, R. A study in judging the opinions of groups. *Archives of psychology.* New York: 1941. No. 266, **37,** 73 pp.

39

Experiments on the Alteration of Group Structure

ALEX BAVELAS, ALBERT H. HASTORF, ALAN E. GROSS, AND
W. RICHARD KITE

A fundamental problem in social psychology is the relationship between an individual's behavior and how that behavior is perceived and evaluated by others. For example, there has been persistent interest in the process which generates a status hierarchy in small face-to-face groups such that some members are perceived as "leaders" and others not. Most of the research on this question has attempted to chart the course of a naturally emerging structure, sociometrically define the leader, and then attempt to define those aspects of his behavior that led to his being perceived as the leader. However, the behavior of the leader is normally so complex that it has been exceedingly difficult to isolate the behaviors that significantly influence the perceptions of the other group members. Bales (3) has explored this approach most thoroughly, with one of the most persistent findings being that the people seen as leaders talk a great deal.

This report will describe a series of studies in which an attempt is made to alter experimentally the verbal behavior of an individual in a group discussion by the use of an operant conditioning procedure. Our primary concern was to develop a workable procedure for increasing one group member's verbal output, to define some of the variables which appear crucial to this procedure, and to explore the other group members' perceptions of this change in behavior on such dimensions as quality of ideas and leadership.

Previous research with operant conditioning techniques in group situations has most commonly made use of confederates. Pepinsky, Hemphill, and Shevitz (7) demonstrated that "accepting" or "rejecting" reactions on the part of confederates influenced

From *Journal of Experimental Social Psychology*, 1965, **1**, 55–70. Reprinted by permission of the authors and Academic Press. This research was supported by a grant from the National Science Foundation.

527

the number of leadership attempts made by a naive subject. By making a straightforward application of a standard verbal conditioning procedure to a group situation, Bachrach, Candland, and Gibson (2) have shown that the verbal output of a naive group member can be increased by the head nods, "umm humms," and agreements of two confederates. It should be noted that in both of these studies, the "group" aspects of the experimental situations were severely attenuated by the use of confederates. In such an experimental set-up it is impossible to obtain data on other group members' perceptions of the "target" subject whose behavior was being altered.

Oakes, Droge, and August (6) demonstrated that verbal behavior can be either increased or decreased by the use of lights as reinforcers or punishers. Aiken (1) has described a similar procedure in which lights as reinforcers or punishers were used for subjects in a group situation where each subject is provided with private feedback on his performance. This procedure has the significant advantage of bringing about a change in the verbal behavior of a subject in the presence of other subjects who are unaware of the exact nature of the reinforcements given the "target" person.

The studies reported below are directed toward answering the following questions. When lights are used as signals or reinforcers in a group situation, how much change in verbal behavior can be obtained? Must the reinforcing lights be directly contingent on talking or will a random pattern of lights also increase verbal output in a group discussion atmosphere? If an increase in the verbal output of a group member is obtained, will that person maintain his new verbal level in a following session where no lights are expected? Finally, how do the other group members evaluate the contributions of the "target" person? Do they increase his status on such dimensions as quality of ideas and leadership?

EXPERIMENT I

METHOD

Subjects

Seventy-two male students from industrial psychology and industrial engineering classes at Stanford University were recruited "to participate in

group discussions of case problems." The subjects were divided into eighteen four-man groups, half of which were assigned to the Experimental condition and half to the Control condition. Group members were not well acquainted with each other prior to the experimental session.

Apparatus

Each of four positions at a discussion table was equipped with a reflector box which contained two small lights, one green and one red. These boxes were flared toward each participant so that only he could see the lights facing his position. The lights were controlled from an observation room which was separated from the discussion room by one-way glass. Clocks and counters were used to record talking time and frequency for each subject. Whenever a subject talked, or whenever a red or green light was turned on, an Esterline-Angus pen recorder was activated, thereby providing a sequential event record.

Procedure

The subjects were told that the discussions would be observed and recorded from behind the one-way glass. The experimenter explained that he was interested in the study of group discussion techniques from an educational viewpoint. It was further explained that several different human relations problems would be discussed so that the dynamics of the group discussion process could be analyzed. Following these brief and purposely vague introductory remarks, the four subjects read the first case problem and were instructed to begin a ten-minute discussion period during which they "should discuss the pertinent facts which will affect a decision."

This initial discussion was intended to provide an operant level or baseline measurement of verbal activity. An observer operated the clocks and counters, which provided, respectively, a record of cumulative talking time and a record of the total number of times each subject talked. This recording procedure was also followed in the two subsequent discussions.

At the end of each discussion period, the experimenter re-entered the discussion room and administered a short sociometric questionnaire. The subjects were required to rank all group members, including themselves, on four key items: amount of participation, quality of ideas, effectiveness in guiding the discussion, and general leadership ability.

After reading the second case problem, the groups were given further oral instructions. The experimenter stated that, in contrast to the usual nonfeedback procedure, group discussions might be more effective "if the participants are given an occasional sign that they are doing the kinds of things that will help the group arrive at intelligent solutions while at the same time yielding the maximum educational benefit to the group." The subjects were then told that some discussion groups work on their own and some groups "are provided with feedback information as to how they are doing as the discussion proceeds." At this point the experimental groups were told that they would be receiving feedback. The experimenter directed attention to the small red and green lights, which had previously been dismissed as extraneous equipment that "we won't be using now," and told the group that these lights would serve as the source of the feedback information. Control groups were told that they would receive no feedback.

Both Experimental and Control groups received vague descriptions of the criteria that were to be used in evaluating their discussion:

Many psychologists have studied group discussion of problems such as this one. Most of these investigators have found that maximum benefit is gained from such discussions when the group proceeds in an orderly way through various stages of development. For instance, one psychologist has cautioned against proceeding into the problem-solving stage of discussion too rapidly before there has been enough orientation. Other research has given us clues as to the value of cooperation, suggestion, conciliation, and other forms of group behavior during certain stages of the discussion process.

The case you have just read has been thoroughly analyzed in terms of how it can be discussed most effectively. Although, of course, there is no single correct solution to the problem, we have developed a definite set of principles, such as those I have just mentioned, which enable us to know whether or not you are following the best course—that is, using the best techniques in contributing to the discussion for the benefit of the group. Note that although this will be a group discussion, it will be your individual contributions to the discussion that will be judged.

At this point the Control groups were reminded that they would not receive any feedback as to how they were being evaluated. However, the Experimental groups were told that they would receive feedback which would be contingent upon the vaguely defined quality of their contributions:

Thus, whenever you make a contribution to the discussion which is helpful or functional in facilitating the group process, your green light will go on like this (*green lights turned on*). Are all your green lights on? Fine. Whenever you behave in a way which will eventually hamper or hinder the group process, your red light will go on like this

(*red lights turned on*). Are all your red lights on? Good. It is conceivable that even remaining silent when you might have been clarifying a point that had been made earlier is a dysfunctional or hindering type of behavior. This would rate a red light, indicating you should have said something at that point. On the other hand, silence might be good when talking would serve to confuse a good point that had already been made.

Since it is often impossible for us to determine the effect that a single statement or thought will have on the group discussion, a feedback light might be referring to the cumulative effect of two or three successive contributions to the discussion. Of course much of the time neither of your lights will be on, indicating that your behavior has been neither helping nor hindering the group, or that we simply can't validly analyze what has been going on in the group at that time.

Note that the discussion table is constructed so that each participant can see only the lights directly in front of him. During the discussion the fact that your lights are either on or off should not be mentioned. This would, of course, tend to disrupt the natural discussion atmosphere.

Group members in both conditions were told the discussion would last for twenty minutes and that they should "try to bring in the various possible facts that can be considered relevant to the problem in the case."

At the end of the first discussion period, the subjects were rank-ordered on the basis of objective behavior measured by the clocks and counters and on the basis of the perceptions of the group members measured by the responses to the four sociometric items. There was usually a close correspondence between amount of talking and average ranking on the four sociometric items. In the few cases in which these measures were inconsistent or contradicted each other, the ranking adopted was made on the basis of total talking times.

The third or fourth ranked man in this hierarchy was designated as the target person (*TP*). One of the less talkative men was selected so that there would be "room" to effect a relatively large change in verbal behavior. An exceedingly quiet man was not selected as the *TP* because it was felt that if he had been extremely quiet it would be difficult to alter his behavior. The man who was ranked first was designated *M-1;* the other two men were labeled *M-2* and *M-3*, respectively.

The experimental manipulation consisted of flashing *TP's* green light whenever he made declarative statements or stated an opinion, and flashing the others' red lights if they (*M-1, M-2, M-3*) engaged in these same behaviors. Occasionally *TP* received a red light for remaining silent, and other group members received green lights for interacting with *TP*, especially for agreeing with him.

No definite criteria or set of rules were followed for administering lights or for controlling the number of lights distributed. The light operator's task was to increase the *TP*'s verbal output during the second discussion and to decrease or inhibit talking by the other group members. The operator was to select for reinforcement those statements by the *TP* which would intuitively appear to result in increased sociometric status.

After the second discussion, the subjects again completed the sociometry questionnaire and then read the third case problem. The Experimental groups were told that the lights would "not be operating—just as in the first case discussion; so don't pay any attention to the equipment." At the end of this final ten-minute discussion, the last sociometric questionnaire was administered, followed by a postsession questionnaire. Each man was asked to rank the three case problems from most to least liked and to indicate whether he felt that he had talked more, less, or about the same as usual during each of three discussions. Experimental subjects responded to items which asked how much attention was paid to the lights and whether the lights were perceived as helping or hindering the discussion.

After this questionnaire was completed, the purpose and design of the experiment was fully explained to the participants and questions were answered.

RESULTS

The experimental procedure is clearly effective in altering both the distribution of verbal outputs and the sociometric structure of the group. In all nine Experimental groups, *TP*'s talking time and frequency of talking increased during the second discussion when lights were being used. Furthermore, this change was strongly reflected in the sociometric votes of the other group members: all nine Experimental *TP*s received higher average rankings after the second discussion than after the first discussion (Table 1). Frequency of talking data, which are correlated with total talking time ($r = .91$) are omitted from Table 1. Since the rankings for guidance, best ideas, participation, and leadership turned out to be highly correlated, the sociometric data are reported as the mean ranking of these four items. The *TP*s' self-rankings are excluded from these averages.

In eight of nine cases *TP*s' ratings drop somewhat following the discussion of the third case, but in only one group do the ratings the *TP* receives drop back below the baseline level of the first period.

TABLE 1. *Sociometric Rank and Verbal Output of Target Person*[a]

Experiment	Mean rankings received by TP from Other Group Members (1 to 4)			Time talked by TP Expressed as a Percentage of Total Group Talking Time		
	Discussion Period			Discussion Period		
	1	2	3	1	2	3
Control (N = 9 groups)	3.05	2.81	2.80	17.3	20.2	19.5
I (N = 9 groups)	3.23 1 vs. 2 & 3, $p < .01$ 2 vs. 3, $p < .05$	1.70	2.30	15.7 1 vs. 2 & 3, $p < .01$ 2 vs. 3, $p < .01$	37.0	26.9
II (N = 7 groups)	3.18 1 vs. 2 & 3, $p < .02$	2.13	2.36	17.4 1 vs. 2, $p < .05$ 1 vs. 3, $p = .02$	31.1	29.0
III (N = 7 groups)	3.12	2.80	2.75	19.8	20.4	20.9
IV (N = 7 groups)	3.24	2.95	3.11	20.9	22.2	18.6
V (N = 7 groups)	3.08	2.66	2.82	19.3	24.3	22.2

[a] Only *p* values of less than 0.10 are indicated. All *p* values are two-tailed. Differences for experimental groups between first and second discussions were compared with corresponding differences for control groups by the Mann-Whitney Test. Significance levels for differences between the second and third discussions and first and third discussions were computed by the sign test.

TABLE 2. *Mean Self-Rankings of Target Person*

Experiment		Discussion Period	
	1	2	3
Control	2.67	2.31	2.39
I	2.91	1.36	2.05
	1 vs. 2, $p < .02$		
	2 vs. 3, $p < .05$		
II	2.79	1.64	1.64
	1 vs. 3, $p < .05$		
III	2.93	2.64	2.79
IV	3.04	2.14	2.50
V	2.68	2.07	2.39

Increased sociometric ratings and length of talking time in the second period for Experimental *TP*s are significantly greater than the slight increase shown for Control group *TP*s. The drop-off from the second to third discussions is significant for the objective talking measures and the sociometric data. Despite the drop-off, *TP*s' level of output and sociometric ratings remain significantly higher than they were after the first discussion.

The *TP*s' perception of their own behavior as reflected in their self-ratings followed a similar pattern. Their self-ratings also rose after the second period and then dropped off somewhat when the lights were not used in the third period. The *TP*s' self-ratings are presented in Table 2. Although mean self-ratings for each discussion period are slightly higher than ratings received from others, the magnitude of change between discussions is very similar to changes in ratings made by others.

Data from the postsession questionnaire are presented in Table 3. These data indicate: (*a*) a strong liking for the second case problem among Experimental *TP*s, while no such consistent preference exists for any one case among the other group members; (*b*) *TP*s were aware that they talked a great deal during the second discussion: six of nine felt that they talked "more than usual" during this period while all but one of the other group members felt that they had talked "less than usual" or "about the same"; (*c*) eight of nine *TP*s responded that the feedback lights had "helped" them during the second discussion while the others were split between feelings of being "helped" and being "hindered."

EXPERIMENTS II AND III

In Experiment I red and green lights were distributed to the subjects on the basis of the experimenter's intuitive judgments as to what behaviors should be encouraged or discouraged. It was thought that such a procedure would be most effective in bringing about the desired changes in the behavior of the participants. When the effectiveness of this procedure was demonstrated, the question arose as to how crucial were the experimenter's choices of which behaviors to reinforce in producing the observed effect. Did the *TP*'s increase in sociometric status result from an increase in certain categories of verbal output, or was it simply the result of his talking more in general? Experiments II and III represent an attempt to answer this question by eliminating the experimenter's judgments from the administering of the lights. Fifty-six undergraduate men were assigned to fourteen four-man groups. Seven groups were run in each experiment.

EXPERIMENT II

Procedure

Experiment II was an exact replication of Experiment I in terms of the general procedure followed. The only modification was in the manner in which the red and green lights were administered during their second case discussion. All "feedback" lights were administered automatically by a preprogrammed event-controlling unit which was activated by the same switches used to record the subjects' verbal output. In this way it was possible to make the lights contingent upon the subjects' talking without regard to its content.

TABLE 3. *Postsession Questionnaire Data*

Experiment	N	Case Preference (1 = Most Liked; 3 = Least Liked)			Estimate of Talking (1 = More; 0 = Same; −1 = Less)			Influence of Lights (Frequencies)		
		Case 1	Case 2	Case 3	Period 1	Period 2	Period 3	Help	No diff.	Hinder
Control										
TP	9	2.56	1.56	1.89	−0.22	+0.33	−0.11	a	a	a
Others	27	2.30	1.81	1.89	−0.04	+0.07	−0.04	a	a	a
I										
TP	9	2.56	1.00	2.44	−0.33	+0.67	+0.22	8	0	1
Others	27	2.15	2.07	1.78	+0.04	−0.37	+0.07	8	9	10
II										
TP	7	2.43	1.86	1.71	−0.43	+0.43	+0.57	4	3	0
Others	21	1.86	2.67	1.48	+0.19	−0.48	+0.05	7	4	10
III										
TP	7	2.29	2.14	1.57	−0.29	−0.29	+0.29	1	4	2
Others	21	2.14	2.05	1.81	−0.04	+0.07	−0.04	3	12	6
IV										
TP	7	2.17	1.50	2.33	−0.50	+0.33	.00	4[b]	2	0
Others	21	2.17	2.17	1.67	−0.22	−0.05	−0.05	a	a	a
V										
TP	7	2.14	2.14	1.71	+0.14	−0.29	−0.14	a	a	a
Others	21	1.85	2.29	1.86	.00	−0.29	−0.10	4	7	10

[a] Did not receive feedback.

[b] One group did not complete postsession questionnaires.

The program unit was connected to a 25-position stepping switch which moved to the next position with the recording of each discrete utterance by any of the participants. Each man had a fixed sequence of 25 events programmed for him: he could receive a green light, a red light, or no lights each time he talked. TP received a "leadership-encouraging" schedule of 15 green lights with the remaining 10 positions blank. A separate timing device was connected to the TP's circuit which delivered a red light to him for every 45 seconds of continuous silence. The other three members received identical "followership encouraging" schedules consisting of 7 red lights, 2 green lights, and 16 blanks. These two schedules were intended to approximate the schedules administered in Experiment I in terms of both absolute number of lights and ratios of red to green.

Instructions regarding the onset of the "feedback lights" prior to the second discussion were the same as in Experiment I. Subjects also filled out the same sociometric questionnaire after each of the three discussions and the same postexperimental questionnaire as were administered in Experiment I.

RESULTS

Although it was the intention of the experimenters to provide subjects with schedules of red and green lights which at least approximated those received by their counterparts in Experiment 1, this objective was not achieved. The actual mean numbers of lights received by the men in both experiments are shown in Table 4. It is obvious that all members in Experiment II received considerably fewer lights of both kinds than did the comparable persons in Experiment I.

This deficit appears to have been mainly due to the fact that the programmed schedules were simply too sparse, particularly in terms of green lights. There is also, however, a methodological probem inherent in the design of this study. In order for the TP to receive green lights, it was necessary for him to talk. If the programmed schedule of green lights was insufficient to produce a sizeable increase in his talking over time, then this placed an obvious limitation on the number of green lights he would receive over the course of the entire discussion.

The major results of Experiment II are presented in Table 1. When compared with TPs in the Control groups, it can be seen that even making the green lights contingent upon sheer talking produces an increase in both the socio-

TABLE 4.   *Number of Lights Received*

Experiment	TP	M-1	M-2	M-3
I				
Green	38.1	15.2	15.1	13.8
Red	7.6	7.8	9.6	9.3
II				
Green	15.4	1.7	1.7	0.4
Red	5.3	9.7	6.0	3.3
III				
Green	38	15	16	14
Red	7	8	10	9
IV				
Green	14.0			
Red	5.0			
V				
Green		7.9	7.9	5.1
Red		6.4	7.7	5.6

metric rankings received from others and verbal output. These increases are not, however, as great as those obtained in Experiment I.

From the first to the second discussion the *TP* shows a significant increase in sociometric rankings received from others and a significant increase in talking time. These gains in sociometry and talking time are maintained by the *TP* to a significant extent throughout the third discussion.

Unfortunately, the fact that fewer lights were given to the participants in Experiment II than in Experiment I makes it impossible to give an unequivocal answer to the question of how much the experimenter's judgments contributed to the overall effect. It does appear safe to conclude, however, that such judgments as were being made in Experiment I were at least not indispensable in producing significant changes in both verbal behavior and sociometric rankings.

EXPERIMENT III

Procedure

As a second method of eliminating the experimenter's judgments from the administration of lights, seven groups received red and green lights on a time-contingency basis. A leadership schedule was derived by averaging the number of red and green lights received by *TPs* in Experiment I within each successive five-minute interval and then distributing this number randomly over an equal period of time. In a like manner a different schedule was derived for *M-1*, *M-2*, and *M-3* on the basis of the average number of lights received by their counterparts in Experiment I.

These schedules were administered manually by a single experimenter who viewed a large clock with a sweep-second hand in conjunction with the four schedules written out on large sheets of cardboard. This procedure allowed subjects to receive the same number and ratio of lights received in Experiment I, but without regard to whether or not they were talking at the time. In all other respects, the procedure was the same as that followed in Experiment I.

RESULTS

Table 4 shows the numbers of lights received by all men in Experiment III. It can be seen that these numbers correspond to the averages of Experiment I.

The changes in sociometric status and verbal output that resulted from this procedure were no greater, and in some cases were smaller, than those obtained in the control groups (see Table 1).

EXPERIMENTS IV AND V

The experiments described thus far have all involved an attempt to alter the verbal behavior of all four group members. This procedure consisted of essentially two operations: (*a*) an attempt to increase the *TP's* output by rewarding his talking and punishing him for being silent and (*b*) an attempt to decrease the other members' output by punishing their talking and rewarding their silence. Although these two operations can be conceptualized separately, they did not function independently in the experiments reported above. The behavior change of the *TP* in Experiments I and II may have been due to one or the other of these two techniques or to an interaction of the two.

In order to determine the independent effects of these two operations, two additional experiments were conducted. Experiment IV provided only the *TP* with feedback, while Experiment V provided only the three non-target members with feedback.

EXPERIMENT IV

Procedure

To provide only the *TP* with feedback during the second discussion, it was necessary to instruct the other three members of the group in such a way that they would not anticipate any feedback while at the same time instructing the *TP* in the usual manner. To achieve this, two sets of written instructions were prepared and were passed out to the group just prior to the second discussion. The instructions that the *TP* read were a written version of the standard instructions given to all subjects in the experimental condition of Experiment I. The other three members were given a written version of the control instructions of Experiment I. Both sets of instructions were carefully prepared so as to appear identical in terms of location of paragraph indentations, margins, and other typographical aspects. No subjects in any of the groups reported awareness of this difference in the instructions.

A single experimenter administered the red and green lights to the *TP* in the same manner that they were given to the *TP*s in Experiment I. No explicit attempt was made to replicate the mean numbers of each kind of light given in Experiment I.

RESULTS

The sociometric and verbal output measures for Experiment IV show virtually no changes over the three discussions and do not differ from the results obtained in the control condition (Table 1). The mean number of lights received by the *TP* are reported in Table 4. In comparison with the figures for Experiment I, the number of green lights received by the *TP*s is much smaller. This was due mainly to the fact that the *TP*s did not markedly increase their verbal output in the second discussion.

EXPERIMENT V

Procedure

This experiment was essentially the complement of Experiment IV. Instead of encouraging the *TP* to talk more, the procedure of Experiment V consisted of discouraging the other three members of the group and withholding all feedback from the *TP*. Written instructions were again used to instruct the men differentially with regard to the administration of feedback in the second discussion. The *TP* received the control version while the other three were given the experimental version.

The experimenter who administered the feedback lights to the three nontarget members followed the same general rules that were observed in Experiment I in attempting to decrease their verbal output in the second discussion.

RESULTS

The *TP*s in Experiment V increased slightly in sociometric ranking and verbal output from the first to the second discussion (Table 1). None of these increases were significant, however. As shown in Table 4, the nontarget subjects received slightly fewer red lights and about half as many green lights as did the nontarget subjects in Experiment I.

DISCUSSION

The results of Experiment I clearly demonstrate that the procedure used is an effective method of changing the verbal output of selected group members in a desired direction. Furthermore, changes in the sociometric structure of the group are highly correlated with verbal output changes ($r = .84$). It had been anticipated that a crucial element necessary for the success of this manipulation was the manner in which the experimenters determined the appropriate times to reinforce group members. Therefore, the results of Experiment II were somewhat surprising in that the programmed machine produced not only an increase in the *TP*'s verbal output but also a significant rise in his sociometric status.

One possible explanation for the similarity in the results of Experiments I and II is that the same general class of behaviors was being reinforced by both the experimenters and the

TABLE 5.   *Sociometric Rank and Verbal Output Changes from Discussion Period 1 to Discussion Period 2*

Experiment	TP	M-1	M-2	M-3
Control				
Sociometric rank[a]	+0.24	−0.12	−0.35	+0.25
Verbal output (%)	+2.9	−2.3	−3.9	+3.3
I				
Sociometric rank	+1.53	−0.72	−0.61	−0.31
Verbal output (%)	+21.3	−15.7	−5.0	−0.7
II				
Sociometric rank	+1.05	−0.36	−0.56	−0.05
Verbal output (%)	+13.7	−10.3	−7.1	+3.6
III				
Sociometric rank	+0.32	+0.06	−0.32	+0.10
Verbal output (%)	+0.6	−2.3	−0.2	+2.1
IV				
Sociometric rank	+0.29	−0.45	+0.11	−0.08
Verbal output (%)	+1.3	−3.5	+1.7	+0.6
V				
Sociometric rank	+0.42	−0.14	−0.38	+0.08
Verbal output (%)	+5.0	−4.8	−1.3	+1.2

[a] Total positive and negative sociometric changes are not necessarily equal because self-rankings have been excluded from the averages which are presented in Table 1.

striction, it is of some interest to explore the dynamics of the change situation. For instance, one might ask which group member loses when *TP* gains. It would be reasonable to predict that each man loses sociometric votes and talking time in proportion to what he has to lose; i.e., *M-1*, the man who was originally ranked the highest, would lose the most, and *M-2* and *M-3* should lose proportionally less. An analysis of ratings received by *M-1*, *M-2*, and *M-3* (Table 5) shows that in Experiment I *M-1*'s losses alone account for *TP*'s gains. In Experiment II, although *M-1* suffers the greatest loss, *M-2* also talks somewhat less and receives lower ratings on the questionnaires.

It might also be asked if the increase in the *TPs*' sociometric rank from the first to the second discussion was largely due to the other members assigning lower ranks to themselves. This would result in an artificial elevation of the *TPs*' rank. The data were analyzed with all self-rankings eliminated and each subject's ratings of the other group members reranked from 1 to 3. This analysis revealed substantially the same pattern of results as those presented in Table 1.

Two opposing hypotheses may be entertained regarding the *TPs*' affective response to the experimental manipulation. It could be predicted that participants who are rewarded for talking will gain more satisfaction from the discussion and will generalize some of this affect to the case problem, or alternatively that the *TP* will feel uncomfortable in the unfamiliar role of a high participator. The postsession questionnaire results clearly support the former prediction in that *TPs* enjoyed participating in the second discussion and indicated strong preference for the second case problem. During the first discussion, before any lights were administered, high participators showed no more preference for the case than did low participators.

In summary, the experiments described above provide a workable technique for the alteration of verbal output and sociometric structure in a group situation and define some of the necessary conditions to obtain such changes.

Two problems emerge that are of significance to the understanding of social interaction. The first relates to the perseveration and the generalization of behavior change. What are the conditions under which behavior change would perseverate and generalize to other conditions? We have obtained evidence of some perseveration to a session which immediately followed the acquisition session. An important variable in this respect is the way in

programmed machine. Although there are no data to confirm this notion, it was the opinion of the experimenters that all discussions were relatively homogeneous in content and highly task-oriented, with very few irrelevant or disruptive statements being made by any of the participants. This being the case, it seems reasonable to assume that the majority of the TPs' statements that were reinforced in both Experiments I and II were task relevant in nature, and, therefore, that an increase in such verbal output would result in higher sociometric rankings for the TPs.

Some indirect support for this contention is provided by Oakes (5), who used a reinforcement technique similar to the one described in this report in an attempt to determine which of the twelve Bales' categories of response are most susceptible to reinforcement. His findings show that only one of these categories, "giving opinion, evaluation, analysis, expresses feeling, wish," could be increased significantly during a group discussion. It should be noted that more than 50% of the total responses were coded in this one category. These findings appear to coincide with our contention that discussion content was both relevant to the case discussion and homogeneous across groups. Therefore, it is not surprising that the experimenter function of selecting statements to "reinforce" in Experiment I is not critical in the alteration of group structure. At the same time, the results of Experiment III indicate that lights must be contingent upon verbal behavior to be effective. Receiving encouraging lights at predetermined intervals did not prove sufficient to significantly alter the initial group structure.

The technique which was used successfully to modify group structure can be considered as two separate operations. One operation consisted of positively reinforcing or encouraging the target person to step up his verbal output. A complementary operation was employed simultaneously to depress the verbal output of the other group members except when they complied or agreed with the TP. It could be argued that one or the other of these two operations alone might account for most of the behavioral and sociometric changes. Experiments IV and V were designed to test the independent effects of each of these two component techniques. The results suggest that both operations are necessary to produce mod-

ification of the group behavior. The ineffectiveness of either operation used separately indicates that without some encouragement quiet group member will not spontaneously increase his output when other members are artificially depressed; and conversely it is not enough to encourage a quiet individual to participate more unless "room" is provided for his increased verbal output. It is also possible that when both techniques are employed, agreeing and complying behaviors of other group members may increase and provide additional social reinforcement for the TP.

The previously mentioned high correlation between sociometric rankings and total talking time deserves further consideration. Given a situation in which four strangers are brought together, allowed to interact for a brief period and then asked to evaluate one another on characteristics such as "best ideas," "guidance," and "leadership," one might expect that sheer amount of talking would be a salient factor in determining these evaluations. It would be misleading, however, to conclude that such a high correlation between talking and sociometry always obtains in group situations, or that talking, regardless of its quality or appropriateness, always leads to the perception of good ideas and leadership ability. Such a hypothesis would have to be tested under a wider variety of situations than the present experimental design affords. For instance, other group members may rate a talkative man highly on "best ideas" if he is perceived as talking a great deal because he had earned encouragement from expert evaluators. On the other hand, others may not positively evaluate a talkative man's ideas if they are aware that experimenters are manipulating rather than evaluating his behavior.

The results of Experiments I and II show that the increase in the TP's verbal output from the first to the second discussion is partly carried over to the third period when the lights are not used. The question of how long the effect lasts and whether or not it will generalize to other similar situations is unanswered. A series of experiments to test the perseveration and generalization of these effects is in progress.

If TP gains in sociometry and talks more, some one person or combination of other participants must lose sociometric votes and talk less. Because of this "degrees of freedom" re-

which the *TP* himself views the situation. We would hypothesize that the more an individual perceives changes in his behavior as being self-caused and not the result of external forces (in Heider's (4) sense of the word), the more likely he will maintain some of this behavior change.

The second general problem concerns the perception and evaluation of one person's behavior change by others. In the experiments described above, when a *TP*'s verbal output was markedly changed the other group members attributed high quality to the output. It is our hypothesis that observers who are able to see the rewarding or punishing lights would be more likely to attribute the change in behavior to the influence of the lights and would thus be less willing to attribute such qualities as leadership to the *TP*.

References

1. Aiken, E. G. Interpersonal behavior changes perceived as accompanying the operant conditioning of verbal output in small groups. *Technical Report Number 2*, Western Behavioral Sciences Institute, 1963.
2. Bachrach, A. J., Candland, D. K., and Gibson, J. T. Group reinforcement of individual response experiments in verbal behavior. In I. A. Berg and B. M. Bass (Eds.), *Conformity and deviation*. New York: Harper, 1961. Pp. 258–285.
3. Bales, R. F. *Interaction process analysis: A method for the study of small groups.* Cambridge, Mass.: Addison-Wesley, 1950.
4. Heider, F. *The psychology of interpersonal relations.* New York: Wiley, 1958.
5. Oakes, W. F. Reinforcement of Bales' categories in group discussion. Psychological Reports, 1962, **11**, 427–435.
6. Oakes, W. F., Droge, A. E., & August, B. Reinforcement effects on participation in group discussion. *Psychological Reports*, 1960, **7**, 503–514.
7. Pepinsky, P. N., Hemphill, J. K., & Shevitz, R. N. Attempts to lead, group productivity, and morale under conditions of acceptance and rejection. *Journal of Abnormal and Social Psychology*, 1958, **57**, 47–54.

40

On "Status-Liability"

JAMES A. WIGGINS, FORREST DILL, AND RICHARD D. SCHWARTZ

In the past, several empirical investigations have concerned themselves with the effect of the status of a frustration- or interference-agent on the aggression or punishment he receives from those he frustrated. In experimental investigations, Worchel (8) and Reiser (6) found that verbal aggression toward a frustration-agent decreased with his increasing status (faculty vs. student; captain vs. private). Similarly, in a correlational study, Cohen (1) found that in hypothetical situations aggression toward a frustration-agent decreased with his status (authority figures vs. peers). The rationale in each case was that a high-status individual could counter-aggress or punish if aggressed against. Schwartz and Skolnick (7) found similar results in the differential sanctioning of lower-class unskilled workers charged with assault and medical doctors accused of malpractice. In an experimental investigation, Hollander (4) found that status (past task competence) protected a frustrating nonconformist from punishment (lost influence), a phenomenon he called "idiosyncrasy credit."

At the same time, only one investigation has attempted to vary simultaneously the status of the interference-agent and the intensity of the frustration. In a correlational study, Graham *et al.* (3) found that in hypothetical situations the strength of the positive relationship between frustration-intensity and aggression toward the frustration-agent decreased as the latter's status increased (and if the frustration-agent was a parent, the relationship completely disappeared).

The purpose of the present investigation is to examine this relationship experimentally. Three levels of interference-intensity and two levels of status are used in the experiment. The former is conceived as the degree to which a group member's behavior decreases the probability of the group achieving its goal. The three levels range from

From *Sociometry*, 1965, **28**, 197–209. Reprinted by permission of the authors and the American Sociological Association.

behavior having little effect on the probability of goal-achievement (low interference-intensity) to behavior appreciably decreasing the probability of goal-achievement (medium interference-intensity) to behavior practically eliminating the possibility of goal-achievement (high interference-intensity). Following Hollander, "status" is conceived as a group member's past competence at group tasks. In order to isolate the effect of high status more exactly, the experiment examines the difference between "high" and "medium status" as opposed to the more usual concern with "high" and "low status."

The specific propositions tested are:

1. The greater the interference-intensity the greater the punishment of the interference-agent.
2. The greater the status of the interference-agent the less the punishment he receives.
3. The relationship between punishment and the status of the interference-agent is negative under low- and medium-interference and positive under high-interference.

Proposition 3 is the major focus of the investigation. It asserts that the group members will show little inclination to punish a high-status interference-agent as long as he does not step too far out of bounds. As long as there is still hope of achieving the group goal, the group will bear with him because of (*a*) his past performance and (*b*) their future need of his services. However, if his behavior interferes to the degree that the group's goal is jeopardized, the members will punish him more than a lower-status member who interferes to the same degree. The rationale for this "status-liability" proposition will be treated in the discussion section below.

METHOD

Experimental Setting

Thirty-four-person groups were randomly assigned to one of six experimental variations by the use of a die. The subjects were student volunteers from psychology and sociology classes in the summer session at Northwestern University.

The subjects were ushered into the experimental room and each settled in an enclosed working space. Although subjects were unable to see one another, the experimenter could observe all subjects from his position at a table in the middle of the room. The subjects were read the following instructions:

When you volunteered to participate in this experiment, you couldn't have known that you stood to gain some money as well as two hours of credit for participating in it. I can now tell you that your group is one of twelve groups which are in competition for a prize of $50. The competition for this $50 prize operates very simply; the group with the highest scores on the five tasks that you are about to undertake wins the $50.

(*More extemporaneously, they were told the following.*) In actuality, you are competing with one other group. Your group is the last in one complete series of twelve groups which are competing for the $50. The other eleven groups have been completed. Since yours is the last group in this series, you will know what score you will have to beat to win the $50 and at the end of this session we will know whether your group has won the $50.

(*Returning to the more obvious reading of instructions.*) We are specifically interested in some factors which affect task performance in a competitive setting, and you will probably be able to see what these factors are as the experiment progresses. If not, I'll explain them to you at the end of the experiment.

The design of the experiment is quite simple. Each of you will work five tasks of varying degrees of difficulty and of varying natures. You will be graded on how well you perform these tasks. Following your completion of each task, they will be collected and graded as quickly as possible. The tasks have been constructed with this in mind: each is easily graded by means of a scoring key. When I have finished scoring the particular task, I will give you your scores on a scoresheet, which I will replicate here on the blackboard. You will notice that the scoresheet will also contain some information of importance to you: the best scores that any one of the previous groups in your series has achieved on each of the tasks. By comparing your group's performance with these scores, you will be able to estimate your group's chances of winning the $50. (*Extemporaneously:* Since yours is the last group in this series, you are assured of winning the $50 if your group accumulative score at the end of the five tasks is higher than the score of the other group.) If, at the end of the five tasks your score is lower than the score of the best group, you will still be eligible for a second prize of $15. If you should win either prize, the money will be sent to you within a week.

On the scoresheet, I will list your individual

performances as well as the total score of your group on each task. Two things should be noted about this scoring procedure. First, the scores that I post will be standardized to a perfect score of 20 for each task. This procedure is followed so that each task will be comparable with each other task in terms of arriving at a total score across all five tasks. No task is worth more than another task. Thus, for example, on the first task, there are 75 items. A person who answers all 75 items correctly would receive a standardized score of 20. A person who gets 45 items right would receive a standardized score of 12. The other tasks work exactly the same way. The second thing about these scores is that you will be primarily interested in the accumulative score of your group. On the blackboard, you will notice that the accumulative score of the best group after the first task is 63, the accumulative score after the second task is 93, after the third task it is 128, and so on. (*Extemporaneously:* If your final group accumulative score is the least bit higher than the best accumulative score—that is, higher than the 222 score achieved by this group—then you will win the $50.) Each of you will be designated by a letter, A, B, C, or D. As this has not been done on the basis of your sitting order, you will not know which individual is designated by a particular letter.

After the scores for each of the tasks has been posted, you will each be given a short questionnaire form and a distribution sheet to complete. The questionnaire concentrates on the factors in which I am interested and is a very important part of the experiment. It is urgent that you answer the items as honestly as possible, since the worth of the experiment depends to a great extent on your honest answers. Equally important is the distribution sheet which you will fill out. On this distribution sheet, you will be asked how you would divide the $50 should your group win it. Your honesty and accuracy is as important to you as to us as the distribution you designate will actually determine what share of the $50 each group member will receive. This will be determined by the average of the distributions indicated by each of you.

One final point. While we are grading your tasks, you are to work on a special task. This task will have nothing to do with your competition for the $50. However, it is an important aspect of this study.

Now are there any questions?

After the answering of any questions, the subjects turned to the first task.

Task #1: A six-minute, 75-word, synonym-antonym test.

Task #2: A four-minute, 200-item, number-translation test in which a code number was to be added to all odd numbers and subtracted from all even numbers.

Task #3: A six-minute, 20-item, logic and math test.

Task #4: A ten-minute, 25-item, reading-comprehension test.

Task #5: A four-minute, 500-item, symbol-for-number substitution test.

Intervening task: A task to construct different shapes from several pieces of cardboard.

The Manipulation of the Independent Variables

The variable of interference was manipulated by the cheating of a fictitious subject and the resulting removal of points from the group score. During task #4, the experimenter interrupted the subjects and in a somewhat emotional and confused manner told the subjects the following:

> On this last task, I had to stop the task early because I observed Member C looking back to the first page consistently through the period. . . . As carefully specified in the instructions this is against the rules. . . . (*After some pondering, he began again.*) In fairness to the other groups in this series, I think I should subtract some points from your score. I think . . . (*so many points*) is fair enough. This is difficult to judge as it has never happened before. (*The written instructions for task #4 specified that one could not look back at the first page.*)

Now, there was no Member C. Although there were four subjects and letters A, B, C, and D were used in reporting performance, none of the subjects was actually lettered C. Instead there were two A's, one B, and one D. Of course, the subjects were not aware of this. The intensity of the interference was manipulated by the number of points that were subtracted from the group score. In the low-intensity variation, 4 points were subtracted (leaving the group only 4 points behind the "best group"); in the medium-intensity variation, 20 points were subtracted (at the same time leaving the group 20 points behind the "best group"); and in the high-intensity variation, 36 points were subtracted (leaving the group 36 points behind the "best group"). The latter deficit was virtually impossible to make up on the last task.

The variable of status was manipulated by the use of standardized scores given to each group member. The scores were such that one member usually received about two-thirds of a perfect score (high status), two members received about one-half of a perfect score (medium status), and one member received about one-third of a perfect score (low status). Which group member received which score was determined by their actual rank order on their performance on the first task. The fictitious Member C was assigned to either the "high-status" or "medium-status" position in order to effect the desired manipulation. The scores were then manipulated so that each subject maintained the same rank on all five tasks. The ambiguity of the scoring procedures and the standardization of all scores to a maximum score of 20 maintained the authenticity of the scores.

Measurements

The effectiveness of the independent variables was measured by two items on the post-task questionnaire. "Perceived status" was measured by the following item:

Who has the greatest ability to affect the group's chances of winning the competition from this point on? List the members by their letters in the appropriate categories shown below.

a. High ability   (3)
b. Medium ability   (2)
c. Low ability   (1)

"Perceived interference-intensity" was measured by the following item:

How did the performance of the other group members on the last task affect your group's chances of winning the competition? List the members by their letters in the appropriate categories shown below.

a. Helped a lot
b. Helped some
c. Helped a little
d. Neither helped nor hindered   (1)
e. Hindered a little   (2)
f. Hindered some   (3)
g. Hindered a lot   (4)

The dependent variable, "punishment," was independently measured by the following items:

How do you feel about the other persons? List each one of them by their letters in the appropriate categories below:

a. Strongly like   (1)
b. Like   (2)
c. Indifferent   (3)
d. Dislike   (4)
e. Strongly dislike   (5)

If you were to participate again in a similar experiment, how would you feel about participating with friends of your own choosing rather than the present members of the group? List the members of the group by their letters in the appropriate categories below.

a. Would strongly favor friend of my own choosing rather than member(s)   (5)
b. Would prefer friend of my own choosing rather than member(s)   (4)
c. Have no preference   (3)
d. Would prefer group member(s)   (2)
e. Would strongly favor group member(s)   (1)

In the spaces provided alongside the letters, indicate how much of the total reward you wish to allocate to each member—including yourself. Please use percentages, e.g., 40%, 30%, etc. Be sure that the total adds up to 100%.

Member A   _____
Member B   _____
Member C   _____
Member D   _____
                100%

This last index was considered the principal index of punishment. The index scores obtained at the end of task #4 were used in the analysis.

RESULTS

THE EFFECTIVENESS OF THE INDEPENDENT VARIABLES

Table 1 shows the average scores of the "perceived status" index for the six experimental variations just prior to the interference manipulation. The average index score is 2.9 in the high-status variation and 1.8 in the medium-status variation. The between-variation difference is statistically significant beyond the .05 level. The differences between the interference-intensity variations are not significant.

Table 2 shows the average scores of the "perceived interference-intensity" index for the six experimental variations just after the interference manipulation. The average index score is 3.8 in the high-intensity variation, 2.9 in the medium-intensity variation, and 1.6 in the low-intensity variation. The between-variation differences are statistically significant beyond the .05 level. The differences between the status variations are not significant.

THE TESTS OF THE PROPOSITIONS

Punishment increases as interference-intensity increases. Tables 3, 4, and 5 show the

TABLE 1.   *Mean Perceived Status Score for All Experimental Variations*

Status of Interference-Agent	Interference-Intensity			Total Mean
	(1) High	(2) Medium	(3) Low	
High	2.9	3.0	2.8	2.9
Medium	1.9[a]	1.8[a]	1.8[a]	1.8[a]
Total mean	2.4	2.4	2.3	

[a] Differences between high and medium status statistically significant at $p < .05$, using the *t*-test (for all cells, $N = 20$).

mean scores of the punishment indices for the six experimental variations. The total mean scores for the three interference-intensity variations are presented in the last row of each table. The difference between the high- and low-interference variation is statistically significant using each of the three indices. The difference between the high- and medium-interference variations is significant using two of the indices. The difference between the medium- and low-interference variations is insignificant using each of the three indices.

Punishment decreases as the status of the interference-agent increases. The total mean scores of the punishment indices for the two status variations are presented in the last column of Tables 3, 4, and 5. Using each of the three punishment indices, the small between-variation differences are in the predicted direction but each fails to reach statistical significance.

The relationship between punishment and the status of the interference-agent is negative under low- and medium-interference and positive under high-interference. As shown in Table 3, the first punishment index (disliking) shows differences between the high- and medium-status variations that are statistically significant for all three interference variations. In both the low- and medium-interference variations, the punishment score is higher for the

medium-status interference-agent. In the high-interference variation, the punishment score is higher for the high-status interference-agent. An analysis of variance test shows an F value with $p < .05$ for the status-interference interaction. As shown in Table 4, the differences for the second punishment index (non-participation), between the high- and medium-status variations, are insignificant for all three interference variations. As shown in Table 5, the differences for the third punishment index (reward distribution), the principal index, are statistically significant for all three interference variations. As with the first punishment index, in both the low- and medium-interference variations, the punishment score is higher for the medium-status interference-agent. In the high-interference variation, the punishment is again higher for the high-status interference-agent. An analysis of variance yields an F value with $p < .05$ for the status-interference interaction.

To look at the data within status variations and across interference variations clarifies the picture. Within the high-status variation, the first and third indices show a significant increase in punishment from the low-interference variation to the high-interference variations and from the medium-interference variation to the high-interference variation. They do not show a significant increase in punish-

TABLE 2.   *Mean Perceived Interference Score for All Experimental Variations*

Status of Interference-Agent	Interference-Intensity			Between-Variation Differences			Total Mean
	(1) High	(2) Medium	(3) Low	1–2	2–3	1–3	
High	3.9	2.9	1.5	1.0[a]	1.4[a]	2.4[a]	2.8
Medium	3.6	2.8	1.7	0.8[a]	1.1[a]	2.9[a]	2.7
Total mean	3.8	2.9	1.6	0.9[a]	1.3[a]	2.2[a]	

[a] Statistically significant at $p < .05$ using the *t*-test.

TABLE 3. *Mean Dislike Score for All Experimental Variations*

Status of Interference-Agent	Interference-Intensity			Between-Variation Differences			Total Mean
	(1) High	(2) Medium	(3) Low	1–2	2–3	1–3	
High	4.8	2.6	2.0	2.2[a]	0.6	2.8[a]	3.1
Medium	3.8	3.7	2.9	0.1	0.8[a]	0.9[a]	3.5
Between-status difference	1.0[a]	−1.1[a]	−0.9[a]				
Total Mean	4.3	3.2	2.4	1.1[a]	0.8	1.9[a]	

[a] Statistically significant at $p < .05$ using the t-test. The status-interference interaction is statistically significant at $p < .05$ (F = 3.49) using the analysis of variance test.

ment from the low- to the medium-interference variation. Within the medium-status variation, the same indices show a significant increase in punishment from the low- to the medium-interference variation and from the low- to the high-interference variation. They do not show a significant increase in punishment from the medium- to the high-interference variation. The only significant difference demonstrated by the second index is the increase in punishment from the low- to the high-interference variation. This is found in both the high- and medium-status variations.

DISCUSSION

The interesting finding in this study is the evidence that high-status persons are punished less for minor, but more for major, interference than middle-status persons. In analysis of variance terms, there is a significant interaction between status and interference in determining punishment. Interactive relationships, in this case, are of special interest because they indicate that a variable which works one way under a given condition works the opposite way when the condition is changed. In seeking an explanation, we must ask what it is about the change in condition which reverses the effect of the variable. Why, in this case, does an increase in interference change high status from a shield to a target?

The problem can best be approached by breaking it into two questions. Why are persons of high status relatively free of penalties when they make a minor or moderate error? Why are they punished more severely than persons of middle status for a major error?

There are several possible explanations of the cloak afforded by high status. Persons who have contributed unusually well to the group in the past may have earned the gratitude of the group, which is usually expressed by giving them extra rewards. This seems especially likely in a situation, such as the experimental one, where the basis for evaluation is largely limited to quantitative scores on a single scale representing contributions to the group goal. In this situation, if not generally, punishment for interference with these goals can be imposed only by a reduction in these rewards, an action which would run counter to the response of expressing appreciation. Therefore, it may be reasonable to suppose that this interference would be discounted as long as it still left the interferer as the highest single contributor to the group. In the condition of low interference, this was the case. The high-status person had, by the end of the third trial, con-

TABLE 4. *Mean Non-Participation Score for All Experimental Variations*

Status of Interference-Agent	Interference-Intensity			Between-Variation Differences			Total Mean
	(1) High	(2) Medium	(3) Low	1–2	2–3	1–3	
High	4.6	3.9	2.8	0.7	1.1[a]	1.8[a]	3.8
Medium	4.6	4.1	3.6	0.5	0.5	1.0[a]	4.1
Total mean	4.6	4.0	3.2	0.6	0.8	1.4[a]	

[a] Statistically significant at $p < .05$ using the t-test.

TABLE 5.   *Mean Reward-Differentiation Score for All Experimental Variations*

Status of Interference-Agent	Interference-Intensity			Between-Variation Differences			Total Mean
	(1) High	(2) Medium	(3) Low	1–2	2–3	1–3	
High	08	32	36	−24[a]	−04	−28[a]	25
Medium	16	17	25	−01	−08[a]	−09[a]	19
Between-status difference	−08[a]	15[a]	11[a]				06
Total mean	12	24	30	−12[a]	−06	−18[a]	

[a]Statistically significant at $p < .05$ using the *t*-test. The status-interference interaction is statistically significant at $p < .05$ ($F = 4.65$) using analysis of variance test.

tributed about 12 points more to the group score than did any of the other participants. By the end of the fifth session, it could be anticipated that he would have contributed in all about 20 "extra" points. Against this total contribution, the loss of four points would still leave him as the outstanding contributor. If his fellow members operated on the principle of distributive justice, they would have a continuing basis for rewarding him differentially.

This explanation does not work as satisfactorily for the reaction to medium interference, however. There, the loss to the group (20 points) was sufficient to wipe out the differential contribution of the high-status person even if he continued to perform as well in the final trials as he had in the first three. Yet he is penalized little more for medium interference than he was for low. He continues to be protected by his high status.

Involved here may well be some subtler social processes. The high-status person may benefit from the sentiment of respect which is associated with a demonstration of skill. One is reminded of the answer given to Dickens when he asked about the respect in which a particular American was held, despite the fact that he was known by all to be a blackguard: "Well, sir, he is a smart man."

Underlying such a sentiment may well be the perception that such persons can retaliate against those who punish them. The fear of retaliation might be heightened in the situation, since punishment had to be called for by the individual without his knowing whether the same decision would be made by others in the group. (The fear of retaliation against the individual might have been lessened by uncertainty as to whether the punitive judgments would be disclosed at the end of the session, but the possibility was left open. Even if the

realistic danger of disclosure were eliminated, habits learned in other situations might have generalized to this one.) Another form of retaliation which might have been feared is that the high-status person would diminish his potential contribution to the group on the final trial. Since his efforts had been demonstrated to be important to the group, there would be good reason to avoid such an effect as long as victory was still possible. Moreover, retaliation by the punished person—in addition to hurting the group more because of the skill of the high-status man—might have been considered more likely. In a society which does award idiosyncrasy credits, high-status persons accept them as their due. When they are denied, as they would be by severe punishment in this case, a sense of injustice is to be expected. A characteristic reaction to perceived injustice is alienation from the group and retaliation against it. Whatever their own perceptions of justice, the other members of the group might accordingly refrain from punishment if only to keep the group in the running.

Most of these considerations would not serve to protect the high-status person where his interference ruins the chance of group success. In this situation, his action had the effect of wiping out his great contribution. Even if he continued to score as he had in the past, his net contribution would be about the same as that of the lowest scorer. It would hardly merit gratitude. Also, retaliation against the punitive individual would be less likely, since everyone in the group would be more likely to punish the offender. (It might also be less serious if the offender were conceived to have lost moral stature as a result of the censure implied in the larger penalty imposed by the experimenter.) Retaliation against the group, through lessened effort on the next trial, would be meaningless since the group had lost its chance of winning already. Thus, gratitude, distributive justice, and the fear of retaliation would not afford the high-status person protection from punishment where his interference destroyed the chance of group success.

Thus, the above factors possibly explain the decrease in the protection afforded by high status, but they do not necessarily explain the intensity of the punishment received by an individual of high status relative to that received by those of lesser status. What about respect for skill, the kind of sentiment Dickens described? It may be less of an asset than at first appears. When it serves the perceived interest of the group, it may heighten acceptance and offset minor failings. When it stands alone, it may work the other way. Homans (5, 148) suggests just such an interaction. "Indeed a man who could supply a service, in the sense that the signs associated with him resemble those of other men who have supplied the service, but who does not in fact supply it, will not reap approval but resentment. He had deprived his fellows of an expected reward." The process is beautifully illustrated in Britten's opera, *Peter Grimes*. The hero, a fisherman who ventures farther and catches more fish for himself than others in the village, is hounded to death for this reason.

There is some social science research which supports this view. Evidence of considerable personal dislike of doctors was discovered in a questionnaire study by Gamson and Schuman (2). A striking finding in that study was that dislike correlated directly with respect. Similar conclusions were reached in the small group studies by Borgatta, Bales, and Slater. They discovered that, with the rare exception of the "great man," persons skilled at providing good ideas or guiding the group were unable to remain or become best-liked and, on the contrary, were disproportionately disliked.

A second possible explanation involves yet another notion of distributive justice, one which suggests that an individual is punished in proportion to the rewards he has received in the past. An individual who has already been awarded more for his contributions to the group should be "fined" more for deviations which seriously jeopardize the group's chances of achieving its goal.

This notion may or may not be supported by the rationale that small punishments will not effectively alter the behavior of an individual who has accumulated great rewards and can therefore "afford" to take some losses. Only correspondingly large punishments can possibly serve this function. Therefore, an individual who has reaped large rewards for major contributions to the group may reap correspondingly large punishments for major depletions.[1]

In many social situations, punitive tendencies toward persons of high status are likely to be obscured by a variety of factors, such as the ones we have discussed. Accordingly, behavior toward such persons tend to be deferential. Where high status is disentangled from these protective factors, however, it appears to establish its possessor as a preferred target for aggression. To the student of revolutions, this conclusion will come as no surprise. The justification for investigating it further in the laboratory lies in the possibility of isolating the process by which it occurs and understanding its consequences more fully.

References

1. Cohen, A. Social norms, arbitrariness of frustration, and status of the agent of frustration in frustration-aggression hypothesis. *Journal of Abnormal and Social Psychology*, 1955, **51**, 222–226.
2. Gamson, W., & Schuman, H. Some undercurrents in the prestige of physicians. *American Journal of Sociology*, 1963, **68**, 463–470.
3. Graham, F., *et al.* Aggression as a function of the attack and the attacker. *Journal of Abnormal and Social Psychology*, 1951, **46**, 512–520.
4. Hollander, E. Competence and conformity in the acceptance of influence. *Journal of Abnormal and Social Psychology*, 1960, **61**, 365–370.

[1] An analysis of the data showed that the high-status person was given an average proportion of the $50 that was significantly higher than that given to the middle-status person through tasks 1, 2, and 3. The other two indices did not show such differences.

5. Homans, G. *Social behavior: Its elementary forms.* New York: Harcourt, Brace & World, 1961.

6. Reiser, M., Reeves, R., & Armington, J. Effect of variations in laboratory procedure and experiments upon ballistocardiogram, blood pressure, and heart rate in healthy young men. *Psychosomatic Medicine,* 1955, **17,** 185–199.

7. Schwartz, R., & Skolnick, J. Two studies of legal stigma. *Social Problems,* 1962, **10,** 133–142.

8. Worchel, P. Catharsis and the relief of hostility. *Journal of Abnormal and Social Psychology,* 1957, **55,** 238–243.

41

Stabilities Underlying Changes in Interpersonal Attraction

THEODORE M. NEWCOMB

It is a safe prediction that individuals who are initially strangers to one another will, under conditions assuring that they will become well acquainted, experience many changes in the degree of their attraction toward one another. Such changes, like any others that scientists investigate, presumably occur in orderly ways, and the principles governing both change and nonchange correspond to constancies. Lewin (5), paraphrasing Cassirer (2), notes that "throughout the history of mathematics and physics problems of constancy of relations rather than of constancy of elements have gained importance and have gradually changed the picture of what is essential." The present report points to a few such constancies of relations that have been observed on the part of two populations of initial strangers over a four-month period, while their attitudes (elements involved in the relations) toward one another were characterized by a good deal of inconstancy.

As reported more fully elsewhere (9), two sets of 17 male students served in two successive years as subjects in an investigation of the phenomena of getting acquainted. They had been successfully selected as total strangers to one another, and lived and took their meals together in a house reserved for them. During each of 16 weeks they responded to a selected set of questionnaires, attitude scales, or other instruments, many of which were repeated from time to time. In particular, they rated or ranked each other as to favorability of interpersonal attitudes (henceforth referred to as *attraction*) during almost every week. In addition, they frequently estimated one anothers' attitudes of various kinds. The present paper partially summarizes and also supplements findings reported in the original monograph, for the specific purpose of noting constancies that underlie inconstancies.[1]

From *The Journal of Abnormal and Social Psychology*, 1963, **66**, 376–386. Reprinted by permission of the author and the American Psychological Association.

[1] There were, of course, individual instances of nonchange, but as population variables most of the attitudes here considered were highly inconstant.

The theoretical considerations from which the investigation stemmed were direct descendants from Heider's (4) theory of "balanced states." For the purposes of this study, the elements among which a balanced relationship may exist for an individual are: his degree of attraction, positive or negative, toward another individual; his attitude, favorable or unfavorable, toward some object (in the inclusive sense, referring to persons, issues, and abstractions like general values); and the second individual's attitude, as perceived by the first individual, toward the same object. A balanced state exists among these elements insofar as attraction is positive and the individual perceives that his own and the others' attitudes are similar. Perceived dissimilarity together with positive attraction represents an imbalanced state; negative attraction (with which this paper does not specifically deal) together with perceived similarity of attitudes may be either imbalanced or merely nonbalanced (a matter of indifference); together with perceived dissimilarity, negative attraction may be either balanced or merely nonbalanced.[2] These rules of balanced relationships include the specification of certain conditions, most important of which are that the attitude objects be of relatively high importance and be considered to have common impact upon self and others, in similar ways.[3]

The significant feature, for present purposes, of balanced and imbalanced states is, in Heider's (4) words, that "if a balanced state does not exist, then forces toward this state will arise. If a change is not possible, the state of imbalance will produce tension." Thus balanced states tend to be stable and imbalanced ones unstable. In either case we are dealing with relations, in Lewin's terms, and not merely with elements attitudes.

[2] This description of balance as associated with negative attraction differs from Heider's position, according to which negative attraction together with dissimilarity is balanced and imbalanced together with perceived similarity. Theoretical considerations suggest that the former combination need not be rewarding nor the latter distressing; and empirical findings from the investigation here reported indicate that the former combination often does not have the stability that is characteristic of balanced relationships, while the latter does not necessarily have the instability characteristic of imbalanced relationships.

[3] For a fuller statement concerning this theoretical approach see Newcomb (6, 7).

INDIVIDUALS' ATTITUDES

It is to be expected that individuals' attraction to the remaining group members will at first be unstable, because initial attraction responses (made on the third day) are necessarily based upon first impressions only; and that week-to-week changes should be in the direction of increased stability—that is, that the rate of change will be a declining one, because in successive weeks the amount of "new" information that individuals receive about one another will decline. The kinds of information about another person that are relevant to attraction toward him are, in general, those that result in the attribution to him of properties that are regarded as rewarding. These are not necessarily persistent or "inherent" personal properties; they may equally well include properties that are elicited only in interaction with specific other persons and they may, of course, be idiosyncratically attributed. Changes in attraction result not only from new discoveries of what characteristics another person already has, but also from observing qualities that, whether one knows it or not, one has oneself helped to elicit in him.[4]

TABLE 1. *Means of Seventeen Individual Correlations* (rho's) *for Pairs of Adjacent Weeks*[a]

Weekly Interval[b]	Year I	Year II
0–1	.51	.65
1–2 through 4–5[c]	.82	.84
5–6 through 9–10[c]	.86	.91
10–11 through 14–15[c]	.88	.90

[a] In rank ordering attraction toward other 16 subjects.
[b] Week numbers refer to the number of preceding weeks of acquaintance.
[c] Variations within these sets of adjacent weeks are so slight that values for the pairs of weeks have been averaged, rather than presenting each one.

Table 1 presents means of week-to-week "reliability coefficients"; each subject's rank ordering of the other 16 subjects in attraction at each week was correlated with his rank ordering for the following week. Table 2 shows similar coefficients, computed over longer intervals. The two tables together provide strong

[4] Certain distinguishable sources of interpersonal reward, and thus of attraction, have been elsewhere described by Newcomb (8).

TABLE 2. *Means of Seventeen Individual Correlations (rho's) over Varying Intervals of Time*[a]

Weekly Interval	Year I	Year II
0–15	.29	.31
0–10	.32	.35
0–5	.38	.43
5–15	.66	.70
5–10	.82	.84
10–15	.83	.85

[a] In rank ordering attraction toward other 16 subjects.

support for both predictions: initial responses have little predictive value even for so short a period as five weeks, whereas Week 5 responses predict almost as well to Week 15 as to Week 10 ($p < .001$ in either case). Change continues throughout the entire period, but the rate of change declines hardly at all after the first five or six weeks. Except for very unpopular subjects, whose high attraction choices are not reciprocated and continue to be relatively erratic, attraction choices show comparatively little change after the first six weeks.

Such changes should occur, hypothetically, in spite of the individual's tendency to maintain a constant relationship between degree of perceived agreement and attraction to others concerning objects of importance to himself. If it may be assumed that the self is such an object, and in general a positively valued one, then it is to be expected that high attraction toward others will be associated with the perception of reciprocation of high attraction toward oneself. Table 3 supports this prediction for Year I, and results for Year II are almost identical. All estimates of reciprocation by

TABLE 3. *Relationship Between Giving High Attraction and Perception of Receiving High Attraction from Same Persons (Year I)*

	Number of Subjects Estimating Reciprocation from Their Rank 1 Choices at Level Indicated		
Estimated Rank of Reciprocated Attraction	Week 1	Week 5	Week 15
1–2 (very high)	14	14	12
3–4 (high)	3	2	2
5–8 (second quarter)	0	1	3
9–16 (lower half)	0	0	0
Total	17	17	17

Rank 1 choices are at all times in the upper half of the distribution, and most of them in the upper eighth. There is a very strong tendency (not necessarily warranted) to assume that one's highest ranked associates return the compliment.

It is to be expected, on similar grounds, that attraction to other individuals will be paralleled by perceived agreement with them as to the relative attractiveness of the remaining House members. As shown in Table 4, which

TABLE 4. *Summary of Relationships Found Between Level of Attraction to Other Subjects and Perceived Agreement with Them About Attractiveness of Remaining Subjects*

Time of Response	χ^2	df
Year I, week 1	55.81[b]	2
Year I, week 5	31.13[b]	2
Year I, week 14	38.94[b]	2
Year II, week 2[a]	17.54[b]	1
Year II, week 5[a]	6.73[d]	1
Year II, week 12[a]	9.95[c]	1

[a] In Year II only 5% of all possible estimates, based on a randomly drawn sample, were made. The somewhat lower significance levels in Year II result, in part at least, from the smaller Ns in that year.
[b] $p < .001$.
[c] $p < .005$.
[d] $p < .01$.

summarizes relationships between level of attraction to others and degree of perceived agreement with them about the relative attractiveness of other House members, there is in both populations, at all stages of acquaintance, a significant relationship between these two variables.

A special instance of this tendency is to be found in the almost universal tendency to assume that one's two most preferred sociometric choices are highly attracted toward each other. (In view of the fact that reciprocated attraction from Rank 1 and Rank 2 choices is also perceived as very high, this set of phenomena may be labeled "the perception of perfect triads.") According to the Year I data, which for this purpose are more complete than in Year II but which are well supported by the latter, the relationships shown in Table 5 are typical of all stages of acquaintance. It seemed to be almost unthinkable to these subjects that their two most-preferred choices should be hostile to each other and

TABLE 5. *Summary of Significance Levels at Which Two Highest Ranking Choices by All Subjects Are Judged to Be Highly Attracted to Each Other (Year I, Week 5)*

Category of Estimated Attraction	Number of Estimates		χ^2	df
	Obtained	Expected		
Highest quarter	22	8.5	26.51 [a]	1
Upper half	33	17.0	28.30 [a]	1
"Favorable"	34	23.6	13.68 [a]	1

[a] $p < .001$.

almost so that they should be merely "neutral." Early estimates to this effect were in several cases quite inaccurate; lack of information invites autistic judgments. Later ones were highly accurate; as earlier perceptions of perfect triads were discovered to be erroneous, preferences shifted in such manner as to justify the perception of perfect triads.

Balance inducing forces should also result, at all times, in the perception of closest agreement with most attractive others with respect to objects other than the self and House members. The data most suitable for testing this prediction are subjects' rankings of the six Spranger values in Year II, together with their estimates of how each other subject would rank them. Both at Week 2 and at Week 14 the relationships between attraction toward other subjects and estimates of agreement with them were highly significant; x^2 values are 17.19 and 11.63, respectively, corresponding p values being $<.001$ and $<.005$, $df = 2$. The slight decline in this relation, from Week 2 to Week 14, is also found in other tests of the same prediction; it reflects in part the countereffects of greater accuracy with increasing acquaintance.

Thus the data show a continuing increase, though at a rapidly declining rate, in the stability of attraction toward others. They also show that at all times, to about the same degree, attraction toward others is related to perceived agreement with them concerning a variety of things.

DYAD RELATIONSHIPS: MUTUAL ATTRACTION AND ACTUAL AGREEMENT

Insofar as subjects were alert to increments of information about one another with continued interaction among them, it is predictable that estimates of others' attitudes will become increasingly accurate with continued acquaintance and that actual relationships between mutual attraction and agreement will increasingly approach the perceived relationships. The latter prediction presumes that, with increasing accuracy, subjects will discover that some of their assumptions about agreement with attractive others are not justified and will tend either to modify their own attitudes or to shift their attraction preferences to individuals with whom they are in fact more closely in agreement.

With respect to the self as an object, the data do not support the first prediction: estimates of others' attraction toward oneself do not become more accurate with increasing acquaintance, and this is true at all levels of expressed attraction. Frequencies and magnitudes of inaccuracies are quite constant, although they are at all times predominantly in the direction of overestimating the true level of reciprocated attraction. Estimates are in general fairly accurate, especially at the extremes of expressed attraction. Most subjects, apparently, are rather sensitive to others' indications of attraction toward themselves, at all times, and at all times there is a constant tendency to exaggerate the degree to which one's own attraction toward another person is reciprocated at about the same level.

The accuracy with which subjects estimate each others' attraction preferences toward other House members does increase. During the early period (Weeks 0–5) this increase is significant only for the estimator's highest attraction ranks, representing individuals with whom he is likely to have associated frequently enough after five weeks to estimate their preferences reasonably well. By Week 15 the trend is unmistakable at all attraction ranks: in Year I (the population in which these data are most nearly complete) 15 of 17 subjects were more accurate than at Week 1—the binomial probability of which is beyond .001.

Subjects' accuracy in estimating others' rank ordering of Spranger values increases at a high level of significance, as shown in Table 6, in which the indices of accuracy represent rank-order correlations between each subject's estimated rank ordering of each other subject's responses and the latter responses as actually made. The mean accuracy of 272 estimates, according to this index, is .25 at Week 2 and .49 at Week 14.

Turning now to actual dyadic relationships,

TABLE 6. *Relative Accuracy of Estimating Others' Rank Ordering of Spranger Values, Early and Late*[a]

Accuracy Level[b]	Number of Estimates at Indicated Levels of Accuracy		
	Week 2	Week 14	Total
≥ .60	66	110	176
< .60, > .14	103	95	198
< .14	103	67	170
Total	272	272	544

[a] $\chi^2 = 17.92$, $p = .001$, $df = 2$.
[b] Rho between each estimated rank with actual rank.

it is to be expected that sensitivity to others' responses to oneself will increasingly result in similar levels of attraction on the part of dyad members, whatever that level may be. Insofar as forces toward balance with regard to the self are tempered with considerations of reality, dyad members should come to assign about the same degree of attraction to one another. Table 7 shows that this is indeed the

TABLE 7. *Ns of Dyads Whose Members' Attractions to Each Other Differ by Three (of Sixteen) Ranks or Less*

Time of Response	Obtained	Expected	χ^2	df
Year I, week 0	51	50	.00	1
Year II, week 0	59	53	.61	1
Year I, week 15	77	53	10.61[a]	1
Year II, week 15	72	53	6.46[b]	1

[a] $p < .002$.
[b] $p < .02$.

case. A large proportion of the dyads whose members accord very different levels of attraction to each other include a very popular or a very unpopular individual or both. Apart from this consideration, the tendency toward increasing reciprocation of attraction by dyad members at closely similar levels is almost universal. This fact about objective dyadic relationships, combined with the unchanging tendency to perceive favorably reciprocated attraction, reflects shifts in actual attraction preferences: changes are such that increasingly accurate judgments of others' attraction toward oneself result in increasingly close reciprocation.

With respect to Spranger values, also, the effects of increased accuracy in judging others, together with constant forces toward balance, are that actual agreement is increasingly associated with high mutual attraction. At Week 2,

when these responses were first obtained, there was no relationship between pair agreement and mutual pair attraction ($x^2 = 1.17$, $p < .50$, $df = 1$). At Week 14, however (when responses were last obtained), the relationship had become highly significant, as shown in Table 8. The x^2 value of this distribution, with both variables equally dichotomized, is 9.52, $df = 1$, and $p < .001$ by a one-tailed test.

TABLE 8. *Relationship Between Degree of Agreement About Spranger Values and Mutual Pair Attraction (Week 14, Year II)*

Level of Agreement	Number of Dyads at Attraction Level Indicated[a]				Total
	Highest Quarter	Second Quarter	Third Quarter	Lowest Quarter	
Highest quarter	12	6	9	6	33
Second quarter	10	16	6	4	36
Third quarter	9	4	8	11	32
Lowest quarter	7	4	10	14	35
Total	38	30	33	35	136

[a] For reasons described in the full report, dyad scores are routinely categorized according to proportions of expected, not obtained, frequencies, which typically show slight differences.

It happened that there were almost no changes in subjects' ranking of the six Spranger values between early and late acquaintance; it was therefore possible to predict later dyad attraction from initial agreement nearly as well from early as from late agreement; early agreement did not, however, predict to early attraction. Similar results were obtained with two other sets of attitude items, each quite wide-ranging in content, from which indices of dyad agreement were computed; first responses to these items were made on the third day of acquaintance in Year I, and by mail one month before subjects arrived at the university in Year II. As shown in Table 9, in neither case did preacquaintance agreement bear any relationship to early scores of mutual attraction, but high preacquaintance agreement in each year predicted significantly to high mutual attraction 4 or 5 months later.

In view of the general increase in accuracy of estimating others' attitudes and in view of the constant tendency to prefer balanced to unbalanced states, it follows that with increasing acquaintance there should be an increasing tendency toward relationships that are balanced not merely phenomenologically but

TABLE 9. *Predictive Value of High Attitudinal Agreement at Early Periods for High Mutual Attraction at Early and Late Periods*

Nature of Attitudes	Year	Week of Attitude Response	Week of Attraction Response	χ^2	df
Miscellaneous	I	0	0	.46	1
Miscellaneous	II	−4	0	.00	1
Spranger values	II	2	2	1.17	1
Miscellaneous	I	0	13	8.78 [a]	1
Miscellaneous	II	−4	13	11.68 [b]	1
Spranger values	II	2	14	9.52 [b]	1

[a] $p < .005$.
[b] $p < .001$.

also in fact. This means that, except in the case of attitudes that show little or no change, change in mutual attraction between dyad members should be accompanied by change in their actual agreement. This prediction is best tested with respect to agreement about the relative attractiveness of House members. As shown in Table 10, the early relationship be-

TABLE 10. *Summary of Mean Correlations Between Mutual Attraction and Actual Agreement About Other House Members on the Part of 136 Dyads*

Week	Year I	Year II
0–1	.15	.18
2–5	.45	.37
6–9	.52	.40
10–13	.50	.43
14–15	.46	.58

tween mutual dyad attraction and agreement about House members approached zero in both populations, and increased to a significant level in the later weeks. Typically, there was a good deal of shifting about during the earlier weeks, both with respect to mutual attraction and to preferences among other House members, with the result that the relationship between attraction and actual agreement becomes a highly significant one. It can also be shown, by more detailed analysis, that among dyads at a high level of mutual attraction in early weeks there is significantly higher agreement three months later on the part of dyads whose mutual attraction remains at the same high level than on the part of dyads whose mutual attraction has decreased.

Change or nonchange in these two respects proceeds together and interdependently.

HIGH ATTRACTION STRUCTURING WITHIN POPULATIONS

Both a rationale and supporting evidence have been presented for the expectation that with increasing acquaintance subjects will shift their attraction preferences in such manner as to satisfy constant preferences for balance (that is, agreement with attractive others about objects of importance) and to take into account considerations of reality, with continuing increments of information about one another. With specific reference to dyad members' agreement about the attractiveness of other House members, this expectation leads to the prediction of increasing numbers of high attraction triads and larger subgroups, for the following reasons. Dyad members will tend to find one or more other individuals toward whom each of them is strongly attracted; dyads in which this does not occur will tend to be unstable. It is likely, as has been shown, that this high attraction will be reciprocated in kind by a third individual; if so, a high attraction triad has been formed, composed of the three mutually attracted pairs; if not, in the case of some particular person, it is likely to occur with a different one. Once a high attraction triad has been formed, similar processes tend toward further accretion, with the attendant formation of high attraction tetrads and larger subgroups.

With respect to triads, such processes did occur, in both populations. Since our principal interest lies in stable triads we took, as a criterion of stability, triads all three of whose component dyadic relationships maintained a high level of mutual attraction for three consecutive weeks. During the first three weeks of acquaintance only 2 of 17 possible triads remained stable by this criterion in Year I and 3 of 13 in Year II. During the last three weeks, however, 7 of 13 in Year I and 14 of 19 in Year II remained stable; the respective *p* values, by exact test, based on Ns of early and late triads that were stable and that were unstable, were .036 and .017. Numbers of stable triads do increase with acquaintance; there were too few high attraction tetrads and pentads at any time to be studied.

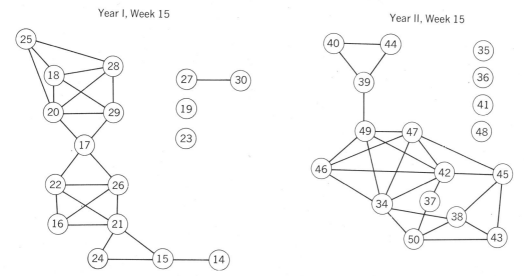

FIGURE 1. High attraction structure of two populations on final acquaintance. Circles represent individuals; connecting lines represent mutual attraction at high levels.

The attraction structuring of the total populations can be described in various ways, which might include numbers of high attraction subgroups of various sizes, the attraction relationships among them, and the number of isolates (individuals who have no mutually high attraction relationships at all). The two population structures did not differ in important ways at first, but interesting differences later appeared, as suggested by the sociograms presented in Figure 1, which show all subgroups of two or more whose members' levels of mutual attraction reached a rather high criterion. The visual appearance of these two sociograms, together with certain other evidence not here reported, suggests differences along a dimension that might be called centrality versus divisiveness—a difference not predicted on the basis of any theoretical considerations. A rather simple index of divisiveness confirmed the appearance, and a post hoc hypothesis was formulated concerning the sources of this difference. This hypothesis rests upon the contribution of two variables to centrality: the degree of interconnectedness among high, mutual attraction dyads on the part of the individuals having the highest attraction power ("popularity"), and the amount of attraction power concentrated in these individuals. It was found that among the most popular six individuals in each population, who together accounted for somewhat more than half of the attraction power in each population, 20% of all such dyads met the criterion of interconnect-

edness in Year I as compared with 53% in Year II. Moreover, there was more attraction power concentrated in the six most popular individuals in Year II than in Year I. Thus each variable contributes to the greater centrality in Year II. It is, in fact, an artifactual necessity that whichever of two populations of the same size has these characteristics will be the more centrally structured: greater interconnectedness at high levels of mutual attraction among individuals having most attraction power and greater attraction power on the part of the same number of popular individuals. These are not necessarily the only variables that contribute to centrality, but they do necessarily contribute to it, for the following reasons. Popular individuals who are multiply-connected by high mutual attraction constitute a triad or larger subgroup that serves as a core substructure, each of whose members brings with him several "hangers-on" who are thus added onto the core structure. And the more "hangers-on" thus added, the larger the substructure becomes.

Our post hoc hypothesis as to why so few popular subjects were multiply interconnected in Year I and so many in Year II is simply that there was more agreement among the six popular individuals in the latter than in the former year; the evidence abundantly supports it.

1. The most nearly comparable attitude responses made by both populations were to miscellaneous batteries of items; in Year I the

15 dyads among the six popular subjects agree with each other no more closely than did all other pairs, whereas in Year II their agreement was significantly closer than that of other pairs ($p < .05$).

2. In authoritarianism (F score), five of the six popular subjects in Year II were extremely low, ranking 1, 2, 3, 4, and 5 in a low-scoring population; in Year I, on the other hand, the six popular subjects covered nearly the entire range, from 2 to 17.

3. Although no comparable data are available for Year I, five of the six popular subjects in Year II were in extraordinarily close agreement in Spranger values—and they knew it: the mean of their ten intercorrelations in actual response was .72, and the mean of their estimated agreements with each other was .75. (The sixth, who disagreed with all of the others both in F score and in Spranger values, was Number 39, the only one of the six not having high mutual attraction with more than one of the others.) Thus the central proposition concerning balance accounts for the close interconnectedness of six popular subjects in one year and for the absence of it in the other year and thus accounts for the different attraction structurings in the two populations. It does not, of course, account for the fact that in Year II but not in Year I popularity was pretty much concentrated among a set of five closely agreeing individuals. Our general theory has nothing to say about the characteristics which led to popularity in these populations, and we can only say that our random methods of selecting subjects had this consequence.

INDIVIDUAL CHARACTERISTICS OF SUBJECTS

Several theoretically derived expectations have been shown to be supported by empirical findings. Our tests, however, have been statistical ones, pertaining to populations or subpopulations and not to individuals. There are two relevant questions concerning the manner in which individuals' characteristics contribute to the findings.

First, it is possible that a comparatively few individuals contribute all or most of the variances that account for the statistically significant findings; if so, the generalizability of the findings is severely limited. The findings depend rather heavily on assumptions concern-

ing two kinds of individual tendencies: to prefer balanced to imbalanced relationships and at the same time to take account of "reality" in the form of accretions of information that may disturb existing states of balance. Individual indices of both of these tendencies (sensitivity to balance, and accuracy in judging others) were therefore constructed. Results of intensive analyses of all 34 subjects may be summarized as follows:

1. Individual differences are clearly apparent, with respect to both balance and accuracy.

2. In estimating others' attitudes toward varying kinds of objects there are in each population typically one or two individuals who show little or no sensitivity to balance or no greater-than-chance accuracy in making estimates.

3. The subjects who are deviant in these ways with respect to one attitude object at a particular stage of acquaintance are not necessarily deviant with respect to other attitude objects or at other times.

In sum, the tendencies to be sensitive to balanced relationships and to judge others' attitudes more accurately with increasing acquaintance, which underlie our theoretically derived predictions, appear to be present, at least in some degree, in all of our subjects.

As to measured individual characteristics, authoritarianism (as measured by the F Scale) seemed most likely to be relevant to the problems of this investigation. Our expectations concerning authoritarianism stem from several studies suggesting that F Scale scores (1) are related to "perceptiveness of others" (3). Such evidence leads to the expectation that low F scorers should be relatively accurate in estimating others' attitudes. With one exception (estimates of others' ordering of attraction toward House members in Year I), the prediction is supported with respect to various attitude objects, and according to different indices of accuracy, in both populations. The data that best lend themselves to detailed analysis of accuracy consist of estimates of others' rank ordering of Spranger values, made in identical manner at Weeks 2 and 14 of Year II. These data show that on the rather difficult task of ranking other subjects according to agreement with the estimator, the nonauthoritarians excel the authoritarians in accuracy on late but not on early acquaintance; the correlation of .56

between F score and accuracy at the later time is significant at $< .01$.

Inaccurate estimates of others' attitudes may represent distortions either in the balance promoting direction or in the opposite direction; the former may be considered autistic, and if we assume that imbalanced relationships represent a form of ambiguity, of which authoritarians are relatively intolerant, then it is to be expected that high F scorers' inaccuracies will be in the autistic direction, relative to low F scorers. No difference in this respect appears at Week 2, when autistic errors are relatively frequent at all $\bar{F}$ score levels; but the prediction is well supported at Week 14: comparisons of autistic, accurate, and contra-autistic estimates for low, intermediate, and high F scorers yield a x^2 of 13.02 in the predicted direction, significant at $< .01$, $df = 4$, by a one-tailed test.[5]

These and other findings are consistent with the following interpretation. The greater sensitivity of the very low F scorers enables them to select as most attractive those with whom they are in fact most closely in agreement about a rather wide range of values. The nonauthoritarians' characteristic solution to imbalance is nonautistic: they tend to achieve balance not by exaggerating actual agreement with those to whom they are attracted (on other grounds), but by judging rather accurately who is in agreement with them and letting their highest attractions be determined accordingly. The characteristic solution of the more authoritarian subjects tends to be just the reverse: instead of letting their personal preferences be determined by accurate perceptions of agreement, they tend to perceive more agreements than actually exists with those toward whom they are already attracted.

NATURE OF CONSTANT RELATIONS

Three kinds of elements, in Lewin's (5) sense, have been considered: an individual's attraction toward another person; his attitude toward some object other than that person; and that person's attitude, as he perceives it,

toward the same object. Under the conditions of the investigation here reported, the stability curves of these three kinds of elements were quite different: attitudes toward nonperson objects (especially toward general values) showed little change from first to last acquaintance; attraction toward other House members, on the part of most subjects, became relatively stable by the end of the first six weeks or so; and estimates of others' attitudes were relatively slow in stabilizing, though with individual differences. If the study had been concerned only with subjects' own attitudes and attractions, it might well have been terminated after six rather than 16 weeks. But in view of the crucial place, in the present formulation, of perceptions of others' attitudes, and in view of the relatively slow and continuing changes in estimates of others' attitudes it might be argued that the study should have been continued for another several weeks.

What does remain relatively constant, in spite of these differential rates of stability and change, is the second-order relationship between the relationship of two of them (own and other's perceived attitude) and attraction. With regard to such diverse attitude objects as the individual subject himself, other group members, and a range of nonperson objects, such a relationship, described as a balanced one, is found at all stages of acquaintance. This constant relationship is maintained despite the fact that all of the related elements are changing or some of them are changing while others are not. Eventually, the single elements tend to become stable, but the level at which they do so is governed by the same constancy of relationships that prevailed throughout the earlier periods of change.

The psychological processes by which intrapersonal states of balance are maintained may be described as follows. As group members interact with one another, each of them selects and processes information—about objects of common interest, about one another as sources of attitudes toward those objects, and about one another as objects of attraction—in such ways that the inconsistencies and conflicts involved in imbalanced relationships tend to be avoided. Both autistic processes ("balance at all costs") and realistic ones ("the truth, whatever it costs") are involved, their respective weightings being determined both by individual differences and by the strength of the attitudes involved. When interaction begins with

[5] If the "accurate" estimates are ignored, in order to compare autistic and contra-autistic responses only, the inverse relationship between autism and authoritarianism is still significant at the .05 level.

total strangership, increments of information are inevitable; attitude change results from the necessity to adapt simultaneously to increments of information and to constant preferences for balanced relationships.

Interacting members of dyads and larger groups necessarily make such adaptations to one another simultaneously. Insofar as they do so realistically, the consequence of reciprocal adaptation is a mutual relationship that is in fact maximally satisfying to both or all of them—that is, maximally within the limits of what is possible. Realism tends to increase with acquaintance and, combined with constant tendencies toward balance, the inevitable trend is toward mutuality of attraction. Stable relationships tend to persist, and relationships that are in fact balanced tend to be stable because they are mutually rewarding and not likely to be disturbed by increments of information with continued interaction.

Viewed intrapersonally, the generalizable constancies underlying changes in interpersonal attraction that apply to all individuals— regardless of their differences in preferring some personal properties to others and regardless of the personal traits that others present— are preferences for balanced relationships and tendencies to adapt to information regarded as valid. Viewed interpersonally, the generalizable constancies are the necessities (which may become internalized as preferences) confronting each of a set of interacting persons to make successive adaptations to one another, simultaneously and reciprocally, in the direction of establishing relationships that are both realistic and balance-promoting for each. It is relationships that are simultaneously rewarding to each and realistically apprehended by each that tend to be stable. Such relationships are both psychologically (intrapersonally) balanced and objectively (interpersonally) balanced.

Attitude changes that are governed by these constancies stem from a triple confrontation that is characteristic of *la condition humaine.* Each of us must somehow come to terms, simultaneously, with the other individuals and groups of which our interpersonal environment is constituted; with the world that we have in common with those persons and groups; and with our own, intrapersonal demands, including the preference for balanced states. Insofar as the individual's confrontation is characterized by changing input of information, the elements that correspond to his attitudes are subject to inconstancy, but the lawfulness with which they change corresponds to certain constancies in relationships among the elements. It is such constancies that make possible viable adaptations, simultaneously, to multiple confrontations.

References

1. Adorno, T. W., *et al. The authoritarian personality.* New York: Harper, 1950.
2. Cassirer, E. *Substance and function.* Chicago: Open Court, 1923.
3. Christie, R., & Cook, P. A guide to published literature relating to the authoritarian personality through 1956. *Journal of Psychology,* 1958, **45,** 171–199.
4. Heider, F. *The psychology of interpersonal relations.* New York: Wiley, 1958.
5. Lewin, K. Frontiers in group dynamics: Concept, method, and reality in social science; social equilibria and social change. *Human Relations,* 1947, **1,** 5–41.
6. Newcomb, T. M. An approach to the study of communicative acts. *Psychological Review,* 1953, **60,** 293–404.
7. Newcomb, T. M. Individual systems of orientation. In S. Koch (Ed.), *Psychology: A study of a science.* Vol. 3. New York: McGraw-Hill, 1959. Pp. 384–422.
8. Newcomb, T. M. Varieties of interpersonal attraction. In D. Cartwright & A. Zander (Eds.), *Group dynamics: research and theory.* (2nd ed.) Evanston, Ill.: Row, Peterson, 1960. Pp. 104–119.
9. Newcomb, T. M. *The acquaintance process.* New York: Holt, Rinehart, and Winston, 1961.

42

A Formal Theory of Social Power

JOHN R. P. FRENCH, JR.

This formal theory is a small part of the later stages of a program of empirical research on social influence. It tries to integrate previous findings into a logically consistent theory from which one can derive testable hypotheses to guide future research.[1] The more specific purpose of the theory is to explore the extent to which the influence process in groups can be explained in terms of patterns of interpersonal relations.

In discussing the effects of the majority on conformity by the individual deviate, Asch states (14, 186), "The effects obtained are not the result of a summation of influences proceeding from each member of the group; it is necessary to conceive the results as being relationally determined." Both Heider (17) and Newcomb (28) have treated patterns of opinion and of interpersonal relations as a single system of relations, though they have discussed only two-person groups. The present theory reduces the process of influence in N-person groups to a summation of interpersonal influences which takes into account three complex patterns of relations: (a) the power relations among members of the group, (b) the communication networks or patterns of interaction in the group, and (c) the relations among opinions within the group. Thus propositions which have been conceptualized at the group level (e.g., that the strength of group standards increases with increasing cohesiveness of the group) are deduced from concepts at the interpersonal level.

From *The Psychological Review*, 1956, **63**, 181–194. Reprinted by permission of the author and the American Psychological Association. The work reported in this paper was financed in part by a grant from the Rockefeller Foundation and by a contract with the Group Psychology Branch of the Office of Naval Research.

[1] Similar current attempts to construct mathematical theories of social influence include unpublished papers by Ardie Lubin, by Harold Guetzkow and Herbert Simon, and by Solomon Goldberg.

The deductive power and the internal consistency of a mathematical model stem from a set of explicit definitions and postulates stated with enough precision so that one can apply the rules of logic. But the construction of theory by coordinating mathematical definitions and postulates to psychological constructs and assumptions leads to a dilemma: the very precision which gives power to the theory also tends to oversimplify it. For reasons of mathematical convenience one tends to make simple assumptions which so restrict the theory that it may seem unrealistic compared to the complexity observed in social behavior. Game theory, for example, describes certain aspects of how "the rational economic man" ought to behave, but actual economic behavior often departs widely from this simple ideal (19).

The present theory deals with this dilemma partly by utilizing a kind of mathematics, the theory of directed graphs, which does not require the making of precise quantitative assumptions about empirical variables.[2] In addition, the basic concepts and postulates of this theory were chosen to conform to the results of experiments on social influence. Frequently, however, our present knowledge was not adequate for making these choices in precise detail. At these points we attempted to choose postulates which would be essentially correct in their main outlines even though some details would have to be changed as new empirical knowledge accumulates. It is not surprising, therefore, that many of the theorems are quite similar to previous findings about influence on opinions and attitudes, even though no research has been done specifically to test this theory. Nevertheless we have intentionally oversimplified the process of social influence by omitting many important determinants and by making very restrictive assumptions about others. It seemed wise to start by examining the implications of a small number of postulates before proceeding to more complex theories.

[2] The theory of directed graphs, which is an extension of graph theory (15, 16) has been studied by Frank Harary, Robert Norman, and Dorwin Cartwright with a view toward utilization by social scientists. The author is indebted to these colleagues for specific help in proving the theorems of this theory as well as for their work on the theory of digraphs upon which it is based.

THE MODEL

Following the theory of quasi-stationary equilibria of Lewin (22), changes in opinion, attitude, or judgment are conceptualized in terms of forces operating along a unidimensional continuum (5). Social influences are coordinated to force fields induced by person A on person B, and the strength of these forces is assumed to vary with the power of A over B. The potential force field corresponding to this power relation will be actualized only if A communicates to B or interacts with him. When A expresses his opinion or argues for it in a way that influences B, then the force field operating on B has a central position corresponding to A's position along the continuum of opinion. All the forces operating on B are directed toward this central position, so B will tend to change his opinion in a direction which brings him closer to A. Similarly, other members, C, D, E, etc., who communicate to B may set up force fields on him with central positions corresponding to their own opinions. The actual changes in B's opinion will be in accordance with the resultant force from all these induced forces plus a force corresponding to his own resistance.

In order to derive the exact amount of influence that each member will have on the opinion of every other, let us assume that we are dealing with a unidimensional continuum of opinion which can be measured with a ratio scale. We might think, for example, of the classic experiment on social norms by Sherif (31), where the members of the group were asked to state their opinions about how many inches the light moved as they viewed the autokinetic effect. We shall denote the members of the group by A, B, C, . . . and their initial opinions by a, b, c, . . . respectively, where a is the distance of A's opinion from the zero point on the scale. The abscissa of Figure 1 shows such a scale of opinion together with the initial opinions of A and B. The ordinate indicates the strength of the forces. The gradient of forces around A represents the forces he can induce on B to agree with his opinion, while the gradient of forces around B represent his tendency to resist changing his opinion. Where these two gradients intersect, a distance of $\frac{1}{2}(a + b)$ from the origin, there is an equilibrium point where the two forces are equal in strength and opposite in direction. At all points to the right of this equilibrium the

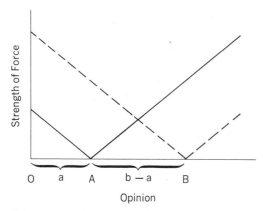

FIGURE 1. The force fields influencing opinion.

forces induced by A are stronger than B's resistance, so B will move toward the point of equilibrium. Conversely, at all points to the left of the equilibrium, B's resistance forces are stronger than A's inductions, so B will still move toward the point of equilibrium. Similar calculations of the resultant force and consequent changes of opinion can be made for A and for groups with any number of members by placing all members on the same scale and by assuming that the gradient of forces around each member represents both forces he can induce on others and forces he can set up as resistance against others.

The process of influence in a group takes place gradually over a period of time. As one member changes his position and begins to influence others toward his new position, the force fields corresponding to his influence will also shift their central positions. It will be convenient, therefore, to divide the influence process into a sequence of units defined in terms of opinion change rather than in terms of physical time. A *unit* is defined as the time required for all members who are being influenced to shift their opinions to the point of equilibrium of all the forces operating at the beginning of that unit. At the end of the unit, after this shift has taken place, we assume that the members now start to argue for their new opinions. It should be noted that this definition implies that all members respond at the same rate to the forces impinging on them. One possible operational definition of a unit might be a single trial in an experiment such as Sherif's.

This conception of influence as a process over time implies a distinction between direct and indirect influence. In a typical organization the president usually influences indirectly a person at the bottom of the chain of command through orders which are handed down through several subordinates. *Direct* influence is exerted on another person by direct communication which is not channeled through a third person. *Indirect influence* is exerted on another through the medium of one or more other persons. Therefore the direct influence of A on B always occurs during the same unit, whereas indirect influence requires two or more units. For example, A influences B directly during the first unit, and B influences C toward his new opinion during the second unit. Thus A has indirectly influenced C by transmitting his opinion via B. In this model, the power structure and the communication channels of the group are translated into a process of influence over time. In the first unit any member, A, influences only those recipients of his communication over whom he has direct power; in the second unit A's influence is also transmitted to all those over whom these intermediaries have power; in the third unit A's influence is transmitted to those who are three steps removed from him in the power structure, etc.

THE POSTULATES

Three main postulates are involved in this model. The first is concerned with interpersonal power. The definition of *power* used in this postulate is the same as that given by Cartwright (6): the power of A over B (with respect to a given opinion) is equal to the maximum force which A can induce on B minus the maximum resisting force which B can mobilize in the opposite direction.

The *basis* of interpersonal power is defined as the more or less enduring relationship between A and B which gives rise to the power. French and Raven (see Chap. 20) have discussed five bases: a *traction power* based on B's liking for A, *expert power* based on B's perception that A has superior knowledge and information, *reward power* based on A's ability to mediate rewards for B, *coercive power* based on A's ability to mediate punishments for B, and *legitimate power* based on B's belief that A has a right to prescribe his behavior or opinions. Any basis of power can vary in strength: there may be variations in how much B likes A, in how much B respects A's expertness, etc. Postulate 1 is general enough to refer to all bases of social power.

POSTULATE 1

For any given discrepancy of opinion between A and B, the strength of the resultant force which an inducer A can exert on an inducee B, in the direction of agreeing with A's opinion, is proportional to the strength of the bases of power of A over B.

Attraction as a basis for interpersonal influence has been demonstrated in experiments by Back (**2**) and by French and Snyder (**12**), and in field studies by Lippitt, Polansky, and Rosen (**24**).

Expertness as a basis for interpersonal power has been demonstrated in the latter two studies as well as in many others (**18, 26, 27**). In unpublished experiments French and Raven and French, Levinger, and Morrison have demonstrated that legitimacy and the ability to punish are bases for social power. Heider (**17**) and Newcomb (**28**) state their theories in terms of "positive relations," a more general conception which combines several types of power. In most real groups the power relations probably do combine several of the bases discussed here and others too. Postulate 1 refers to all of these bases combined.

Resistance, as a part of the social power discussed in Postulate 1, has not been treated separately nor in detail in this model. In a further development it might be coordinated to such factors as "certainty of own opinion" (**12**), or as Kelman (**20**) and Mausner (**25**) call it, "prior reinforcement," and to various personality characteristics such as rigidity and authoritarianism (**8**).

POSTULATE 2

The strength of the force which an inducer A exerts on an inducee B, in the direction of agreeing with A's opinion, is proportional to the size of the discrepancy between their opinions.

This postulate combines two effects which have been demonstrated in previous research. (*a*) More influence is attempted toward the member who is more discrepant (**9, 10, 29**). These studies also show, however, that this effect holds only under conditions where the inducee is not rejected. Too great a deviation leads to changes in the attraction power structure of the group and hence to changes in the effects implied by Postulate 1. (*b*) If the amount of influence attempted is held constant, the amount of change in the inducee increases with increasing size of discrepancy. For this latter relation, French and Gyr (in a study as yet unpublished) found correlations of .77, .62, .65, and .83 in different experimental groups. Goldberg (**13**) also reports a strong tendency for the amount of change to increase with increasing discrepancy, with the inducee moving 30 per cent of the way toward the inducer for discrepancies of all sizes. In a subsequent unpublished theoretical paper, Goldberg [3] also assumes that change in opinion is a direct function of discrepancy until the inducee rejects the credibility (expert power) of the inducer, after which it becomes an inverse function of discrepancy. Again the data support Postulate 2 within the range where the expert power structure of the group is not changed.

Postulate 2 is represented in Figure 1 by the two increasing gradients of forces around A's opinion and around B's opinion. The two gradients are assumed to be linear, though the evidence cited above would suggest that they are curvilinear. We have made the more convenient assumption because it appears to be true as a first approximation and because it seems to be possible to revise the postulate later, if subsequent empirical data do show curvilinearity, with only minor quantitative changes in the theorems.

POSTULATE 3

In one unit, each person who is being influenced will change his opinion until he reaches the equilibrium point where the resultant force (of the forces induced by other members at the beginning of the unit and the resisting force corresponding to his own resistance to change) is equal to zero.

Postulate 3 is an application of a basic assumption of Lewin (**21**) that locomotion or restructuring will take place in the direction of the resultant force whenever that force is greater than zero. Though consistent with a great many empirical studies, this assumption is close to a conceptual definition which cannot be directly tested.

[3] S. C. Goldberg. Some cognitive aspects of social influence: A hypothesis.

THEOREMS

For lack of space, no attempt will be made to state all the theorems which have been proven nor to give the formal proofs of those presented. Instead we will select some representative theorems and indicate informally the nature of the derivations. In making empirical predictions from these theorems, this theory, like any other, must always assume "other things being equal," including all extrasystem influences and the many factors within the group which are not part of the theory.

THE EFFECTS OF THE POWER STRUCTURE OF THE GROUP

This section presents some theorems concerning the effects of the power structure of the group on the influence process and its outcome. These theorems illustrate how the present theory explains a well-known proposition about groups in terms of concepts about interpersonal relations.

This proposition—that the strength of group standards increases with increasing cohesiveness of the group—has been substantiated in several studies (2, 4, 10, 29, 30). A group standard has been defined conceptually as group-induced pressures toward uniformity of behavior or belief, and it may be measured by the degree of conformity of members produced by these pressures. *Cohesiveness* has been defined conceptually as the resultant forces on members to belong to the group, but it has been operationalized in many of these experiments as the attraction of members for one another (7, 23). Festinger, Schachter, and Back (10) have shown that the hypothesized relation is stronger when cohesiveness is operationalized in a way which takes account of the pattern of the sociometric structure instead of a simple summation of choices. But each sociometric choice measuring the attraction of member B toward member A is, according to Postulate 1, a basis for A's power over B. Thus the sociogram of a group can be transformed into the attraction power structure of the group by simply reversing the direction of each arrow. The attraction power structure of the group is a special type of power structure, and hence it is treated in these theorems about power structure and trends toward uniformity of opinion within the group.

The power structure of a group may be rep-resented conceptually in terms of the mathematical theory of directed graphs, called "digraphs." A digraph is a finite set of points. A, B, C, . . . and a subset of the directed lines $\overrightarrow{AB}$, $\overrightarrow{BA}$, $\overrightarrow{AC}$, $\overrightarrow{CA}$, $\overrightarrow{BC}$, $\overrightarrow{CB}$, . . . between distinct points. In representing power structures as digraphs, we shall coordinate points to members and directed lines to power relations between members. In this coordination we shall make only relatively crude distinctions in differences of power: if "A has power over B," there is a directed line $\overrightarrow{AB}$ in the digraph representing the power structure of the group; if "A does not have power over B," there is no such line.

Various properties of digraphs may be used to characterize power structures of groups. We shall be concerned here primarily with the "degree of connectedness" of power structures. In order to discuss this property we need two definitions: *complete digraph* and *directed path*. A digraph is complete if there exists a directed line from each point to every other point. A power structure would be complete, then, if each member had power over each other member. If we assume that when A chooses B sociometrically B has power over A, then it follows that when every member of a group chooses every other member, the digraph representing the power structure of the group will be complete (e.g., No. 5 in Figure 2). A *directed path* is a collection of distinct points A, B, C, . . . together with the lines $\overrightarrow{AB}$, $\overrightarrow{BC}$, ... If in the power structure of a group there is a directed path from A to C, it follows that A can exert influence on C even though A may not have direct power over C (there must be a sequence of directed lines originating at A and going to C even though there is no line $\overrightarrow{AC}$).

In their work on digraphs, Harary, Norman, and Cartwright (16) have defined four degrees of connectedness. Their definitions are as follows: (*a*) A digraph is *strongly connected* (or *strong*) if for every pair of distinct points, A and B, there exists a directed path from A to B *and* a directed path from B to A. It follows that every complete digraph is strong, but not every strong digraph is complete. (*b*) A digraph is *unilaterally connected* (or *unilateral*) if for every pair of points, A and B, there is a directed path from A to B *or* from B to A. (*c*) A digraph is *weakly connected* (or *weak*) if it

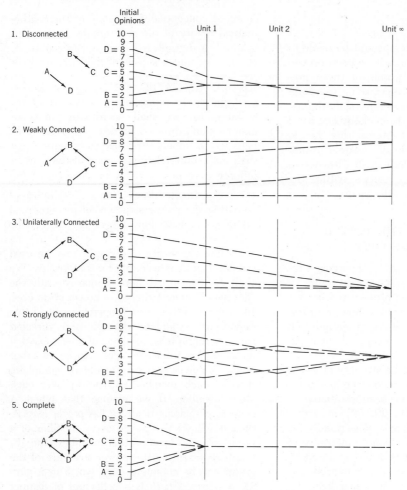

FIGURE 2. The effects of connectedness on opinion changes in the group.

is impossible to separate the points of the digraph into two classes such that no line of the digraph has one end point in one class and the other end point in the other class. Thus, for every possible separation of all of the points of a weak digraph into two disjoint, nonempty classes, there must be at least one line having one end point in one class and the other end point in the other class. (*d*) A digraph is *disconnected* if it is not weak. Thus a disconnected digraph may be separated into two (or more) disjoint classes of points such that no line goes from one class to the other. From these definitions it is clear that all strong digraphs are unilaterally and weakly connected and that all unilateral digraphs are weakly connected. It is also clear that all weak digraphs are *not* strongly connected. For this reason it is useful to define a digraph as *strictly unilateral* if it is unilateral but not strong, and to define a digraph as *strictly weak*

if it is weak but not unilateral. In our discussion here, when we speak of unilateral or weak digraphs we shall mean "strictly unilateral" and "strictly weak."

In groups where each member communicates to all others over whom he has direct power during every unit of the influence process, the amount of uniformity achieved and the speed of achieving it tend to vary with the degrees of connectedness of the power structure, except that no differences were proved for weak versus disconnected digraphs.

The effect is illustrated in Figure 2 and generalized later in the first four theorems. In Figure 2 five different types of structures (complete, strong, unilateral, weak, and disconnected) are illustrated by digraphs of four-person groups. To the right of each structure are curves showing some of the theoretically predicted changes of opinion. The ordinate gives the scale of opinion and, at the left, the initial opinion of members A, B, C, and D. The line labeled "Unit 1" gives the distribution of opinion after the first unit; the line labeled "Unit 2" gives the distribution of opinion after the second unit; and the line labeled "Unit ∞" gives the equilibrium of opinions reached in an infinite number of units.

The disconnected structure is composed of two cliques, AD and BC. Between these two cliques there are no paths of influence, regardless of direction. Consequently neither clique can influence the other, and each will eventually end up with a different opinion. Within the AD clique, influence is all in one direction, so A will eventually swing D over to his opinion. Since D only moves half-way in each unit, however, he will require an infinite number of units to move all the way. Accordingly the dotted lines show D's opinion converging to A's at infinity, while A's opinion remains unchanged. Within the BC clique, influence is mutual, so in the first unit B will influence C to move half-way from 5 to 2 on the opinion scale, and likewise C will influence B to move half-way from 2 to 5. Therefore both B and C will arrive at 3½ on the opinion scale in the first unit and will remain in agreement thereafter.

The weakly connected structure is more highly connected but still does not result in unanimous agreement. In this case there is no directed path, for example, between A and D, so neither can influence the other.

The unilaterally connected structure has a directed path in at least one direction between every possible pair of points. Because it has a higher degree of connectedness, it shows more convergence of opinion.

The strongly connected structure has directed paths in both directions between every possible pair of points. In this example the strongly connected digraph is a cycle, yielding a final common opinion which reflects more equal influence of all members.

The completely connected structure has direct, one-step paths in both directions between the members of every possible pair. It converges in only one unit to a final common opinion.

Theorem 1. For all possible patterns of initial opinion, in a completely connected power structure the opinions of all members will reach a common equilibrium level equal to the arithmetic mean of the initial opinions

of all the members, and this final common opinion will be reached in one unit.

Under these conditions where the power and the resistance of all members is equal, we have already illustrated in Figure 1 that the new opinion of A is equal to $\frac{1}{2}(a+b)$, i.e., the arithmetic mean of the opinions of both members. B's opinion at the end of the first unit b_1 is also equal to $\frac{1}{2}(a+b)$, according to Postulates 2 and 3. Thus this two-person group reaches agreement in one step. The proof of Theorem 1 for an N-person group is a simple extension of this example.

Theorem 2. In an N-person cycle (which is a strongly connected group) the members will reach a final common opinion at the arithmetic mean $(1/N)(a+b+c+\ldots)$, in an infinite number of units.

If A has power over B, then $b_1 = \frac{1}{2}(a+b)$ and b_2, the opinion of B at the end of the second unit, $= \frac{1}{2}(a_1+b_1)$. In general B's opinion at the end of any unit will be half-way between his own and A's opinion at the beginning of the unit; so the general difference equation describing B's change of opinion in any unit, n, is: $b_n = \frac{1}{2}(a_n+b_{n-1})$. Solving these general difference equations for all members constitutes a proof of Theorem 2.

Theorem 3. In a unilaterally connected group the opinions of all members will converge to a final common opinion in an infinite number of steps.

It is an obvious theorem of digraph theory that no strictly unilateral digraph can have more than one point of input zero, i.e., with no directed lines leading to it (because then these two or more points could not have a directed path between them—which violates the definition of a unilateral digraph). It follows that, during every unit, at least one of the two members at the extremes of the range of opinion will be subject to the power of another and will move toward the center, thus restricting the range of opinion still further. Eventually, therefore, all members will arrive at the same opinion. If there is one person in the group with input zero, then all members will eventually agree with his initial opinion, for he will influence the others but no one will influence him.

Theorem 4. In a weakly connected group the members will not reach common agreement except under special conditions in the distribution of initial opinions.

A (strictly) weak digraph contains at least one pair of points with no directed path between them. Thus there are at least two members who cannot influence each other either directly or indirectly.

The Disconnected Group. When the final equilibrium has been reached, a disconnected group will tend to have at least as many different opinions as there are cliques (i.e., disjoint classes of members), because no clique can influence any other. If all the cliques are themselves either completely connected, strongly connected, or unilaterally connected, it follows from Theorems 1, 2, and 3 that there will be uniformity of final opinions within each clique; but there will be differences among them except under special conditions in the distribution of initial opinion.

Summarizing the theorems illustrated in Figure 2, we can say that there is a "funneling effect," a tendency for the opinions of individuals to converge toward one another, and the strength of this tendency increases with increasing connectedness in the power structure of the group. Since the power structure includes the special case of the attraction power of the group, we have a more general group of theorems consistent with the finding that the strength of group standards is determined by the cohesiveness of the group. Additionally the model predicts the exact level of the group standard as well as the precise degree of conformity at each unit. Thus we have rigorously derived a more differentiated statement of the empirically well-established relation between cohesiveness and group standards.

So far we have considered only all-or-none variations in the power of A over B; now we will illustrate the effect of continuous variation.

Theorem 5. The greater the bases of power of A over B (B's attraction to A, B's acceptance of A as an expert, etc.), the more influence A will have on B and subsequently on any other person P for whom there exists a directed path from B to P.

According to Postulates 1 and 3, increases in the basis of power of A over B will increase the strength of the resultant force exerted by A on B and therefore the amount of change produced in B. Similarly in subsequent units this influence will be transmitted, though in a weakened form, from B to P.

THE EFFECTS OF COMMUNICATION PATTERNS

In the preceding section we have dealt with the restricted case of groups of persons whose power is always utilized in every unit.[4] Earlier we noted that the head of an organization may not communicate to all those over whom he has direct power but will instead follow the established channels of communication. Likewise in a face-to-face group a member may remain silent or may attempt to influence some but not others over whom he has power. These patterns of interaction often become stabilized so that they may be treated as more-or-less consistent channels of communication. It is also clear that the strength of influence attempted can vary continuously, but we shall here treat the communication from A to B as an all-or-none variable so that we can utilize digraph theory.

Now, if we reverse the conditions of Theorems 1 through 4 and consider only completely connected power structures with variations in the degree of connectedness of the communication channels, we can apply the same four theorems and proofs. For example:

Theorem 1a. For all possible patterns of initial opinion, in a completely connected communication network, the opinions of all members will converge to a common equilibrium level equal to the arithmetic mean of the initial opinions of all the members, and this final common opinion will be reached in one unit.

Similarly, theorems analogous to 2, 3, and 4 can be stated for strong, unilateral, and weak communication networks, respectively. All possible networks in experiments of the Bavelas type (3) are included in these theorems.

Even where stable communication channels do not exist, this model may be applied provided the interaction pattern is specified for each unit. Consider a strongly connected cycle

[4] It is probable that B will respond partly to the relationships among successive influence attempts by A, for example to the consistency among his various arguments or to the simple fact of too much reiteration of the same influence attempt; these factors are omitted from the present model.

of three persons. Theorem 2 states that opinions in this group will converge to a final common opinion equal to ⅓ $(a + b + c)$. In Theorem 6 we assume a particular communication pattern: A exerts influence in the first unit, B and C exert influence in the second unit, A exerts influence in the third unit, B and C in the fourth unit, and so on.

Theorem 6. In a group where the power structure is a three-person cycle in which A has power over B, B has power over C, and C has power over A, and the communication pattern is A, BC, A, BC, . . . , the final common opinion in the group equals ⅕ $(2a + b + 2c)$.

We note that a change in the interaction pattern changes the outcome considerably. Furthermore, B and C no longer have equal influence, even though they have equal interaction patterns and similar positions in the power structure; it is the interaction of these two factors which produces the difference. A has more influence than B because he comes first in the sequence of interaction, but C has more influence than B because he has direct power over A, whereas B's power over A is indirect. Intuitively it would appear that the "primacy effect" shown in this theorem can be generalized: the sooner a person speaks the more influence he will have.

THE EFFECTS OF PATTERNS OF OPINION

In an experiment like Sherif's, each member communicates to every other and the members probably have relatively equal power. In such a completely connected power structure with completely connected communication channels, what happens to the opinion of a single deviate member?

Theorem 7. The amount of change of the deviate toward the opinions of the majority is proportional to the sum of the deviations of all other members from the deviate.

By Theorem 1 the amount of change by the deviate D equals $d_1 - d$ which is equal to $1/N$ $(d + a + b + c + . . .) - d$. Thus the more members in the group the more they will influence the deviate. Also the larger each deviation, the more D will change. Though these predictions are generally congruent with Asch's findings, they probably do not agree in detail (**1, 14**). However, the conditions of

Asch's experiment do not fit the model very well.

LEADERSHIP

To a large extent leadership consists of a member's ability to influence others both directly and indirectly by virtue of his position in the power structure, including the structure of legitimate authority. Thus leadership may be distributed among many members or concentrated in a few; the pattern of leadership is a distribution which describes the whole group rather than an attribute of single individuals. Figure 2 illustrates the dependence of influence on the total structure of the group.

Compare the influence of member A in the weakly connected group with the influence of member A in the unilaterally connected group. Both groups start out with the same distribution of opinion, and in both groups A has direct influence over only B. However, A's influence is markedly different in the two cases; in the weakly connected group the opinions of others diverge more and more from his, whereas in the unilaterally connected group the opinion of all other members converges completely to A's opinion.

The complete distribution of direct plus indirect leadership in a group with any power structure and any communication network may be calculated by matrix multiplication.[5] We may represent the power structure of the group as a matrix where each row shows the power applied to a member and each column shows the power exerted by a member. A 0 in the cell corresponding to the ath row and the bth column shows that B does not have power over A, whereas a 1 in the cell corresponding to the cth row and the dth column shows that D does have power over C. Thus the number in a cell represents the number of directed lines from the person in that column to the person in that row (under the conditions assumed in this paper, always 1 or 0). If this matrix M is multiplied by itself, then the resulting squared matrix M^2 shows in each cell the number of sequences consisting of two directed lines between the person in the column and the person in the row. The cubed matrix

[5] See Harary, Norman, and Cartwright (**16**) for a review of some related applications of matrix algebra to sociometric data.

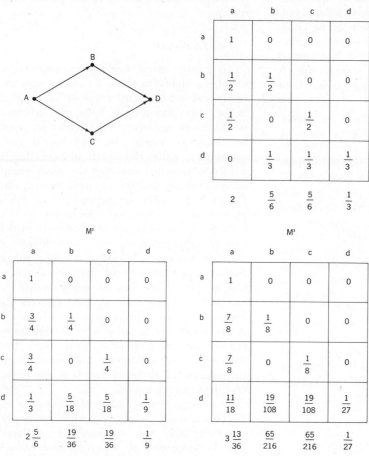

FIGURE 3. The distribution of leadership in a weakly connected group.

M^3 shows the number of three-line sequences between each pair of persons. By raising the matrix to successively higher powers, we can thus determine the number of directed line sequences, of various lengths, from each member to every other. The matrix M gives the directed lines which will result in influence in the first unit; M^2 gives the two-line sequences through which influence will be exerted by the end of the second unit; M^3 gives the three-line sequences through which influence will be exerted by the end of the third unit; etc.

In order to apply this process to Group G in Figure 3, we construct a matrix of opinion M where the columns a, b, c, d represent influence exerted by the initial opinions a, b, c, d of persons A, B, C, D, respectively. The rows represent the influence received by these opinions from all the opinions in the group. Thus the cell entries must show the amount by which an opinion is changed by another opin-

ion during one unit; and these values are given by the coefficients in the right hand side of the general difference equations. For Group G these equations are:

$$a_n = a_{n-1} \tag{1}$$
$$b_n = \tfrac{1}{2}\left(a_{n-1} + b_{n-1}\right) \tag{2}$$
$$c_n = \tfrac{1}{2}\left(a_{n-1} + c_{n-1}\right) \tag{3}$$
$$d_n = \tfrac{1}{3}\left(b_{n-1} + c_{n-1} + d_{n-1}\right) \tag{4}$$

The cell a, a has an entry of 1, indicating that in any unit A's opinion is completely determined by his previous opinion; accordingly the remaining cells in row a have entries of 0, showing that opinions b, c, d do not influence a, since there are no directed paths from B, C, or D to A. Cells b, a, and b, b have entries of ½ because b_n is a compromise half-way between the previous opinions of A and B, etc.

It will be noted that each row in M (and in M^2 and M^3) sums to 1 because it represents the total opinion of a member, and the frac-tions along the row represent the proportion of that opinion determined by each person. The sum of a column in M, on the other hand, represents the total influence of a person's opinion during the first unit on the opinions of all members (including the influence of his initial opinion on his second opinion—which we have called "resistance").

In M^2 the column sum shows the total influence of a person's initial opinion at the end of the second unit (including the changes produced in both the first and second units). Similarly M^3 shows the cumulative influence at the end of the third unit. The same procedure can obviously be extended to any number of units.

Thus the column totals of the successive powers of M give the distribution of leadership over time, as predicted by this theory. In Group G, we can see that A, the only member with input 0 in the power structure, contin-uously increases his influence at the expense of the other members. B and C, having symmetrical positions in the structure, show the same curves of decreasing influence; but D, who is influenced by all other members, has the least influence.

CONCLUSIONS

This theory illustrates a way which many complex phenomena about groups can be deduced from a few simple postulates about interpersonal relations. By the application of digraph theory we are able to treat in detail the *patterns of relations* whose importance has long been noted by the field theorists. Even if this treatment does not turn out to be empirically correct, it illustrates the need for some such conceptual and mathematical tools if we are to make progress toward the theoretical integration of psychology and sociology.

References

1. Asch, S. *Social psychology*. New York: Prentice-Hall, 1952.
2. Back, K. Influence through social communication. *Journal of Abnormal and Social Psychology*, 1951, **46**, 9–23.
3. Bavelas, A. Communication patterns in task-oriented groups. *Journal of Acoustical Society of America*, 1950, **22**, 725–730.
4. Berkowitz, L. Group standards, cohesiveness, and productivity. *Human Relations*, 1955, **7**, 509–519.
5. Biddle, B., French, J., & Moore, J. Some aspects of leadership in the small work group. USAF Technical Report (Contract 33 [038]–14091), 1953.
6. Cartwright, D. (Ed.), *Studies in social power*. Ann Arbor, Mich.: Institute for Social Research, 1959.
7. Cartwright, D., & Zander, A. *Group dynamics: research and theory*. Evanston, Ill.: Row, Peterson, 1953.
8. Crutchfield, R. Conformity and character. *The American Psychologist*, 1955, **10**, 191–198.
9. Festinger, L., *et al*. The influence process in the presence of extreme deviates. *Human Relations*, 1952, **5**, 327–346.
10. Festinger, L., Schachter, S., & Back, K. *Social pressures in informal groups*. New York: Harper, 1950.
11. Festinger, L., & Thibaut, J. Interpersonal communication in small groups. *Journal of Abnormal and Social Psychology*, 1951, **46**, 92–99.
12. French, J. R. P., Jr., & Snyder, R. Leadership and interpersonal power. In D. Cartwright (Ed.), *Studies in social power*. Ann Arbor, Mich.: Institute for Social Research, 1959.
13. Goldberg, S. Three situational determinants of conformity to social norms. *Journal of Abnormal and Social Psychology*, 1954, **49**, 325–329.
14. Guetzkow, H. (Ed.), *Groups, leadership, and men*. Pittsburgh: Carnegie Press, 1951.
15. Harary, F., & Norman, R. *Graph theory as a mathematical model in the social sciences*. Ann Arbor, Mich.: Institute for Social Research, 1953.
16. Harary, F., Norman, R., & Cartwright, D. *Structural models*. New York: Wiley, 1965.
17. Heider, F. Attitudes and cognitive organization. *Journal of Psychology*, 1946, **21**, 107–112.

18. Hovland, C., & Weiss, W. The influence of source credibility on communication effectiveness. *Public Opinion Quarterly*, 1952, **15**, 635–650.
19. Katona, G. Rational behavior and economic behavior. *Psychological Review*, 1953, **60**, 307–318.
20. Kelman, H. Effects of success and failure on "suggestibility" in the autokinetic situation. *Journal of Abnormal and Social Psychology*, 1950, **45**, 267–285.
21. Lewin, K. The conceptual representation and measurement of psychological forces. *Contributions to Psychological Theory*, 1938, **1**, 1–247.
22. Lewin, K. *Field theory in social science.* New York: Harper, 1951.
23. Libo, L. *Measuring group cohesiveness.* Ann Arbor, Mich.: Institute for Social Research, 1953.
24. Lippitt, R., Polansky, N., & Rosen, S. The dynamics of power. *Human Relations*, 1952, **5**, 37–64.
25. Mausner, B. The effect of prior reinforcement on the interaction of observer pairs. *Journal of Abnormal and Social Psychology*, 1954, **49**, 65–68.
26. Mausner, B. The effect of one partner's success or failure in a relevant task on the interaction of observer pairs. *Journal of Abnormal and Social Psychology*, 1954, **49**, 557–560.
27. Moore, H. The comparative influence of majority and expert opinion. *American Journal of Psychology*, 1921, **32**, 16–20.
28. Newcomb, T. An approach to the study of communicative acts. *Psychological Review*, 1953, **60**, 393–404.
29. Schachter, S. Deviation, rejection, and communication. *Journal of Abnormal and Social Psychology*, 1951, **46**, 190–207.
30. Schachter, S., *et al.* An experimental study of cohesiveness and productivity. *Human Relations*, 1951, **4**, 229–238.
31. Sherif, M. A study of some social factors in perception. *Archives of Psychology*, 1935, **27** (187).

INDEXES

Index of Names

Index of Subjects